South India

David Stott

South India is a spellbinding intersection of old and new, and is the best place to grasp the nature of the colossus that is modern-day India. The thriving southern cities, where fast-talking graduate professionals ride the crest of the globalization wave against a backdrop of wide British-built boulevards and Gothic architecture, are prime engines of India's recent economic growth. But beyond these cities of software chips, biotech booms and shopping malls lies a land singularly unmoved by the upheaval of burgeoning business. There is the tropical calm of Kerala's bucolic backwaters, the splendid insouciance of Goa's Portuguese-steeped villages and the riotous exuberance of Hindu temples teeming with gaudy gods and braying demons. Streaming bazars bustle and dusty markets are crammed with marigold garlands and spice sacks. Sacked Hindu empires exude their bewitching beauty while all that remains of spent Muslim dynasties are brooding tombs.

From paddy fields, coconut groves and mangrove thickets come enchanting glimpses of meringue-white churches and blue-tiled synagogues. Between spice plantations and hill stations lies parkland overrun with elephants and monkeys, while giddying waterfalls crash to the floor of forests packed with precious flora and fauna. Along the spectacular coastline beaches are lapped by the warm waters of the Andaman Sea and Indian Ocean.

As with the whole subcontinent, expect excess in everything. Come prepared for a colour palette running riot in its vibrancy, a lush and relaxed kaleidoscope of what India has been and what India is bracing herself to become.

THIS PAGE The stucco of the ancient Meenakshi Temple towers over the town of Madurai
PREVIOUS PAGE A slow ride through Kerala's backwaters

iii

1 Mumbai
Pune
Nizamabad
MAHARASHTRA
TELANGANA
Solapur
Hyderabad 9
Bhima
Kolhapur
Bijapur
Guntur
Krishna
Panjim
Hampi 8
GOA
Gooty
Kavali
Gokarna
KARNATAKA
ANDHRA
PRADESH
Penar
Tunga
Arabian
Sea
Tirupati 10

Bengaluru
Chennai
12 Vagator
Vellore
Palar
Anjuna 11
Panjim
Mangalore
Kanchipuram
GOA
Mysore
Ponnaiyar
7 Nagarhole
National Park
2
Thalassery
(Tellicherry)
Wayanad
Puducherry
5
6
Salem
Udhagamandalam
TAMIL NADU
(Ooty)
Kaveri
KERALA
Tiruchirappalli

Thrissur
Dindigul
Chettinad
Fort Kochi
Madurai 3
Vaigai
Rameswaram

Kollam
Tamraparni
Palayamkottai
Tuticorin
Thiruvananthapuram
SRI
4
LANKA
Kanniyakumari

N

Indian Ocean

100 km
100 miles
The Government of India states that
"the external boundaries of India
are neither correct nor authenticated"

Harvesting coconuts in Puducherry

Don't miss...
See colour maps at end of book

**Bay of
Bengal**

1 **Mumbai** ▶▶page 33
India's economic capital and melting pot.

2 **Puducherry** ▶▶page 104
A beguiling fusion of French, Tamil and Utopian ideas.

3 **Meenakshi Temple, Madurai** ▶▶page 164
An outstanding Vijayanagar temple.

4 **Kanniyakumari** ▶▶page 181
Where three seas meet at India's toe tip.

5 **Thalassery (Tellicherry)** ▶▶page 265
Clashing swords in martial arts practice rooms.

6 **Wayanad** ▶▶page 267
Stunning hill district with tea plantations and rainforest.

7 **Nagarhole National Park** ▶▶page 311
Former maharaja reserve inhabited by elephants,
monkeys and flying squirrels.

8 **Hampi** ▶▶page 341
Hindu capital strewn with boulders and desolate temples.

9 **Hyderabad** ▶▶page 372
Stone-carved bazaars and crumbling palaces.

10 **Tirupati** ▶▶page 405
India's most revered temple, famed for head-shaving rituals.

11 **Anjuna flea market** ▶▶page 439
One of the world's biggest bring-and-buy sales.

12 **Vagator** ▶▶page 441
Trance parties, Ayurveda centres and stunning beaches.

v

Mumbai's streets are aswarm with colourful traffic.

Itineraries for South India

Try not be too ambitious as distances are huge (individual states are as big as countries in Western Europe); your best bet is to limit yourself and properly explore one region in depth rather than trying to notch up the sights against an exhaustive inventory. Three weeks is just enough to see some of the South's highlights. Consider internal flights but to curb carbon emissions pursue road and rail routes and see much more of the landscape. Travel in India, regardless of budget, is tiring so take breaks; Mahabalipuram, Kovalam, the hill stations or Goa make ideal R&R stops.

Anjuna flea market.

ITINERARY ONE: 2-3 weeks
Karnataka and Malabar

It makes sense to combine Bengaluru (Bangalore) and Mysore – and Tipu Sultan's palace at Srirangapatnam – with a trip to Hassan, the wonderful Hindu temples at Belur and Halebid and the monolithic freestanding Jain sculpture at Sravanabela-gola. From here head for the old Kodagu (Coorg) capital Madikeri, south of Hassan, an excellent place to relax and get a feel of the unspoilt hill country. Stay in the mountains for Sultan's Battery and the Wayanad, Kerala's little-explored jungle coffee planta-tion country, crossing over to Tamil Nadu for Ooty and Coonoor and clipped tea trees; or, if you've already had your fill of the high country, slip straight down into North Kerala to Malabar. Telicherry, Kannur and

Calicut all offer a fascinating insight into the Moplah community. Don't skip Fort Kochi and the backwaters country that begins on the city's fringes – the Christian belt of Kottayam and its environs.

Temple trail

You can really overdose on temples in Tamil Nadu: start off at Chennai for nearby seaside Mahabalipuram with its rock-cut and structural temples. If you are feeling energetic you can take a day trip to see either the great temples of Kanchipuram, also famous as a silk-making town, or the fort at Gingee and the magnificent temple at Tiruvanna-malai. Continue to the centres of ancient Tamil culture, with remarkable temples at Chidambaram, and stop at Swamima-

A Hindu temple of the Vijayanagara kingdom, Hampi.

The Upper Sivalaya Temple, Badami.

vii

lai, where exquisite deities are still cast in solid bronze.,to visit Darasuram, Kumbakonam and Gangaikondacholapuram en route to Thanjavur and Madurai. Return via Trichy and Srirangam to Chennai.

ITINERARY TWO: 3 weeks
Sampling the south

From Chennai head to Swamimalai before continuing south to the ancient Tamil temples at Thanjavur and Madurai. Stop at Padmanabhapuram Palace on the way across to Kerala to relax on the beach at Kovalam, near Thiruvananthapuram. Take a boat along the backwaters as you move to Kochi, a fascinating meeting point

of Eastern and European cultures. Then explore the tea estates of Munnar, high in the Western Ghats, before dropping to the Tamil plains to visit the ancient fort and temples at Trichy and Srirangam. Make time for a stop by the sea to visit the rock-cut cave temples at Mahabalipuram.

ITINERARY THREE: 1 month
Goa and the Deccan

India's Latin quarter is Goa, with easy living, relaxed dress codes, excellent food and experienced tourist infrastructure. Once you've had a swim, shopped at the flea market and had a good look at the Portuguese churches of Old Goa, Chandor, you can push on into Karnataka and south to Gokarna, for a beautiful beach-cum-seething pilgrim centre, or east for prize culture in the ruins of a home-grown vanquished empire at Hampi, stone-masonry cut like lace at Badami, Pattadakal and Aihole and the onion tombs of the Deccan's Islamic

TRAVEL TIP

Use the travel agents listed in this guide for booking transport. Their fees are negligible, and they can save you a substantial amount of time.

The beach at the pilgrimage centre of Varkala is backed by dramatic cliffs

Malabar is one of the best places to see the ritual temple dance, Theyyam

Kerala is synonymous with its idyllic backwaters

rulers at Bijapur. Keep east to pursue the Muslim trail: Gulbarga and Bidar make fascinating stops on the road to the old fort of Golconda, the Qutb Shahi tombs, taking you to the one-time capital of the Nizam's princely state in the hi-tech city of Hyderabad. From here fly to Chennai and the British Fort Area, then catch your breath at Mahabalipuram's shore temple before stopping at Puducherry for a slice of Gallic India. Great Hindu temples are scattered across Tamil Nadu's central plains, and Srirangam near Trichy and Madurai offer access to some of the most spectacular examples of these. From Madurai you can climb the Western Ghats to Periyar's tiger reserve. From Periyar, travel to Kerala's west coast port of Kochi and sample the idyllic backwaters by boat.

TRAVEL TIP
Trains can now be booked online which cuts down queuing immeasurably.

The 16th-century Church of the Immaculate Conception, Goa

Munnar's tea plantations

Contents

MUMBAI

TELANGANA & ANDHRA PRADESH

GOA

KARNATAKA

TAMIL NADU

KERALA

Contents

Essentials

Best time to visit South India

By far the most comfortable time to visit South India is from October to March, when the weather is dry and relatively cool. April and May are intensely hot, especially on the Deccan Plateau and the Tamil Nadu plains – South India's hill stations fill to bursting during this time – with humidity building up as the monsoon approaches. The southwest monsoon hits Kerala in early June, sweeping northward to reach Mumbai about 10 days later; the heaviest rain comes in July and can see large parts of the west coast knee-deep in water for hours at a time. A second monsoon travels up the east coast during September and October. If you're travelling during the monsoon you need to be prepared for extended periods of torrential rain and disruption to travel. The post-monsoon period comes with cool air and clear skies – this is the best time for mountain views – while winter temperatures can drop close to zero in the high points of the Western Ghats. Autumn and winter are also the time of some of India's great festivals, including the wild **Ganesh Charturthi** in Mumbai, **Dussehra** and **Diwali**.

Getting to South India

Air

South India is accessible by air from virtually every continent. By far the most common arrival point is Mumbai, though excellent connectivity through the Gulf and Southeast Asia makes it just as easy to fly directly into Chennai, Bengaluru, Hyderabad, Kochi or Thiruvananthapuram. Several carriers permit 'open-jaw' travel, arriving in and departing from different cities. In 2014 the cheapest return flights to Mumbai from London started from around £550, but went up to £650+ as you approached the high seasons of Christmas, New Year and Easter.

Once you're on the ground India's comprehensive internal flight network can get you to destinations throughout the south.

From Europe
Despite the increases to Air Passenger Duty, Britain remains the cheapest place in Europe for flights to India. **British Airways**, **Virgin Atlantic**, **Jet Airways** and **Air India** fly direct from London to Mumbai, while BA also flies direct to Chennai, Bengaluru and Hyderabad. **Air India** and **Jet Airways** also serve several airports in mainland Europe, while major European flag carriers including **KLM** and **Lufthansa** fly to Mumbai from their respective hub airports. In most cases the cheapest flights are with Middle Eastern or Central Asian airlines, transiting via airports in the Gulf. Several airlines from the Middle East (eg **Emirates**, **Etihad**, **Gulf Air**, **Kuwait Airways**, **Qatar Airways** and **Oman Air**) offer good discounts to Indian regional capitals from London via their hub cities. This adds a couple of hours to the journey

Packing for India

You can buy most essentials in larger cities and shops in five-star hotels. Items you might find useful include a loose-fitting, light cotton clothes including a sarong (women should dress modestly at all times; brief shorts and tight vest tops are best avoided, though on the beach modest swimwear is fine). It can be cold in the north from December to February and everywhere over 1500 m, where warmer clothing is essential. Comfortable shoes, sandals or trainers are essential. Take high-factor sun screen and a sun hat. Earplugs and an eyemask are also essential. Indian pharmacies can be very cheap but aren't always reliable, so take a supply of medicines from home, including inhalers and anti-malarial drugs. For protection against mosquitoes, take repellent. See also Health, page 22.

Photocopies of documents, passport ID and visa pages, and spare photos are useful when applying for permits or in case of loss or theft.

For budget travellers: moquito nets aren't always provided in cheap hotels so take one with you. Take a good padlock to secure your budget room too, though these are cheaply bought in India. A cotton or silk sheet sleeping bag is useful when you can't be sure of clean linen.

time, but makes it possible to fly to less obvious gateway cities such as Kochi and Thiruvananthapuram, avoiding the more fraught route via Mumbai (which involves long immigration queues and shuttling from the international to domestic terminal). Consolidators in the UK can quote some competitive fares, such as: www.skyscanner.net, www.ebookers.com; **North South Travel** ① *T01245-608291, www.northsouthtravel.co.uk (profits to charity)*.

From North America

From the east coast, several airlines including **Air India, Jet Airways, Continental** and **Delta** fly direct from New York to Mumbai. **American** flies from Chicago. Discounted tickets on **British Airways, KLM, Lufthansa, Gulf Air** and **Kuwait Airways** are sold through agents although they will invariably fly via their country's capital cities. From the west coast, **Air India** flies from Los Angeles to Mumbai, and **Jet Airways** from San Francisco to Mumbai via Shanghai. Alternatively, fly via Hong Kong, Singapore or Bangkok using one of those countries' national carriers. **Air Canada** operates between Vancouver and Delhi, with internal connections to airports in the South. **Air Brokers International** ① *www.airbrokers.com*, is competitive and reputable. **STA** ① *www. statravel.co.uk*, has offices in many US cities, Toronto and Ontario. Student fares are also available from **Travel Cuts** ① *www.travelcuts.com*, in Canada.

From Australasia

Qantas, Singapore Airlines, Thai Airways, Malaysian Airlines, Cathay Pacific and **Air India** are the principal airlines connecting the continents, although none have direct flights to the south. **Singapore Airlines** offer the most flexibility, with subsidiary **Silk Air** flying to airports in Tamil Nadu and Kerala. Low-cost carriers including **Air Asia** (via Kuala Lumpur), **Scoot** and **Tiger Airways** (Singapore) offer a similar choice of arrival airports at substantial savings, though long layovers and possible missed connections make this a slightly more risky venture than flying with the mainstream airlines. STA and Flight Centre offer discounted tickets from their branches in major cities in Australia and New Zealand. **Abercrombie & Kent** ① *www.abercrombiekent.co.uk*, **Adventure World** ① *www.adventure world.net.au*, **Peregrine** ① *www.peregrineadventures.com*, and **Travel Corporation of India** ① *www.tcindia.com*, organize tours.

Airport information

The formalities on arrival in India have been increasingly streamlined during the last few years and the facilities at the major international airports greatly improved. However, arrival can still be a slow process. Disembarkation cards, with an attached customs declaration, are handed out to passengers during the inward flight. The immigration form should be handed in at the immigration counter on arrival. The customs slip will be returned, for handing over to the customs on leaving the baggage collection hall. You may well find that there are delays of over an hour at immigration in processing passengers who need help with filling in forms. When departing, note that you'll need to have a printout of your itinerary to get into the airport, and the security guards will only let you into the terminal within three hours of your flight. Many airports require you to scan your bags before checking in, and in rare cases you may also be asked to identify your checked luggage after going through immigration and security checks.

Departure charges

Several airports, including Bengaluru and Hyderabad, have begun charging a Passenger Service Fee or User Development Fee to each departing passenger. This is normally included in international tickets, but some domestic airlines have been reluctant to incorporate the charge. Keep some spare cash in rupees in case you need to pay the fee on arriving at the terminal.

Transport in South India

Air

India has a comprehensive network linking the major cities of the different states. Deregulation of the airline industry has had a transformative effect on travel within India, with a host of low-budget private carriers with a host of low-cost private carriers jockeying to provide the lowest prices or highest frequency on popular routes. On any given day, booking a few days in advance, you can expect to fly from Mumbai to Goa, Bengaluru, Chennai or Kochi for around US$100 one way including taxes, while booking a month in advance can reduce the price to US$60-70.

Competition from the efficiently run private sector has, in general, improved the quality of services provided by the nationalized airlines. It also seems to herald the end of the two-tier pricing structure, meaning that ticket prices are now usually the same for foreign and Indian travellers. The airport authorities too have made efforts to improve handling on the ground.

Although flying is comparatively expensive, for covering vast distances or awkward links on a route it is an option worth considering, though delays and re-routing can be irritating. For short distances (eg Thiruvananthapurm–Kochi), and on some routes where you can sleep during an overnight journey (eg Aurangabad–Hyderabad) it makes more sense to travel by train.

The best way to get an idea of the current routes, carriers and fares is to use a third-party booking website such as www.cheapairticketsindia.com (toll-free numbers: UK T0800-101 0928, USA T1-888 825 8680), www.cleartrip.com, www.makemytrip.co.in, or www.yatra.com. Booking with these is a different matter: some refuse foreign credit cards outright, while others have to be persuaded to give your card special clearance. Tickets booked on these sites are typically issued as an email ticket or an SMS text message – the simplest option if you have an Indian mobile phone, though it must be converted to a paper ticket at the relevant carrier's airport offices before you will be allowed into the terminal. Makemytrip.com and Travelocity.com both accept international credit cards.

Rail

Trains can still be the cheapest and most comfortable means of travelling long distances saving you hotel expenses on overnight journeys. It gives access to booking station Retiring Rooms, which can be useful from time to time. Above all, you have an ideal opportunity to meet local travellers and catch a glimpse of life on the ground.

High-speed trains
There are several air-conditioned 'high-speed' Shatabdi (or 'Century') Express for day travel, and Rajdhani Express ('Capital City') for overnight journeys. These cover large sections of the network but due to high demand you need to book them well in advance (up to 90 days). Meals and drinks are usually included.

Classes
A/c First Class, available only on main routes, is the choice of the Indian upper crust, with two- or four-berth carpeted sleeper compartments with washbasin. As with all a/c sleeper accommodation, bedding is included, and the windows are tinted to the point of being almost impossible to see through. A/c Sleeper, two and three-tier configurations (known as 2AC and 3AC), are clean and comfortable and popular with middle class families; these are the safest carriages for women travelling alone. A/c Executive Class, with wide reclining seats, are available on many Shatabdi trains at double the price of the ordinary a/c Chair Car which are equally comfortable. First

Class (non-a/c) is gradually being phased out, and is now restricted to a handful of routes through Tamil Nadu and Kerala, but the run-down old carriages still provide a very enjoyable combination of privacy and windows you can open. **Second Class (non-a/c)** two and three-tier (commonly called **Sleeper**), provides exceptionally cheap and atmospheric travel, with basic padded vinyl seats and open windows that allow the sights and sounds of India (not to mention dust, insects and flecks of spittle expelled by passengers up front) to drift into the carriage. On long journeys Sleeper can be crowded and uncomfortable, and toilet facilities can be unpleasant; it is nearly always better to use the Indian-style squat loos rather than the Western-style ones as they are better maintained. At the bottom rung is **Unreserved Second Class**, with hard wooden benches. You can travel long distances for a trivial amount of money, but unreserved carriages are often ridiculously crowded, and getting off at your station may involve a battle of will and strength against the hordes trying to shove their way on.

Indrail passes

These allow travel across the network without having to pay extra reservation fees and sleeper charges but you have to spend a high proportion of your time on the train to make it worthwhile. However, the advantages of pre-arranged reservations and automatic access to 'Tourist Quotas' can tip the balance in favour of the pass for some travellers.

Tourists (foreigners and Indians resident abroad) may buy these passes from the tourist sections of principal railway booking offices and pay in foreign currency, major credit cards, travellers' cheques or rupees with encashment certificates. Fares range from US$57 to US$1060 for adults or half that for children. Rail-cum-air tickets are also to be made available.

Indrail passes can also conveniently be bought abroad from special agents. For people contemplating a single long journey soon after arriving in India, the Half- or One-day Pass with a confirmed reservation is worth the peace of mind; two- or four-day passes are also sold.

The UK agent is SDEL ① *103 Wembley Park Dr, Wembley, Middlesex HA9 8HG, UK, T020-8903 3411, www.indiarail.co.uk.* They make all necessary reservations and offer excellent advice. They can also book Air India and Jet Airways internal flights.

Cost

A/c first class costs about double the rate for two-tier shown below, and non a/c second class about half. Children (aged five to 12) travel at half the adult fare. The young (12-30 years) and senior citizens (65 years and over) are allowed a 30% discount on journeys over 500 km (just show your passport).

Period	US$ A/c 2-tier	Period	US$ A/c 2-tier
½ day	26	21 days	198
1 day	43	30 days	248
7 days	135	60 days	400
15 days	185	90 days	530

Fares for individual journeys are based on distance covered and reflect both the class and the type of train. Higher rates apply on the Mail and Express trains and the air-conditioned Shatabdi and Rajdhani Expresses.

Internet services Much information is available online via www.railtourismindia. com, www.indianrail.gov.in, www.erail.in and www.trainenquiry.com, where you can check timetables (which change frequently), numbers, seat availability and even the running status of your train. Internet e-tickets can be bought and printed on www.irctc.in though it's a fiendishly frustrating system to use, and paying with a foreign credit card is fraught with difficulty. If you plan to do a lot of train travel on popular routes (eg Hospet–Goa or Goa–Mumbai) it might be worth the effort to get your credit card recognized by the booking system. This process changes often, so your best option is to consult the very active India transport forums at www. indiamike.com. An alternative is to seek a local agent who can sell e-tickets, which can cost as little as Rs 10 (plus Rs 20 reservation fee, although some agents charge up to Rs 150 a ticket), and can save hours of hassle; simply present the printout to the ticket collector. However, it is tricky if you then want to cancel an e-ticket which an agent has bought for you on their account.

Tickets and reservations It is possible to reserve tickets for virtually any train on the network from one of the 1000 computerized reservation centres across India. It is always best to book as far in advance as possible (usually up to 60 days). To reserve a seat on a particular train, note down the train's name, number and departure time and fill in a reservation form while you line up at the ticket window; you can use one form for up to four passengers. At busy stations the wait can take an hour or more. You can save a lot of time and effort by asking a travel agent to get your tickets for a fee of Rs 50-100. If the class you want is full, ask if tickets are available under any of Indian Rail's special quotas. **Foreign Tourist Quota** (FTQ) reserves a small number of tickets on popular routes for overseas travellers; you need your passport and either an exchange certificate or ATM receipt to book tickets under FTQ. The other useful special quota is **Tatkal**, which releases a last-minute pool of tickets at 1000 on the day before the train departs. If the quota system can't help you, consider buying a 'wait list' ticket, as seats often become available close to the train's departure time; phone the station on the day of departure to check your ticket's status. If you don't have a reservation for a particular train but carry an Indrail Pass, you may get one by arriving three hours early. Be wary of touts at the station offering tickets, hotels or exchange.

Timetables Regional timetables are available cheaply from station bookstalls; the monthly *Indian Bradshaw* is sold in principal stations. The handy *Trains at a Glance* (Rs 40) lists popular trains likely to be used by most foreign travellers and is available at stalls at Indian railway stations and in the UK from SDEL (see page 8).

Road

Road travel is sometimes the only choice for reaching many of the places of outstanding interest, particularly national parks or isolated tourist sites. For the uninitiated, travel by road can also be a worrying experience because of the apparent absence of conventional traffic regulations. Vehicles drive on the left – in theory. Routes around the major cities are usually crowded with lorry traffic, especially at night, and the main roads are often poor and slow. There are a few motorway-style expressways, but most main roads are single track. Some district roads are quiet, and although they are not fast they can be a good way of seeing the country and village life if you have the time.

Bus

Buses now reach virtually every part of India, offering a cheap, if often uncomfortable, means of visiting places off the rail network. Very few villages are now more than 2-3 km from a bus stop. Services are run by the State Corporation from the State Bus Stand (and private companies which often have offices nearby). The latter allow advance reservations, including booking printable e-tickets online (check www. redbus.in and www.viaworld.in) and, although tickets prices are a little higher, they have fewer stops and are a bit more comfortable.

Bus categories Though comfortable for sightseeing trips, apart from the very best 'sleeper coaches' even **air-conditioned luxury coaches** can be very uncomfortable for really long journeys. Often the air conditioning is very cold so wrap up. Journeys over 10 hours can be extremely tiring so it is better to go by train if there is a choice. If you must take a sleeper bus (a contradiction in terms), choose a lower berth near the front of the bus. The upper berths tend to be really uncomfortable on bumpy roads. **Express buses** run over long distances (frequently overnight), these are often called 'video coaches' and can be an appalling experience unless you appreciate loud film music blasting through the night. Ear plugs and eye masks may ease the pain. They rarely average more than 45 kph. **Local buses** are often very crowded, quite bumpy, slow and usually poorly maintained. However, over short distances, they can be a very cheap, friendly and easy way of getting about. Even where signboards are not in English someone will usually give you directions. Many larger towns have **minibus** services which charge a little more than the buses and pick up and drop passengers on request. Again very crowded, and with restricted headroom, they are the fastest way of getting about many of the larger towns.

Bus travel tips Some towns have different bus stations for different destinations. Booking on major long-distance routes is now computerized. Book in advance where possible and avoid the back of the bus where it can be very bumpy. If your destination is only served by a local bus you may do better to take the Express bus and 'persuade' the driver, with a tip in advance, to stop where you want to get off. You will have to pay the full fare to the first stop beyond your destination but you will get there faster and more comfortably. When an unreserved bus pulls into a bus station, there is usually an unholy scramble for seats, whilst those arriving have to struggle to get off! In many areas there is an unwritten 'rule of reservation' using handkerchiefs or bags thrust through the windows to reserve seats. Some visitors may feel a more justified right to a seat having fought their way through the crowd, but it is generally best to do as local people do and be prepared with a handkerchief. As soon as it touches the seat, it is yours! Leave it on your seat when getting off to use the toilet at bus stations.

Car

A car provides a chance to travel off the beaten track, and gives unrivalled opportunities for seeing something of India's great variety of villages and small towns. Until recently, the most widely used hire car was the romantic but notoriously unreliable Hindustan Ambassador. You can still find them for hire in parts of Tamil Nadu and Kerala, but they're gradually giving way to more efficient (and boring) Tata and Toyota models with mod cons such as optional air conditioning – and seat belts. A handful of international agencies offer self-drive car hire (Avis, Sixt), but India's majestically anarchic traffic culture is not for the faint-hearted, and emphatically not a place for those who value such quaint concepts as lane discipline, or indeed driving on your assigned side of the road. It's much more common, and comfortable, to hire not just the car but someone to drive it for you.

Car hire If you fancy the idea of being Lady Penelope and gadding about with your own chauffeur, dream no more. Hiring a car and driver is the most comfortable and efficient way to cover short to medium distances, and although prices have increased sharply in recent years car travel in India is still a bargain by Western standards. Even if you're travelling on a modest budget a day's car hire can help take the sting out of an arduous journey, allowing you to go sightseeing along the way without looking for somewhere to stash your bags.

Local drivers often know their way around an area much better than drivers from other states, so where possible it is a good idea to get a local driver who speaks the state language, in addition to being able to communicate with you. The best way to guarantee a driver who speaks good English is to book in advance with a professional travel agency, either in India or in your home country. Recommended operators with English speaking drivers include **Milesworth Travel** ① *Tamil Nadu, www.milesworth.com*, **Skyway** ① *Karnataka, www.skywaytour.com*, and **Intersight** ① *Kerala, www.intersighttours.com*. You can, if you choose, arrange car hire informally by asking around at taxi stands, but don't expect your driver to speak anything more than rudimentary English.

On pre-arranged overnight trips the fee you pay will normally include fuel and inter-state taxes – check before you pay – and a wage for the driver. Drivers are responsible for their expenses, including meals (and the pervasive servant-master culture in India means that most will choose to sit separately from you at meal times). Some tourist hotels provide rooms for drivers, but they often choose to sleep in the car overnight to save money. In some areas drivers also seek to increase their earnings by taking you to hotels and shops where they earn a handsome commission; these are generally hugely overpriced and poor alternatives to the hotels recommended in this book, so don't be afraid to say no and insist on your choice of accommodation. If you feel inclined, a tip at the end of the tour of Rs 100 per day is perfectly acceptable.

	Tata Indica non-a/c	Tata Indigo non-a/c	Hyundai Accent a/c	Toyota Innova
8 hrs/80 km	Rs 1200	Rs 1600	Rs 2200	Rs 2500
Extra km	Rs 8	Rs 10	Rs 15	Rs 15
Extra hour	Rs 80	Rs 100	Rs 200	Rs 180
Out of town				
Per km	Rs 8	Rs 10	Rs 15	Rs 15
Night halt	Rs 200	Rs 200	Rs 300	Rs 250

Taxi

Taxi travel in India is a great bargain, and in most cities in the south you can take a taxi from the airport to the centre for under US$10. Yellow-top taxis in cities and large towns are metered, although tariffs change frequently. These changes are shown on a fare conversion chart which should be read in conjunction with the meter reading. Increased night time rates apply in most cities, and there might be a small charge for luggage. Insist on the taxi meter being flagged in your presence. If the driver refuses, the official advice is to contact the police. When a taxi doesn't have a meter, you will need to fix the fare before starting the journey. Ask at your hotel desk for a guide price. As a foreigner, it is rare to get a taxi in the big cities to use the meter – if they are eager to, watch out as sometimes the meter is rigged and they have a fake rate card. Also, watch out for the David Blaine-style note shuffle: you pay with a Rs 500 note, but they have a Rs 100 note in their hand. This happens frequently at the prepaid booth outside New Delhi train station too, no matter how small the transaction.

Most airports and many major stations have booths where you can book a **prepaid taxi**. For slightly more than the metered fare these allow you to sidestep overcharging and give you the security of knowing that your driver will take you to your destination by the most direct route. You might be able to join up with other travellers at the booth to share a taxi to your hotel or a central point. It's OK to give the driver a small tip at the end of the journey.

At night, always have a clear idea of where you want to go and insist on being taken there. Taxi drivers may try to convince you that the hotel you have chosen 'closed three years ago' or is 'completely full'. Say that you have a reservation.

Rickshaw

Auto-rickshaws (autos) are almost universally available in towns across South India and are the cheapest and most convenient way of getting about. It is best to walk a short distance away from a hotel gate before picking up an auto to avoid paying an inflated rate. In addition to using them for short journeys it is often possible to hire them by the hour, or for a half or full day's sightseeing. In some areas younger drivers who speak some English and know their local area well may want to show you around. However, rickshaw drivers are often paid a commission by hotels, restaurants and gift shops so advice is not always impartial. Drivers generally refuse to use a meter, often quote a ridiculous price (Chennai's 'rickshaw mafia' are particularly notorious for overcharging) or may sometimes stop short of your destination. If you have real problems it can help to note down the vehicle licence number and threaten to go to the police. Beware of some rickshaw drivers who show the fare chart for taxis.

Cycle-rickshaws and **horse-drawn tongas** are more common in the more rustic setting of a small town or the outskirts of a large one. You will need to fix a price by bargaining. The animal attached to a tonga usually looks too undernourished to have the strength to pull the driver, let alone passengers.

Where to stay in South India

India has an enormous range of accommodation, and you can stay safely and very cheaply by Western standards right across the country.

The mainstay of the budget traveller is the ubiquitous Indian 'business hotel': within walking distance to train and bus stations, anonymous but generally decent value, with en suite rooms of hugely variable cleanliness and a TV showing 110 channels of cricket and Bollywood MTV. At the top end, alongside international chains like **ITC Sheraton** (ostentatious) and **Radisson Blu** (dependable), India boasts several home-grown hotel chains, best of which are the exceptional heritage and palace hotels operated by the Taj group. Meanwhile, Kerala and Tamil Nadu offer abundant opportunities to stay in fine style in converted mansions and farmhouses – a great way to help preserve architectural heritage while keeping your money in the local economy. And while the coastal holiday belts of Goa and Kerala have their share of big and bland resorts, you'll also find a huge variety of individual lodgings, from porous coconut-fibre beach shacks that don't even come with a lock to luxuriously restored forts overlooking the Arabian Sea and minimalist Zen retreats hidden in paddy fields.

In the high season (October to April, peaking at Christmas/New Year and again at Easter) bookings can be extremely heavy in popular destinations. It is generally possible to book in advance by phone, fax or email, sometimes on payment of a deposit, but double check your reservation a day or two beforehand and always try to arrive as early as possible in the day to iron out problems.

Hotels

Price categories The category codes used in this book are based on prices of double rooms excluding taxes. They are **not** star ratings and individual facilities vary considerably. Modest hotels may not have their own restaurant but will often offer 'room service', bringing in food from outside. In temple towns, restaurants may only serve vegetarian food. Expect to pay more in Mumbai and, to a lesser extent, Chennai for all categories. Prices away from large cities tend to be lower for comparable hotels.

Off-season rates Large reductions are made by hotels in all categories out-of-season in many resorts. Always ask if any is available. You may also request the 10-15% agent's commission to be deducted from your bill if you book direct. Clarify whether the agreed figure includes all taxes.

Price codes

Where to stay

$$$$ over US$150 $$$ US$66-150

$$ US$30-65 $ under US$30

For a double room in high season, excluding taxes.

Restaurants

$$$ over US$12 $$ US$6-12 $ under US$6

For a two-course meal for one person, excluding drinks and service charge.

Taxes In general most hotel rooms rated at Rs 3000 or above are subject to a tax of 10%. Many states levy an additional luxury tax of 10-25%, and some hotels add a service charge of 10% on top of this. Taxes are not necessarily payable on meals, so it is worth settling your meals bill separately. Most hotels in the $$ category and above accept payment by credit card. Check your final bill carefully. Visitors have complained of incorrect bills, even in the most expensive hotels. The problem particularly afflicts groups, when last-minute extras appear mysteriously on some guests' bills. Check the evening before departure, and keep all receipts.

Hotel facilities You have to be prepared for difficulties which are uncommon in the West. It is best to inspect the room and check that all equipment (air conditioning, TV, water heater, flush) works before checking in at a modest hotel. Many hotels try to wring too many years' service out of their linen, and it's quite common to find sheets that are stained, frayed or riddled with holes. Don't expect any but the most expensive or tourist-savvy hotels to fit a top sheet to the bed.

In some states **power cuts** are common, or hot water may be restricted to certain times of day. The largest hotels have their own generators but it is best to carry a good torch.

In some regions **water supply** is rationed periodically. Keep a bucket filled to use for flushing the toilet during water cuts. Occasionally, tap water may be discoloured due to rusty tanks. During the cold weather and in hill stations, hot water will be available at certain times of the day, sometimes in buckets, but is usually very restricted in quantity. Electric water heaters may provide enough for a shower but not enough to fill a bath tub. For details on drinking water, see below.

Hotels close to temples can be very **noisy**, especially during festivals. Music blares from loudspeakers late at night and from very early in the morning, often making sleep impossible. Mosques call the faithful to prayers at dawn. Some find ear plugs helpful.

Some hotels offer 24-hour checkout, meaning you can keep the room a full 24 hours from the time you arrive – a great option if you arrive in the afternoon and want to spend the morning sightseeing.

Homestays

At the upmarket end, increasing numbers of travellers are keen to stay in private homes and guesthouses, opting not to book large hotel chains that keep you at arm's length from a culture. Instead, travellers get home-cooked meals in heritage houses and learn about a country through conversation with often fascinating hosts. Kerala in particular has embraced the homestay model – though the term is increasingly abused as a marketing term by small hotels – while Chennai has a number of smart family-run B&Bs. Tourist offices have lists of families with more modest homestays. Companies specializing in homestays include **Home & Hospitality** ⓘ *www.homeandhospitality.co.uk*, **MAHout** ⓘ *www.mahoutuk.com*, and **Sundale Vacations** ⓘ *www.sundale.com*.

Food and drink in South India

Food

You find just as much variety in dishes crossing India as you would on an equivalent journey across Europe. Combinations of spices give each region its distinctive flavour.

The South has given rise to a particularly wide variety of cuisine. Most ubiquitous are the humble snacks that appear on the menu in South Indian cafés the length and breadth of India: *masala dosa*, a crispy rice pancake folded over and stuffed with a lightly spiced potato filling; *uttapam*, a cross between a pancake and a pizza, topped with tomato and onion or slices of banana; and *idli*, soft steamed rice cakes served with a spicy stew called *sambar* and coconut chutney. Every town in the south has a slew of places serving these staples, and for less than US$1 you can fuel yourself up for a full morning's sightseeing.

Vegetarian food is still prevalent throughout the Hindu-dominated states of Maharashtra, Tamil Nadu, Kerala and Karnataka. Along the Kerala coast, with its largely Christian and Muslim population, you'll find excellent seafood and fish dishes, which might be served grilled or stewed in a potent coconut-laden curry with tapioca. Goa, meanwhile, is the birthplace of the vindaloo – a more subtle, sweet-sour ancestor to the highly flammable offerings found in your local curry house – and also does a nice line in Portuguese pastries. And if you find yourself in Hyderabad, don't miss the opportunity to try India's most famous biryani, a succulent mound of rice and spices piled high with chunks of lamb or goat.

Throughout India the best value food comes in the shape of the traditional *thali*, a complete meal served on a large stainless steel plate, or on a banana leaf in traditional Brahmin restaurants. Several preparations, placed in small bowls, surround the central serving of wholewheat chapati and rice. A typical vegetarian *thali* will include dhal (lentils), two or three curries (which can be quite hot) and crisp poppadums. A variety of pickles are offered – mango and lime are two of the most popular. These can be exceptionally hot, and are designed to be taken in minute quantities alongside the main dishes. Plain *dahi* (yoghurt), or *raita*, usually acts as a bland 'cooler', and there's usually a bowl of sweet *kheer* (rice pudding) to finish off.

If you're unused to spicy food, go slow. Food is often spicier when you eat with families or at local places, and certain cuisines (notably those of Andhra Pradesh and the Chettinad region of Tamil Nadu) are notorious for going heavy on the chilli. Most restaurants are used to toning things down for foreign palates, so if you're worried about being overpowered, feel free to ask for the food to be made less spicy.

Food hygiene has improved immensely in recent years. However, you still need to take extra care, as flies abound and refrigeration in the hot weather may be inadequate and intermittent because of power cuts. It is safest to eat only freshly prepared food by ordering from the menu (especially meat and fish dishes). Be suspicious of salads and cut fruit, which may have been lying around for hours or washed in unpurified tap water – though salads served in top-end hotel restaurants and places primarily catering to foreigners (eg in Goa and Puducherry) can offer a blissful break from heavily spiced curries.

Choosing a good restaurant can be tricky if you're new to India. Many local eateries sport a grimy look that can be off-putting, yet serve brilliant and safe food, while swish four-star hotel restaurants that attract large numbers of tourists can dish up buffet food that leaves you crawling to the bathroom at 0200. A large crowd of locals is always a good sign that the food is freshly cooked and good. Even fly-blown *dhabas* on the roadside can be safe, as long as you stick to freshly cooked meals and avoid timebombs like deep-fried samosas left in the sun for hours.

Many city restaurants and backpacker eateries offer a choice of so-called European options such as toasted sandwiches, stuffed pancakes, apple pies, fruit crumbles and cheesecakes. Italian favourites (pizzas, pastas) can be very different from what you are used to. Ice creams, on the other hand, can be exceptionally good; there are excellent Indian ones as well as some international brands.

India has many delicious tropical fruits. Some are seasonal (eg mangoes, pineapples and lychees), while others (eg bananas, grapes and oranges) are available throughout the year. It is safe to eat the ones you can wash and peel.

Don't leave India without trying its superb range of indigenous sweets. *Srikhand* is a popular dessert in Maharashtra, and is a thick yoghurt laden with sugar, while a piece or two of milk-based *peda* or Mysore *pak* make a perfect sweet postscript to a cheap dinner.

Drink

Drinking water used to be regarded as one of India's biggest hazards. It is still true that water from the tap or a well should never be considered safe to drink since public water supplies are often polluted. Bottled water is now widely available although not all bottled water is mineral water; most are simply purified water from an urban supply. Buy from a shop or stall, check the seal carefully and avoid street hawkers; when disposing bottles puncture the neck which prevents misuse but allows recycling.

There is growing concern over the mountains of plastic bottles that are collecting and the waste of resources needed to produce them, so travellers are being encouraged to carry their own bottles and take a portable water filter. It is important to use pure water for cleaning teeth.

Tea and **coffee** are safe and widely available. Both are normally served sweet, and with milk. If you wish, say 'no sugar' (*chini nahin*), 'no milk' (*dudh nahin*) when ordering. Alternatively, ask for a pot of tea and milk and sugar to be brought separately. Freshly brewed coffee is a common drink in South India, but in the North, ordinary city restaurants will usually serve the instant variety. Even in aspiring smart cafés, espresso or cappuccino may not turn out quite as you'd expect in the West.

Bottled **soft drinks** such as Coke, Pepsi, Teem, Limca and Thums Up are universally available but always check the seal when you buy from a street stall. There are also several brands of fruit juice sold in cartons, including mango, pineapple and apple – Indian brands are very sweet. Don't add ice cubes as the water source may be contaminated. Take care with fresh fruit juices or *lassis* as ice is often added.

Indians rarely drink **alcohol** with a meal. In the past wines and spirits were generally either imported and extremely expensive, or local and of poor quality. Now, the best Indian whisky, rum and brandy (IMFL or 'Indian Made Foreign Liquor') are widely accepted, as are good Champagnoise and other wines from Maharashtra. If you hanker after a bottle of imported wine, you will only find it in the top restaurants or specialist liquor stores for at least Rs 1000.

For the urban elite, refreshing Indian beers are popular when eating out and so are widely available. 'Pubs' have sprung up in the major cities. Elsewhere, seedy, all-male drinking dens in the larger cities are best avoided for women travellers, but can make quite an experience otherwise – you will sometimes be locked into cubicles for clandestine drinking. If that sounds unsavoury then head for the better hotel bars instead; prices aren't that steep. In rural India, local rice, palm, cashew or date juice *toddy* and *arak* is deceptively potent.

Most states have alcohol-free dry days or enforce degrees of Prohibition. Some upmarket restaurants may serve beer even if it's not listed, so it's worth asking. In some states there are government approved wine shops where you buy your alcohol through a metal grille. For information on liquor permits, see page 32.

Festivals in South India

India has a wealth of festivals with many celebrated nationwide, while others are specific to a particular state or community or even a particular temple. Many fall on different dates each year depending on the Hindu lunar calendar; there's an amazingly thorough calendar of upcoming major and minor festivals at www.drikpanchang.com.

The Hindu calendar
Hindus follow two distinct eras: The *Vikrama Samvat* which began in 57 BC and the *Salivahan Saka* which dates from AD 78 and has been the official Indian calendar since 1957. The *Saka* new year starts on 22 March and has the same length as the Gregorian calendar. The 29½-day lunar month with its 'dark' and 'bright' halves based on the new and full moons, are named after 12 constellations, and total a 354-day year. The calendar cleverly has an extra month (*adhik maas*) every 2½ to

three years, to bring it in line with the solar year of 365 days coinciding with the Gregorian calendar of the West.

Some major national and regional festivals are listed below. A few count as national holidays: **26 January**: Republic Day; **15 August**: Independence Day; **2 October**: Mahatma Gandhi's Birthday; **25 December**: Christmas Day.

Jan New Year's Day (1 Jan) is accepted officially when following the Gregorian calendar but there are regional variations which fall on different dates, often coinciding with spring/harvest time in Mar and Apr. **Makar Sankranti** (14 Jan), marks the end of winter and is celebrated with kite flying. In the south, particularly Tamil Nadu, this date marks the 4-day festival of **Pongal**, when houses are decorated with colourful *kolam* designs and cows are worshipped to promote a good harvest.

Feb Vasant Panchami, the spring festival when people wear bright yellow clothes to mark the advent of the season with singing, dancing and feasting.

Feb-Mar Maha Sivaratri marks the night when Siva danced his celestial dance of destruction (*Tandava*), which is celebrated with feasting and fairs at Siva temples, but preceded by a night of devotional readings and hymn singing.

Mar Holi, the festival of colours, marks the climax of spring. The previous night bonfires are lit symbolizing the end of winter (and conquering of evil). People have fun throwing coloured powder and water at each other and in the evening some gamble with friends. If you don't mind getting covered in colours, you can risk going out but celebrations can sometimes get very rowdy (and unpleasant). Some worship Krishna who defeated the demon Putana.

Apr/May Kerala's *pooram* season reaches full swing, with elephant parades, fireworks and cacophonous drumming in honour of the goddess Kali. **Buddha**

Jayanti, the 1st full moon night in Apr/May marks the birth of the Buddha.

Jul/Aug Raksha (or Rakhi) Bandhan symbolizes the bond between brother and sister, celebrated at full moon. A sister says special prayers for her brother and ties coloured threads around his wrist to remind him of the special bond. He in turn gives a gift and promises to protect and care for her. Sometimes *rakshas* are exchanged as a mark of friendship. **Narial Purnima** on the same full moon. Hindus make offerings of *narial* (coconuts) to the Vedic god Varuna (Lord of the waters) by throwing them into the sea. **Independence Day** (15 Aug), is a national secular holiday marked by special events.

Aug/Sep Ganesh Chaturthi was established just over 100 years ago by the Indian nationalist leader Lokmanya Tilak. The elephant-headed God of good omen is shown special reverence. On the last of the 5-day festival after harvest, clay images of Ganesh are taken in procession with dancers and musicians, and are immersed in the sea, river or pond. Kerala celebrates the 10-day harvest festival of **Onam** with processions, snake boat races and sumptuous feasts.

Janmashtami, the birth of Krishna, is celebrated at midnight at Krishna temples.

Sep/Oct Dasara has many local variations. Celebrations for the 9 nights (*navaratri*) are marked with **Ramlila**, various episodes of the Ramayana story are enacted with particular reference to the battle between the forces of good and evil. In some parts of India it celebrates *Rama*'s victory over the Demon king *Ravana* of Lanka with the help of loyal *Hanuman* (Monkey). On the 10th day (**Dasara** or **Dussehra**) huge effigies of Ravana made of bamboo and paper are burnt in public open spaces. Mysore has South India's most spectacular Dussehra, with the final day marked by a parade led by caparisoned elephants.

Oct/Nov Gandhi Jayanti (2 Oct), Mahatma Gandhi's birthday, is remembered with prayer meetings and devotional singing.

   Diwali/Deepavali (*Sanskrit ideepa* lamp), the festival of lights. Some Hindus celebrate Krishna's victory over the demon *Narakasura*, some Rama's return after his 14 years' exile in the forest when citizens lit his way with oil lamps. The festival falls on the dark *chaturdasi* (14th) night (the one preceding the new moon), when rows of lamps or candles are lit in remembrance, and *rangolis* are painted on the floor as a sign of welcome. Fireworks have become an integral part of the celebration which are often set off days before Diwali. Equally, Lakshmi, the Goddess of Wealth (as well as Ganesh) is worshipped by merchants and the business community who open the new financial year's account on the day. Most people wear new clothes; some play games of chance.

   Guru Nanak Jayanti commemorates the birth of Guru Nanak. **Akhand Path** (unbroken reading of the holy book) takes place and the book itself (*Guru Granth Sahib*) is taken out in procession.

Dec Christmas Day (25 Dec) sees Indian Christians celebrate the birth of Christ in much the same way as in the West; many churches hold services/mass at midnight, particularly in Goa and the Christian belt of central Kerala. There is an air of festivity in city markets which are specially decorated and illuminated. Over **New Year's Eve** (31 Dec) hotel prices peak and large supplements are added for meals and entertainment in the upper category hotels. Some churches mark the night with a Midnight Mass.

Muslim holy days

These are fixed according to the lunar calendar. According to the Gregorian calendar, they tend to fall 11 days earlier each year, dependent on the sighting of the new moon.

Ramadan, known in India as 'Ramzan', is the start of the month of fasting when all Muslims (except young children, the very elderly, the sick, pregnant women and travellers) must abstain from food and drink, from sunrise to sunset.

Id ul Fitr is the 3-day festival that marks the end of Ramzan.

Id-ul-Zuha/Bakr-Id is when Muslims commemorate Ibrahim's sacrifice of his son according to God's commandment; the main time of pilgrimage to Mecca (the Hajj). It is marked by the sacrifice of a goat, feasting and alms giving.

Muharram is when the killing of the Prophet's grandson, Hussain, is commemorated by Shi'a Muslims. Decorated *tazias* (replicas of the martyr's tomb) are carried in procession by devout wailing followers who beat their chests to express their grief. Lucknow is famous for its grand *tazias*. Shi'as fast for the 10 days.

Responsible travel

As well as respecting local cultural sensitivities, travellers can take a number of simple steps to reduce, or even improve, their impact on the local environment. Environmental concern is relatively new in India. Don't be afraid to pressurize businesses by asking about their policies.

Litter Many travellers think that there is little point in disposing of rubbish properly when the tossing of water bottles, plastic cups and other non-biodegradable items out of train windows is already so widespread. Don't follow an example you feel to be wrong. You can immediately reduce your impact by refusing plastic bags and other excess packaging when shopping – use a small backpack or cloth bag instead – and if you do collect a few, keep them with you to store other rubbish until you get to a litter bin.

Plastic mineral water bottles, an inevitable corollary to poor water hygiene standards, are a major contributor to India's litter mountain. However, many hotels, including nearly all of the upmarket ones, most restaurants and bus and train stations, provide drinking water purified using a combination of ceramic and carbon filters, chlorine and UV irradiation. Ask for *'filter paani'*; if the water tastes like a swimming pool it is probably quite safe to drink, though it's best to introduce your body gradually to the new water. If purifying water yourself, bringing it to a boil at sea level will make it safe, but at altitude you have to boil it for longer to ensure that all the microbes are killed. Various sterilizing methods can be used that contain chlorine or iodine and there are a number of mechanical or chemical water filters available on the market.

Bucket baths or showers The biggest issue relating to responsible and sustainable tourism is water – particularly relevant in arid areas such as the Deccan plateau where a poor monsoon can result in severe drought. The traditional Indian 'bucket bath', in which you wet, soap then rinse off using a small hand-held plastic jug dipped into a large bucket, uses on average around 15 litres of water, as compared to 30-45 for a shower. These are commonly offered except in four- and five-star hotels.

Support responsible tourism Spending your money carefully can have a positive impact. Sleeping, eating and shopping at small, locally owned businesses directly supports communities, while specific community tourism concerns, such as those operated by **Be The Local** ① *Mumbai, www.bethelocaltoursandtravels.com*, **The Blue Yonder** ① *north Kerala, www.theblueyonder.com*, and the **Ex-Vayana Bark Collectors Eco Development Commitee** ① *Periyar Tiger Reserve, www.periyartigerreserve.com*, provide an economic motivation for people to stay in remote communities, protect natural areas and revive traditional cultures, rather than exploit the environment or move to the cities for work.

Transport Choose walking, cycling or public transport over fuel-guzzling cars and motorbikes and travel by train rather than plane wherever possible.

Essentials A-Z

Accident and emergency

Contact the relevant emergency service (police T100, fire T101, ambulance T102) and your embassy. Make sure you obtain police/medical reports required for insurance claims.

Customs and duty free

Duty free

Tourists are allowed to bring in all personal effects 'which may reasonably be required' without charge. The official customs allowance includes 200 cigarettes or 50 cigars, 0.95 litres of alcohol, a camera and a pair of binoculars. Valuable personal items and professional equipment including jewellery, special camera equipment and lenses, laptop computers and sound and video recorders must in theory be declared on a **Tourist Baggage Re-Export Form (TBRE)** in order for them to be taken out of the country, though in practice it's relatively unlikely that your bags will be inspected beyond a cursory X-ray. Nevertheless, it saves considerable frustration if you know the equipment serial numbers in advance and are ready to show them on the equipment. In addition to the forms, details of imported equipment may be entered into your passport. Save time by completing the formalities while waiting for your baggage. It is essential to keep these forms for showing to the customs when leaving India, otherwise considerable delays are very likely at the time of departure.

Prohibited items

The import of live plants, gold coins, gold and silver bullion and silver coins not in current use are either banned or subject to strict regulation. Enquire at consular offices abroad for details.

Drugs

Be aware that the government takes the misuse of drugs very seriously. Anyone charged with the illegal possession of drugs risks facing a fine of Rs 100,000 and a minimum 10 years' imprisonment. Several foreigners have been imprisoned for drugs-related offences in the last decade.

Electricity

India's supply is 220-240 volts AC. Some top hotels have transformers. There may be pronounced variations in the voltage, and power cuts are common. Power back-up by generator or inverter is becoming more widespread, even in humble hotels, though it may not cover a/c. Socket sizes vary so take a universal adaptor; low-quality versions are available locally. Many hotels, even in the higher categories, don't have electric razor sockets. Invest in a stabilizer for a laptop.

Embassies and consulates

For information on visas and immigration, see page 31. For a comprehensive list of embassies (but not all consulates), see http://india. gov.in/overseas/indian_missions.php or http://embassy.goabroad.com. Many embassies around the world are now outsourcing the visa process which might affect how long the process takes.

Health

Local populations in India are exposed to a range of health risks not encountered in the Western world. Many of the diseases cause major problems for the local poor and destitute and, although the risks to travellers is more remote, they cannot be ignored. Obviously 5-star travel is going to carry less risk than backpacking on a budget.

Health care in the region is varied. There are many excellent private and government clinics/hospitals. As with all medical care, first impressions count. It's worth contacting your embassy or consulate on arrival and asking where the recommended clinics are (ie those used by diplomats). You can also ask about locally recommended medical dos and don'ts. If you do get ill, and you have the opportunity, you should also ask your medical insurer whether they are satisfied that the medical centre/hospital you have been referred to is of a suitable standard.

Before you go

Ideally, you should see your GP or travel clinic at least 6 weeks before your departure for general advice on travel risks, malaria and vaccinations. Make sure you have travel insurance, get a dental check (especially if you are going to be away for more than a month), know your own blood group and if you suffer a long-term condition such as diabetes or epilepsy make sure someone knows or that you have a Medic Alert bracelet/necklace with this information on it. Remember that it is risky to buy medicinal tablets abroad because the

doses may differ and India has a huge trade in counterfeit drugs.

Vaccinations

If you need vaccinations, see your doctor well in advance of your travel. Most courses must be completed by a minimum of 4 weeks. Travel clinics may provide rapid courses of vaccination, but are likely to be more expensive. The following vaccinations are recommended: typhoid, polio, tetanus, infectious hepatitis and diphtheria. For details of malaria prevention, contact your GP or local travel clinic.

The following vaccinations may also be considered: rabies, possibly BCG (since TB is still common in the region) and in some cases meningitis and diphtheria (if you're staying in the country for a long time). Yellow fever is not required in India but you may be asked to show a certificate if you have travelled from Africa or South America. Japanese encephalitis may be required for rural travel at certain times of the year (mainly rainy seasons). An effective oral cholera vaccine (Dukoral) is now available as 2 doses providing 3 months' protection.

Websites

Blood Care Foundation (UK), www.bloodcare.org.uk A Kent-based charity 'dedicated to the provision of screened blood and resuscitation fluids in countries where these are not readily available'. They will dispatch certified non-infected blood of the right type to your hospital/clinic. The blood is flown in from various centres around the world.
British Travel Health Association (UK), www.btha.org This is the official website of an organization of travel health professionals.

Fit for Travel, www.fitfortravel.scot. nhs.uk This site from Scotland provides a quick A-Z of vaccine and travel health advice requirements for each country.
Foreign and Commonwealth Office (FCO) (UK), www.fco.gov.uk This is a key travel advice site, with useful information on the country, people, climate and lists the UK embassies/ consulates. The site also promotes the concept of 'know before you go' and encourages travel insurance and appropriate travel health advice. It has links to Department of Health travel advice site.
The Health Protection Agency, www. hpa.org.uk Up-to-date malaria advice guidelines for travel around the world. It gives specific advice about the right drugs for each location. It also has useful information for those who are pregnant, suffering from epilepsy or planning to travel with children.
Medic Alert (UK), www.medicalalert. com This is the website of the foundation that produces bracelets and necklaces for those with existing medical problems. Once you have ordered your bracelet/necklace you write your key medical details on paper inside it, so that if you collapse, a medic can identify you as having epilepsy or a nut allergy, etc.
Travel Screening Services (UK), www.travelscreening.co.uk A private clinic dedicated to integrated travel health. The clinic gives vaccine, travel health advice, email and SMS text vaccine reminders and screens returned travellers for tropical diseases.
World Health Organization, www. who.int The WHO site has links to the *WHO Blue Book* on travel advice. This lists the diseases in different regions of the world. It describes vaccination schedules and makes clear which countries have yellow fever vaccination certificate requirements and malarial risk.

Books

International Travel and Health, World Health Organization Geneva.
Lankester, T, *The Travellers Good Health Guide.*
Warrell, D and Anderson, A (eds), *Expedition Medicine (The Royal Geographic Society).*
Young Pelton, R, Aral, C and Dulles, W, *The World's Most Dangerous Places.*

Language → See also page 574.

Hindi, spoken as a mother tongue by over 400 million people, is India's official language, but in the South it is only widely spoken in Mumbai, Maharashtra and Goa. The regional languages you'll come across in South India are mostly from the Dravidian family, with Telugu spoken by 8.2% of Indians (mainly in Andhra Pradesh), Tamil (Tamil Nadu, 7%), Kannada (Karnataka, 4.2%) and Malayalam (Kerala, 3.5%). Of the Indo-Aryan languages, Marathi (Maharashtra, 8%) and Urdu (Hindi's almost-identical twin, spoken by Muslims throughout the country) are the most common, with Konkani spoken only in Goa and coastal Maharashtra.

Owing to India's linguistic diversity, English is also enshrined in the Constitution for a wide range of official purposes, notably communication between Hindi and non-Hindi speaking states. It is widely spoken in towns and cities and even in quite remote villages it is usually not difficult to find someone who speaks at least a little English. Outside of major tourist sites, other European languages are almost completely unknown. The accent in which English is spoken is often affected strongly by the mother tongue of the speaker and there have been changes in common grammar which sometimes make it sound unusual. Many of these changes have become standard Indian English usage, as valid as any other varieties of English used around the world. It is possible to study a number of Indian languages at language centres.

Money → *Up-to-the-minute currency rates can be found on www.xe-com.*

Indian currency is the Indian Rupee (Re/Rs). It is **not** possible to purchase these before you arrive. If you want cash on arrival it is best to get it at the airport bank, although see if an ATM is available as airport rates are not very generous. Rupee notes are printed in denominations of Rs 1000, 500, 100, 50, 20, 10. The rupee is divided into 100 paise. Coins are minted in denominations of Rs 10, 5, Rs 2, Rs 1 and (the increasingly uncommon) 50 paise. **Note** Carry money, mostly as TCs or currency card, in a money belt worn under clothing. Have a small amount in an easily accessible place.

Currency cards

If you don't want to carry lots of cash, prepaid currency cards allow you to preload money from your bank account, fixed at the day's exchange rate. They look like a credit or debit card and are issued by specialist money changing companies, such as **Travelex** and **Caxton FX**. You can top up and check your balance by phone, online and sometimes by text.

Traveller's cheques (TCs)

TCs issued by reputable companies (eg **Thomas Cook**, **American Express**) are widely accepted. They can be easily exchanged at small local travel agents and tourist internet cafés but are rarely used directly for payment. Try to avoid changing at banks, where the process can be time consuming; opt for hotels and agents instead, take large denomination cheques and change enough to last for some days.

Credit cards

Major credit cards are increasingly accepted in the main centres, though in smaller cities and towns it is still rare to be able to pay by credit card. Payment by credit card can sometimes be more expensive than payment by cash, whilst some credit card companies charge a premium on cash withdrawals. **Visa** and **MasterCard** have an ever-growing number of ATMs in major cities and several banks offer withdrawal facilities for Cirrus and Maestro cardholders. It is however easy to obtain a cash advance against a credit card. Railway reservation centres in major cities take payment for train tickets by Visa card which can be very quick as the queue is short, although they cannot be used for Tourist Quota tickets.

ATMs

By far the most convenient method of accessing money, ATMs are all over India, usually attended by security guards, with most banks offering some services to holders of overseas cards. Banks whose ATMs will issue cash against Cirrus and Maestro cards, as well as Visa and MasterCard, include **Bank of Baroda**, **Citibank**, **HDFC**, **HSBC**, **ICICI**, **IDBI**, **Punjab National Bank**, **State Bank of India (SBI)**, **Standard Chartered** and **UTI**. A withdrawal fee is usually charged by the issuing bank on top of the conversion charges applied by your own bank. Fraud prevention measures quite often result in travellers having their cards blocked by the bank when unexpected overseas transactions occur; advise your bank of your travel plans before leaving.

Changing money

The **State Bank of India** and several others in major towns are authorized to deal in foreign exchange. Some give cash against Visa/MasterCard (eg **ANZ**). American Express cardholders can use their cards to get either cash or TCs in Mumbai. The larger cities have licensed money changers with offices usually in the commercial sector. Changing money through unauthorized dealers is illegal. Premiums on the currency black market are very small and highly risky. Large hotels change money 24 hrs a day for guests, but banks often give a substantially better rate of exchange. It is best to exchange money on arrival at the airport bank or the Thomas Cook counter. Many international flights arrive during the night and it is generally far easier and less time consuming to change money at the airport than in the city. You should be given a foreign currency encashment certificate when you change money through a bank or authorized dealer; ask for one if it is not automatically given. It allows you to change Indian rupees back to your own currency on departure. It also enables you to use rupees to pay hotel bills or buy air tickets for which payment in foreign exchange may be required. The certificates are only valid for 3 months.

Cost of living

The cost of living in India remains well below that in the West. The average wage per capita is about Rs 68,700 per year (US$1200). Manual, unskilled labourers (women are often paid less than men), farmers and others in rural areas earn considerably less. However, thanks to booming global demand for workers who can provide cheaper IT and technology support functions and many Western firms transferring office functions or call centres to India, salaries in certain sectors have sky rocketed. An IT specialist can earn an average Rs 500,000 per year and upwards – a rate that is rising by around 15% a year.

Cost of travelling

Most food, accommodation and public transport, especially rail and bus, is exceptionally cheap, although the price of basic food items such as rice, lentils, tomatoes and onions have skyrocketed. There is a widening range of moderately priced but clean hotels and restaurants outside the big cities, making it possible to get a great deal for your money. Budget travellers sharing a room, taking public transport, avoiding souvenir stalls, and eating nothing but rice and dhal can get away with a budget of Rs 400-600 (about about US$7-11 or £6-7) a day. This sum leaps up if you drink alcohol (still cheap by European standards at about US$2, £1 or Rs 80 for a pint), smoke foreign-brand cigarettes or want to have your own wheels (you can expect to spend between Rs 150 and 300 to hire a scooter per day). Those planning to stay in fairly comfortable hotels and use taxis sightseeing should budget at US$50-80 (£30-50) a day. Then again you could always check into the **Falaknuma Palace** for Christmas and notch up an impressive US$600 (£350) bill on your B&B alone. India can be a great place to pick and choose, save a little on basic accommodation and then treat yourself to the type of meal you could only dream of affording back home. Also, be prepared to spend a fair amount more in Mumbai, where not only is the cost of living significantly higher but where it's worth coughing up extra for a half-decent room: penny-pinch in places like Hampi where, you'll be spending precious little time indoors anyway. A newspaper costs Rs 5 and breakfast for two with coffee can come to as little as Rs 100 in a basic 'hotel', but if you intend to eat banana pancakes or pasta in a backpacker restaurant, you can expect to pay more like Rs 100-150 a plate.

Opening hours

Banks are open Mon-Fri 1030-1430, Sat 1030-1230. Top hotels sometimes have a 24-hr money changing service. **Government offices** open Mon-Fri 0930-1700, Sat 0930-1300 (some open on alternate Sat only). **Post offices** open Mon-Fri 1000-1700, often shutting for lunch, and Sat mornings. **Shops** open Mon-Sat 0930-1800. Bazars keep longer hours.

Safety

Personal security

In general the threats to personal security for travellers in India are remarkably small. However, incidents of petty theft and violence directed specifically at tourists have been on the increase so care is necessary in some places, and basic common sense needs to be used with respect to looking after valuables. Follow the same precautions you would when at home. There have been much-reported incidents of severe sexual assault in Delhi, Kolkata and some more rural areas in the last few years. Avoid wandering alone outdoors late at night in these places. During daylight hours be careful in remote places, especially when alone. If you are under threat, scream loudly. Be cautious before accepting food or drink from casual acquaintances, as it may be drugged – though note that Indians on a long train journey will invariably try to share their snacks with you, and balance caution with the opportunity to interact.

The left-wing Maoist extremist Naxalites are active in east central India. They have a long history of conflict with state and national authorities, including attacks on police and government officials. The Naxalites have not specifically targeted Westerners, but have attacked symbolic targets including Western companies. As a general rule, travellers are advised to be vigilant in the lead up to and on days of national significance, such as Republic Day (26 Jan) and Independence Day (15 Aug) as militants have in the past used such occasions to mount attacks.

Following a major explosion on the Delhi to Lahore (Pakistan) train in Feb 2007 and the Mumbai attacks in Nov 2008, increased security has been implemented on many trains and stations. Similar measures at airports may cause delays for passengers so factor this into your timing. Also check your airline's website for up-to-date information on luggage restrictions.

That said, in the great majority of places visited by tourists, violent crime and personal attacks are extremely rare.

Travel advice

It is better to seek advice from your consulate than from travel agencies. Before you travel you can contact: **British Foreign & Commonwealth Office Travel Advice Unit**, T0845-850 2829, www.fco.gov.uk. **US State**

Department's **Bureau of Consular Affairs**, Overseas Citizens Services, Room 4800, Department of State, Washington, DC 20520-4818, USA, T202-647 1488, www.travel.state.gov. **Australian Department of Foreign Affairs Canberra**, Australia, T02-6261 3305, www.smartraveller.gov.au. Canadian official advice is on www.voyage.gc.ca.

Theft

Theft is not uncommon. It is best to keep TCs, passports and valuables with you at all times. Don't regard hotel rooms as being automatically safe; even hotel safes don't guarantee secure storage. Avoid leaving valuables near open windows even when you are in the room. Use your own padlock in a budget hotel when you go out. Pickpockets and other thieves operate in the big cities. Crowded areas are particularly high risk. Take special care of your belongings when getting on or off public transport.

If you have items stolen, they should be reported to the police as soon as possible. Keep a separate record of vital documents, including passport details and numbers of TCs. Larger hotels will be able to assist in contacting and dealing with the police. Dealings with the police can be very difficult and in the worst regions, such as Bihar, even dangerous. The paperwork involved in reporting losses can be time consuming and irritating and your own documentation (eg passport and visas) may be demanded.

In some states the police occasionally demand bribes, though you should not assume that if procedures move slowly you are automatically being expected to offer a bribe. The traffic police are tightening up on traffic offences in some places. They have the right to make on-the-spot fines for speeding and illegal parking. If you face a fine, insist on a receipt. If you have to go to a police station, try to take someone with you.

If you face really serious problems (eg in connection with a driving accident), contact your consular office as quickly as possible. You should ensure you always have your international driving licence and motorbike or car documentation with you.

Confidence tricksters are particularly common where people are on the move, notably around railway stations or places where budget tourists gather. A common plea is some sudden and desperate calamity; sometimes a letter will be produced in English to back up the claim. The demands are likely to increase sharply if sympathy is shown.

Telephone

The international code for India is +91. International Direct Dialling is widely available in privately run call booths, usually labelled on yellow boards with the letters 'PCO-STD-ISD'. You dial the call yourself, and the time and cost are displayed on a computer screen. Cheap rate (2100-0600) means long queues may form outside booths. Telephone calls from hotels are usually more expensive (check price before calling), though some will allow local calls free of charge. Internet phone booths, usually associated with cybercafés, are the cheapest way of calling overseas.

A double ring repeated regularly means it is ringing; equal tones with equal pauses means engaged (similar to the UK). If calling a mobile, rather than ringing, you might hear music while you wait for an answer.

One disadvantage of the tremendous pace of the telecommunications revolution is the fact that millions of telephone numbers go out of date every year. Current telephone directories themselves are often out of date and some of the numbers given in this book will have been changed even as we go to press. Our best advice is if the number in the text does not work, add a '2'. **Directory enquiries**, T197, can be helpful but works only for the local area code.

Mobile phones are for sale everywhere, as are local SIM cards that allow you to make calls within India and overseas at much lower rates than using a 'roaming' service from your normal provider at home – sometimes for as little as Rs 0.5 per min. Arguably the best service is provided by the government carrier **BSNL/MTNL** but security provisions make connecting to the service virtually impossible for foreigners. Private companies such as **Airtel**, **Vodafone**, **Reliance** and **Tata Indicom** are easier to sign up with, but the deals they offer can be befuddling and are frequently changed. To connect you'll need to complete a form, have a local address or receipt showing the address of your hotel, and present photocopies of your passport and visa plus 2 passport photos to an authorized reseller – most phone dealers will be able to help, and can also sell top-up. **Univercell**, www.univercell.in, and **The Mobile Store**, www.themobilestore. in, are a few widespread and efficient chains selling phones and Sim cards.

India is divided into a number of 'calling circles' or regions, and if you travel outside the region where your connection is based, you will pay higher 'roaming' charges for making and receiving calls, and any problems that may occur – with 'unverified' documents, for example – can be much harder to resolve.

Time

India doesn't change its clocks, so from the last Sun in Oct to the last Sun in Mar the time is GMT +5½ hrs, and the rest of the year it's +4½ hrs (USA, EST +10½ and +9½ hrs; Australia, EST -5½ and -4½ hrs).

Tipping

A tip of Rs 10 to a bellboy carrying luggage in a modest hotel (Rs 20 in a higher category) would be appropriate. In upmarket restaurants, a 10% tip is acceptable when service is not already included, while in places serving very cheap meals, round off the bill with small change. Indians don't normally tip taxi drivers but a small extra is welcomed. Porters at airports and railway stations often have a fixed rate displayed but will usually press for more. Ask fellow passengers what a fair rate is.

Tour operators

UK
Ace Study Tours, T01223-841055, www.acestudytours.co.uk. Expert-led cultural study tours.
Adventure Company, Cross and Pillory House, Cross and Pillory Lane, Alton, GU34 1HL, T0808-250 7088, www. adventurecompany.co.uk. Adventure tours, small groups.
Asian Explorations, Afex House, Holwell, Burford, Oxfordshire, OX18 4JS, T01367-850566, www.asianexplorations. com. Bespoke holidays, including to the Andaman Islands and Rajasthan.
Colours Of India, Marlborough House, 298 Regent's Park Rd, London, N3 2TJ, T020-8347 4020, www.partnershiptravel. co.uk. Tailor-made cultural, adventure, spa and cooking tours.

Cox & Kings (Taj Group), T020-7873 5000, www.coxandkings.co.uk.
Dragoman, T01728-861133, www.dragoman.com. Overland, adventure, camping.
Exodus, T0845-867 5585, www.exodus. co.uk. Small group overland and trekking tours.
Greaves Tours, 53 Welbeck St, London, T020-7487 9111, www.greavesindia. com. Luxury, tailor-made tours using only scheduled flights. Traditional travel such as road and rail preferred to flights between major cities.
Kerala Connections, School House Lane, Horsmonden, Kent, TN12 8BP, T01892-722440, www.keralaconnections.co.uk. Excellent tailor-made tours specializing in South India, including Lakshadweep, with great homestays.
Kerala Vacations, Roper Rd, Canterbury, CT7 7EX, T07931-104010, www.kerala vacations.com. Individually designed holidays to South India.
MAHout, The Manor, Manor Rd, Banbury, T01295-758 150, www.mahoutuk.com. Boutique hotels representation specialist.
Master Travel, T020-7501 6742, www. mastertravel.co.uk. History, Ayurveda.
On the Go Tours, 68 North End Rd, London, W14 9EP, T020-7371 1113, www.

onthegotours.com. Legendary tours and tailor-made itineraries at amazing prices.
Pettitts, T01892-515966, www.pettitts. co.uk. Unusual locations.
STA Travel, T0871-230 0040, www.sta travel.co.uk. Student and young persons' travel agent.
Steppes Discovery, The Travel House, 51 Castle St, Cirencester, GL7 1QD, T01285-643333, www.steppesdiscovery. co.uk. Wildlife safaris, tiger study tours and cultural tours with strong conservation ethic.
Trans Indus, 75 St Mary's Rd and the Old Fire Station, Ealing, London, W5 5RH, T0844 879 3960, www.transindus. com. Upmarket India travel specialists offering tailor-made and group tours and holidays. Unusual locations.
Tropical Locations, Welby House, 96 Wilton Rd, London, SW1V 1DW, T0845-277 3310, www.tropical-locations.com. Specialist tour company covering India and the Indian Ocean.

India
Banyan Tours and Travels, www. banyantours.com. Pan-Indian operator specializing in bespoke, upmarket travel, with strength in culture, heritage, adventure and wildlife.

The Blue Yonder, 23-24 Sri Guru Nivas, 2nd floor, No 6, Amar Jyoti Layout, Nagashetty Halli, Sanjay Nagar, Bengaluru, T080-4115 2218, www.theblueyonder.com. Highly regarded and award-winning sustainable and community tourism operators, active in Kerala, Sikkim, Orissa and Rajasthan.

Ibex Expeditions, 30 Community Centre, East of Kailash, New Delhi 110065, T011-2646 0246, www.ibexpeditions.com. Award-winning eco-aware tour operator for tours, safaris and treks.

Indebo India, New Delhi, T011-4716 5500, www.indebo.com. Customized tours and travel-related services throughout India.

Paradise Holidays, 312 Ansals Classique Tower, Rajouri Garden, New Delhi, T011-4552 0735, www.paradiseholidays.com. Wide range of tailor-made tours, from cultural to wildlife.

Peter and Friends Classic Adventures, Casa Tres Amigos, Assagao, Goa, T0832-226 8467, www.classic-bike-india.com. An Indo-German company which arranges high-octane tours around South India, Rajasthan and the Himalaya and Nepal on Enfield motorbikes.

Pyramid Tours, Bangalore, T080-2286 7589, www.pyramidsdeccan.com.

Academics as guides, conservationists on heritage, nature, culture and rejuvenation packages.

Royal Expeditions Pvt Ltd, New Delhi, T011-2623 8545 (UK T020-8150 6158; USA T1-609-945 2912), www.royalexpeditions.com. Tailor-made tours in culture, wildlife and photography. Specializes in easy options for senior travellers.

Shanti Travel, C-66 Okhla, 2nd floor, Okhla Phase 1, New Delhi 110020, T011-4607 7800, www.shantitravel.com. Tailor-made tours throughout India.

Shoestring, T01306-744797, www.shoestring.com. Group leisure and adventure tours.

Weeks Tour, 'Weeks Wilson', 6/253C, Jewtown, Mattancherry, Kochi-682 002, Kerala, T094-4702 2370, www.weekswilson.in. Tailor-made cultural, arts and nature tours throughout India.

North America
Absolute Asia, New York, T1-212-627 1950, www.absolute asia.com. Luxury custom-designed tours: culinary, pilgrimage of the south, honey-moon, 'Jewish India' tour plus Tamil tour combining Tamil Nadu with Sri Lanka.

Adventures Abroad, T1-800-665 3998, www.adventures-abroad.com.

Alexander and Roberts, T1-800-221-2216, www.alexanderroberts.com. Packages include Kerala spas, houseboats and wildlife, South India and Karnataka, South India and Tamil Nadu, Goa.
Greaves Tours, T1-800-318 7801. See under UK entry, above.
Myths and Mountains, T1-800-670 6984, www.mythsandmountains.com. Culture, crafts and religion.
Original World, T1888-367 6147, www.originalworld.com. General and spirituality-focused tours, local experts.
Sita World Travel, T1-800-421-5643, www.sitatours. com. Top-end packages like 7-day Ayurveda programmes and Trails of South India tour.

Australia and New Zealand
Adventure World, T1300-295049, www.adventureworld.com.au. Independent tour operator with packages from 7 nights in Kerala. Also in Auckland, T+64-9524 5118, www.adventureworld.co.nz.
Classic Oriental Tours, T02-9657 2020, www.classic oriental. com.au. Travel for groups and independent travellers, all standards from budget to deluxe.
India Unbound, T1300-889513, www.india unbound. com.au. Intriguing range of small-group trips and bespoke private tours.
Intrepid Travel, T1300-797010, www.intrepid travel.com. Cookery courses to village stays.
Peregrine Adventures, Australia, T1300-854445, www.peregrine adventures.com. Small group overland and trekking tours.

Continental Europe
Academische Reizen, Amsterdam, T020-589 2940, www.academische reizen.nl. All-India group culture tours.
Chola Voyages, 190, rue du Faubourg St Denis, 75010 Paris, T01-4034 5564, www.cholatravels.fr.
La Maison Des Indes, Paris, T01-5681 3838, www.maisondes indes.com. Bespoke or group cultural tours.

Tourist information

There are **Government of India** tourist offices in the state capitals, as well as state tourist offices (sometimes **Tourism Development Corporations**) in some towns and places of tourist interest. They produce their own tourist literature, either free or sold at a nominal price, and some also have lists of city hotels and paying guest options. The quality of material is improving though maps are often poor. Many offer tours of the city, neighbouring sights and overnight and regional packages. Some run modest hotels and midway motels with restaurants and may also arrange car hire and guides. The staff in the regional and local offices are usually helpful.

Visas and immigration

For embassies and consulates, see page 21. Virtually all foreign nationals, including children, require a visa to enter India. Nationals of Bhutan and Nepal only require a suitable means of identification. The rules regarding visas change frequently and arrangements for application and collection also vary from town to town so it is essential to check details and costs with the relevant embassy or consulate. These remain closed on Indian national holidays. Now many consulates and embassies are outsourcing the visa process, it's best to find out in advance how long it will take. For example, in London where you used to be able to get a visa in person in a morning if you were prepared to queue, it now takes 3-5 working days and involves 2 trips to the office.

At other offices, it can be much easier to apply in advance by post, to avoid queues and frustratingly low visa quotas. Postal applications take 10-15 working days to process.

Visitors from countries with no Indian representation may apply to the resident British representative, or enquire at the **Air India** office. An application on the prescribed form should be accompanied by 2 passport photographs and your passport which should be valid 6 months beyond the period of your visit. Note that visas are valid from the date granted, not from the date of entry.

Tourist visa Normally valid for 3-6 months from date of issue, though some nationalities may be granted visas for up to 5 years. Multiple entries permitted, and it is worth requesting this on the application form if you wish to visit neighbouring countries.

Liquor permits

Periodically some Indian states have tried to enforce prohibition. When applying for your visa you can ask for an All India Liquor Permit. Foreigners can also get the permit from any Government of India Tourist Office in Delhi or the state capitals. Instant permits are issued by some hotels.

Weights and measures

Metric is in universal use in the cities. In remote areas local measures are sometimes used. One lakh is 100,000 and 1 crore is 10 million.

Contents

At a glance

◎ **Getting around** Ride the suburban railway network in Mumbai. Cabs and motor rickshaws are plentiful.

◐ **Time required** Allow 48 hrs for Mumbai.

☀ **Weather** Hot all year, with a heavy monsoon.

✖ **When not to go** Jun and Jul when rainfall is torrential.

Mumbai

Mumbai (Bombay)

Maximum City, the City of Dreams, India's economic capital and melting pot. You can throw epithets and superlatives at Mumbai until the cows come home, but it refuses to be understood on a merely intellectual level. Like London and New York, it's a restless human tapestry of cultures, religions, races, ways of surviving and thriving, and one that evokes palpable emotion; whether you love it or hate it, you can't stay unaffected.

From the cluster of fishing villages first linked together by the British East India Company in 1668, Mumbai has swelled to sprawl across seven islands, which now groan under the needs of 19 million stomachs, souls and egos. Its problems – creaking infrastructure, endemic corruption coupled with bureaucratic incompetence, and an ever-expanding population of whom more than two thirds live in slums – are only matched by the enormous drive that makes it the centre of business, fashion and film-making in modern India, and both a magnet and icon for the country's dreams, and nightmares.

The taxi ride from the airport shows you both sides of the city: slum dwellers selling balloons under billboards of fair-skinned models dripping in gold and reclining on the roof of a Mercedes; the septic stench as you cross Mahim Creek, where bikers park on the soaring bridge to shoot the breeze amid fumes that could drop an elephant; the feeling of diesel permeating your bloodstream and the manically reverberating mantra of *Horn OK Please* as you ooze through traffic past Worli's glitzy shopping malls and the fairytale island mosque of Haji Ali. And finally the magic moment as you swing out on to Chowpatty Beach and the city throws off her cloak of chaos to reveal a neon-painted skyscape that makes you feel like you've arrived at the centre of all things.

Getting there

Chhatrapati Shivaji International Airport is 30 km from Nariman Point, the business heart of the city. The domestic terminals at Santa Cruz are 5 km closer. Pre-paid taxis to the city centre are good value and take 40-90 minutes; buses are cheaper but significantly slower. If you arrive at night without a hotel booking it is best to stay at one of the hotels near the airports. If you're travelling light (and feeling brave), local trains head into the city from Vile Parle (International) and Santa Cruz (Domestic) stations, but these are daunting at any time (passengers leap off while the train is still moving and will 'help' you if you're in their way) and become impossibly crowded during the morning and evening rush hours.

Getting around

The sights are spread out and you need transport. Taxis are metered and good value. Older taxis carry a rate card to convert the meter reading to the correct fare. You can download the rate card in advance from www.hindustantimes.com/farelist, and various fare conversion apps are available for smartphones. There are frequent buses on major routes, and the two suburban railway lines are useful out of peak hours, but get horrendously crowded. Auto-rickshaws are only allowed in the suburbs north of Mahim Creek.

Tourist information

Government of India ⓘ *123 M Karve Rd, opposite Churchgate, T022-2207 4333, Mon-Sat 0830-1730 (closed 2nd Sat of month from 1230); counters open 24 hrs at both airports; Taj Mahal Hotel, Mon-Sat 0830-1530 (closed 2nd Sat from 1230).* **Maharashtra Tourist Development Corporation (MTDC)** ⓘ *CDO Hutments, Madam Cama Rd, T022-2204 4040, www.maharashtratourism.gov.in; Koh-i-Noor Rd, near Pritam Hotel, Dadar T022-2414 3200; Gateway of India, T022-2284 1877.* Information and booking counters at international and domestic terminals and online.

Background

Hinduism made its mark on Mumbai long before the Portuguese and British transformed it into one of India's great cities. The caves on the island of Elephanta were excavated under the Kalachuris (AD 500-600). Yet, only 350 years ago, the area occupied by this great metropolis comprised seven islands inhabited by Koli fishermen. The British acquired these marshy and malarial islands as part of the marriage dowry paid by the Portuguese when Catherine of Braganza married Charles II in 1661. Four years later, they took possession of the remaining islands and neighbouring mainland area and in 1668 the East India Company leased the whole area from the crown for £10 a year, which was paid for nearly 50 years. The East India Company shifted its headquarters to Mumbai in 1672.

1 Central Mumbai

To ① ② ③ ⑤
① ② ③ ④ ⑦ ⑧ & Airports
Sivaji Park

To Matunga Road, Santa Cruz, Mahim & Vile Parle Stations

To Matunga Station

Mahim Bay

WORLI

Dadar

Wadala

Arabian Sea

Ranade Rd

Gokhale Rd (South)

Senapati Bapat Marg

Dadasaheb Phalke Marg

Dr Babasaheb Ambedkar Rd

Pandurang Budhkar Marg
Elphinstone Road

Parel

Rafi Ahmed Kidwai Rd

Sewri

Khan A G K Marg

Annie Besant Rd

Ganpatrao Kadam Marg
Lower Parel

Dr E Moses Rd

➡ Mumbai maps
1 Central Mumbai, page 36
2 Gateway of India & Colaba, page 39
3 CST, Churchgate & Fort, page 42

⑦

Phoenix Mills

Curry Rd

Dr Ambedkar Rd

Pai Marg (Reay Rd)

Chinchpokli

Cotton Green

Stadium

Dhobi Ghats

Mahalaxmi Race Course

Lala Lajpat Rai Rd

Mahalaxmi

Keshavrao Khade Rd

SG Maharaj Chowk

Dr Babasaheb

M Azad Rd

NM Joshi Rd

Bhau Daji Lad (Victoria & Albert Museum)

Barrister Nath Pai Marg

Reay Road

Haji Ali's Tomb

Mahalaxmi Temple

A/C Market

Tardeo Rd

Mumbai Central

④

Byculla

Victoria Gardens

Sant Savta Marg

B Desai Rd

Tata Garden

⑥

J B Behram Marg

Interstate Bus Terminus

Catholic Cathedral

Dockyard Rd

Breach Candy

Kemp's Corner

Grant Road

PAK

Christ Church

Towers of Silence

L Jagmohandas Rd

Gandhi Museum

Grant Rd (M Saukat Ali Rd)

Jamshedji Boman

Chor Bazar

Babulnath Temple

S Patel Rd

NSC Bose Rd

Charni Road

Sandhurst Road

Frere Rd

Masjid

Hanging Gardens

Ali Saints

Malabar Hill

Walkeshwar Temple

Walkeshwar

Chowpatty Beach

Mangaldas

Raj Bhavan

Taraporewala Aquarium

Marine Lines

Back Bay

Malabar Point

Marine Drive

Mahatma Gandhi Rd

Dr Dadabhai Naoroji Rd

P D Mello Rd

CST

Churchgate

Vir Nariman Rd

Madam Cama Rd

②

Nariman Point

Shahid Bhagat Singh Rd

Gateway of India

③

N

⊙

|—— 1 km
|—— 1 mile

Where to stay 🛏
Juha Residency 1
Leela 2
Orchid 3
Regency 7
Transit 5
YMCA International House 4

World Trade Centre

Tata Institute for Fundamental Research

Backbay Bus Terminus

St John's

Sassoon Dock

Colaba Bus Terminus

Naval Colony

Catholic Church

Dr N M Marg

Observatory

Restaurants 🍴
Gajalee 1
Olive Bar & Kitchen 4
Out of the Blue 2
Pali Village Café 3
Swati Snacks 6

Bars & clubs 🍸
Aurus 7
Bling 8

Isolated by the sharp face of the Western Ghats and the constantly hostile Marathas, Mumbai's early fortunes rested on the shipbuilding yards established by progressive Parsis. It thrived entirely on overseas trade and, in the cosmopolitan city this created, Parsis, Sephardic Jews and the British shared common interests and responded to the same incentives.

After a devastating fire on 17 February 1803, a new town with wider streets was built. Then, with the abolition of the Company's trade monopoly, the doors to rapid expansion were flung open and Mumbai flourished. Trade with England boomed, and under the governorship of Sir Bartle Frere (1862-1869) the city acquired a number of extravagant Indo-Gothic landmarks, most notably the station formerly known as the Victoria Terminus. The opening of the Suez Canal in 1870 gave Mumbai greater proximity to European markets and a decisive advantage over its eastern rival Kolkata. It has since become the headquarters for many national and international companies, and was a natural choice as home to India's stock exchange (BSE). With the sponsorship of the Tata family, Mumbai has also become the primary home of India's nuclear research programme, with its first plutonium extraction plant at Trombay in 1961 and the establishment of the Tata Institute for Fundamental Research, the most prestigious science research institute in the country.

Mumbai is still growing fast, and heavy demand for building space means property value is some of the highest on earth. As in Manhattan, buildings are going upward: residential skyscrapers have mushroomed in the upscale enclaves around Malabar Hill. Meanwhile, the old mill complexes of Lower Parel have been rapidly revived as shopping and luxury apartment complexes. An even more ambitious attempt to ease pressure on the isthmus is the newly minted city of Navi Mumbai, 90 minutes east of the city, which has malls, apartments and industrial parks, but little of the glamour that makes Mumbai such a magnet.

The latest project is the controversial redevelopment of Dharavi, a huge chunk of prime real estate that's currently occupied by Asia's biggest slum – home to one third of Mumbai's population, in desperately squalid makeshift hovels originally designed to house migrant mill workers. In addition, an uncounted number live precariously in unauthorized, hastily rigged and frequently demolished corrugated iron or bamboo-and-tarpaulin shacks beside railways and roads, while yet more sleep in doorways and on sheets across the pavement.

In recent decades, the pressure of supporting so many people has begun to tell on Mumbai. Communal riots between Hindus and Muslims have flared up several times since the destruction by militant Hindus of the Babri Masjid in 1992, and the disastrous 2005 monsoon, which dumped almost a metre of rainfall on the city overnight and left trains stranded with water up to their windows, laid bare the governmental neglect which had allowed drainage and other infrastructure to lag behind the needs of the populace.

The unprecedented attacks of 26 November 2008, when Lashkar-e-Taiba terrorists held staff and foreign guests hostage in the Taj Mahal and Oberoi hotels, have been widely read as a strike against the symbols of India's overseas business ambitions. They further served to illustrate that money cannot buy protection from the harsh realities of Indian life. Yet the citizens did not vent their anger on each other, but at the government that had failed to deal effectively with the attacks. Within weeks the front of the Taj had been scrubbed clean and tourists were packing out the Leopold Café, while CST station emerged from the bullets a cleaner, calmer, less chaotic place. Somehow, whether through economic imperative or a shared mentality of forward thinking, the city always finds a way to bounce back.

Gateway of India and Colaba → *For listings, see pages 50-60.*

The Indo-Saracenic-style Gateway of India (1927), designed by George Wittet to commemorate the visit of George V and Queen Mary in 1911, is modelled in honey-coloured basalt on 16th-century Gujarati work. The great gateway is an archway with halls on each side capable of seating 600 at important receptions. The arch was the point from which the last British regiment left on 28 February 1948, signalling the end of the empire. The whole area has a huge buzz at weekends. Scores of boats depart from here for **Elephanta Island**, creating a sea-swell which young boys delight in diving into. Hawkers, beggars and the general throng of people all add to the atmosphere. A short distance behind the Gateway is an impressive **statue of Shivaji**.

The original red-domed **Taj Mahal Hotel** was almost completely gutted by fire in the aftermath of the 26/11 terrorist attacks, which saw guests and staff of the hotel taken hostage and several killed, but the outside has been swiftly restored to normal and has fully reopened for business. It is worth popping into the Taj for a bite to eat or a drink, or to go to the nightclub with its clientele of well-heeled young Indians. Unfortunately, drug addicts, drunks and prostitutes frequent the area behind the hotel, but you can also find couples and young families taking in the sea air around the Gateway at night.

South of the Gateway of India is the crowded southern section of Shahid (literally 'martyr') Bhagat Singh Marg, or Colaba Causeway, a brilliantly bawdy bazar and the epicentre of Mumbai's tourist scene; you can buy everything from high-end jeans to cheaply made *kurtas* and knock-off leather wallets at the street stalls, and the colourful cast of characters includes Bollywood casting agents, would-be novelists plotting a successor to *Shantaram* in the **Leopold Café** (another bearer of bullet scars from 26/11), and any number of furtive hash sellers. The Afghan Memorial **Church of St John the Baptist** (1847-1858) is at the northern edge of Colaba itself. Early English in style, with a 58-m spire, it was built to commemorate the soldiers who died in the First Afghan War. Fishermen still unload their catch early in the morning at **Sassoon Dock**, the first wet dock in India; photography prohibited. Beyond the church near the tip of the Colaba promontory lie the **Observatory** and **Old European cemetery** in the naval colony (permission needed to enter). Frequent buses ply this route.

Fort → *For listings, see pages 50-60.*

The area stretching north from Colaba to CST (Victoria Terminus) is named after Fort St George, built by the British East India Company in the 1670s and torn down by Governor Bartle Frere in the 1860s. Anchored by the superb Chhatrapati Shivaji Museum to the south and the grassy parkland of Oval Maidan to the west, this area blossomed after 1862, when Sir Bartle Frere became governor (1862-1867). Under

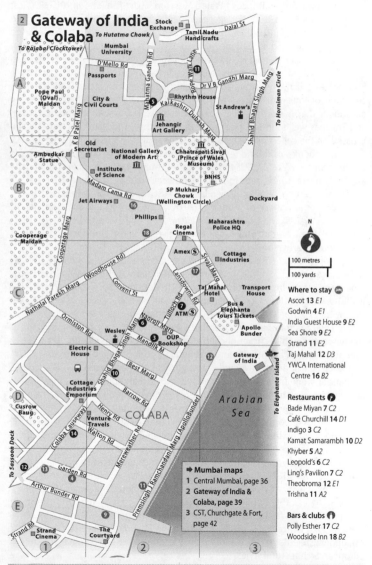

2 Gateway of India & Colaba

To Hutatma Chowk
To Rajabai Clocktower
Stock Exchange
Tamil Nadu Handicrafts
Dalal St
Mumbai University
D'Mello Rd
Passports
Bora Walk Lane
Mahatma Gandhi Rd
Dr V B Gandhi Marg
To Horniman Circle
Shahid Bhagat Singh Marg

A

Pope Paul (Oval) Maidan
City & Civil Courts
Kaikashru Dubash Marg
Rhythm House
St Andrew's
Jehangir Art Gallery

Old Secretariat
National Gallery of Modern Art
Chhatrapati Sivaji (Prince of Wales Museum)
Ambedkar Statue
Institute of Science
BNHS

B

Madam Cama Rd
SP Mukharji Chowk (Wellington Circle)
Dockyard
Jet Airways
Phillips
Regal Cinema
Maharashtra Police HQ

Cooperage Maidan
Cooperage Marg
Amex
Cottage Industries

N
100 metres
100 yards

C

Nathalal Parekh Marg (Woodhouse Rd)
Convent St
Lansdowne Rd
Sivaji Marg
Tulloch Rd
Taj Mahal Hotel
Transport House
Ormiston Rd
Naoroji Marg
Wesley
ATM
Bus & Elephanta Tours Tickets
Apollo Bunder
Electric House
Mandlik M
OUP Bookshop
Shahid Bhagat Singh Marg
(Best Marg)
Gateway of India
To Elephanta Island

D

Cottage Industries Emporium
Barrow Rd
Arabian Sea
Cusrow Baug
Venture Travels
Henry Rd
Colaba Causeway
Merewather Rd
COLABA
Walton Rd
Premsingh J Ramchandani Marg (Apollo Bunder)

E

To Sassoon Dock
Garden Rd
Strand Rd
Arthur Bunder Rd
Strand Cinema
The Courtyard

Where to stay
Ascot **13** *E1*
Godwin **4** *E1*
India Guest House **9** *E2*
Sea Shore **9** *E2*
Strand **11** *E2*
Taj Mahal **12** *D3*
YWCA International Centre **16** *B2*

Restaurants
Bade Miyan **7** *C2*
Café Churchill **14** *D1*
Indigo **3** *C2*
Kamat Samarambh **10** *D2*
Khyber **5** *A2*
Leopold's **6** *C2*
Ling's Pavilion **7** *C2*
Theobroma **12** *E1*
Trishna **11** *A2*

Bars & clubs
Polly Esther **17** *C2*
Woodside Inn **18** *B2*

➡ Mumbai maps
1 Central Mumbai, page 36
2 Gateway of India & Colaba, page 39
3 CST, Churchgate & Fort, page 42

his enthusiastic guidance Mumbai became a great civic centre and an extravaganza of Victorian Gothic architecture, modified by Indo-Saracenic influences. This area is worth exploring at night, when many of the old buildings are floodlit.

Chhatrapati Shivaji (Prince of Wales) Museum ⓘ *Oct-Feb Tue-Sun 1015-1800, last tickets 1645; foreigners Rs 300 (includes audio guide), Indians Rs 15, camera Rs 15 (no flash or tripods), students Rs 10, children Rs 5, avoid Tue as it is busy with school visits*, is housed in an impressive building designed by George Wittet to commemorate the visit of the Prince of Wales to India in 1905. The dome of glazed tiles has a very Persian and Central Asian flavour. The archaeological section has three main groups: Brahminical; Buddhist and Jain; Prehistoric and Foreign. The art section includes an excellent collection of Indian miniatures and well displayed *tankhas* along with a section on armour that is worth seeing. There are also works by Gainsborough, Poussin and Titian as well as Indian silver, jade and tapestries. The Natural History section is based on the collection of the Bombay Natural History Society, founded in 1833. Good guidebooks, cards and reproductions on sale. **Jehangir Art Gallery** ⓘ *within the museum complex, T022-2284 3989*, holds short-term exhibitions of contemporary art. The **Samovar café** is good for a snack and a chilled beer in a pleasant, if cramped, garden-side setting. Temporary members may use the library and attend lectures.

The **National Gallery of Modern Art** ⓘ *Sir Cowasji Jehangir Hall, opposite the museum, T022-2285 2457, foreigners Rs 150, Indians Rs 10*, is a three-tiered gallery converted from an old public hall which gives a good introduction to India's contemporary art scene.

St Andrew's Kirk (1819) ⓘ *just behind the museum, daily 1000-1700*, is a simple neoclassical church. At the south end of Mahatma Gandhi (MG) Road is the renaissance-style **Institute of Science** (1911) designed by George Wittet. The Institute, which includes a scientific library, a public hall and examination halls, was built with gifts from the Parsi and Jewish communities.

The **Oval Maidan** has been restored to a pleasant public garden and acts as the lungs and public cricket pitch of the southern business district. On the east side of the **Pope Paul Maidan** is the Venetian Gothic-style **old Secretariat** (1874), with a façade of arcaded verandas and porticos that are faced in buff-coloured porbander stone from Gujarat. Decorated with red and blue basalt, the carvings are in white *hemnagar* stone. The **University Convocation Hall** (1874) to its north was designed by Sir George Gilbert Scott in a 15th-century French decorated style. Scott also designed the adjacent **University Library** and the **Rajabai clock tower** (1870s) next door, based on Giotto's campanile in Florence. The sculpted figures in niches on the exterior walls of the tower were designed to represent the castes of India. Originally the clock could chime 12 tunes including *Rule Britannia*. The **High Court** (1871-1879), in early English Gothic style, has a 57-m-high central tower flanked by lower octagonal towers topped by the figures of Justice and Mercy. The Venetian Gothic **Public Works Office** (1869-1872) is to its north. Opposite, and with its main façade to Vir Nariman Road, is the gorgeously wrought former **General Post Office** (1869-1872). Now called the Telegraph Office, it stands next to the original Telegraph Office adding romanesque to the extraordinary mixture of European architectural styles.

From here you can walk east and delve into the dense back lanes of the Fort district, crossing the five-way junction of **Hutatma Chowk** ('Martyrs' Corner'), in the centre of which stands the architecturally forgettable but useful landmark of the Flora Fountain (1869). This is an interesting area to explore although there are no particular sights.

Vir Nariman Road cuts through to the elegant tree-shaded oval of **Horniman Circle**, laid out in 1860 and renamed in 1947 after Benjamin Horniman, editor of the pro-independence *Bombay Chronicle* – one of the few English names remaining on the Mumbai map. The park in the middle is used for dance and music performances during the **Kala Ghoda Arts Festival**, held in January. On the west edge are the Venetian Gothic **Elphinstone Buildings** (1870) in brown sandstone, while to the south is the **Cathedral Church of St Thomas** (1718), which contains a number of monuments amounting to a heroic 'Who's Who of India'.

South of Horniman Circle on Shahid Bhagat Singh Marg, the **Custom House** is one of the oldest buildings in the city, believed to incorporate a Portuguese barrack block from 1665. Over the entrance is the crest of the East India Company. Remnants of the old Portuguese fort's walls can be seen and many Malabar teak 'East Indiamen' ships were built here. Walk north from here and you'll reach the **Town Hall** (1820-1823), widely admired and much photographed as one of the best neoclassical buildings in India. The Corinthian interior houses the **Assembly Rooms** and the **Bombay Asiatic Society**. Immediately north again is the **Mint** (1824-1829) ① *visit by prior permission from the Mint Master, T022-2270 3184, www.mumbaimint. org*, built on the Fort rubbish dump, with Ionic columns and a water tank in front of it. The nearby **Ballard Estate** is also worth a poke around while you're in the area, with some good hotels and restaurants, as well as Hamilton Studios, the swanky offices of *Vogue* magazine, and the Mumbai Port Authority.

Around the CST (VT) → *For listings, see pages 50-60.*

Chhatrapati Shivaji Terminus (1878-1887), formerly Victoria Terminus and still known to many elder taxi drivers as 'VT', is far and away the most remarkable example of Victorian Gothic architecture in India. Opened during Queen Victoria's Golden Jubilee year (1887), over three million commuters now swarm through the station daily, though the bustling chaos of old has been reined in somewhat since November 2008's terror attacks, when at least 50 people were shot dead here. Several scenes from *Slumdog Millionaire* were filmed on the suburban platforms at the west end of the station.

The station was built at a time when fierce debate was taking place among British architects working in India as to the most appropriate style to develop to meet the demands of the late 19th-century boom. One view held that the British should restrict themselves to models derived from the best in Western tradition. Others argued that architects should draw on Indian models, trying to bring out the best of Indian tradition and encourage its development. By and large, the former were dominant, but the introduction of Gothic elements allowed a blending of Western

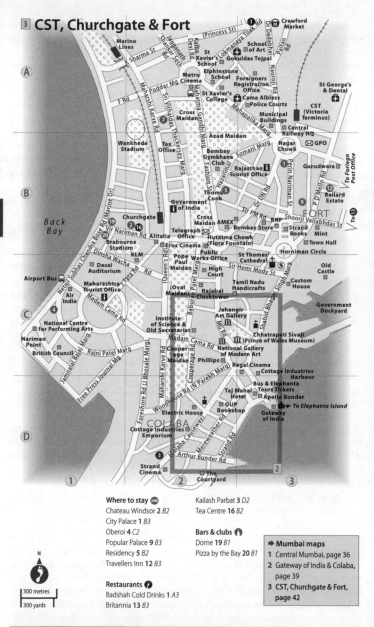

3 CST, Churchgate & Fort

Where to stay 🛏
Chateau Windsor **2** *B2*
City Palace **1** *B3*
Oberoi **4** *C2*
Popular Palace **9** *B3*
Residency **5** *B2*
Travellers Inn **12** *B3*

Kailash Parbat **3** *D2*
Tea Centre **16** *B2*

Bars & clubs 🍸
Dome **19** *B1*
Pizza by the Bay **20** *B1*

Restaurants 🍴
Badshah Cold Drinks **1** *A3*
Britannia **13** *B3*

➡ **Mumbai maps**
1 Central Mumbai, page 36
2 Gateway of India & Colaba, page 39
3 CST, Churchgate & Fort, page 42

N

300 metres
300 yards

traditions with Indian (largely Islamic) motifs, which became known as the Indo-Saracenic style. The station that resulted, designed by FW Stevens, is its crowning glory: a huge, symmetrical, gargoyle-studded frontage capped by a large central dome and a 4-m-high statue of Progress, with arcaded booking halls, stained glass and glazed tiles inspired by St Pancras. The giant caterpillar-like walkway with perspex awnings looks truly incongruous against the huge Gothic structure.

There are many more Victorian buildings in the area around CST, particularly along Mahapalika Marg (Cruickshank Road), which runs northwest of the station past the grand **Municipal Buildings** (also by Stevens, 1893), and Lokmanya Tilak Marg (Camac Road), which joins Mahapalika Marg at the Metro Cinema traffic circle – a landmark known to every Mumbai cabbie.

Immediately to the north of CST lies **Crawford Market** (1865-1871), now renamed **Mahatma Jyotiba Phule Market** after a Maharashtran social reformer, designed by Emerson in 12th-century French Gothic style, with paving stones imported from Caithness and fountains carved by Lockwood Kipling. The market is divided into bustling sections for fruit, vegetables, fish, mutton and poultry, with a large central hall and clock tower.

Running northwest of Crawford Market towards Mumbai Central Railway Station is **Falkland Road**, the centre of Mumbai's red-light district. Prostitutes stand behind barred windows, giving the area its other name, 'The Cages' – many of the girls are sold or abducted from various parts of India and Nepal. AIDS is very widespread, and a lot of NGOs are at work in the area educating the women about prevention.

North of Crawford Market is **Masjid Station**, the heart of the Muslim quarter, where agate minarets mingle with the pollution-streaked upper storeys of 1960s residential towers. The atmosphere here is totally different from the crumbling colonial architectural glory of the Colaba and Fort area: balconies on faded apartment blocks are bedecked with fairy lights, laundry dries on the window grilles, and at sunset the ramshackle roads hum with taxis, boys wielding wooden carts through traffic and Muslim women at a stroll. One of the city's most interesting markets, the **Chor Bazar** (Thieves' Market) ① *Sat to Thu 1100-1900*, spreads through the streets between the station and Falkland Road. The bazar is a great place to poke around in with tonnes of dealers in old watches, film posters, Belgian- or Indian-made temple lamps, enamel tiles and door knobs. The area around Mutton Street is popular with film prop-buyers and foreign and domestic bric-a-brac hunters.

Marine Drive to Malabar Hill → *For listings, see pages 50-60.*

When the hustle of the city becomes too much, do as the Mumbaikars do and head for the water. The 3-km sweep of **Marine Drive** (known as the 'Queen's Necklace' for the lines of streetlights that run its length) skirts alongside the grey waters of the Arabian Sea from Nariman Point in the south to exclusive Malabar Hill in the north. This is where you'll see Mumbai at its most egalitarian: servants and *babus* alike take the air on the esplanades in the evening. For an interesting half-day trip, start downtown at Churchgate Station and follow the curving course of the Queen's Necklace to the

Walkeshwar Temple out on the end of Malabar Hill; start at lunchtime and you can be strolling back down Marine Drive, ice cream in hand, among the atmospheric sunset crush of power-walking executives and festive families.

Churchgate Station (1894-1896), on Vir Nariman Road at the north end of the Oval Maidan, was the second great railway building designed by FW Stevens. With its domes and gables, Churchgate has an air of Byzantine simplicity that contrasts with CST's full-tilt Gothic overload, but the rush hour spectacle is no less striking: Sebastiao Salgado's famous photograph of commuters pouring out of suburban trains was taken here.

A block to the west is Netaji Subhash Road, better known as **Marine Drive**, which bends northwest past Wankhede cricket stadium, several luxury hotels and the run-down Taraporewala Aquarium. At the north end in the crook of Malabar Hill is **Chowpatty Beach**, a long stretch of grey-white sand that looks attractive from a distance, but is polluted. Swimming here is not recommended but there is a lot of interesting beach activity in the evening. Chowpatty was the scene of a number of important 'Quit India' rallies during the Independence Movement. During important festivals, like **Ganesh Chaturthi** and **Dussehra**, it is thronged with jubilant Hindu devotees.

Mahatma Gandhi Museum (Mani Bhavan) ① *west of Grant Rd station at 19 Laburnum Rd, www.gandhi-manibhavan.org, 0930-1800, Rs 10, allow 1 hr*, is north of Chowpatty on the road to Nana Chowk. This private house, where Mahatma Gandhi used to stay on visits to Mumbai, is now a memorial museum and research library with 20,000 volumes. There is a diorama depicting important scenes from Gandhi's life, but the display of photos and letters on the first floor is more interesting, and includes letters Gandhi wrote to Hitler in 1939 asking him not to go to war, and those to Roosevelt, Einstein and Tolstoy.

At the end of Chowpatty, Marine Drive becomes Walkeshwar Road and bends southwest to pass the **Jain Temple** (1904), built of marble and dedicated to the first Jain Tirthankar. Much of the colourful decoration depicts the lives of the Tirthankars. Visitors can watch various rituals being performed. Jains play a prominent part in Mumbai's banking and commerce and are one of the city's wealthiest communities. Beyond, on the tip of Malabar Point, is **Raj Bhavan**, now home to the Governor of Maharashtra.

Behind the Jain Temple, Gangadhar Kher Rd (Ridge Road) runs up Malabar Hill to the **Hanging Gardens (Pherozeshah Mehta Gardens)** so named since they are located on top of a series of tanks that supply water to Mumbai. The gardens are well kept with lots of topiary animals and offer an opportunity to hang out with Mumbai's elite, whose penthouse apartments peer down on the park from all sides; there are good views over the city and Marine Drive from the **Kamala Nehru Park** across the road. It's worth a visit after 1700 when it's a bit cooler, but it's reputed to be unsafe after nightfall. Immediately to the north are the Parsi **Towers of Silence**, set in secluded gardens donated by Parsi industrialist Sir Jamshetji Jeejeebhoy. This very private place is not accessible to tourists but it can be glimpsed from the road. Parsis believe that the elements of water, fire and earth must not be polluted by the dead, so they lay their 'vestments of flesh and bone' out on the top of the towers to be picked clean by vultures. The depletion in the number of vultures is a cause for concern, and more and more agiarys now opt for solar panels to speed up the process of decay.

At the end of the headland behind Raj Bhavan stands the **Walkeshwar Temple** ('Lord of Sand'), built about AD 1000 and one of the oldest buildings in Mumbai. In legend this was a resting point for Lord Rama on his journey from Ayodhya to Lanka to free Sita from the demon king Ravana. One day Rama's brother failed to return from Varanasi at the usual time with a *lingam* that he fetched daily for Rama's worship. Rama then made a *lingam* from the beach sand to worship Siva. You'd also do well to visit **Banganga**, a freshwater tank that's part of an 12th-century temple complex. Legend has it that when Rama got thirsty Lakshman raised his bow and shot a *baan* (arrow) into the ground, bringing forth fresh water from the Ganga in this ocean locked island. The site is being renovated and is regularly used as a venue for concerts, festivals and pilgrimages alike.

Central Mumbai → *For listings, see pages 50-60. See map on page 36.*

Other than to catch a train from Mumbai Central Station, relatively few visitors venture into the area north of Marine Drive, yet it contains some fascinating only-in-Mumbai sights which, with judicious use of taxis and the odd suburban train, can easily be combined into a day trip with the coastal sights described above.

On the coast, 1 km north of the Ghandi Museum on Bhulabhai Desai (Warden Road), are the **Mahalakshmi temples**, the oldest in Mumbai, dedicated to three goddesses whose images were found in the sea. Lakshmi, goddess of wealth, is the unofficial presiding deity of the city, and the temple is host to frenzied activity – pressing a coin into the wall of the main shrine is supposed to be a sign of riches to come. Just to the north, **Haji Ali's Mosque** sits on an islet 500 m offshore. The mosque, built in 1431, contains the tomb of Muslim saint Haji Ali, who drowned here while on pilgrimage to Mecca, and as a last request demanded that he be buried neither on land nor at sea. A long causeway, usable only at low tide, links the mosque and tomb to the land, and is lined by Muslim supplicants. The money changers are willing to exchange one-rupee coins into smaller coins, enabling pilgrims to make several individual gifts to beggars rather than one larger one, thereby reputedly increasing the merit of the gift.

From Haji Ali's Tomb go east along Keshavrao Khade Road, passing the **Mahalakshmi Race Course** ① *racing season Nov-Apr, www.rwitc.com*, to SG Maharaj Chowk (**Jacob's Circle**), and turn north to Mahalakshmi Bridge, reachable by local trains from Churchgate. From the bridge there is a view across the astonishing Municipal **dhobi ghats**, where Mumbai's dirty laundry is soaked, smacked in concrete tubs and aired in public by the *dhobis* (washerfolk); vistas unfold in blocks of primary colours, though you may have to fend off junior touts to enjoy them in peace. A short distance further north are the disused Victorian cotton mills of **Lower Parel**. Closed in 1980 after an all-out strike, some remain standing in a state of picturesque ruin (local residents may offer to show you round for Rs 50-100) while others, notably the Phoenix, Mathuradas and Bombay Dyeing mill compounds, have been converted into slick new malls, nightclubs and studio spaces popular with publishers and advertising agencies.

Southeast of Mahalakshmi station in Byculla are the **Veermata Jijibai Bhonsle Udyan** gardens, formerly Victoria Gardens. The attractive 19-ha park is home to Mumbai's **zoo** ① *Thu-Tue 0900-1800, Rs 5*, be warned though, the signboards are missing and while the birds are gorgeous – they have birds of paradise, white peacocks and pink pelicans among others – there's no indication of what you're looking at. The gardens share space with the newly renovated **Bhau Daji Lad Museum (Victoria and Albert Museum)** ① *www.bdl museum.org, Thu-Tue, 1000-1730, foreigners Rs 100, Indians Rs 10, children half price.* Inspired by the V&A in London and financed by public subscription, it was built in 1872 in a palladian style and is the second oldest museum in India. The collection covers the history of Mumbai and contains prints, maps and models that show how the seven disjointed islands came to form Mumbai.

Bandra, Juhu Beach and Andheri → *For listings, see pages 50-60.*

If you really want to get under the skin of the city, a jaunt into the far-flung northern suburbs is essential. Close to the airports and relatively relaxed compared to living in the city centre, Bandra and Juhu are popular with Mumbai's upper crust, and most Bollywood A-listers have at least one of their homes here. **Bandra** is a lively suburb, full of the young and wealthy, with some exciting places to eat and some of the coolest bars, coffee shops, gyms and lounges in the city. Linking Road is home to a long open-air shoe bazar where you can find cheap, colourful sandals and knock-offs of every brand of clothing. Bandra's two seaside promenades, one at Bandra Bandstand by the Taj Lands End Hotel and one at Carter Road, the next bay northwards, feature sea-facing coffee shops with spectacular sunset views.

Juhu Beach, 20 km north of the centre, used to be an attractive and relaxed seaside area, but one sniff of the toxic water oozing out of Mahim Creek is enough to dissuade anyone from dipping so much as a toe in the ocean. Hordes of people still visit every day to walk on the beach, eat *bhel puri* and other spicy street food that delicate stomachs had best avoid, while kids buy balloons and take rides on horse-driven chariots. Beyond the beach Juhu is primarily a residential area, full of luxurious apartments, elegant old bungalows (Bollywood megastar Amitabh Bachchan has a place here) and day spas.

Andheri, spreading north of the airports, is the biggest suburb in Mumbai: it covers 50 sq km, is home to between 1.5 million and four million people depending on who's counting, and has sprung up from villages and mangrove swamps in a mere 30 years. There are few sights of note, but as a city within a city, with its own social subdivisions (mega-trendy residential enclaves and malls to the west, business parks and down-at-heel slums to the east, and even a suburban monorail system in construction), Andheri may well come to represent Mumbai's second city centre. If you want to explore, the areas to know about are Lokhandwala, New Link Road and Seven Bungalows/Versova; all are in Andheri West.

Ten kilometres east of the Gateway of India, the heavily forested **Elephanta Island**, barely visible in the haze from Mumbai, rises out of the bay like a giant whale. The setting is symbolically significant; the sea is the ocean of life, a world of change (Samsara) in which is set an island of spiritual and physical refuge. The 'caves', excavated over 1000 years ago in the volcanic lava high up the slope of the hill, saw Hindu craftsmen express their view of spiritual truths in massive carvings of extraordinary grace. Sadly a large proportion have been severely damaged, but enough remains to illustrate something of their skill.

Background

The vast majority of India's 1200 **cave sites** were created as temples and monasteries between the third century BC and the 10th century AD. Jain, Buddhist and Hindu caves often stand side by side. The temple cave on Elephanta Island, dedicated to Siva, was probably excavated during the eighth century by the Rashtrakuta Dynasty which ruled the Deccan AD 757-973, though the caves may have had earlier Buddhist origins. An earlier name for the island was Garhapuri ('city of forts') but the Portuguese renamed it after the colossal sculpted elephants when they captured Mumbai from the Sultan of Gujarat in 1535, and stationed a battalion there. They reportedly used the main pillared cave as a shooting gallery causing some of the damage you see. Muslim and British rulers were not blameless either.

Arriving in Elephanta Caves

Boats to Elephanta Island leave every few minutes from 0900, from the jetty in front of the Gateway of India. The crossing takes about an hour. From the landing place, a 300-m unshaded path along the quayside and then about 110 rough steps lead to the caves at a height of 75 m. The walk along the quay can be avoided when the small train functions (Rs 10 return). The climb can be trying for some, especially if it is hot, though *doolies* (chairs carried by porters) are available for Rs 300 return, Rs 200 one-way. At the start of the climb there are stalls selling refreshments, knick-knacks and curios (including models of the Eiffel Tower), but if you're carrying food watch out for aggressive monkeys. **Maharashtra Tourism** normally organizes a festival of classical music and dance on the island in the third week of February. Early morning is the best time for light and also for avoiding large groups with guides which arrive from 1000. The caves tend to be quite dark so carry a powerful torch.

The site

① *Tue-Sun, sunrise to sunset; foreigners Rs 250, Indians Rs 10, plus Rs 5 passenger tax. Weekends are very busy.*

Entrance Originally there were three entrances and 28 pillars at the site. The entrances on the east and west have subsidiary shrines which may have been excavated and used for different ceremonies. The main entrance is now from the north. At dawn, the rising sun casts its rays on the approach to the *garbagriha* (main shrine), housed in a square structure at the west end of the main hall. On your right is a carving of Siva as

Nataraj. On the left he appears as Lakulisa in a much damaged carving. Seated on a lotus, the Buddha-like figure is a symbol of the unconscious mind and enlightenment, found also in Orissan temples where Lakulisa played a prominent role in attempting to attract Buddhists back into Hinduism. From the steps at the entrance you can see the *yoni-lingam*, the symbol of the creative power of the deity.

Main Hall The ribbed columns in the main hall, 5- to 6-m high and in a cruciform layout, are topped by a capital. At the corner of each pillar is a dwarf signifying *gana* (the earth spirit), and sometimes the figure of Ganesh (Ganapati). To the right, the main **Linga Shrine** has four entrances, each corresponding to a cardinal point guarded by a *dvarpala*. The sanctum is bare, drawing attention to the *yonilingam* which the devotee must walk around clockwise.

Wall panels To the north of the main shrine is **Bhairava killing the demon Andhakasura**. This extraordinarily vivid carving shows Siva at his most fearsome, with a necklace of skulls, crushing the power of Andhaka, the Chief of Darkness. It was held that if he was wounded each drop of his blood would create a new demon. So Siva impaled him with his sword and collected his blood with a cup, which he then offered to his wife Shakti. In winter this panel is best seen in the early afternoon.

Opposite, on the south side of the main shrine is the damaged panel of **Kalyan Sundari**, in which Siva stands with Parvati on his right, just before their wedding (normally a Hindu wife stands on her husband's left). She looks down shyly, but her body is drawn to him. Behind Parvati is her father Himalaya and to his left Chandramas, the moon god carrying a gift – *soma*, the food of the gods. On Siva's left is Vishnu and below him Brahma.

At the extreme west end of the temple are **Nataraja** (left) and **Yogisvara Siva** (right). The former shows a beautiful figure of Ganesh above and Parvati on his left. All the other gods watch him. Above his right shoulder is the four-headed God of Creation, Brahma. Below Brahma is the elephant-headed Ganesh.

On the south wall, opposite the entrance are three panels. **Gangadhara** is on the west. The holy River Ganga (Bhagirathi) flowed only in heaven but was brought to earth by her father King Bhagiratha (kneeling at Siva's right foot). Here, Ganga is shown in the centre, flanked by her two tributaries, Yamuna and Saraswati. These three rivers are believed to meet at Allahabad.

To the left of these is the centre piece of the whole temple, the remarkable **Mahesvara**, the Lord of the Universe. Here Siva is five-headed, for the usual triple-headed figure has one face looking into the rock and another on top of his head. Nearly 6 m high, he unites all the functions of creation, preservation and destruction. Some see the head on the left (your right) as representing Vishnu, the Creator, while others suggest that it shows a more feminine aspect of Siva. To his right is Rudra or Bhairava, with snakes in his hair, a skull to represent ageing from which only Siva is free, and he has a look of anger. The central face is Siva as his true self, Siva Swarupa, balancing out creation and destruction. In this mode he is passive and serene, radiating peace and wisdom like the Buddha. His right hand is held up in a calming gesture and in his left hand is a lotus bud.

The panel to the left has the **Ardhanarisvara**. This depicts Siva as the embodiment of male and female, representing wholeness and the harmony of opposites. The female half is relaxed and gentle, the mirror in the hand symbolizing the woman reflecting the man. Siva has his 'vehicle', Nandi on the right.

To the east, opposite the *garbha-griha*, was probably the original entrance. On the south is Siva and Parvati **Playing chaupar on Mount Kailash**. Siva is the faceless figure. Parvati has lost and is sulking but her playful husband persuades her to return to the game. They are surrounded by Nandi, Siva's bull, celestial figures and an ascetic with his begging bowl.

On the north is **Ravana Shaking Mount Kailash** on which Siva is seated. Siva is calm and unperturbed by Ravana's show of brute strength and reassures the frightened Parvati. He pins down Ravana with his toe, who fails to move the mountain and begs Siva's forgiveness which is granted.

Kanheri Caves → *For listings, see pages 50-60.*

Sanjay Gandhi National Park, north of the city at Goregaon, is worth a visit in itself for its dense deciduous and semi-evergreen forest providing a beautiful habitat for several varieties of deer, antelope, butterflies, birds and the occasional leopard. However, the main reason for visiting is for the **Kanheri Caves** situated in the heart of the park.

Some 42 km north of Mumbai, the caves (also known as Mahakali Caves) are on a low hill midway between Borivli and Thane. The hills used to form the central part of Salsette Island, but the surrounding land has long since been extensively built on. Further up the ravine from the caves there are some fine views across the Bassein Fort and out to sea. Still shaded by trees, the entrance is from the south. There are 109 Buddhist caves, dating from the end of the second to the ninth century AD with flights of steps joining them. The most significant is the **Chaitya Cave** (cave 3) circa sixth century. The last Hinayana chaitya hall to be excavated is entered through a forecourt and veranda. The pillared entrance has well carved illustrations of the donors, and the cave itself comprises a 28 m x 13 m colonnaded hall of 34 pillars. At one end these encircle the 5-m-high *dagoba*. Some of the pillars have carvings of elephants and trees. Some 50 m up the ravine is **Darbar of the Maharajah Cave** (Cave 10). This was a *dharamshala* (resthouse) and has two stone benches running down the sides and some cells leading off the left and back walls. Above Cave 10 is **Cave 35** which was a *vihara* (monastery), which has reliefs of a Buddha seated on a lotus and of a disciple spreading his cloak for him to walk on. All the caves have an elaborate drainage and water storage system, fresh rainwater being led into underground storage tanks.

Above the cave complex is **Ashok Van**, a sacred grove of ancient trees, streams and springs. From there, a three-hour trek leads to 'View Point', the highest in Mumbai. There are breathtaking views. Photography is prohibited from the radar station on top of the hill; there are excellent opportunities just below it.

The park is also home to hyena and panther, though rarely seen, while three lakes have ducks, herons and crocodiles. Nature trails lead from Film City (reached by bus from Goregaon station). A lion safari leaves from **Hotel Sanjay** near Borivli station.

For hotel and restaurant price codes and other relevant information, see pages 13-17.

Where to stay

Room prices in Mumbai are stratospheric by Indian standards, and there's no such thing as low-season: if possible make reservations in advance or arrive as early in the day as you can. Most hotels are concentrated in the downtown area, between **Colaba** and **Marine Dr**, and around the airport in the suburbs of **Santa Cruz**, **Juhu**, **Bandra** and **Andheri**. There are also several options around Mumbai Central and Dadar stations – handy for a quick getaway or an un-touristy view of the city.

Backpackers usually head for the **Colaba** area, which has some of the cheapest rooms in the city. **Arthur Bunder Rd** is a hotspot, with several places hidden away on upper floors of apartment blocks, usually with shared facilities, cold water and sometimes windowless rooms; arrive early and inspect room first. For a more personal view of the city, consider staying in a private home: browse the listings on **Airbnb** (www.airbnb.com), or contact **India Tourism**, 123 M Karve Rd, Churchgate, T022-2203 3144.

Gateway of India and Colaba *p38, map p39*
$$$$ Ascot, 38 Garden Rd, Colaba, T022-6638 5566, www.ascothotel.com. The tan-wood rooms, shoehorned into a graceful 1930s building, veer dangerously close to IKEA anonymity, but they're generously proportioned and new, with safe deposit boxes, work desks and granite shower stalls.

Great views from the upper floors. Breakfast included.
$$$$ Taj Mahal, Apollo Bunder, T022-6665 3366, www.tajhotels.com. The grand dame of Mumbai lodging, over a century old. The glorious old wing has been fully restored and updated after the 26/11/08 attacks, joining the 306 rooms in the **Taj Mahal Intercontinental** tower. Several top-class restaurants and bars, plus fitness centre, superb pool and even a yacht on call.
$$$ Godwin, 41 Garden Rd, Colaba, T022-2287 2050, hotelgodwin@mail. com. 48 large, clean, renovated, a/c rooms with superb views from upper floors, mostly helpful management and a good rooftop restaurant – full of wealthy Mumbaikars on Fri and Sat night.
$$$ Strand, 25 PJ Ramchandani Marg, T022-2288 2222, www.hotelstrand.com. Friendly. Clean rooms, some with bath and sea view.
$$$ YWCA International Centre, 18 Madame Cama Rd, Colaba, T022-2202 0598, www.ywcaic.info. For both sexes, 34 clean and pleasant rooms with bath, and breakfast and buffet dinner included in the price. A reliable and sociable budget option, though the deposit required to hold your booking is a slight hassle.
$ India Guest House, 1/49 Kamal Mansion, Arthur Bunder Rd, T022-2283 3769. 20 rooms along long corridor, white partitions that you could, at a push, jump over. Fan, no toilet or shower. The corner room has a neat panorama over the bay. Sound will travel.
$ Sea Shore, top floor, 1/49 Kamal Mansion, Arthur Bunder Rd, T022-2287 4238. Kitsch as you like, 15 bright gloss-pink rooms and purple corridors with

plastic flowers, shower in room but no sink, 7 with window and TV and fan, 8 without. Sea-view room has 4 beds. 2 rooms come with toilet, TV and hot water.

Fort *p38, map p42*
$$$ Residency, corner of Rustom Sidhwa Marg and DN Rd, T022-6667 0555, www.residencyhotel.com. Clean and modern rooms in an interesting 19th-century building halfway between Flora Fountain and CST. Great location and good value.
$$-$ Traveller's Inn, 26 Adi Murzban Path, Ballard Estate, Fort, T022-2264 4685, www.hoteltravellersinn.co.in. A relatively new addition to Mumbai's backpacker repertoire, with simple, clean rooms, a 3-bed dormitory, internet and Wi-Fi, and friendly staff.
$ Popular Palace, 104-106 Mint Rd, near GPO, Fort Market, T022-2269 5506. Small but clean rooms with bath (hot water), some a/c, helpful staff, good value.

Around the CST (VT) *p41, map p42*
$$ City Palace, 121 City Terrace (Nagar Chowk), opposite CST Main Gate, T022-2261 5515. Decrepit guesthouse with tiny but functional rooms bang opposite the station. An OK place to crash before catching an early train.

Marine Drive to Malabar Hill *p43, map p42*
$$$$-$$$ Regency, 73 Nepean Sea Rd, T022-66571234, www.regencymumbai.com. 80 modest but immaculate rooms in quiet spot close to the sea at the base of upmarket Malabar Hill. Personable, friendly staff and free breakfast.
$$$$ The Oberoi, Nariman Pt, T022-6632 5757, www.oberoimumbai.com. Newly renovated and reopened, with beautiful sea-view rooms, glass-walled bathrooms, and 3 top-class restaurants.

$$$ Chateau Windsor Guest House, 86 Vir Nariman Rd, T022-6622 4455, www.cwh.in. Friendly and helpful place in a great location. The rooms on the 1st and 3rd floors are the best, newly renovated with large spotless bathrooms, marble tiles and balconies. Some of the older rooms are small, poky and dark. Recommended.

Central Mumbai *p45, map p36*
$$ YMCA International House, 18 YMCA Rd, near Mumbai Central, T022-6154 0100. Decent rooms, shared bath, meals included, temp membership Rs 120, deposit Rs 1300, good value, book 3 months ahead.

Bandra, Juhu Beach and Andheri *p46, map p36*
$$$$ Leela, near International Terminal, T022-6000 2233, www.theleela.com. One of the best of the airport hotels, with 460 modern rooms, excellent restaurants, pricey but excellent bar (residents only after 2300), all-night coffee shop, happening nightclub.
$$$$ Orchid, 70C Nehru Rd, Vile Parle (east), 5 mins' walk from domestic terminal, T022-2616 4040, www.orchidhotel.com. Refurbished, attractive rooms, eco-friendly. **Boulevard** restaurant boasts a good midnight buffet and '15-min lightning' buffet. Recommended.
$$$ Juhu Residency, 148B Juhu Tara Rd, Juhu Beach, T022-6783 4949, www.juhuresidency.com. Across the road from Juhu Beach, with just 28 attractive refurbished rooms, free Wi-Fi, friendly efficient staff and 2 excellent restaurants. A decent deal by Mumbai standards.
$$$ Transit, off Nehru Rd, Vile Parle (east), T022-6693 0761, www.hoteltransit.in. Modern, 54 rooms, reasonable overnight halt for airport, excellent

restaurant (draught beer), airport transfer. Special rates for day use (0800-1800).

🍴 Restaurants

Gateway of India and Colaba *p38, map p39*

$$$ Indigo, 4 Mandlik Rd, behind **Taj Hotel**, T022-6636 8999. Excellent Mediterranean in smart restaurant, good atmosphere and wine list, additional seating on rooftop.

$$$ Khyber, 145 MG Rd, Kala Ghoda, T022-4039 6666. North Indian. For an enjoyable evening in beautiful surroundings, outstanding food, especially lobster and *reshmi* chicken kebabs, try *paya* soup (goats' trotters).

$$$ Ling's Pavilion, 19/21 KC College Hostel Building, off Colaba Causeway (behind **Taj** and Regal Cinema), T022-2285 0023. Stylish decor, good atmosphere and delightful service, colourful menu, seafood specials, generous helpings. Recommended.

$$$ Trishna, Sai Baba Marg, next to Commerce House, T022-2270 3213. Good coastal cuisine, seafood, excellent butter garlic crab. Recommended.

$$ Café Churchill, 103-8, East West Court Building, opposite Cusrow Baug, Colaba Causeway, T022-2284 4689. Open 1000-2330. A tiny little café with 7 tables crammed with people basking in a/c, towered over by a cake counter and a Winston Churchill portrait. Great breakfasts, club sandwiches, seafood, fish and chips, lasagne and Irish stew.

$$ Leopold's, Colaba, T022-2282 8185. An institution among Colaba backpackers and Mumbai shoppers. The food, predominantly Western with a limited choice of Indian vegetarian, is average and pricey (similar cafés nearby are far better value) but **Leo's** gained cachet from its cameo role in the novel *Shantaram*, and was the first target of the terror attacks in Nov 2008.

$ Bade Miyan, Tullock Rd behind Ling's Pavilion. Streetside kebab corner, but very clean. Try *baida roti*, *shammi* and *boti* kebabs. The potato *kathi* rolls are excellent veg options.

$ Kailash Parbat, 1st Pasta La, Colaba. Excellent snacks and *chats*, in an old-style eatery also serving Punjabi *thalis*. The milky-sweet *pedas* from the counterare a Mumbai institution.

$ Kamat Samarambh, opposite Electric House, Colaba Causeway. Very good and authentic South Indian food, *thalis* and snacks. Try the moist, fluffy *uttapam* and *upma*. Clean drinking water.

Cafés and snacks

Theobroma, Colaba Causeway, next to **Cusrow Baug**. Decent coffee and terrific egg breakfasts. The brownies here are to die for – try the millionaire brownie or the rum-and-raisin with coffee. Egg-free cakes available.

Fort *p38, map p42*

$$ Britannia, Wakefield House, Sprott Rd, opposite New Custom House, Ballard Estate, T022-22615264. Mon-Sat 1200-1600. Incredible Parsi/Iranian fare with a delicious berry *pullav* made from specially imported Bol berries (cranberries from Iran). Try the *dhansak* and the egg curry. Recommended.

Around the CST (VT) *p41, map p42*

$$ Badshah Cold Drinks & Snacks, opposite Crawford Market. Famous for its *kulfi* (hand-churned ice cream) and fresh fruit juices (drink without ice), it's a default stop for everyone shopping . at Crawford Market. Good and fast *pav-bhaji* (mixed veg with buttered rolls).

Marine Drive to Malabar Hill p43, map p42

$ Tea Centre, 78 Vir Nariman Rd, near Churchgate. A little old-fashioned and colonial, but dozens of refreshing tea options, and a menu of heavy Indian food. Good value and a/c.

Central Mumbai p45, map p36

$$$ Olive, Union Park, Pali Hill, Bandra, T022-2605 8228. 'Progressive Mediterranean' food, served in an upscale environment to a cast of Bollywood celebs. Packed on Thu, when there's live music, and for brunch on Sun. Also has a branch at Mahalaxmi racecourse, T022-4085 9595.

$$$ Pali Village Cafe, Ambedkar Rd, Bandra (W), T022-2605 0401. Super-trendy new restaurant done out in shabby-chic industrial style, cascading across different rooms and levels. Good desserts and tapas-style starters, though the wine list and general vibe outweigh the quality of food and service.

$ Swati Snacks, Tardeo Rd, opposite Bhatia Hospital, T022-6580 8405. Gujarati and Parsi snacks along with street foods made in a hygienic fashion: try *khichdi*, *sev puri*, *pav bhaji*, *dahi puri* here. Be preparedfor a 20- to 40-min wait, but it's worth it.

Bandra, Juhu Beach and Andheri p46, map p36

$$ Gajalee, Kadambari Complex, Hanuman Rd, Vile Parle (E), T022-6692 9592, www.gajalee.com; also in Phoenix Mills. Fine coastal cuisine, try fish tikka, stuffed bombay duck and shellfish with the traditional breads *ghawne* and *amboli*.

$$ Out of the Blue, 14 Union Park, off Carter Rd, Khar West, T022-2600 3000. Romantic candlelit restaurant with a Goan beach-shack vibe. Great sizzlers, and live music most nights.

⊙ Bars and clubs

Gateway of India and Colaba p38, map p39

Polly Esther, Gordon House Hotel. A reggae, pop, rock disco, retro-themed club, where anything goes. Open late, most people come here after they finish partying elsewhere.

Woodside Inn, opposite Regal Cinema Colaba. Cramped pub carved out of stone Gothic building, with decent retro music, good dining upstairs (pizzas and sandwiches are surprisingly decent) and good selection of whiskies. Free Wi-Fi too.

Marine Drive to Malabar Hill p43, map p42

Dome, Intercontinental Hotel, Marine Dr, T022-6639 9999. Rooftop restaurant and lounge bar with a stunning view of the Queen's Necklace. Try the grilled prawns with your cocktails.

Pizza by the Bay, 143 Marine Dr, T022-2285 1876. Fun place near Churchgate, with live music, karaoke, good food menu (great starters and desserts), generous portions, wide selection of drinks. Loud and lively.

Bandra, Juhu Beach and Andheri p46, map p36

Aurus, Juhu Tara Rd, Juhu. Trendy seaside patio bar where Bollywood stars rub shoulders with the glitterati. Avant garde DJs, some international, spin inside. Expensive appetizers, good signature drinks and ocean views. Free entry, easier for couples.

Bling, Leela Hotel (see Where to stay, page 51). Club that lives up to its name, stays open late so attracts the spillover from the other clubs. Entry Rs 700-2500 depending on the time, the night and the bouncers.

Toto's, 30th Rd, off Pali Naka, Bandra (W). Retro music, regular clients, and no attitude amid funky automotive decor.

⊛ Festivals

Mumbai *p34, maps p36, p39 and p42*
In addition to the national Hindu and Muslim festivals (see pages 17 and 19) there are the following:

Feb Elephanta Cultural Festival at the caves. Great ambience. Contact **MTDC**, T022-2202 6713, for tickets Rs 150-200 including launch at 1800. **Kala Ghoda Arts Festival**, held in various locations around Colaba and Fort, T022-2284 2520, showcases of all forms of fine arts.

Mar Jamshed Navroz. This is New Year's Day for the Parsi followers of the Fasli calendar. The celebrations, which include offering prayers at temples, exchanging greetings, alms-giving and feasting at home, date back to Jamshed, the legendary King of Persia.

Jul-Aug Janmashtami celebrates the birth of Lord Krishna. Boys and young men form human pyramids and break pots of curd hung up high between buildings.

Aug Coconut Day. The angry monsoon seas are propitiated by devotees throwing coconuts into the ocean.

Aug-Sep Ganesh Chaturthi. Massive figures of Ganesh are towed through the streets to loud techno and storms of coloured powder, before a final *puja* at Chowpatty Beach where they're finally dragged out into the sea. The crowds making their way on foot to the beach cause immense traffic pile ups, and the scene at Chowpatty is chaotic, with

priests giving *puja* to Ganesh and roaring crowds of men psyching themselves up for the final push into the ocean. A similar celebration happens shortly after at **Durga Pooja**, when the goddess Durga is worshipped and immersed.

Sep-Oct Dussehra. Group dances by Gujarati women in all the auditoria and residents have their own *garba* and *dandiya* dance nights in the courtyards of their apartment buildings. There are also **Ram leela** celebrations at Chowpatty Beach, where the story of the *Ramayana* is enacted in a dance drama. **Diwali** (The Festival of Lights) is particularly popular in mercantile Mumbai when the business community celebrate their New Year and open new account books. **Eid ul-Fitr**, the celebration when Ramzan with its 40 days of fasting is also observed. Since both the Hindu and Islamic calendar are lunar, there is often overlap between the holidays.

25 Dec Christmas. Christians across Mumbai celebrate the birth of Christ. A pontifical High Mass is held at midnight in the open air at the Cooperage Grounds, Colaba.

○ Shopping

Mumbai *p34, maps p36, p39 and p42*
Most shops are open Mon-Sat 1000-1900, the bazars sometimes staying open as late as 2100. Mumbai prices are often higher than in other Indian cities, and hotel arcades tend to be very pricey but carry good-quality select items. Best buys are textiles, particularly tie-dye from Gujarat, hand-block printed cottons, Aurangabad and 'Patola' silks, gold-bordered saris from Surat and Khambat, handicrafts, jewellery and leather goods. It is illegal to take

anything over 100 years old out of the country. CDs of contemporary Indian music in various genres make good souvenirs as well as gifts.

Bazars
Crawford Market, Ambedkar Rd (fun for bargain hunting) and **Mangaldas Market**. Other shopping streets are South Bhagat Singh Marg, M Karve Rd and Linking Rd, Bandra. For a different experience try **Chor (Thieves') Bazar**, on Maulana Shaukat Ali Rd in Central Mumbai, full of finds from Raj leftovers to precious jewellery. Make time to stop at the **Mini Market**, 33-31 Mutton St, T022-2347 2425, minimarket@rediffmail.com, nose through the Bollywood posters, lobby cards, and photo-stills. On Fri, 'junk' carts sell less expensive 'antiques' and fakes.

Books
There are lines of second-hand stalls along Churchgate St and near the University. An annual book fair takes place at the Cross Maidan near Churchgate each Dec.
Crossword, under the flyover at Kemps Corner bridge (east of Malabar Hill). Smart, spacious, good selection.
Nalanda, Taj Mahal Hotel. Excellent art books, Western newspapers/magazines.
Strand Books, off Sir PM Rd near HMV, T022-2206 1994. Excellent selection, best deals, reliable shipping.

Clothes
Benzer, B Desai Rd, Breach Candy. Daily. Good saris and Indian garments.
The Courtyard, 41/44 Minoo Desai Marg, Colaba. Very elite and fashionable mini-mall includes boutiques full of stunning heavy deluxe designs (Swarovski crystal-studded saris, anyone?) by **Rohit Bal** and

Rabani & Rakha (Rs 17,000 for a sari) but probably most suitable to the Western eye is textile designer **Neeru Kumar's Tulsi**, a cotton textiles designer from Delhi. Beautiful linen/silk stoles and fine *kantha* thread work. There's also a store from top menswear designer **Rajesh Pratap Singh**.
Ensemble, 130-132 South Bhagat Singh Marg, T022-2287 2882. Superb craftsmanship and service for women's clothes – Indian and 'East meets West'.
Fabindia, Jeroo Building, 137MG Rd, Kala Ghoda, and 66 Pali Hill, Bandra, www.fabindia.com. Fair-trade handloom Western and Indian wear including *kurtas*, pants, etc, for men, women and children (also bamboo, earthenware and jute home furnishings, *khadi* and *mulmul* cloth).

Crafts and textiles
Government emporia from many states sell good handicrafts and textiles; several at **World Trade Centre**, Cuffe Parade. In Colaba, a street **Craft Market** is held on Sun (Nov-Jan) in K Dubash Marg.
Anokhi, 4B August Kranti Marg, opposite Kumbala Hill Hospital. Gifts and handicrafts.
Bombay Electric, 1 Reay House, BEST Marg, Colaba, T022-2287 6276, www.bombayelectric.in. Pricey, chic, trendsetter art and couture.
Bombay Store, Western India House, 1st floor, PM Rd, Fort, www.bombaystore. com. Daily. Ethnic lifestyle supplies, from home decor and fancy paper to clothing, gifts; best one-stop shop, value for money.
Cottage Industries Emporium, Apollo Bunder, Colaba. A nationwide selection, especially Kashmiri embroidery, South Indian handicrafts and Rajasthani textiles. Colaba Causeway,

next to **BEST**, for ethnicware, handicrafts and fabrics.

Curio Cottage, 19 Mahakavi Bhushan Rd, near the Regal Cinema, Colaba, T022-2202 2607. Silver jewellery and antiques. Natesan in Jehangir Gallery basement; also in Taj Hotel. For fine antiques and copies.

Phillips, Madame Cama Rd, Colaba. A pricey Aladdin's cave of bric-a-brac and curios.

Sadak Ali, behind **Taj Hotel**, Colaba. Good range of carpets, but bargain hard.

Jewellery

The **Cottage Industries Emporium**, near Radio Club, Colaba Causeway, has affordable silver and antique jewellery from across India.

Popli Suleman Chambers, Battery St, Apollo Bunder, Colaba, T022-2285 4757. Semi-precious stones, gems, garnets and pearls.

Music

Musical instruments on VB Patel Rd, **RS Mayeka** at No 386, **Haribhai Vishwanath** at No 419 and Ram Singh at Bharati Sadan.

Planet M, opposite CST station; smaller branches in most malls. Also has book/poetry readings, gigs.

Rhythm House, next to Jehangir Gallery. Excellent selection of jazz and classical CDs. Also sells tickets for classical concerts.

Silks and saris

Biba, next to Crossword, Kemp's Corner, Phoenix Mills, Lower Parel, Bandra (W). Affordable designer wear for ladies, alterations possible.

Nalli, Shop No 7, Thirupathi Apartments, Bhulabhai Desai Rd, T022-2353 5577. Something for every budget.

⏱ What to do

Mumbai *p34, maps p36, p39 and p42*
Adventure tourism
Maharashtra Tourism, www. maharashtratourism.gov.in. Actively encourages adventure tourism (including jungle safaris and water sports) by introducing 'rent-a-tent', hiring out trekking gear and organizing overnight trips; some accommodation included. Prices range from US$35-150 per day/ weekend depending on season and activity. It has also set up 27 holiday resorts around the state providing cheap accommodation at hill stations, beaches, archaeological sites and scenic spots. Details from tourist offices.

Odati Adventures, T(0)9820-079802, www.odati.com. Camping, weekend hiking, bike rides, rock climbing and waterfall rappelling around the Mumbai area. If you go rappelling in Maljesh Ghat during the monsoon, you'll glimpse thousands of flamingos. Bikes can be hired. Call or book online. Weekend cycle tours are Rs 2000-3000.

Body and soul

Aquarium, Marine Dr, T022-2281 8417. Good therapeutic yoga classes.

Iyengar Yogashraya, Elmac House,126 Senapati Bapat Marg (off Tulsi Pipe Rd opposite Kamla Mills), Lower Parel, T022-2494 8416, www.bksiyengar.com. Iyengar drop-in centre. Call before dropping in.

Kerala Ayurvedic Health Spa, Prabhadevi, next to Subway and Birdy's, T022-6520 7445. Very reasonable rates for massage, Rs 900 for 45 mins. Call for an appointment.

Tour operators
If you wish to sightsee independently with a guide, ask at the tourist office. See page 35.
Be the Local, T(0)9930-027370, www.be thelocaltoursandtravels.com. Fascinating walking tours of Dharavi, which take you through some of the cottage industries – from traditional Gujarati pottery to plastic – which sustain Mumbai from within Asia's largest slum. Owned and run by local students, the tours are neither voyeuristic nor intrusive, and photography is prohibited. Rs 400 per person includes transport from Colaba; private tours Rs 3500 for up to 5 people.
Bombay Heritage Walks, T022-2369 0992, www.bombayheritagewalks.com. Informative walking tours specializing in Mumbai's built history, founded by a pair of local architects.
City sightseeing Approved guides from the **India tourist office**, T022-2203 6854. City tour usually includes visits to The Gateway of India, the Chhatrapati Shivaji (Prince of Wales) Museum, Jain temple, Hanging Gardens, Kamla Nehru Park and Mani Bhavan (Gandhi Museum). Suburban tour includes Juhu Beach, Kanheri Caves and Lion Safari Park.
MTDC, Madam Cama Rd, opposite LIC Building, T022-2202 6713. City tour Tue-Sun 0900-1300 and 1400-1800, Rs 100. Evening open-top bus tour of Colaba, Marine Drive and Fort, runs Sat and Sun at 1900 and 2015; Rs 150 (lower deck Rs 50). Elephanta tours from Gateway of India. Boat 0900-1415, Rs 130 return; reserve at Apollo Bunder, T022-2284 1877.
Mumbai Magic, T(0)98677-07414, www.mumbaimagic.com. A vast range of tours covering every inch of the city from Colaba to Bandra and beyond. Highlights include South Indian cuisine tours of Matunga, a walk through the Chor Bazaar, and the Mumbai Local tour which hops you around the city by taxi, local train and bus. Personalized itineraries available. Professional and highly recommended.

⊖ Transport

Mumbai *p34, maps p36, p39 and p42*
Mumbai is one of the 2 main entry points to India, with daily international flights from Europe, North America, the Middle East, Asia, Australia and Africa, and frequent domestic connections with every major city in India, and most minor ones. All touch down at **Chhatrapati Shivaji International Airport**, enquiries T022-6685 0222, www.csia.in. The recently smartened-up international terminal is 30 km north of the city. There are exchange counters, ATMs, tourist offices, domestic airline and railway reservation counters, and a cloakroom for left luggage.

The domestic airport, recently renovated with 2 separate terminals – 1A for **Air India** (enquiries T022-6685 1351), 1B for **Jet Airways** and all budget airlines (enquiries T022-2626 1149), is 4 km closer to the city in Santa Cruz and has most of the same facilities. Free shuttle buses link the domestic and international terminals every few mins.
Transport to and from the airport Pre-paid taxis, from counters at the exits, are the simplest way of getting downtown. Give the exact area or hotel and the number of pieces of luggage, and pay at the booth. On the receipt will be scribbled the number of your taxi: ask the drivers outside to help you find it, and hand the receipt to the driver at the end of the journey. There is no need to tip, though drivers will certainly drop heavy hints. To **Nariman Point** or

Gateway of India, about Rs 430, 1-2 hrs depending on traffic. To **Juhu Beach** Rs 290. Metered taxis picked up outside the terminal should be marginally cheaper than a pre-paid, but make sure the driver starts the meter when you get in. The cheaper alternatives – crowded and slow **BEST** buses that connect both terminals with the city, and even more crowded local **trains** – have only economy in their favour. The closest railway stations are **Vile Parle** (for international) and **Santa Cruz** (domestic), both on the Western line to Mumbai Central and Churchgate.

Airline offices

The easiest way to comparison shop for domestic fares is online, though not all sites accept international credit cards. One that does is www.cleartrip.com.

Air India (Indian Airlines) and **Jet Airways** are full-service airlines and have the most comprehensive networks; budget carriers such as **Go Air**, **Indigo** and **Spicejet** serve major routes and charge for extras. During the winter, prepare for a 'congestion charge' on certain domestic routes, including Mumbai–Delhi.

Bus

Local Red **BEST** (Brihanmumbai Electrical Supply Co) buses are available in most parts of Greater Mumbai. There's a handy route finder at http://bestundertaking.com/transport/index.htm. Fares are cheap, but finding the correct bus is tricky as the numbers and destinations on the front are only in Marathi. English signs are displayed beside the back doors. Ask locals to help point out a bus going your way.
Long distance Maharashtra SRTC operates from the Mumbai Central Bus

Stand, T022-2307 4272, http://msrtconline.in/timetable.aspx, to most major centres in the state as well as several destinations in Goa.

Private buses also serve long-distance destinations: most leave from the streets surrounding Mumbai Central, where there are ticket agents, while others leave from Dadar; information and tickets from **Dadar Tourist Centre**, outside Dadar station, T022-2411 3398. The most popular company is **Neeta Volvo**, T022-2890-2666. Some private buses can be booked in advance on www.redbus.in.

Car

Costs for hiring a car are (for 8 hrs or 80 km): luxury a/c cars Rs 1500; **Indica/ Indigo**, a/c Rs 1000, non-a/c Rs 800. Companies include: **Auto Hirers**, 7 Commerce Centre, Tardeo, T022-2494 2006. **Blaze**, Colaba, T022-2202 0073. **Budget**, T022-2494 2644, and **Sai**, Phoenix Mill Compound, Senapati Bapat Marg, Lower Parel, T022-2494 2644. Recommended. **NRI Services**, Chowpatty, T(0)9821-252287, www.nriservicesindia.com. **Wheels**, T022-2282 2874.

Auto-rickshaw

Not available in Central Mumbai (south of Mahim). Metered; about Rs 9 per km, revised tariff card held by the driver, 25% extra at night (2400-0500). Some rickshaw drivers show the revised tariff card for taxis!

Taxi

Metered yellow-top cabs and more expensive a/c Cool Cabs are easily available. Meter rates are Rs 16 for the 1st km and Rs 10 for each extra kilometre. Drivers should carry tariff cards that convert the meter fee into current prices; a new fleet of yellow-top Indica cars have digital meters that show the correct price. Always get a pre-paid taxi at the airport.

A/c radio taxis can be pre-booked. They charge Rs 15 per km and provide metered receipts at the end of your journey. Tip the driver about 10% if you feel they had to do a lot of waiting. **Megacab**, T022-4242 4242. **Meru Cab**, T022-4422 4422.

Train

Local Suburban electric trains are economical. They start from **Churchgate**for the western suburbs and from **CST (VT)** for the east but are often desperately crowded; stay near the door or you may miss your stop. There are 'ladies' cars' in the middle and ends. Avoid peak hours (south-bound 0700-1100, northbound 1700-2000), and keep a tight hold on valuables. The difference between 1st and 2nd class is not always obvious although 1st class is 10 times more expensive. Inspectors fine people for travelling in the wrong class or without a ticket. If you're travelling frequently, invest in a smart card that lets you avoid queues at the ticket counter by printing tickets from a machine.

Long distance Many daily trains travel down the coast from Mumbai to **Madgaon**, the main jumping-off point for Goa; some stop at intermediate stations (such as **Pernem** and **Thivim**) closer to the northern beaches. The most convenient departures are the *Mandovi Exp 10103*, 0710, 11½ hrs; *Konkan Kanya Exp 10111*, 2305, 11½ hrs; and *Mangalore Exp 12133*, 2210, 9 hrs. These all depart from CST (enquiries T134/135; reservations T022-2265 9512, 0800-1230, 1300-1630), while all other trains leave from far flung suburban stations in the suburbs: **Lokmanya Tilak** terminus, 13 km northeast of the centre,

has the *Netravati Exp 16345*, 1140, 12 hrs. **Dadar**, 6 km north, has the *Madgaon Jan Shatabdi Exp, 12051*, 0525, 8¾ hrs.

Mumbai–Goa is one of India's busiest train routes and advance bookings are imperative, especially during holiday season. Night trains tend to fill up faster than daytime departures.

There's a useful **Foreign Tourist** counter at CST (opens 0900 – arrive early) for Indrail Passes and ticket bookings under Foreign Tourist Quota; bring your passport and an ATM receipt or currency encashment certificate.

❻ Directory

Mumbai *p34, maps p36, p39 and p42*
Banks **ATMs** are now ubiquitous in all parts of the city, including at the airports and stations, and most take foreign cards. For other services, branches open Mon-Fri 1000-1400, Sat 1000-1200. It's more efficient to change money at the airport, or at specialist agents, eg **Bureau de Change**, upstairs in Air India Building, Nariman Pt; **Thomas Cook**, 324 Dr DN Rd, T022-2204 8556; also at 102B Maker Tower, 10th floor, F Block, Cuffe Pde, Colaba. **Credit cards** **American Express**, Oriental Building, 364 Dr DN Rd; **Diners Club**, Raheja Chambers, 213 Nariman Pt; **MasterCard**, C Wing, Mittal Tower, Nariman Pt; **Visa**, Standard Chartered Grindlays Bank, 90 MG Rd, Fort. **Embassies and consultes** For up-to-date details of foreign embassies and consulates in India, go to embassy.goabroad.com. **Emergencies** Ambulance T102. Fire T101. Police T100. **Internet** Internet cafés are increasingly strict about demanding photo ID. There are several on the back streets of Colaba near Leopold Café. **Medical services** The

larger hotels usually have a house doctor, the others invariably have a doctor on call. Ask hotel staff for prompt action. The telephone directory lists hospitals and GPs. Admission to private hospitals may not be allowed without a large cash advance (eg Rs 50,000). Insurers' guarantees may not be sufficient. **Prince Aly Khan Hospital**, Nesbit Rd near the harbour, T022-2377 7800/900, **Jaslok Hospital**, Peddar Rd, T022-6657 3333; **Hinduja Hospital**, T022-2444-0431; **Lilavati Hospital**, in Bandra (W), T022-2642 1111 are recommended. **Chemists**: several open day/night, especially opposite **Bombay Hospital**. **Wordell**, Stadium House, Churchgate; **New Royal Chemist**, New Marine Lines. **Useful contacts** Commissioner's Office, Dr DN Rd, near Phule Market. **Foreigners' Regional Registration Office**, 3rd floor, Special Branch Building, Badruddin Tayabji Lane, Behind St Xaviers College, T022-2262 1169. **Passport office**, T022-2493 1731.

Contents

Footprint features

Tamil Nadu

At a glance

◉ **Getting around** Frequent buses between the temple towns, otherwise hire a cab or join a tour group. The rack-and-pinion train to Ooty is a treat. City bus tours from the tourism office recommended for Chennai.

◉ **Time required** A week for the temples, 4 days for the hills, as little as possible in Chennai, 3 days in Pondicherry; 2 days for Mahabalipuram, allow more for beach R&R. Optional 2-day detour to Chettinad.

☼ **Weather** Monsoon Oct-Dec. Warm year round but oppressively hot from the end of Mar. Hill stations are cool all year but wet from Jun.

✖ **When not to go** Cyclones Nov and Dec. Avoid the hottest months between Apr and Jul.

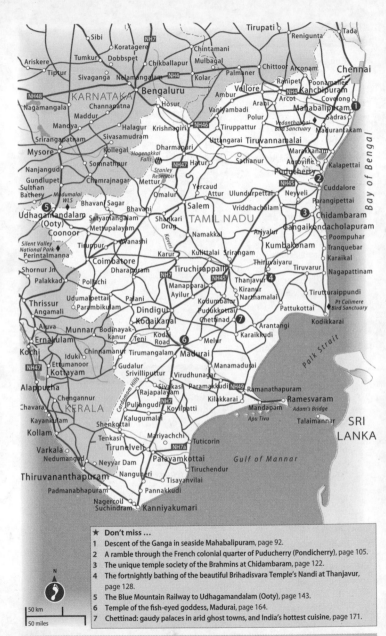

★ **Don't miss ...**

1 Descent of the Ganga in seaside Mahabalipuram, page 92.
2 A ramble through the French colonial quarter of Puducherry (Pondicherry), page 105.
3 The unique temple society of the Brahmins at Chidambaram, page 122.
4 The fortnightly bathing of the beautiful Brihadisvara Temple's Nandi at Thanjavur, page 128.
5 The Blue Mountain Railway to Udhagamandalam (Ooty), page 143.
6 Temple of the fish-eyed goddess, Madurai, page 164.
7 Chettinad: gaudy palaces in arid ghost towns, and India's hottest cuisine, page 171.

50 km
50 miles

Tamil Nadu smells of sacrificial burning camphor and the perfume from jasmine garlands piled up before its beautifully carved granite gods, well oiled with gingelly smeared from the palms of centuries of devotees, then reddened with sandal powder and washed with devotional milk baths.

About 90% of the 60-million-strong Tamil population is Hindu and religious ritual here is lived and breathed: men's entire foreheads are daubed with potash, huge horizontal sweeps or fingernail-thin red edges drawn from the hair's centre-parting sideways, while women sprinkle intricate geometric designs of ground rice powder on their hearths every dawn. It's rare to find a temple that has outlived its religious purpose – seldom the shrine that is mere monument. But nor is worship confined to the feats of architecture that dot Tamil Nadu. Banyan trees are festooned with dangling sacred talismens; tridents are slammed into the ground to create makeshift mounds of worship; village gods in life-size stucco renderings bare their teeth and brandish knives at every roadside, and files of pilgrims pick their way along baked dirt tracks.

Here, then, is the heady temple trail: Kanchipuram, Mahabalipuram, Chidambaram, Thanjavur, Madurai, the second Varanasi of Rameswaram, and the holy toe-tip of India in Kanniyakumari. Here too, for serious seekers and dilettante yogis, the contrasting ashram atmospheres of introspective Tiruvannamalai, futuristic utopian Auroville, and the industrious urban campus of Sri Aurobindo in Puducherry.

Welcome antidotes to temple fatigue come in the form of Puducherry's charming French domestic architecture and the crumbling palatial homes of Chettinad, or in big breaths of nature in the blue Nilgiri mountains around the celebrated hill stations of Ooty and Kodaikanal.

Chennai (Madras)

Chennai, South India's sprawling metropolis and India's fourth largest city, is dubbed 'India's Detroit' thanks to its chiefly automotive industrial revolution. The analogy is apt in more ways than one. Chennai's beautiful Indo-Saracenic buildings now stand like islands of elegance in a sea of concrete sprawl, and seen from the back of a taxi crawling along Anna Salai in the rush hour, the city can seem to be little more than a huge, sweltering traffic jam.

Nevertheless, modern Chennai remains the de facto capital of Indian high culture – complex dances such as Bharatnatyam are still widely taught and practised here – and the city retains an air of gentility that's missing from the other Indian metros. Despite attempts to carpet-bomb the southern suburbs with IT parks and malls, you'll find little here of the boom of Mumbai or the overheated dynamism of Bengaluru. Chennai's urban elite of textile magnates, artists and web entrepreneurs still maintain their networks around the bars and walking tracks of the city's Raj-era clubs, where chinos and loafers rule and *churidars* and *lungis* are checked at the door.

Outside the gates of these green refuges, Chennai can be a hard city to love. It's polluted, congested, tricky to negotiate and lacks anything resembling a centre. Nevertheless, there are reasons to stick around for more than the customary pre- or post-flight overnight stay, particularly if you base yourself near the old Brahmin suburb of Mylapore, which with its beautiful temple towers, old-time silk emporia and dingy cafés, makes a worthy introduction or postscript to the Tamil temple circuit.

Getting there Chennai's international and domestic air terminals are next to each other about 15 km from the city: allow 50 minutes, although it may take as little as half an hour. Airport buses run the circuit of the main hotels, and include Egmore station; otherwise it's best to get a pre-paid taxi: either yellow-topped government taxis or the more comfortable and expensive private cabs (note the number written on your charge slip). Trains from the north and west come into the Central Station behind the port, while lines from the south terminate at Egmore; both stations have abundant hotels nearby. State-owned buses terminate at the Koyembedu Moffusil terminus, 10 km west of the centre, and private buses at the nearby Omni terminus; it's worth asking whether the driver can drop you closer to your destination.

Getting around Chennai is very spread out and walking is usually uncomfortably hot so it's best to find an auto-rickshaw. Chennai's autos, once a notorious rip-off, are now required by law to run by the meter, though the rule is flexibly followed. With patience you should be able to find a driver who will use the meter.

Taxis are comparatively rare and a bit more expensive. The best option are call/radio taxis, which you call and book in advance rather than hail on the street. You can use these simply to get from one point to another, or for a set number of hours – a cheap (as little as Rs 100 per hour) and convenient way to cover a lot of sights in a morning or a day. There are a number of companies, all charging similar rates; **Fast Track** ① *T044-24732020*, is a reliable one. The bus network is extensive with frequent services, but it's often very crowded. ▸ *See Transport, page 87*.

Orientation Chennai is far from an 'organized' city. The main harbour near the old British military zone of **George Town** is marked by cranes for the cargo business. Nearby is the **fort**, the former headquarters of the British and now the Secretariat of the Tamil Nadu Government, and the High Court. The **Burma bazar**, a long line of pokey shops, runs between the two near Parry's Corner, while the two main rail stations lie to the west of George Town. From the fort, **Anna Salai** (Mount Road of old) cuts a southwestward swathe through the city, passing through or near to most areas of interest to visitors: **Triplicane**, where most of Chennai's cheap accommodation can be found; **Thousand Lights** and **Teynampet**, where ritzier hotels and malls dominate; and the commercial free-for-all of **T Nagar**. Just south of the central area between Anna Salai and the long sweep of Marina Beach lies **Mylapore**, older than Chennai itself and the cultural heart of the city. Further south still, industrial and high-tech sprawl stretches down the coast almost as far as Mahabalipuram.

Tourist information Most tourist offices are located in the the new **Tourism Complex** ① *2 Wallajah Rd, near Kalaivanar Arangam*. **Tamil Nadu Tourism (TN)** ① *T044-2536 8358, www.tamilnadutourism.org*, also has offices opposite Central station (T044-2535 3351), in Egmore (T044-2819 2165), and at the Domestic and International airports. **Tamil Tourist Development Corporation (TTDC)** ① *T044-2538 9857, www.ttdconline.com*.

Possibly the best organized office is **Government of India Tourism** ① *154 Anna Salai, T044-2846 0285, Mon-Fri 0915-1745, Sat until 1300.* **India Tourism Development Corporation (ITDC)** ① *29 Ethiraj Salai, T044-2821 1782, Mon-Sat 1000-1800, Sun closed.* For city information see also **www.chennaionline.com**.

Background

Armenian and Portuguese traders had settled the San Thome area before the arrival of the British. In 1639, **Francis Day**, a trader with the East India Company, negotiated the grant of a tiny plot of sandy land to the north of the Cooum River as the base for a warehouse or factory. The building was completed on 23 April 1640, St George's Day. The site was chosen partly because of local politics – Francis Day's friendship with Ayyappa Nayak, brother of the local ruler of the coast country from Pulicat to the Portuguese settlement of San Thome – but more importantly by the favourable local price of cotton goods.

By 1654 the patch of sand had grown into Fort St George, complete with a church and English residences – the 'White Town'. To its north was 'Black Town', referred to locally as Chennaipatnam, after Chennappa Nayak, Dharmala Ayyappa Nayak's father. The two towns merged and Madraspatnam grew with the acquisition of neighbouring villages of Tiru-alli-keni (meaning Lily Tank, and Anglicized as Triplicane), in 1676. In 1693, Governor Yale (founder of Yale University in the USA) acquired Egmore, Purasawalkam and Tondiarpet from Emperor Aurangzeb, who had by then extended Mughal power to the far south. In 1746 Madras was captured by the French, to be returned to British control as a result of the Treaty of Aix-la-Chapelle in 1748. Villages like Nungambakkam, Ennore, Perambur, San Thome and Mylapore (the 'city of the peacock') were absorbed by the mid-18th century with the help of friendly Nawabs. In 1793, the British colonial administration moved to Calcutta, but Madras remained the centre of the East India Company's expanding power in South India.

It was more than 150 years after they had founded Fort St George at Madras (in 1639) before the East India Company could claim political supremacy in South India. Haidar Ali; who mounted the throne of Mysore in 1761, and his son Tipu Sultan, allied with the French, won many battles against the English. The 1783 Treaty of Versailles forced peace. The English took Malabar in 1792, and in 1801 Lord Wellesley brought together most of the south under the Madras Presidency.

The city continues to grow, although many services, including water and housing, are stretched to breaking point. Since Independence an increasing range of heavy and light goods industries, particularly automotive, has joined the long-established cotton textiles and leather industries.

Places in Chennai → For listings, see pages 77-90.

Apart from anomalous little pockets of expats, such as Chetpet's Jamaican and South African communities, life in Chennai continues much as it always has done:

brahminical neighbourhoods still demand strict vegetarianism of all tenants; and flat sharing, a commonly accepted practice among the young in Bengaluru (Bangalore), is taboo. Superstition is important here too: rents are decided according

1 Chennai city

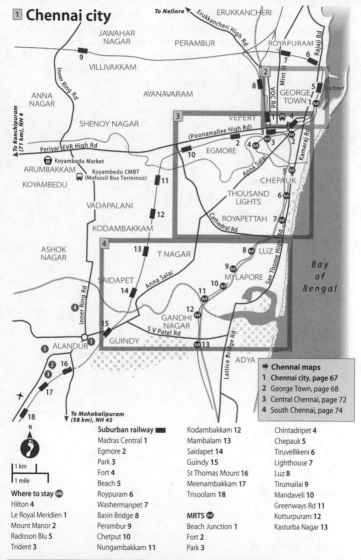

Chennai maps
1 Chennai city, page 67
2 George Town, page 68
3 Central Chennai, page 72
4 South Chennai, page 74

Suburban railway ▬
Madras Central 1
Egmore 2
Park 3
Fort 4
Beach 5
Roypuram 6
Washermanpet 7
Basin Bridge 8
Perambur 9
Chetput 10
Nungambakkam 11

Kodambakkam 12
Mambalam 13
Saidapet 14
Guindy 15
St Thomas Mount 16
Meenambakkam 17
Trisoolam 18

MRTS Ⓜ
Beach Junction 1
Fort 2
Park 3

Chintadripet 4
Chepauk 5
Tiruvellikeni 6
Lighthouse 7
Luz 8
Tirumailai 9
Mandaveli 10
Greenways Rd 11
Kotturpuram 12
Kasturba Nagar 13

Where to stay 🛏
Hilton 4
Le Royal Meridien 1
Mount Manor 2
Radisson Blu 5
Trident 3

to vasthu, India's equivalent of feng shui, and a wrong-facing front door can slash your payments.

You have to squint hard today to picture the half-empty grandeur that was the Madras of the East India Presidency. Triplicane has some of the finest architectural remains but the derelict district is better known today as 'Bachelors' Neighbourhood' due to its popularity with young men who come to make their fortune in the city.

The long expanse of Marina Beach, just seaward of Triplicane, made Chennai's residents tragically vulnerable to the 2004 tsunami, which devastated this public land – the city's cricket pitch, picnic ground and fishing shore. There's no trace of the ferocity of the waves today, but here alone it took about 200 lives.

The fort and port: St George and George Town

Madras began as nothing more than a huddle of fishing villages on the Bay of Bengal, re-christened Madras by British 17th-century traders after they built the Factory House fortifications on the beach. The present fort dates from 1666. The

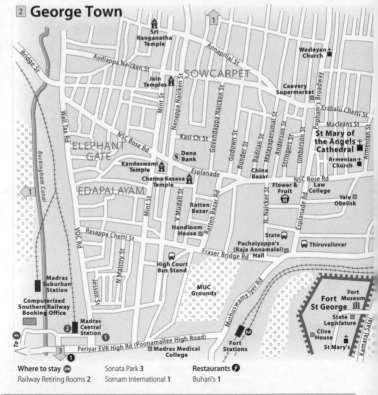

② **George Town**

Where to stay 🛏
Railway Retiring Rooms **2**
Sonata Park **3**
Sornam International **1**

Restaurants 🍽
Buhari's **1**

24 black **Charnockite pillars**, were reclaimed by the British in 1762 after the French had carried them off to Puducherry in 1746. Now the site of state government, the **State Legislative Hall** has fine woodwork and black and white stone paving. You can also see the old barracks and officers' quarters including Lord Clive's house, which he rented from an Armenian merchant. One room, Clive's Corner, has small exhibits. The house once occupied by Arthur Wellesley, the future Duke of Wellington, is 100 m further along.

The fort's governor Streynsham Master was responsible for the most interesting building in the compound, **St Mary's Church** ① T044-2538 2023. Built between 1678 and 1680, it ranks as the first English church in India and the oldest British building to survive. It's unusually well fortified for a house of God – all solid masonry with semi-circular cannon-proof roofs and 1.3-m-thick walls – so that in times of siege it could function as a military dormitory and storehouse, and had to be almost entirely rebuilt in 1759 after military action in a siege. **Governor Elihu Yale** and **Robert Clive** were both married in the church. Yale, an American (born to English parents), who worked as a writer for the East India Company from the ages of 24 to 39, rose to become governor; his son David is buried under the Hynmers Obelisk in the old burial ground. The famous missionary **Schwartz**, at one time the intermediary between the British and Haidar Ali, is also celebrated here for his role just 'going about doing good'. Job Charnock is commemorated for carrying a Hindu widow from the funeral pyre she was about to burn herself on and whereupon he took her as his wife. You can also learn the unhappy end of poor Malcolm McNeill, a colonel of the Madras Light Cavalry, who died at Rangoon in 1852 from neither battle nor disease but from a case of sunstroke. Nor is he alone: many Britishers appear to have fallen "a martyr to an ungenial climate".

The original black font, made from 3000-million-year-old Charnockite from Pallavaram, has been in continuous use since the church was consecrated. Outside the west entrance lies one of the oldest British inscriptions in India: the tombstone of Elizabeth Baker.

Also in the compound is an 18th-century building housing the **Fort Museum** ① Sat-Thu 1000-1700, US$2,

Kalikambar
Kameshwarar
Temple
Post Office St

M. Nalla Muthu St

Thambu Chetty St

Lingi Chetty St

Rajaji Rd (North Beach Rd)

Burma Bazar

Shipping Corp of India (Tickets for Andaman Islands)

Beach Station

Beach Junction

Thomas Cook

Parry's Corner

City High Court

Esplanade Lighthouse

PORT AREA

➡ **Chennai maps**
1 Chennai city, page 67
2 George Town, page 68
3 Central Chennai, page 72
4 South Chennai, page 74

N

200 metres
200 yards

photography prohibited, with exhibits from 300 years of British Indian history including brilliant portraits of Madras governors. It includes prints, documents, paintings, sculpture, arms (medieval weapons with instructions on their use) and uniforms. The Indo-French gallery has some Louis XIV furniture and clocks. Clive Corner, which includes letters and photographs, is particularly interesting. The building itself was once an exchange for East India Company merchants, becoming an officers' mess later.

Within walking distance of the compound, to the north, is the city's long-standing commercial centre, **George Town**. The area was renamed after the future King George V when he visited India in 1905. You first reach the grand Indo-Saracenic complex of the **High Court** ① *Mon-Sat 1045-1345, 1430-1630, contact registrar for visit and guide, Rs 10*, developed in the style of the late 19th-century architects like **Henry Irwin**, who was also responsible for the National Art Gallery. You are allowed to visit the courtrooms by using the entrance on the left. A fine example is Court No 13 which has stained glass, fretted woodwork, carved furniture, silvered panels and a painted ceiling. The huge red central tower, nearly 50 m tall (you can climb to the top), built like a domed minaret to serve as a lighthouse, can be seen 30 km out at sea. It was in use from 1894 until 1977. The original **Esplanade Lighthouse** ① *open to visitors Tue-Sun 1000-1300 and 1500-1700, Rs 10*, southeast of the High Court, is in the form of a large Doric pillar and took over from the fort lighthouse in 1841.

Cross NSC Bose Road from the High Court's north gate to walk up Armenian Street for the beautiful Armenian **Church of the Holy Virgin Mary** (1772) ① *0930-1430, bells rung on Sun at 0930*. Solid walls and massive 3-m-high wooden doors conceal the pleasant open courtyard inside, which contains a pretty belltower and many Armenian tombstones, the oldest dating from 1663. The East India Company praised the Armenian community for their 'sober, frugal and wise' lifestyle and they were given the same rights as English settlers in 1688. Immediately north again is the Roman Catholic cathedral, **St Mary of the Angels** (1675). The inscription above the entrance (1642) celebrates the date when the Capuchin monks built their first church in Madras.

Popham's Broadway, west from the St Mary cathedral, takes its name from a lawyer called Stephen (in Madras 1778-1795) who was keen to improve the city's sanitation, laying out what was to become Madras's main commercial street. Just off Popham's Broadway in Prakasham Road is the **Wesleyan Church** (1820).

In the 18th century there was major expansion between what is now First Line Beach (North Beach Road) and **Mint Street** to the west of George Town. The Mint was first opened in 1640, and from the late 17th century minted gold coins under licence for the Mughals, but did not move to Mint Street until 1841-1842.

The 19th-century growth of Madras can be traced north from **Parry's Corner**. **First Line Beach**, built on reclaimed land in 1814 fronted the beach itself. The **GPO** (1844-1884) was designed by Chisholm. The completion of the harbour (1896), transformed the economy of the city.

Central Chennai and the marina

Triplicane and **Chepauk** contain some of the finest examples of late 19th-century Indo-Saracenic architecture in India, concentrated in the area around the University of Madras. The Governor of Madras, Mountstuart Elphinstone Grant-Duff (1881-1886), decided to develop the marina as a promenade, since when it has been a favourite place for thousands of city inhabitants to walk on a Sunday evening.

Until the harbour was built at the end of the 19th century the sea washed up close to the present line of Kamaraj Salai (South Beach Road). However, the north-drifting current has progressively widened **Marina Beach**, which now stands as one of the longest urban beaches in the world – a fact that fills Chennai with great pride, if little sense of urgency about keeping the beach itself clean. The area just south of the malodorous mouth of the River Cooum is dedicated to a series of memorials to former state governors: **Anna Park** is named after the founder of the DMK party, CN Annadurai, while pilgrims converge on the **MGR Samadhi** to celebrate **MG Ramachandran** – the charismatic 1980s film star-turned-chief minister. **Chepauk Palace**, 400 m away on South Beach Road, was the former residence of the Nawab of the Carnatic. The original four-domed Khalsa Mahal and the Humayun Mahal with a grand *durbar* hall had a tower added between them in 1855. The original building is now hidden from the road by the modern Public Works Department (PWD) building, Ezhilagam. Immediately behind is the Chepauk **cricket ground** where test matches are played. Further south, opposite the clunky sculpture entitled 'the Triumph of Labour', the elegant circular **Vivekenanda Illam** was Madras' first ice house, and now hosts a **museum** ① *Thu-Tue 1000-1200, 1500-1900, yoga and meditation classes are currently stopped, may resume from Jan 2014, Rs 2*, devoted to the wandering 20th-century saint, Swami Vivekananda. There are weekend yoga classes at the ice house (weekends, 0630-0830) and regular meditation classes (T044-2844 6188, Wednesday at 1900) run by the Sri Ramakrishna Math.

Inland from here lies the **Parthasarathi Temple** ① *0630-1300, 1500-2000*, the oldest temple structure in Chennai. It was built by eighth-century Pallava kings, then renovated in the 16th by Vijayanagara rulers. Dedicated to Krishna as the royal charioteer, it shows five of Vishnu's 10 incarnations, and is the only temple dedicated to Parthasarathi. Further north in the heart of Triplicane, the **Wallajah Mosque** ① *0600-1200, 1600-2200*, or 'Big Mosque', was built in 1795 by the Nawab of the Carnatic. There are two slender minarets with golden domes on either side. North again, near the Round Thana which marks the beginning of Anna Salai, is the Greek temple-style banqueting hall of the old Government House, now known as **Rajaji Hall** (1802), built to mark the British victory over Tipu Sultan.

Egmore

A bridge across the Cooum at Egmore was opened in 1700, and by the late 18th century, the area around Pantheon Road became the fulcrum of Madras's social and cultural life, a 'place of public entertainment and balls'. Egmore's development, which continued for a century, started with the building of Horden's garden house in 1715. The original pantheon (public assembly rooms) was completely replaced by one of India's National Libraries. The **Connemara Library** (built 1896) traces its roots back to 1662, when residents exchanged a bale of Madras calico for books from London. At the southwest corner of the site stands Irwin's Victoria Memorial Hall,

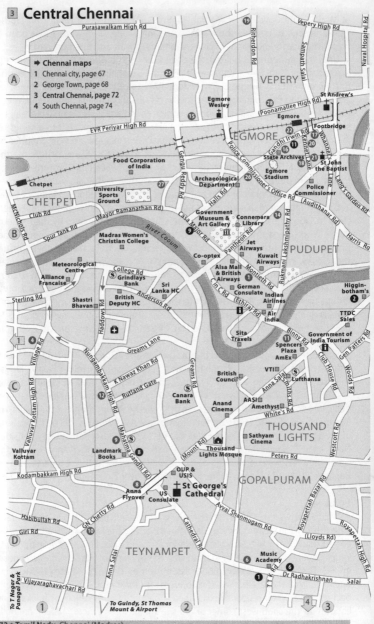

3 Central Chennai

➡ Chennai maps
1 Chennai city, page 67
2 George Town, page 68
3 Central Chennai, page 72
4 South Chennai, page 74

Purasawalkam High Rd

Vepery High Rd

Naval Hospital Rd

VEPERY

St Andrew's

Egmore Wesley

Poonamallee High Rd

Egmore

Footbridge

EVR Periyar High Rd

EGMORE

Gandhi Irwin Rd

St John the Baptist

Police Commissioner's Office Rd

State Archives

Kennet Lane

Lang's Garden Rd

Food Corporation of India

Chetpet

Police Commissioner's Office Rd

Egmore Stadium

Police Commissioner

Archaeological Department

Halls Rd

(Audithanar Rd)

CHETPET

University Sports Ground

Casa Major Rd

Government Museum & Art Gallery

Connemara Library

Club Rd

McNichols Rd

Spur Tank Rd

River Cooum

Pantheon Rd

Jet Airways

PUDUPET

Harris Rd

Madras Women's Christian College

Co-optex

Kuwait Airways

Rukmani Lakshmipathy Rd

Meteorological Centre

College Rd

Grindlays Bank

Alsa Mall & British Airways

Higginbotham's

Alliance Francaise

Sri Lanka HC

In C Rd

German Consulate

Indian Airlines

Sterling Rd

Shastri Bhavan

British Deputy HC

Anderson Rd

(Ethiraj Rd)

Air India

TTDC Sales

Haddows Rd

Greams Lane

Sita Travels

Binny Rd

Government of India Tourism

Village Rd

Greams Rd

Spencers Plaza

Club House Rd

Gen Patter Rd

Pls spool Rd

Nungambakkam High Rd

K Nawaz Khan Rd

Rutland Gate

British Council

AmEx

VTI

Lufthansa

Valluvar Kottam High Rd

Canara Bank

Anna Salai

Smiths Rd

AASI

Amethyst

Valluvar Kottam

Landmark Books

Mahatma Gandhi Rd

Anand Cinema

White's Rd

THOUSAND LIGHTS

Mount Rd

Thousand Lights Mosque

Sathyam Cinema

Peters Rd

Westcott Rd

Kodambakkam High Rd

OUP & USIS

St George's Cathedral

GOPALPURAM

Anna Flyover

US Consulate

Avvai Shanmugam Rd

Royapettah Bazar Rd

Royapettah High Rd

Habibullah Rd

GN Chetty Rd

Giri Rd

(Lloyds Rd)

TEYNAMPET

Music Academy

Dr Radhakrishnan Salai

To T Nagar & Panagal Park

Vijayaraghavachari Rd

Anna Salai

Cathedral Rd

TTK Rd

To Guindy, St Thomas Mount & Airport

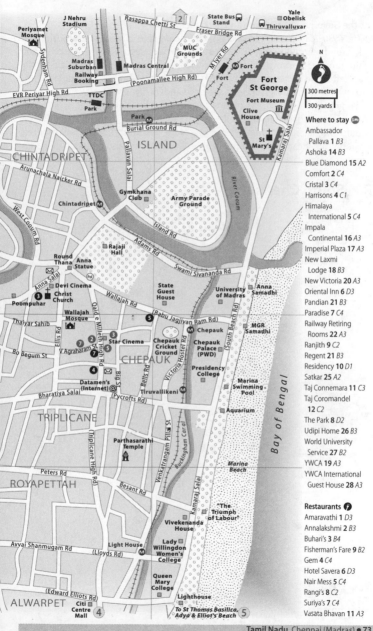

Where to stay

Ambassador Pallava **1** B3
Ashoka **14** B3
Blue Diamond **15** A2
Comfort **2** C4
Cristal **3** C4
Harrisons **4** C1
Himalaya International **5** C4
Impala Continental **16** A3
Imperial Plaza **17** A3
New Laxmi Lodge **18** B3
New Victoria **20** A3
Oriental Inn **6** D3
Pandian **21** B3
Paradise **7** C4
Railway Retiring Rooms **22** A3
Ranjith **9** C2
Regent **21** B3
Residency **10** D1
Satkar **25** A2
Taj Connemara **11** C3
Taj Coromandel **12** C2
The Park **8** D2
Udipi Home **26** B3
World University Service **27** B2
YWCA **19** A3
YWCA International Guest House **28** A3

Restaurants

Amaravathi **1** D3
Annalakshmi **2** B3
Buhari's **3** B4
Fisherman's Fare **9** B2
Gem **4** C4
Hotel Savera **6** D3
Nair Mess **5** C4
Rangi's **8** C2
Suriya's **7** C4
Vasata Bhavan **11** A3

now the **Government Museum and Art Gallery** ⓘ *486 Pantheon Rd, T044-2819 3238, Sat-Thu 0930-1630, closed Fri, foreigners Rs 250, Indians Rs 15, camera Rs 500.* The red-brick rotunda surrounded by an Italianate arcade was described by Tillotson as one of "the proudest expressions of the Indo-Saracenic movement". There are locally excavated Stone and Iron Age implements and striking bronzes including a 11th-century Nataraja from Tiruvengadu, seated images of Siva and Parvati from Kilaiyur, and large figures of Rama, Lakshmana and Sita from Vadak-kuppanaiyur. Buddhist bronzes from Nagapattinam have been assigned to Chola and later periods. The beautiful Ardhanariswara statue here is one of the most prized of all Chola bronzes: Siva in his rare incarnation as a hermaphrodite. There are also good old paintings including Tanjore glass paintings, Rajput and Mughal miniatures and 17th-century

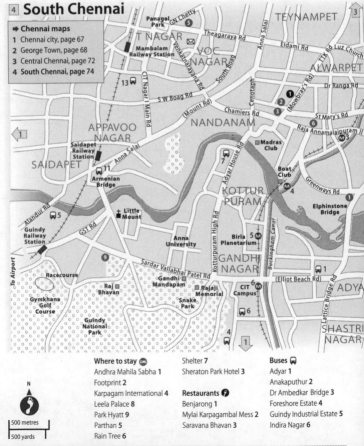

4 South Chennai

➡ **Chennai maps**
1 Chennai city, page 67
2 George Town, page 68
3 Central Chennai, page 72
4 South Chennai, page 74

Where to stay	Shelter **7**	Buses
Andhra Mahila Sabha **1**	Sheraton Park Hotel **3**	Adyar **1**
Footprint **2**		Anakaputhur **2**
Karpagam International **4**	**Restaurants**	Dr Ambedkar Bridge **3**
Leela Palace **8**	Benjarong **1**	Foreshore Estate **4**
Park Hyatt **9**	Mylai Karpagambal Mess **2**	Guindy Industrial Estate **5**
Parthan **5**	Saravana Bhavan **3**	Indira Nagar **6**
Rain Tree **6**		

Deccan paintings. Contemporary art is displayed at the **Gallery of Modern Art** ① *Government Museum, T044-2819 3035.*

Egmore has other reminders of the Indo-Saracenic period of the 19th and early 20th centuries, the station itself being one of the last to be built, in the 1930s. Northeast of the station is the splendid **St Andrew's Church** ① *Poonamalle High Rd, T044-2561 2608*. With a façade like that of London's St Martin-in-the-Fields, it has a magnificent shallow-domed ceiling. Consecrated in 1821, it has an active congregation.

Mylapore and South Chennai

Mylapore, which is technically older than Chennai and is the seat of city's urban elite, is more charming than the city centre. The present **Basilica of San Thomas** (1898) ① *24 San Thome High Rd, T044-2498 5455*, surrounded now by the tenement rehousing scheme of a fishermen's colony, is claimed as one of the very few churches to be built over an apostle's tomb. St Thomas Didymus (Doubting Thomas) is believed to have come to India in AD 52. According to one legend, he crossed the peninsula from his landing on the west coast to reach Mylapore (the 'town of peacocks') where he proceeded to live and preach, taking shelter from persecution in Little Mount (see page 76). An alternative story argues King Gondophernes invited him to Taxila, where he converted the king and his court before moving to South India. Some claim that his body was ultimately buried in the Italian town of Ortona. Marco Polo in his travels in 1293 recorded the chapel on the seashore and a Nestorian monastery on a hill to the west where the apostle was put to death. In 1523, when the Portuguese started to rebuild the church they discovered the tomb containing the relics consisting of a few bones, a lance head and an earthenware pot containing bloodstained earth. The church was replaced by the neo-Gothic structure which has two spires and was granted the status of a basilica in 1956. The relics are kept in the sacristy and can be seen on request. There are 13th-century

Kotturpuram **7**
Mandaveli **8**
Mylapore **9**
Queen Mary Art
   College **10**
Saidapet **11**
Taramani **12**
T Nagar **13**

MRTS ⓜ
Luz **1**
Thirumaila **2**
Mandaveli **3**
Greenways Rd **4**
Kotturpuram **5**
Kasturba Nagar **6**

wall plaques, a modern stained glass window, a 450-year-old Madonna brought from Portugal and a 16th-century stone sundial. The basilica is now subject to an ambitious US$164,400 restoration project. To stop the Mangalore tile roof leaking, concrete reparations are being peeled back and replaced with original lime mortar.

Kapaleeswarar Temple ① *0600-1300, 1600-2200*, to the west, is a 16th-century Siva temple with a 40-m *gopuram* (gateway), built after the original was destroyed by the Portuguese in 1566. Sacred to Tamil Shaivites, non-Hindus are only allowed in the outer courtyard. It's absolutely worth a visit, especially at sunset when worshippers gather for the evening *puja*, conducted amidst ropes of incense smoke and swirling pipe music.

The nearby **Sri Ramakrishna Math** ① *31 Ramakrishna Mutt Rd, www. sriramakrishnamath.org, 0500-1145, 1500-2100*, is one of the city's more appealing quiet corners, with a spectacular multi-faith temple, a quieter memorial to Ramakrishna in a prettily tiled Chettinad-style house, and a bookshop packed with writings by Ramamkrishna and notable devotees, including Swami Vivekananda.

The diminutive Portuguese **Luz Church**, 1547-1582 (the 1516 date in the inscription is probably wrong), is possibly the oldest church in Chennai. Its Tamil name, *Kattu Kovil*, means 'jungle temple'. Legend has it that Portuguese sailors lost at sea in a storm followed a light to the shore, where it disappeared. In gratitude they built the church. There are a number of 19th-century marble plaques to wives of the Madras civil service in the church and an ornate crypt.

To the south of Elphinstone Bridge, the **Theosophical Society** ① *Mon-Fri 0830-1000, 1400-1600, Sat 0830-1000, bus 5 from Central Chennai, ask taxi for Ayappa Temple on San Thome High Rd*, is set in large and beautifully quiet gardens. There are several shrines of different faiths and a Serene Garden of Remembrance for Madame Blavatsky and Colonel Olcott who founded the society in New York in 1875 and moved its headquarters to Madras in 1882. There's a huge 400-year-old banyan past the kitchen garden, a library and a meditation hall. The brackish river attracts waders and seabirds.

Tucked away near Saidapet is the **Little Mount** area. The older of the two churches (1551), with its small vaulted chapel, was built by the Portuguese. The modern circular church was built in 1971. St Thomas is believed to have been martyred and bled to death in AD 52 on the **Great Mount**, though others believe he was accidentally killed by a hunter's arrow. On top of the 90-m-high 'mount' is the **Church of Our Lady of Expectation**. The altar marks the spot where, according to legend, Thomas fell. Some legends suggest that after St Thomas had been martyred on the Little Mount, near Saidapet Bridge, his body was brought back to the beach which had been his home and was buried there.

For hotel and restaurant price codes and other relevant information, see pages 13-17.

● Where to stay

Chennai has seen a major increase of luxury accommodation options in the last few years, all pitched at the city's ever-growing business sector. These include the **ITC Grand Chola**, **Leela Palace**, **Hyatt Regency**, **Park Hyatt**, **Hilton** and the **Westin**. There continue to be excellent mid-range options, including a slew of service apartments and 1 solitary but wonderful B&B. Cheap hotels congregate around Central and Egmore stations and on hectic Triplicane High Rd, but even here you'll tramp a long way to find an acceptably clean room for under Rs 400. For more atmosphere, up your budget a little and stay near the temple in Mylapore.

Chennai airport
These hotels offer free airport transfers. Other hotels are 12-15 km from the airport.
$$$$ Hilton, JN Salai, near the Kathipara Grade Separator, T044-2225 5555, www. chennaiguindy.hilton.com. Flashy design, great restaurants, popular rooftop bar, and just 15 mins from the airport.
$$$$ Trident, 1/24 GST Rd, T044-2234 4747. 166 rooms in characterless but functional hotel. Pleasant swimming pool in the garden.
$$$ Le Royal Meridien, 1 GST Rd, St Thomas Mount, T044-2231 4343, www.leroyalmeridien-chennai.com. Plush hotel with all facilities including good restaurants and bars.
$$$ Radisson Blu, 531 GST Rd, St Thomas Mount, T044-2231 0101, www. radissonblu.com. Excellent value if rather

anonymous rooms just 2 km from the airport. With amenable staff and a good variety of restaurants and bars, plus free airport pick-up, this is a good choice if you just want to flop for a night off the plane.
$$ Mount Manor, 14, GST Rd, St Thomas Mount, T044-2231 0975. New business-style hotel with modern facilities and free airport transfers, but guests warn drivers may try to take you to inferior nearby hotels (eg Mount Heera) for commission.

George Town *p68, map p68*
Good location for Central Station and State bus stands. Many cheap hotels are along VOC (Walltax) Rd, while slightly more salubrious places jostle for space with cheap restaurants and travel agencies along EVR Periyar (Poonamallee) High Rd.
$ Railway Retiring Rooms, Central Station, T044-2535 3337. Some a/c rooms, dorms.
$ Sonata Park, 41 Sydenhams Rd, T044-4215 2272. Simple but well-looked-after rooms and excellent-value suites, within walking distance of the station, but away from the usual budget hotel belt.
$ Sornam International, 7 Stringer St, T044-2535 3060. Pleasant, 50 rooms with TV and balcony, hot water, rooftop vegetarian restaurant.
$ Youth Hostel (TTDC), EVR Park (near Central Railway Station), T044-2538 9132. Reasonably quiet.

Central Chennai *p70, map p72*
Many accommodation options are within 1 km of Anna Salai (Mount Rd). **$$$-$** hotels charge an extra 19.42% tax.
$$$$ The Park, 601 Anna Salai, T044-4267 6000, www.theparkhotels.com. Converted from the site of the Gemini

Film Studios, this is a quintessentially film hotel. Conran interiors, original film posters on the walls, world-class business facilities and restaurants and lovely rooftop pool with magnificent views over Chennai.

$$$$ Taj Connemara, 2 Binny Rd (off Anna Salai), T044-6600 0000, www.tajhotels.com. Supremely comfortable hotel with 148 renovated rooms that retain splendid art deco features. Excellent restaurants, bar and good **Giggles** bookshop – so heavily stocked you can't get in the door. Heavily booked Dec-Mar.

$$$$ Taj Coromandel, 37 Mahatma Gandhi Rd, Nungambakkam, T044-6600 2827, www.tajhotels.com. 201 rooms, fine restaurants, good pool. Recommended but Western tours dominate.

$$$ Ambassador Pallava, 53 Montieth Rd, T044-2855 4476, www.ambassador india.com. Enormous, frumpy wedding cake of a hotel, with 120 rooms split between 'Heritage' (red carpet, quirky old furniture, antique bathroom fittings) and slightly cheaper, tile-floored 'Executive'. Neither are brilliant value, but good restaurants (especially Chinese), a pool and health club make it a viable choice if you want a taste of retro Indian high-end hospitality.

$$$ Harrisons, 315 Valluvar Kottam High Rd, T044-4222 2777, www.harrisons hotels.com. A new 4-star tower bock stands on the site of one of the city's classic hotels. Though it's all a bit slick and soulless, the rooms are large and new enough to qualify as spotless, with great views from the upper floors, and there are 2 good restaurants (South Indian and Chinese) plus a bar.

$$$-$$ Oriental Inn, 71 Cathedral Rd, T044-2811 4941, www.orientalgroup. in. The older rooms here come with crisp sheets and unusually fragrant bathrooms, but the studio apartments in the new wing are the real steal, with huge amounts of space and designer fittings. Wi-Fi available in both wings, and a slew of good restaurants right downstairs. Price includes breakfast.

$$ Ranjith, 15 Nungambakkam High Rd, T044-2827 0521, hotelranjith@yahoo. com. 51 threadbare but spacious and cool rooms, some a/c, restaurant (good non-vegetarian continental), reasonable bar, travel desk.

$$ Residency, 49 GN Chetty Rd (convenient for airport), T044-2825 3434, www.theresidency.com. 112 very comfortable spacious rooms, 4th floor upwards have good views (9th floor, plush **$$$** suites). Excellent **Ahaar** restaurant (good buffet lunches), exchange, car hire with knowledgeable drivers. Better rooms and service than some more expensive hotels. Highly recommended, book ahead.

$ Comfort, 22 Vallabha Agraharam St, Triplicane, T044-2858 7661. 40 rooms, some a/c, friendly and a good deal more salubrious than most other options in the area.

$ Cristal, 34 CNK Rd, Triplicane, T044-2851 3011. Clean basic rooms with tiled bath, very helpful service, better and cheaper than some others in the area.

$ Himalaya International, 91 Triplicane High Rd, T044-2854 7522. Modern, bright, welcoming, 45 rooms with nice bath, some a/c, clean. No food but available from **Hotel Gandhi** next door.

$ Paradise, 17/1 Vallabha Agraharam St, Triplicane, T044-2859 4252, paradisegh@ hotmail.com. Spacious clean rooms with fans (some with 2), shower, good value, very friendly and helpful owners. A firm budget-traveller favourite.

Egmore *p71, map p72*

Many hotels (including several good budget options) are around the station and along EVR Periyar (Poonamallee) High Rd, an auto-rickshaw ride away to the north of the railway line. Try to book ahead as budget hotels opposite the station and down Kennet Lane often fill up by midday.

$$$-$$ New Victoria, 3 Kennet Lane (200 m from station), T044-2819 3638. 51 a/c rooms, restaurant (excellent breakfast), bar, spacious, quiet, ideal business hotel. Recommended.

$$ Ashoka, 47 Pantheon Rd, T044-2855 3377, www.ballalgrouphotels.com. The funky 1950s flavour and encouraging whiff of disinfectant run out of steam before they make it to the rooms, but this is one of Egmore's more appealing mid-range options, set back from the street and right opposite the museum, with an in-house restaurant and 'Ice Cream Park'. Popular wedding venue, so ring ahead.

$$ Pandian, 15 Kennet Lane, T044-2819 1010, www.hotelpandian.com. A decent budget choice that's cornered the foreign-traveller market, with a host of handy facilities including travel desk, multiple internet cafés and an a/c restaurant and bar. But the 90 rooms are small and poky for what you're paying, and the whole place could do with a lick of paint.

$$-$ Udipi Home, Udipi Junction (corner of Hall's Rd and Police Commissioner's Rd), T044-6454 6555, uhome@redifmail.com. Some excellent business-class 'Deluxe' rooms with colourful glass dividers separating sleeping and meeting areas, plus more basic doubles, some windowless, at the cheaper end. There's an internet café and a superb restaurant downstairs. Book ahead – walk-ins rarely get a room.

$ Blue Diamond, 934 EVR Periyar High Rd, T044-2641 2244. 33 rooms, some a/c, quieter at rear, good a/c restaurant (busy at peak times), exchange.

$ Impala Continental, opposite station, T044-2819 1778. Near **Vasanta Bhavan** restaurant, 50 excellent clean rooms with TV, good service.

$ Imperial Plaza, 6 Gandhi Irwin Rd, T044-4214 7362. A friendly mid-priced option, set back from the street in a complex of 5 'Imperial' hotels, each owned by a different member of the same family. Rooms are average for the area – clean enough, but don't expect sparkling value, and there's a huge markup if you want the a/c switched on.

$ New Laxmi Lodge, 16 Kennet Lane, T044-2819 4576. Old building, set back in garden, with 50 rooms around courtyard.

$ Railway Retiring Rooms, Egmore Station, T044-2819 2527.

$ Regent, 11 Kennet Lane, T044-2819 1801. 45 renovated clean rooms set motel-style around a leafy courtyard/car park. The friendly owner makes this the pick of the Egmore cheapies.

$ Satkar, 65 Ormes Rd (junction of Flowers Rd and Miillers Rd), T044-2642 5179. Spotless rooms with bath, some a/c, good vegetarian **Suryaprakash** restaurant, helpful staff, good value but very noisy.

$ Silver Star, 5 Purasawalkam High Rd, T044-2642 6818. Set back from the road, 38 simple clean rooms, open-air restaurant in courtyard, helpful and friendly staff.

$ World University Service, East Spur Tank Rd, T044-2836 4422. Some rooms with bath, dorm, International student cards needed, couples not allowed to share a room, cheap canteen for Indian snacks, good value, well situated for Egmore and south central Chennai.

$ YMCA, 74 Ritherdon Rd, T044-2532 2628. Good rooms and an extensive range of sports facilities including badminton, snooker, table tennis.
$ YWCA International Guest House, 1086 EVR Periyar High Rd, T044-2532 4234. Restaurant (rate includes breakfast), 60 rooms with bath and a/c, available to both men and women, popular so book early, excellent value, also campsite and plenty of parking – good for bikers.

South Chennai *p75, map p74*
$$$$ The Leela Palace, Adyar Seaface, M.R.C Nagar, T044-3366 1234, www.the leela.com. Chennai's only luxury hotel with an ocean view offers the gorgeous, over-the-top glamour for which Leela hotels are renowned. Rooms have lovely views of the Adyar River Estuary and Bay of Bengal. Recommended.
$$$$ Park Hyatt, Velachery Rd near the Governors residence, T044-7177 1234. Chennai's uber-cool design hotel is understated, elegant and packed with the young and beautiful. Their multi-level restaurant and lounge bar, **Flying Elephant**, is all the rage, and the rooftop pool has spectacular views over Guindy National Park. Highly recommended.
$$$$-$$$ Sheraton Park Hotel & Towers (Adyar Gate Hotel), 132 TTK Rd, T044-2499 4101. Good pool, 160 rooms, **Dakshin Chettinad** restaurant.
$$$$-$$$ Rain Tree, 120 St Mary's Rd, T044-4225 2525, www.raintree hotels.com. Beautiful luxury hotel, and Chennai's 1st to be run on an environmentally sustainable basis.
$$$ Footprint Bed and Breakfast, behind **Park Sheraton**, off TTK Rd, T(0)98400-37483, www.chennaibed andbreakfast.com. Beautifully cool, peaceful and intimate retreat from

the city, with 9 stylish but unfussy rooms, decorated with handmade paper from Auroville, spread over 2 floors of a residential apartment block. Indian and continental breakfasts come with fresh newspapers, and there's a small library, free internet and Wi-Fi. Owner, Rucha, pops in every day to check on things, and will negotiate weekly and monthly rates if you want to stay longer. Highly recommended.
$$ Parthan, 75 GN Chetty Rd (near Panagal Park), T044-2815 8792. Restaurant (Chinese), 29 clean, large, comfortable and quiet rooms, exchange. Recommended.
$$ Shelter, 19-21 Venkatesa Agraharam St, T0411-2495 1919, T(0)9840-037483, www.hotelshelter.com. Business hotel located in Mylapore. Clean rooms with hot water, central a/c, very helpful staff, internet café, exchange, restaurant.
$ Andhra Mahila Sabha, 12 D Deshmukh Rd, T044-2493 8311. Some a/c rooms, vegetarian restaurant.
$ Karpagam International, 41 South Mada St, Mylapore, T044-2495 9984. Basic but clean rooms amid the Mylapore temple madness; the best ones face straight across the lake. Book 2 weeks in advance.

❼ Restaurants

Central Chennai *p70, map p72*
Most restaurants are in Central Chennai and are open 1200-1500, 1900-2400. Those serving non-vegetarian dishes are often more expensive.
$$$ 601, The Park (see Where to stay). Possibly the best choice in town for a night out, with fantastic fusion food in a super elegant setting. Also at The Park, **Aqua**, serves excellent Mediterranean dishes and cocktails in poolside cabanas,

and lays on a barbeques with live music on Wed nights.

$$$ Copper Chimney, Oriental Inn (see Where to stay). Rich Mughlai and tandoori offerings in very clean setting. In the same building you can eat Chinese at **Chinatown** and good Spanish tapas at **Zara** (see Bars and clubs).

$$$ Hotel Savera, 146 Dr Radhakrishnan Rd, T044-2811 4700. Atmospheric rooftop restaurant with superb views, excellent Indian food, friendly service and live Indian music in the evenings. The hotel pool is open to non-residents, Rs 150.

$$$ Raintree, Taj Connemara (see Where to stay). Romantic outdoor restaurant with good food, atmosphere and ethnic entertainment but cavalier service. Very good buffet dinner on Sat night.

$$$ Southern Spice, Taj Coromandel (see Where to stay). Very good South Indian, along with evening dance recitals and freezing a/c.

$$ Annalakshmi, Anna Salai (near **Higginbotham's** bookshop). Wholesome, health-restoring offerings, Southeast Asian specialities (profits to charity, run by volunteers). Closed Mon. Recommended.

$$ Buhari's, 83 Anna Salai, and EVR Periyar Rd opposite Central Station. Good Indian. Dimly lit a/c restaurant, with terrace and unusual decor. Try crab curry, egg *rotis* and Muslim dishes; also in Park Town near Central Station.

$$ Dynasty, Harrisons (see Where to stay). Highly regarded Chinese, a popular venue for business lunchers.

$$ Rangi's, Continental Chambers, 142 Nungambakkam High Rd. Tiny but excellent hole-in-the-wall Chinese bistro.

$ Amaravathi, corner of TTK Rd and Cathedral (Dr Radhakrishan) Rd. Great value for spicy Andhra food, but relatively little joy for vegetarians.

$ Gem, Triplicane High Rd. Tiny non-veg Muslim place.

$ Nair Mess, 22 Mohammed Abdullah 2nd St, Chepauk. Fast and furious Kerala 'meals' joint, dishing out rice and *sambhar* in mountain-sized portions until 2100 sharp.

$ Saravana Bhavan, branches all over the city including Cathedral Rd opposite **Savera Hotel**, both railway stations, **Spencer Plaza Mall** and **Pondy Bazar**. Spotlessly clean Chennai-based chain restaurant, serving excellent snacks and 'mini tiffin', fruit juices (try pomegranate), sweetmeats, all freshly made.

$ Suriyas, 307 Triplicane High Rd. Shiny and clean vegetarian restaurant, with North and South Indian options.

Egmore *p71, map p72*

$$ Jewel Box, Blue Diamond (see Where to stay). Cool a/c, good for breakfasts, snacks and main courses.

$ Fisherman's Fare, 21 Spur Tank Rd. Outstanding value fish and seafood cooked in Indian, Chinese and Western styles.

$ Mathsya, Udipi Home, 1 Hall's Rd (corner of Police Commissioner's Rd). Chennai's night-owl haunt par excellence has been burning the oil (the kitchen stays open until 0200) by government order since the Indo-Chinese war. It also happens to serve some of the city's best pure veg food; their Mathsya *thali* comes with tamarind and sweetened coconut *dosas* and will keep you going all day. Recommended.

$ Vasanta Bhavan, 1st floor, 10 Gandhi Irwin Rd, opposite Egmore station. Very clean and super cheap, excellent food, friendly staff, downstairs bakery does delicious sweets.

South Chennai *p75, map p74*

$$$ Dakshin, Sheraton Park Hotel **(Adyar Gate Hotel)** (see Where to stay). High on the list of the best South Indian restaurants in the city, with Kanchipuram silk draped everywhere and a huge range of veg and non-veg choices. Book ahead.

$$ Benjarong & Teppan, 537 TTK Rd, Alwarpet, T044-2432 2640. 2 great restaurants in the same building: one an upscale Thai affair, doing very passable renditions of *tom kha* and *pad thai* (and plenty of vegetarian options) amid a collection of Buddhas in glass cases; the other a smart new teppanyaki restaurant with live cooking.

$ Mylai Karpagambal Mess, 80 East Mada St, Mylapore. If you can handle the all-round dinginess, this place serves superb, simple food – *vada*, *dosas* and a sweet *pongal* to die for – to an avid Tamil Brahmin crowd.

$ Saravana Bhavan, north of the temple tank, Mylapore. Similarly excellent food in a more salubrious if less interesting environment.

✪ Bars and clubs

Central Chennai *p70, map p72*
Alcohol can be purchased only through government-run TASMAC shops. Generally unsavoury locations with a street-bar on the side. Not recommended for women travellers. Instead go to TASMAC a/c shops located at Alsa Mall in Egmore or at Parsns Complex near Park Hotel Chennai.

10 Downing, Kences Inn, BN Rd, T Nagar, T044-2815 2152. Noisy and popular bolthole, with live jazz and classic rock bands, but not a place for a quiet conversation.

365 A.S, Hyatt Regency, 365 Anna Salai, Teynampet, T044-6100 1234. Want to meet the city's expats? Head out to this popular centrally located lounge bar on the weekend. Lots of intimate seating options and excellent, well-priced drinks and snacks.

Bike and Barrel, Residency Towers, Sri Thyagaraya Rd, T044-2815 6363. Split-level restaurant and bar, playing rock, trance and house.

Dublin, Sheraton Park Hotel & Towers (see Where to stay). A notionally Irish pub by day, at night Dublin turns into a pulsating nightclub, pumping out the tunes until the early hours.

Flying Elephant, Park Hyatt, Velachery, T044-7177 1234. Chennai's hottest restaurant, built on 3 floors with central sunken bar. Converts into a nightclub from Thu-Sat after 2300. Move over Leather Bar (Park Hotel), Chennai's young and hip congregate at this watering hole now. Reservations needed.

Havana, Rain Tree (see Where to stay). Lounge bar with dance floor, hosts various theme nights.

Leather Bar, The Park (see Where to stay). Not as kinky as the name suggests, but this dark womb of a bar, with black leather floors and olive suede walls, is still one of the city's sexiest.

Oakshott Bar, Taj Connemara (see Where to stay). A large, bright bar, offering huge tankards of beer, great snacks and a huge TV.

Pasha, The Park (see Where to stay). The city's sleekest dance club.

The Tapas Bar, Oriental Inn (see Where to stay). Cocktails and Indian-style Spanish classics are the order of the day at this buzzing tapas bar, where you can lounge on leather banquettes with the trendies of Chennai.

🌐 Entertainment

Chennai *p64, maps p67, p68, p72 and p74*
Although Chennai is revered for its
strong cultural roots, much of it is
difficult for tourists to access. Events
are often publicized only after they
have passed. Check the free *Cityinfo*
guide, published fortnightly, and www.
explocity.com, for upcoming events.

Cinemas

Cinemas showing foreign (usually
English-language) films are mostly in the
centre of town on Anna Salai.
Escape, Express Avenue Mall, Whites Rd.
Sathyam's swanky new multiplex located
on the top-floor of Chennai's new city-
centre mall. 30 mins from both Central
and Egmore stations, the food-court and
restaurants make this a great place to
while away an afternoon with food and
a movie before your train.
Sathyam, 8 Thiru-vi-ka Rd, Royapettah,
T044-4392 0200. Chennai's first multiplex
is also India's highest grossing cinema,
with 6 screens and a mix of new-release
Hollywood, Bollywood and Tamil films.
Worth visiting if only to overload on
chocolate and caffeine at Michael Besse's
Ecstasy bakery.

Music, dance and art galleries

Sabhas are membership societies that
offer cultural programmes 4 times a
month to their members, but occasionally
tickets are available at the door.
Chennai Music Academy, TTK Rd, T044-
2811 2231, www.musicacademymadras.in.
The scene of many performances of Indian
music, dance and theatre, not only during
the prestigious 3-week music festival from
mid-Dec but right through the year.
FOCUS Art Gallery, 59 TTK Rd (close to
Amaravathi Restaurant/Hotel Savera),

T044-2498 6611. Good place to pick
up affordable contemporary art by
South Indian artists and prints of famous
Indian painters.
Kalakshetra, Tiruvanmiyur, T044-2446
1943. Daily 0900-1700, entry Rs 50.
A temple of arts founded by Rukmani
Devi Arundale in 1936 to train young
artists to revive the dance form
Bharatnatyam. The foremost exponents
of the art are now trained here, and you
can have a peek at lessons in progress
between 0930 and 1130.
Shree Bharatalaya, Mylapore. One
of the key dance fine arts institutes
run by respected guru Sudharani
Raghupathy, Sura Siddha, 119 Luz
Church Rd, T044-2499 4460.

🌐 Festivals

Chennai *p64, maps p67, p68, p72 and p74*
Jan 14 Pongal Makara Sankranti,
the harvest thanksgiving, is celebrated
all over Tamil Nadu for 3 days (public
holiday). After ritually discarding old
clothes and clay pots, festivities begin
with cooking the first harvest rice
in a special way symbolizing good
fortune, and offering it to the Sun god.
The 2nd day is devoted to honouring
the valuable cattle; cows and bulls
are offered special 'new rice' dishes
prepared with jaggery or nuts and
green lentils. You will see them decorated
with garlands, bells and balloons, their
long horns painted in bright colours,
before being taken out in procession
around villages. Often they will pull
carts decorated with foliage and flowers
and carrying children, accompanied by
noisy bands of musicians. On the final
day of feasting, it is the turn of the
'workers' to receive thanks (and bonuses)
from their employers.

O Shopping

Chennai *p64, maps p67, p68, p72 and p74*
The main shopping areas are **Parry's Corner** in George Town and **Anna Salai. Khader Nawaz Khan Rd** is a very pleasant and (for a change) walkable street, with several elegant boutiques.

Note that many drivers – even those from reputable agents and companies – see little wrong in collecting a sweetening kickback from Kashmiris staffing huge shopping emporia, in exchange for dumping you on their doorstep. These are expert salesmen and although they do have some beautiful items, will ask at least double. The commission comes out of whatever you buy, so exercise restraint.

Most shops open Mon-Sat 0900-2000, some close for lunch 1300-1500. Weekly holidays may differ for shops in the same locality. There are often discount sales during the festival seasons of Pongal, Diwali and Christmas. The weekly *Free Ads* (Rs 5, Thu) has listings for second-hand cameras, binoculars, etc, which travellers might want to buy or sell.

Books
Most bookshops open 0900-1900; many upmarket hotels also have a selection of books for sale.
Higginbotham's, 814 Anna Salai and F39 Anna Nagar East, near Chintamani Market.
Landmark, Apex Plaza, 3 Nungambakkam High Rd, T044-2822 1000.

Clothes and crafts
Amethyst, next to Corporation Bank, Whites Rd, Royapettah, T044-6499 3634. Open 1100-2000. Elegant Indian couture and jewellery, plus a lovely café set in a converted factory warehouse, surrounded by fabulous gardens and foliage. Don't miss the delicious ginger-lime sugarcane juice!
Atmosphere, K Nawaz Khan Rd. Beautiful modern furniture, fabrics and curtains – mostly silks – which can be shipped anywhere within India within 72 hrs.
Central Cottage Industries, 118 Nungambakkam High Rd, opposite **Taj Coromandel**. Wide variety of handicrafts, fixed prices.
Chamiers, 85 Chamiers Rd. Home to the beloved Anokhi store, for tribal-style block print fabrics and jewellery, plus a nice-looking but terrible-value outdoor café.
Evoluzione, 30 Khader Nawaz Khan Rd. High-end brands and cutting-edge Indian designers.
Fabindia, Besant Nagar/Woods Ro/Express Ave Mall. India's best loved ethnic apparel brand. Their biggest choice is on the 2-storied outlet located opposite the Velankani Church off Elliots Beach in Besant Nagar in South Chennai.
Habitat, K Nawaz Khan Rd nearby. Good for special, unusual gifts.
Kalakshetra at Thiruvanmiyur (see Entertainment). Excels in *kalamkari* and traditional weaving, good household linen.
Kalpa Druma, 61 Cathedral Rd (opposite **Chola Sheraton**). Attractive selection of wooden toys and panels.
Khazana, Taj Coromandel (see Where to stay). Good for special, unusual gifts.
Naturally Auroville, Khader Nawaz Khan Rd. Products from the new-age colony of Auroville, including incense, handmade papers, clothing and delicious breads and cheeses.
New Kashmir Arts, 111 Anna Salai. Good carpets.
Poompuhar, 818 Anna Salai. Tamil Nadu crafts store, specializes in first-class bronzes.
Tiffany's, 2nd floor, Spencer's Plaza. Antiques and bric-a-brac.

Vatika, 5 Spur Tank Rd. Good for special, unusual gifts.

Victoria Technical Institute, Anna Salai near **Taj Connemara** hotel and opposite the Life Insurance Corporation of India. This fixed-rate, government-backed operation is the best for South Indian handicrafts (wood carving, inlaid work, sandalwood). Other government emporia are along Anna Salai.

Department stores and malls
Most open 1000-2000.

Burma Bazar, Rajaji Salai, George Town. For imports, especially electronic. Bargain hard.

Citi Centre, 10-11 Dr Radhakrishnan Salai, Mylapore. Huge new mall packed with international names, plus **Lifestyle** department store, bookshop, food court.

Express Avenue Mall, Whites Rd, Royapettah. Centrally located, fabulous new mall with a luxury good section, but also excellent Indian brands. Well-maintained, a/c, and has the city's best multiplex cinema on the top floor. Great for whiling away time between hotel check-out and your overnight train!

Ispahani Centre, 123/4 Nungambakkam High Rd. Where the hip Madrasis hang out. Very snazzy designer 'ethnic' clothes shops.

Phoenix Market City Mall, Velachery. Located about 25 mins from the airport, this is Chennai's newest and largest mall, with several luxury brands and excellent international chain restaurants. Again, a good place to spend time between flights.

Spencer's Plaza, Anna Salai near **Taj Connemara**, is a dizzyingly huge mall with loads of choice, but suffering from power cuts and poor maintenance. Patronage from locals has declined, but there are plenty of small independent stores that offer good bargains.

Supermarket, 112 Davidson St and TNHB Building, Annanagar (closed Fri).

Fabrics
Chennai was founded because of the excellence of the local cotton.

Co-optex (government run) shops, 350 Pantheon Rd. These stock handloom silks and cottons. The alleyway directly to the north is Cotton St, where piles of export surplus fabrics are sold at less than half the normal shop prices.

Khadi, 44 Anna Salai. Stores specialize in handspun and handwoven cotton.

Shilpi or **Urvashi**, TTK Rd. Good for cottons.

Jewellery
Radha Gold Jewellers, 43 North Mada St, Mylapore, T044-249 1923. Open 0930-1300 and 1600-2100. 'Antique'-finished items and dance jewels.

Sri Sukra Jewels, 42 North Mada St, Mylapore, T044-2464 0699, www.sukra. com. Brilliant temple and costume jewellery. Fixed price.

Silk and saris
Look out for excellent Kanchipuram silk and saris. Recommended for quality and value:

Handloom House, 7 Rattan Bazar.

Nalli, opposite Panagal Park, with excellent selection, both in T Nagar.

Radha, 1 Sannadhi St, Mylapore (near east gate of temple). 4 floors of silk and cotton saris, *salwar kameez* sets, men's *kurtas* and children's clothes. Great old-fashioned department store atmosphere.

Rupkala, 191 Anna Salai. Good prices, helpful.

☀ What to do

Chennai *p64, maps p67, p68, p72 and p74*
Body and soul
Krishnamacharya Yoga Mandiram,
New No 31 (Old No13), Fourth Cross St, R K
Nagar (near Tirumailai MRT station), T044-
2493 7998, www.kym.org. Runs 2- and
4-week intensive courses in yoga, plus
an extended Diploma course, and a very
well-regarded yoga therapy program.

Cultural centres
These have libraries, daily
newspapers from home and
cultural programs including film
shows and photo exhibitions.
Alliance Française, 24 College Rd,
Nungambakkam, T044-2827 9803.
American Center, 561 Anna Salai, T044-
2827 7825. Library 0930-1800, closed Sun.
British Council, 737 Anna Salai, T044-
4205 0600. Tue-Sun 1000-1900.
InKo, 51 6th Main Rd, Raja
Annamalaipuram, T044-2436 1224.
Run workshops in traditional Korean
arts, eg calligraphy.
Max Müeller Bhawan, 4 5th St,
Rutland Gate, T044-2833 1314.
Mon-Sat 0900-1900.

Golf
Cosmopolitan Club, 334 Anna Salai,
T044-2432 2759. The best course in town,
though you may need an invitation to
play. Also offers tennis, billiards, library
and bar.
   There's another, less exclusive golf
course at **Guindy Race Course**.

Sports clubs and associations
Most clubs are members-only domains,
though temporary membership may
be available for sports facilities. The
Chennai Cricket Club in Chepauk and

the **Gymkhana Club** at the racecourse
on Anna Salai both offer tennis,
swimming, cricket, billiards, library and a
bar – definitely worth experiencing if you
can make friends with a member.
Chennai Riders' Club, Race View, Race
Course, Velachery Rd. Riding (including
lessons) throughout the year except Jun.
Tamil Nadu Sailing Association, 83 East
Mada Church Rd, Royapuram, T044-2538
2253. Open to the public.
Wildertrails Adventure Club, T044-
2644 2729. Camping and hiking trips.

Swimming
The pool at the **Savera** hotel is open to
non-residents. Others open to the public
are at Marina Beach and the YMCA pool
at Saidapet. Sea bathing is safe at Elliot's
Beach, though no longer attractive.

Tennis
Clubs allowing members' guests and
temporary members to use courts are:
Chennai Club, **Gymkhana Club**, **Cricket
Club**, **Cosmopolitan Club**, **Presidency
Club** and **Lady Willingdon Club**. YMCA
at Saidapet also has courts.

Tours and tour operators
Cox & Kings, 10 Karuna Corner, Spur
Tank Rd, T044-2820 9500.
Mercury, 191 Anna Salai, T044-2852 2993.
Milesworth Holidays, RM Towers,
108 Chamiers Rd, T044-2432 0522,
www.milesworth.com. Tamil Nadu
specialists, but cover all of India.
Favourite among Chennai's expats.
STIC, 672 Anna Salai, T044-2433 0211
Surya, 1st floor, Spencer's Plaza, Anna
Salai, T044-2849 3934. Very efficient,
friendly, personal service.
Tamil Nadu Tourism, sales counters
at: Tourism Complex, 2 Wallajah Rd,
T044-2536 8358; 4 EVR Periyar High Rd

(opposite Central Station), T044-2536 0294; and Express Bus Stand near High Ct compound, T044-2534 1982 (0600-2100). You can book the some tours online, www.ttdconline.com. The following tours are on deluxe coaches and accompanied by a guide.

City sightseeing half-day, daily 0800-1300, 1330-1830. Fort St George, Government Museum (closed Fri), Valluvar Kottam, Snake Park, Kapaleeswarar Temple, Elliot's Beach, Marina Beach. Rs 120, a/c Rs 170.

Mahabalipuram and Kanchipuram, 0730-1900, Rs 200 (a/c Rs 350) and Tirupati, 0630-2200, Rs 375 (a/c Rs 600).

Hop-On Mahabalipuram tours leave hourly 0900-1600, returning 1040-1740; the ticket (Rs 250) lets you stop at several points along the way, eg at Dakshinachitra and the Crocodile Bank, and catch a later bus.

Thomas Cook, 45 Monteith Rd, opposite Ambassador Pallava hotel, T044-2855 4600.

Welcome, 150 Anna Salai, near India Tourist Office, T044-2846 0614. Open 24 hrs.

Walking tours

Detours, T(0)9000-850505, www.detours india.com. Off-beat walking and car-based thematic city experiences covering British history, religions and spirituality, food and bazaars. Exclusive and guided by local experts.

Story Trails, T(0)9940-040215, www. storytrails.in. Themed walking tours that allow the city to unfold through its stories, including Spice Trail, Mystic Trail and Bazar Trail.

⊖ Transport

Chennai *p64, maps p67, p68, p72 and p74*
Air
The **Arignar Anna International Airport** (named after CN Annadurai), T044-2234 6013 with 2 terminals and the **Kamaraj Domestic Airport**, T044-2256 0501, are on one site at Trisulam in Meenambakkam, 12 km from the centre. Enquiries, T140, arrivals and departures, T142. **Pre-paid taxis** from both; to Chennai Central or Egmore, Rs 600-800 (yellow taxis are cheaper than private), 45-60 mins; Rs 1500-1800 to Mahabalipuram. Buses to centre Rs 75 (day), Rs 100 (night). **Auto-rickshaws** to Chennai Central, Rs 200, but you have to walk to the main road to catch one. **Suburban railway** the cheapest way into town, from Trisulam suburban line station to Egmore and Fort, but trains are often packed. Free phone in the main concourse, after collecting baggage in the international airport, to ring hotels. Railway bookings 1000-1700.

Domestic Flights to **Bengaluru (Bangalore)**, **Bhubaneswar**, **Coimbatore**, **Delhi**, **Goa**, **Hyderabad**, **Kochi**, **Kolkata**, **Madurai**, via **Tiruchirappalli**; **Mumbai**, **Port Blair** and **Pune**, **Puttaparthy**, **Thiruvananthapuram**, **Visakhapatnam**.

Indian Airlines (Marshalls Rd, Egmore, T044-2345 3301 (daily 0800-2000). Reservations, all 24 hrs: T044-2855 5209, airport T044-2256 6065.

International Connections with: **Abu Dhabi**, **Bangkok**, **Colombo**, **Doha**, **Dubai**, **Frankfurt**, **Hong Kong**, **Kuala Lumpur**, **Kuwait**, **London**, **Male**, **Mauritius**, **Muscat**, **Paris**, **Reunion** and **Singapore**.

Air France, 42 Kubers, Pantheon Rd, T1800-180 0044. Air India, 19 Rukmani

Lakshmipathy Rd (Marshalls Rd), T044-2345 3301 (0930-1730, avoid 1300-1400), airport T044-2256 6065. **British Airways**, 10/11 Dr Radha Krishnan Salai, T98-4037 7470. **Cathay Pacific**, 47 Spur Tank Rd, T044-4298 8400; airport, T044-2256 1229. **Emirates**, 12 Nungambakkam High Rd, T044-6683 4444. **Gulf Air**, 52 Montieth Rd, T044-2815 6244. **Jet Airways**, 43 Montieth Rd, Egmore, T044-3989 3333, airport T044-2256 1818. **Kuwait Airways**, 476, Anna Salai, Nandanam, T044-2431 5162. **Malaysian Airlines**, 90 Dr Radha Krishnan Salai, T044-4219 1919. **Singapore Airlines**, 108 Dr Radhakrishna Rd, T044-4592 1921; airport, T044-2256 0409. **Sri Lankan**, 4 Vijaya Towers, Kodambakkam High Rd, T044-4392 1100. **Thai**, at ITC Park Sheraton, TTK Rd, T044-4206 3311.

General Sales Agents (GSA): **Air Kenya**, **Garuda Airways**, **Japan Airlines**, Global Travels, 703 Anna Salai, T044-4295 9633. **Air Canada**, **Bangladesh Biman** and **Royal Jordanian**, Thapar House, 43 Montieth Rd, T044-2856 9232. **Delta**, at Interglobe, 1, 4th St, Dr Radhakrishnan Salai, T044-2824 0073. **Continental**, **Iberian** and **Royal Nepal Airlines**, at STIC Travels, 672 Anna Salai, T044-2433 0211.

Bus

Local The cheap and convenient local bus service is not overcrowded and offers a realistic alternative to auto-rickshaws and taxis outside the rush hour (0800-1000, 1700-1900). Make sure you know route numbers as most bus signs are in Tamil (timetables from major bookshops).

Metropolitan Transport Corp (MTC), Anna Salai, runs an excellent network of buses from 0500-2300 and a skeleton service through the night. 'M' service on mini-buses are good for the route between Central and Egmore stations and journeys to the suburban railway stations. The 'V' service operates fast buses with fewer stops and have a yellow board with the route number and LSS (Limited Stop Service). PTC has a half-hourly 'luxury' mini-bus service between Egmore Station, Indian Airlines' Marshall's Rd office and the airports at Meenambakkam picking up passengers from certain hotels (inform time keeper at Egmore in advance, T044-2536 1284). The fare is about Rs 20.

Long-distance For long-distance journeys, the state highways are reasonably well maintained but the condition of other roads varies. The fast new highways leading north and south of Chennai and the East Coast Rd (ECR) have helped to cut some journey times. Fast long-distance a/c buses now run on some routes, giving a comfortable ride on air-cushioned suspension.

Chennai is amazingly proud of its bus station – Asia's biggest, with 30 arrival and 150 departure terminals. Officially titled the **Chennai Mofussil Bus Terminus (CMBT)** it is known to rickshaw drivers as Koyambedu CMBT, Jawaharlal Nehru Rd near Koyambedu Market, T044-2479 4705.

Tamil Nadu Govt Express, T044-2534 1835, offers good connections within the whole region and the service is efficient and inexpensive. Best to take a/c coaches or super deluxe a/c. Bookings 0700-2100. Other state and private companies cover the region but you may wish to avoid their video coaches which make listening, if not viewing, compulsory as there are no headphones.

Beware of children who 'help' you to find your bus in the expectation of a tip; they may not have a clue. There have also been reports of men in company uniforms selling tickets, which turn out to be invalid; it is best to buy on the bus. The listings given are for route number, distance. **Coimbatore** *No 460*, 500 km; **Chidambaram** and **Nagapattinam** *326*; **Kanchipuram** *76B*; **Kanniyakumari** *282 and 284*, 700 km; **Kumbakonam** *303F*, 289 km, 6½ hrs; **Madurai** *137*, 447 km, 10 hrs; **Mahabalipuram** *109*, Rs 19, 1½ hrs (*108B* goes via Meenambakkam airport, 2½ hrs) can be very crowded; **Nagercoil** *198*, 682 km, 14 hrs; **Ooty** *468*, 565 km, 13 hrs; **Puducherry** *803,* 106 km, 3 hrs; **Thanjavur** *323*, 320 km, 8 hrs; Tiruchirappalli *123*, 320 km and Route *124*, 7 hrs; **Tiruvannamalai** 180 km, 5 hrs; **Yercaud** *434*, 360 km, 8 hrs; **Bengaluru** (**Bangalore**) via **Vellore** and **Krishnagiri** *831*, 360 km, 8 hrs; **Bengaluru** (via **Kolar**) 350 km, 7½ hrs; **Tirupati** via **Kalahasti** *802*, 150 km, 3½ hrs.

Car
A/c or ordinary cars with drivers are good value and convenient for sightseeing, especially for short journeys out of the city when shared between 3 and 5 people. Large hotels can arrange, eg **Ganesh Travels**, 35/1 Police Commisioner Office Rd, T044-2819 0202; **Milesworth**, 108 Chamiers Rd, Alwarpet, T044-2436 2557, vacations@milesworth. com. Efficient and friendly company, good touring cars and English speaking drivers); **Regency** (Rs 600 per 8 hrs; Rs 750 for Mahabalipuram). **TTDC**, 2 Wallajah Rd, T044-2536 8358.

Ferry
Passenger ships leave every 7-10 days to the **Andaman** and **Nicobar Islands**, taking 3 days, and as visas are now issued on arrival at Port Blair the process of getting a ticket is less complicated than it used to be. Ships are operated by the **Shipping Corporation of India**, Jawahar

Building, Rajaji Salai, T044-2523 1401, and the **Deputy Directorate of Shipping Services**, 6 Rajaji Salai, T044-2522 6873. Check sailing schedules, then take 4-5 passport photos, originals plus 3 copies of your passport and visa, and queue up for a ticket, 1000-1300. Women have an advantage when queuing.

Motorbike hire or purchase
Southern Motors, 995A Koleth Court, 11th Main Rd, 2nd Av, Anna Nagar, T044-2616 4666, T044-2499 0784, is a good modern garage with efficient service. The **YWCA**, EVR Periyar Rd, is a good hotel for bikers and has a big shaded garden to park bikes securely.

MRTS
The **Mass Rapid Transit System** (raised, above-ground railway) runs from Chennai Beach south to Velacheri in the IT belt, passing through Chepauk, Triplicane (Thiruvallikeni) and Mylapore on the way. Station facilities are minimal, and there's little information about when the next train might depart.

Rickshaws
Three-wheeler scooter taxis are the most common form of transport around the city. A recent court ruling has forced rickshaw drivers, in defiance of the age-old Chennai tradition of radical price gouging, to charge by the meter. Look out for the Namma Auto-rickshaw fleet (reliable and safe). Minimum charge Rs25 for up to 1.8 km, additional km Rs 12. As always, drivers get kickbacks from emporium owners to encourage detours via shops.

Taxi
Taxis are better than rickshaws for extended trips and sightseeing. Many

companies offer 'packages' of fixed times and distances – Rs 700 for 40 km and 4 hrs, Rs 1200 for 80 km and 8 hrs, plus Rs 100 for each extra hour. Expect to pay more for a/c. **Bharati Call Taxi**, T044-2814 2233. **Chennai Call Taxi**, T044-2598 4455. **Fast Track**, T044-2473 2020. **Thiruvalluvar Travels**, T044-2474 5807.

Train
Suburban railway Inexpensive and handy, but very crowded at peak times. Stops between Beach Railway Station and Tambaram (every 5 mins in rush hour) include Fort, Park, Egmore, Chetpet, Nungambakkam, Kodambakkam, Mambalam, Saidapet, Guindy, St Thomas Mt. Also serves suburbs of Perambur and Villivakkam. Convenient stop at Trisulam for the airports, 500-m walk from the terminals.
Long distance Chennai has 2 main stations **Chennai Central (MC)** for broad-gauge trains to all parts of India and **Egmore (ME)** for trains to the south; a few significant trains also start from Tambaram, in the southern suburbs. Egmore and Central are linked by minibus; taxis take 5 mins. There is a reservations counter at the domestic airport, as well as at the stations. **Chennai Central** enquiry, T131, reservations, T132, arrivals and departures, T133, then dial train no. Advance Reservations Centre, Mon-Sat 0800-1400, 1415-2000, Sun 0800-1400, is in a separate building in front of the suburban station, to the left of the main station. Indrail Passes and booking facilities for foreigners and NRIs on the 1st floor. From Chennai Central to **Coimbatore** *Kovai Exp 12675*, 0615, 7¾ hrs; *West Coast Exp 16627*, 1100, 8¾ hrs; *Cheran Exp 12673*, 2145, 8½ hrs. **Kochi**

(**Cochin**) *Chennai-Aleppey Exp 16041*, 1945, 13¾ hrs; *Guwahati Cochin Exp 15624*, 1210, Fri, 14¾ hrs. **Mettupalayam** *Nilgiri Exp 16605*, 2015, 10 hrs.

Egmore enquiry, T135, arrivals and departures, T134. No counter for foreign tourist quota bookings. To **Kanniyakumari** *Chennai-Kanniyakumari Exp 16121*, 1900, 15 hrs. **Madurai** *Chennai-Kanniyakumari Exp 16121*, 1815, 10 hrs; *Vaigai Exp 12635*, 1225, 8 hrs; *Pandyan Exp 16717*, 2100, 9½ hrs via Kodai Rd (this connects with the bus service at **Kodaikanal** arriving at midday). **Tiruchirappalli** *Vaigai Exp 12635*, 1225, 5½ hrs; *Pallavan Exp 12606*, 1530, 5½ hrs.

ⓘ Directory

Chennai *p64, maps p67, p68, p72 and p74* **Embassies and consulates** For Indian visa extensions go to **Foreigners' Registration Office**, Shastri Bhavan Annexe, 26 Haddows Rd, T044-2345 4970, Mon-Fri 0930-1800. For details of foreign embassies in Chennai, go to embassy.goabroad.com. **Medical services** Ambulance (Government), T102; **St John's Ambulance**, T044-2819 4630, 24-hr. **Dental hospital (Government)**, T044-2534 0441; **All-in-One**, 34 Nowroji Rd, T044-2641 1911, 0400-2000, 0900-1200 Sun. **Chemists**: **Apollo Pharmacy**, many branches including 320 Anna Salai, Teynampet; 52 Usman Rd South, T Nagar. **SS Day & Night Chemists**, 106D, 1st Main Rd, Anna Nagar. **Hospitals**: **Apollo Hospital**, 21 Greams Rd, T044-2829 3333. **CSI Rainey**, GA Rd, RA Puram, T044-2595 3322, with 24-hr pharmacy. **Deviki Hospital**, 148 Luz Church Rd, Mylapore, T044-2499 2607. **National Hospital**, 2nd Line Beach Rd, T044-2524 0131.

Around Chennai

South of the capital, easily reached in a day but worthy of at least a weekend, lies Mahabalipuram, an intriguing little beachside town given over entirely to sculpture, both ancient and modern. Part open-air museum and part contemporary workshop, its seventh-century bas-reliefs are some of the world's largest and most intricate, telling the Indian flood myth, the *Descent of the Ganga*. Within earshot of the old shore temples you can find modern-day masons industriously piling their shacks and yards high with freshly and beautifully chiselled deities. Inland from Chennai, the former Pallava capital of Kanchipuram is one of India's seven sacred cities, chock-full of temples and overflowing with silks spun straight from the loom.

Chennai to Mahabalipuram → *For listings, see pages 100-103.*

If travelling from Chennai, there are three good stop-off points before Mahabalipuram.

Cholamandal Artists' Village
ⓘ *East Coast Rd, Enjampakkam, T044-2449 0092, 0900-1900, free.*
The first of three good stop offs, travelling from Chennai to Mahabalipuram, is 19 km from Chennai. The artists' community, started in 1969, gives living, working and exhibition space for artists creating sculptures, pottery and batik. They sometimes hold dance performances in a small open-air theatre, and there are some simple cottages for hire if you want to stick around for a workshop or residency.

Dakshinchitra
ⓘ *East Coast Rd, T044-2747 2603, www.dakshinachitra.net, Wed-Mon 1000-1830, Rs 200, Indians Rs 75.*
The second stop is the Madras Craft Foundation's model village, which showcases the rich cultural heritage of the four southern states against a backdrop of 17 authentic buildings, each relocated piece by piece from their original homes around South India. There's a regular programme of folk performances, including puppet shows, plus a newly opened art gallery with an excellent collection of tribal art from across India, a small textile museum, a restaurant and a fortune-telling parrot.

Madras Crocodile Bank
ⓘ *Tue-Sun 0830-1730, RRs 35, camera Rs 20, video Rs 100.*
Finally, 14 km before Mahabalipuram, is Romulus Whitaker's captive breeding centre for Indian crocodiles. Established by the American-born herpetologist

(known as the Snake Man of India), you can now see several rare species from India and beyond, including Siamese and African dwarf crocodiles, basking around the open pools. There's a small extra charge to visit the snake venom bank, where snakes donate small quantities of poison for use in antivenins before being released back to the wild.

Mahabalipuram (Mamallapuram) → *For listings, see pages 100-103.*

Mahabalipuram's mix of magnificent historic rock temples, exquisite alfresco bas reliefs and inviting sandy beach bestows a formidable magnetism, and it has matured into a buzzing backpacker hamlet, complete with all the high-power Kashmiri salesmanship and insistent begging that such a role implies. Though the beach and ocean are dirty enough to make you think twice about swimming, the craftsmanship that built the temples continues today and the whole place echoes with the sound of chisels tapping industriously on stone.

Arriving in Mahabalipuram → *Phone code: 044. Population: 12,345.*
Getting there Buses from Chennai take around 1½ hours to the bus stand in the centre of the small village. They may stop at hotels north of Mahabalipuram, on the way, otherwise autos from anywhere in the village will ferry you there for Rs 50. Arriving by car, you may have to pay a Rs 20 toll at the booth near the post office on Kovalam Road.

Getting around The town is small enough to explore on foot, but hiring a bike can get you further afield. ▸▸ *See Transport, page 103.*

Tourist information Tamil Nadu Tourist Office ⓘ *Kovalam Rd, 300 m north of Othavadai St, T044-2744 2232, Mon-Fri 1000-1745,* can arrange guides, car and cycle hire. The best time to visit is early morning, for the best light on Bhagiratha's Penance. Allow two hours for a circuit. It's hard to get lost but the paths on the top of the rock are not always clear.

Background
The coastal temple town Mahabalipuram is officially known as Mamallapuram after 'Mamalla' ('great wrestler'), the name given to Narasimhavarman I Pallavamalla (ruled AD 630-668). The Pallava ruler made the port famous in the seventh century and was largely responsible for the temples. There are 14 cave temples and nine monolithic *rathas* (shrines in the shape of temple chariots), three stone temples and four relief sculptured rock panels.

The **Dravida** or Dravidian style underwent several changes over the course of the different dynasties that ruled for about 1000 years from the time of the Pallavas who laid its foundations. In Mahabalipuram, rock-cut cave temples, *mandapas* (small excavated columned halls), and *rathas* were carved out by the early Pallavas. These were followed by structural temples and bas relief sculptures on giant rocks.

The Ekambaresvara Temple in Kanchipuram (see page 97) shows the evolution of the Dravidian style – the shrine with its pyramidal tower and the separate *mandapa* (pillared portico) all within the courtyard with its high enclosure wall made up of cells. Six centuries later the two separate structures were joined by the *antarala* (covered hall). A large subsidiary shrine, which took the place of an entrance gateway, also hinted at the later *gopuram*.

A characteristic feature of the temples here was the system of water channels and tanks, drawn from the **Palar River**, which made it particularly suitable as a site of religious worship. The *naga*, or serpent cult associated with water worship, can be seen to be given prominence at Bhagiratha's Penance.

Mahabalipuram

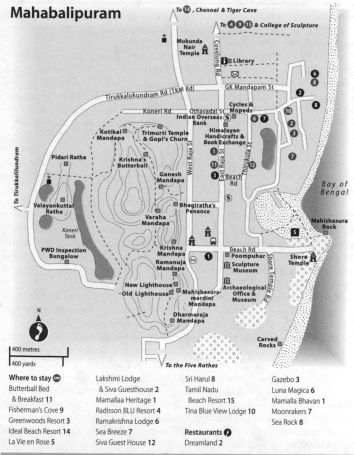

Where to stay 🛏
Butterball Bed
 & Breakfast 11
Fisherman's Cove 9
Greenwoods Resort 3
Ideal Beach Resort 14
La Vie en Rose 5

Lakshmi Lodge
 & Siva Guesthouse 2
Mamallaa Heritage 1
Radisson BLU Resort 4
Ramakrishna Lodge 6
Sea Breeze 7
Siva Guest House 12

Sri Harul 8
Tamil Nadu
 Beach Resort 15
Tina Blue View Lodge 10

Restaurants 🍴
Dreamland 2

Gazebo 3
Luna Magica 6
Mamalla Bhavan 1
Moonrakers 7
Sea Rock 8

Carving in stone is still a living art; stone masons can be heard chipping away from dawn to dusk along the dusty roadsides, while students at the **Government School of Sculpture** ① *near the bus stand, Wed-Mon 0900-1300, 1400-1830,* continue to practise the skills which flourished centuries ago.

Places in Mahabalipuram

Bhagiratha's Penance *Descent of the Ganga,* also called **Arjuna's Penance**, is a bas relief sculpted on the face of two enormous adjacent rocks, 29 m long and 7 m high. It shows realistic life-size figures of animals, gods and saints watching the descent of the river from the Himalaya. Bhagiratha, Rama's ancestor, is seen praying to Ganga. A man-made waterfall, fed from a collecting chamber above, issues from the natural crack between the two rocks. Some see the figure of an ascetic (to the top left-hand side of the rock, near the cleft) as representing Arjuna's penance when praying for powers from Siva, though this is disputed. There are scenes from the fables in the *Panchatantra* and a small shrine to Vishnu.

A path north goes to the double-decker rectangular **Ganesh** *ratha* with a highly decorative roof and two pillars with lions at their base – an architectural feature which was to become significant. The Ganesh image inside is mid-20th century. To the west are the **Valayankuttai** and twin **Pidari** *rathas*. The path continues past the precariously balanced **Krishna's Butterball** through some huge boulders at the north end of the hillock to the **Trimurti Temple** caves that hold three shrines to Brahma, Vishnu and Siva, the last with a lingam.

Mandapas The 10 *mandapas* are shallow, pillared halls or porticos in the rocky hillside which hold superb sculptures from mythological tales, and illustrate the development of the Dravidian (South Indian) temple style.

On the south is a **Durga niche** (AD 630-660), while next door is the **Gopi's Churn**, a Pallava cistern. Walk back along the ridge, passing Krishna's Butterball on your left and boulders with evidence of incomplete work. The **Varaha Mandapa** (AD 640-674) on the left of the ridge shows two incarnations of Vishnu – Varaha (boar) and Vamana (dwarf) – among scenes with kings and queens. The base forms a narrow water pool for pilgrims to use before entering the temple. From here you can walk to the top of Bhagiratha's Penance.

Krishna Mandapa (mid-seventh century) has a bas relief scene of Krishna lifting Mount Govardhana to protect a crowd of his kinsmen from the anger of the Rain God, Indra. The cow licking its calf during milking is remarkably realistic.

Kotikal Mandapa (early seventh century) may be the earliest of the *mandapas*, roughly carved with a small shrine with no image inside. **Ramanuja Mandapa** was originally a triple-cell Siva temple, converted later into a Vaishnava temple.

South of the new lighthouse the simple **Dharmaraja cave** (early seventh century) contains three empty shrines. To its west is **Isvara Temple** (or Old Lighthouse), a truncated Siva temple still standing like a beacon on the highest summit, with a view for miles around. (To the south, across the Five Rathas, is the nuclear power station of Kalpakkam; to the west is the flat lagoon and the original port of Mahabalipuram.)

Stone temple pilot

When the British Council sponsored Bristol-born artist Stephen Cox to scout India for a place to make his huge-scale stone works for the national art prize, the Indian Triennale, he chose not the country's best art schools, but a little fishing village on the Coromandel coast of Tamil Nadu. It may sound bloody minded, until you arrive in Mahabalipuram, where the whole air clatters with the sound of chisel on rock. It must be the most industrious seat of Hindu idol-making the world over; everywhere you look masons sit on their haunches hammering away at the local dolerite rock.

As Cox explains: "I didn't go to India to work with like-minded contemporary artists, I wanted people who could work with great big blocks of stone without fear. Mahabalipuram is totally unique in having this unbroken, living tradition of making idols for people to pray to, and that means that they are also used to working with huge monolithic stone so no-one's daunted by making my 14-tonne sculptures." Although he has kept a studio there from that first year, 1986, you won't find any of his sculpture in the town itself – these are mainly kept for cities: the British High Commission at Delhi, the British Council's office in Chennai and dotted about London's Square Mile. Indeed his work – too minimalist for Hindu temple carving purists – has been received with something less than gusto by some of the local craftsman, and

journalist Mark Tully, branded Cox's use of Indian labour a form of 'neo-colonialism'. One sculpture alone can take up to a year to make and will have passed through, on average, 20 pairs of Indian hands before being shipped for exhibition. "At the end of the day of course, I wouldn't be working in India over Carrara in Italy if it wasn't economically viable," Cox concedes, but he also says "my raison d'être for working in India is because, in working amongst and with the temple carvers, I can immerse myself in a living antique tradition. It is not just the cost factor. The hand skills of the silpies have been lost to the rest of the world."

The town has changed dramatically since he arrived in 1986, but Cox spares the burgeoning tourist industry infrastructure to reserve his criticism for the Architectural Survey of India's maintenance of the monuments themselves. "Since it was declared a World Heritage Site, they've buggered the Shore Temple up; it's not a shore temple anymore, instead it sits in a bijou plot of grassland, while the five *rathas* are fenced off, destroying the whole beauty of these wonderful monuments in a natural environment."

And his favourite piece of sculpture in a town teeming with them? It's the Pallava's flair for observation that still gets him: "the naturalism that Giotto was supposed to have invented you find in a ninth-century relief carving here. It is amazing. I only hope fewer and fewer people come."

Mahishasuramardini Mandapa (mid-seventh century) is immediately below. It has fine bas relief and carved columns with lion bases. The main sculpture shows the goddess Durga slaying the buffalo demon Mahishasura while another relief shows Vishnu lying under Adishesha, the seven-hooded serpent.

Pancha Rathas ① *Rs 250, Indians Rs 10*. These mid-seventh-century monolithic temples, 1.5 km south of the Old Lighthouse, were influenced by Buddhist architecture as they resemble the *vihara* (monastery) and *chaitya* (temple hall). They imitate in granite temple structures that were originally built of wood and are among the oldest examples of their type.

The five *rathas* to the south of the hill are named after the Pancha Pandava (five Pandava brothers) in the epic *Mahabharata* and their wife Draupadi. The largest is the domed **Dharmaraja** with many images including an interesting Ardhanarishvara (Siva-Parvati) at the rear. The barrel-vaulted **Bhima** nearby has a roof suggestive of a thatched hut, while next to it the dome-shaped ratha **Arjuna** imitates the Dharmaraja. **Draupadi ratha** is the smallest and simplest and is again in the form of a thatched hut. The base, now covered by sand, conceals a lion in front which appears to carry it, which suggests that it may be a replica of a portable shrine. Immediately east is a large unfinished *Nandi*. To its west is the apsidal **Nakula-Sahadeva ratha** with a freestanding elephant nearby. The Bhima and Nakula-Sahadeva follow the oblong plan of the Buddhist *chaitya* hall and are built to two or more storeys, a precursor to the *gopuram*, the elaborate entrance gateway of the Dravidian temple.

Shore Temple ① *0900-1730, foreigners Rs 250, Indians Rs 10, video Rs 25, includes Panch Rathas if visited on same day*. This beautiful sandstone World Heritage Site, built in the seventh century by King Rajasimha, is unusual for holding shrines to both Siva and Vishnu. Its gardens have been laid out to ape their ancient antecedents. Its base is granite and it has a basalt *kalasha* at its top. Its position on the water's edge, with an east-facing altar designed to catch the rising sun and a stone pillar to hold the beacon for sailors at night, meant that there was no space for a forecourt or entrance gateway, but two additional shrines were built to the west. The second smaller spire adds to the temple's unusual structure. The outer parapet wall has lines of *Nandi* (Siva's sacred bull) and lion pilasters.

Saluvankuppam Some 5 km north of Mahabalipuram, on the coast, is the temple at Saluvankuppam. It holds the **Tiger Cave** *mandapa* with carvings of tiger heads. The cave, not signposted from the beach, is secluded and peaceful – perfect for a picnic. On the way you will see the **Mukunda Nayar Temple**.

Beaches Mahabalipuram's beach is far from pristine, particularly north of the temples towards the **Ashok** and in the rocky area behind the Descent of the Ganga where it serves as an open latrine. To sunbathe undisturbed by hawkers pay Rs 200 to use the small pools at **Crystal Shore Palace** or **Sea Breeze**, or the bigger pool, 1 km north at **Tamil Nadu Beach Resort**.

Around Mahabalipuram

Tirukkalukundram is a small Siva temple dedicated to Vedagirishvara on top of the 3000-million-year-old rock, 14 km west of Mahabalipuram. About 400 steps take you to the top of the 160-m hill which has good views, plus money-conscious priests and 'guides'. Be prepared for a hot barefoot climb, 'donations' at several shrines and Rs 10 for your shoes. The Bhaktavatsleesvara in town with its *gopuram* (gateway) stands out like a beacon. The tank is considered holy and believed to produce a conch every 12 years. Small shops in the village sell cold drinks. Buses from Mahabalipuram take 30 minutes or you can hire a bike.

Sriperumbudur, 44 km from Chennai on National Highway 4, is the birthplace of the 11th-century Hindu philosopher Ramanuja, and is where Rajiv Gandhi was assassinated on 21 May 1991. There is a memorial at the site in a well-kept garden.

Kanchipuram → *For listings, see pages 100-103.*

What Darjeeling is to tea, and Cheddar is to cheese, so Kanchipuram is to silk. One of Hinduism's seven most sacred cities, 'the Golden City of a Thousand Temples', dates from the early Cholas in the second century. The main temple complexes are very spacious and only a few of the scattered 70 or so can be seen in a day's visit. The town itself is relatively quiet except for crowds of pilgrims. **Tourist information** ⓘ *Hotel Tamil Nadu, T044-2722 2553, 1000-1700.*

Background

The **Pallavas** of Kanchi came to power in the fourth century AD and were dominant from AD 550 to 869. Possibly of northern origin, under their control Mahabalipuram became an important port in the seventh century. Buddhism is believed to have reached the Kanchipuram area in the third century BC. Successive dynasties made it their capital and built over 100 temples, the first as early as the fourth century. As well as being a pilgrimage site, it was a centre of learning, culture and philosophy. Sankaracharya and the Buddhist monk Bodhidharma lived and worked here.

Places in Kanchipuram → *Phone code: 044. Population: 153,000.*

ⓘ *Temples are usually open from 0600 and closed 1200-1600, but very few allow non-Hindus into the inner sanctum. Have change ready for 'donations' to each temple you visit.*
Ekambaresvara Temple ⓘ *small entry fee, cameras Rs 3, only Hindus are allowed into the inner sanctuary.* The temple has five enclosures and a 'Thousand-pillared Hall' (if you're pedantically inclined, the number is actually 540). Dedicated to Siva in his ascetic form it was begun by the Pallavas and developed by the Cholas. In the early 16th century the Vijayanagara king Krishna Deva Raya built the high stone wall which surrounds the temple and the 59-m-tall *rajagopuram* (main tower) on which are sculpted several figures of him and his consort.

The main sanctuary has a *lingam* made of earth (Siva as one of the elements) and the story of its origin is told on a carved panel. The teasing Parvati is believed to have unthinkingly covered her husband Siva's eyes for a moment with her hands which resulted in the earth being enveloped in darkness for years. The enraged Siva ordered Parvati to do severe penance during which time she worshipped her husband in the form of an earth *lingam* which she created. When Siva sent a flood to test her, she clung to the *lingam* with her hands until the waters subsided. Some believe they can see her fingerprints on the *lingam* here. On 18 April each year the sun's rays enter the sanctum through a small square hole.

Kailasanatha Built in the early seventh century, this is considered to be the most beautiful of the town's temples. It was built of sandstone by the Pallava king Narasimha

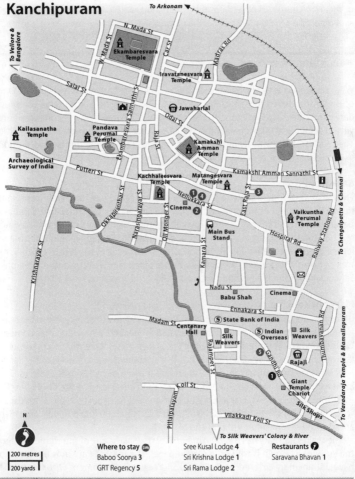

Kanchipuram

Where to stay 🛏
Baboo Soorya **3**
GRT Regency **5**

Sree Kusal Lodge **4**
Sri Krishna Lodge **1**
Sri Rama Lodge **2**

Restaurants 🍴
Saravana Bhavan **1**

Varman II with the front completed by his son Mahendra III. The outer structure has a dividing wall with a shrine and doorways, separating a large courtyard from a smaller one. The unusual enclosure wall has 58 small raised shrines with a *Nandi* in most pavilions and some frescoes have survived. The seven shrines in the temple complex have images of different Siva forms. The intricately carved panels on the walls depict legends about Siva with accompanying text in ancient Grantha script. It has been extensively restored. The festival **Mahashivaratri** is held here in February.

Vaikuntha Perumal Eighth century and dedicated to Vishnu, this temple was built by the Pallava king Nandivarman just after the Kailasanatha and illustrates the progress of Dravidian temple architecture. The sanctuary is separated from the *mandapa* by an open space. The cloisters are built from rows of lion pillars. Panels of bas relief accompanied by lines in old Tamil trace the history of the wars between the Pallavas and Chalukyas. There is an unusual *vimana* (tower) with shrines in three tiers with figures of Vishnu in each.

Varadaraja (Devarajasvami) ① *0630-1200, 1530-2000, Rs 5, camera Rs 5, video Rs 100.* Built by the Vijayanagara kings (circa 16th century), 3 km southeast of town, it has superb sculpture in its marriage hall (with 96 pillars). Figures on horseback wear half North Indian/half South Indian costumes. Note the rings at each corner and the massive flexible chain supposedly carved out of one piece of granite, although it is no longer in one piece. The main shrine is on an elephant-shaped rock, Hastagiri. The **Float Festival** is in February and November, **Brahmotsavam** in May and **Garuda Sevai** in June.

Chengalpattu (Chingleput) The fort here was built by the Vijayanagar king Thimmu Raya after his defeat at the Battle of Talikotta in 1565. After 1687 it was absorbed into the Mughal Empire. Then in 1750 it was taken by the French, who held it until it was captured by Clive in 1752; British control was only finally established after the defeat of Haidar Ali in 1781. Although the fort is now almost totally destroyed (the railway runs through the middle of it), the Raja Mahal ('King's Palace') remains.

Around Kanchipuram
On the Trichy Road, 87 km from Chennai and 60 km from Mahabalipuram, the **Vedanthangal Bird Sanctuary** ① *0530-1800, Rs 5, camera Rs 50, see Transport, page 103*, and **Karikili Tank** are thought to have existed as a protected area for about 250 years. The marshy site attracts numerous water fowl and provides their main nesting place. Visitors and residents include crested cormorants, night herons, grey pelicans, sand pipers, white wagtails, open-billed storks, white ibis, egrets, little grebe and purple moorhens. The best time to visit is November to February, at dawn and from 1500 to 1800; avoid weekends and holidays. Afternoons are best because the sun is behind you for clear views, and you get to see large flocks of birds returning home to roost.

Marakkanam, mentioned in Roman records as an important port in the first century AD, has an ancient Siva temple with many inscriptions. Immediately inland is the Kaliveli Tank, an extremely important staging post and wintering area for about 40,000 migratory water fowl, including over 200 pelicans.

For hotel and restaurant price codes and other relevant information, see pages 13-17.

● Where to stay

Mahabalipuram *p92, map p93*
Even modest hotels charge 20% luxury tax. Several new places in the Othavadai St area. It's busy during the Jan dance festival.
$$$$ Fisherman's Cove (Taj), Kovalam Rd, 8 km north, T044-6741 3333, www.tajhotels.com. A beautiful resort, recently expanded and given a sleek and thoroughly modern fit-out. Pick of the rooms are the beachfront cottages with private sit-outs and open-air showers.
$$$$ Radisson BLU Resort, off the northern entry point into town, T044-27443636, www.radissonblu.com. 100 rooms on 18 ha, beachfront. Best luxury resort in town. Top-notch service and food. Excellent seafood restaurant on the beach. Best rooms are the Pool View Chalets.
$$$$-$$$ Ideal Beach Resort, Kovalam Rd (3.5 km north), T044-2744 2240, www.idealresort.com. 30 rooms in cottages, some a/c (limited hours), good restaurant, exchange, spa with Ayurvedic massage, pool and gardens, clean, comfortable.
$$$-$$ Sea Breeze, Othavadai Cross, T044-2744 3035, www.hotelseabreeze.in. Clean, spacious, well-furnished rooms (some a/c with fridge, Rs 700), direct beach access, pool (non-residents Rs 200), good food. Iffy 'hot water', mediocre upkeep. Next door annexe is cheaper, see below.
$$ Butterball B&B, East Raja St, T(0)9094-792525, bbbb@gatsby.in. 9-room B&B located in town centre next to Nilgiris Supermarket. Rooms are small but clean. Holds music and art events, a weekly sandhai (flea market). Good food

at their restaurant called **Burger Shack**. Avoid rooms at the rear which face Krishna's butterball – big noisy coaches park there. Recommended.
$$-$ Lakshmi Lodge, Othavadai St, T044-2744 2463. Friendly, popular with backpackers, 26 clean rooms in main building, upstairs small but light, downstairs dark and poor, plus an annexe out the back with larger, brighter a/c rooms and a pool (which you pay extra to use if you stay in the cheap rooms). Restaurant with beach view.
$ Greenwoods Beach Resort, 7 Othavadai Cross St, T044-2744 2212, greenwoods_resort@yahoo.com. Basic but good and clean rooms with mosquito nets in a rambling building lushly shaded by banana and mango trees. The family owners are genuinely welcoming, and there's a well-regarded Ayurvedic clinic on site.
$ La Vie en Rose, 9 Old College Rd, near bus stand, T(0)9444-877544. Small, quiet hotel slowly going to rack and ruin, but it's a genuine cheapie and the manager is friendly.
$ Mamalla Heritage, 104 East Raja St, T044-2744 2060. Spotless, friendly and reasonable value, 43 clean spacious rooms, 17 a/c, nice balconies, pool, excellent vegetarian restaurant, exchange, travel, 24-hr hot water, and complimentary toiletries. Recommended.
$ Ramakrishna Lodge, 8A Othavadai St, T044-2744 2431. Friendly, good value, 31 well-kept, clean rooms with fan, shower, Western toilets, no nets, courtyard, good rooftop restaurant with travellers' menu and music; contact Vijay for informal yoga classes. Possibly the best cheap deal in town.

$ Sea Breeze Annexe, see above. Clean doubles with fan and deck, but rates don't include access to the **Sea Breeze** hotel pool.
$ Siva Guest House, 2 Othavadai Cross St, T044-2744 3534, www.sivaguesthouse. com. 11 very clean rooms, taxi hire, internet, friendly. Highly recommended.
$ Sri Harul Guest House, 181 Bajanai Koil St, T(0)9384-620173, lings6@rediffmail. com. Friendly little guesthouse right on the beach, with interesting views over the fishermen's colony. Rooms on the ground floor have private balconies.
$ Tamil Nadu Beach Resort, north of town on Covelong Rd, T044-2744 2361. Beautiful setting, 48 cottages, some a/c but neglected, damp, restaurants, bar (limited hours), exchange, good pool (non-residents Rs 75).
$ Tina Blue View Lodge, 1 Othavadai St, T044-2744 2319. Very friendly, 25 rooms with bath and balcony (Room 9 best), cottages for long-term stays, garden and rooftop restaurant, massage. Recommended.

Kanchipuram *p97, map p98*
$$-$ Baboo Soorya, 85 East Raja St, T044-2722 2555. Set back off main road down palm-fringed lane. 38 clean, spacious rooms, some a/c, restaurant, snack bar, glass 'bubble' lift, friendly staff, quiet.
$$-$ GRT Regency, Gandhi Rd, T044-2722 5250, www.grthotels.com. The best in town by a long chalk, with smart, spotless rooms and all the facilities of a luxury business hotel.
$ Sree Kusal Lodge, 68C Nellukkara St, T044-2722 3356. 25 clean and good-value rooms, TV, vegetarian restaurant.
$ Sri Krishna Lodge, 68A Nellukkara St, T044-2722 2831. Helpful, friendly manager, 28 good, clean rooms, some with bath.

$ Sri Rama Lodge, 20 Nellukkara St, near Bus Stand, T044-2722 2435. Fairly basic rooms, some a/c and TV, a/c restaurant, relatively quiet, helpful staff.

Around Kanchipuram *p99*
$$ Karadi Malai Camp, 5 km east of Chengalpattu, T(0)8012-033087, www. draco-india.com. Wildlife film-maker and croc man Romulus Whittaker and his wife Janaki have opened up their home and farm in the Vallam Reserve Forest. There are just 3 bamboo cottages here, plus a campsite and a delightful pool. Rich in small mammals (and the occasional leopard), birds, amphibians and reptiles. Set camera traps, search for snakes and other critters with Irula tribal guides. The best base for visiting Vedanthangal Sanctuary too.
$ Forest Rest House, 1 km from Vedanthangal Sanctuary gates, contact Wildlife Warden, T044-2432 1471 in Chennai, or ask a local agency to help with bookings. Rest house with 4 well-kept rooms (2 with a/c), meals available on request.

🍴 Restaurants

Mahabalipuram *p92, map p93*
Beachside cafés are pleasant for a drink: **Sea Rock** and **Luna Magica** in particular. In top hotels waterfront cafés are especially attractive in the evening.
$$ Curiosity, Othavadai St. Wide range, excellent food, very willing to please.
$$ Gazebo, East Raja St. Charcoal-grilled fish, pleasant seating.
$$ Moonrakers, Othavadai St, www.moonrakersrestaurant.com. Long-established backpacker favourite. Pleasant and friendly vibe during the week, but very rushed at weekends – you may be ordered out of your seat to make way for incoming diners.

$$ Temple View, GRT Temple Bay Kovalam Rd, T044-2744 3636. Multi-cuisine restaurant overlooking shore temple, breakfast lunch and dinner, plus less formal, open-air **Beach Comber** and **High Tide** bars (1000-2200).
$ Dreamland, Othavadai St. Western favourites, very friendly, relaxed.
$ Mamalla Bhavan, opposite bus stand. Classic high-ceilinged South Indian restaurant, excellent for cheap breakfasts.

Kanchipuram *p97, map p98*
Baboo Soorya (see Where to stay). A/c, cheap Indian vegetarian restaurant, good *thalis*.
Bakery Park Place, Odai St. Cakes and sweets.
Saravana Bhavan, next to Jaybala International 504 Gandhi Rd (50 m off the road). "Best in town".
Sri Rama Lodge, a/c, and **Sri Vela**, Station Rd. Good breakfasts.

⊛ Festivals

Mahabalipuram *p92, map p93*
Dec-early Feb 6-week **Dance Festival** starting on 25 Dec; at Bhagiratha's (Arjuna's) Penance, classical 1800-2030, folk 2030-2100, every Sat, Sun and holidays. Long speeches in Tamil on opening (full moon) night.
Mar Masi Magam attracts large crowds of pilgrims.
Apr-May Brahmotsava lasts for 10 days.
Oct-Nov The **Palanquin Festival** is held at the Stalasayana Perumal Temple.

Kanchipuram *p97, map p98*
Mar-Apr The **Panguni Uthiram Festival** is the largest of Kanchipuram's festivals, very atmospheric. Celebrated all over Tamil Nadu.

○ Shopping

Mahabalipuram *p92, map p93*
Hidesign, 138 East Raja St. Excellent Western-style leather goods, very reasonable. Recommended.
Himalayan Handicrafts, 21 East Raja St, also has 900 books for exchange.
JK Books, off the beach on Othavadai St. Books and newspapers.
Silver Star, 51 East Raja St, good tailor.

Kanchipuram *p97, map p98*
Silk and cotton fabrics with designs of birds, animals and temples or in plain beautiful colours, sometimes 'shot', are sold by the metre in addition to saris. It's best to buy from government shops or Co-operative Society stores.
AS Babu Shah, along Gandhi Rd. High-quality silks.
BM Silks, 23G Yadothagari, Sannathi St. Worth a look.
Murugan Silk Weavers' Co-operative, 79 Gandhi Rd.
Sreenivas, 135 Thirukatchi Nambi St (Gandhi Rd).

⊙ What to do

Mahabalipuram *p92, map p93*
Tour operators
Hi Tours, 123 East Raja St, T044-2744 3360, www.hi-tours.com. Train/air tickets, tours, foreign exchange, Kerala house boats.
Tamil Nadu Tourism runs a hop-on-hop-off bus service from Chennai, departing the Tourism Complex (2 Wallajah Rd) at 0900, 0930, 1000, 1100, returning from Mahabalipuram at 1600, 1700, 1730 and 1800; stops include the Crocodile Bank and Dakshina Chitra; tickets Rs 250. Also day tours to Kanchipuram and Mahabalipuram.

0630-1900. Tiring, but good value if you don't mind being rushed. It also includes a stop at the appallingly garish Indian kitsch, **VGP Beach Resort**.

⊖ Transport

Mahabalipuram *p92, map p93*
Bicycle/car hire Bicycle hire from tourist office and shops in East Raja St and hotels, Rs 40-50 per day. Recommended for **Tirukkalukundram** – from Dec to Feb a comfortable and very attractive ride. The same shops also hire out mopeds and motorbikes at around Rs 200-300. Car hire from the tourist office.

Bus The bus stand in the centre has buses to **Tirukkalukundram**, and further afield to **Chennai**, **Puducherry** and **Tiruvannamalai**.

Taxi Taxis charge Rs 1000-1200 for a 1-day excursion from Chennai, around Rs 1000 from Mahabalipuram to the airport.

Train The nearest train station is Chengalpattu, 29 km away, which has express trains to **Chennai** and south Tamil Nadu; buses from here to Mahabalipuram take an hour.

Kanchipuram *p97, map p98*
Auto-rickshaws Available for visiting temples. Also cycle rickshaws.

Bicycle hire The town is flat and easy to negotiate so the best and cheapest way to get about is by hiring a bike from near the bus stand or off East Raja St.

Bus The bus station in the middle of town with direct Govt Express to **Chennai** (*No 828*) 2½ hrs, **Bengaluru**

(**Bangalore**) (*No 828*), **Kaniyakumari** (*No 193*), **Puducherry** (*No 804*, 109 km) 3½ hrs, and **Tiruchirappalli** (*No 122*). For **Mahabalipuram** (65 km) 2 hrs, direct bus or take a bus to Chengalpattu (35 km) and catch one from there. Frequent buses to **Vellore**, other buses go to **Tirupati**, **Tiruttani** and **Tiruvannamalai**.

Train The train station, on a branch line, is under 1 km to the northeast of the bus stand. There are 3 direct passenger trains to **Chennai** (**Egmore**), at 0715, 1750 and 1900, 2 hrs; for long-distance trains, it's better to go by bus to **Arakkonam**, 28 km to the north, which is on the main Chennai–Bengaluru line.

Around Kanchipuram *p99*
Vedanthangal Bird Sanctuary is best accessed by car; an overnight taxi from Chennai will cost around Rs 2500, less from Mahabalipuram. The closest major town and railway station is Chengalpattu, which has several daily buses to the sanctuary and frequent connections to Chennai and Mahabalipuram.

⊙ Directory

Mahabalipuram *p92, map p93*
Banks Cherry, Beach St, for exchange. LKP, 130 East Raja St. Good rate, speedy. **Prithvi Securities**, opposite **Mamalla Heritage**, no commission, transfers money. **Libraries** English-language dailies. Book exchange at **Himalayan Handicrafts**. **Post** Post office on a back street off Kovalam Rd.

Kanchipuram *p97, map p98*
Banks State Bank of India, Gandhi Rd, with ATM. Amex TCs not accepted; **Indian Overseas Bank**, Gandhi Rd. **Post** Head Post Office, 27 Gandhi Rd.

Puducherry and Auroville

Pretty little Puducherry (still widely known by its old name of Pondicherry) has all the lazy charm of a former French colony: its stately whitewashed 18th-century homes froth with bright pink bougainvillea and its kitchens still smack gloriously of Gaul – excellent French breads, hard cheese and ratatouilles that run with olive oil, accompanied by real French wines. The primly residential French quarter contrasts wonderfully with the dog-eared heritage houses of the Tamil districts, whose streets were built to tilt towards Mecca, while the scores of pristine grey mansions indicate the offices of the Sri Aurobindo Ashram, headquarters of one of India's liveliest spiritual schools of thought.

Up the road is the 1960s Westernized branch of Sri Aurobindo's legacy, Auroville, the 'City of Dawn', which was conceived as "a place where human beings could live freely as citizens obeying one single authority, that of the supreme Truth". This is the industrious fulcrum of people seeking an alternative lifestyle – a place of spirulina, incense and white cotton weeds – and while many tourists visit Auroville on a rushed day trip from Puducherry, if you're of a meditative mindset and can forgo your fix of Gallic good cheer, it can be far more interesting to do it the other way round.

Puducherry is the archetypal ambling town: cleaved in two with the **French quarter** along the beach, boasting pretty high-ceilinged wood-slatted residential houses with walled gardens and bougainvillea, and with the markets, mess, businesses and 'talking streets' of the **Tamil** ('black') town to its west. While the French area, with 300 heritage buildings, is well maintained (the majority owned by the ashram), the Tamil area, despite its 1000 homes now classified as heritage, is dangerously dilapidated. The European Commission has funded the restoration of Calve Subraya Chettiar (Vysial) street (between Mission and Gandhi streets), while Muslim domestic architecture is clearly visible in the streets of Kazy, Mulla and Tippu Sultan, in the southern part of the Tamil quarter.

Many people come to Puducherry to visit the campus-like ashram of **Sri Aurobindo Ghosh** and his chief disciple Mirra Alfassa ('The Mother'). Ghosh was an early 20th-century Bengali nationalist and philosopher who struggled for freedom from British colonial power and wrote prodigiously on a huge variety of subjects, particularly Integral Yoga and education. In his aim to create an ashram utopia he found a lifelong *compadre* in the charismatic Frenchwoman Alfassa, who continued as his spiritual successor after his death in 1950. It was Alfassa who pushed into practice Sri Aurobindo's ideas on integral schooling, the aim of which is to develop all aspects of the student's being – "mind, life, body, soul and spirit". In the ashram school, class sizes are limited to eight students, and both pupils and teachers enjoy an extraordinary freedom to alter classes according to individual needs. Alfassa died in 1973 at the age of 93. Both Sri Aurobindo and Alfassa live on as icons, their images gazing down from the walls of almost every building in Puducherry.

Arriving in Puducherry → *Phone code: 0413. Population: 220,700.*
Getting there Buses take under four hours from Chennai on the East Coast Road. The well-organized bus stand is just west of the town, within walking distance, or a short auto-ride from the centre (expect the usual hassle from rickshaw-wallahs). The train station, on a branch line from Villupuram which has trains to major destinations, is a few minutes' walk south of the centre.

Getting around Puducherry is lovely to explore on foot, but hiring a bike or moped will give you the freedom to venture further along the coast. ➤ *See Transport, page 113.*

Tourist information Puducherry Tourism ① *40 Goubert Salai, T0413-233 9497, http://tourism.puducherry.gov.in, 0845-1300, 1400-1700.* Well run with maps, brochures and tours. The **Indian National Trust for Art and Cultural Heritage** (INTACH) ① *62 rue Aurobindo St, T0413-222 5991, http://intachpuducherry.org*, is particularly active in Puducherry and runs heritage walks from its offices. **La Boutique d'Auroville** ① *38 JL Nehru St, T0413-233 7264.* Provides information on visiting Auroville.

Puducherry

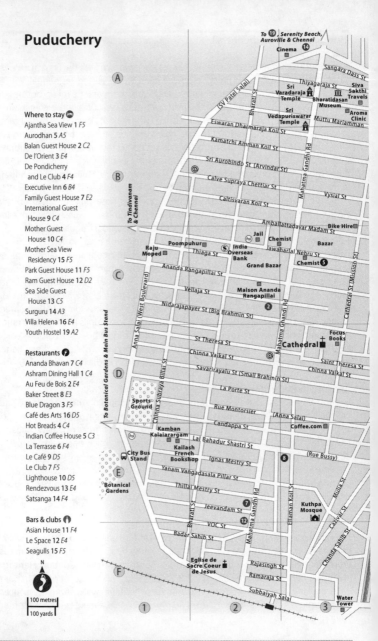

Where to stay

Ajantha Sea View 1 *F5*
Aurodhan 5 *A5*
Balan Guest House 2 *C2*
De l'Orient 3 *E4*
De Pondicherry
  and Le Club 4 *F4*
Executive Inn 6 *B4*
Family Guest House 7 *E2*
International Guest
  House 9 *C4*
Mother Guest
  House 10 *C4*
Mother Sea View
  Residency 15 *F5*
Park Guest House 11 *F5*
Ram Guest House 12 *D2*
Sea Side Guest
  House 13 *C5*
Surguru 14 *A3*
Villa Helena 16 *E4*
Youth Hostel 19 *A2*

Restaurants

Ananda Bhavan 7 *C4*
Ashram Dining Hall 1 *C4*
Au Feu de Bois 2 *E4*
Baker Street 8 *E3*
Blue Dragon 3 *F5*
Café des Arts 16 *D5*
Hot Breads 4 *C4*
Indian Coffee House 5 *C3*
La Terrasse 6 *F4*
Le Café 9 *D5*
Le Club 7 *F5*
Lighthouse 10 *D5*
Rendezvous 13 *E4*
Satsanga 14 *F4*

Bars & clubs

Asian House 11 *F4*
Le Space 12 *E4*
Seagulls 15 *F5*

N

100 metres
100 yards

Background

Ancient Vedapuri was where the sage **Agastya Muni** had his hermitage in 1500 BC and in the first century AD Romans traded from nearby Arikamedu. The French renamed the area Puducherry in 1673. In 1742, Dupleix, newly named Governor of the French India Company, took up residence. In 1746 the British lost Fort St George in Madras to Dupleix but in 1751 Clive counter-attacked by capturing Puducherry in 1761. Puducherry was voluntarily handed over to the Indian government in 1954 and became the Union Territory of Puducherry.

Places in Puducherry

The **French Quarter**, which extends from the seafront promenade inland to the canal, contains most of Puducherry's sights, and wandering the quiet streets, stopping into antique shops and colonial mansions, is a pleasure in itself.

The **Sri Aurobindo Ashram** ① *rue de la Marine, 800-1200, 1400-1800, free, meditation Mon-Wed, Fri 1925-1950*, has its main centre in rue de la Marine. Painted in neat grey and white like most of the ashram's buildings, it contains the flower-bedecked marble Samadhi (resting place and memorial) of both Sri Aurobindo and the Mother.

The **French Institute** ① *rue St Louis*, was set up in 1955 for the study of Indian culture and the 'Scientific and Technical Section' for ecological studies. There's a French and English library looking over the sea, and the colonial building is an architectural treat in its own right.

Puducherry Museum ① *next to the library, rue St Louis, Tue-Sun 0940-1300 and 1400-1720, closed public holidays, free,* has a good sculpture gallery and an archaeological section with finds discovered at the Roman settlement at Arikamedu. The French gallery charts the history of the colony and includes Dupleix's four-poster bed.

Another place worth seeking out is the grand whitewashed **Lycée Français** ① *rue Victor Simonel*, with its lovely shady courtyard and balconies.

The French Catholic influence is evident in a number of churches, notably the **Jesuit Cathedral** (Notre Dame de la Conception, 1691-1765). The attractive amber and pink **Church of Our Lady of Angels** (1855) holds an oil painting of Our Lady of Assumption given to the church by King Louis Napoleon III.

The **Government (Puducherry) Park**, laid out with lawns, flower beds and fountains (one at the centre is of the Napoleon III period), lies in front of the Raj Niwas, the residence of the lieutenant governor. This was the original site of the first French garrison, Fort Louis, which was destroyed in Clive's raid of 1761.

Auroville → *For listings, see pages 109-114. Phone code: 0413. Population 1700.*

① *Visitor centre, International Zone, T0413-262 2239, www.auroville.org, Mon-Sat 0900-1300 and 1400-1730, Sun 1000-1200 and 1400-1730. All visitors are expected to report here first. Passes for visits to Matrimandir gardens and Amphitheatre are issued here (Mon-Sat 0930-1230 and 1400-1600, Sun 0930-1230; gardens open daily 1000-1250 and 1400-1630), and a 5-min video about the Matrimandir is shown according to demand. Visitors may enter the Inner Chamber for 10 mins' silent 'concentration' with at least 1 day's notice; apply in person at the Visitor Centre 1000-1100 or 1400-1500 any day except Tue. A useful information booklet, The Auroville Handbook, is available here and at La Boutique d'Auroville, 38 JL Nehru St, Puducherry.*

Futuristic Auroville, 'City of Dawn', was founded in 1968 by 'The Mother' (Mirra Alfassa) as a tribute to Sri Aurobindo, and remains a fascinating experiment in communal living and spiritual evolution. The founding charter reads: "To live in Auroville one must be a willing servitor of the Divine Consciousness," and describes it as belonging "to humanity as a whole … the place of an unending education, of constant progress … a bridge between the past and the future … a site of material and spiritual researches for a living embodiment of actual human unity".

A baked and desolate plateau when the first residents moved here, Auroville has been transformed into a lush forest, among which are scattered 100 distinct hamlets, housing a permanent population of 2200 people plus a regular throughflow of international eco-warriors, holistic therapists and spiritually inclined intellectuals. It's a place where concepts that would be deemed too flakey to fly in the outside world are given free rein: the town plan is based on the shape of a spiralling galaxy, with the Matrimandir – an extraordinary 30-m-high globe-shaped meditation chamber clad in shimmering discs of gold leaf, with a lotus bud shaped foundation urn and a centrepiece crystal said to be the largest in the world – at its spiritual and geographic fulcrum. The main buildings are based on principles espoused in Sri Aurobindo's philosophical tracts. And a town that can't provide enough housing to accommodate all its would-be residents has found the money to build a gleaming pavilion dedicated to study of Aurobindo's epic poem Savitri.

Yet there's a great deal of serious and earnest work going on here, in the fields of sustainable architecture, reforestation, education, organic agriculture, renewable energy and self-development.

Residents are quick to point out that Auroville is not a tourist attraction, and a casual day trip here can be as much an exercise in frustration as inspiration. Tours from Puducherry visit the Matrimandir gardens for a view of the dome, but to experience the unforgettable womb-like interior and spend 10 minutes in silent 'concentration' you have to request permission in person at the Matrimandir office, at least 24 hours in advance.

On the other hand, the community welcomes visitors who have a genuine interest in its philosophy – all the more so if you can find a project you'd like to work on – and an extended stay here makes a very pleasant retreat. An ideal way to get to know the place is to take the three-day orientation tour, which guides you around many of Auroville's 'villages' by bike and provides a good opportunity to interact with Aurovilians.

⊙ Puducherry and Auroville listings

For hotel and restaurant price codes and other relevant information, see pages 13-17.

⊙ Where to stay

Puducherry *p105, map p106*
$$$$-$$$ The Dune, 15 km from Puducherry, T0413-265 5751, www. thedunehotel.com. Funky beachside eco-hotel with 36 themed villas and 15 colourful, clean and comfortable rooms spread amongst 12 ha of landscaped grounds. Yoga, reflexology, Ayurvedic massage, organic food and optional detox programmes are on offer, along with a pool, tennis and free bike hire.
$$$ Ajantha Sea View, 1C 50 Goubert Salai, T0413-234 9032, www.ajantha seaviewhotel.com. The best-value sea views in town (other than the ashram guesthouses, see below). Not the most modern rooms, but they're clean, bright and have huge balconies gazing straight out into the Bay of Bengal.
$$$ Aurodhan, 33 rue François Martin, T0413-222 2795, www.aurodhan.com. 16 superb rooms stuffed with top-quality

art and quirky antique furniture in an otherwise undistinguished building, with art galleries on the lower floors, Wi-Fi, a kitchen for home cooking and great views from the rooftop.
$$$-$$ Hotel de l'Orient, 17 Romain Rolland St, T0413-234 3067, www. neemranahotels.com. Beautifully renovated 19th-century school now a small exclusive hotel, with 16 tastefully decorated rooms in colonial style with objets d'art. Mixed reviews of the restaurant (French/Creole) and service, but achingly beautiful location. Recommended.
$$ Hotel de Pondichery, 38 rue Dumas, T0413-222 7409, www.hotelde pondichery.com. Simple, clean, tastefully decorated 10 rooms (some with no windows but private courtyard), in the same colonial-style building as the popular French bistro Le Club (so can get noisy). Very friendly and efficient staff. A/c. Babysitting service available.
$$ Mother Sea View Residency, 1-C rue Bazar St Laurent, T0413-222 5999, mother_residency@yahoo.co.in.

A handful of spacious, airy, marble-floored rooms with balconies pointing seawards.
$$ Villa Helena, 14 Suffren St, T0413-222 6789, www.villa-helena-pondicherry.com. 5 comfortable rooms with antique furniture set around large shady courtyard, suite on the 1st floor, includes breakfast.
$$-$ Executive Inn, 1a Perumal Koil St, T0413-233 0929, www.executiveinn.biz. 11 a/c suites, TV, restaurant, internet, no smoking, no alcohol, quiet yet short walk from the beachfront and bazar, good value. Recommended.
$$-$ Surguru, 104 Sardar Patel Rd, T0413-233 9022. Good, clean rooms, some a/c, excellent South Indian restaurant, bit noisy.
$ Balan Guest House, 20 Vellaja St, T0413-233 0634. 17 immaculate rooms with bath, clean linen.
$ Family Guest House, 526 MG Rd, T0413-222 8346, fghpondy@yahoo.co.in. 4 rooms, TV, hot water, bit cramped but very clean, roof terrace, hall, dining area, friendly.
$ Mother Guest House, 36 Ambur Salai, T0413-233 7165. Well-located cheap dive just off the JL Nehru shopping strip, with dark but clean enough rooms squirrelled away along labyrinthine corridors above a clothes shop.
$ Ram Guest House, 546 MG Rd, 278 Avvai Shanmugam (Lloyds) Rd, T0413-222 0072, ramguest@hotmail.com. 20 excellent rooms set back from the main road, maintained to European standards, spotless, good breakfast from clean kitchen. Recommended.
$ Youth Hostel, Solaithandavan Kuppam, T0413-222 3495, north of town. Dorm beds (Rs 30), close to the sea among fishermen's huts. Bicycle or transport essential.

Ashram guesthouses

Though these are mainly for official visitors and guests associated with the ashram, they are open to the public. Gates close by 2230 (late-comers may be locked out) and alcohol and smoking are prohibited. Book well in advance.
$ International Guest House, Gingee Salai, T0413-233 6699, ingh@aurosociety.org. 57 very clean and airy rooms, some a/c, huge for the price, very popular so often full.
$ Park Guest House, near Children's Park, T0413-222 4644. 93 excellent sea-facing rooms, breakfasts, clean, quiet, great garden, reading room, ideal for long stays. Recommended.
$ Sea Side Guest House, 14 Goubert Salai, T0413-223 1700, seaside@aurosociety.org. 25 excellent, large rooms, hot showers, breakfast, spotless, sea views. Recommended.

Auroville *p108*

For details of the 20-odd guesthouses scattered around Auroville, see www.aurovilleguesthouses.com. Accommodation ranges from basic thatched huts with shared toilets to self-contained studios, with rooms available in 4 distinct zones: Centre (close to the Matrimandir, theatres and cafés), Residential, Forest and Beach. The **Auroville Guest Service**, T0413-262 2704, can also help with finding a room. Costs vary from **$$-$**, though some operate a kibbutz-type arrangement.
$ Centre Guest House, T0413-262 2155. Most short-stay visitors are accommodated here ("welcomes those who wish to see and be in Auroville, but not to work there"), lovely setting under a huge banyan treee. Bikes and scooters for rent, famous weekly pizza.

🍴 Restaurants

Puducherry *p105, map p106*

$$$ Le Club, 38 rue Dumas, T0413-233 9745. Tue-Sun 0830-1830. French and Continental. Smart, excellent cuisine (Rs 400 for a splurge), French wine (Rs 1000). Mixed reviews: "we could have been in a French Bistro!" to "dearest but not the best".

$$$ Lighthouse, on the roof of **Promenade Hotel**, 23 Goubert Salai, T0413-222 7750. Superb barbecue fare, including some quite adventurous veg options alongside the expected seafood and meat options, served on a glassed-in terrace with front-row sea views. Good cocktails, too.

$$ Blue Dragon, 30 rue Dumas near New Pier (south end of Goubert Salai). Chinese. Excellent food, antique furniture.

$$ Café des Arts, 1 rue Labourdonnais. Very pleasant courtyard café serving good coffees and sandwiches, attached to an art gallery. Also has free Wi-Fi and clean toilets.

$$ La Terrasse, 5 Subbaiyah Salai, T0413-222 7677. Open 0830-2000, closed Tue. Excellent Continental. Good value, huge salads, no alcohol.

$$ Rendezvous, 30 Suffren St. French and Continental. Attractive, modern, reasonable food but overpriced wine, nice roof terrace, pleasant atmosphere: the owner worked for a wealthy American family for 20 years and so his continental grub is first rate.

$$ Salad Bar, 13 rue Surcouf. Delivers what it promises: fresh, hygienic and delicious salads, as well as falafel wraps, burgers and crepes. There's free Wi-Fi too.

$$ Satsanga, 32 rue Mahe de Labourdonnais, T0413-222 5867. Closed Thu. Continental (quite expensive wine), friendly, French atmosphere with art 'gallery'. Garden setting and staff make up for mediocre food.

$ Ananda Bhavan, 15 Nehru St. Big, buzzy and modern pure veg place, excellent for sweets and *thalis*, and good fun if you don't mind elbowing your way to the front of the queue.

$ Ashram Dining Hall, north of Government Place. Indian vegetarian. Simple, filling, meals (Rs 30 per day) in an unusual setting, seating on cushions at low tables, farm-grown produce, non-spicy and non-greasy. Buy a ticket (from ashram guesthouses or Central Bureau), then turn up at 0640, 1115, 1745 or 2000. Recommended, though non-ashramites can expect a grilling before being sold a ticket.

$ Au Feu de Bois, rue Bussy. Pizzas, salads, crêpes at lunchtime.

$ Baker Street, 123 rue Bussy. Closed Mon. Excellent new French sandwich shop and patisserie, with good but pricey coffee and handmade chocolates.

$ Hot Breads, Ambur Salai. Open 0700-2100. Good burgers, chicken puffs, pizzas, pastries, sandwiches and shakes.

$ Indian Coffee House, 41 Nehru St. Real local vegetarian fare from 0700.

$ Le Café, Goubert Salai, by Gandhi statue. Cute beachside pavilion in a grassy garden, great for hanging out with a milkshake or ice cream, though service is stretched and you'll be in for a long wait if it's busy.

🍸 Bars and clubs

Puducherry *p105, map p106*

Asian House, 7 Beach Blvd. Slick Bali-themed disco-pub, with a Buddha presiding over the bartenders and a DJ playing Euro house until the lights come on at 2300.

Le Space, 2 rue de la Bourdonnais. Sociable hippy-chic roof terrace hideaway strung with lanterns, with cheap drinks and music that's not too loud to talk over. Draws a mixed crowd of backpackers, Chennai hipsters and Pondy's young and beautiful. **Seagulls**, near Children's Park. Recently renovated, but the old formula of cheap beer and sea views remains unchanged.

⊕ Festivals

Puducherry *p105, map p106*
4-7 Jan International Yoga Festival held at Kamban Kalairangam, contact Puducherry Tourism for full details.
Jan Pongal is a 3-day harvest, earth and sun festival, popular in rural areas.
Feb/Mar Masi Magam on the full moon day of the Tamil month of Masi, pilgrims bathe in the sea when deities from about 40 temples from the surrounding area are taken in colourful procession for a ceremonial immersion. 'Fire walking' sometimes accompanies the festival.
14 Jul Bastille Day.
Aug Fete de Puducherry cultural programme.

⊙ Shopping

Puducherry *p105, map p106*
The shopping areas are along Nehru St and Mahatma Gandhi Rd. *Experience! Puducherry* booklet has a good shopping guide.

Dolls of papier mâché, terracotta and plaster are made and sold at Kosapalayam. Local grass is woven into *korai* mats. Craftsmen at the Ashram produce marbled silk, hand-dyed cloths, rugs, perfumes and incense sticks.

Antiques
Geethanjali, 20 rue Bussy. Pricey but well selected and restored pieces. **Heritage Art Gallery**, rue Romain Rolland.

Books
Focus, 204 Mission St. Good selection of Indian writing in English, cards, stationery, CDs, very helpful. **Kailash French Bookshop**, 87 Lal Bahadur Shastri St. Large stock.

Clothes and crafts
Several Ashram outlets on Nehru St. **Aurosarjan**, rue Bussy. Auroville clothes and crafts. **Cluny Centre**, 46 Romain Rolland St, T0413-233 5668. This is run by a French order in a lovely colonial house where nuns both design and oversee high quality embroidery. **Curio Centre**, 40 Romain Rolland St. Some fine antiques and good reproduction colonial furniture. **Kalki**, 134 Mission St, T0413-233 9166. Produces exceptional printed and painted silk scarves, hangings, etc. **Pondy Cre'Art**, 53B Suffren St. Intriguing variety of locally handmade products, from pencil cases and notebooks to pottery, cushion covers and bespoke bamboo fountains. Also some fantastic clothes. Highly recommended. **Red Courtyard**, 4 Chetty St. Floaty, feminine, boho clothing in silks, linens and cottons by local designer Virginie Malé, plus artworks, bags and jewellery by other local creators. **Sri Aurobindo Handmade Paper Factory**, 44 Sardar Patel Rd. Shop sells attractive products.

Auroville *p108*
Shops at the visitor centre sell products made in the hive of industry that is Auroville, including handmade paper, incense, wind chimes and the like. **La Boutique d'Auroville** has excellent clothes and accessories, cut to suit Western tastes.

⏻ What to do

Puducherry *p105, map p106*
Swimming
Pools in **Hotel Blue Star** and **Calve Bungalow**, Kamaraj Salai open to non-residents for a fee.

Tours and tour operators
Auro Travels, Karikar Building, Nehru St, T0413-233 5560. Efficient, quick service. **PTDC**, T0413-233 9497. Full-day sightseeing, 0930-1730, Rs 200 including lunch: Ashram, Govt Museum, Botanic Gardens, Sacred Heart church, Auroville and Matrimandir. Half day covers ashram, museum and Auroville, 1430-1730, Rs 100. Departs from tourist office on Goubert Salai.

Yoga
Ananda Ashram, on Yoga Sadhana Beach, 16 Mettu St, Chinna Mudaliarchavadi, Kottakuppam, T0413-224 1561. It runs 1-, 3- and 6-month courses starting in Jan, Apr, Jul and Oct; or book through **Puducherry Tourism**, Rs 1500 for 10 lecture modules.

Auroville *p108*
Body and soul
With a guest pass to Auroville you can participate in retreat activities from Indian dance to ashtanga yoga. There's also a Quiet Healing Centre on the nearby beach, well known for its underwater body treatments. The hydrotherapy treatment tank is a little public so it may be best to stick to the good Ayurvedic massages.

Tours
Available 0830-1100 from **Ashram**, Puducherry, autocare@auroville.org.in; 1430-1745 from **Cottage Complex**, Ambur Salai, includes Auroville Visitor Centre and Matrimandir. Visitors recommend going independently. A 5-day residential introduction to Auroville is available through the **Guest Service**, T0413-262 2704, www.aurovilleguestservice.org.

⊘ Transport

Puducherry *p105, map p106*
Bicycle/scooter hire Bike hire is well worthwhile as the streets are broad, flat and quiet. The best choice of mopeds and bikes is on Mission St between Amballattadavar Madam St and Caltisvaran Koil St. Day rates start from Rs 30 for a bike, Rs 100 for a scooter, Rs 200 for a motorbike, plus photo ID (some places ask to keep it) and Rs 500 deposit.

Bus Local bus stand: T0413-233 6919, 0430-1230, 1330-2130. **Main bus stand:** a few hundred metres west of the junction of Anna Salai and Lal Bahadur Shastri, T0413-233 7464, serves all State bus companies. Computerized Reservations: 0700-2100 (helpful staff). **Puducherry Tourism Corporation** (PTC), T0413-233 7008, 0600-2200, also runs long-distance services. Left luggage, Rs 20 per 24 hrs, at cloakroom on Platform 5. Auto-rickshaw to town Rs 30-40.

    Bengaluru (Bangalore): 7½ hrs, overnight Volvo service with PTC; **Chennai**: frequent express buses via East Coast Rd, 3 hrs; **Chidambaram**: frequent, 1½ hrs; **Coimbatore** via **Salem** and **Erode**: 8½-9½ hrs; **Kanniyakumari**: overnight service; **Kannur** and **Mahé**: 15 hrs; **Karaikal**: 4 hrs; **Madurai** via **Tiruchirappalli**: 6½-8 hrs overnight; **Mahabalipuram**: several, 4 hrs; **Tirupati**: 6½-7 hrs; **Tiruvannamalai** (via **Villupuram** or **Tindivanam**, 1 hr, and **Gingee**, 2 hrs): regular buses between 0600-2000, 3½-4 hrs; **Kottakarai**, frequent service from **Town Bus Stand**.

Car hire One-way and round trips to many destinations can be arranged at roughly Rs 10 per km (though be aware that even if you travel only one way you'll be charged the cost of returning to Puducherry) eg **Bengaluru (Bangalore)** (310 km) Rs 5500; **Chidambaram** (74 km), Rs 3300; **Chennai** (166 km), Rs 3500; **Mahabalipuram** (130 km), Rs 2600; **Tiruvannamalai**, Rs 2400. Also available for multi-day trips, eg **Madurai**, 2 days, Rs 3500; **Ooty**, 3 days, Rs 5300; **Cochin**, 4 days, Rs 6000. Add 20% for a/c, plus extra charges for driver (Rs 200 per day), hill driving (Rs 350), tolls and parking.

Companies include: **Siva Sakthi**, 66 Perumal Koil St, T0413-222 1992, www.sivasakthitravels.com, helpful but with limited English. **Praveen Cabs**, 63 Laporte St, T0413-222 9955.

Taxi Easiest to find along the canal. For local sightseeing, expect to pay around Rs 400 for 4 hrs (40 km), Rs 800 for 8 hrs (80 km).

Train Reservations: T0413-233 6684, Mon-Sat 0800-1400 and 1500-1900, Sun 0800-1400. Pondy has virtually no direct express trains, but is connected by branch line to Villupuram, which has good connections towards Chennai and Madurai.

Direct express trains: to **Chennai**, *Auroville Exp 16116*, 0535; *Chennai Pass 56038*, 1435, 5 hrs. To **Villapuram**: 6 trains daily at 0535, 0805, 1325 (continues to Tirupati, 9 hrs), 1515, 1600 and 1935; 45 mins. Also frequent buses, which drop off at the bus stop 100 m from Villlupuram station.

Express trains from Villupuram: **Chennai** several daily; **Madurai**: *Vaigai Exp 12635*, 1550, 6 hrs, via **Trichy**, 3 hrs, and **Kodaikanal Rd**, 5½ hrs. It's possible to make computerized reservations from Pondy station to any other station, and there is a quota on major trains leaving from Chennai Central.

Auroville *p108*
Bicycle hire Rent a bicycle (Rs 25 per day, though at some guesthouses they are free) and take advantage of the many cycle paths. **Centre Guest House** is one of several places renting bikes/mopeds.

Rickshaw/taxi Either of the 2 roads north from Puducherry towards Chennai leads to Auroville. A rickshaw from **Puducherry** will cost around Rs 200, a taxi costs around Rs 500 return.

⊙ Directory

Puducherry *p105, map p106*
Banks Many ATMS along Nehru St, Mission St and MG Rd. **Andhra Bank**, 105 Easwaran Koil St, offers cash against Visa. **State Bank of India**, 5 Suffren St, changes cash and TCs (Amex, Thomas Cook), 24-hr ATM. **LKP**, 185 Mission St. No commission. **Cultural centres** French Institute, rue St Louis, close to the north end of Goubert Salai. **Alliance Française**, southern end of Goubert Salai for cultural programmes, Mon-Fri 0800-1230, 1500-1900, Sat 0830-1200. **Embassies and consulates** French Consulate, 2 Marine St. **Internet** Coffee.com, 236 Mission St, plays DVDs, great coffee and real Italian pasta, but service and connection are equally slow. **Shreenet**, 54 Mission St. High speed, good computers, scanning. **Medical services** General Hospital, rue Victor Simone, T0413-233 6050; JIPMER, T0413-227 2381. **Ashram Dispensary**, Depuis St, near seaside. **Post** Head Post Office, northwest corner of Govt Place, T0413-233 3051. **CTO**, Rangapillai St. **Useful contacts** Foreigners' Regional Registration Office, Goubert Salai.

Palar Valley

Running between the steep-sided northern Tamilnad hill range is the broad, flat bed of the River Palar, an intensively irrigated, fertile and densely populated valley cutting through the much poorer and sometimes wooded high land on either side. The whole valley became the scene of an Anglo-French-Indian contest at the end of the 18th century. Today it is the centre of South India's vitally important leather industry and intensive agricultural development.

Vellore → *For listings, see pages 119-121. Phone code: 0416. Population: 177,400.*

The once strategically important centre of Vellore, pleasantly ringed by hills, is in the process of converting itself from the dusty market town of old into an unmissable stop on the Tamil Nadu temple circuit, complete with its own airport. The reason for this transformation is the glittering new **Sripuram Temple** ① *12 km south of town at the base of the Thirumalaikodi hills, www.sripuram.org, 0700-2000, free entry*, which opened in late 2007 with funding from the local Sri Narayani Peedam trust, headed by Sri Sakthi Amma. The central temple building is covered in 1.5 tonnes of gold leaf – more than adorns the Golden Temple in Amritsar – which is laid over sheets of copper embossed with figures of gods. The temple has attracted no small measure of controversy, largely because of the huge sum of money ploughed into its construction – an estimated 600 million rupees – which some feel would have been better spent on poverty alleviation programs. Sri Sakthi Amma has defended the temple on the basis that it will serve as an attraction to people from all over the world, with lasting financial benefits to the area's people – from increased tourism spending as well as from donations to the trust's various beneficent activities – and spiritual benefits to visitors. To reach the temple you have to negotiate a 2-km-long covered walkway, modelled after the star-shaped Sri Chakra and festooned with quotes from the Vedas, Bible and Koran. The inner sanctum contains a granite idol of Mahalaxmi, the goddess of wealth, draped in golden adornments.

Before Sripuram, Vellore was best known for its **Christian Medical College Hospital**, founded by the American missionary Ida Scudder in 1900. Started as a one-room dispensary, it extended to a small hospital through American support. Today it is one of the country's largest hospitals with over 1200 beds and large outpatients' department which caters for over 2000 patients daily. The college has built a reputation for research in a wide range of tropical diseases. One of its earliest and most lasting programmes has been concerned with leprosy and there is a rehabilitation centre attached. In recent years it has undertaken a wide-ranging programme of social and development work in villages outside the town to back up its medical programmes.

Vijayanagar architecture is beautifully illustrated in the temple at **Vellore Fort**, a perfect example of military architecture and a *jala durga* (water fort). Believed to have been built by the Vijayanagara kings and dating from the 14th century, the fort has round towers and huge gateways along its double wall. The moat, still filled with water by a subterranean drain, followed ancient principles of defence: it was home to a colony of crocodiles. A wooden drawbridge crosses the moat to the southeast. In 1768 Vellore came under the control of the British, who defended it against Haidar Ali. After the victory in Seringapatnam in 1799, Tipu Sultan's family was imprisoned here and a mutiny of 1806, in which many British and Indian mutineers were killed, left many scars. In the fort is a parade ground, the CSI church, the temple and two-storeyed *mahals*, which are used as government offices.

Jalakantesvara Temple ① *bathing Rs 2*, with a 30-m-high seven-storeyed granite *gopuram*, has undergone considerable restoration. Enter from the south and inside

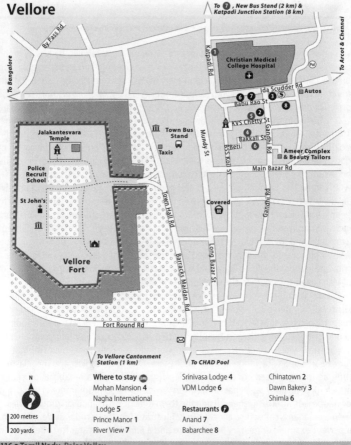

Vellore

To ⑦, New Bus Stand (2 km) & Katpadi Junction Station (8 km)

By Pass Rd

To Bangalore

To Arcot & Chennai

Katpadi Rd

① Christian Medical College Hospital

Ida Scudder Rd
⑥ ⑦ ③ ⑤
Babu Rao St
⑤ ②
KVS Chetty St
Bakkali St
⑥
Gandhi Rd
Autos ⑧
Ameer Complex & Beauty Tailors

Jalakantesvara Temple
Police Recruit School
St John's
Vellore Fort

Town Bus Stand
Taxis
Mundy St
Bss Koil St
Main Bazar Rd
Covered M
Gandhi Rd
Long Bazar St

Town Hall Rd
Barracks Maidan Rd

Fort Round Rd

To Vellore Cantonment Station (1 km)
To CHAD Pool

N
200 metres
200 yards

Where to stay
Mohan Mansion 4
Nagha International Lodge 5
Prince Manor 1
River View 7

Srinivasa Lodge 4
VDM Lodge 6

Restaurants 🍴
Anand 7
Babarchee 8

Chinatown 2
Dawn Bakery 3
Shimla 6

on the left, the *kalyana mandapa* (wedding hall), one of the most beautiful structures of its kind, has vivid sculptures of dragons and 'hippogryphs' on its pillars. The temple consists of a shrine to Nataraja in the north and a lingam shrine in the west.

Gingee → *For listings, see pages 119-121. Phone code: 04145.*

Gingee (pronounced *Senjee*), just off the NH45, situated between Chennai and Tiruvannamalai, has a remarkable 15th-century Vijayanagar fort with much to explore. It is well off the beaten track, very peaceful and in beautiful surroundings. Spend the night here if you can. Lovers come here at the weekends; it's on the domestic tourist map because it is often used as a film location. The landscape is made up of man-sized boulders, like Hampi, piled on top of each other to make mounds the texture of cottage cheese.

The fort ① *0900-1700, allow 2½ hrs for Rajagiri, and 2 hrs for Krishnagiri (if you have time), foreigners Rs 100, Indians Rs 20, camera Rs 50, video Rs 250, includes both forts,* was intensely contested by successive powers before being captured by an East India Company force in 1762, by the end of the century, however, it had lost its importance. Although it had Chola foundations, the 'most famous fort in the Carnatic' was almost entirely rebuilt in 1442. It is set on three strongly fortified Charnockite hills: Krishnagiri, Chakklidrug and Rajagiri. In places the hills on which the fort stands are sheer cliffs over 150 m high. The highest, Rajagiri ('King's Hill'), has a south-facing overhanging cliff face, on top of which is the citadel. The inner fort contains two temples and the Kalyana Mahal, a square court with a 27-m breezy tower topped by pyramidal roof, surrounded by apartments for the women of the governor's household. On top of the citadel is a huge cannon and a smooth granite slab known as the Raja's bathing stone. An extraordinary stone about 7 m high and balanced precariously on a rock, surrounded by a low circular brick wall, it is referred to as the Prisoner's Well. There are fine Vijaynagara temples, granary, barracks and stables and an 'elephant tank'. A caretaker may unlock a temple and then expect a tip.

The Archaeological Survey of India Office is just off the main road towards the fort. They may have guides to accompany you to the fort. Carry provisions, especially plenty of drinks; a few refreshments are sold, but only at the bottom of the hill. The climb is only for the fit and healthy; it's cooler in the morning and the views are less hazy.

Tiruvannamalai → *For listings, see pages 119-121. Phone code: 04175. Population: 130,300.*

At the foot of rocky Arunachala Hill, revered by Hindus across South India as the physical manifestation of Siva, Tiruvannamalai is one of Tamil Nadu's holiest towns. It is a major pilgrimage centre, focused around the enormous and fascinating Arunachaleshwar Temple whose tall *gopurams* stand dazzling white against the blue sky, and for the first half of the 20th century was home to one of India's most beloved saints, the clear-eyed Sri Ramana Maharishi.

One of the largest temples in South India, the 16th- and 17th-century **Arunachala Temple** was built mainly under the patronage of the Vijayanagar kings and is dedicated to Siva as God incarnate of Fire. Its massive bright white *gopurams*, the tallest of which is 66 m high, dominate the centre of the town. The temple has three sets of walls forming nested rectangles. Built at different periods they illustrate the way in which many Dravidian temples grew by accretion. The east end of each is extended to make a court, and the main entrance is at the east end of the temple. The lower parts of the *gopurams*, built of granite, date from the late Vijayanagar period but have been added to subsequently. The upper 10 storeys and the decoration are of brick and plaster. There are some remarkable carvings on the *gopurams*. On the outer wall of the east *gopuram*, for example, Siva is shown in the south corner dancing, with an elephant's skin. Inside the east doorway of the first courtyard is the 1000-pillared *mandapa* (hall, portico) built in the late Vijayanagar period. To the south of the court is a small shrine dedicated to Subrahmanya. To the south again is a large tank. The pillars in the *mandapa* are typically carved vigorous horses, riders and lion-like *yalis*. The middle court has four much earlier *gopurams* (mid-14th century), a large columned *mandapa* and a tank. The innermost court may date from as early as the 11th century and the main sanctuary with carvings of deities is certainly of Chola origin. In the south is Dakshinamurti, the west shows Siva appearing out of a lingam and the north has Brahma. The outer porch has small shrines to Ganesh and Subrahmanya. In front of the main shrine are a brass column lamp and the *Nandi* bull.

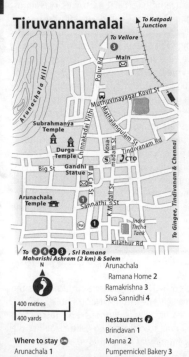

Some 2 km southwest of the centre, the **Sri Ramanasramam** ① *T04175-237292*, *www.sriramanamaharshi.org*, was founded by Sri Ramana Maharishi, the Sage of Arunachala (1879-1950). Aged 16, he achieved spontaneous self-realization and left his family to immerse himself in *samadhi* at the foot of the holy mountain. He spent 20 years in caves, steadily accumulating followers, one of whom was his own mother, who died at the base of the mountain in 1922. Recognized as a saint herself, Sri Ramana chose his mother's shrine as the site for his ashram.

The peacock-filled ashram grounds, which attract a sizeable community of Westerners between December and April, contain a library with 30,000 spiritual books and many photos of

Maharishi, the last of which were taken by Henri Cartier-Bresson, who photographed him when he was alive and also the morning after his death in April 1950. Apart from the two daily *pujas* (1000 and 1815) the ashram organizes few daily programs; the focus here is on quiet self-enquiry and meditation. Foreigners wishing to stay need to write to the ashram president with proposed dates.

A gate at the back of the ashram gives access to the hillside, from where you can begin the 14-km *pradakshina* (circuit) of Arunachala. The hike is done barefoot – no shoes should be worn on the holy mountain – and takes four to five hours; on full moon nights, particularly during the annual **Karthikai Deepam** festival (November-December), the trail fills with crowds of pilgrims who chant the name of Siva and make offerings at the many small temples along the way. Another track, branching off to the right shortly after the ashram gate, climbs to Skandasramam, a shady hermitage dug into the rock at which Sri Ramana lived from 1916 to 1922. From here there's a wonderful view over the town, best at sunrise when the temples rise out of the haze like a lost Mayan city. The challenging trek to the summit of Arunachala continues beyond Skandasramam (allow six hours up and down).

◉ Palar Valley listings

For hotel and restaurant price codes and other relevant information, see pages 13-17.

◐ Where to stay

Vellore *p115, map p116*
$ Mohan Mansion, 12 Beri Bakkali St, T0416-222 7083, 15 mins' walk from bus stand. Small, basic and clean, quieter than others.
$ Nagha International Lodge, 13/A KVS Chetty St, T0416-222 6338. Some a/c rooms.
$ Prince Manor, 41 Katpadi Rd, T0416-222 7106. Comfortable rooms, excellent restaurant.
$ River View, New Katpadi Rd, T0416-222 5251, 1 km north of town. 31 rooms, some a/c (best on tank side), modern, pleasant courtyard with mature palms, 3 good restaurants.
$ Srinivasa Lodge, Beri Bakkali St, T0416-222 6389. Simple and clean.
$ VDM Lodge, T0416-222 4008. Very cheap, pleasant, helpful staff.

Gingee *p117*
Avoid **Aruna Lodge**, near bus stand.
$ Shivasand, M Gandhi Rd, opposite bus stand, T04145-222218. Good views of fort from roof, 21 clean rooms with bath, some a/c, veg restaurant, a/c bar, helpful manager.

Tiruvannamalai *p117, map p118*
The best areas to stay are around the temple and in the streets opposite the ashram; hotels opposite the bus stand are uniformly grim. At full moon pilgrims arrive to walk around Arunachala Hill and hotels are overbooked.
$ Arunachala, 5 Vadasannathi St, T04175-228300. 32 clean, rooms, 16 a/c, TV, hot water, best away from temple, can get noisy during festivals, great vegetarian food downstairs.
$ Arunachala Ramana Home, 70 Ramana Nagar, off Chengam Rd, near ashram, T04175-236120. Friendly place with clean, good-value rooms. The owners can arrange bike hire and taxis,

and also hand out a home-made map of the ashram area and mountain circuit.
$ Ramakrishna, 34F Polur Rd, T04175-250005, info@hotelramakrishna.com. Modern, 42 rooms, 21 a/c, TV, hot water, excellent vegetarian tandoori restaurant, parking, helpful and friendly staff. Recommended.
$ Siva Sannidhi, Siva Sannidhi St, opposite ashram, T04175-236972. Spacious, simple and clean rooms, some with balconies overlooking Arunachala, slightly institutional feel of this large complex. Free veg meals.

Restaurants

Vellore *p115, map p116*
$ Anand, Ida Scudder Rd. Excellent breakfasts.
$ Babarchee, Babu Rao St. Good fast food and pizzas.
$ Best, Ida Scudder Rd. Some meals very spicy, nice parathas, 0600 for excellent breakfast.
$ Chinatown, Gandhi Rd. Small, friendly, a/c. Good food and service.
$ Dawn Bakery, Gandhi Rd. Fresh bread and biscuits, cakes, also sardines, fruit juices.
$ Geetha and **$ Susil**, Ida Scudder Rd. Rooftop or inside, good service and food.
$ Shimla, Ida Scudder Rd. Tandoori, naan very good.

Tiruvannamalai *p117, map p118*
This town is a *thali* lover's paradise with plenty of 'meals' restaurants.
$ Brindavan, 57 A Car St. Great *thali*.
$ Manna, next to **Arunachala Ramana Home** (see Where to stay). Super-relaxed place for salads and snacks, with free Wi-Fi and a noticeboard listing upcoming events.

$ Pumpernickel Bakery, Agni Nilam St, near ashram. Western-orientated place split between 2 neighbouring rooftops, serving good breakfasts, soups and fantastic pastries.

Festivals

Tiruvannamalai *p117, map p118*
Nov-Dec Karthikai Deepam, full moon day. A huge beacon is lit on top of the hill behind the temple. The flames, which can be seen for miles around, are thought of as Siva's lingam of fire, joining the immeasurable depths to the limitless skies. A cattle market is also held.

Shopping

Vellore *p115, map p116*
Most shops are along Main Bazar Rd and Long Bazar St. Vellore specializes in making 'Karigari' glazed pottery in a range of traditional and modern designs. Vases, water jugs, ashtrays and dishes are usually coloured blue, green and yellow.
Beauty, Ameer Complex, Gandhi Rd. Cheapest good-quality tailoring.
Mr Kanappan, Gandhi Rd. Very friendly, good-quality tailors, bit pricier.

What to do

Vellore *p115, map p116*
Hillside Resort, CHAD (Community Health and Development), south of town. Open early morning to late evening, closed Mon and 1200-1500. Excellent pool, Rs 250 per day.

Transport

Vellore *p115, map p116*
Bus The new long-distance bus stand is 2 km north of the town centre, which

can be reached by local buses 1 and 2 or auto-rickshaw. Buses to **Tiruchirappalli**, **Tiruvannamalai**, **Bengaluru** (**Bangalore**), **Chennai**, **Ooty**, **Thanjavur** and **Tirupathi**. The regional state bus company **PATC** runs frequent services to **Kanchipuram** and **Bengaluru** from 0500 (2½ hrs) and **Chennai**. From the **Town-Bus Stand**, off Long Bazar Rd near the fort, buses 8 and 8A go to the Sripuram temple.

Train Vellore Town station has daily passenger trains to **Tirupati** at 1015 and 1800. The main station, **Katpadi Junction**, 8 km north of town, is on the broad gauge line between **Chennai** and **Bengaluru**. Buses and rickshaws (Rs 35) into Vellore. **Chennai** (**C**): dozens of trains a day; *West Coast Exp 16628*, 1245, 2½ hrs. **Bengaluru** (**C**): *Brindavan Exp 12639*, 0903, 4¼ hrs; *Lalbagh Exp 12607*, 1745, 4 hrs. **Tirupati**: *Seshadri Exp 17209*, 1755, 2 hrs; also unreserved passenger trains at 0610, 1030, 1415, 1820 and 2100. It is also on the metre gauge line to **Villupuram** to the south, with 1 or 2 trains per week to **Puducherry** mostly at inconvenient hours of the night.

Gingee *p117*
Bicycles There are bicycles for hire next to the bus station.

Bus Buses to/from **Puducherry**, infrequent direct buses (2 hrs); better via Tindivanam (45 mins). To/from **Tiruvannamalai**, 39 km: several buses (1 hr), Rs 13; Express buses will not stop at the fort. TPTC bus *122* to/from **Chennai**.

Rickshaw To visit the fort take a cycle-rickshaw from the bus stand to the hills; Rs 30 for the round trip, including a 2-hr wait. There are bicycles for hire next to the bus station.

Tiruvannamalai *p117, map p118*
Bicycle Cycling can be hazardous in this very busy small town, but it's a practical way to get around the ashram area. Bikes for hire from a stand just east of the **Amman Rooftop Café**, Rs 20 per day.

Bus Buses to major cities in **Tamil Nadu**, **Kerala** and **Karnataka**. Local people will point out your bus at the bus stand; you can usually get a seat although they do get crowded. To **Gingee**, frequent, 1 hr; **Chennai**, 5 hrs, Rs 30, including 4 non-stop a/c buses per day; **Puducherry**, 3-3½ hrs.

Train At present there are no trains to Tiruvannamalai. The closest useful stations are Tindivanam, on the Chennai–Trichy line, and Katpadi on the Chennai–Bengaluru line. Frequent buses to both.

❶ Directory

Vellore *p115, map p116*
Banks Central Bank, Ida Scudder Rd, east of hospital exit, is at least 10 mins faster at changing TCs than the State Bank of India. **Internet** Net Paradise, north of bus stand. **Medical services** CMC Hospital, Ida Scudder Rd, T0416-228 2066. **Post** CMC Hospital has PO, stamps, takes parcels.

Tiruvannamalai *p117, map p118*
Bank ATM on South Sannadhi St. Vysya Bank, Sannathi St. Quick for cash and TCs. **Internet** Sri Bhagavan Net Park, 18/7 Manakkula Vinayagar St (near ashram), good connection, Wi-Fi, cold drinks. **Post** A Car St.

Chola Heartland and the Kaveri Delta

Chidambaram, Trichy and Tanjore together represent the apotheosis of Tamilian temple architecture: the great temples here act as *thirthas*, or gateways, linking the profane to the sacred. This pilgrim's road boasts the bare granite Big Temple in the charming agricultural town of Tanjore, which was for 300 years the capital of the Cholas; Trichy's 21-*gopuram*, seven-walled island city of Srirangam, a patchwork quilt of a temple built by successive dynastic waves of Cholas, Cheras, Pandyas, Hoysalas, Vijayanagars and Madurai Nayaks; and the beautiful Nataraja Temple at Chidambaram, with its two towers given over to bas reliefs of the 108 *mudras*, or gestures, of classical dance.

Chidambaram → *For listings, see pages 133-139. Phone code: 04144.*

The capital of the Cholas from AD 907 to 1310, the temple town of Chidambaram is one of Tamil Nadu's most important holy towns. The town (population 59,000) has lots of character and is rarely visited by foreigners. Its main attraction is the temple, one of the only ones to have Siva in the cosmic dance position. It is an enormously holy temple with a feeling all its own.

The **Nataraja Temple** ① *0400-1200, 1630-2200, visitors may be asked for donations, entrance into the inner sanctum Rs 50, men must remove their shirts,* was the subject of a supreme court battle that ended in Delhi, where it was decided that it should remain as a private enterprise. All others fall under the state, with the Archeological Survey of India's sometimes questionable mandate to restore and maintain them. The unique brahmin community, with their right forehead shaved to indicate Siva, the left grown long and tied in a front top knot to denote his wife Parvati, will no doubt trot this out to you. As a private temple, it is unique in allowing non-Hindus to enter the sanctum (for a fee); however, the brahmins at other shrines will ask you to sign a book with other foreign names in it, supposedly having donated Rs 400. The lack of state support does make this temple poorer than its neighbours, but if you want to give a token rupee coinage instead then do so. The atmosphere of this temple more than compensates for any money-grabbing tactics, however. Temple lamps still hang from the hallways, the temple music is rousing and the *puja* has the statues coming alive in sudden illumination. The brahmins themselves have a unique, stately presence too. The evening *puja* at 1800 is particularly interesting. At each shrine the visitor will be daubed with *vibhuti* (sacred ash) and paste. It is not easy to see some of the sculptures in the interior gloom. You may need patience and persuasive powers if you want to take your own time but it is worth the effort.

There are records of the temple's existence before the 10th century and inscriptions from the 11th century. One legend surrounding its construction suggests that it was built by 'the golden-coloured emperor', Hiranya Varna Chakravarti, who suffered from leprosy. He came to Chidambaram on a pilgrimage from Kashmir in about AD 500. After bathing in the temple tank he was reputed to have recovered from the disease and in gratitude offered to rebuild and enlarge the temple.

On each side are four enormous *gopurams*, those on the north and south being about 45 m high. The east *gopuram* (AD 1250), through which you enter the temple, is the oldest. The north *gopuram* was built by the great Vijayanagar king **Krishna Deva Raya** (1509-1530). Immediately on entering the East Gate is the large **Sivaganga Tank**, and the **Raja Sabha**, a 1000-columned *mandapa* (1595-1685). In the northwest of the compound are temples dedicated to Subrahmanya (late 13th century), and to its south the 12th century shrine to Sivakumasundari or Parvati (circa 14th century). The ceiling paintings are 17th century. At the southern end of this outer compound is what is said to be the largest shrine to **Ganesh** in India. The next inner compound has been filled with colonnades and passageways. In the innermost shrine are two images of Siva, the Nataraja and the lingam. A later Vishnu shrine to Govindaraja was added by the Vijayanagar kings. The **inner enclosure**, the most sacred, contains four

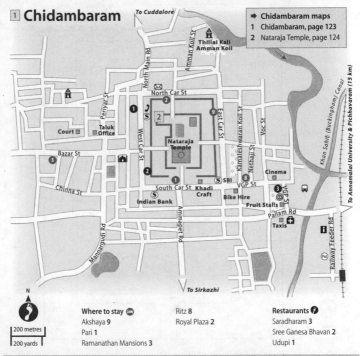

① **Chidambaram**   To Cuddalore

➡ **Chidambaram maps**
1 Chidambaram, page 123
2 Nataraja Temple, page 124

Thillai Kali Amman Koil

North Car St

Nataraja Temple

Court Taluk Office

Bazar St

West Car St

Chinna St

South Car St   Khadi Craft   SBI

Indian Bank   Bike Hire   Cinema   VGP St

Mamangudi Rd   Annapet Rd   Fruit Stalls

Pallam Rd

Taxis

To Sirkazhi

To Annamalai University & Pichavaram (15 km)

Khan Sahib (Buckingham) Canal

Railway Feeder Rd

N

200 metres
200 yards

Where to stay
Akshaya 9
Pari 1
Ramanathan Mansions 3

Ritz 8
Royal Plaza 2

Restaurants
Saradharam 3
Sree Ganesa Bhavan 2
Udupi 1

important *Sabhas* (halls), the **deva sabha**, where the temple managers hold their meetings; the **chit sabha** or *chit ambalam* (from which the temple and the town get their names), meaning the hall of wisdom; the **kanakha sabha**, or golden hall; and the **nritta sabha**, or hall of dancing. Siva is worshipped in the *chit ambalam*, a plain wooden building standing on a stone base, in his form as Lord of the Dance, Nataraja. The area immediately over the deity's head is gold plated. Immediately behind the idol is the focus of the temple's power, the Akasa Lingam, representing the invisible element, 'space', and hence is itself invisible. It is known as the Chidambaram secret.

Around Chidambaram
The Danish king Christian IV received permission from Raghunath Nayak of Thanjavur to build a fort here at **Tranquebar** (Tharangampadi) in 1620. The Danish Tranquebar Mission was founded in 1706 and the Danesborg **fort** and the old **church** still survive. The Danes set up the first Tamil printing press, altering the script to make the casting of type easier and the Danish connection resulted in the National Museum of Copenhagen today possessing a remarkable collection of 17th-century

2 Nataraja Temple, Chidambaram

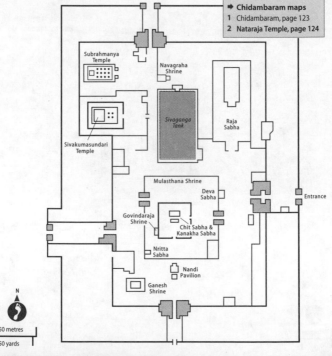

➡ **Chidambaram maps**
1 Chidambaram, page 123
2 Nataraja Temple, page 124

Thanjavur paintings and Chola bronzes. There is a **museum** and a good beach, plus the evocatively ruined 14th-century Masilamani Nathar temple on the seashore. From Chidambaram most transport requires a change at Sirkazhi. From Thanjavur there are some direct buses; other buses involve a change at Mayiladuthurai (24 km).

Gangaikondacholapuram → *For listings, see pages 133-139.*

Once the capital of the Chola king Rajendra (1012-1044), this town (whose name means 'The city of the Chola who conquered the Ganga') has now all but disappeared. The temple and the 5-km-long 11th-century reservoir embankment survive.

The **temple** ① *0700-1200, 1600-2100,* that Rajendra built was designed to rival the Brihadisvara temple built by Rajendra's father Rajaraja in Thanjavur. Unlike the *Nandi* in Thanjavur, the huge *Nandi* facing the *mandapa* and sanctuary inside the compound by the ruined east *gopuram* is not carved out of one block of stone. As in Thanjavur, the *mandapa* and sanctuary are raised on a high platform, orientated from west to east and climbed by steps. The whole building is over 100 m long and over 40 m wide. Two massive *dvarapalas* (doorkeepers) stand guard at the entrance to the long closed *mandapa* (the first of the many subsequent *mandapas* which expanded to 'halls of 1000 pillars'); the plinth is original. A *mukha-mandapa* (narrow colonnaded hall) links this hall to the shrine. On the east side of this hall are various carvings of Siva for example bestowing grace on Vishnu, who worships him with his lotus-eye. On the northeast is a large panel, a masterpiece of Chola art, showing Siva blessing Chandikesvara, the steward. At the centre of the shrine is a huge *lingam* on a round stand. As in Thanjavur there is a magnificent eight-tiered, pyramidal *vimana* (tower) above the sanctuary, nearly 55 m high. Unlike the austere straight line of the Thanjavur Temple, however, here gentle curves are introduced. Ask the custodian to allow you to look inside (best for light in the morning). Immediately to the north of the *mandapa* is an excellently carved shrine dedicated to Chandikesvara. To north and south are two shrines dedicated to Kailasanatha with excellent wall sculptures. The small shrine in the southwest corner is to Ganesh.

Kumbakonam → *For listings, see pages 133-139. Phone code: 0435. Population: 140,000.*

This very pleasant town, 54 km from Thanjavur, was named after the legend where Siva was said to have broken a *kumbh* (water pot) after it was brought here by a great flood. The water from the pot is reputed to have filled the Mahamakam Tank. High-quality betel vines, used for chewing *paan*, are grown here.

Places in Kumbakonam

The temples in this region contain some exceptional pieces of jewellery – seen on payment of a small fee. There are 18 **temples** ① *closed 1200-1630, no photography,* in the town centre and a monastery of the Kanchipuram Sankaracharya. The oldest is the **Nagesvara Swami Temple**, a Shaivite temple begun in AD 886. The small

Nataraja shrine on the right before you reach the main sanctum is designed to look like a chariot being pulled by horses and elephants. Superb statues decorate the outside walls of the inner shrine; Dakshinamurti (exterior south wall), Ardinarisvara (west facing) and Brahma (north) are in the central panels, and described as being among the best works of sculpture of the Chola period. The temple has a special atmosphere and is definitely worth a visit.

Sarangapani is the largest of Kumbakonam's shrines. Dedicated to Vishnu (one of whose avatars is Krishna the cowherd), it is also one of the few temples in Tamil Nadu where you will see devotees actively paying reverence to cows. Beyond the 11-storey main *gopuram* that towers above the entrance lies a cattle shed, where visitors can offer gifts of leaves before tiptoeing in (barefoot, naturally) to touch the hindquarters of the closest cow. The Nayaka *mandapa*, with huge beams of beautifully carved stone, leads through a second, smaller *gopuram* to a further *mandapa* carved in the form of a chariot, towed by horses and elephants.

The **Kumbesvara Temple** dates mainly from the 17th century and is the largest Siva temple in the town. It has a long colonnaded *mandapa* and a magnificent collection of silver *vahanas* (vehicles) for carrying the deities during festivals. The **Ramasvami Temple** is another Nayaka period building, with beautiful carved rearing horses in its pillared *mandapa*. The frescoes on the walls depict events from the *Ramayana*. The **Navaratri Festival** is observed with great colour.

Kumbakonam

To Swamimalai & Gangaikondacholapuram

To Chidambaram

To Darasuram & Thanjavur

BAZAR

Kaveri River

College Rd

Banadurai Rd

Kamatchi Josier St

Chakkarapani Temple

Town Hall Rd

Big Bazar St

State Bank of India

TSR Big St

Besant Rd

Town Hall

Tiruvidamarudat Rd

Sarangapani Temple

East St

Ayekulam Rd

Kumbesvara Temple

Poothamari Tank

Nagesvaran North St

Khadi Gramadyog

Head PO Rd

Nagesvara Swami Temple

Ramasvami Temple

Gandhi Adikal Salai

BAZAR

Clock Tower

Kamaraj Rd

Mahamakam Tank

N

300 metres
300 yards

Where to stay	Pandian 3	Restaurants
ARK International 1	Raya's 4	Sri Venkkatramana 1
Femina 2	Raya's Annexe 5	

The terrifying guardian deities

Many Hindu villagers in Tamil Nadu believe in guardian deities of the village – Ayyanar, Muneeswaram, Kaliamman, Mariamman and many more. Groups of larger-than-life images built of brick, wood or stone and covered in *chunam* (brightly painted lime plaster) guard the outskirts of several villages. They are deliberately terrifying, designed to frighten away evil spirits from village homes, but villagers themselves are also very frightened of these gods and try to keep away from them. The deities are supposed to prevent epidemics, but if an epidemic does strike, special sacrifices are offered, mainly of rice. Firewalking, often undertaken in fulfilment of a vow, is a feature of the special festivals at these shrines. Disease is also believed to be held at bay by other ceremonies, including piercing the cheeks and tongue with wire and the carrying of *kavadis* (special carriages or boxes, sometimes designed like a coffin).

The **Mahamakam Tank** is visited for a bathe by huge numbers of pilgrims every 12 years, when 'Jupiter passes over the sign of Leo'. It is believed that on the day of the festival nine of India's holiest rivers manifest themselves in the tank, including the Ganga, Yamuna and Narmada.

Darasuram

About 5 km south of Kumbakonam is Darasuram with the **Airavatesvara Temple** ① *open 0600-1200,1600-2000*, after Thanjavur and Gangaikondacholapuram, the third of the great Chola temples, built during the reign of **Rajaraja II** (1146-1172). The entrance is through two gateways. A small inner gateway leads to a court where the mainly granite temple stands in the centre. The *gopuram* is supported by beautifully carved *apsaras*. Inside, there are friezes of dancing figures and musicians. The *mandapa* is best entered from the south. Note the elephant, ridden by dwarfs, whose trunk is lost down the jaws of a crocodile. The pillars illustrate mythological stories for example 'the penance of Parvati'. The five gods Agni, Indra, Brahma, Vishnu and Vayu in the niches are all shown paying homage to Siva. The **main mandapa**, completely enclosed and joined to the central shrine, has figures carved in black basalt on the outside. The ceilings are also richly decorated and the pillars have the same flower emblems as in the outer *mandapa*. The main shrine has some outstanding sculptures; the guardians on the north are particularly fine. Sculpted doorkeepers with massive clubs guard the entrance to the main shrine, which has a *Nandi* at the entrance. Some of the niches inside contain superb early Chola sculptures of polished black basalt, including a unique sculpture of Ardhanarisvara with three faces and eight arms, a four-armed Nagaraja and a very unusual sculpture of Siva destroying Narasimha. The **outer walls** are also highly decorative. Siva as Dakshinamurti on the south wall, Brahma on the north wall and Siva appearing out of the lingam on the west wall. The inner wall of the *prakara* (encircling walkway) is divided into cells, each originally to house a deity. The corners of the courtyard have been enlarged to make four *mandapas*, again with beautiful decoration.

Thanjavur is a mathematically perfect Brihadisvara Temple. A World Heritage Site, it is one of the great monuments of South India, its huge Nandi bull washed each fortnight with water, milk, turmeric and gingelly in front of a rapt audience that packs out the whole temple compound. In the heart of the lush, rice-growing delta of the Kaveri, the upper echelons of Tanjore life are landowners, rather than industrialists, and the city itself is mellow in comparison with Trichy, especially in the old town surrounding the Royal Palace.

Arriving in Thanjavur → *Phone code: 04362. Population: 215,700.*
Getting there Most long-distance buses stop at the New Bus Stand 4 km southwest of the centre, from where there are frequent buses and autos (Rs 60) to town. There's a second, more central bus stand off South Rampart Street, close to several budget hotels, which has some direct buses to Chennai. The train station is at the south end of the town centre, about a 20-minute walk from the Brihadisvara Temple, with connections to Tiruchirappali, Chennai and Bangalore.

Getting around Most hotels are within a 15-minute walk of the temple. Auto-rickshaws charge Rs 20-30 for trips around town. ▸▸ *See Transport, page 138.*

Tourist information ① *In the grounds of Hotel Tamil Nadu, Railway Station Rd (aka Gandhiji Rd), T04362-230984.*

Places in Thanjavur
Brihadisvara Temple ① *0600-2030, inner sanctum closed 1230-1600*, known as the Big Temple, was the achievement of the Chola king Rajaraja I (ruled AD 985-1012). The magnificent main temple has a 62-m-high *vimana* (the tallest in India), topped by a dome carved from an 80-tonne block of granite, which needed a 6.5-km-long ramp to raise it to the top. The attractive gardens, the clean surroundings and well-lit sanctuaries make a visit doubly rewarding, especially in the evening. The entrance is from the east. After crossing the moat you enter through two *gopurams*, the second guarded by two *dvarapalas* typical of the early Chola period, when the *gopurams* on the outer enclosure walls were dwarfed by the scale of the *vimana* over the main shrine. An enormous Nandi, carved out of a single block of granite 6 m long, guards the entrance to the sanctuary. According to one of the many myths that revolve around the image of a wounded Nandi, the Thanjavur Nandi was growing larger and larger, threatening the temple, until a nail was driven into its back. The temple, built mainly with large granite blocks, has superb inscriptions and sculptures of Siva, Vishnu and Durga on three sides of the massive plinth. Siva appears in three forms, the dancer with 10 arms, the seated figure with a sword and trident, and Siva bearing a spear. The carvings of dancers showing the 81 different Bharat Natyam poses are the first to record classical dance form in this manner. The main shrine has a large lingam. In the inner courtyard are Chola frescoes on walls prepared with lime plaster, smoothed and polished, then painted while the surface was wet. These were hidden

under later Nayaka paintings. Since music and dance were a vital part of temple life and dancing in the temple would accompany the chanting of the holy scriptures which the community attended, Rajaraja also built two housing colonies nearby to accommodate 400 *devadasis* (temple dancers). Subsidiary shrines were added to the main temple at different periods. The Vijayanagara kings built the Amman shrine, the Nayakas the Subrahmanya shrine and the Marathas the Ganesh shrine.

The **palace** ① *1000-1700, foreigners Rs 50, Indians Rs 5, camera Rs 30*, built by the Nayakas in the mid-16th century and later completed by the Marathas, is now partly in ruins, its walls used as makeshift hoardings for the latest Tamil movie release or political campaign. Still, there's evidence of its original splendour in the ornate

Thanjavur

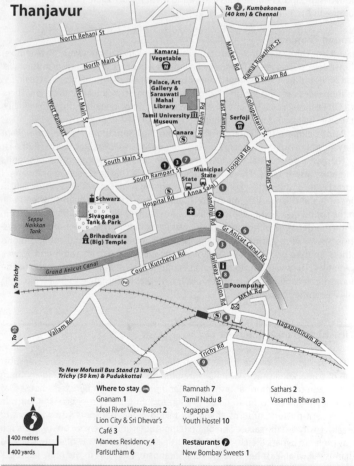

Where to stay 🛏
Gnanam **1**
Ideal River View Resort **2**
Lion City & Sri Dhevar's
  Café **3**
Manees Residency **4**
Parisutham **6**

Ramnath **7**
Tamil Nadu **8**
Yagappa **9**
Youth Hostel **10**

Sathars **2**
Vasantha Bhavan **3**

Restaurants 🍴
New Bombay Sweets **1**

Durbar Hall. The towers are worth climbing for a good view; one tower has a whale skeleton which was washed up in Chennai. The **art gallery** ① *0900-1300, 1500-1800, foreigners Rs 20, Indians Rs 5, camera Rs 30*, with bronze and granite sculptures, **Sangeeta Mahal** (the Hall of Music, where musicians and dancers performed before the Chola kings) with excellent acoustics, and the **Tamil University Museum** are here, together with some government offices. The pokey **Saraswati Mahal Library** ① *Thu-Tue 1000-1300, 1330-1700*, is brilliant. Among its 40,000 rare books are texts from the medieval period, beautiful botanical pictures from the 18th century, palm leaf manuscripts of the *Ramayana*, intricate 250-year-old miniatures, and splendid examples of the gaudy Tanjore style of painting. It also has old samples of dhoti cloth design, and 22 engravings illustrating methods of torture from other oriental cultures in the 'Punishments of China'.

Around Thanjavur

A visit to **Thiruvaiyaru**, 13 km away, with the Panchanatheswara Siva temple, known for its **Thyagaraja Music Festival**, gives a glimpse of South Indian rural life. Hardly visited by tourists, music connoisseurs arrive in large numbers in January. Performances vary and the often subtle music is marred by loud amplification. There is a **Car Festival** in March. Catch one of the frequent, crowded buses from the old bus station in Thanjavur, taking 30 minutes.

Point Calimere (Kodikkarai) Wildlife and Bird Sanctuary ① *open throughout the year, best season mid-Dec to Feb, Rs 5, camera Rs 5, video Rs 50*, is 90 km southeast of Thanjavur. The coastal sanctuary, half of which is tidal swamp, is famous for its migratory water birds. The Great Vedaranayam Salt Swamp (or 'Great Swamp') attracts one of the largest colonies of flamingos in Asia (5000-10,000) especially in December and January. Some 243 different bird species have been spotted here. In the spring green pigeons, rosy pastors, koels, mynahs and barbets can be seen. In the winter vegetables and insects attract paradise flycatchers, Indian pittas, shrikes, swallows, drongos, minivets, blue jays, woodpeckers and robins among others. Spotted deer, black buck, feral horses and wild boar are also found, as well as reptiles. The swamp supports a major commercial fishing industry. Jeeps can be booked at reception. Exploring on foot is a pleasant alternative to being 'bussed'; ask at reception for a guide.

Tiruchirappalli (Trichy) → *For listings, see pages 133-139.*

Trichy, at the head of the fertile Kaveri Delta, is an industrial city and transport hub of some significance, with its own international airport connecting southern Tamil Nadu to Singapore and the Gulf. Land prices are high here, and houses, as you'll see if you climb up to its 84-m-high rock fort, are densely packed, outside the elegant doctors' suburbs. If you are taking public transport you will want to break here to visit the sacred Srirangam temple but if you have your own wheels you may prefer to bypass the city, which has little else to offer by way of easily accessed charms. Allow at least half a day to tour Srirangam, then stay in the more laid-back agricultural centre of Tanjore to the north or the more atmospheric temple madness of Madurai further south.

Tiruchirappalli

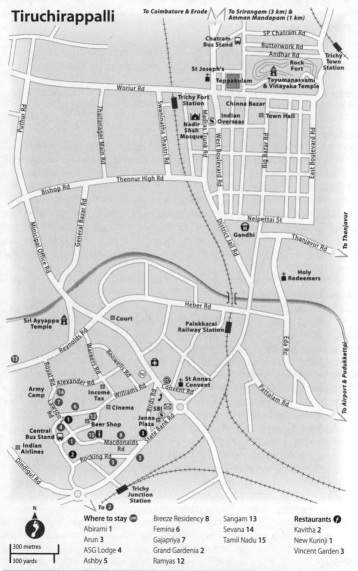

To Coimbatore & Erode
To Srirangam (3 km) & Amman Mandapam (1 km)
SP Chatram Rd
Chatram Bus Stand
Butterwork Rd
Andhar Rd
Trichy Town Station
St Joseph's
Teppakulam
Rock Fort
Tayumanasvami & Vinayaka Temple
Woriur Rd
Trichy Fort Station
Chinna Bazar
Thailanager Main Rd
Swainatha Shastri Rd
Madras Trunk Rd
Nadir Shah Mosque
Indian Overseas
Town Hall
West Boulevard Rd
East Boulevard Rd
Big Bazar Rd
Puthur Rd
Bishop Rd
Thennur High Rd
General Bazar Plaza
Nelpettai St
Municipal Office Rd
Gandhi
To Thanjavur
District Jail Rd
Thanjavur Rd
Holy Redeemers
Heber Rd
Sri Ayyappa Temple
Court
Palakkarai Railway Station
Reynolds Rd
Eda Rd
Warners Rd
Royal Rd
Bewells Rd
Pol
St Annes Convent
Convent Rd
Bharti Rd
To Airport & Pudukkottai
Army Camp
Alexander Rd
Income Tax
Williams Rd
Cinema
SBI
Pattalam Rd
Larson Rd
Beer Shop
Jenna Plaza
State Bank Rd
Central Bus Stand
Macdonalds Rd
Indian Airlines
Rocking Rd
Dindigul Rd
Trichy Junction Station
To 2

N
300 metres
300 yards

Where to stay 🏨
Abirami 1
Arun 3
ASG Lodge 4
Ashby 5

Breeze Residency 8
Femina 6
Gajapriya 7
Grand Gardenia 2
Ramyas 12

Sangam 13
Sevana 14
Tamil Nadu 15

Restaurants 🍴
Kavitha 2
New Kurinji 1
Vincent Garden 3

Arriving in Tiruchirappalli → *Phone code: 0431.*
Getting there Trichy airport, 8 km from the centre, has flights to Madurai and Chennai. With good transport connections to major towns, the Junction Railway Station and the two bus stations are in the centre of the main hotel area, all within walking distance.

Getting around Much of Trichy is quite easy to see on foot, but plenty of autos and local buses run to the Rock Fort and Srirangam. » *See Transport, page 139.*

Tourist information Tourist office ① *New Central Bus Stand, T0431-246 0136.* Also counters at the railway station and airport.

Background
Trichy was mentioned by Ptolemy in the second century BC. A Chola fortification from the second century, it came to prominence under the Nayakas from Madurai who built the fort and the town, capitalizing on its strategic position. In legend its name is traced to a three-headed demon, Trisiras, who terrorized both men and the gods until Siva overpowered him in the place called Tiruchi. Cigar making became important between the two world wars, while the indigenous *bidis* continue to be made, following a tradition started in the 18th century. Trichy is the country's largest artificial diamond manufacturing centre. Jaffersha Street is known as Diamond Bazar. The town is also noted for its high-quality string instruments, especially veenas and violins.

Places in Tiruchirappalli
Rock Fort (1660), stands on an 84-m-high rock. **Ucchi Pillayar Koil (Vinayaka Temple)** ① *Tue-Sun 0600-1200, 1600-2100, camera Rs 10, video Rs 50,* approached from Chinna Bazar, is worth climbing for the stunning panoramas but don't expect much from the temple. At the top of the first flight of steps lies the main 11th-century defence line and the remains of a thousand-pillared hall, destroyed in 1772. Further up is a hundred-pillared hall where civic receptions are held. At the end of the last flight is the **Tayumanasvami Temple**, dedicated to Siva, which has a golden *vimana* and a lingam carved from the rock itself. There are further seventh-century Pallava cave temples of beautiful carved pillars and panels.

Try to make time to explore the atmospheric old city, particularly **Big Bazar Street** and **Chinna Bazar**. The **Gandhi Market** is a colourful vegetable and fruit market.

Among the dozen or so mosques in the town, the **Nadir Shah Mosque** near the city railway station stands out with its white dome and metal steeple, said to have been built with material taken from a Hindu temple. **St Joseph's College Church** (Church of our Lady of Lourdes), one of several Catholic churches here, was designed as a smaller version of the Basilica at Lourdes in France. It has an unusual sandalwood altar but is rather garish inside. The grounds are a peaceful spot. The 18th-century **Christ Church**, the first English church, is north of the Teppakulam, while the early 19th-century **St John's Church** has a memorial plaque to Bishop Heber, one of India's best known missionary bishops, who died in Trichy in 1826.

Srirangam

The temple town on the **Kaveri**, just north of Trichy, is surrounded by seven concentric walled courtyards, with magnificent gateways and several shrines. On the way to Srirangam is an interesting river *ghat* where pilgrims take their ritual bath before entering the temple. The countryside to the west of the temple is an excellent place to sample rural Indian life and a good way to spend a couple of hours.

Sri Ranganathasvami Temple ① *0700-1300, 1400-1800, camera Rs 50, video Rs 100 (Rs 10 for the rooftop viewing tower), allow about 2 hrs, guides will greet you on arrival (their abilities are highly variable; some tell you that the staircase to the viewpoint will close shortly, which is usually a scam to encourage you to use their services),* is one of the largest in India and dedicated to Vishnu. It has some fine carvings and a good atmosphere. The fact that it faces south, unlike most other Hindu temples, is explained by the legend that Rama intended to present the image of Ranganatha to a temple in Sri Lanka but this was impossible since the deity became fixed here, but it still honours the original destination. The temple, where the Vaishnava reformer **Ramanuja** settled and worshipped, is famous for its superb sculpture, the 21 impressive *gopurams* and its rich collection of temple jewellery. The 'thousand' pillared hall (904 columns) stands beyond the fourth wall, and fifth enclosure there is the unusual shrine to Tulukka Nachiyar, the god's Muslim consort. Non-Hindus are not allowed into the sanctuary but can enter the fourth courtyard where the famous sculptures of *gopis* (*Radha's* milk maids) in the Venugopala shrine can be seen.

Nearby, on the north bank of the Kaveri, **Amma Mandapam** is a hive of activity. The *ghats*, where devotees wash, bathe, commit cremated ashes and pray, are interesting to visit, although some may find the dirt and smell overpowering.

So named because a legendary elephant worshipped the lingam, **Tiruvanaikkaval** is located 3 km east of Srirangam. It has the architecturally finer **Jambukesvara Temple** ① *200 m east off the main Tiruchi–Chennai road, a short stroll from Srirangam or easily reached by bus, officially 0600-2045, camera Rs 10, non-Hindus are not allowed into the sanctuary,* with its five walls and seven splendid *gopurams* and one of the oldest and largest Siva temples in Tamil Nadu. The unusual lingam under a *jambu* tree always remains under water.

◉ Chola Heartland and the Kaveri Delta listings

For hotel and restaurant price codes and other relevant information, see pages 13-17.

● Where to stay

Chidambaram *p122, map p123*
The overall quality of hotels partly explains why most people visit the

town on day trips, but there are plenty of lower-bracket choices around the temple, particularly on East Car St (also known as East Sannithi).
$ Akshaya, 17-18 East Car St, T04144-220191, www.hotelakshaya.com.
Comfortable small hotel right in the centre (can be noisy) with 24 well-swept

rooms and a rooftop overlooking the temple grounds.

$ Pari, 1 South Car St, T04144-220733. With a great atmospheric location near the temple's south gate and relatively grime-free rooms, this is the pick of the rock-bottom options. A/c available in 3- and 4-bed rooms.

$ Ramanathan Mansions, 127 Bazar St, T04144-222411. Away from busy temple area, quieter than most, 28 rooms with bath, spacious and airy (no power sockets), friendly.

$ Ritz, 2 VGP. (Venugopal Pillai) St, T04144-223312, alritzhotel@gmail.com. Drab and decrepit-looking from the outside, but the all-a/c rooms and suites are cleaner than most in town, and service is enthusiastic – especially when tips might be in the offing.

$ Royal Plaza, North Car St, T04144-222179. Good and friendly cheapie, with most rooms boasting Indian toilets and no pretence of hot water, on the rarely tourist-trod northern edge of the temple.

Kumbakonam *p125, map p126*
Luxury Tax of 10-12.5% is always added. Most places offer 24-hr checkout.

$$-$ Raya's Annexe, 19 Head PO Rd, near Mahamaham tank, T0435-242 3270, www.hotelrayas.com. The shiny exterior conceals the best and cleanest rooms in town: 'Standard' rooms are a/c, light and spacious with good bathrooms; 'Elite' and 'Studio' rooms offer extra space and dining/sitting areas. Interesting views across temple roofs from upper floor lobbies.

$ ARK International, 21 TSR Big St, T0435-242 1234, www.hotelark.in. 50 good-size a/c rooms, some cleaner and brighter than others (some barely clean at all), all with bathroom and TV. Pure veg restaurant, room service meals.

$ Femina, 15/8 Head PO Rd, T0435-242 0369. Typically grim budget choice, with dank, grimy and musty rooms, but tolerable if you can snare one of the end rooms with outward-facing windows.

$ Pandian, 52 Sarangapani East Sannathi St, T0435-243 0397. The very cheap rooms here come with bath and TV, but little in the way of light and air. Chiefly popular with Tamil men, whose conversations echo along the corridor.

$ Raya's, 18 Head PO Rd, T0435-242 3170. Older and dingier than the annexe opposite, but OK at the price, and the otherwise uninspiring 'garden villas' are family-friendly with 1 double and 1 single bedroom. A/c restaurant downstairs, exchanges cash.

Thanjavur *p128, map p129*
Even modest hotels charge 20% Luxury Tax. Cheapies congregate near the railway station and opposite the Central Bus Stand on South Rampart Rd, but cleanliness standards are, with the odd notable exception, awful.

$$$$ Parisutham, 55 GA Canal Rd, T04362-231801, www.hotelparisutham. com. The poshest place in town, with 52 well-kept but wildly overpriced a/c rooms in a 1980s building. Passable restaurants, massages in cabin by pretty coconut-shaded pool, free internet (and claims of free Wi-Fi in rooms), relatively peaceful location, but derives most of its custom from package tours.

$$$ Ideal River View Resort, Vennar Bank, Palli Agraharam, 6 km north of centre, T04362-250533, www.idealresort. com. Clean, comfortable cottages (some a/c) in large grounds overlooking a branch of the Kaveri. A peaceful alternative to staying in Thanjavur, with boating, a big pool, restaurant and shuttles into town. Recommended.

$$ Gnanam, Anna Salai (Market Rd), T04362-278501, www.hotelgnanam.com. The mid-range sister hotel to **Parisutham** lacks the pool and top-end facilities, but offers much better value. 30 sparkling clean a/c rooms, some with balcony, vegetarian multi-cuisine restaurant, safety deposit lockers and travel desk, free Wi-Fi in lobby. Recommended.

$ Lion City, 130 Gandhiji Rd, T04362-275650, hotellioncity@hotmail.com. 25 well-appointed but unremarkable rooms in a fairly convenient but noisy location. TV, hot water, acceptably clean, spacious, good service.

$ Manees Residency, 2905 Srinivasam Pillai Rd (next to train station), T04362-271574, www.maneesresidency.com. The cleanest, newest and most pleasant in a row of similarly priced places on this street, with a veg restaurant downstairs.

$ Ramnath, 1335 South Rampart St, T04362-272567. Modern and friendly choice in the hectic bus stand area, with bright artworks adorning the corridors and pleasant, spacious, well-scrubbed rooms, plus a clean and popular restaurant downstairs.

$ Tamil Nadu I (TTDC), Gandhiji Rd, 5-min walk from railway station, T04362-231325. Pleasant setting around a cool inner courtyard, 32 moderately clean rooms with bath, some a/c, a bit mosquito-ridden, simple restaurant, bar, tourist office.

$ Yagappa, off Trichy Rd, south of station, T04362-230421. Good size, comfortable rooms with bath, restaurant, bar, good value.

$ Youth Hostel, Medical College Rd, T04362-235097. Dorm Rs 40.

Around Thanjavur p130

Nov-Dec are busy at Point Calimere (Kodikkarai) Wildlife Sanctuary, 3 Main St, Thanjavur.

$ Poonarai Illam, Point Calimere Sanctuary reservations via the Wildlife Warden, Collectorate, Nagapattinam, T04365-253092. 14 simple rooms with bath and balcony, caretaker may be able to arrange a meal with advance notice, intended for foreign visitors, rooms are often available.

$ PV Thevar Lodge, 40 North Main St, Vedaranyam, 50 m from bus station (English sign high up only visible in daylight), T04369-250330. Good value, 37 basic rooms with bath and fan, can be mosquito-proofed, fairly clean, very friendly owners. Indian vegetarian meals in the bazar near bus stand.

Tiruchirappalli p130, map p131

$$$$-$$$ Sangam, Collector's Office Rd, T0431-241 4480. Very friendly, 58 comfortable a/c rooms, restaurants (great tandoori), good breakfast in coffee shop, pleasant bar, exchange, pool, spacious lawns.

$$$ Breeze Residency, 3/14 Macdonalds Rd, T0431-241 4414, www.breezehotel. com. Pool (non-residents Rs 100), 93 a/c rooms, those in newer wing smaller but in better condition, good restaurants, excellent travel desk, exchange, beauty salon.

$$$ Grand Gardenia, Mannarpuram Junction (1 km south of station), T0431-404 5000, www.grandgardenia. com. Excellent new business hotel with spacious, sparkling clean rooms and good Chettinadu restaurant. Currently the best upscale deal in town.

$$$-$$ Femina, 14C Williams Rd, T0431-241 4501, www.feminahotels.in. 157 clean rooms, 140 a/c, vegetarian restaurants for great breakfasts, bar, pool in new block, good value, modern, comfortable 4-storey hotel.

$$-$ Kanchana Towers, 50 Williams Rd, 2-min walk from bus stand, T0431-420 0002. 90 spacious, comfortable rooms with bath, 26 a/c, restaurant, bar, travel agent, very quiet, new and clean.
$$-$ Ramyas, 13D/2 Williams Rd, T0431-400 0400, www.ramyas.com. 78 spotless rooms, 24 a/c, restaurants, bar.
$$-$ Tamil Nadu (TTDC), Macdonalds Rd, Cantt, T0431-241 4346. Run-down, 36 rooms, some a/c or bath, restaurant, bar, tourist office.
$ Abirami, 10 Macdonalds Rd, T0431-241 5001. Old fashioned, noisy location, 55 rooms, some a/c with bath, good busy a/c restaurant (vegetarian), exchange.
$ Arun, 24 State Bank Rd, T0431-241 5021. 40 rooms in garden setting, restaurant, bar, TV, excellent value.
$ ASG Lodge, opposite **Arun**. Very noisy but quite clean (from Rs 100).
$ Ashby, 17A Junction Rd, T0431-246 0652. Set around courtyard, 20 large a/c rooms with bath, good restaurants, bar. The oldest hotel in town, plenty of Raj character and a bit noisy and scruffy, but excellent friendly staff, good value.
$ Gajapriya, 5 Royal Rd, T0431-241 4411. 66 good-value rooms, 28 a/c (no twin beds), restaurant, bar, library, parking, spacious hotel, quieter than most.
$ Sevana, 5 Royal Rd, Cantt, T0431-241 5201. Quiet, friendly, 44 rooms, some a/c with bath, a/c restaurant (Indian), bar.

Restaurants

Chidambaram *p122, map p123*
$$ Hotel Saradharam, 10 VGP St. Popular, a/c. Excellent range of meals, pizzas and European dishes. Good variety and value.
$ Sree Ganesa Bhavan, West Car St. South Indian vegetarian. Friendly, helpful staff.

$ Udupi, West Car St. Good vegetarian, clean.

Kumbakonam *p125, map p126*
$$ Sri Venkkatramana Hotel, 40 Gandhi Park North St. Excellent vegetarian restaurant, with pure veg *thali*-style meals (complete with digestive *paan* package to finish) served in Brahmnical cleanliness in a/c hall, and the usual gamut of snacks in the somewhat fly-blown main room.

Thanjavur *p128, map p129*
$$ Parisutham (see Where to stay). Good North Indian meat dishes, excellent vegetarian *thalis* ("best of 72 curries"), service can be slow.
$ New Bombay Sweets, South Rampart St. Tasty Indian snacks including pakora and kachori, and good sweets.
$ Sathars, Gandhiji Rd. Excellent for biryani and tandoori, both veg and meat variants.
$ Sri Dhevar's Café, Gandhiji Rd below **Lion City Hotel**. Widely recommended for pure veg meals.
$ Vasantha Bhavan, 1338 South Rampart Rd, near **Hotel Ramnath**. Wide range of South and North Indian and Chinese dishes, good juices bursting with sugar, very popular.

Tiruchirappalli *p130, map p131*
Good Indian vegetarian places in Chinna Bazar are: **$ New Kurinji**, below Hotel Guru Lawson's Rd, a/c vegetarian; and **$ Ragunath** and **Vasantha Bhavan**, *thalis*, good service.
$$ Abirami's (see Where to stay), T0431-246 0001. A/c, Vasantha Bhavan at the back, serves excellent vegetarian; front part is a meals-type eatery.
$$ Breeze Residency (see Where to stay). Good Chinese, extensive menu,

attentive service but freezing a/c. Also **Wild West** bar.
$$ Kavitha, Lawson's Rd. A/c. Excellent breakfasts and generous vegetarian *thalis*.
$$ Sangam's, T0431-246 4480. Indian and continental.
$$ Vincent Garden, Dindigul Rd. Pleasant garden restaurant and pastry shop, lots of coloured lights but on a busy road.

🎭 Entertainment

Thanjavur *p128, map p129*
Bharat Natyam, 1/2378 Krishanayar Lane, Ellaiyamman Koil St, T04362-233759. Performances by Guru Herambanathan from a family of dancers.
South Zone Cultural Centre Palace, T04362-231272. Organizes programmes in the Big Temple, 2nd and 4th Sat; free.

✹ Festivals

Chidambaram *p122, map p123*
Feb/Mar Natyanjali Dance Festival for 5 days starting with **Maha Sivaratri**.
Jun/Jul Ani Tirumanjanam Festival.
Dec/Jan Markazhi Tiruvathirai Festival.

Tiruchirappalli *p130, map p131*
Mar Festival of Floats on the Teppakulam when the temple deities are taken out onto the sacred lake on rafts.

Around Tiruchirappalli *p133*
Srirangam
Dec/Jan Vaikunta Ekadasi (bus No 1 (C or D) from Trichy or hire a rickshaw), and associated temple car festival, draws thousands of pilgrims who witness the transfer of the image of the deity from the inner sanctum under the golden *vimana* to the *mandapa*.

Tiruvanaikkaval
Special festivals in Jan and the spring.
Aug Pancha Piraharam is celebrated and in the month of **Panguni** the images of Siva and his consort Akhilandesvari exchange their dress.

🛍 Shopping

Kumbakonam *p125, map p126*
Kumbakonam and its surrounding villages are renowned centres of bronze sculpture, some still practicing the traditional *'pancha loha'* (5 metals – gold, silver, lead copper and iron) technique reserved for casting temple idols. You can visit workshops in Kumbakaonam itself, and in Swamimalai to the west and Nachiyar Koil to the southeast.

Thanjavur *p128, map p129*
You may not export any object over 100 years old. Thanjavur is known for its decorative copper plates with silver and brass relief (*repoussé*) work, raised-glass painting, wood carving and bronze/brass casting. Granite carving is being revived through centres that produce superb sculpted images. Craft shops abound in Gandhiji Rd Bazar.
Govindarajan's, 31 Kuthirai Katti St, Karandhai (a few kilometres from town), T04362-230282. A treasure house of pricey old, and affordable new, pieces; artists and craftspeople at work.

⏱ What to do

Thanjavur *p128, map p129*
TTDC, enquire at tourist office. Mon-Fri 1000-1745. Temple tour of Thanjavur and surroundings by a/c coach.

Tiruchirappalli *p130, map p131*
Indian Panorama, 5 Anna Av, Srirangam, T0431-422 6122, www.indianpanorama. in. Tours from Chennai, Bengaluru (Bangalore), Kochi, Madurai and Thiruvananthapuram. Recommended for tours (good cars with drivers), ticketing, general advice.

⊖ Transport

Chidambaram *p122, map p123*
Bus The bus station is chaotic with daily services to **Chennai**, **Madurai**, **Thanjavur**, and to **Karaikal** (2 hrs), **Nagapattinam** and **Puducherry** (2 hrs).

Train Reservations T04144-222298, Mon-Sat 0800-1200, 1400-1700; Sun 0800-1400. **Chennai** (**E**) *Cholan Exp 16854*, 1200, 6 hrs. **Rameswaram**: *Rameshwaram Exp 16701*, 0130, 10½ hrs, via **Chettinad** (6 hrs). **Tiruchirappali**: *Cholan Exp 16853*, 1255, 3½ hrs, via **Kumbakonam**, 1½ hrs, and **Thanjavur**, 2 hrs.

Gangaikondacholapuram *p125*
Bus Frequent buses shuttle back and forth from Kumbakonam, and a few buses between **Trichy** and **Chidambaram** also stop here.

Kumbakonam *p125, map p126*
Car hire Half day for excursions, Rs 400.

Bus TN Govt Express buses to **Chennai**, *No 305*, several daily (7½ hrs); half hourly to **Thanjavur**. The railway station is 2 km from town centre. Trains to **Chennai** (**Egmore**), 1010-2110, change at Tambaram (8½-9 hrs), **Chidambaram** (2 hrs), **Thanjavur** (50 mins) and **Tiruchirappalli**, 0600-1555 (2½ hrs).

Thanjavur *p128, map p129*
Bus
Most long-distance buses use the **New Bus Stand**, T04362-230950, 4 km south of town off Trichy Rd. Daily services to **Chennai** (8 hrs), **Chidambaram** (4 hrs), **Kumbakonam** (1 hr), **Madurai** (3½ hrs), **Puducherry** (6 hrs), **Tirupathi**, **Tiruchirappalli** (1½ hrs). Also to **Vedaranyam** (100 km) for Point Calimere, about hourly, 4-4½ hrs. Buses to Kumbakonam, and the odd one to Chennai and Puducherry, also leave from the **State Bus Stand** on South Rampart St.

Taxi
Taxis wait at the railway station and along South Rampart St, but drivers quote high rates, eg **Puducherry** Rs 3500, **Madurai** Rs 2500, **Chidambaram** Rs 2000.

Train
Reservations, T04362-231131, Mon-Sat 0800-1400, 1500-1700; Sun 0800-1400. For **Madurai** and points south, it's better to go to Trichy and change. **Chennai** (**ME**): *Rockfort Exp 16878*, 2030, 9 hrs. **Tiruchirappalli**: several fast passenger trains throughout the day.

Around Thanjavur *p130*
Point Calimere (Kodikkarai)
Bus Buses via Vedaranyam, which has services to/from **Thanjavur**, **Tiruchirappalli**, **Nagapattinam**, **Chennai**, etc. From Thanjavur buses leave the **New Bus Stand** for **Vedaranyam** (100 km) hourly (4-4½ hrs); buses and vans from there to **Kodikkarai** (11 km) which take about 30 mins. Avoid being dropped at 'Sri Rama's Feet' on the way, near a shrine that is of no special interest.

Tiruchirappalli *p130, map p131*
Air
The airport, T0431-234 0551, is 8 km from the centre (taxi Rs 100-150). **Air India**, Dindigul Rd, 2 km from Express Bus Stand, T0431-248 3800, airport T0431-234 1601; flies to **Chennai** daily except Mon and Fri. **Sri Lankan**, 14 Williams Rd, T0431-246 0844, (0900-1730) to **Colombo**. **Air Asia**, www.airasia.com, no-frills flights to **Kuala Lumpur**.

Bus
Local Good City Bus service. From airport, Nos 7, 63, 122, 128, take 30 mins. The **Central State Bus Stand** is across from the tourist office (Bus *No 1* passes all the sights); 20 mins to **Chatram Bus Stand**.
Long distance The bus stands are 1 km from the railway station and are chaotic; TN Govt Express, T0431-246 0992, Central, T0431-246 0425. Frequent buses to **Chennai** (6 hrs), **Coimbatore** 205 km (5½ hrs), **Kumbakonam** 92 km, **Madurai** 161 km (3 hrs), **Palani** 152 km (3½ hrs), **Thanjavur** (1½ hrs). Also 2 to **Kanniyakumari** (9 hrs).

Taxi
Unmetered taxis, and tourist taxis from **Kavria Travels**, Hotel Sangam, Collector's Office Rd, T0431-246 4480.

Train
Enquiries, T131. **Bengaluru (Bangalore):** *Mayiladuturai Mysore Exp 16232*, 2040, 9½ hrs, continues to **Mysore**, 3¼ hrs. **Chennai:** several throughout the day, including *Pallavan Exp 12606*, 0630, 5½ hrs; *Vaigai Exp 12636*, 0850, 5¼ hrs;

all go via Villupuram (for Puducherry), 3 hrs. **Kollam:** *Nagore-Quilon Exp 16361*, 1615, 12½ hrs. **Madurai:** *Vaigai Exp 12635*, 1745, 2¾ hrs.

❶ Directory

Chidambaram *p122, map p123*
Banks Changing money can be difficult. **City Union Bank**, West Car St has exchange facilities. **Indian Bank**, 64 South Car St. **Post** Head Post Office, North Car St.

Kumbakonam *p125, map p126*
Banks Changing money is difficult. **State Bank of India**, TSR Big St. **Internet** End of Kamaraj Rd, close to clock tower. **Post** Near Mahamakam Tank.

Thanjavur *p128, map p129*
Banks ATMs at the station, along South Rampart St, and opposite the tourist office on Gandhiji Rd. **Canara Bank**, South Main St, changes TCs. **Medical services** Govt Hospital, Hospital Rd, south of the old town. **Post** Head Post and Telegraph Office are off the Railway Station Rd. **Useful contacts** Police, south of the Big Temple between the canal and the railway, T04362-232200.

Tiruchirappalli *p130, map p131*
Banks Lots of ATMs around the bus stands. Exchange is available at Western Union money transfer in Jenne Plaza, Cantonment. Mon-Sat 0900-1730. Quick; good rates. **Internet** Mas Media, Main Rd, 6 terminals; **Central Telegraph Office**, Permanent Rd.

The Tamil Hill Stations

The Tamil ghats were once shared between shola forest and tribal peoples. But the British, limp from the heat of the plains, invested in expeditions up the mountains and before long had planted eucalyptus, established elite members' clubs and substituted jackals for foxes in their pursuit of the hunt. Don't expect to find the sheer awe-inspiring grandeur of the Himalaya, but there is a charm to these hills where neatly pleated, green tea plantations run like contour lines about the ghats' girth, bringing the promise of a restorative chill and walking tracks where the air comes cut with the smell of eucalyptus.

Arriving in the Tamil Hill Stations

The northern Nilgiris or the more southerly Palani Hills offer rival opportunities for high-altitude stopovers on the route between Tamil Nadu, Karnataka and Kerala. The most visited towns of Ooty and Kodai both have their staunch fan bases – Ooty tends to attract nostalgic British and rail enthusiasts, while Kody gets the American vote, thanks in part to its international schools. Both are well connected by road: Kody is best approached from Madurai; Ooty makes a good bridge to Kerala from Mysore or Tamil Nadu's more northern temple towns. The famous narrow-gauge rack-and-pinion Nilgiri Mountain Railway is most dramatic between Coonoor and Mettupalayam, which in turn has trains from Coimbatore and Chennai. The roads worsen dramatically when you cross the Tamil border from Kerala, reflecting the different levels of affluence between the two states. ▶▶ *See Transport, page 158.*

Udhagamandalam (Ooty) → *For listings, see pages 150-161.*

Ooty has been celebrated for rolling hills covered in pine and eucalyptus forests and coffee and tea plantations since the first British planters arrived in 1818. A Government House was built, and the British lifestyle developed with cottages and clubs – tennis, golf, riding – and tea on the lawn. But the town is no longer the haven it once was; the centre is heavily built up and can be downright unpleasant in the holiday months of April to June, and again around October. It's best to stay either in the grand ruins of colonial quarters on the quiet outskirts where it's still possible to steal some serenity or opt instead for the far smaller tea garden town of Coonoor (see page 143), 19 km down the mountain. **Tamil Nadu Tourism** ① *Wenlock Rd, T0423-244 3977,* is not very efficient.

Places in Udhagamandalam → *Phone code: 0423. Population 93,900. Altitude: 2286 m.*
The **Botanical Gardens** ① *3 km northeast of railway station, 0800-1800, Rs 25, camera, Rs 50, video Rs 500*, house more than 1000 varieties of plant, shrub and tree including orchids, ferns, alpines and medicinal plants, but is most fun for watching giant family groups picnicking and gambolling together among beautiful lawns and glass houses. To the east of the garden in a Toda *mund* is the Wood House made of logs. The **Annual Flower Show** is held in the third week of May. The **Rose Garden** ① *750 m from Charing Cross, 0830-1830*, has over 1500 varieties of roses.

Ooty Lake was built in 1825 as a vast irrigation tank and is now more than half overgrown with water hyacinth, though it is still used enthusiastically for boating and **pedalo hire** ① *0900-1800, Rs 60-110 per hr.*

Kandal Cross ① *3 km west of the railway station*, is a Roman Catholic shrine considered the 'Jerusalem of the East'. During the clearing of the area to make way for a graveyard in 1927, an enormous 4-m-high boulder was found and a cross was

Udhagamandalam (Ooty)

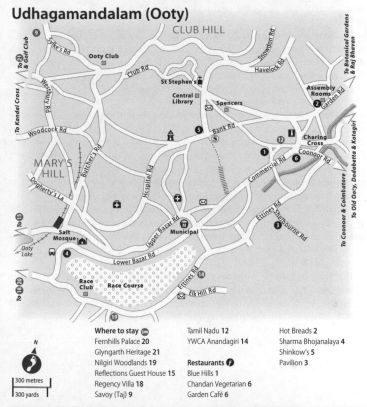

Where to stay ⌂	Tamil Nadu **12**	Hot Breads **2**
Fernhills Palace **20**	YWCA Anandagiri **14**	Sharma Bhojanalaya **4**
Glyngarth Heritage **21**		Shinkow's **5**
Nilgiri Woodlands **19**	**Restaurants** 🍴	Pavilion **3**
Reflections Guest House **15**	Blue Hills **1**	
Regency Villa **18**	Chandan Vegetarian **6**	
Savoy (Taj) **9**	Garden Café **6**	

300 metres
300 yards

erected. Now a relic of the True Cross brought to India by an Apostolic delegate is shown to pilgrims every day. The annual feast is in May.

St Stephen's Church was Ooty's first church, built in the 1820s. Much of the wood is said to be from Tipu Sultan's Lal Bagh Palace in Srirangapatnam. The inside of the church and the graveyard at the rear are worth seeing.

Dodabetta ① *1000-1500, buses from Ooty, autos and taxis (Rs 200 round trip) go to the summit*, is 10 km east of the railway station off the Kotagiri road. Reaching 2638 m, the 'big mountain' is the second highest in the Western Ghats, sheltering Coonoor from the southwest monsoons when Ooty gets heavy rains. The top is often shrouded in mist. There is a viewing platform at the summit. The telescope isn't worth even the nominal Rs 2 fee.

Walks and hikes around Ooty

Hiking or simply walking is excellent in the Nilgiris. It is undisturbed, quiet and interesting. Climbing Dodabetta or Mukurti is hardly a challenge but the longer walks through the *sholas* are best undertaken with a guide. It is possible to see characteristic features of Toda settlements such as *munds* and *boas*.

Dodabetta–Snowdon–Ooty walk starts at Dodabetta Junction directly opposite the 3 km road to the summit. It is a pleasant path that curves gently downhill through a variety of woodland (mainly eucalyptus and conifers) back to Ooty and doesn't take more than a couple of hours. For longer treks, contact **Nilgiris Trekking Association** ① *Kavitha Nilayam, 31-D Bank Rd, or R Seniappan, 137 Upper Bazar, T0423-244 4449, sehi appan@yahoo.com*.

Mukurti Peak ① *buses from Ooty every 30 mins from 0630 or you can take a tour (see page 157), book early as they are popular*, is 36 km away, off the Gudalur road. After 26 km you reach the 6-km-long Mukurti Lake. Mukurti Peak (the name suggests that someone thought it resembled a severed nose), not an easy climb, is to the west. The Todas believe that the souls of the dead and the sacrificed buffaloes leap to the next world from this sacred peak. It is an excellent place to escape for walking, to view the occasional wildlife, to go fishing at the lake or to go boating.

Avalanche ① *24 km from town, bus from Ooty at 1110*, a valley, is a beautiful part of the *shola*, with plenty of rhododendrons, magnolias and orchids and a trout stream running through it, and is excellent for walking. The **Forestry Department Guest House** is clean and has good food. Contact the **Wildlife Warden** ① *1st floor, Mahalingam Building, Ooty, T0423-244098*.

The **River Pykara** ① *19 km from Ooty, several buses 0630-2030, or take a car or bicycle*, has a dam and power plant. There is breathtaking scenery. The **waterfalls**, about 6 km from the bridge on the main road, are best in July though it is very wet then, but they are also worth visiting from August to December.

Blue Mountain Railway

Ever since 15 June 1899, the narrow-gauge steam *Mountain Railway*, in its blue and cream livery, has chugged from Mettupalayam to Ooty via Coonoor, negotiating 16 tunnels and 31 major bridges and climbing from 326 m to 2193 m. This was the location for the railway scenes of the *Marabar Express* in the film *A Passage to India*.

It's a charming 4½-hour (46-km) journey through tea plantations and forest, but – outside first class – be prepared for an amiable Indian holidaymakers' scrum. There are rest stops at Hillgrove (17 km) and Coonoor (27 km).

For enthusiasts, the pricier and more spacious *Heritage Steam Chariot* runs between Ooty and Runneymede picnic area, 23 km away, at weekends (more often in high season). The drawback is that you can be stranded for hours when the engine breaks down; some decide to scramble to the nearest road to flag down a bus.

Coonoor → *For listings, see pages 150-161. Phone code: 0423. Altitude: 1800 m. Population 50,100.*

ⓘ *When you arrive by train or bus (which doesn't always stop at the main bus stand if going on to Ooty), the main town of Lower Coonoor will be to the east, across the river. Upper Coonoor, with the better hotels 2-3 km away, is further east.*

Smaller and much less developed than Ooty, Coonoor is an ideal starting point for nature walks and rambles through villages. There's no pollution, no noise and very few people. The covered market, as with many towns and cities in South India, is almost medieval and cobblers, jewellers, tailors, pawn brokers and merchants sell everything from jasmine to beetroot. The picturesque hills around the town are covered in coffee and tea plantations.

The real attraction here is the hiking, though there are a couple of sights in town. The large **Sim's Park** ⓘ *0800-1830, Rs 5*, named after a secretary to the Madras Club, is a well-maintained botanical garden on the slopes of a ravine with over 330 varieties of rose but is only really worth the journey for passionate botanists. Contact the **United Planters' Association of South India (UPASI)** ⓘ *Glenview House, Coonoor, T0423-223 0270, www.upasi.org*, to visit tea and coffee plantations.

The **Wellington Barracks**, 3 km northeast of Lower Coonoor, which are the raison d'être for the town, were built in 1852. They are now the headquarters of the Indian Defence Services Staff College and also of the Madras Regiment, which is over 250 years old, the oldest in the Indian Army.

Lamb's Rock, on a high precipice, 9 km away, has good views over the Coimbatore plains and coffee and tea estates on the slopes. At **Dolphin's Nose** (12 km away, several buses 0700-1615), you can see **Catherine Falls**, a further 10 km away (best in the early morning). **Droog** (13 km away, buses 0900, 1345) has ruins of a 16th-century fort used by Tipu Sultan, and requires a 3-km walk.

Kotagiri ⓘ *29 km from Ooty, frequent services from Coonoor, Mettupalayam Railway Station and Ooty*, has an altitude of 1980 m. It sits on the northeast crest of the plateau overlooking the plains. It has a milder climate than Ooty. The name comes from Kotar–Keri, the street of the *Kotas* who were one of the original hill tribes and who have a village to the west of the town. You can visit some scenic spots from here: **St Catherine Falls** (8 km) and **Elk Falls** (7 km), or one of the peaks, **Kodanad Viewpoint** (16 km) – reached through the tea estates or by taking one of the several buses that run from 0610 onwards – or **Rangaswamy Pillar**, an isolated rock, and the conical Rangaswamy Peak.

Mettupalayam and the Nilgiri Ghat Road → *For listings, see pages 150-161.*

The journey up to Coonoor from Mettupalayam is one of the most scenic in South India, affording superb views over the plains below. Between Mettupalayam and the start of the Ghat road, there are magnificent groves of tall, slender areca nut palms. Mettupalayam has become the centre for the areca nut trade as well as producing synthetic gems. The palms are immensely valuable trees: the nut is used across India wrapped in betel vine leaves – two of the essential ingredients of India's universal after-meal digestive, *paan*.

The town is the starting point of the ghat railway line up to Ooty (see box, page 143). If you take the early-morning train you can continue to Mysore by bus from Ooty on the same day, making a very pleasant trip.

Mudumalai Wildlife Sanctuary → *For listings, see pages 150-161.*

ⓘ *Minibus safaris 0630-0900, 1530-1800, Rs 45, still camera Rs 25, video Rs 150; Reception Range Office, Theppakadu, T0423-252 6235, open 0630-1800, is where buses between Mysore and Ooty stop. There is a Ranger Office at Kargudi. The best time to visit is Sep-Dec and Mar-May when the undergrowth dies down and it's easier to see animals, especially at dawn when they're on the move. Forest fires can close the park temporarily during Feb-Apr.*

The sanctuary adjoins Bandipur National Park beyond the Moyar River, its hills (885-1000 m), ravines, flats and valleys being an extension of the same environment. The park is one of the more popular and is now trying to limit numbers of visitors to reduce disturbance to the elephants.

There are large herds of elephant, gaur, sambar, barking deer, wild dog, Nilgiri langur, bonnet monkey, wild boar, four-horned antelope and the rarer tiger and leopard, as well as smaller mammals and many birds and reptiles. **Elephant Camp**, south of Theppakadu, open 0700-0800 and 1600-1700, tames wild elephants. Some are bred in captivity and trained to work for the timber industry. You can watch the elephants being fed in the late afternoon, learn about each individual elephant's diet and the specially prepared 'cakes' of food.

You can hire a jeep for about Rs 10 per km but must be accompanied by a guide. Most night safaris are best avoided. Elephant rides from 0700-0830 and 1530-1700 (Rs 50 per person for 30 minutes); check timing and book in advance in Theppakadu or with the **Wildlife Warden** ⓘ *Mount Stuart Hill, Ooty, T0423-244 4098*. They can be fun even though you may not see much wildlife. There are *machans* near waterholes and salt licks and along the Moyar River. With patience you can see a lot, especially rare and beautiful birds. Treks and jeep rides in the remoter parts of the forest with guides can be arranged from some lodges, including **Jungle Retreat** (see page 151). You can spend a day climbing the hill and bathe at the impressive waterfalls. The core area is not open to visitors.

Coimbatore and the Nilgiri Hills → *For listings, see pages 150-161.*

Coimbatore → *Phone code: 0422. Population: 923,000.*
As one of South India's most important industrial cities since the 1930s development of hydroelectricity from the Pykara Falls, Coimbatore holds scant charm to warrant more than a pit stop. It was once the fulcrum of tussles between Tamilian, Mysorean and Keralite coastal rulers (the word *palayam* crops up tellingly often in Coimbatore – its translation being 'encampment') and sadly violence continues today. You are likely to stay here only if fascinated by the cotton trade or stuck for an onward bus or train.

Salem → *Phone code: 0427. Population: 693,200.*
Salem, an important transport junction, is surrounded by hills: the Shevaroy and Nagaramalai Hills to the north and the Jarugumalai Hills to the southeast. It is a busy, rapidly growing industrial town – particularly for textiles and metal-based industries – with modern shopping centres. The old town is on the east bank of the River Manimutheru. Each evening around Bazar Street you can see cotton carpets being made. The **cemetery**, next to the Collector's office, has some interesting tombstones. To the southeast of the town on a ridge of the Jarugumalai Hills is a highly visible *Naman* painted in *chunam* and ochre. On the nearby hill the temple (1919) is particularly sacred to the weavers' community. Some 600 steps lead up to excellent views over the town.

Yercaud and the Shevaroy Hills → *Phone code: 04281. Altitude: 1515 m.*
The beautiful drive up the steep and sharply winding ghat road from Salem quickly brings a sharp freshness to the air as it climbs to over 1500 m. The minor resort has a small artificial lake and Anna Park nearby. Some attractive though unmarked walks start here. In May there is a special festival focused on the **Shevaroyan Temple**, on top of the third highest peak in the hill range. Many tribal people take part but access is only possible on foot. Ask for details in the **Tamil Nadu Tourist Office** in Chennai, see page 65. There's also a tourist information office in the Tamil Nadu hotel in town.

Just outside town is **Lady's Seat**, overlooking the ghat road, which has wonderful views across the Salem plains. Near the old Norton Bungalow on the Shevaroyan Temple Road is another well-known local spot, **Bear's Cave**. Formed by two huge boulders, it is occupied by huge colonies of bats. The whole area is full of botanical interest. There is an orchidarium and a horticultural research station.

The climb up the Palanis starts 47 km before Kodaikanal (Kodai) and is one of the most rapid ascents anywhere across the ghats. The views are stunning. In the lower reaches of the climb you look down over the Kambam Valley, the Vaigai Lake and across to the Varushanad Hills beyond, while higher up the scene is dominated by the sawn-off pyramid of Perumal Malai. Set around a small artificial lake, the town has crisply fresh air, even at the height of summer, and the beautiful scent of pine and eucalyptus make it a popular retreat from the southern plains. Today Kodai is a fast-growing resort, yet it retains a relatively low-key air that many feel gives it an edge over Ooty.

Arriving in Kodaikanal → *Phone code: 04542. Population: 32,900. Altitude: 2343 m.*
Buses make the long climb from Madurai and other cities to the Central Bus Stand, which is within easy walking distance from most hotels. The nearest train station is Kodai Road. Kodai is small enough to walk around, though for some of the sights it is worth getting an unmetered taxi. There's a **Tamil Nadu Tourist Office** ① *Hospital Rd next to bus stand, T04542-241675, 1000-1745 except holidays*, with helpful staff and maps available. ⏩ *See Transport, page 160.*

Background
The Palani Hills were first surveyed by British administrators in 1821, but the surveyor's report was not published until 1837, 10 years after Ooty had become the official sanatorium for the British in South India. A proposal to build a sanatorium was made in 1861-1862 by Colonel Hamilton, who noted the extremely healthy climate and the lack of disease, but the sanatorium was never built because the site was so inaccessible. So it was that Kodaikanal became the first hill station in India to be set up not by heat-sick Britons but by American missionaries.

The American Mission in Madurai, established in 1834, had lost six of their early missionaries within a decade. The missionaries had been eyeing a site in the Sirumalai Hills, at around 1300 m, but while these were high enough to offer respite from the heat of the plains they were still prone to malaria. Isolated Kodai, almost 1000 m higher, proved to be the ticket, and the first two bungalows were built by June 1845. Kodai's big transformation came at the turn of the 20th century with the arrival of the car and the bus. In 1905 it was possible to do the whole journey from Kodai Road station to Kodai within the hours of daylight. The present road, up Law's Ghat, was opened to traffic in 1916.

Places in Kodaikanal
Star-shaped **Kodaikanal Lake** covers 24 ha and is surrounded by gentle wooded slopes. The walk around the lake takes about one hour; you can also hire pedal boats and go fishing (with permission from the Inspector of Fisheries), although the water is polluted. The International School, established in 1901, has a commanding position on the lakeside, and provides education for children from India and abroad between the ages of five and 18.

The view over the plains from **Coaker's Walk**, built by Lieutenant Coaker in the 1870s, can be magnificent; on a rare clear day you can see as far as Madurai. It is reached from a signposted path just above the bazar, 1 km from the bus stand.

Kurinji Andavar Temple, northeast of the town past Chettiar Park, is dedicated to Murugan and associated with the Neelakurinji flower that carpets the hills in purple flowers once every 12 years (the next mass flowering is due in 2018). There are excellent views of the north and southern plains, including Palani and Vaigai Dams.

The small but interesting **Shenbaganur Museum** ⓘ *5 km down Law's Ghat road, open 1000-1130; 1500-1700*, at the Sacred Heart College seminary, is the local flora and fauna museum, exhibiting 300 orchid species as well as some archaeological remains. It's an attractive walk downhill from the town passing a number of small waterfalls. Some 4 km west of the bus stand at a height of 2347 m, the **Solar Physical**

Kodaikanal

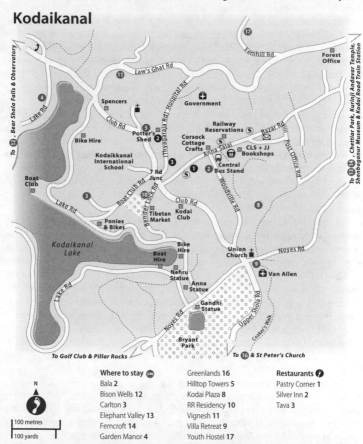

Where to stay	Greenlands **16**	**Restaurants**
Bala **2**	Hilltop Towers **5**	Pastry Corner **1**
Bison Wells **12**	Kodai Plaza **8**	Silver Inn **2**
Carlton **3**	RR Residency **10**	Tava **3**
Elephant Valley **13**	Vignesh **11**	
Ferncroft **14**	Villa Retreat **9**	
Garden Manor **4**	Youth Hostel **17**	

Observatory ① *T04542-240588, open Fri 1000-1230, 1900-2100*, is one of the oldest in the world, established in 1899.

Bear Shola Falls, named because it once attracted bears, is a favourite picnic spot about 2 km from the bus stand. The falls, like most others around Kodai, have been reduced to a trickle outside monsoon season. A pleasant walk or bike/scooter ride leads southwest from the lake along leafy avenues, past the golf course where wild deer and gaur are sometimes seen, to the striking viewpoint at Valley View; a further 3 km away are Pillar Rocks, a trio of impressive granite formations over 120 m high.

Around Kodaikanal → *For listings, see pages 150-161.*

If you're in the mood for an adventure there's a popular semi-official trekking route that links Kodaikanal to Munnar, roughly following the now-overgrown Escape Road built by the British Army in anticipation of a Japanese invasion in 1942. The route follows the Pillar Rocks road, then descends to beautiful Berijam Lake, 21 km southwest of Kodaikanal, where there's an adequate Forest Rest House. You can visit the lake on a day trip with permission from the **Forestry Department Office** ① *Law's Ghat Rd, Kodaikkanal, T04542-240287; only 10 permits are granted a day so arrive at the office before 1000*. The next day you continue through pine and eucalypt plantations, patches of shola forest and the occasional village to Top Station in Kerala (five to six hours), where there is a Forest Hut and shops and tea stalls selling snacks. From here you can catch a bus or jeep to Munnar, 41 km away. You'll need permission from the Forestry Department in both Kodai and Munnar to complete the trek, and cross-border bureaucratic wrangling can makes this hard to come by. Local guides can help with permits and transport at a charge: try **Raja** ① *T(0)9842-188893*, or the semi-legendary **Kodai Mani** ① *T(0)9894-048493*, who knows the trails well and charges accordingly.

The ghat road running north from Kodaikanal to **Palani** passes through smallholdings of coffee, oranges and bananas. Inter-planting of crops such as pepper is further increasing the yields from what can be highly productive land, even on steep slopes. The shrine to **Murugan** (Subrahmanya) on top of Palani (or Sivagiri) Hill is a very important site of pilgrimage. At full moon in January to February pilgrims walk from as far afield as Chettinad and Munnar to climb the 659 steps to the shrine. Many carry shoulder poles with elaborate bamboo or wooden structures on each end, living out the myth of Idumban, who carried the twin hills of Sivagiri and Shaktigiri from Mount Kailash to their present locations on either end of a bamboo *kavadi*. Around the temple, Palani presents a chaotic but compelling pastiche of pilgrim fervour, religious souvenir shopping and decaying flower garlands.

Pollachi, in a key strategic position on the east to west crossing of the ghats through the Palakkad Gap, has been an important trading centre for over 2000 years, as witnessed by the finds of Roman silver coins bearing the heads of the emperors Augustus and Tiberias. Today its main appeal is as the gateway to the small but very attractive Anamalai (Indira Gandhi) National Park (see below).

Anamalai (Indira Gandhi) Wildlife Sanctuary

ⓘ *0600-1800, Rs 15, camera Rs 25, video Rs 150; best time to visit Dec-Jun, closed mid-Feb to mid-Apr, avoid Sun. Reception and Information Centre at Top Slip organizes bus rides, elephant safaris and trekking guides. Day permits from entrance gate at Sethumadai; for overnight stays advance written permission is needed from Wildlife Warden (1176 Meenakalai Salai, Pollachi, 1.5 km out of town on road towards Top Slip, T04259-225356).*

This beautiful, unspoilt park covering 960 sq km of grassland, rainforest and mountain shola forest, is rarely visited except by Indian day trippers. Wildlife includes Nilgiri langur, lion-tailed macaque, elephant, gaur, tiger, panther, sloth, wild boar, birds – including pied hornbill, drongo, red whiskered bulbul, black-headed oriole – and a large number of crocodiles in the Amaravathi reservoir. There is an elephant camp, claimed to be the largest in Asia, reached by a two- to three-hour minibus ride through the forest (0615, 1130 and 1515, Rs 25), and short elephant rides can be arranged. Birdwatching is good from Kariam Shola watchtower, 2 km from Topslip.

There are some **trekking** routes that vary from easy treks to Pandaravara (8 km), Kozhikamuthi (12 km) and Perunkundru peak (32 km), which is demanding. Permits can be obtained from the **Range Officer** ⓘ *Top Slip, Rs 150-300 per person*. Private guides charge upwards of Rs 100 for a three-hour trek.

Dindigul → *For listings, see pages 150-161.*

Now a large market town, Dindigul, north of Madurai, commands a strategic gap between the Sirumalai Hills to its east and the Palani Hills to the west. The market handles the produce of the Sirumalai Hills, including a renowned local variety of banana. Dindigul is particularly known for its cheroots.

The massive granite rock and **fort** ⓘ *2 km west of the bus stand, 0730-1730, foreigners Rs 100, Indians Rs 5, autos Rs 20*, towers over 90 m above the plain. The Mysore army captured it in 1745 and Haidar Ali was appointed governor in 1755. It was ceded to the British under the Treaty of Seringapatam. There are magnificent views of the town, valley and hills on either side from the top of the rock fort. **Our Lady of Dolours Church**, one of several churches in the town, is over 250 years old and was rebuilt in 1970. The Old City is interesting to walk around; you can walk up to the fort from there. The station is 2 km south of the bus stand that has cheap lodges nearby.

For hotel and restaurant price codes and other relevant information, see pages 13-17.

◉ Where to stay

Udhagamandalam (Ooty) *p140, map p141*

Rates quoted are for the high season. Good discounts Jul-Mar except during *puja* and Christmas (add 30% tax in upper categories). Winter nights can be bitterly cold and hotel fireplaces are often inadequate. Avoid the budget accommodation round Commercial Rd and Ettines Rd, particularly if you are a woman travelling alone.

$$$$ Fernhills Palace, Fernhill Post, T0423-244 3910, www.fernhillspalace. co.in. After years of stop-start renovation, Wadiyar, the current Mysore maharaja has opened his ancestral palace as a luxury heritage hotel. It offers 30 suites, with teak furniture, wooden panelling, fireplaces and jacuzzis. Spa, gym, plus correspondingly high price tags.

$$$$ Savoy (Taj), 77 Sylkes Rd, T0423 222 5500. 40 well-maintained cottage rooms with huge wooden doors, open fires and separate dressing areas. Even if you're not staying it's worth a teatime visit for the building's interesting history and lovely gardens, and the wood-panelled dining room serves excellent takes on traditional Tamil food.

$$ Glyngarth, Golf Club Rd, Fingerpost (2 km from centre), T0423-244 5754, www.glyngarthvilla.com. Just 5 huge double rooms with period furniture plus original fittings including all-teak floors and fireplaces in a Raj building – complete with metal roof – dating from 1853. Modern bathrooms, meals made from fresh garden produce, large grounds, clean, excellent service, tremendously characterful (too much for some) good value. Walking distance to golf course. Recommended.

$$ Regency Villas, Fernhill Post, T0423-244 2555, regency@sancharnet.in. The maharaja of Mysore's staff had some of the best sunset views of the blue hills from their bungalows. The 19 villas here were under much-needed renovation at time of updating – hopefully not at the risk of the appealing air of ramshackle and rows of dog-eared colonial photos.

$$-$ The Nilgiri Woodlands, Race Course Rd, T0423-244 2551, nilgiris_ woodlands@yahoo. com. 22 rooms ranging from paint-peeling doubles to spacious cottages. Shared veranda outside racecourse-facing rooms that give onto a garden and the pink/green/blue bungalows of Ooty central. Quiet and spacious rooms tucked round the back (without views) are best value.

$ Reflections Guest House, North Lake Rd, T0423-244 3834, www. reflectionsguesthouseooty.com. Clean, homely, quiet, with good views of the lake, 9 rooms (cheaper dorm beds), pleasant dining and sitting room serving good food, friendly owners. Rs 50 for wood for the fire or to use the stove for your own cooking, dodgy plumbing, can get chilly, restricted hot water.

$ Tamil Nadu (TTDC), Charing Cross, up the steps by the tourist office, T0423-244 4370. Spotless rooms and penthouse with good views, restaurant, bar, exchange, pleasant hotel tucked away. Avoid the food.

$ YWCA Anandagiri, Ettines Rd, T0423-244 2218, www.ywcaagooty.com. It's basic and a little institutional, and the hot water can be iffy, but this is the most atmospheric budget accommodation in Ooty, with high-ceilinged 1920s cottages in an extensive garden complex surrounded by tall pines and superb views.

Coonoor *p143*

Most hotels are 3-5 km from the station and bus stand.

$$$$-$$$ Gateway Hotel, Church Rd, Upper Coonoor, T0423-223 0021, www.tajhotels.com. This wonderful quiet place offers spectacular mountain views and a wide choice of rooms, including cool stone-walled cottages with private terraces, romantic open-sided treehouses, simple bamboo huts and a well-swept dorm (Rs 700). The friendly owners keep high standards and can arrange safaris, good treks with local guides and elephant rides. There's an excellent swimming pool, and somewhat pricey food.

$$$ The Tryst, Carolina Tea Estate, T0423-220 7057, www.trystindia.com. The shelves at this homestay groan under years of hoarding. 5 double rooms with well-stocked library, snooker table, games galore and gym, plus a huge cottage that sleeps 10. Unexpected and in an outstanding location away from all other accommodation cradled in the nape of a rolling tea estate. Excellent walking. Book in advance.

$ Blue Star, Kotagiri, next to bus station, T04266-274454. Rooms with shower and toilet in modern building.

$ Tamil Nadu (TTDC), Ooty Rd, Mt Pleasant (1 km north of station), T0423-223 2813. Simple rooms, TV, restaurant, bar and dorm.

$ 'Wyoming' Holiday Home (YWCA), near Hospital, Upper Coonoor (auto from bus stand Rs 25), T0423-223 4426. Set in a house with character and idyllic views, 8 large rooms and 2 dorms (8-bedded), excellent food (no alcohol) but some

warn you should check bill and watch out for the neurotic labrador who is known to bark through the night. Garden, friendly, helpful, popular. Manager qualified in alternative therapies (runs clinic and courses). Book ahead.

Mettupalayam *p144*

$ EMS Mayura, 212 Coimbatore Main Rd, T04254-227936. Set back from the main road a 5-min walk from the station, this makes a decent overnight choice with clean rooms, a decent restaurant and bar.

$ Surya International, 345 Ooty Main Rd, T04254-223502, fairly clean rooms (Rs 150), rooftop restaurant, often empty, quiet, but characterless.

Mudumalai Wildlife Sanctuary *p144*

Advance booking is essential especially during the season and at weekends. Accommodation is better near Masinagudi which also has restaurants and shops but there is some in Bokkapuram, 3 km further south. Ask private lodges for pick-up if arriving by bus at Theppakadu.

$$$ Bamboo Banks Farm Guest House, Masinagudi, T09443-373201, www.bamboobanks.in. 6 clean rooms, 4 in cottages in a fine setting, attractive garden, good food, birdwatching, riding, jeep.

$$$-$$ Jungle Hut, near Bokkapuram, T0423-252 6463, www.junglehut.in. In valley, 12 clean, simple rooms with bath in 3 stone cottages plus a few small tents, good food ("lovely home cooking"), pool, jeep hire, game viewing and treks, very friendly welcome. Recommended.

$$$-$ Jungle Retreat, Bokkapuram, T0423-252 6469, www.jungleretreat.com. This wonderful, quiet place offers spectacular mountain views and a wide choice of rooms, including cool stone-walled cottages with private terraces, romantic open-sided treehouses, simple bamboo huts and a well-swept dorm (Rs 700). The friendly owners keep high standards and can arrange safaris, good treks with local guides and elephant rides. There's an excellent swimming pool, and somewhat pricey food.

$$ New Mountania, Masinagudi, T0423-252 6267, www.newmountania.com. Rooms in cottages (prices vary), "nice but a bit overpriced", restaurant, jeep tour to waterfalls, easy animal spotting (evening better than morning).

$$-$ Monarch Safari Park, Bokkapuram, on a hill side, T0423-252 6250. Large grounds, with 14 rooms in twin *machan* huts on stilts with bath (but rats may enter at night), open-sided restaurant, cycles, birdwatching, good riding (Rs 150 per hr), some sports facilities, meditation centre, "lovely spot", management a bit slack but friendly, if slow, service.

$ Forest Department Huts, reserve in advance through Wildlife Warden, Mudumalai WLS, Mt Stuart Hill, Ooty, T0423-244 4098, or Reception Range Officer, Theppakadu, T0423-252 6235. Most have caretakers who can arrange food.

$ Forest Hills Farm, 300 m from **Jungle Hut**, T0423-252 6216, www.foresthills india.com. Friendly, 6 modern rooms with bath. Good views, good food, game viewing. Recommended.

$ Tamil Nadu (TTDC hostel), Theppakadu, T0423-252 6249. 3 rooms, 24 beds in dorm (Rs 45), restaurant, van for viewing.

Abhayaranyam Rest House, Kargudi. 2 rooms.

Abhayaranyam Annexe, Kargudi. 2 rooms. Recommended.

Minivet and **Morgan**, Kargudi. Dorm, 8 and 12 beds.

Peacock, Kargudi. 50-bed dorm, excellent food.

Rest House and **Annexe**, Kargudi. Ask for deluxe rooms.

Log House, Masinagudi, 5 rooms.
Rest House, Masinagudi, 3 rooms.

Coimbatore *p145*

$$$ Heritage Inn, 38 Sivaswamy Rd, T0422-223 1451, www.hotelheritage inn.in. Standard hotel with good restaurants, internet, excellent service, 63 modern, a/c rooms, good value.

$$ City Tower, Sivaswamy Rd (just off Dr Nanjappa Rd), Gandhipuram, near bus stand, T0422-223 0681, www.hotelcity tower.com. 91 excellent redecorated rooms, some a/c, small balconies, 2 restaurants (rooftop tandoori), no alcohol, superb service. Recommended.

$$ Sabari Nest, 739-A Avanashi Rd, 2 km from railway, T0422-450 5500, www.sabarihotels.com. 38 a/c rooms, some small, restaurant, bar, amazing supermarket downstairs (for Western snacks and last stop for supplies), business facilities, roof garden. Recommended.

$ Channma International, 18/109 Big Bazar St, T0422-239 6631. Oldish art deco-style hotel, 36 spacious clean rooms, tiny windows, restaurant, internet, health club and pool next door.

$ KK Residency, 7 Shastri Rd, by Central Bus Stand, Ramnagar, T0422-430 0200. 42 smallish but clean rooms, 6 a/c, good condition, restaurant, friendly service. Recommended.

$ Meena, 109 Kalingarayar St, T0422-223 5420. Small family hotel with 30 clean and pleasant rooms, vegetarian restaurant.

Salem *p145*

Choose a room away from the road if possible.

$$ Salem Castle, A-4 Bharati St, Swarnapuri, 4 km from railway station, T0427-244 8702. Rather brash modern hotel with 64 comfortable, very clean a/c rooms. Restaurants (good Chinese but expensive, the rest are Indian-style), coffee shop, bar, exchange, pool.

$ City View, Omalur Main Rd, T0427-233 4232. Rooms with bath, some clean, strong a/c, meals, travel. **Shree Saravanabhavan** in the same block does good south Indian veg.

$ Ganesh Mahal, 323 Omalur Rd, T0427-233 2820, www.ganeshmahal.com. Modern and comfortable, 45 pleasant rooms, TV, good restaurant, bar.

$ Railway Retiring Rooms. Battered but with olde-worlde feel.

$ Raj Castle, 320 Omalur Rd, T0427-233 3532. 21 nicely fitted rooms, 4 a/c, some with balcony, TV, hot water mornings, tourist car.

$ Selvam, T0427-233 4491. Clean rooms with bath, some a/c, good restaurant.

Yercaud p145

Most hotels offer off-season discounts Jan-Mar, Aug-Dec.

$$ Sterling Resort, near Lady's Seat, T04281-222700. 59 rooms, modern, excellent views.

$ Shevaroys, Main (Hospital) Rd, near lake, T04281-222288. 32 rooms, 11 **$$** cottages with baths, restaurant, bar, good views.

$ Tamil Nadu (TTDC), Salem-Yercaud Ghat Rd, near lake, behind Panchayat Office, T04281-222273. 12 rooms, restaurant, garden.

Kodaikanal p146, map p147

Room rates are high in Kody compared to the rest of Tamil Nadu, but so are standards of cleanliness, in every price category. Off-season rates are given here: prices rise by 30-100% Apr-Jun and 12.5% tax is charged everywhere. On Anna Salai cheap basic lodges, mostly with shared bathroom, can charge Rs 800 in season.

$$$ Carlton, Boat Club Rd, T04542-248555, www.carlton-kodaikanal.com. Fully modernized but colonial-style hotel with 91 excellent rooms, many with private terraces overlooking the lake. Excellent restaurant, billiards, tennis, golf and boating, often full in season. Recommended.

$$$ Elephant Valley, Ganesh Puram village (20 km from Kodai off Palani road), T0413-265 5751. This tranquil eco-resort comprises 13 cute rustic stone cottages (some in converted village houses) dotted across a 30-ha organic farm on either side of a rocky river, visited by wild boar, gaur and elephants (best sightings Apr-Jun). Restaurant serves good food based on home-grown veg and herbs, fantastic salads, plus superb coffee which is grown, roasted and ground entirely on-site. Highly recommended.

$$ Bison Wells Jungle Lodge, Camp George Observatory, T04542-240566, www.wilderness-explorer.in. A cottage for the nature purist, with no electricity and space for only 3, a whole mountain range away from the rest of the hill station. Jeep transport from Kody arranged on request at extra cost.

$$ Ferncroft, 17 km from town on Palani Rd, T04542-230242, jfmfernando33@ yahoo.com. Simple, rustic lodgings on the ground floor of Tamil-Scots couple Jo and Maureen Fernando's stone built house, set among trees heavy with peaches, passion fruit and avocado. There's a small but comfortable bedroom, a kitchenette and living room with wicker chairs, plus a parcel of lush lawn with beautiful views down the valley. Far from town, but hard to beat for peace and quiet.

$$ RR Residency, Boathouse Rd, T04542-244300, residency@rediffmail. com. 7 well-furnished, top-quality rooms in newish hotel, though views are lacking and there's potential olfactory disturbance from adjacent petrol pump. Vegetarian restaurant next door.

$$-$ Garden Manor, Lake Rd (10-min walk from bus station), T04542-240461. Good location in pleasant gardens overlooking lake, with 7 rooms (including a 4-bed), restaurant with outdoor tables.

$$-$ Villa Retreat, Coaker's Walk, T04542-240940, www.villaretreat. com. 8 deluxe rooms in an old house, 3 cottages (open fireplace), rustic, good service. Garden setting, excellent views, clean but overpriced.

$ Bala, 11/49 Woodville Rd, opposite the bus station (entrance tucked away in private courtyard), T04542-241214, www.balagroups.com. Friendly and well-kept hotel, with 57 rooms (ask for one on 2nd or 3rd floor as lower rooms look out on neighbouring walls), good vegetarian restaurant, friendly staff.

$ Greenlands, St Mary's Rd, Coaker's Walk end, T04542-240899, www. greenlandskodaikanal.com. Clean, small and friendly budget traveller choice. 15 very basic, clean rooms (jug and bucket of hot water 0700-0900), amazing views. A few newish rooms are less atmospheric but have hot water on tap. Pleasant gardens, 62-bed dorm (Rs 55-65).

$ Hilltop Towers, Club Rd, T04542-240413, www.hilltopgroup.in. 26 modern, properly cleaned and comfortable rooms, some noise from passing buses and limited hours for hot water, but the management are very obliging and the complex contains a slew of good restaurants. Recommended.

$ Kodai Plaza, St Anthoia Koil St (walk uphill from bus stand and turn left down steep narrow lane), T04542-240423. The cheapest choice around the bus stand, rooms not the cleanest but survivable,

and some have good views of distant peaks framed by fluttering prayer flags.

$ Vignesh, Laws Ghat Rd, near lake, T04542-244348. Old period-style house, 6 spacious rooms (can interconnect), good views, garden setting. Recommended.

$ Youth Hostel (TTDC), Fernhill Rd, T04542-241336. Rooms and dorm beds.

Anamalai (Indira Gandhi) Wildlife Sanctuary p149

There are several Forest Department rest houses scattered around Top Slip and other parts of the sanctuary including Mt Stuart, Varagaliar, Sethumadai and Amaravathinagar. May allow only 1 night's stay. Reservations: District Forest Officer, Coimbatore S Div, 176 Meeanakalai Salai, Pollachi, T04259-225356. The friendly canteen in Top Slip serves good *dosa* and *thalis* for lunch.

$ Sakti, 144 Coimbatore Main Rd, T04259-223050, Pollachi. Newish, large and smart, rooms, vegetarian restaurant.

Dindigul p149

$$ Cardamom House, Athoor village, Kamarajar Lakeside, T0451-255 6765, www.cardamomhouse.com. This pretty home of a retired British doctor from Southsea introduces you to Tamil village life in Athoor and is a good bridge for journeys between either Kerala and Tamil Nadu or Trichy and Madurai. Tucked out of the way at the foothills of the Palani hills overlooking the lake, which is rich in birdlife, 7 rooms spread across 3 buildings all with lake views.

$$-$ Maha Jyothi, Spencer Compound, T0451-243 4313, hotelmahajyothi@ rediffmail.com. Range of rooms, a/c, clean, modern, 24-hr check out.

$ Prakash, 9 Thiruvalluvar Salai, T0451-242 3577. 42 clean, spacious rooms. Recommended.

$ Sukanya Lodge, 43 Thiruvallur Salai (by bus stand), T0451-242 8436. Small, rather dark a/c rooms, but very clean, friendly staff, good value.

$ Venkateshwar Lodge, near bus stand, T0451-242 5881. Very cheap, 50 rooms, basic, clean, vegetarian restaurant next door.

🍴 Restaurants

Udhagamandalam (Ooty) *p140, map p141*

There are usually bars in larger hotels. **Southern Star** is recommended, but pricey.

$$$ Savoy (see Where to stay). Old-world wood-panelled dining hall serving up good food. Also has bar, café, snooker and table tennis halls.

$$ Chandan Vegetarian, Nahar Nilgiris, Charing Cross, T0423-244 2173. 1230-1530, 1900-2230. Roomy restaurant inside the **Nahar** hotel complex serving up vegetarian North Indian and Chinese food.

$$ The Pavilion, **Fortune Hotel**, 500 m from town, Sullivan Court, 123 Shelbourne Rd, T0423-244 1415. In modern hotel, good multi-cuisine plus separate bar.

$ Blue Hills, Charing Cross. Good-value Indian and continental, non-vegetarian.

$ Garden Café, Nahar Nilgiris, Charing Cross. 0730-2130. Lawn-side coffee shop and snack bar with South Indian menu: *iddli*, *dosa* and *chats* from Rs 30.

$ Hot Breads, Charing Cross. Tasty hot dogs, pizzas, etc.

$ Hotel Ooty Saravanaa's, 302 Commercial Rd. 0730-1000, 1130-2230. The place for super-cheap south Indian breakfast: large mint green place that does a fast trade in *iddli*, *dosa* and meals.

$ Sharma Bhojanalaya 12C Lower Bazar Rd. Gujarati and North Indian food served upstairs in comfortable (padded banquettes) but not aesthetically

pleasing venue, overlooks race course, good vegetarian lunch *thali* (Rs 40).

$ Shinkow's, 38/83 Commissioner's Rd (near Collector's Office) T0423-244 2811. 1200-1545, 1830-2145. Authentic Chinese, popular, especially late evening. Chicken chilli Rs 120. Tartan tablecloths and fish tank. Highly recommended.

Cafés

Try local institutions **Sugar Daddy** and **King Star** (established in 1942), 1130-2030, for brilliant home-made chocolates such as fruit'n'nut and fudges.

Coonoor *p143*

$$ Velan Hotel Ritz, Bedford, T0423-223 0632. Open 0730-1030, 1230-1530, 1930-2230. Good multi-cuisine restaurant overlooking the Ritz's lawns – don't expect speedy service, though.

$ The Only Place, Sim's Park Rd. Simple, homely, good food.

$ Sri Lakshmi, next to bus station. Freshly cooked, quality vegetarian; try paneer butter masala and Kashmiri naan.

Mettupalayam *p144*

Karna Hotel in the bus station is good for *dosas*.

Coimbatore *p145*

$$$ Cloud Nine, City Tower Hotel (see Where to stay). Excellent views from rooftop of one of city's tallest buildings, good international food (try asparagus soup), buzzing atmosphere especially when it's full of families on Sun evening, pleasant service but slightly puzzling menu.

$$ Dakshin, **Shree Annapoorna Hotel Complex**, 47 East Arokiasamy Rd, RS Puram. International. Very smart, good food.

$$ Solai Drive-in, Nehru Stadium, near VOC Park. Chinese, Indian food and good ice creams.

$ Indian Coffee House, Ramar Koil St. South Indian snacks.
$ Royal Hindu, opposite Junction station. Indian vegetarian.

Kodaikanal *p146, map p147*
$$$ Carlton Hotel, set in very pleasant grounds overlooking lake and Garden Manor. Good for tea and snacks.
$$ Royal Tibet Hotel, J's Heritage complex, PT Rd. Noodle soup and momos.
$$ Silver Inn, Hospital Rd. Travellers' breakfasts and Indian choices. Popular but slow service.
$$ Tava, Hospital Rd. Very good Indian.
$$ Tibetan Brothers Hotel, J's Heritage Complex. 1200-2200 (closed 1600-1730). Serves excellent Tibetan, homely atmosphere, good value. Recommended.

Bakeries and snacks
Eco-Nut, J's Heritage Complex. Good wholefoods, brown bread, jams, peanut butter, etc (cheese, yoghurts, better and cheaper in dairy across the road).
Hot Breads, J's Heritage Complex. For very good pastries.
Pastry Corner, Anna Salai Bazar. Brown bread, pastries and chocolate brownies, plus a couple of tables out the front.
Philco's Cold Storage, opposite Kodai International School. For home-made chocolate, cakes, frozen foods, delicatessen. Also internet.
Spencer's Supermarket, Club Rd. Wide range of local and foreign cheeses.

Dindigul *p149*
Cascade Roof Garden, at Sree Arya Bhavan, 19 KHF Building, near the bus stand. Serves very good vegetarian.
Janakikarm, near new Roman Catholic church. Don't miss their pizzas, sweets and snacks, surprisingly good value, "*channa samosa* to die for".

⊛ Festivals

Udhagamandalam (Ooty) *p140, map p141*
Jan Pongal.
May The **Annual Flower and Dog Shows** in the Botanical Gardens.
Summer Festival of cultural with stars from all over India.

Kodaikanal *p146, map p147*
May Summer Tourist Festival: boat race, flower show, dog show, etc.

O Shopping

Udhagamandalam (Ooty) *p140, map p141*
Most shops open 0900-1200, 1500-2000. The smaller shops keep longer hours.
Higginbotham's, Commercial Rd, T0423-244 3736. Open 0930-1300, 1550-1930, closed Wed. Bookseller.
Toda Showroom, Charing Cross. Sells silver and tribal shawls.
Variety Hall, Silver Market. Old family firm (1890s) for good range of silk, helpful, accepts credit cards.

Kodaikanal *p146, map p147*
Belgian Convent Shop, east of town. Hand-embroidered linen.
Cottage Crafts Shop, Anna Salai (Council for Social Concerns in Kodai). Mon-Sat 0900-1230, 1400-1830. Volunteer-run.
Govt Sales Emporium, near Township Bus Stand. Only open in season.
Kashmir Handicrafts Centre, 2 North Shopping Complex, Anna Salai. Jewellery, brass, shawls, walnut wood crafts and Numdah rugs.
Potter's Shack, PT Rd. Lovely earthy cups and vases made by local potters Subramaniam and Prabhu under tutelage of Ray and Deborah Meeker of

Puducherry. Visits to the workshop can be arranged, and proceeds go to help disadvantaged children.

⚙ What to do

Udhagamandalam (Ooty) p140, map p141
Horse riding
Gymkhana Club, T0423-244 2254. Big bar open 1130-1530 or 1830-2300. Temporary membership; beautifully situated amidst superbly maintained 18-hole golf course. Riding from Regency Villa: Rs 500 for 2 hrs with 'guide'; good fun but no helmets.

Tour operators
Tours can be booked through the **TTDC**, at Hotel Tamil Nadu, T0423-244 4370. Ooty and Mudumalai: Ooty Lake, Dodabetta Peak, Botanical Gardens, Mudumalai Wildlife Sanctuary. 0830-2000. Rs 150. Kotagiri and Coonoor: Kotagiri, Kodanad View Point, Lamb's Rock, Dolphin's Nose, Sim's Park. 0830-1830. Rs 130.
Blue Mountain, Nahar Complex, Charing Cross, T0423-244 3650. Luxury coach bookings to neighbouring states.
George Hawkes, 52C Nahar Complex, T0423-244 2756. For tourist taxis.
Sangeetha Travels, 13 Bharathiyar Complex, Charing Cross, T0432-244 4782. Steam train.
Woodlands Tourism, Race Course Rd, T0423-244 2551. Ooty and Coonoor. 0930-1730. Rs 130. Stunning views.

Yoga
Rajayoga Meditation Centre, 88 Victoria Hall, Ettines Rd.

Coonoor p143
TTDC from Ooty (reserve in Ooty Tourist Office). Coonoor–Kotagiri Rs 120, 6 hrs; visiting Valley View, Sim's Park, Lamb's Rock, Dolphin's Nose, Kodadu viewpoint.

Coimbatore p145
Alooha, corner near **Heritage Inn**. Helpful travel agency.

Kodaikanal p146, map p147
Boating
Boat Club, T04542-241315. Rents out pedal boats, 6-seater row boats and romantic Kashmir-style *shikaras*, Rs 40-160 per 30 mins plus boatman fees. The boatmen here are friendly and speak good English. 0900-1730.
TTDC Boat House, next door. Similar services and prices. 0900-1730.

Golf
Golf club, T04542-240323. Kodai's forest-swathed course is one of the most beautiful and (out of season) peaceful in the world, and the greens and fairways are maintained with minimal watering and no chemical pesticides. A round costs Rs 200-250, club hire Rs 200.

Horse riding
Ponies for hire near the Boat House, Rs 300 per hr.

Tour operators
Several tour operators around town book similar sightseeing tours, at around Rs 85 for a half day, Rs 150 full day.
Vijay Tours, Anna Salai, T04542-241137.

Trekking
A reputable local guide is **Vijay Kumar**, T(0)9994-277373.

⊖ Transport

Udhagamandalam (Ooty) *p140, map p141*
Arrive early for buses to ensure a seat. They often leave early if full. Ghat roads have numerous hairpin bends which can have fairly heavy traffic and very bad surfaces at times. The Gudalur road passes through Mudumalai and Bandipur sanctuaries. You might see an elephant herd and other wildlife, especially at night.

Air The nearest airport is at Coimbatore, 105 km away. Taxis available.

Bus State government and private Cheran buses (T0423-244 3970) pull in to the bus stand, just south of the railway station and a 10-min walk from the town centre. Frequent buses to **Coimbatore** (every 20 mins, 0530-2000, 3½ hrs), **Coonoor** (every 10 mins, 0530-2045), and **Mettupalayam** (0530-2100, 2 hrs). Daily buses to **Bengaluru** (**Bangalore**) (0630-2000), **Mysore** (0800-1530, 3½-5 hrs), **Kozhikode** (0630-1515), **Chennai** (1630-1830), **Palani** (0800-1800), **Kanniyakumari** (1745), **Kodaikanal** (0630, 9½ hrs via magnificent route through Palani); **Puducherry** (1700); **Salem** (1300). Check timings. Several on the short route (36 km) to **Masinagudi** in Mudumalai, 1½ hrs on a steep and bendy but interesting road.

Train Ooty is the terminus of the Nilgiri Mountain Railway. 4 diesel trains a day run from Ooty to **Coonoor**, at 0915, 1215, 1400 and 1800; the 1400 *Ooty-Mettupalayam Passenger 56137* swaps to a steam loco at Coonoor and continues down the wonderfully scenic track to **Mettupalayam**. This train connects with the *Nilgiri Exp* to **Chennai** (for trains to Ooty, see Mettupalayam transport below). Book tickets well in advance. Railway station, T0423-244 2246. From **Mettupalayam** *Blue Mountain* (steam to **Coonoor**; then diesel to Ooty), 1 return train daily, see Mettupalayam transport, below.

Coonoor *p143*
Bus Frequent buses to **Ooty** (every 10 mins from 0530) some via Sim's Park and many via Wellington. Also regular services to **Kotagiri** and **Coimbatore** (every 30 mins) through **Mettupalayam**. Direct bus to **Mysore** (or change at Ooty).

Train Coonoor sits at the top of the most scenic section of the Nilgiri Mountain Railway; steam locos from Mettupalayam terminate here, switching to diesel for the run into Ooty. Trains leave to **Ooty** at 0745, 1040, 1235 and 1630 (1½ hrs); and to **Mettupalayam** at 1515 (2½ hrs).

Mettupalayam *p144*
Train The *Nilgiri Express* from Chennai Central arrives in Mettupalayam at 0615, triggering a mad dash for tickets and seats on the tiny 'toy train' of the Nilgiri Mountain Railway, which departs for **Ooty** at 0710 (5 hrs). Only 30 tickets are available for same-day purchase on the toy train, so book as far in advance as possible. Note that the line is subject to landslides and washouts that can close the route for some months; check before travelling. If you're coming from Coimbatore, it is better to arrive in advance at Mettupalayam by bus (quicker and more frequent than local trains). If you have time to spare the engine sheds are interesting to look around. For **Chennai**: *Nilgiri Exp 12672*, 1945, 10½ hrs.

Mudumalai Wildlife Sanctuary *p144*
Bus Theppakadu is on the main Mysore–Ooty bus route. From **Mysore**, services from 0615 (1½-2 hrs); last bus to Mysore around 2000. From **Ooty** via **Gudalur** on a very winding road (about 2½ hrs); direct 20 km steep road used by buses, under 1 hr. Few buses between Theppakadu and Masinagudi.

Jeeps are available at bus stands and from lodges.

Coimbatore *p145*
Air Peelamedu Airport, 12 km centre, runs airport coach into town, Rs 25; taxis Rs 150-200; auto-rickshaw Rs 85. On Trichy Rd: **Air India**, T0422-239 9833, airport T0422-257 4623, 1000-1300, 1345-1730, to **Bengaluru** (**Bangalore**), **Chennai**, **Delhi**, **Kochi**, **Kozhikode**, **Mumbai**. **Jet Airways**: 1055/1 Gowtham Centre, Avinashi Rd, T0422-221 2034, airport T0422-257 5375, to **Bengaluru** (**Bangalore**), **Chennai**, **Mumbai**.

Bus City buses run a good service: several connect the bus stations in Gandhipuram with the Junction Railway Station 2 km south. No 20 goes to the airport (Rs 20).

There are 4 long-distance bus stations, off Dr Nanjappa Rd.

City or '**Town**' **Bus Stand** in Gandhipuram. **Thiruvallur Bus Stand**, Cross Cut Rd. Computerized reservations T0422-226700, 0700-2100. Frequent Government Express buses to **Madurai** (5 hrs), **Chennai** (12 hrs), **Mysore** (6 hrs), **Ooty** (3 hrs), **Tiruchirappalli** (5½ hrs).

'**Central**' **Bus Stand** is further south, on corner of Shastri Rd. State buses to **Bengaluru** (**Bangalore**) and **Mysore**; **Ooty** via **Mettupalayam** (see below for train connection) and **Coonoor** every 20 mins, 0400-2400, 5 hrs.

Ukkadam Bus Stand, south of the city, serves towns within the state (**Pollachi**, **Madurai**) and in north Kerala (**Pallakad**, **Thrissur**, **Munnar**).

Taxi Tourist taxis and yellow top taxis are available at the bus stations, railway station and taxi stands. Rs 2.5 per km; for out-station hill journeys, Rs 3 per km; minimum Rs 30.

Train Junction Station, enquiries, T132, reservations, T131, 0700-1300, 1400-2030. **Bengaluru** (**Bangalore**): *Tilak Exp 11014*, 0800, 7¼ hrs; *Bangalore Exp 12678*, 1245, 7 hrs; **Kanniyakumari**: *Kanyakumari Exp 16381*, 0010, 9 hrs. **Chennai**: *West Coast Exp 16628*, 0630, 9 hrs; *Kovai Exp 12676*, 1420, 7½ hrs. **Kochi** (**HT**): *Ernakulam Exp 12677*, 1310, 4hrs; *Hyderabad-Kochi Exp 17030*, 0935, daily, 5½ hrs.

For **Ooty** best to take the bus to Mettupalayam (see above).

Salem *p145*
Bus The **New Bus Stand**, north of the hospital, off Omalur Rd, T0427-226 5917, has buses to all major towns in Tamil Nadu, Kerala and South Karnataka.

Train Salem Junction is the main train station. Enquiries, T132. Reservations, T131, 0700-1300, 1400-2030. **Bengaluru** (**Bangalore**): *Tilak Exp 11014*, 1040, 4½ hrs; *Bangalore Exp 12678*, 1535, 4 hrs. **Chennai** (**C**): *Coimbatore–Chennai Exp 12680*, 0835, 5 hrs. **Madurai**: *Tuticorin Exp 16732*, not Tue, Wed, Sun, 0200, 5 hrs. For **Ooty**, *Nilgiri Exp 12671*, 0135, connects with narrow-gauge steam train from Mettupalayam.

Yercaud *p145*
Bus There are no local·buses but some from Salem (1 hr) continue to nearby villages.

Kodaikanal *p146, map p147*
Bicycle hire There are several bike hire stands around the lake, charging Rs 10 per hr, Rs 100 per day for good new bikes.

Bus Check timings; reservations possible. To **Bengaluru (Bangalore)**, overnight, 12 hrs; **Chennai** (497 km) 12 hrs; **Coimbatore** (171 km) 6 hrs; **Dindigul** (90 km) 3½ hrs, via Kodai Rd; **Madurai** (120 km), 0730-1830, 4 hrs; **Kumily** (for Periyar NP), 5½ hrs, change buses at Vatigundu; **Palani** (65 km) 3 hrs; **Tiruchirappalli** (197 km) 6 hrs. To **Munnar** by bus takes 8 hrs, changing at Palani and Udhamalpet.

Taxi Unmetered taxis available for sight-seeing. Tourist taxis from agencies including **Raja's**, near Pastry Corner on Anna Salai, T04542-242422. Taxi transfer to **Munnar** costs around Rs 2200, or Rs 450 for a seat in a shared taxi.

Train Reservations counter off Anna Salai behind **Anjay** hotel, 0800-1200, 1430-1700, Sun 0800-1200. No Foreign Tourist Quota bookings. The nearest station is Kodai Rd, 80 km away. Taxi drivers at the station quote Rs 1000 to drop you in Kodai, but this price drops if you cross the road and look determined to catch a bus. **Hotel Tamil Nadu**, just south of the station, has rooms if you get stuck.

Anamalai (Indira Gandhi) Wildlife Sanctuary *p149*
Bus 3 daily buses connect **Top Slip** with Pollachi, which has connections to **Coimbatore** and **Palani**. To Top Slip: 0600, 1100, 1500 (but check timings); from Top Slip: 0930, 1300, 1830.

Dindigul *p149*
Bus Good and frequent bus service to **Tiruchirappalli**, **Chennai**, **Salem** and **Coimbatore** and long-distance connections.

Train Train to **Chennai (ME)** *Vaigai Exp 12636 (AC/CC)*, 0730, 6¾ hrs via **Tiruchirappalli** 1½ hrs. To **Madurai** *Vaigai Exp 12635 (AC/CC)*, 1905, 1¼ hrs.

❶ Directory

Udhagamandalam (Ooty) *p140, map p141*
Banks ATMs congregate along Bank Rd and Commercial Rd. **State Bank of India**, on Bank Rd, deals in foreign exchange. **Internet** Gateways, 8/9 Moosa Sait Complex, Commercial Rd. Excellent, fast, ISDN lines, Rs 30 per hr. **Medical services** Govt Hospital, Hospital Rd, T0423-244 2212. **Post** Head Post Office, Collectorate and Telegraph Office, Town W Circle. **Useful contacts** Police, T100. **Wildlife Warden**, 1st floor, Mahalingam Building, T0423-244098, 1000-1730. Closed 1300-1400.

Coonoor *p143*
Banks Travancore Bank, Upper Coonoor (Bedford Circle) changes cash. **South Indian Bank**, Mount Rd, 1000-1400 changes cash and TCs. **Medical services** Lawley Hospital, Mt Rd, T0423-223 1050.

Coimbatore *p145*
Banks Several on Oppankara St. **State Bank of India** (exchange upstairs), and **Bank of Baroda** are on Bank Rd. **Medical services** Government Hospital, Trichy Rd. **Post** Near flyover, Railway Feeder Rd. **Useful**

contacts Automobile Association, 42 Trichy Rd, T0422-222 2994.

Yercaud *p145*
Banks Banks with foreign exchange are on Main Rd. **Medical services** Govt Hospital, 1 km from bus stand; **Providence Hospital**, on road to Lady's Seat. **Post** On Main Rd.

Kodaikanal *p146, map p147*
Banks Several branches with ATMs on Anna Salai. **Indian Bank** does foreign exchange **Hotel Tamil Nadu**, has a counter for foreign exchange counter.
Medical services Van Allan Hospital, T04542-241273, is recommended. Consultations (non-emergency): Mon-Fri 0930-1200, 1530-1630. Sat 1000-1200. Clean and efficient, good doctors. **Government Hospital**, T04542-241292. **Post** Head Post Office on Post Office Rd.

Madurai and around

Madurai is a maddening whirl of a temple town: the red-and-white striped sanctuary of the 'fish-eyed goddess' is a towering edifice crested by elaborate gaudy stucco-work *gopurams*, soundtracked by tinny religious songs, peopled by 10,000 devoted pilgrims prostrating themselves at shrines, lighting candles and presenting flower garlands to idols, seeking blessings from the temple elephant or palmistry on the shores of the Golden Lotus Tank. Even the city's town planning reflects the sanctity of the spot: surrounding streets radiate like bicycle spokes from the temple in the mandala architectural style, a sacred form of geometry. The centre seems all dust and cycle-rickshaws, but Madurai, as the second biggest city in Tamil Nadu, is also a modern industrial place that never sleeps. Around the city the area of fertile agricultural land is dotted with exotically shaped granite mountain ranges such as Nagamalai (snake hills) and Yanaimalai (elephant hills).

Madurai → *For listings, see pages 173-179. Phone code: 0452. Population: 922,900.*

There is the usual combination of messy crumbling buildings harking back to times of greater architectural aspirations, modern glass-and-chrome palaces, internet cafés, flower sellers, tailors and tinkers and Kashmiri antique and shawl dealers. Further out, in the leafy suburbs to the west and north across the Vaigai River, are museums, lakes and temple tanks. Allow at least two days to explore everything.

Arriving in Madurai
Getting there The airport is 12 km from town and is linked by buses, taxis and autos to the city centre. The railway station is within easy walking distance of many budget hotels (predatory rickshaw drivers/hotel touts may tell you otherwise). Hire an auto to reach the few north of the river. Most intercity buses arrive at the Mattuthavani Bus Stand 6 km northeast of the centre; those from Kodaikanal and destinations to the northwest use the Arapalayam Bus Stand, 3 km northwest. Both are linked to the centre by bus and auto.▸▸ *See Transport, page 177.*

Getting around The city centre is compact and the temple is within easy walking distance of most hotels. Prepare for hordes of touts. To visit the sights around the city, buses and taxis are available.

Tourist information ① *W Veli St, T0452-233 4757, Mon-Fri 1000-1745*, has useful maps, tours (arranged through agents), guides for hire. Also at **Madurai Junction Railway Station** ① *Main Hall, 0630-2030*, and the airport counter during flight times.

Background
According to legend, drops of nectar fell from Siva's locks on this site, so it was named Madhuram or Madurai, 'the Nectar City'. The city's history goes back to the sixth century BC. Ancient Madurai, which traded with Greece and Rome, was a centre of Tamil culture, famous for its writers and poets during the last period of the three *Sangam* (Tamil 'Academies') nearly 2000 years ago.

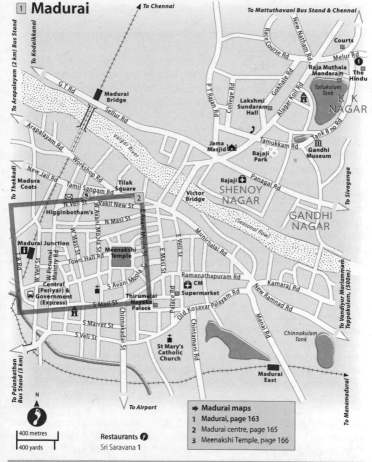

1 Madurai

→ **Madurai maps**
1 Madurai, page 163
2 Madurai centre, page 165
3 Meenakshi Temple, page 166

Restaurants ❼
Sri Saravana 1

By the fourth century, Madurai, Tirunelveli and a part of southern Kerala were under the **Pandiyas**, a major power from the sixth to the early 10th century. The Pandiyas made Madurai their capital and remained here for 300 years, staying on even during the rule of the **Cholas**; after Chola power declined in the late 12th century the Pandiyas regained control of Madurai, and they presided over a period of flourishing international trade until Malik Kafur destroyed the city in 1310.

For a period Madurai became a sultanate, but Muslim rule in Tamil Nadu proved as short-lived as it was tenuous. In 1364 the city was recaptured by the Hindu Vijayanagar kings, who remained until 1565, when the defeat of the Vijayanagar Empire by a confederacy of Muslim states forced their leaders to take refuge in Madurai. As the **Nayaka** kings, they continued to rule well into the 17th century. The Nayakas have been seen essentially as warriors, given an official position by the Vijayanagar rulers, but in Sanskrit the term applied to someone of prominence and leadership. Burton Stein comments, "the history of the Vijayanagara is essentially the history of the great Telugu Nayakas" from Madurai.

The Vijayanagar had been great builders, preserving and enriching the architectural heritage of the town, and the Nayakas held true to their legacy. They laid out the old town in the pattern of a lotus, with narrow streets surrounding the Meenakshi Temple at the centre, and took up the Vijayanagar predilection for building temple complexes with tall *gopurams*. These increased in height to become dominating structures covered profusely with plaster decorations. The tall *gopurams* of Madurai were built by Thirumalai (ruled 1623-1655), the greatest of the Nayaka rulers, and may have served a strategic purpose as they moved away from the earlier Chola practice of giving the central shrine the tallest tower. The *kalyana mandapa* or marriage hall with a 'hundred' or 'thousand' pillars, and the temple tank with steps on all four sides, were introduced in some southern temples, along with the *Nandi* bull, Siva's vehicle, which occupies a prominent position at the entrance to the main Shaivite shrine.

In 1840, after the Carnatic Wars, the British destroyed the fort, filling in the surrounding moat; its original course is now followed by the four Veli streets. The inner streets encircling the central temple are named after the festivals which take place in them and give their relative direction: South 'Chitrai Street, East 'Avani Moola' Street and West 'Masi Street'.

Places in Madurai

Meenakshi Temple ① *Inner Temple 0500-1230, 1600-2130, foreigners Rs 50, camera Rs 50, tickets from counters near South Entrance and Thousand-Pillared Hall (valid for multiple entries on same day); art museum 0600-2030, Rs 5, camera fee Rs 50. Metal detectors and body searches at entrance gates. Sanctuaries of Meenakshi and Sundareswarar are open only to Hindus. Offers of good viewpoints made by helpful bystanders will invariably turn out to be from the roofs of nearby shops.* This is an outstanding example of Vijayanagar temple architecture and an exact contemporary of the Taj Mahal in Agra. Meenakshi, the 'fish-eyed goddess' and the consort of Siva, has a temple to the south, and Sundareswarar (Siva), a temple to the west. Since she is the presiding deity the daily ceremonies are first performed in her shrine and, unlike the practice at other temples, Sundareswarar plays a secondary role. The temple's nine towering *gopurams* stand out with their colourful stucco images of gods, goddesses and animals which are renewed and painted every 12 years – the most recent touch-up having been completed in February 2009. There are about 4000 granite sculptures on the lower levels. In addition to the Golden Lotus tank and various pillared halls there are five *vimanas* over the sanctuaries.

The temple is a hive of activity, with a colourful temple elephant, flower sellers and **musical performances** ① *1800-1930, 2100-2130*. There is an evening ceremony (arrive by 2100), when an image of Sundareswarar is carried in procession, to a heady accompaniment of whirling pipe and drum music and clouds of incense, from the shrine near the east *gopuram* to Meenakshi, to 'sleep' by her side; he is returned first thing the next morning. The procession around the temple is occasionally led by the elephant and a cow. During the day the elephant is on continual duty, 'blessing' visitors with its trunk and then collecting a small offering.

The main entrance is through a small door of the **Ashta Sakthi Mandapa (1)** (Porch of the Eight Goddesses) which projects from the wall, south of the eastern *gopuram*. Inside to the left is the sacred **Tank of the Golden Lotus (2)**, with a lamp in the centre, surrounded by pillared cloisters and steps down to the waters. The Sangam legend speaks of the test that ancient manuscripts had to undergo: they were thrown into the sacred tank, and only if they floated were they considered

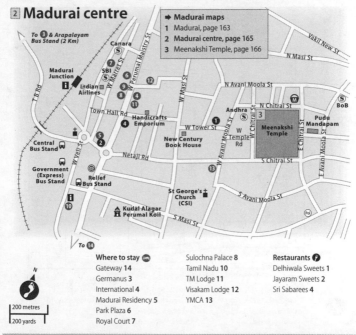

2 **Madurai centre**

➡ Madurai maps
1 Madurai, page 163
2 Madurai centre, page 165
3 Meenakshi Temple, page 166

Where to stay
Gateway **14**
Germanus **3**
International **4**
Madurai Residency **5**
Park Plaza **6**
Royal Court **7**

Sulochna Palace **8**
Tamil Nadu **10**
TM Lodge **11**
Visakam Lodge **12**
YMCA **13**

Restaurants
Delhiwala Sweets **1**
Jayaram Sweets **2**
Sri Sabarees **4**

worthy of further study. The north gallery has murals (under restoration at the time of writing) relating 64 miracles said to have been performed by Siva, and the southern has marble inscriptions of the 1330 couplets of the *Tamil Book of Ethics*. To the west of the tank is the **Oonjal Mandapa (3)**, the pavilion leading to the Meenakshi shrine. Here the pillars are carved in the form of the mythical beast *yali* which recurs in temples throughout the region. Golden images of Meenakshi and Sundareswarar are brought to the *oonjal* or swing each Friday evening where they are worshipped. Cages with parrots, Meenakshi's green bird that brings luck, hang from the ceiling of the neighbouring **Kilikootu Mandapam (4)**, which is flanked by finely carved columns. The **Meenakshi shrine (5)** with the principal image of the goddess, stands in its own enclosure with smaller shrines around it.

To the north of the tank is another enclosure with smaller *gopurams* on four sides within which is the **Sundareswarar shrine (6)** guarded by two tall *dwarapalas*. In the northeast corner, the superb sculptures of the divine marriage of Meenakshi and Sundareswarar being blessed by Vishnu and Brahma, and Siva in his 24 forms are in the 19th-century **Kambathadi Mandapa (7)**, around the golden flagstaff.

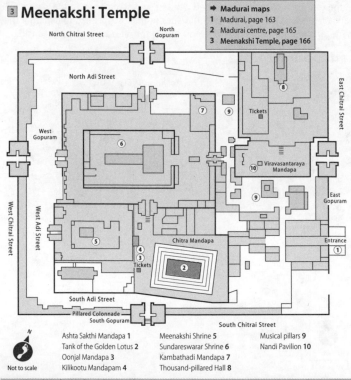

③ Meenakshi Temple

➡ **Madurai maps**
1 Madurai, page 163
2 Madurai centre, page 165
3 Meenakshi Temple, page 166

Ashta Sakthi Mandapa **1**
Tank of the Golden Lotus **2**
Oonjal Mandapa **3**
Kilikootu Mandapam **4**

Meenakshi Shrine **5**
Sundareswarar Shrine **6**
Kambathadi Mandapa **7**
Thousand-pillared Hall **8**

Musical pillars **9**
Nandi Pavilion **10**

Not to scale

The mid-16th century **Thousand-pillared Hall (8)** is in the northeast corner of the complex. The 985 exquisitely carved columns include a lady playing the *vina*, a dancing Ganesh, and a gypsy leading a monkey. The art museum here exhibits temple art and architecture, fine brass and stone images, friezes and photos (the labelling could be improved). Just inside the museum to the right is a cluster of five **musical pillars (9)** carved out of a single stone. Each pillar produces a different note which vibrates when tapped. Nayaka musicians could play these as an instrument.

The **Nandi pavilion (10)** is to the east and is often packed with market stalls peddling flowers, trinkets and coconuts. The long *Pudu Mandapa* (New Mandapa), across the road from the East Tower, is lined with yet more beautiful sculptures of *yalis*, Nayaka rulers and elephants. Beyond lies the base of the unfinished *Raya Gopuram* which was planned to be the tallest in the country.

Northeast of the Meenakshi Temple, off N Avani Moola Street, is the **flower market**, a profusion of colour and activity at its best 0500-0730. It is a two-storey hall with piles of jasmine of all colours, lotuses, and huge jumbles of floral prettiness amid a sea of decomposing mulch of flowers trampled underfoot.

Thirumalai Nayaka Palace ① *0900-1300, 1400-1700, bus 17, 17A, 11, 11A*. Built in 1636 in the Indo-Mughal style, its 15 domes and arches are adorned with stucco work while some of its 240 columns rise to 12 m. Its *Swarga Vilasam* (Celestial Pavilion), an arcaded octagonal structure, is curiously constructed in brick and mortar without any supporting rafters. Special artisans skilled in the use of traditional lime plaster and powdered seashell and quartz have renovated parts. The original complex had a shrine, an armoury, a theatre, royal quarters, a royal bandstand, a harem, a pond and a garden but only about a quarter survives since Thirumalai's grandson removed sections to build another palace in Tiruchirappalli, and the original *Ranga* Vilasam was destroyed by Muslim invaders. It is a bit run down.

Vandiyur Mariammam Teppakulam ① *Buses 4 and 4A take 10 mins from the bus stand and railway station*. To the southeast of town, this has a small shrine in its centre where the annual **Float Festival** takes place in January/February.

Gandhi Museum ① *1000-1300, 1400-1730, free*. Located in the 300-year-old Rani Mangammal Palace, this is Madurai's best museum: informative, interesting and well laid out. It contains an art gallery, memorabilia (including the *dhoti* Gandhi was wearing when he was shot) and traces the history of the Independence struggle and the Quit India movement. It also has sections for Khadi and Village Industries and some stunning examples of South Indian handicrafts. Yoga classes are held daily (though only in Tamil) at 0630. Excellent bookshop.

Ramesvaram and around → *For listings, see pages 173-179.*

The conch-shaped island of Ramesvaram is normally lapped by the limpid blue waters of the Gulf of Mannar, but cyclones can whip the sea here into ferocious stormy waves. This is where Rama is believed to have worshipped Siva, making it sacred to both Shaivites and Vaishnavites, and so a pilgrim to Varanasi is expected to visit Ramesvaram next if he is to reach salvation. The great Ramalingesvara temple, which forms the core of the scrappy town, is one of India's most memorable, as much for the sight of priests spattering pilgrims with holy water from each of 22 sacred wells as for its cavernous, echoing corridors.

Arriving in Ramesvaram → *Phone code: 04573. Population: 38,000.*
Getting there Ramesvaram is connected to Madurai and other centres by regular bus and train services. The bus stand is 2 km from the centre, the railway station 1 km southwest of the great temple. There are also daily tours from Madurai.

Getting around Local buses and auto-rickshaws link the bus and train stations to the temple, where there are a few places to stay. ▶▶ *See Transport, page 178.*

Tourist information Tourist office ① *at bus stand, T04573-221371, 1000-1700.* Also at the **Railway Station** ① *T04573-221373, open (with some breaks) 0700-2030.* The **Temple Information** is on the east side of the temple.

Background
The *Ramayana* tells how the monkey king Hanuman built the bridges linking Ramnad to Pamban and Danushkodi (a spot where Rama is believed to have bathed) to help Rama rescue Sita from the demon king Ravana. When Rama returned he was told by the *rishis* that he must purify himself after committing the sin of murdering a Brahmin, for *Ravana* was the son of a Brahmin. To do this he was advised to set up a *lingam* and worship Siva. The red image of Hanuman north of the main East Gate illustrates this story.

The original shrine long predates the present great Ramesvaram temple. It is one of India's most sacred shrines and is visited by pilgrims from all over India. The temple benefited from huge donations from the 17th-century *Setupatis* (the so-called guardians of the causeway), who derived their wealth from the right to levy taxes on crossings to the island. The temple stands on slightly higher ground, surrounded by a freshwater lake.

To Ramesvaram and Adam's Bridge
Seen from the air the plains of the Vaigai River form one of the most remarkable landscapes in India, for there are over 5000 tanks, and irrigation has been so developed that barely a drop of water is wasted. The coastal districts of Ramnad have their own highly distinct economy and society. For the Hindus the sandbanks barely concealed in the Palk Strait are like giant stepping stones linking India and Sri Lanka: Adam's Bridge. Both Hindu and Muslim communities have long-established trading links across the Bay of Bengal, to Malaysia and Southeast Asia and to Sri Lanka. Small settlements along the coast like Kilakkarai have long been associated with smuggling. The civil war in Sri Lanka has made it a sensitive region.

Ramesvaram

The **Ramalingesvara** (or **Ramanathasvami**) **Temple** was founded by the Cholas but most of the temple was built in the Nayaka period (16th-17th centuries). It is a massive structure, enclosed by a huge rectangular wall with *gopurams* in the middle of three sides. Entrances through the east wall are approached through columned *mandapas* and the east *gopuram* is on the wall of the inner enclosure rather than the outer wall. Over 45 m high, it was begun in 1640 but left incomplete until recently. On entering, you see the statue of Hanuman, then the *Nandi* flanked by statues of the Nayaka kings of Madurai, Visvanatha and Krishnama. The north and south *gopurams* were built by Keerana Rayar of the Deccan in about AD 1420; the west *gopuram* is comparatively new.

The most remarkable feature of the temple is its pillared *mandapas*, the longest of which is over 200 m long. The pillars lining the four corridors, nearly 4 m tall, give an impression of almost unending perspective: those on the north and south sides are particularly striking. Tragically, however, the original stone pillars, decorated with scrollwork and lotus motifs, are being progressively phased out in favour of graceless grey concrete facsimiles. You're only likely to see the original versions lying on the ground in piles.

Ramesvaram

To gandhamadhana Parvatam (2 km)

Temple Bus Stand

N Car St
E Car St

SBI (S)

Ramalingesvara Temple

Indian (S)

Car St

S Car St

To Central Bus Stand (2 km), Pomban & Mandapam

HPO

Mela St

Palk Bay

Jetty

Port Station

Ramesvaram

N

500 metres (approx)
500 yards (approx)

Where to stay 🛏
Maharaja 1
Railway Retiring Rooms 2

Swami Ramanatha
  Tourist Home 3
Tamil Nadu 4
Venkatesh 5

Restaurants 🍴
Abbirami 1
Devasthanam Trust 2
Snack Stalls 3

There are two gateways on the east side which give access to the Parvati and Ramalinga shrines at the centre; the masonry shrine is probably the oldest building on the site, going back to 1173. Non-Hindus are generally turned away, but you might be able to enter if you can tag along with a group of pilgrims doing the holy well circuit (see box, page 170).

Gandhamadana Parvatam

Gandhamadana Parvatam, 2 km north of Ramesvaram, takes its name from the Sanskrit words *gandha* (fragrance) and *mad* (intoxicate), 'highly fragrant hill'. Dedicated to Rama's feet, this is the spot from which Hanuman is believed to have surveyed the area before taking his leap across the narrow Palk strait to Sri Lanka. You can get an excellent view from the top of the *mandapa*.

Dhanuskodi

Dhanuskodi ('the end of the bow') is the island's toe-tip where the Bay of Bengal meets the Indian Ocean, so named because Rama, at the request of Vibishana, his friend, destroyed the

Holy dips

Having bathed in the Ganga at Varanasi, Hindu pilgrims head straight for Ramesvaram, where a bath in the 22 *theertham* (holy wells) dotted within and around the Ramalingesvara temple promise a final release from the chains of *karma*.

The *theertham* circuit is a festive event for the pilgrims, complete with much cheering and song as buckets are emptied over heads, and as a visitor it can offer one of the most atmospheric and memorable temple experiences in Tamil Nadu, especially if you can get yourself adopted by a group of Indian visitors. The locals tend to bring along a change of clothes and submit to a thorough drenching, but if you come overdressed it is possible to request a light sprinkle. It's also traditional, but not obligatory, to taste of the waters; each apparently has a distinct flavour.

Brahmin priests wait at the train and bus stations and along the shoreline east of the temple to greet new arrivals, but the haggling of old has now been replaced by a standard charge of Rs 51 per person, which includes a dunking in each of the wells and access to the inner sanctum. Non-Hindus are traditionally prevented from entering the sanctum, but if you dress appropriately and arrive with a group (day tours from Madurai are an all-but-guaranteed way to join one) there's a good chance the priests will allow you in. If you do the circuit alone, it's best to leave valuables outside the temple: bystanders who offer to watch your bags are not all trustworthy.

bridge to Sri Lanka with the end of his bow. Some 20 km to the east of Ramesvaram island, it is considered particularly holy. There is a good beach, on which pilgrims will be making *puja*, and beautiful flat turquoise waters in which they take their holy bath, not to mention excellent views. A trip across the scrappy sand dunes is only recommended for the really hardy – get a local person to go with you. Travel by bus, and then join a pilgrim group on a jeep or lorry for the last desolate few miles (this should cost Rs 50 for a round trip but establish the price up front). Alternatively, take an auto to Adam's Bridge; insist on going as far as the radio mast for beach and fishing shack photos.

Cardamom Hills → For listings, see pages 173-179.

To the south of Madurai is a series of modest towns situated in the lee of the southern ranges of the Western Ghats. From Madurai to Thiruvanathapuram is a comfortable day's drive either via Tirunelveli or over the ghats, but there are several interesting places on the way if you wish to take your time.

Rajapalayam
ⓘ *To Sankaracoil, Rs 12, 30 mins; from there to Kalugumalai, Rs 8, 30 mins, buses to and from Tenkasi, Rs 30, 2 hrs.*

The town originated on the dispersal of the Vijayanagar families after 1565. The Sankarankovil temple is worth visiting. The Western Ghats rise to heights of over 1200 m immediately behind the town. Wild elephants still come down through the forests, devastating farmland.

Tenkasi

ⓘ *To Courtallam Falls frequent buses, Rs 8, to Courtallam Bus Stand, then walk through the grey arch to the 'Main Falls'. See Rajapalayam, above, for transport to Tenkasi.*

Literally the 'Kashi (Varanasi) of the South', Tenkasi is the nearest town to the Kuttalam (Courtallam) Falls, 6 km away. The impressive 16th-century Visvanatha temple dedicated to Siva has some fine carvings inside. The temple flagstaff is believed to be 400 years old. From Tenkasi the road goes through a low pass into the densely forested hills of Kerala.

Courtallam (Kuttalam)

With average temperatures of 22-23°C, Courtallam is a very popular health resort, especially during the monsoon. The impressive **Main Falls** is in town where the river Chittar cascades over 92 m. The approach is lined with spice, banana chips and knick-knack stalls and at the falls you'll find pilgrims washing themselves and their clothes. The waters, widely believed to have great curative powers, draw big crowds at the **Saral Festival** in July. The **Thirukutralanathar Temple** contains old inscriptions while the small **Chitra Sabha Temple** nearby contains religious murals.

Virudhunagar

The name Virudhupatti (Hamlet of Banners) was changed to Virudhunagar (City of Banners) in 1915, and was upgraded to a full municipality in 1957, reflecting the upwardly mobile social status of the town's dominant local caste, the Nadars. Originally low caste toddy tappers, they have established a wide reputation as a dynamic and enterprising group. The powerful Congress leader, Kamaraj Nadar, was chiefly responsible for Indira Gandhi's selection as prime minister.

Kalugumalai

Some 6 km south of Kovilpatti, Kalugumalai (Kazhugumalai) has a profusion of magnificent fifth-century bas-relief Jain figures on a huge rock which are well worth the detour. The Jain temple is to the north of the rock and is easily missed. There is also an unfinished monolithic cave temple to Siva (circa AD 950).

Chettinad → *For listings, see pages 173-179.*

The magnificent palaces of South India's old merchant and banking classes rise from the hot and dusty plains to stand as strong as fortresses and as gaudy as a packet of French Fancies. As the merchants, bankers and money-lenders of the British Empire, the Nattukottai Chettiars raked in enormous riches on their postings to places such as Burma, Sri Lanka, Indochina and South Africa, wealth they ploughed into these glorious architectural pastiches that explode in a profusion of colour in the arid desert-scape.

Now their monumental arches and long processional corridors open onto empty halls, the bats are more at home here than princes and shafts of light break on empty, cob-webbed dining rooms. The Nattukottai Chettiars saw their riches contract with the Second World War and the wanton palaces they built turned into tombstones, the series of south Indian villages they stand in left as virtual ghost towns. Architectural salvage merchants in the main town of Karaikkudi now sell off the portraits and granite pillars this proud caste have been forced to surrender to stave off financial hardship, while Bollywood crews make regular pilgrimages to the old mansions, propping up the owners with *lakhs* of studio rupees in return for the right to daub their chosen colour scheme across the walls.

Karaikkudi is in the heart of Chettinad, and has several typical mansions, particularly along the back lanes leading off busy Sekkalai Road (ask for the Thousand Window House, a well-known landmark). From here you can walk south to the local *santhai* (market), where you can find gold and silversmiths in their workshops, as well as antique and textile shops and several colourful temples.

Devakottai, 18 km south of Karaikkudi, is Chettinad's second largest town and offers similarly rich pickings in the way of old mansions and palaces: look out for the particularly grand Periya Minor's *veedu*.

Kanadukathan, 12 km north of Karaikkudi, has a number of magnificent mansions – some still inhabited by friendly owners (who'll let you have a look around for a Rs 100 donation), others are empty except for bats, monkeys and antique dealers. It has been estimated that the Burma teak and satinwood pillars in a single Chettiar house weighs 300 tonnes, often superbly carved. The plaster on the walls is made from a mixture of lime, egg white, powdered shells and myrobalan fruit (the astringent fruit of the tree *Phyllantles emblica*), mixed into a paste which, when dried, gives a gleaming finish. Most houses have the goddess of wealth, Lakshmi, made of stucco over the main arch.

The **Raja of Chettinad's Palace** ① *0930-1630, free, caretakers provide brief free tours*, is an amazing place overlooking the town's pond and full of sepia, larger-than-life-size portraits of stern family members, the frames garlanded with heavy yellow flowers. Next door is **Visalakshi Ramaswamy's house**, with a museum of local crafts, artefacts and handlooms upstairs. The raja's waiting room at the railway station is also pretty special.

Athangudi, 9 km away, is renowned for its tiles, which grace the floors of most Chettiar mansions; ask locally if you want to visit one of the 30-40 workshops in town. Nearby is Pillaiyarpatti, one of the most important temples in Chettinad, dedicated to Ganesh (known as Pillaiyaru in Tamil Nadu) and with an inner sanctum carved into a natural boulder.

At **Avudayarkoil**, 30 km northeast of Karaikkudi, the **Athmanathar Temple** has one of the most renowned sites in Tamil history. A legend tells that Manickavaskar, a Pandyan prime minister, redirected money intended for the purchase of horses to build the temple. However, his real fame lies as author of the *Thiruvasakam* ('Holy Outpourings'), one of the most revered Tamil poetic texts. Completely off the beaten track, the temple has superb sculptures, and is noted for the absence of any images of Siva or Parvati, the main deities, whose empty pedestals are worshipped. The woodcarvings on the temple car are notable too.

Pudukkottai and around

Pudukkottai, on the northern edge of Chettinad, 50 km south of Trichy, was the capital of the former princely state ruled by the Tondaiman Rajas, founded by Raghunatha Raya Tondaiman in 1686. At one entrance to the town is a ceremonial arch raised by the raja in honour of Queen Victoria's jubilee celebrations. The town's broad streets suggest a planned history; the temple is at the centre, with the old palace and a tank. The new palace is now the District Collector's office.

Thirukokarnam, 5 km north of the railway station, is the site of the rock-cut Sri Kokarnesvarar Temple ⓘ *closed 1200-1600*, dates from the Pallava period. The natural rock shelters, caves, stone circles, dolmens and Neolithic burial sites show that there was very early human occupation. The local museum ⓘ *Big St, open daily except except Fri, 2nd Sat of the month, public holidays, 0930-1700, free, allow 40 mins, recommended*, has a wide range of exhibits including sections on geology, zoology and the economy as well as sculptures and the arts. The archaeology section has some excellent sculptures from nearby temples. There is a notable carving of Siva as *Dakshinamurti* and some fine bronzes from Pudukkottai itself.

Sittannavasal, 13 km away, has a Jain cave temple (circa eighth century) with sculptures, where monks took shelter when they fled from persecution in North India. In a shrine and veranda there are some fine frescoes in the Ajanta-style and bas-relief carvings. You can also see rock-hewn beds of the monks. The *Brahmi* inscriptions date from the second century BC.

⊛ Madurai and around listings

For hotel and restaurant price codes and other relevant information, see pages 13-17.

◉ Where to stay

Tax of up to 20% is added even by modest hotels. Cheap hotels along and around West Peramul Maistry St, 2 blocks east of the railway station, but rooms can be hard to find by late afternoon. Most offer 24-hr checkout. Although there are slick hotels across the Vaigai these are not good value as they lack character and are away from the town's atmosphere. It's best to visit Madurai either from the charming remove of the

hilltop **Taj**, or abandon yourself to the throng and take a room near the temple.

Madurai *p162, maps p163 and p165*
$$$$ Gateway (Taj), Pasumalai Hills, 7 TPK Rd, 5 km southwest of centre on NH7, T0452 663 3000, www.thegateway hotels.com. A real oasis, set on top of a hill with great views over surrounding country. The 30 rooms (some set in an old colonial house) set among shady gardens full of peacocks. There's a good bookshop and lovely pool.
$$$ Heritage Madurai, 11, Melakkal Main Road, Kochadai, T0452-238 5455, www.heritagemadurai.com. Stunning

new resort set in the banyan-shaded refuge of the Madurai Club. Standard rooms are big and full of light, while the good value villas come with your own pool and personal chef. A spectacular step-well pool and good restaurants are well worth the 4-km trek to the temple.

$$$-$$ Germanus, 28 By-Pass Rd, T0452-435 6999, www.hotelgermanus. com. Functional and well-run though slightly dated business hotel with quiet, bright and well-equipped rooms. Excellent rooftop restaurant (1900-2300) serves Chettinad specialities. Choose rooms at the rear to save you from the busy roundabout in front.

$$$-$$ Park Plaza, 114 W Perumal Maistry St, T0452-301 1111. Some of the 56 smart, 60s-print, stylish a/c rooms offer temple views, breakfast included, excellent rooftop restaurant (1700-2300), bar, all facilities. Free pick-up from airport/railway station.

$$$-$$ Royal Court, 4 West Veli St, T0452-435 6666, www.royalcourtindia. com. 70 extremely clean a/c rooms with bath, satellite TV and great views from rooftop (open 1900-2300), good value.

$$ Supreme, 110 W Perumal Maistry St, T0452-234 3151, www.hotelsupreme.in. 69 slightly tatty but adequately clean rooms with marble and plastic furniture, 31 a/c, good rooftop restaurant, **Surya**, with temple views, bar, 24-hr travel desk, exchange, internet booths in the basement, a bit noisy and a mite overpriced. Security and service both wanting.

$$-$ The Madurai Residency, 14-15 West Marret St, T0452-438 0000, www.madurai residency.com. Rather grand for Madurai: 75 rooms over 7 floors, glass lift. Economy rooms better than a/c due to musty smell.

$ Hotel Tamil Nadu, West Veli St, T0452-233 7471, htn-mdu1@ttdconline.

com. Mint-coloured guesthouse dating from 1968 set around courtyard attached to the friendly TN tourist office. In bad need of a new lick of paint – it's pretty grubby – but there are TVs, huge rooms and the staff are charming.

$ International, 46 W Perumal Maistry St, T0452-437 7463. Friendly, 34 clean and tidy rooms with TV and views from upper floors. Tends to have rooms when others are full.

$ Sulochna Palace, 96 W Perumal Maistry St, T0452-234 1071. Good-value, clean rooms, and slightly more salubrious than the nearby bottom-bracket options. Avoid lower floors where generator noise is obtrusive.

$ TM Lodge, 50 W Perumal Maistry St, T0452-234 1651. 57 rooms (hot water), some a/c, some with TV, balcony, very clean, bookings for rail/bus journeys.

$ YMCA International Guest House, Main Guard Sq, near temple, T0452-234 0861, www.ymcamadurai.com. A great option within spitting distance of the temple. The double rooms here are simple but spacious and clean, the staff are friendly, and profits go to worthwhile projects.

$ Visakam Lodge, 9 Kakathope St, T0452-234 1241. Good-value place with 18 clean rooms, very popular with Indian tourists.

Ramesvaram *p167, map p169*
$ Hotel Tamil Nadu (TTDC), 14 East Car St, T04573-221064. Sea-facing balconies, 53 rooms (2-6 beds), some a/c, clean, grubby restaurant (breakfast from 0700), bar, sea bathing nearby, exchange. Very popular; book well in advance.

$ Maharaja, 7 Middle St, west of the Temple, T04573-221271. 30 rooms, some a/c with bath, exchange, temple music broadcast on loudspeakers, otherwise recommended.

$ Railway Retiring Rooms, T04573-221226. 9 rooms and dorm.
$ Swami Ramanatha Tourist Home, opposite museum, T04573-221217. Good clean rooms with bath, best budget option.

Chettinad p171

Chettinad is still largely uncharted territory, and the few really good places to stay are priced towards the higher end. A handful of cheaper options exist in Karaikkudi and other towns, but they do not have the guides on hand to gain access to the old private homes (without whose help the Raja of Chettinad's palace may be the only house you look inside).
$$$$ Visalam, Kanadukathan, T04565-273302, www.cghearth.com. Romantic and supremely comfortable high-celinged rooms, sparely furnished with Chettiar writing desks and 4-posters, in a beautifully restored art deco mansion – the only one in Chettinad built for a girl. The chef serves banana-leaf lunches and does cooking demonstrations, good local guides are available for walking and bike tours, plus there's a huge pool and lawns.
$$$ The Bangala, Senjai, T04565-220221, www.thebangala.com. 8 bright and spacious a/c rooms with period colonial furniture, in restored 1916 bungalow, a heritage guesthouse of character set amidst orchards and palms, serves full-on, totally authentic Chettinad feasts for a fair whack at Rs 800 per meal (must be booked in advance, rest stop facilities for day visitors and a full-board option. The family here wrote the (coffee table) book on Chettinad architecture.
$$$ Chettinadu Mansion, behind the raja's palace, Kanadukathan, T04565-273080; book through **Deshadan Tours and Travels**, T0484-232 1518,

www.chettinadumansion. com. Dating back to 1902, this stunning house takes up half the block, with courtyard after courtyard stretching back from the street. Huge rooms, with a quirky green-brown colour scheme, heavy painted shutters and private rooftop sit-outs, encircle the upper floor. Downstairs is still used for family *pujas* and storing the wedding dowry. Simple Chettinad-style meals, served in the colonnaded dining room or under stars in the courtyard, cost Rs 450, and the charming Mr Chandramouli, who was born in the house, is often on hand to share stories or sharp business advice.
$ Golden Singar, 100 Feet Rd, Karaikuddi, T04565-235521. Remarkably clean and good-value marble-floored rooms (fan-cooled half the price of a/c), handy for bus stand though a bit distant from the market and temples. Clean restaurant downstairs and cheap internet cafés nearby.
$ Hotel Udhayam, A-333 Sekkalai Rd, Karaikuddi, T04565-234068. Another decent cheap option, similar to the **Golden Singar** but closer to the action.
$ Nivaas, Devakottai, 1st left from bus station coming from the north (no sign in English), T04561-272352. Basic (no electric sockets), no English spoken.

⓪ Restaurants

Madurai *p162, maps p163 and p165*
$$ Surya, **Supreme** (see Where to stay). Open 1600-2400. 7th-floor rooftop restaurant with international as well as Indian menu. Excellent Andhra *thalis*, very busy Sun evenings.
$$ Temple View, **Park Plaza** (see Where to stay). Excellent rooftop venue.
$ Delhiwala Sweets, W Tower St. Delicious Indian sweets and snacks.

$ Jayaram Sweets, 6-7 Netaji Rd. Good salty namkeens and fantastic coconut buns.

$ Sri Sabarees, corner of W Perumal Maistry St and Town Hall Rd. Serves simple South Indian fare – *thalis* (lunchtime only), *pongal*, *iddli* and *dosai* – but the 2 dining halls are perpetually packed, as is the coffee stall out front.

$ Sri Saravana, 7 Melur Rd, opposite Court. Delicious sweets (try the spectacular milk *peda*) and decent meals, across the river from town. Worth a diversion if you're at the Gandhi Museum.

Ramesvaram *p167, map p169*
Don't expect anything other than *thalis* here. There are several popular snack stands, with signs only in Tamil, on the road between Mela St and the museum.
Abbirami Hotel, off East Car St on road towards beach. Neat place churning out lunchtime meals and tiffin (*dosas, vada* and the like) after 1500.
Devasthanam Trust has a canteen opposite the east gate of the temple.

⊕ Entertainment

Madurai *p162, maps p163 and p165*
Folk performances, in the 4 'Chitrai' streets by the temple, every Sat 1700-1800, free.
Meenakshi Temple: 'Bedtime of the God' 2100, is not to be missed (see page 164).
Thirumalai Nayaka Palace: Sound and Light show: English 1845-1930; Rs 5 (take mosquito repellent), sadly, "poor, faded tape". During the day, dance drama and concerts are held in the courtyard.

⊛ Festivals

Madurai *p162, maps p163 and p165*
Jan **Jallikattu Festival** (Taming the Bull).
Jan/Feb The annual **Float Festival** marks the birth anniversary of Thirumalai Nayaka. Many temple deities in silks and jewels, including Meenakshi and Sundareswarar, are taken out on a full moon night on floats decorated with hundreds of oil lamps and flowers. The floats carry them to the central shrine to the accompaniment of music and chanting.
Apr/May The 10-day **Chitrai Festival** is the most important at the Meenakshi Temple, celebrating the marriage of Siva and Meenakshi.
Aug/Sep The **Avanimoolam** is the Coronation Festival of Siva when the image of Lord Sundareswarar is taken out to the river bank dressed as a worker.

Pudukkottai *p173*
Jan/Feb Bullock races (*manju virattu*) are held in the area.

○ Shopping

Madurai *p162, maps p163 and p165*
Kashmiri emporia pay 40-50% commission to touts who lure you into their shops with spurious promises of views into the temple. Best buys are textiles, wood and stone carvings, brass images, jewellery and appliqué work for temple chariots. Most shops are on South Avani Moola St (for jewellery), Town Hall Rd, Masi St and around the temple.

Books

Higginbotham's Book Exchange, near the temple.
New Century Book House, 79-80 West Tower St. Recommended.

Handicrafts

Handicrafts Emporium, 39-41 Town Hall Rd. Also try: **Khadi Gramodyog Bhandar** and **Surabhi** on W Veli St.

Textiles and tailors

The market near Pudu Mandapam, next to Meenakshi East Gate. Sells fabric and is a brilliant place to get clothes made.
Femina, 10 W Chitrai St. Similar to the market (you can take photos of the Meenakshi Temple from their rooftop).
Hajee Moosa, 18 E Chitrai St. Tailoring in 8 hrs; 'ready-mades' at **Shabnam**, at No 17.

Chettinad *p171*
Antiques

Muneesvaran Kovil St in Karaikkudi is lined with antiques shops selling old sepia photographs, temple lamps, old advertising posters, scrap book matter, religious paintings and Czech pewter jars.
Kattu Raja's, Palaniappa Chettiar St.
Old Chettinad Crafters, Murugen Complex, 37/6 Muneesvaran Kovil St, Karaikkudi, T(0)98428-223060, chettinaduantiques@yahoo.co.in. One of the best.
VJ Murugesan, sells old wooden furniture, household articles, wooden pillars, glass.
Venkateswara Furniture and Timber Merchant, No 8 Keela Oorani West, Karaikkudi, T(0)98424-232112. If you're in the market for bigger objects and weight is no object, this architectural salvage yard is a good starting point. Bargain hard.

Cotton and fabrics

MM Street and The Weavers' Lane beside the Bangala have Chettinad cotton for sale straight off the loom. Ask locally for the next *sandais*, the colourful local weekly markets.

◑ What to do

Madurai *p162, maps p163 and p165*
Body and soul

Yoga classes at **Gandhi Museum**, T0452-248 1060. Daily at 0630.

Tour operators

Tours can be arranged with **TTDC**, via Hotel Tamil Nadu, West Veli St, T0452-233 7471, or through most hotel desks. **Temple tour** of Madurai and attractive surroundings by a/c coach; half day, 0700-1200, 1500-2000. Rs 125. Recommended for an overview. Apr-Jun: **Courtallam**, Rs 300; **Kodaikanal**, 0700-2100, Rs 300; **Rameswaram**, Rs 275.
Ex-Serviceman Travels, 1 Koodalalagar, Perumal Kovil St, T0452-273 0571, City tour, half day, 0700, 1500, Rs 140; Kodaikanal or Rameswaram 0700-1900, Rs 275; overnight to Kanniyakumari, Rs 350.
Indian Panorama (Trichy), T0431-422 6122, www.indianpanorama.in. Tours from Madurai (and other towns). The Pandians are very helpful, efficient, South India tours, car with excellent driver. Highly recommended.
Siraj, 28 T P K Rd, opposite Periyar Bus Stand, T097 8859 6388. Ticketing, good multilingual guides, cars.

⊖ Transport

Madurai *p162, maps p163 and p165*
Air

Madurai's small airport is 12 km south of the centre. There are daily direct flights from Chennai, Bengaluru and Hyderabad, with connecting flights from Mumbai and New Delhi; you can also fly cheaply to Colombo with **Spicejet**. The 10A bus runs from the airport to the central Periyar bus stand. Taxis to the centre charge around Rs 375; an auto should cost Rs 150-200.

Airport to city centre (12 km) by Pandiyan coach (calls at top hotels); taxi (Rs 375) or auto-rickshaw (Rs 150). **Air India**, 7A W Veli St, T0452-234 1234. 1000-1300, 1400-1700; Airport, T0452-269 0433. **Jet Airways**, T0452-252 6969; airport T0452-269 0771.

Bus
Local There is a good network within the city and the suburbs. **Central (Periyar) Bus Stands**, near W Veli St, are now used for buses around town and destinations nearby. Approaching on a bus from the south, to get to the centre, change to a city bus at Tirumangalam (15 km south).
Long distance Most intercity buses use the well-organized **New Central Bus Stand** (Mattuthavani Bus Terminal), 6 km northeast of town (continuation of Alagar Koil Rd), T0452-258 0680; Rs 100 by rickshaw, or catch city buses 3, 48 or 700. Buses leave from here for **Bengaluru (Bangalore)** (11 hrs), **Ernakulam (Kochi)**, **Chennai** (10 hrs), **Puducherry** (9 hrs), **Thiruvananthapuram** (8 hrs), **Kumbakonum, Ramesvaram** (under 4 hrs, every 15 mins), **Thanjavur** (4 hrs), **Tiruchirappalli** (2½ hrs), **Tirunelveli** (4 hrs, Rs 40). Buses for the west and northwest leave from the Arapalayam Bus Stand, 3 km northwest of centre (Bus route No 7A, auto-rickshaws Rs 40), T0452-236 1740. Destinations include **Kodaikkanal** (3½ hrs, buses crowded in peak season Apr-Jul), **Coimbatore** (5 hrs,

change for Mettupalayam and Ooty, **Periyar/Kumily** (4 hrs), **Salem** (5½ hrs), **Dindigul** (2 hrs).

Rickshaw
Auto-rickshaw rates are theoretically Rs 10-15 per km, but drivers quote excessive rates for trips around town. A cycle rickshaw from the station area to temple should cost around Rs 30.

Taxi/car hire
Most taxis are unmetered. Local car hire rates begin at 4 hrs/40 km Rs 700, 8 hrs/80 km Rs 1200. **FastTrack** T0452-288 8999.

Train
Madurai Junction is the main station: enquiries, T131. 0700-1300, 1330-2000. New Computer Reservation Centre to south of main entrance. Left-luggage facilities. Pre-paid auto-rickshaw kiosk outside. **Chennai** (ME) via Villupuram for **Puducherry**: *Vaigai Exp 12636*, 0630, 8 hrs; *Pandiyan Exp 12638*, 2045, 10 hrs. **Coimbatore**: *Coimbatore Exp 16609*, 0040, 7 hrs. **Kanniyakumari**: *Chennai-Guruvayoor Exp 16127*, 1640, 5 hrs. **Ramesvaram**: 3 unreserved passenger trains a day, at 0010, 0615 and 1815, 3-4 hrs. **Tiruchirappalli**: several, *Vaigai Exp 12636*, 0630, 2½ hrs (beautiful countryside); *Pandiyan Exp 12638*, 2045, 3½ hrs.

Ramesvaram p167, map p169
Bicycle hire
Bike hire from West Car or East Car St.

Bus
Local Marudhu Pandiyan Transport Corporation (MPTC) covers the town and area around. Bus station is 2 km west of town. Take a bus from the train

station to the Ramalingesvara Temple, to Pamban or to Dhanuskodi. From the temple's east gate to Dhanuskodi roadhead and to Gandhamadana Parvatam, both every 2 hrs.

Long distance State, MPTC and private bus companies run regular services via **Mandapam** to several towns nearby. **Govt Express Bus Reservations**, North Car St, 0700-2100. Frequent buses to **Madurai**, 173 km (4½ hrs); tourist coaches (hotel-to-hotel) are better.

Taxi
A few cars and jeeps are available from the train station and hotels.

Train
Ramesvaram Railway Station, enquiries and reservations, T226. 0800-1300, 1330-1730. **Chennai**: *Sethu Exp 16714*, 2000, 12½ hrs, via **Karaikkudi**, 4 hrs, and **Villupuram** (for Puducherry), 9 hrs. **Madurai**: 3 unreserved passenger trains a day, at 0005, 0525, 1735. **Tiruchirappalli**: *Chennai Egmore Exp 16702*, 1700, 5½ hrs.

Virudhunagar *p171*
Bus Leave Madurai early morning to catch the Kollam train; get off at police station and go to the end of the road opposite and turn left; the railway station is about 1 km on the right (take a rickshaw if carrying heavy luggage).

Train To **Kollam** and **Thiruvananthapuram**, Platform 3 across the bridge.

Chettinad *p171*
Bus Bus routes link **Karaikkudi** with every part of the state. Auto-rickshaws

provide slow but relatively cheap transport between towns – Karaikkudi to Kanadukathan should cost around Rs 150.

Train Chennai: *Sethu Exp 16714*, 2340, 9 hrs; **Rameswaram**: *Boat Mail Express 16101*, 0715. **Tiruchirappali**: passenger trains at 0620, 0940, 1450, 1815, 2½ hrs.

Pudukkottai *p173*
Bus to Tiruchirappalli, Thanjavur, Karaikkudi via Kanadukathan (for Chettinad), Madurai, Ramnad, Ramesvaram, and to Sittanavasal.

Train Pudukkottai is 1 hr north of Karaikkudi on the Chennai-Rameswaram line. All trains listed for Karaikkudi stop here.

① Directory

Madurai *p162, maps p163 and p165*
Banks Several on East Avani Moola St. **Alagendran Finance**, 182D N Veli St, good rate for cash US$ but not for TCs. **Andhra Bank**, W Chitrai St, accepts credit cards; **Canara Bank**, W Veli St, cashes Amex and sterling TCs. **Internet** Many west of the temple and in the budget hotel area charge Rs 20 per hr. **Medical services** Christian Mission Hospital, East Veli St; **Grace Kennet Hospital**, 34 Kennet Rd. **Post** The town GPO is at the north end of W Veli St (Scott Rd). In Tallakulam: Head Post Office and Central Telegraph Office, on Gokhale Rd.

Pudukkottai *p173*
Banks State Bank of India, East Main St.

Far south

India's southernmost point is a focus of pilgrimage that captures the imagination of millions of Hindus on a daily basis. Kanniyakumari occupies a beautiful headland site where the waters of the Bay of Bengal, the Indian Ocean and the Arabian Sea mingle together and crash upon the rocks. An hour further towards Kerala is Padmanabhapuram Palace, the painstakingly maintained ancient seat of the Travancore rulers. Tirunelveli, one-time capital of the Pandyas, is now a market and educational centre that is often passed over on the trail towards Madurai.

Tirunelveli and Palayamkottai → *For listings, see pages 184-186.*
Phone code: 0462. Population: 411,300.

On the banks of the Tamraparni, the only perennial river of the south, **Tirunelveli** is an attractive town surrounded by a belt of rice fields (*nelveli* means 'paddy-hedge') irrigated from the river's waters. Rising only 60 km to the east, at an altitude of over 1700 m, the river benefits from both the southwest and southeast monsoons; it tumbles down to the plains where it is bordered by a narrow strip of rich paddy land. Tirunelveli is now joined with the twin settlement of Palayamkottai. It is a market town and one of the oldest Christian centres in Tamil Nadu. St Francis Xavier settled

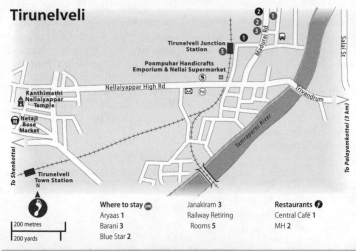

Tirunelveli

Tirunelveli Junction Station

Poompuhar Handicrafts Emporium & Nellai Supermarket

Nellaiyappar High Rd

Kanthimathi Nellaiyappar Temple

Netaji Bose Market

Tamraparni River

Trivandrum

To Shenkottai

Tirunelveli Town Station

To Palayamkottai (3 km)

Sarai St

Madurai Rd

200 metres
200 yards

Where to stay
Aryaas 1
Barani 3
Blue Star 2

Janakiram 3
Railway Retiring
Rooms 5

Restaurants
Central Café 1
MH 2

here to begin his ministry in India in the early 16th century, but it has also been a centre of Protestant missionary activity. In 1896 it became the head of an Anglican diocese, now Church of South India.

Places in Tirunelveli and Palayamkottai

Kanthimathi Nellaiyappar Temple ① *closed 1230-1600, no photography*, is worth visiting; it is a twin temple, with the north dedicated to Siva (Nellaiyappar) and the south to Parvati (Kanthi). Each section has an enclosure over 150 m by 120 m. The temples have sculptures, musical pillars, valuable jewels, a golden lily tank and a 1000-pillared *mandapa*. There is a large white Nandi at the entrance. There is a **car festival** in June/July. The old town area around the temple is well worth a few hours of anyone's time, with the blue-painted houses reminiscent of Jodhpur (but without the tourist crowds). **Palayamkottai** has **St John's Church** (Church Missionary Society) with a spire 35 m high, a landmark for miles around. The town is known for its palm-leaf crafts.

Around Tirunelveli

Tiruchendur, 50 km east of Tirunelveli, has a famous **shore temple** ① *Rs 50 for 'fast darshan', men must remove shirts*, dedicated to Subrahmanya, and considered to be one of his six 'abodes'. It is a hive of activity during festivals. There are caves with rock-cut sculptures along the shore.

Manapad, the predominantly Roman Catholic coastal village 18 km south of Tiruchendur, is where St Francis Xavier is said to have landed and lived in a cave near the headland. The **Holy Cross Church** (1581) close to the sea is believed to house a fragment of the True Cross from Jerusalem.

Kanniyakumari → *For listings, see pages 184-186.*

Kanniyakumari's grubby streets come alive in the hour before dawn, as thousands throng the shoreline to witness the sunrise over the southern tip of India. This important pilgrimage site is centred on worship of the Goddess Kumari, 'the protector of India's shores'. The new day is heralded in by the scent of jasmine garlands, the wail of temple music and the whoops and applause of excited children as the sun finally crawls its way over the sea. It's an early-morning party that everyone is invited to join. The view offshore is dominated by India's answer to the Statue of Liberty: a 133-ft sculpture of the Tamil poet Thiruvalluvar. Just behind is a memorial to the philosopher Swami Vivekananda, a spiritual leader inspired by the Devi. Both can be reached by a quick ferry ride. In April, at full moon, special *chithra pournami* celebrations are held at sunset and the town heaves with crowds who come to see the simultaneous setting and rising of the sun and moon.

Places in Kanniyakumari → *Phone code: 04652. Population: 19,700.*

The **Kanniyakumari Temple** ① *0400-1200, 1600-2000, non-Hindus are not allowed into the sanctuary, shoes must be left outside and men must wear a* dhoti *to enter,* overlooks the shoreline. The Devi Kumari, an incarnation of Parvati, vowed to remain a virgin to her dying day after meddling gods prevented her marriage to Siva. Legend tells that the exceptionally brilliant diamond in the deity's nose ring is visible even from the sea, and the sea-facing temple door is kept closed to prevent ships being misguided by the gem's shimmer.

The **Vivekananda Memorial** ① *0800-1600, Rs 10, ferry Rs 20, 15 mins (see page 186), allow 1 hr for the visit, smoking and eating prohibited, take off shoes before entering*, stands on one of two rocks, about 500 m from the mainland. The Bengali religious leader and philosopher Swami Vivekananda swam out here when a simple monk and devotee of the Devi, to sit in long meditation on this rock in 1892. He left convinced that religion could be a powerful instrument of social regeneration and individual development and was inspired to speak on Hinduism at the Parliament of Religions in Chicago, preaching that "the Lord is one, but the sages describe Him differently". On his return, he founded the Ramakrishna Mission in Chennai, which now has spread across the world. The rock was renamed Vivekananda Rock and a memorial was built in 1970. The design of the *mandapa* incorporates different styles of temple architecture from all over India and houses a statue of Vivekananda. People also come to see Sri Pada Parai, where the 'footprint' of the Devi has been enshrined on the rock.

The massive **Thiruvalluvar Statue** ① *0800-1600, free, ferry Rs 20, 15 mins*, immortalizes the writer of the Tamil classic, *Thirukkural*. The statue is exactly 133 ft (40 m) tall, to correspond with the 133 chapters of his most famous work. Stairs allow visitors to stand at his giant feet.

In 1948 some of Mahatma Gandhi's ashes were brought here for public display before being immersed in the sea. The **Ghandi Mandapam** ① *0700-1900, free*, was built as a memorial to this event. At midday on Gandhi's birthday, 2 October, the sun shines on the spot where his ashes were placed.

Kanniyakumari

To Trivandrum (NH 47) & Madurai (NH 7)

Vivekanandapuram

Guganathan Temple

Church of Our Lady of Ransom

Main Rd

N Car St
Car St
S Car St

Kovalam Rd

Lighthouse

Wandering Monk Museum

Toilet

Beach Rd

Tamil Nadu Sales Emporium

Shops

Jetty

Vinayaka Temple

Gandhi Mandapam

Kanniyakumari Temple & Kumari Ghat

Thiruvalluvar Memorial

Vivekananda Memorial

N

400 metres
400 yards

Where to stay 🛏
Lakshmi **1**
Maadhini & Archana
  Restaurant **2**
Manickam **3**
Parvathi Nivas Lodge **4**

Sankar's Guest House **7**
Saravana Lodge **6**
Seaview **5**
Singaar **9**
Sunrock **8**
Tamil Nadu & TTDC
  Restaurant **10**

Restaurants 🍴
Annapoorna **1**
Sangam **2**
Sravanas **3**

The **Wandering Monk Museum** ① *Main Rd, 0830-1200, 1600-2000, Rs 5,* has an informative exhibition on the life and work of Vivekananda. There is also a photo exhibition, in **Vivekanandapuram**, 1 km north, which can be reached by an easy walk along the beach though there is no access from the north side. The **Yoga Kendra** there runs courses from June to December. Further north there is a pleasant sandy beach, 3.5 km along Kovalam Road.

Around Kanniyakumari

Suchindram Temple ① *open to non-Hindus, priests acting as guides may expect donations,* was founded during the Pandiyan period but was expanded under Thirumalai Nayaka in the 17th century. It was also used later as a sanctuary for the rulers of Travancore to the west and so contains treasures from many kingdoms. One of the few temples dedicated to the Hindu Trinity, Brahma, Vishnu and Siva, it is in a rectangular enclosure that you enter through the massive ornate seven-storeyed *gopuram*. North of the temple is a large tank with a small shelter in the middle while round the walls is the typically broad street used for car festivals. Leading to the entrance is a long colonnade with musical pillars and sculptures of Siva, Parvati, Ganesh and Subrahmanya on the front and a huge Hanuman statue inside. The main sanctuary, with a *lingam*, dates from the ninth century but many of the other structures and sculptures date from the 13th century and after. There are special temple ceremonies at sunset on Friday.

Nagercoil, 19 km from Kanniyakumari, is set with a stunning backcloth of the Western Ghats, reflected from place to place in the broad tanks dotted with lotuses. The landscape begins to feel more like Kerala than Tamil Nadu. It is an important railway junction and bus terminal. It is often a bottleneck filled with lorries so be prepared for delays. The old town of **Kottar**, now a suburb, was a centre of art, culture and pilgrimage. The **temple** ① *0630-0900, 1730-2000,* to Nagaraja, after which the town is named, is unique in that although the presiding deity is the serpent god Naga, there are also shrines to Siva and Vishnu as well as images of Jain Tirthankaras, Mahavira and Parsvanatha on the pillars. The temple is alive with snakes during some festivals. Christian missionaries played an important part in the town's development and left their mark in schools, colleges, hospitals and churches of different denominations. There is also a prominent Muslim community in Kottar, reflected in the shops closing on Fridays and remaining open on Sunday.

Padmanabhapuram → *For listings, see pages 184-186.*

① *Tue-Sun 0900-1300, 1400-1630 (last tickets 1600), Rs 200, child Rs 50 (accredited guide included, but expects a 'donation' after the tour), camera Rs 25, video Rs 1500. Best at 0900 before coach parties arrive.*
Padmanabhapuram, the old palace of the rajas of Travancore, contains some fascinating architecture and paintings but some of the methods employed during its restoration have been criticized. Although decaying somewhat, the Kuthiramalika Palace in Trivandrum – if you are venturing into Kerala – might be

better worth looking round. The name Padmanabhapuram (*Padma*, lotus; *nabha*, navel; *puram*, town) refers to the lotus emerging from the navel of Vishnu. From the ninth century this part of Tamil Nadu and neighbouring Kerala were governed by the Ay Dynasty, patrons both of Jainism and Hinduism. However, the land was always contested by the Cholas, the Pandiyas and the Cheras. By the late 11th century the new Venadu Dynasty emerged from the Chera rulers of Kerala and took control of Kanniyakumari District in AD 1125 under Raja Kodai Kerala Varman. Never a stable kingdom, and with varying degrees of territorial control, Travancore State was governed from Padmanabhapuram between 1590-1790, when the capital was shifted to Thiruvananthapuram. Although the rajas of Travancore were Vaishnavite kings, they did not neglect Siva, as can be seen from various sculptures and paintings in the palace. The King never officially married and the heir to the throne was his eldest sister's oldest son. This form of matrilineal descent was characteristic of the earlier Chera Empire (who ruled for 200 years from the early 12th century). The palace shows the fine craftsmanship, especially in woodworking, characteristic of Kerala's art and architecture. There are also some superb frescoes and excellent stone-sculpted figures. The outer cyclopean stone wall is fitted together without mortar. It encloses a total area of 75 ha and the palace buildings 2 ha.

◉ Far south listings

For hotel and restaurant price codes and other relevant information, see pages 13-17.

⬤ Where to stay

Tirunelveli *p180, map p180*
Hotels are often full during the wedding season (Apr-Jun). Book ahead or arrive early. Several budget hotels are clustered near Junction Railway Station, most with Western toilet and shower.
$$-$ Aryaas, 67 Madurai Rd, T0462-233 9002. 69 rooms, 25 a/c, in dark bordello-style, non a/c better value, restaurants (separate vegetarian one, but it's also a mosquito's heaven), bar. Excellent internet café opposite.
$$-$ Bharani, 29 Madurai Rd, T0462-233 3234. 43 rooms, with hot shower, 10 a/c, clean, well maintained, vegetarian restaurant, in large modern block, lift, ample parking.

$$-$ Janakiram, 30 Madurai Rd, near bus stand, T0462-233 1941. 70 clean rooms, with hot shower, some a/c, lift, smart, brightly lit, outstanding vegetarian rooftop restaurant. Highly recommended.
$ Blue Star, 36 Madurai Rd, T0462-421 0501. 50 rooms with cold shower, 10 a/c, good veg restaurant, Indian style, modern. Good value.
$ Railway Retiring Rooms. Clean, secure rooms and dorm. Excellent value.

Kanniyakumari *p181, map p182*
Hotels are in heavy demand; book well ahead. Cheaper places may only offer squat toilets.
$$$ Seashore Hotel, East Car St, T04652-246704. Good rooms in a swish new hotel. The rooftop restaurant offers Indian and seafood dishes washed down with ocean views.

$$$ Seaview, East Car St, T04652-247841, www.hotelseaview.in. Plush, central hotel with spotlessly clean, a/c rooms. Helpful staff, restaurant, bar. Recommended.
$$ Hotel Singaar, Main Rd, 2 km from attractions, T04652-247992. Smart, popular hotel with comfortable rooms, many with balcony. Nice pool, decent restaurant. Breakfast included.
$$-$ Hotel Tamil Nadu (TTDC), Beach Rd, T04652-246257, www.ttdconline.com. Acceptably decrepit rooms in a superb location, with terraces looking out to sea and a nice garden setting, in a quiet spot away from the busy centre. Popular with Indian families.
$$-$ Maadhini, East Car St, T04652-246887. Wide variety of good-value rooms. A/c rooms have balconies with sea views. Restaurant, bar, central location.
$ Lakshmi, East Car St, T04652-247203. Friendly, family-run hotel with clean rooms, some a/c. Can be noisy as guests arrive at 0500 to see sunrise from the roof. Excellent value.
$ Manickam, North Car St, T04652-246387. Under same management as **Maadhini**, this cheaper option has good-sized rooms but unfriendly staff. Overpriced a/c rooms.
$ Sankar's Guest House, Main Rd, T04652-246260. Best of the cheapies. Quiet and clean rooms all with TV and balcony. Very friendly management. Recommended.
$ Saravana Lodge, Sannathi St, T04652-246007. Moderately clean, basic rooms. Upstairs rooms open onto wide veranda with good sea view. The temple next door provides alarm clock services at 0500. Cheerful, helpful staff.
$ Sunrock, Pillyarkoil St, T04652-246167. Newish hotel tucked away down a back alley. Clean rooms, some a/c, all with terraces, but no views.

Around Kanniyakumari *p183*
$ Parvathi Residency, Nagercoil, T04652-233020. Clean good-sized rooms, some a/c.
$ Rajam, MS Rd, Vadasery, Nagercoil, T04652-276581. Good-value rooms, restaurant, roof garden.

🍴 Restaurants

Tirunelveli *p180, map p180*
$ Central Café, near station. Good vegetarian.
$ MH Restaurant, opposite **Aryaas**. Western fast food, pizzas. Modern.

Kanniyakumari *p181, map p182*
You'll find a dozen tiny restaurants serving cheap and tasty snacks of *dosai, vadai, bhaji* and *pakora* on Main Rd between Sth Car St and the **Sangam Hotel**.
$$ Archana, **Maadhini** (see Where to stay). Good mixed menu of Indian, Chinese and International options.
$ Annapoorna, Sannathi St. Excellent vegetarian food in clean, bright surroundings. Very popular with families.
$ Sangam, Sangam Hotel, Main Rd. Good *thalis*.
$ Sravanas, Sannathi St. Cheap and cheerful vegetarian meals. Recommended.
$ TTDC Restaurant, **Hotel Tamil Nadu** (see Where to stay). Looks like a barracks, but excellent non-vegetarian Indian meals.

✴ Festivals

Kanniyakumari *p181, map p182*
Apr **Chithra Pournami** is a special full moon celebration at the temple usually held in the 2nd week of Apr.
Oct Special **Navarathri** celebrations in 1st week of Oct.

⊖ Transport

Tirunelveli *p180, map p180*
Bus Good bus connections to
Kanniyakumari, **Thiruvananthapuram**,
and to **Madurai** (faster to change
buses at Tirumangalam), **Tiruchirappalli**
and **Chennai**. For **Courtallam**, go
to Tenkasi (1½ hrs) and take bus to
Courtallam (20 mins).

Train Train to **Chennai** (**ME**): *Nellai Exp
12632*, 1845, 12 hrs, via **Madurai** (2½ hrs).
Kanniyakumari: *Kanyakumari Exp 12633*,
0450, 2 hrs.

Kanniyakumari *p181, map p182*
Bus Long-distance buses leave
from the station west of town on
Kovalam Rd, 15 mins' walk from centre,
T04652-271285. There are frequent
services to **Nagercoil** (½ hr, Rs 10) and
Thiruvananthapuram (2½ hrs, Rs 45).
For **Kovalam** and **Varkala** change at
Thiruvananthapuram. There are 4 daily
departures to **Chennai** (16 hrs, Rs 390),
via **Madurai** (6 hrs, Rs 145), at 0930, 1345,
1445 and 1630.

Ferry The ferry to **Vivekananda
Rock** runs every 30 mins, 0700-1100,
1400-1700, Rs 20. Expect long queues
during festivals.

Train The station is to the north,
on Main Rd. Several important trains
arrive and depart from Nagercoil, 15 mins
away. **Chennai**, *Kanyakumari Exp 12634*,
1720, 13½ hrs, via **Madurai** (40½ hrs),
Trichy (7 hrs) and **Villupuram** (for
Puducherry, 11 hrs.

Around Kanniyakumari *p183*
Bus From **Nagercoil** there are
frequent buses to **Thiruvananthapuram**
(2 hrs); **Kanniyakumari** (30 mins); and
Madurai (6½ hrs).

Train At **Nagercoil** the railway station
is 3 km from the bus station. The daily
Kanniyakumari Mumbai Exp 16382, and
Kanniyakumari Bengaluru Exp 16525
both stop here on their way to, and
from **Kanniyakumari**. Frequent bus
connections to **Thiruvananthapuram**,
Kanniyakumari and **Madurai**.

Padmanabhapuram *p183*
Bus Regular buses to
Thiruvananthapuram and
Kanniyakumari. Less frequent buses to
and from **Kovalam**. From Kovalam, depart
approximately 0940 to **Thuckalai**. Return
buses from Thuckalai depart 1445, 1530.
Taxi A taxi from Kovalam or
Thiruvananthapuram costs Rs 800.

❶ Directory

Tirunelveli *p180, map p180*
Banks On Trivandrum High Rd.
Medical services Hospital in High
Ground, Palayamkottai. **Post** GPO,
Trivandrum High Rd.

Kanniyakumari *p181, map p182*
Banks Canara Bank, State Bank of
India and State Bank of Travancore,
are all on Main Rd. All have ATMs.
Internet There are several internet
cafés on Main Rd. All charge around Rs
20 per hr. **Medical services** General
Hospital, off Main Rd, T04652-248505.
Post Head Post Office, Main Rd, 0800-
1600, 1000-1400.

Contents

Kerala

At a glance

◉ **Getting around** Famous for its converted rice boat backwaters tours; take the ferry for a more local route around. Bus/car journeys in the backwaters are picturesque too. Trains from Malabar to Ernakulam and on to Thiruvananthapuram.

● **Time required** 2 days is enough for a backwaters cruise. Allow a couple of days for Fort Kochi and a few in Varkala. A week will make Malabar a worthwhile detour. Add 3 days for inland or ghat nature, such as the Wayanad.

☼ **Weather** Hot year round. Monsoon in Jun, Jul and Aug.

✖ **When not to go** Mar and Apr are stiflingly hot.

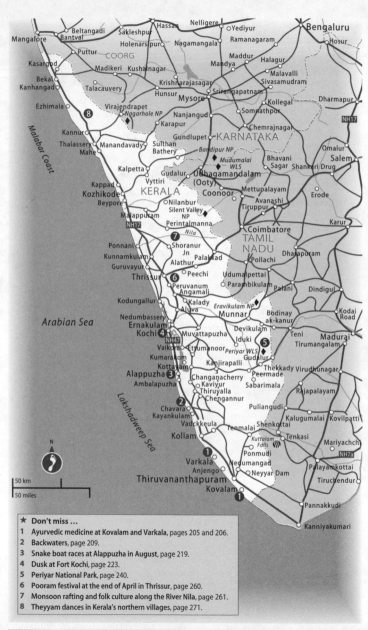

★ **Don't miss ...**
1 Ayurvedic medicine at Kovalam and Varkala, pages 205 and 206.
2 Backwaters, page 209.
3 Snake boat races at Alappuzha in August, page 219.
4 Dusk at Fort Kochi, page 223.
5 Periyar National Park, page 240.
6 Pooram festival at the end of April in Thrissur, page 260.
7 Monsoon rafting and folk culture along the River Nila, page 261.
8 Theyyam dances in Kerala's northern villages, page 271.

Kerala ebbs by at snail's pace, most picturesquely in the slow-flowing networks of lagoons and rivers that make up its backwaters, where nature grows in such overwhelming profusion that canals sit choked with pretty water-lily thickets and dragonflies bunch in clouds over lotus leaves. Dawn mists drift through canopies made by antique mango and teak trees, as farmers slip their oars into the silent waters, and women's dresses glare extra bright in the reflections of the still glass waters.

In the ramshackle port city of Fort Kochi, it's as if the clocks stopped a few centuries back: wizened traders sift spice in the shadows of derelict go-downs, the churches glow lime white, at the harbour's edge lines of cantilevered Chinese fishing nets swoop for their next catch of silvery sprats, and medieval streets and antique shops thread the route between the tiny blue-tiled synagogue and grand Dutch wooden palace of Mattancherry.

The The southern beaches of Kovalam and Varkala are great places to unwind with Ayurvedic massages, but Malabar, in the north, is the real unsung jewel of the state, an outpost of staunch Hindu religiosity and capital of the Muslim Moplah community. Here, hushed families gather at dawn in leafy temple gardens to watch spectacles of the unique, hypnotic temple dance form *Theyyam* and, come nightfall, the precision athletes of the swashbuckling martial art *Kalarippayattu* draw their swords.

Switchback turns bear you from the lush green paddy fields of the plains through spindly rubber plantations and blooming coffee-tree forests up to the thick tea-shrub territory of the high mountain villages of Thekaddy and Munnar, whose nature reserves hide tigers and herds of elephant.

Thiruvananthapuram and the far south

The state capital, a pleasant city built over gently rolling coastal land, is very much a village as soon as you step away from the crowded centre. There's none of the throb, bustle and boom-time of Ernakulam, its opposite city up north, and no one could accuse it of being cosmopolitan; you'll be pushed to find a club, or bar, or even any traffic on the roads after midnight.

It is, however, a stone's throw from here to the white sands of Kovalam, still a working fishing village, albeit one that survives under the lengthening shadow cast by unchecked tourist development. The backpackers who first populated Kovalam have left it to the package holidaymakers and luxury resorts and head instead to Varkala, a pilgrimage village and beach marked out by its sheer red rock face. Inland are the little-visited forests of Ponmudi and just over the southern border lies Kanniyakumari, the sacred toe-tip of India where three seas converge.

Arriving in Thiruvananthapuram and the far south

Getting there
The international airport is 6 km from the centre, a 15-minute drive outside rush hour, and half an hour from Kovalam. It has direct flights from Colombo, the Maldives, Kuala Lumpur, Singapore and the Middle East, as well as most major Indian cities. You can hire a prepaid taxi (Rs 150) or auto (about Rs 100) into town or wait for a local bus. At the southern end of town are the central (long-distance) bus station, with services throughout Kerala and into neighbouring Tamil Nadu, and the railway station from where trains run up and down the coast. Local buses, including those bound for Kovalam, leave from the East Fort City stand opposite the fort entrance, southwest of the station. Buses to Kovalam can drop you at Waller Junction, five minutes' walk from the Samudra Beach hotels. A further 1.5 km on they turn off for the main Kovalam Bus Stand at the Ashok Hotel gate, five minutes from most southern hotels and cafés. Lighthouse Road is steep and narrow, but autos and taxis are able to drive up it. ►► *See Transport, page 206.*

Getting around
Thiruvananthapuram is relatively strung out, though the centre is compact. Autos or taxis are more convenient than the packed buses but bargain hard: businesses have

fast acclimatized to the price naivety that goes hand in hand with package tourism. Minimum charges start at Rs 75 for taxis, Rs 15 for autos; thereafter the rate per running kilometre for cars is Rs 4.50 (non-a/c), Rs 6.50 (a/c), rickshaws Rs 3. Drivers may be reluctant to accept the going rate. If you're heading for Kovalam, budget on around Rs 250 for a taxi and Rs 175 for an auto.

Tourist information

Tourist offices have plenty of leaflets and information sheets and are very helpful. Thiruvananthapuram's main tourist office is **Kerala Tourism** ① *Park View, T0471-232 1132, www.keralatourism.org, Mon-Sat 1000-1700*, where you can book day and half-day tours around the city (Rs 110 and Rs 70 respectively). There are also offices at Thampanoor Central Bus Station, the railway station and the airport.

Thiruvananthapuram (Trivandrum) → *For listings, see pages 197-208.*
Phone code: 0471. Population: 744,739 of 3,234,356 in the Trivandrum District.

According to legend, the **Sri Padmanabhaswamy Temple** ① *East Fort, T0471-245 0233, open 0330-0445, 0630-0700, 0830-1000, 1030-1110, 1145-1200, 1700-1815 and 1845-1920*, was built in stages to house the statue of Vishnu reclining on the sacred serpent Ananta, which was found in the forest. It was rebuilt in 1733 by Raja Marthanda Varma, king of the erstwhile kingdom of Travancore, who dedicated the whole kingdom, including his rights and possessions, to the deity. The full significance of this gift came to light in July 2011, after Kerala's High Court ordered the Travancore royal family to hand over control of the temple and its assets to the State. Upon opening the six *kallaras* (vaults) hidden beneath the temple, a team of archaeologists discovered a hoard of gold- and jewel-encrusted idols estimated to be worth at least US$22 billion in weight alone. The find instantly propelled the temple to the head of the list of India's richest religious institutions. Meanwhile, in a twist fit for Indiana Jones, a sixth vault, guarded by an iron door emblazoned with images of cobras, remains sealed while the Supreme Court and temple astrologers wrestle over legends of a powerful curse set to be unleashed if the door is ever prised open.

Unusually for Kerala, the temple is built in the Dravidian style associated with Tamil Nadu, with beautiful murals, sculptures and 368 carved granite pillars which support the main pavilion or *kulashekhara mandapa*. You can see the seven-storeyed *gopuram* with its sacred pool from outside; otherwise to get a closer look you first have to persuade the famously strict Kerala Brahmins to waive the Hindus-only entry restriction. It becomes easier to do so if men have donned a crisp white *dhoti*, women a sari and blouse.

The Travancore king, Maharajah Swathi Thirunal Balarama Varma, was a musician, poet and social reformer, and his palace, just next door to the temple, **Kuthiramalkia (Puthenmalika) Palace** ① *Temple Rd, East Fort, T0471-247 3952, Tue-Sun 0830-1230 and 1530-1730, Rs 20, camera Rs 15*, is a fine reflection of his patronage of the arts. On the upper level a window gives an angle on scores of fine wood-carved horses that look like a huge cavalry charge, and among the portraits painted in the slightly unsettling Indian/European classical hybrid style is one from an artist who trumped

Thiruvananthapuram (Trivandrum)

To Kollam (NH 17)

Sri Chitra Art Gallery

Zoo

Air India

To Ponmadi

Museum Rd

PMG Circle

Indian Airlines

LMS Junction

Napier Museum & Open Air Theatre

Crafts Design Centre

Swimming Pool

University Stadium

New State Assembly

Main Central Rd

Christ

Public Library

VELLAYAMBALAM

Police Stadium

St Joseph's Cathedral

Nandanam Rd

Palayam Junction

Tagore Theatre

Town Hall

University College

KUNNUKUZHI

Connemara

VAZHUTAKKAD

Central Survey Office

General Hospital Circle

Spencer Junction

Bakery Junction

Canara

Accountant General's Office

Air Lanka

Yoga Centre

Vazhuthacaud Rd

State Bank of India

Statue Rd

Statue Junction

Secretariat

Jaihind Travels

Foreigners' Registration Office

Kairali Handicrafts

Central Stadium

Panavila Junction

CSI Megabyte

Aries Travel

SMSM Handicrafts

Pulimudu Junction

Press Rd

Housing Board Junction

To 7, Beach & Airport (6km)

VANCHIYOOR

THYCAUD

Ayurvedic College

Mahatma Gandhi Rd

Residency

Thycaud Hospital Rd

Ayurvedic College Junction

Lab Supplies

Manjalkulam Rd

S.S Coil Rd

Aristo Rd

THAMPANOOR

(KITTS)

Chettikulangara Rd

KSRTC Thampanoor Bus Stand

Mettukkada Mukku

Taikkad Junction

To 6 & Airport

Central Station Rd

Aristo Junction

Overbridge

Thampanoor Junction

Hospital Rd

VALIYASHALA

Thakaraparambu Rd

Power House Junction

Power House Rd

SRI VENKATESWARAM

Verma Travels

Padmavilasam Rd

Fort Bus Station

EAST FORT

N

200 metres

200 yards

Sri Padmanabhaswamy Temple

FORT

Kuthiramalika Palace

Buses to Kovalam

To Airport

To Kovalam Beach (16 km)

Thamburu International 9
Thapovan Heritage Home 12
Wild Palms Homestay 10
Youth Hostel 7

Where to stay

Asha 11
Capital 4
Chaithram 1
Greenland 2
Highland 3
Manjikulam Tourist Home 6
Residency Tower 8

Restaurants

Arul Jyoti 2
Indian Coffee House 1
Kalavara 5
Kerala House 7
Mascot 3
Queen's 4
Villa Maya 6

his rivals by painting not just eyes that follow you around the room, but also feet. Sadly, it is ill maintained, but a gem nonetheless.

Napier Museum ① *North Park Grounds, city north, T0471-231 8294, Tue-Sun 1000-1645, Wed morning only, closed public holidays*, is a spectacular landmark. The structure designed by RF Chisholm in traditional-Kerala-meets-Indo-Saracenic style, was completed in 1872. Today, it houses a famous collection of eighth to 18th-century South Indian bronzes, mostly from Chola, Vijayanagar and Nayaka periods, a few Jain and Buddhist sculptures and excellent woodcarvings. **Sri Chitra Art Gallery** ① *just north of the museum, 1000-1645, closed Mon and Wed mornings, Rs 5*, has a fine catalogue of Indian art from early to modern schools: works by Raja Ravi Varma, 20th-century pioneer of the radical post-colonial school of painting, sit among paintings from Java, Bali, China and Japan, Mughal and Rajput miniatures. The Tanjore paintings are studded with semi-precious stones. The **Zoological Park** ① *entrance at southwest corner of park, Tue-Sun 0900-1815, Rs 5, cameras Rs 15*, is a hilly woodland of frangipani and jacaranda with a wide collection of animals and a well-labelled botanical garden.

Kovalam and nearby resorts → *For listings, see pages 197-208.*
Phone code: 0471. Population: 25,400.

Local fishermen's boats still sit on Kovalam's narrow strip of sand right next to sunbathing tourists, but the sleepy Lakshadweep seaside village of old has now been almost completely swallowed up by package tourist infrastructure: Ayurveda parlours, trinkets, tailoring shops and tour operators line every inch of the narrow walkways behind the shore. In peak season it's something of an exotic god's waiting room, popular with pensioners, and it's safe and sedate enough for families. Backpackers tend to return off season.

North and south of Kovalam are four main stretches of beach, about 400 m long, divided by a rocky promontory on which sits the Charles Correa-designed Leela Hotel. The area to the north of the promontory, known as **Samudra Beach** and **Pozhikara Beach**, 5 km away offers the most sheltered bathing and the clearest water. The southern beaches, **Lighthouse Beach** and **Eve's Beach**, are more crowded and lively. Lighthouse Beach is far and away the most happening and has a long line of bars screening pirated Hollywood films, cafés selling muesli and pastries and hawkers peddling crafts or drugs; but it is still low-key compared to the costas. Further south still is where the classy resorts are clustered. **Pulinkudi Beach** and **Chowara Beach**, respectively 8 km and 10 km to the south, is where to go for hand-and-foot attentiveness, isolation, heritage-style villas and Ayurveda in luxurious surrounds. Chowara Beach has security staff but some sunbathers still feel plagued by hawkers. **Poovar Island**, 20 km south, is accessible only by boat (Rs 200). There are now lifeguard patrols but you still need to be careful when swimming. The sea can get rough, particularly between April and October with swells of up to 6 m. From May the sea level rises, removing the beach completely in places, and swimming becomes very dangerous.

Within easy walking distance of Kovalam, sandwiched in between Lighthouse and Poovar beaches but scarcely visited by tourists, is **Vizhinjam**, a scruffy town

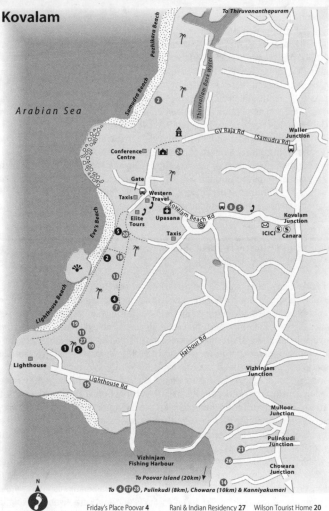

Kovalam

Arabian Sea

Pozhikara Beach

Samudra Beach

To Thiruvananthapuram

Thiruvallam Back Water

GV Raja Rd (Samudra Rd)

Waller Junction

Conference Centre

Gate

Taxis

Western Travel

Kovalam Beach Rd

Upasana

Elite Tours

Taxis

Eve's Beach

Kovalam Junction

ICICI

Canara

Lighthouse Beach

Harbour Rd

Vizhinjam Junction

Lighthouse

Lighthouse Rd

Mulloor Junction

Pulinkudi Junction

Chowara Junction

Vizhinjam Fishing Harbour

To Poovar Island (20km)

To 4 17 28, Pulinkudi (8km), Chowara (10km) & Kanniyakumari

N

200 metres (approx)
200 yards (approx)

Where to stay
Bethsaida Hermitage 26
Coco Land 13
Coconut Bay Beach
  Resort 22

Friday's Place Poovar 4
Greenland 11
Green Valley Cottages 7
Holiday Home Resort 8
Karikkathi Beach House 28
Maharaju Palace 10
Molly's 24
Niraamaya 21
Poovar Island Resort 17

Rani & Indian Residency 27
Rockholm 15
Sea Flower Beach Resort 11
Shirley's Beach
  White House 18
Somatheeram Ayurvedic
  Beach Resort 14
Usha's 19
Vivanta by Taj 2

Wilson Tourist Home 20

Restaurants
Fusion 5
Karuna 3
Lonely Planet 4
Sea Face 2
Suprabhatan 1

with a low-rise string of bangle shops, banana stalls, beauticians and seamstresses sewing jasmine buds onto strings for garlands. It's hard to believe it today but Vizhinjam was once the capital of the Ay rulers who dominated South Travancore in the ninth century AD. In the seventh century they had faced constant pressure from the Pandiyans who kept the Ay chieftains under firm control for long periods. There are rock-cut sculptures in the 18th-century cave temple here, including a rough sculpture of Vinandhara Dakshinamurthi in the shrine and unfinished reliefs of Siva and Parvati on the outer wall. Today Vizhinjam is the centre of the fishing industry and is being developed as a major container port. The traditional boats are rapidly being modernized and the catch is sold all over India, but you can still see the keen interest in the sale of fish, and women taking headloads off to local markets.

Around Kovalam

South of Kovalam in Tamil Nadu is **Padmanabhapuram** ① *Tue-Sun 0900-1300, 1400-1630 (last tickets 1600), Rs 200, child Rs 50 (accredited guide included, but 'donation' expected after the tour), camera Rs 25, video Rs 1500; best at 0900 before coach parties arrive, see page 183*, the old wooden palace of the Rajas of Travancore. Enclosed within a cyclopean stone wall, the palace served as the capital of Travancore from 1490-1790, and is a beautiful example of the Kerala school of architecture, with fine murals, floral carvings and black granite floors. It makes a great day trip, or a neat stopover if you're heading across the Tamil Nadu border to Kanniyakumari.

At the foot of the Western Ghats, 30 km east of Thiruvananthapuram, the **Neyyar Wildlife Sanctuary** ① *free, speedboat for 2 people Rs 100/150, larger boats to view the forests enclosing the lake Rs 20 per person, minibus safari Rs 10*, occupies a beautiful wooded and hilly landscape, dominated by the peak of Agasthya Malai (1868 m). The vegetation ranges from grassland to tropical, wet evergreen. Wildlife includes gaur, sloth bear, Nilgiri tahr, jungle cat, sambar deer, elephants and Nilgiri langur; the most commonly seen animals are lion-tailed macaques and other monkeys. Tigers and leopards have also been reported. **Neyyar Dam** supports a large population of crocodiles and otters; a crocodile farm was set up in 1977 near the administrative complex.

Immediately to the northeast of the Neyyar Wildlife Sanctuary a section of dense forest, **Agasthya Vanam**, was set aside as a biological park in 1992 to recreate biodiversity on a wide scale. Nearby, the **Sivananda Yoga Vedanta Dhanwantari Ashram** ① *T0471-2273093, www.sivananda.org/neyyardam, minimum stay 3 days*, runs highly regarded meditation and yoga courses. It is quite an intensive schedule, with classes that start just after dawn and a strict timetable including karma yoga (meditation or devotion to God through physical labour). It is only really suitable for the hardy; others may find it heavy on Hinduism and Indian diet.

Further north sits **Ponmudi** ① *buses from Trivandrum, Thampanoor Bus Stand 0530-1630; return 0615-1905, 2½ hrs*, the nearest hill station to Thiruvananthapuram, 65 km away. In a spectacular and peaceful setting, the tourist complex, though basic, serves as a good base for trekking, birdwatching and visiting the nearby minimalist deer park.

Like Gokarna in Karnataka, Varkala is a pilgrimage centre for both backpackers and Hindus. The former come for the ruddy beach which lies at the bottom of the dramatic drop of a laterite cliff, the latter for the Vaishnavite **Janardhanaswamy Temple** and the Sivagiri Mutt of social reformer Sree Narayana Guru. The sea is far from calm (it has lifeguards for good reason), and the main beach, **Papanasam**, accessed by steep steps hacked in the cliffs, is shared between holidaymakers and fishermen. Along the cliff path, particularly along the **North Cliff**, is the tourist village high street; sizeable concrete hotels, travel agents, internet cafés, tailors stitching out endless pairs of fisherman's trousers and a huge preponderance of Kashmiri and Tibetan salespeople pushing their customary turquoise, silverware and carpets. Further north, the tourist

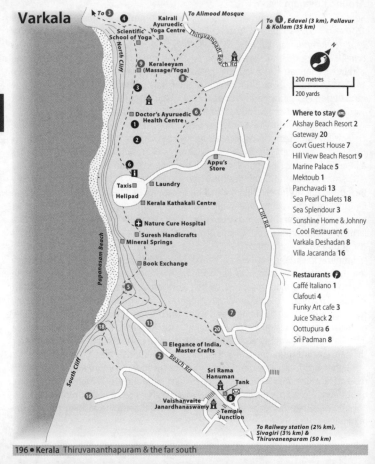

Varkala

To ③ ④
Kairali Ayuruedic Yoga Centre
To Alimood Mosque
Scientific School of Yoga
Thiruvanvadi Beach Rd
To ①, Edavai (3 km), Pallavur & Kollam (35 km)

North Cliff

⑨ Keraleeyam (Massage/Yoga)

③
⑧
⑥

■ Doctor's Ayuruedic Health Centre
①
②

200 metres
200 yards

⑥
ℹ
Appu's Store

Taxis ■
Helipad
■ Laundry
■ Kerala Kathakali Centre

✚ Nature Cure Hospital
■ Suresh Handicrafts
■ Mineral Springs

Cliff Rd

Papanasom Beach

■ Book Exchange

⑤

⑱
⑬
⑦
⑳

■ Elegance of India, Master Crafts
②
Beach Rd

South Cliff

⑯

Sri Rama Hanuman
Tank

⑧

Vaishanvaite Janardhanaswamy
Temple Junction

To Railway station (2½ km), Sivagiri (3½ km) & Thiruvanenpuram (50 km)

Where to stay
Akshay Beach Resort 2
Gateway 20
Govt Guest House 7
Hill View Beach Resort 9
Marine Palace 5
Mektoub 1
Panchavadi 13
Sea Pearl Chalets 18
Sea Splendour 3
Sunshine Home & Johnny
   Cool Restaurant 6
Varkala Deshadan 8
Villa Jacaranda 16

Restaurants
Caffé Italiano 1
Clafouti 4
Funky Art cafe 3
Juice Shack 2
Oottupura 6
Sri Padman 8

shacks bleed into fishing village life around the **Alimood Mosque** (dress modestly). Watch your step around the cliff, particularly at night; carry a torch after dark.

The south, bordered by a golden beach, has a lovely village feel, with traditional houses built around the 13th-century temple dedicated to Vishnu. The **Arratu festival** in March-April draws thousands of visitors.

Opposite is the **Sri Rama Hanuman Temple**, whose large temple tank three wheeler drivers splash through in the morning, while women thwack their *lungis* clean on its steps. The main 'town' area (including the train station) is a further 2 km inland from Temple Junction.

A two-hour excursion takes you to **Golden Island** for a glimpse of local backwaters; there's a small temple here but it's the type of visit you'd make for the atmosphere more than anything else. A boat round the island should cost Rs 50 for the hour.

Lullaby@Varkala, www.lullabyatvarkala.in, runs tours to introduce tourists to *anganwadis*, childcare centres for underprivileged families. The project helps feed, clothe and educate its beneficiaries.

⊙ Thiruvananthapuram and the far south listings

For hotel and restaurant price codes and other relevant information, see pages 13-17.

⊜ Where to stay

Thiruvananthapuram *p191, map p192*
$$$$-$$$ Thapovan Heritage Home, Nellikunnu, T0471-248 0453, www.thapovan.com. 18 km south of town with rooms in beautiful gardens or overlooking Nellikunu beach. Ayurvedic treatments, yoga, restaurant.
$$$ Keys Hotel, Housing Board Junction (opposite the Fire Brigade), T0471-394 4100, www.keyshotels.com. Ultra-modern hotel with high-speed Wi-Fi, gym and all mod cons. Also has a women's-only floor with extra security measures.
$$$-$$ Residency Tower, Press Rd, T0471-233 1661, www.residencytower.com. Top-quality a/c rooms in a business hotel, with full facilities. Highly efficient, good restaurants, bar, rooftop pool (non-residents Rs 350). A bit swish.
$$ The Capital, off MG Rd, near the GPO, Pulimudu, T0471-247 1987,

www.thecapital.in. Renovated business hotel, with smallish but clean rooms and some large, excellent value suites. Excellent rooftop restaurant. Friendly.
$$ Chaithram (KTDC), Station Rd, T0471-233 0977, www.ktdc.com. Very clean decent-sized rooms, some a/c. Next to railway and bus stand so can be noisy. Restaurant, bar.
$$ Wild Palms Homestay, Mathrubhoomi Rd, Vanchiyoor, 10 mins' walk from Statue Junction or ask for pick-up, T0471-247 1175, wildpalm@md3.vsnl.net.in. Modern welcoming guesthouse set in pretty tropical garden in the leafy suburbs. Spacious rooms, some a/c. Price includes breakfast.
$$-$ Highland, Manjalikulam Rd, T0471-233 3416, www.highland-hotels.com. Busy hotel with wide variety of clean rooms. Budget rooms good value.
$$-$ Thamburu International, Aristo Junction, T0471-232 1974, www.thamburu.com. Quiet, well-run hotel with wood-panelled walls and cheesy music in foyer. Rooms (all with TV) tend to be on small side. Some a/c rooms have balcony.

$ Asha, 200 m from airport, T0471-250 1050. Very handy for early departures. Decent rooms with bath.

$ Greenland, Aristo Junction, T0471-232 3485. Great-value rooms in quiet, immaculate, freshly renovated hotel, perfectly located within a couple of mins of both bus and railway stations. Best budget choice in town.

$ Manjalikulam Tourist Home, Manjalikulam Rd, T0471-233 0776, www. manjalikulam.com. Quiet yet central hotel with large, spotlessly clean rooms. Very friendly staff. Good value, recommended.

$ Youth Hostel (YHAI), Veli (10 km from centre), T0471-250 1230. Rooms and a dorm surrounded by coconut groves, with a pretty lagoon and clean beach. Very cheap vegetarian lunches, boating, watersports, good views.

Kovalam and nearby resorts *p193, map p194*

Long power cuts are common here, so a/c often doesn't work. Look for rooms with windows on 2 walls to get a good through-breeze. There are numerous budget cottages and rooms to let with a range of rooms from Rs 150-1000. The alleys behind **Lighthouse Beach** tend to have the cheapest accommodation. Scouts greet arrivals at the bus stand but you may pay considerably more if you use their services. You will find rooms to let, behind bars and restaurants, by walking from the Sea Rock hotel towards the lighthouse, and on the **Samudra Beach** and **GV Raja Rd** (Samudra Rd). Be aware that management of the cheaper hotels often changes hands and hotel names can change from year to year. Rates shown here are for the high season. Prices skyrocket in all hotels for the 3-week peak period (23 Dec-7 Jan), though it still pays to bargain. High season is 1-19 Dec, 11

Jan-28 Feb; in the low season, especially May-Jul, expect 40-75% discounts.

$$$$ Friday's Place Poovar, Poover Island, T(0)9744-161636, www.fridays placekerala.com. Remote, watery eco-hideaway with 3 solar-powered teak and mahogany cottages and a spectacular Ark-like 'Tsunami House', set on an isolated sandbank amid rows of palms and hibiscus, frangipani and bougainvillea, run by British couple Mark and Sujeewa, the latter a Sivananda yoga teacher and reiki healer. Food is fresh, with fruit for breakfast, *thali* lunches, fish and chicken suppers. Kayaking and temple tours.

$$$$ Karikkathi Beach House, near Nagar Bhagavathy Temple at Mulloor Thottam, Pulinkudi, T0471-240 0956, www. karikkathibeachhouse.com. 2 doubles with linked lounge, palm-thatch roof, no a/c or TV, perfect for honeymooners or those used to being kept; the house comes with private beach, chef, waiter and servants. There's a cottage should families or groups need extra beds.

$$$$ Niraamaya, Pulinkudi, near Kovalam, T0471-226 7333, www. niraamaya.in. Sitting high on a rocky bluff between Kovalam and Kannyukamari, this elite resort boasts a world-class spa and offers Ayurveda treatments from its beautifully designed complex. There are just 21 traditional Keralite cottages, with 4-posters, big plantation chairs and open-air bathrooms, spread over 9 ha of jackfruit, bamboo, cinnamon, mango, frangipani, palm and hibiscus trees. Excellent Sivananda yoga on a one-on-one basis at an open-air pavilion overlooking the sea.

$$$$ Poovar Island Resort, Poovar Island, T0471-221 2068, www.poovar islandresort.com. Award-winning boutique hotel with 'floating' cottages where the backwaters meet the sea.

facilities include pool, handicrafts, Ayurveda, watersports.

$$$$ Vivanta by Taj, GV Raja Vattapara Rd, Kovalam, T0471-661 3000, www.vivantabytaj.com. Appealing and luxurious Balinese-flavoured complex set in 4 ha of tropical grounds with superb views of the sea, infinity pool, excellent spa, gym and Wi-Fi.

$$$$-$$$ Bethsaida Hermitage, Pulinkudi, T0471-226 7554, www.bethsaidahermitage.com. Eco-friendly stone and bamboo beach *cabanas* surrounded by coconut groves. Profits support a variety of charitable projects. Family-friendly, informal and unpretentious.

$$$$-$$$ Coconut Bay Beach Resort, Mulloor, T0471-2480 566, www.coconutbay.com. Spacious stone villas on beach, good restaurant, friendly. Secluded location in traditional fishing village. Recommended.

$$$$-$$$ Somatheeram Ayurvedic Beach Resort, Chowara Beach, south of Kovalam, T0471-226 8101, www.somatheeram.in. Kerala's 1st Ayurvedic resort and also the repeat winner of the state's competition to find the best. Its cottages and traditional Keralite houses set in coconut groves are dotted over a steep hill above the beach. If you want more peace, and the use of an oyster-shaped pool with whirlpool, stay at sister resort, **Manaltheeram**. 15 doctors and 90 therapists work in 48 treatment rooms at the shared Ayurvedic facilities. British-based holistic health and beauty therapist, **Bharti Vyas**, T+44(0)20-7935 5312 (UK), www.bharti-vyas.com, leads 10-day retreats here, or join a yoga retreat with uplifting American vinyasa flow teacher, **Shiva Rea**, www.yogaadventures.com.

$$$ Molly's, Samudra Beach Rd, Kovalam, T0471-326 2099, www.mollyskovalam.com. 2-storey hotel set around a pool. Each

room has a terrace overlooking a jungly thicket of coconuts. The restaurant, which serves Mexican, European, Indian and tandoor food, is very popular.

$$$-$$ Maharaju Palace, Lighthouse Beach, T(0)9946-854270, www.maharajupalace.nl. Beautiful, shady garden setting, quiet and set back from beach. 6 very clean rooms inside and outside cottages complete with chandeliers and frou-frou interiors. Genial staff, very popular.

$$$-$ Holiday Home Resort, Beach Rd, T0471-248 0497, www.holidayhomeresort.net. Cute cottages amid a tree-filled, shady garden with hammocks to laze in. Serene location 10 mins' walk from beach. Excellent, friendly service from the helpful manager, Shar. Camping, with own tent, is possible (Rs 150).

$$ Kailasam Yoga and Ayurveda Holidays, Kovalam, T0471-248 4018, book through **Free Spirit Travel**, T+44 (0)127-356 4230 (UK), www.yogaindia.co.uk. Peaceful oasis set up by a yoga teacher and Ayurvedic physician. Yoga classes held in tiled areas under coconut-leaf roofs, surrounded by trees and open-sided to catch the sea breezes. Price includes all yoga classes.

$$ Rockholm, Lighthouse Rd, T0471-248 0406, www.rockholm.com. Very pleasant hotel owned by an Anglo-Indian family with cheerful staff. Good-sized rooms, with balcony, in a wonderful position just above the lighthouse. Direct access to beach. Good terrace restaurant.

$$-$ Coco Land, between Lighthouse Beach and Eve's Beach, T0471-653 3591, cocoheritage@yahoo.com. Bamboo huts and 'luxury' wood cottages in a little garden set back from the beach. Cottages boast TVs, a/c and hot water. Friendly management. Recommended.

$$-$ Hotel Greenland, Lighthouse Beach, T0471-248 6442, hotelgreenland@

yahoo.com. Friendly female manger has a variety of spotlessly clean rooms set amongst her flowery garden. All have porch, fly-screens, 4 have kitchenettes and TV. Cheaper rooms are excellent value. Recommended.

$$-$ Sea Flower Beach Resort, Lighthouse Rd, T0471-248 0554, www.seaflowerkovalam.com. Great location right on the shore. Good-sized rooms with decent bath and balcony. Helpful staff, good value, big discounts for long stays.

$ Green Valley Cottages, between Lighthouse Beach and Eve's Beach, T0471-248 0636, indira_ravi@hotmail.com. Spick and span simple rooms with fly-screens and sit-outs. Good value.

$ Hotel Rani, Lighthouse Beach, T(0)9995-566039, www.hotelrani.com. Basic, well-maintained rooms that open out onto a communal veranda. Friendly owner.

$ Shirley's Beach White House, between Lighthouse Beach and Eve's Beach, T(0)9447-224902, www.shirleysbeach.com. The sea-facing rooms here are a cut above other hotels in this price range. All are breezy and painted a cheerful blue, some with balcony. The owner is a wealth of knowledge. Quiet location, very good value. Recommended.

$ Usha's, Lighthouse Beach, T0471-279 0563. Good little cheapie in the winding alleys behind the beach. Basic rooms, all with bath and fly-screens. Run by the genial Usha and her family.

$ Wilson Tourist Home, up path behind Neelkantha, T0471-248 0052. Clean, quiet rooms with bath, balcony, fan, some with a/c. Open-air restaurant, pretty garden, helpful service. Recommended.

Around Kovalam p195

$$$$ Duke's Forest Lodge, Anappara, near Ponmudi, T0471-226 8822, www.dukesforest.com. 5 luxury villas, each with its own plunge pool, set on organic estate. Great trekking.

$ Government Guest House, Ponmudi, T0471-289 0211. 24 rooms and 10 cottages, in attractive gardens surrounded by wooded hills, spartan facilities but spacious rooms, restaurant serves limited but reasonable vegetarian meals, beer available, also a post office and general store.

Varkala p196, map p196

There are at least 50 guesthouses, plus rooms in private houses. The **North Cliff** area is compact, so look around until you find what you want: the northernmost area is where the most laid-back, budget options are and has the most character, while the far south side has a few fancier places. None, however, is actually on the beach. Outside the high season of Nov-Mar, prices drop by up to 50%. During the monsoon (Jun-Jul) many close.

$$$ Varkala Deshadan, Kurakkanni Cliff, T0470-320 4242, www.deshadan.com. Scrupulously clean Chettinadu-style a/c bungalows set around a large pool. Price includes breakfast.

$$$ Villa Jacaranda, Temple Rd West, South Cliff, T0470-261 0296, www.villa-jacaranda.biz. A delightful guesthouse, home with 5 huge rooms elegantly but sparely decorated. Jasmine, birds of paradise and magnolia blossoms are tucked into alcoves, there's a lotus-filled pond and tropical garden and everything is immaculately maintained. Guests have their own keys and entrance. Really special.

$$$-$ Marine Palace, Papanasam Beach, T0471-260 3204, www.varkalamarine.com. 12 rooms in total with 3 lovely old-style wooden rooms with balconies and a sea view. The honeymoon suite has a truly gigantic bed. Good service and nice tandoori restaurant on the beach. Recommended.

$$ Mektoub, Odayam Beach, T(0)9447-971239. Beautiful rustic-mystic hideaway – a place of candles and incense smoke. Charming owner, utterly peaceful, and a minute from uncrowded sand.

$$-$ Akshay Beach Resort, Beach Rd (about 200 m from beach), T0470-260 2668. Wide variety of bright, clean rooms. Quiet location away from the cliff. Restaurant, TV lounge, good value.

$$-$ Hill View Beach Resort, North Cliff, T0470-260 5744, www.varkalahillview. neehaarika.org. Self-contained cottages and budget rooms in a smart resort. Internet, airport pick-up, hot water.

$$-$ Sea Pearl Chalets, Beach Rd, T0470-260 0105, www.seapearlchalets. com. Circular thatched huts perched scarily near the cliff edge. Great views, breakfast included. Recommended.

$ Government Guest House, towards The Gateway (see Restaurants), T0470-260 2227. Immense, high-ceilinged rooms with marble floors and big baths, in the leafy former summer residence of the maharaja. Isolated, idyllic and quiet. Book in advance, recommended.

$ Panchavadi, Beach Rd, T0470-260 0200, www.panchavadi.com. Excellent location close to beach. Very clean and secure with simple rooms. Budget rooms very good value. Restaurant, helpful staff. Recommended.

$ Sea Splendour, North Cliff end, Odayam Beach, T0470-266 2120, www.seasplendour. com. Homely choice with simple rooms in retired teacher's guesthouse. Excellent home cooking (unlimited and spoilt for choice), very peaceful.

$ Sunshine Home/Johnny Cool & Soulfood Café, North Cliff, Varkala Beach, T(0)9341-201295. Colourful, chilled-out Rasta house set back off the cliff. Bongo drums and Marley posters abound. There's a variety of rooms, some

with balcony, plus a little standalone thatched cottage out the back. The café does pastas, noodles, fish and chips – but in its own sweet time.

🍴 Restaurants

Thiruvananthapuram *p191, map p192*
$$$ Villa Maya, Airport Rd, Subash Nagar, Enchakkal Westfort Rd, T0471-257 8901. One of the most beautiful restaurants in this book, set in a restored 18th-century Dutch villa surrounded by fountains. Dishes span a broad range of cuisines, from traditional Kerala curries to Israeli or Moroccan specials. It's pricey and they don't serve alcohol, but this is a superb choice for a splurge.

$$ Kalavara, Kalavara Hotel, Press Rd, T0471-232 2195. Indian, Continental, Chinese, fast food (burgers, shakes), takeaway. Food average, slow service but good-value buffets in upstairs thatched section with a patch of garden. Good ambience, limited views.

$$ Kerala House, near Statue Junction, T0471-247 6144. Keralite cuisine in the basement of shopping complex. Slow for breakfast but newspapers available, outside seating in the evening in roadside car park area is cheaper. Colourful and fun place to pass some time, even if the food arrives cold. Try *neem, kappa* and rice (delicious fish with tapioca), or inexpensive chicken dishes with coconut; bakery in the complex does excellent samosas and puffs.

$$ Mascot, Mascot Hotel, Museum Rd. Excellent lunchtime buffet, pleasant, 24-hr coffee shop for all types of snacks, good value, a cool haven at midday.

$$ Queen's, Aristo Junction. Indian non-vegetarian. Chilli chicken recommended.

$ Arul Jyoti, MG Rd, opposite Secretariat. South Indian vegetarian. With a/c family room, clean, wide choice of good-value dishes, try jumbo *dosas*. Great Tamil Nadu *thalis*.

$ Indian Coffee House, 2 on MG Rd, with others near YWCA, north of the Secretariat, and near KSRTC Bus Stand (the latter designed by the English architect Laurie Baker). Worth seeing, excellent value coffee and snacks.

Kovalam and nearby resorts *p193, map p194*

There are hundreds of restaurants here. Service can be slow, and quality hit-and-miss since management often changes hands. Below is a very short list of those that have proved consistent. The restaurant at the **Taj** is good, if predictable. **The Leela** hotel Sun brunch has a giant salad counter and loud live music. Avoid 'catch of the day' on Sun – it's unlikely to be fresh. Some restaurants will screen pirated DVDs, sometimes to compensate for underwhelming cuisine.

$$ Fusion, Eve's Beach, T0471-248 4153. Kovalam's take on fusion food doesn't really pull it off but the cold coffees are exceptional and the menu has a nice varied mix of international and Indian food.

$$ Rockholm Hotel, (see Where to stay), Lighthouse Rd. Very good international food and tandooris served on a pleasant terrace with beautiful views, especially early morning.

$$ Sea Face, Eve's Beach. Breezy raised terrace on the beach by a pleasant pool. Varied choice including versatile fish and seafood. Friendly and attentive.

$ Karuna, Lighthouse Beach. Excellent Keralite breakfasts, home-made brown bread, decent coffee.

$ Lonely Planet, between Lighthouse Beach and Eve's Beach. Wholesome, mildly spiced Ayurvedic vegetarian food. Set around a pond with ducks – and

mosquitoes. Sells recipe books and runs cookery courses.

$ Suprabhatan, Lighthouse Beach, opposite **Hotel Greenland**. South and North Indian vegetarian meals.

Varkala *p196, map p196*

There are numerous restaurants along North Cliff, most with facsimile menus, slow service and questionable kitchens; take extra care with drinking water here. 'Catch of the day' splayed out for you to inspect, usually costs Rs 100-150 depending upon the type/size of fish, but make sure you don't get 'catch of yesterday' (fresh fish keep their glassy eyes and bright silvery scales). Many restaurants close out of season.

$$$ The Gateway, **Gateway Hotel**, near **Government Guest House**. Every Sun 1230-1530 (Rs 300, includes pool use). Good-value eat-all-you-want buffet, delicious rich vegetarian cuisine.

$$ Caffé Italiano, North Cliff, T(0)9846-053194. Good Italian and seafood, but quite pricey.

$$ Sri Padman, near Hanuman Temple, T0472-260 5422. **Sri Padman**'s terrace overlooking the temple tank offers the best non-beachfront position in town. Come here for South Indian vegetarian breakfasts served in big stainless steel *thali* trays, and oily *parathas* to sop up spicy curries and coconut chutneys.

$ Clafouti, Clafouti Hotel, North Cliff (see Where to stay). Fresh pastries and cakes, but standards seem to drop when the French-Keralite owners are away.

$ Funky Art Café, North Cliff. Eclectic multi-cuisine menu. Sometimes hosts local bands playing Varkala versions of Western rock songs, which can be an amusing diversion while waiting for the incredibly slow service.

$ The Juice Shack, cliffside Varkala, turn off at Tibetan market. Shady little

spot with healthy juice, good coffee and excellent toasted sandwiches. Brilliant for breakfast – they even have Marmite.
$ Oottupura, cliffside Varkala, near helipad, T0472-260 6994. A Varkala institution. Excellent 100% vegetarian with 60 curries and everything from Chinese to macaroni cheese. Breakfast can be *iddlies* or toasted sandwiches, all served under a giant pistachio tree covered in fairy lights.

⚙ Entertainment

Thiruvananthapuram *p191, map p192*
Performances of *Kalarippayattu*, Kerala's martial art, can be seen through: **CVN Kalari**, East Fort, T0471-247 4182 (0430-0830); and **Balachandran Nair Kalari Martial Arts Gymnasium**, Parasuvaikal, T0471-223 2686, www.kalari.in.

Kovalam and nearby resorts *p193, map p194*
Kalakeli Kathakali Troupe, T0471-248 1818. Daily at hotels including **Ashok** and **Neptune**, Rs 100.

Varkala *p196, map p196*
Varkala is a good place to hang out, chill and do yoga but there's no organized nightlife to speak of, only impromptu campfire parties.
Kerala Kathakali Centre, by the helipad, holds a daily *Kathakali* demonstration (Rs 150, make-up 1700-1800, performance 1830-2000). The participants are generally students of the art rather than masters.

⚙ Festivals

Thiruvananthapuram *p191, map p192*
In 2010 the city hosted an outlier of the **Hay Festival**, featuring authors including Vikram Seth and William Dalrymple and gigs by the likes of Bob Geldof. It's hoped

it will become an annual event. Check out www.hayfestival.com/kerala.
Mar Chandanakuda, at Beemapalli, a shrine on Beach Rd 5 km southwest of the railway station. 10-day festival when local Muslims go to the mosque, holding incense sticks and pots. Marked by sword play, singing, dancing, elephant procession and fireworks.
Mar-Apr (Meenam) and Oct-Nov (Thulam) **Arattu** is the closing festival of the 10-day celebrations of the Padmanabhaswamy Temple, in which the deity is paraded around the temple inside the fort and then down to the sea.
Sep/Oct Navaratri at the special *mandapa* in Padmanabhaswamy Temple. Several concerts are held which draw famous musicians. **Thiruvonam week** in Sep.
1-10 Oct Soorya Dance Festival.
Nov-Mar A similar **Nishangandhi Dance Festival** is held at weekends when all-important classical Indian dance forms are performed by leading artistes at Nishagandhi open-air auditorium, Kanakakkunnu Palace.

⚙ Shopping

If shopping, bear in mind that prices are relatively high here: traders seldom honour the standard rates for 92.5 silver, charging by piece not weight.

Thiruvananthapuram *p191, map p192*
Shopping areas include the **Chalai Bazar**, the **Connemara Market** and the main road from Palayam to the East Fort. Usually open 0900-2000 (some take a long lunch break). Although ivory goods have now been banned, inlay on woodcarving and marquetry using other materials (bone, plastic) continue to flourish. *Kathakali* masks and traditional fabrics can be bought at a number of shops.

The shopping centre opposite East Fort Bus Stand has a large a/c shop with a good selection of silks and saris but is not cheap. *Khadi* recommended from shops on both sides of MG Rd, south of Pulimudu Junction.

Co-optex, Temple Rd. Good for fabrics and *lungis*.

Handloom House, diagonally across from **Partha's**. Has an excellent range of fabrics, clothes and export quality dhurries.

Partha's, towards East Fort. Recommended.

Premier Stationers, MG Rd, opposite Post Office Rd. The best best in town.

Raymonds, Karal Kada, East Fort. Good selection of men's clothing.

Handicrafts

Gift Corner and **Natesan Antique Arts**, MG Rd. High-quality goods including old dowry boxes, carved wooden panels from old temple 'cars', miniature paintings and bronzes.

Gram Sree, MG Rd. Excellent village crafts.

Kairali, MG Rd. Items of banana fibre, coconut, screw pine, mainly utilitarian, also excellent sandalwood carvings and bell-metal lamps, utensils.

Kalanjali, Palace Garden, across from the museum. Recommended.

SMSM Handicrafts Emporium, behind the Secretariat. Government-run, heaps of items reasonably priced.

Kovalam and nearby resorts *p193, map p194*

Numerous craft shops, including Kashmiri and Tibetan shops, sell a wide range of goods. Most are clustered around the bus stand at the gate of the Ashok with another group to the south around the lighthouse. Good-quality paintings, metalwork, woodwork and carpets at reasonable prices. Gems and jewellery are widely available but it is notoriously difficult to be sure of quality.

Tailoring is available at short notice and is very good value with the fabrics available. Charges vary, about Rs 50-80 per piece.

Brother Tailors, 2nd Beach Rd.

Raja, near hotel **Surya**.

Suresh, next to **Garzia** restaurant.

Zangsty Gems, Lighthouse Rd. Sells jewellery and silver and has a good reputation for helpfulness and reliability.

Varkala *p196, map p196*

Most of the handicraft shops are run by Kashmiris, who will tell you that everything (including the tie-dye T-shirts) is an antique from Ladakh.

Elegance of India and **Mushtaq**, Beach Rd. Sell Kashmiri handicrafts, carpets, jewellery, etc, reported as honest, will safely air-freight carpets and other goods.

Satori, T(0)9387-653261. Cliff-top boutique, selling pretty Western clothes made with local fabric and jewelled Rajasthani slippers.

Suresh, on path south from helipad. Handicrafts from Karnataka.

◐ What to do

Thiruvananthapuram *p191, map p192*
Body and soul

Institute of Yogic Culture, Vazhuthacaud, T0471-304 9349, www.pillaisyogicculture.com. Yoga therapy, Ayurvedic massage.

Sivananda Ashram, Neyyar Dam, T0471-227 3093, www.sivananda.org/ndam. One of India's most highly regarded yoga teacher training programs.

Swimming

Mascot Hotel, Cantonment Rd, has a big pool. Small rooftop pool at **Residency Tower** (0700-1900, Rs 250), with great views. **Waterworks**, pool near museum, T0471-231 8990.

Tour operators

IATA-approved agencies include:

Great India Tour Co, New Corporation Building, Palayam, T0471-301 1500, www.gitc.travel. Offers afternoon city tours, among others. Reliable but pricey.

KTDC, **Hotel Chaithram**, Station Rd, T0471-233 0031, www.ktdc.com. Can arrange 2- to 3-day tours to Munnar and Thekkady and also runs the following local tours:

City tour: daily 0730 and 1300, 5½ hrs including Padmanabhapuram, Puthenmalika Palace, Shangumugham beach and Napier Museum, Rs 250 (Padmanabhapuram is closed on Mon).

Kanniyakumari: daily 0730-2100, including Kovalam, Padmanabhapuram and Kanniyakumari, Rs 550. Tours can feel quite rushed with little time spent at sights.

TourIndia, MG Rd, T0471-233 0437, www.tourindiakerala.com. The pioneers of backwater tourism and Periyar's Tiger Trails trekking program, highly recommended for innovative and unusual experiences, eg treehouse holidays or sport fishing off Fort Kochi.

Trekking and birdwatching

Trekking is best Dec-Apr. Obtain permission first from the Chief Conservator of Forests (Wildlife), Forest HQ, Thiruvananthapuram, T0471-232 2217, or the Assistant Wildlife Warden at Neyyar Dam, T0471-227 2182.

Kovalam and nearby resorts *p193, map p194*

Body and soul

Ayurvedic treatments are also offered by most upmarket resorts (a massage will set you back about Rs 700).

Dr Franklin's Panchakarma Institute and Research Centre, Chowara,

T0471-248 0870, www.dr-franklin.com. The good doctor's family have been in Ayurveda for 4 centuries, and he himself is the former district medical officer of the Keralan government. Programmes include treatment for infertility, sluggishness, paralysis and obesity. 15-day body purification therapy (*panchakarma* and *swetakarma*) costs US$714. 21-day *Born To Win* programme US$968. Others include *You and your spine*, *Body Mind Soul*, and there are age-reducing treatments including body immunization and longevity treatments (28 days, US$1290). The slimming programme takes 28 days, US$1200. 51-day *panchakarma*, US$2390. Cheaper treatments include: face pack US$7, 1-hr massage US$17. Also training courses in massage, Ayurveda and *panchakarma*.

Medicus, Lighthouse Rd, T0471-248 0596. Mrs Babu has a loyal clientele, many of whom return year after year.

Padma Nair, Pink Flowers, Lighthouse Beach, T(0)9895-882915, www.yoga shala.in. One of *Kalaripayattu* master Balachandran Nair's students, Padma Nair has 10-day massage programmes at her village home from US$180.

Vasudeva, T0471-222 2510, in the Rohith Hotel (near Green Land). Simple but with experienced professionals.

Fishing

Can readily be arranged through the hotels, as can excursions on traditional catamarans or motor boats. You may be promised corals and beautiful fish just offshore but don't expect to see very much.

Indian martial arts

Guru Balachandran Nair, is the master of the **Indian School of Martial Arts**, Parasuvykal, 20 km from Trivandrum, T0471-272 5140, www.kalari.in. This is a college teaching *Kalaripayattu*, India's traditional martial art, as well as *Kalarichikitsa*, an ancient Indian healing tradition combining Ayurveda with *Marma* therapy, which manipulates the vital pressure points of the body to ease pain. A fighter would have had an intimate knowledge of these points to know what to harm or how to heal. A fascinating place to stay.

Tour operators
There are dozens of tour operators on the roads leading down to the beach and on the beachfront. Nearly all of them offer money exchange, onward travel booking and backwater tours.
East India Premier Tours, behind **Neelkantha Hotel**, between Lighthouse and Eve's Beach, T0471-248 3246. Can suggest unusual hotels.
Great Indian Travel, Lighthouse Rd, T0471-248 1110, www.keralatours.com. Wide range of tours, exchange, eco-friendly beach resorts.
Visit India, Lighthouse Rd, T0471-248 1069. Friendly and helpful, exchange, short backwater tours from Thiruvallam.

Varkala *p196, map p196*
Body and soul
Keraleeyam, North Cliff. One of the best of the many yoga/Ayurvedic massage centres.
Lakshmi Herbal Beauty Parlour, **Clafouti Hotel** (see Where to stay). Individual attention, amazing massages plus waxing, henna, etc.
Nature Cure Hospital, North Cliff. Opened in 1983, treats patients entirely by diet and natural cures including hydrotherapy, chromotherapy (natural sunbath with different filters) and mud therapy, each treatment normally lasting 30 mins.

Naturomission Yoga Ashram, near the helipad. Runs 1-, 2- and 7-day courses in yoga, massage, meditation, and healing techniques. Payment by donation.
Scientific School of Yoga, Naturopathy and Massage, Diana Inn, North Cliff, T0470-320 6294. 10-day yoga and massage course (2 classes daily), Rs 500, professionally run by English-speaking doctor. Also has a shop selling Ayurvedic oils, soaps, etc.

Tour operators
Most hotels offer tours, air tickets, backwater trips, houseboats, etc, as do the many agents along North Cliff.
JK Tours & Travels, Temple Junction Varkala, T0802-668 3334. Money exchange, daily 0900-2100.

⊖ Transport

Thiruvananthapuram *p191, map p192*
Air The airport, T0471-250 1426, is 6 km away from the beach. **Transport to town**: by local bus no 14, prepaid taxi (Rs 150) or auto (about Rs 100, 20 mins). Confirm international bookings and arrive in good time. Expect inflated prices at refreshments counter, though you can get cheap tea and coffee in the final lounge after security check. Banks at the airport are outside arrivals. **Johnson & Co** travel agent opposite domestic terminal, T0471-250 3555. Note that the teminal is closed at night.

Airlines Sri Lankan Airlines, Spencer Building, MG Rd, T0471-247 1810; **Kuwait Airways**, airport, T0471-250 1401; **Indian Airlines**, Mascot Sq, T0471-231 6870 (airport T0471-250 1537), and **Air India**, Museum Rd, Velayambalam, T0471-231 0310 (airport T0471-250 1426).
Domestic departures include: **Indian Airlines** to **Bengaluru**, **Chennai**, **Delhi**

and **Mumbai**. Air India to **Mumbai**. Jet Airways to **Chennai** and **Mumbai**.

International departures include: **Air India Express** to several **Gulf** destinations; **Emirates** to **Dubai**; Etihad to **Abu Dhabi**. Maldivian to **Malé**; Silk Air and Tiger Airways to **Singapore**; Sri Lankan to **Colombo**.

Bus Local: City Bus Stand, T0471-246 3029. Green buses have limited stops; yellow/red buses continue through town up to museum. Blue/white bus (No 888) to **Kovalam** goes from **East Fort Bus Station** (30 mins, Rs 9).
Long distance: Buses leave from KSRTC Bus Station, Station Rd, near railway station, T0471-232 3886. Buses to **Kanniyakumari** via **Nagercoil** or direct, 0530, 0930, 1000, 1200, 1500, 1600 and 1830 (2½ hrs, Rs 40) and frequent departures to **Kozhikode**, (10 hrs, Rs 200) via **Kollam** (2½ hrs, Rs 44), **Alappuzha** (4 hrs, Rs 96), **Ernakulam/Kochi** (5½ hrs, Rs 129), and **Thrissur** (7 hrs, Rs 173). You can include a section of the backwaters on the way to Kochi by getting a boat from Kollam (shared taxis there cost Rs 60 each, see below). TNSTC to **Chennai**, **Coimbatore**, **Cuddalore**, **Erode**, **Kanniyakumari**, **Madurai** from opposite the Central Railway station.

Rickshaw Rickshaws to the Kovalam beach area should cost around Rs 70-100. You will need to bargain. Tell auto-rickshaw drivers which beaches you want to get to in advance, otherwise they will charge much more when you get there.

Taxi Prepaid taxis from the airport charge around Rs 350 to Kovalam. From outside **Mascot Hotel** taxis charge about Rs 7 per km; to **Kovalam**, Rs 175, return Rs 225 (waiting: extra

Rs 50 per hr). From outside train station, Rs 5 per km. To **Kanniyakumari** with a stop at Padmanabhapuram costs about Rs 900/1100.

Train Central Station, T132. Reservations in building adjoining station. Advance, upstairs, open 0700-1300, 1330-1930, Sun 0900-1700; ask to see Chief Reservations Supervisor, Counter 8. **Kochi (Ernakulam)** (5¼ hrs), via **Varkala** and the backwater towns: around 20 trains daily 0500-2145 including: *Kerala Exp 12625*, 1115; and *Trivandrum Ernakulam Exp 16342*, 1710. **Bengaluru**: *Island Exp 16525*, 1255, 18 hrs. **Mangalore**: *Parasuram Exp 16650*, 0630, 14 hrs; and *Malabar Exp 16629*, 1830, via **Kochi**, **Thrissur**, **Kozhikode** and **Kannur**. **Chennai**: *TVC Chennai Exp 12696*, 1710, 15 hrs. **Kanniyakumari**: *Kanyakumari Jayanti Exp 16381*, 1020, 2½ hrs.

Kovalam and nearby resorts *p193, map p194*
There are 3 main points of access to Kovalam's beaches. Remember to specify which when hiring an auto or taxi.
Bus Local: Frequent buses depart 0540-2100 to East Fort, **Thiruvananthapuram**, from bus stand outside **Ashok Hotel** gate on Kovalam Beach (30 mins, Rs 9). From **East Fort bus station**, walk or catch an auto-rickshaw to town centre (Rs 20).
Long distance: To **Kanniyakumari**, **Kochi** via **Kollam** (**Quilon**) and **Kottayam**, **Nagercoil**, **Padmanabhapuram**, **Varkala** and **Thodopuzha** via **Kottayam**.

Rickshaw Auto-rickshaw to **Thiruvanan-thapuram**, Rs 70-80, but bargain hard.

Taxi From taxi stand or through **Ashok** or **Samudra** hotels. One-way to **Thiruvananthapuram** or airport, Rs 200; station Rs 175; city sights Rs 600; **Kanniyakumari**, **Padmanabhapuram**, Rs 1750 (8 hrs); **Kochi**, Rs 2250 (5 hrs); **Kollam**, Rs 1100; **Thekkady**, Rs 2650 (6 hrs).

Varkala *p196, map p196*
Bus To/from **Temple Junction** (not beach) for **Alappuzha** and **Kollam**, but often quicker to go to Paripally on NH47 and catch onward buses from there.

Motorcycle **Kovalam Motorcycle hire**, Voyager Travels, Eye's Beach Rd, T0471-248 1993. Next door to **JA Tourist Home**, Temple Junction; and **Mamma Chompo**, Beach Rd.

Rickshaw/taxi Autos and taxis can be found on Beach Rd and near the helipad. Both charge about Rs 50 to train station. Taxi to **Thiruvananthapuram**, Rs 1000 (1¼ hrs).

Train Varkala sits on the Kochi–Trivandrum line, with at least 20 trains a day in each direction. All northbound trains call at **Kollam**, while many of the southbound trains continue to **Kanniyakumari**.

ⓘ Directory

Thiruvananthapuram *p191, map p192*
Banks Mon-Fri 1000-1400, Sat 1000-1200. Most banks can be found on MG Rd including **Andhra Bank**, **Canara Bank** and **State Bank of India**. All have ATMs. The airport has banks and money exchange facilities including **Thomas Cook**, T0471-250 2470. **Medical services** Many chemists, near hospitals; a few near Statue Junction. **Opticians**: **Lens & Frames**, Pulimudu Junction, T0471-247 1354. **General**

Hospital, Vanchiyoor, T0471-230 7874, **Ramakrishna Ashrama Hospital**, Sasthamangalam, T0471-272 2125, **Cosmopolitan Hospital**, T0471-244 8182 and **Vrindavan Ayurvedic Health Centre**, Kumarapuram, T0471-244 0376. **Useful contacts** Foreigners' Regional Registration Office, City Police Commissioner, Residency Rd, Thycaud, T0471-232 0579; allow up to a week for visas, though it can take less. Mon-Sat 1000-1700. **Wildlife Warden**, PTP Nagar, Vattiyoorkavu, T0471-236 0762.

Kovalam and nearby resorts *p193, map p194*
Banks **Canara Bank**, **ICICI Bank**, both at Kovalam Junction; ATMs. **Catholic Syria Bank**, Kovalam Beach Rd, has an ATM. **Central Bank**, branch in Kovalam Hotel (around the corner near the bookshop) changes money and TCs for non-residents after 1045, T0471-248 0101. Nearly all tour operators and many hotels offer money exchange. Best rates, however, are at the airport. **Wilson's**, T0471-248 1647, changes money, any time, no hassle. **Internet** Several on Lighthouse Beach. **Medical services** Emergency assistance either through your hotel or from **Government Hospital** in Thiruvananthapuram. **Upasana Hospital**, near *Le Meridien* gate, T0471-248 0632, has experienced English-speaking doctor.

Varkala *p196, map p196*
Banks **State Bank of India**, Temple Junction has an ATM. There are several money changers: along the north cliff and around Temple Junction (lower than US$/£ rate at Trivandrum airport), and most will give cash advances on credit cards (at a hefty 5% commission).

Backwaters

Kerala is synonymous with its lyrical backwaters: a watery cat's cradle of endlessly intersecting rivers, streams, lagoons and tanks that flood the alluvial plain between the Indian Ocean and Western Ghats. They run all the way from Kollam via Alappuzha and Kottayam to Kochi to open up a charming slow-tempo window onto Keralite waterfront life: this is the state's lush and fertile Christian belt, Arundhati Roy country, with lakes fringed by bird sanctuaries, idyllic little hamlets, beside huge paddy ponds rustling in the breeze.

The silent daybreak is best, as boats cut through the mist, geese and ducks start to stir along banks, plumes from breakfast fires drift out across the lagoons. As the hamlets and villages wake, Kerala's domestic scene comes to life: clothes are pounded clean, teeth brushed, and smartly turned out primary school children swing their ways to class.

Luxury houseboats are the quintessential way of seeing the waterfront, but they can be shocking polluters, and if your budget or attention span won't stretch that far the state-operated ferries will give you much the same access for a fraction of the fee. Alternatively, borrow a bicycle or move around by car; the roads and canals are interchangeable. Both thread their way through flood plains the size of football pitches, brown lakes with new shoots prodding out and netted fields that protect prawns and fish from snooping white egrets. At dusk young men sit about on bridges or congregate by teashops made of corrugated iron, while others shimmy up coconut palms to tap a fresh supply of sour moonshine toddy, and kids catch fish with poles.

Arriving in the backwaters

Getting there and around The chief embarkation point for houseboat trips through the backwaters is **Alappuzha** (Alleppey), 64 km south of Kochi on the shore of Lake Vembanad. Trains pull in at the station 3 km west of the town centre, while the bus stand is right on the waterfront, a short walk from several budget hotels and the main houseboat jetty. The other main centres are **Kumarakom**, across the lake from Alappuzha and a short taxi ride from the railway station at Kottayam; and **Kollam**, 70 km north of Trivandrum on the southern end of Lake Ashtamudi, linked to Alappuzha by road, rail and ferry.

Buses, trains and taxis link the main backwaters towns, but the most appealing ways to explore are by bike and boat. A cheap alternative to the full houseboat experience is to spend a few hours riding the ferries that ply across Lake Vembanad and south to Kollam. The 'tourist boat' from Alappuzha to Kollam gives you eight hours on the water at a bargain price of Rs 300, but it's a long day and lacks the peace of the best houseboats.➨ *See Transport, page 221.*

Tourist information In Kollam: **District Tourism Promotion Council (DTPC)** ① *Govt Guest House Complex, T0474-275 0170; also at DTPC bus station, T0474-274 5625, train station and ferry jetty, www.dtpckollam.com*, offers cruises, coach tours, and details of *Kathakali* performances. In Alappuzha: **KTDC** ① *Motel Araam, T0477-224 4460;* **ATDC**, *Komala Rd, T0477-226 4462, info@atdcalleppey.com;* **DTPC** ① *KSRTC bus station near jetty, T0477-225 3308, 0830-2000*, is helpful and offers good backwaters trips. In Kottayam: **tourist office** ① *Government Guest House, Nattakom, T0481-256 2219.* In Kumarakom: **Responsible Tourism Travel Desk** ① *T0481-252 4343*, books tours to meet local craftsmen.

Kollam (Quilon) → *For listings, see pages 215-222. Phone code: 0474. Population 361,400.*

Kollam is a busy shaded market town on the side of the Ashtamudi Lake and the headquarters of India's cashew nut trading and processing industry. It is congested and there's little reason to linger, but its position at the south end of Kerala's backwaters, where the waterways are less crowded than those further north, make it a good alternative starting point for boat trips up the canals.➨ *See What to do, page 219.*

Known to Marco Polo as 'Koilum', the port saw trading between Phoenicians, Persians, Greeks, Romans and Arabs as well as the Chinese. Kollam became the capital of the Venad Kingdom in the ninth century. The educated king Raja Udaya Marthanda Varma convened a special council at Kollam to introduce a new era. After extensive astronomical calculations the new era was established to start on 15 August AD 825. The town was associated with the early history of Christianity.

From the KSWTC boat jetty in the city centre you can hire houseboats or sightseeing boats (a houseboat in appearance but with large seating areas instead of bedrooms) to explore the palm-fringed banks of **Ashtamudi Lake**. You might see Chinese fishing nets and large-sailed dugouts carrying the local crops of coir, copra

Kerala backwaters

and cashew. **Munroe Island** is a popular destination for tours, with coir factories, good birdwatching and narrow canals to explore.

Kollam to Alappuzha → *Backwater tours: A ferry leaves for Alappuzha at 1030 (8 hrs).*

Mata   Amritanandamayi   Ashram
ⓘ *10 km north of Kollam at Vallikkavua, accessible by boat or road (through Kayambkulam or Karungappally), www. amritapuri.org, Rs 150 per day*, a giant, pink skyscraper sandwiched on the backwaters between the sea and the river, is the ashram of 'Amma' (the hugging 'Mother'). Thousands, Western and Indian alike, attend *Darshan* in hope of a hug. The ashram feels a bit lacklustre when Amma is on tour. She has hugged around three million people so far. In the early days, these used to last for minutes; now she averages one hug every 1½ seconds, so she can happily hug 30,000 in a day. The ashram has shops, a bank, library and internet. Smoking, sex and alcohol are forbidden.

Mannarsala, 32 km before Alappuzha, has a tremendously atmospheric **Nagaraja Temple** buried deep in a dense jungle forest. Traditionally *naga* (serpent) worshippers had temples in serpent groves. Mannarsala is the largest of these in Kerala with '30,000 images' of snake gods lined up along the path and among the trees, and many snakes living around the temple. Childless women come for special blessing and also return

Where to stay 🛌
Anthraper Home Stay **1**
Coconut Palms **9**
Emerald Isle
  Heritage Villa **7**
Keraleeyan Lakeside
  Ayurvedic Resort **3**
Marari Beach &
  Marari Beach Home **4**
Mata Amritanandamayi
  Ashram **10**
Olavipe **5**
Pooppally's Heritage
  Homestay **6**
Purity **3**
Vembanad House
  Homestay **8**

Preserving the backwaters for the future

The backwaters are lagoons fed by a network of perennial rivers with only two permanent outlets to the sea. The salts are flushed out between May and September, but sea waters rush inland by up to 20 km at the end of the monsoon and the waters become increasingly brackish through the dry season. This alternation between fresh and salt water has been essential to the backwaters' aquatic life. However, as land value has rocketed and reclamation for agriculture has reduced the surface water area, the backwaters' fragile ecology has been put at risk. Many of the original swamps have been destroyed and the waters are becoming increasingly saline.

Tourism, too, is taking its toll. Exploring the backwaters in a traditional *kettuvallam* is the ultimate Kerala experience but the popularity of these trips is having an adverse effect on the waterways. However, there are ways to help prevent further degeneration.

The trend so far has been for houseboat operators to offer larger, more luxurious boats (some even equipped with plunge pools) to meet the demands of tourists. The powerful outboard motors contribute heavily to pollution levels in the canals. Opting for a smaller boat not only helps ease environmental damage but also allows you to venture into the many narrower and less visited lagoons that the larger boats are unable to access.

Some operators are becoming aware of the damage being caused and are putting responsible travel practices in place. Support these efforts by checking that your houseboat is equipped with a chemical toilet (to prevent your waste being dumped into the canals) and if possible, opting for a solar-powered boat. Alternatively consider hiring a hand-propelled *thoni* or canoe as an entirely carbon neutral way of exploring this unique region.

for a 'thanksgiving' ceremony afterwards when the child born to the couple is placed on special scales and gifts in kind equalling the weight are donated. The temple is unusual for its chief priestess.

The village of **Haripad** has one of Kerala's oldest and most important Subrahmanya temples. The four-armed idol is believed to have been found in a river, and in August the three-day **Snake Boat Race** at Payipad, 3 km by bus, commemorates its rescue and subsequent building of the temple. There are boat processions on the first two days followed by competitive races on the third day. There is a guesthouse on **Mankotta Island** on the backwaters; the large comfortable rooms with bath are well kept.

Squeezed between the backwaters and the sea, and 12 km from Haripad station, **Thottapally** makes a good stop on a backwaters trip, two hours from Alappuzha.

About 10 km from Chengannur, **Aranmula** has the Parthasarathi Temple and is known for its unique metal mirrors. The **Vallamkali (or Utthrittathi) festival** on the last day of Onam (August-September) is celebrated with a boat race. The festival celebrates the crossing of the river by Krishna, who is believed to be in all the boats simultaneously, so the challenge is to arrive at the same time, rather than race.

Alappuzha (Alleppey) and around → *For listings, see pages 215-222.*
Phone code: 0477. Population: 177,100.

Alappuzha (pronounced *Alappoorra*) has a large network of canals, choked with the blue flowers of water hyacinth, passing through the town. It's the chief departure point for cruises into the backwaters and the venue for the spectacular **snake boat races** (see Festivals, page 219). **Houseboat trips** can be arranged at any of the numerous tour operators in town or directly, by heading to the boat dock just off VCNB Road. Although the town itself doesn't have many tourist sites, it's a pleasant, bustling place to walk around and there's a lovely stretch of undeveloped beach as well.

Mararikulam, 15 km north of Alappuzha on the coast, is a quiet, secluded beach which, until recently, was only known to the adjoining fishing village. The main village has a thriving cottage industry of coir and jute weaving.

Some 16 km southeast of Alappuzha is the hushed backwaters village of **Champakulam** where the only noise pollution is the odd squeak of a bicycle and

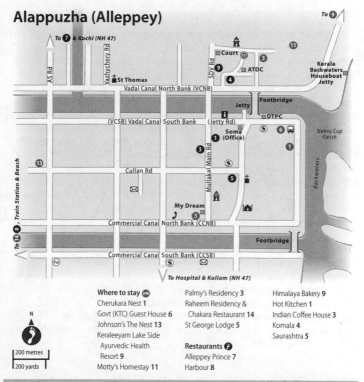

Alappuzha (Alleppey)

Where to stay
Cherukara Nest **1**
Govt (KTC) Guest House **6**
Johnson's The Nest **13**
Keraleeyam Lake Side
  Ayurvedic Health
  Resort **9**
Motty's Homestay **11**

Palmy's Residency **3**
Raheem Residency &
  Chakara Restaurant **14**
St George Lodge **5**

Restaurants
Alleppey Prince **7**
Harbour **8**

Himalaya Bakery **9**
Hot Kitchen **1**
Indian Coffee House **3**
Komala **4**
Saurashtra **5**

the slush of a canoe paddle. The Syrian Christian church of **St Mary's Forane** was built in 1870 on the site of a previous church dating from AD 427. The English-speaking priest is happy to show visitors round. Nearby the **St Thomas Statuary** makes wooden statues of Christ for export round the world: a 2-m-tall Jesus will set you back US$450. To get there, take the Alappuzha–Changanacherry bus (every 30 minutes) to Moncombu (Rs 4), then an auto-rickshaw to Champakulam (4 km, Rs 12). Alternatively the Alappuzha–Edathna ferry leaves at 0615 and 1715 and stops at Champakulam. In the backwater village of **Edathna**, you can visit the early Syrian **St George's Church**.

Kottayam and Kumarakom → *For listings, see pages 215-222. Phone code: 0481. Population: 60,700.*

Around Kottayam lies some of the lushest and most beautiful scenery in the state, with hills to its east and backwaters to its west. Kottayam itself is the capital of Kerala's Christian community, which belonged to the Orthodox Syrian tradition up till the Portuguese arrival. Two churches of the era survive 2 km north of town, in the 450-year-old **Cheria Palli** ('Small' St Mary's Church), which has beautiful vegetable dye mural paintings over its altar, and the **Valia Palli** ('Big' St Mary's Church), from 1550, with two Nestorian crosses carved on plaques behind two side altars. One has a Pallavi inscription on it, the other a Syriac. The cross on the left of the altar is the original and may be the oldest Christian artefact in India; the one to the right is a copy. By the altar there is an unusual small triptych of an Indian St George slaying a dragon. Note the interesting Visitors' Book (1898-1935); a paper cutting reports that "the church has attracted many European and native gentlemen of high position". Mass at Valia Palli at 0900 on Sunday, and Cheria Palli at 0730 on Sunday and Wednesday. The Malankara Syrian Church has its headquarters at Devalokam.

Ettumanoor, just north of Kottayam, has possibly the wealthiest temple in Kerala. The present Mahadeva temple was constructed in 1542, and is famous for its murals depicting scenes from the *Ramayana* and the Krishna legends, both inside and outside the *gopuram*. The typical circular shrine with a copper-covered conical roof encloses a square sanctuary. The **Arattu festival** in March draws thousands of pilgrims when gold elephant statues are displayed. They weigh 13 kg each.

Tucked among the waterways of Vembanad Lake, in mangrove, paddy and coconut groves with lily-studded shores, is **Kumarakom**, 16 km from Kottayam. Here are stacks of exclusive hotels where you can be buffed and Ayurvedically preened, bent into yoga postures, peacefully sunbathe or take to the water: perfect honeymoon territory.

The tourism department has developed an old rubber plantation set around Vembanad Lake into a **bird sanctuary** ① *1000-1800*. A path goes through the swamp to the main bird nesting area. **Pathiramanal** ('midnight sands') **Island** in the middle of the lake can be reached by boat. The best season for birdlife is June-August; to visit in the early morning.

For hotel and restaurant price codes and other relevant information, see pages 13-17.

⊙ Where to stay

Kollam (Quilon) *p210*
$$$$ Fragrant Nature Retreat and Resorts, Paravur, T0474-251 4000, www.fragrantnature. com. A 4-star luxury lakeside resort with spa, swimming pool and jacuzzi. Accommodation in lakeside rooms or villas.
$$$ Aquasserenne, Paravoor, 15 mins from town by road or boat, T0474-251 2410, www.aquasserenneindia.com. Splendid backwaters location, well-furnished chalets (some reassembled Kerala houses) with TV, restaurant, Ayurvedic massage/treatment, boat rides.
$$$-$$ Valiyavila Family Estate, Panamukkam Jetty, Kureepuzha, access by ferry (frequent, Rs 3) from Kollam boat jetty, T0474-270 1546, www.kollamlakeviewresort.com. 6 bright, breezy rooms in large house right on the lakeside. Peaceful location, lovely garden with hammocks, great views. Friendly, attentive staff. Wide selection of meals available. Eccentric 55 ft statue of 'Goddess of Light' in garden means you can't miss this place. Good discounts off-season. Canoe trips. Recommended.
$$ Nani, opposite Clock Tower, Chinnakada, T0474-275 1141, www.hotelnani.com. Swish business hotel close to the railway station, with smart if slightly overpriced rooms and friendly staff.
$$-$ Tamarind (KTDC), Ashramam, T0474-274 5538, www.ktdc.com/tamarind. Newly renovated rooms in a bland block building. All rooms with a/c, TV. Nice views of the waterway. Quiet location, restaurant, boat hire.

$ Government Guest House, Ashramam, T0474-274 3620. Live like the British Raj on a pauper's budget. 12 simply furnished rooms, all with attached bath, in the sprawling former residence of the British governor. More expensive rooms have bathrooms large enough to throw a party in. High ceilings, shady veranda, huge garden, bags of character, friendly staff. Some cheaper rooms are in bland modern building at the back. Meals on request. Recommended.
$ Mahalaxmi Lodge, opposite bus station, T0474-276 3823. Smallish, moderately clean, basic rooms, some with attached bath and TV.

Kollam to Alappuzha *p211, map p211*
$$-$ Coconut Palms, Kumarakodi, T0471-301 8100, www.coconutpalms.co.in. Idyllic 200-year-old traditional house in shaded compound, on backwaters and 100 m from sea. Yoga, Ayurveda and package deals available.
$ Mata Amritanandamayi Ashram, Vallikkavu, T0476-289 6399, www.amritapuri.org. Amma's ashram offers spartan but spacious accommodation in a multi-storey block, with hugs and South Indian meals included in the price. Western canteen (at extra cost) serves American-style meals.

Alappuzha (Alleppey) and around *p213, maps p211 and p213*
Book ahead to avoid the scramble off the ferry. Hotels north of Vadai Canal are quieter.
$$$$ Marari Beach, Mararikulam, Alappuzha, T0478-286 3801, www.cghearth.com. Well-furnished, comfortable, local-style cottages (garden villas,

garden pool villas and 3 deluxe pool villas) in palm groves – some with private pool. Good seafood, pool, Ayurvedic treatment, yoga in the morning, *pranayama* in the evening, shop, bikes, badminton, beach volleyball, boat cruises (including overnight houseboat), farm tours, friendly staff, discounts Apr-Sep. Recommended.

$$$$ Motty's Homestay, Kidangam-parambu Rd, Alappuzha, T(0)9847-032836, motty@alleppeybeach.com. Just 2 double rooms, with old furniture and 4-poster beds, in a private house on Alappuzha's outskirts. Excellent home-cooked breakfast and dinner included.

$$$$ Olavipe, Thekanatt Parayil, Olavipe, 25 km from Kochi, T0478-252 2255, www.olavipe. com. Century-old mansion belonging to family of Syrian Christan notables, on a 16-ha organic farm on the lush island of Olavipe. 5 rooms: 3 in the main house and 2 in a cottage.

$$$$ Purity, Muhamma, Aryakkara, (8 km from Alappuzha town), T0484-221 6666, www.malabarhouse.com. This beautiful Italianate villa, set on an acre of tropical grounds overlooking Lake Vembanad, is the most elegant lodging for miles around, with minimalist decor and a smattering of rare antiques. Huge rooms on the ground floor open out to a grassy lawn, but for the ultimate splurge check in to the huge turquoise-toned suite upstairs, with arched windows hoovering up views of the glassy lake. There's a pool and a discreet spa offering Ayurvedic treatments and yoga classes, and high-class dinners, which the chef can tailor to your wishes, are served around a pond in the courtyard. Superb in every respect and thoroughly recommended.

$$$$ Raheem Residency, Beach Rd, Alappuzha, T0477-223 9767, www.raheemresidency.com. Special luxury heritage hotel housed in a beautifully restored colonial 19th-century bungalow, on a pristine piece of Kerala's coast. 10 immaculate rooms, all with a/c and lovely antique furnishings. Palatial living room, jasmine-scented garden, excellent restaurant and a lovely pool under a velvet apple tree. The Irish journalist owner also offers the property as a writers' retreat (contact for prices). Easily the best address in Alappuzha. Recommended.

$$$$-$$$ Anthraper Home Stay, Cherthala, T0478-281 3211, www.anthrapergardens.com. Charming country house on the backwaters. Sprawling garden, cooking demonstrations, yoga, canoeing, fishing and river walks.

$$$$-$$$ Emerald Isle Heritage Villa, Kanjooparambil-Manimalathan, T0477-270 3899, www.emeraldislekerala.com. 4 rooms on the shores of an island of lush jungle, surrounded by sunken paddy field. Toddy on tap, cookery courses, boat trips, Ayurveda. The magic of the place begins on the 10-km journey from Alappuzha.

$$$ Pooppally's Heritage Homestay, Pooppally Junction, Nedumudy, T0477-276 2034, www.pooppallys.com. Traditional wooden cottage (water bungalow) and rooms, with open-air bathrooms, in 19th-century family farmhouse, shaded by a mango tree, set in a garden stretching down to the River Pampa. Great home-cooked food. Catch the ferry to Alappuzha for 90 mins of free houseboat.

$$$ Vembanad House Homestay, Puthankayal, Alappuzha, T0478-286 8696, www.vembanadhouse.com. 4 spacious rooms in stately heritage house surrounded by a lake in the pretty Muhamma area. Fresh food from the family farm cooked to Kerala recipes. Traditional architecture with modern bathrooms (no a/c). The house is managed by the delightful Balakrishnan family.

$$ Keraleeyam Lakeside Ayurvedic Health Resort, off Thathampally main road, Alappuzha, T0477-223 1468, www. keraleeyam.com. Keraleeyam sits on one of the prettiest nubs of the backwaters and is one of the most reasonable places to embark on a proper Ayurvedic programme. Doctors attend daily, there's no alcohol, and the menu is tailored according to your Ayurvedic body type. Cottages on the lake are better than the drab rooms in the main house.

$$-$ Cherukara Nest, just around the corner from KSRTC bus station, Alappuzha, T0477-225 1509, www. cherukaranest.com. Airy, cool, spotlessly clean rooms in a peaceful traditional family home. Rattan furniture on large shady porches. Pigeon house in the back garden. Very helpful and friendly. Meals available on request.

$ Government Guest House (KTDC), Jetty Rd, Alappuzha, T0477-224 4460. Bright yellow building next door to the KSRTC bus station. More expensive rooms are large but have tired-looking bathrooms. Cheaper bamboo-walled rooms on 3rd floor. Be careful not to trip over the staff members fast asleep on the veranda. Free bike hire, internet.

$ Johnson's The Nest, Lal Bagh Factory Ward (West of Convent Sq), Alappuzha, T0477-224 5825, www.johnsonskerala. com. Friendly family-run guesthouse in a quiet street away from the town centre. 6 rooms, each with balcony. Free pick-up from bus station, internet, houseboat facility, popular.

$ Palmy's Residency, north of new Matha footbridge, Alappuzha, T0477-223 5938, www.palmyresidency.com. Large, clean rooms with fly-screens and fans. Quiet but central location. More expensive rooms have big balconies to lounge in. Local waterway canoe trips (4-5 hrs, Rs 200 per hr). Free bike hire. Recommended.

$ St George Lodge, CCNB Rd, Alappuzha, T0477-225 1620. Don't let the dilapidated façade put you off – this is an excellent cheapie. 80 very basic but clean rooms, some with attached bath. Friendly staff.

Kottayam and Kumarakom *p214*

In Kumarakom 26% taxes are added to bills.

$$$$ Coconut Lagoon, Vembanad Lake Kumarakom (CGH Earth), T0484-301 1711, www.cghearth.com. Comfortable heritage *tharavads* (traditional Keralite wooden cottages), heritage mansions and pool villas. Outdoor restaurant facing lagoon, good dinner buffet, pool, yoga, very friendly, Ayurvedic treatments, attractive waterside location, spectacular approach by boat (10 mins from road). Vechoor cows mow the lawns. Recommended. Discounts Apr-Sep.

$$$$ Philipkutty's Farm, Pallivathukal, Ambika Market, Vechoor, Kottayam, T0482-927 6529, www.philipkuttysfarm. com. 5 immaculate waterfront villas sharing an island on Vembanad Lake. The delightful working farm boasts coconut, banana, nutmeg, coca and vanilla groves. Delicious home cooking and personal attention from all the family. No a/c or TV. Cooking and painting holidays.

$$$$ Privacy at Sanctuary Bay, Kannamkara, opposite Kumarakom, T0484-221 6666, www.malabarhouse. com. Absolute lakeside isolation in a fully staffed but fully self-contained 3-bedroom bungalow. Modern opulent interiors hide behind the old Keralite facade, and there's stunning veranda looking out across the lake.

$$$$ Vivanta by Taj, Kumarakom, T0481-252 5711, www.vivantabytaj.com. 19 a/c rooms, in sensitively renovated 120-year-old 'Bakers' House', as featured in *The God of Small Things*. Also newer cottages and a moored houseboat, good meals. An intimate hotel but packed.

$$$$ Waterscapes (KTDC), Kumarakom, T0481-252 5861. Idyllic cottage experience on the backwaters. All chalets have a/c and cable TV. Pool, bar, restaurant.

$$ GK's Riverview Homestay, Valliadu, Aymanam, T0481-259 7527, www.gk homestay-kumarakom.com. Set amid paddy fields in the heart of *God of Small Things* country, George and Dai's lovely house offers home comforts in the shape of simple immaculate rooms, hammocks lazily overlooking the river, and superb Kerala cooking. The consummate hosts are always on hand to share secrets of the area, and arrange excellent tours.

$$-$ Aida, MC Rd, 2 km from railway, Kottayam, T0481-256 8391, www.hotel aidakerala.com. Clean, pleasant rooms with bath, some with a/c. Front rooms can be noisy. Restaurant, bar, helpful staff.

$$-$ Anjali Park, KK Rd, 4 km from railway, Kottayam, T0481-256 3661. Decent rooms with bath and a/c. Good restaurants.

$ Ambassador Hotel, KK Rd (set back), T0481-256 3293. Friendly Indian-style hotel with good restaurant and bar. Very good value.

$ Green Park, Kurian Uthup Rd, Nagampadam, T0481-256 3331, greenparkhotel@yahoo.co.in. Adequate rooms with bath. A/c rooms noisy, non-a/c at back too hot. Restaurant.

$ Kaycee's Residency, off YMCA Rd, Kottayam, T0481-256 3440. Good value, clean, decent-sized rooms.

$ PWD Rest House, on hill 2 km south of Kottayam, T0481-256 8147. Remarkable late 19th-century building with superb furniture, overlooking vista of paddy fields.

$ Venad Tourist Complex, Ancheril Building, near State Bus Stand, Kottayam, T0481-258 1383. Modern building with clean rooms. Restaurant. Recommended.

❼ Restaurants

Kollam (Quilon) *p210*
$ Eat N Pack, near Taluk Office, Main St. Excellent value, clean, good choice of dishes, friendly. Recommended.

$ Indian Coffee House, Main Rd. For good coffee and vegetarian and non-vegetarian South Indian food. Nice waiter service and good atmosphere.

$ Suprabhatam, opposite clock tower, Main St. Adequate vegetarian.

Alappuzha (Alleppey) and around
p213, maps p211 and p213
$$$ Chakara, Raheem Residency, Beach Rd. Rooftop dining with attentive service and excellent multi-cuisine food. The 4-course set dinner menu (pegged at rupee equivalent to 11) is unbeatable value. Alcohol available.

$$ Alleppey Prince Hotel, AS Rd (NH47), 2 km from town. International, comfortable a/c restaurant, reasonable food, alcohol in bar only.

$ Harbour, Beach Rd. Specializes in seafood, also has Indian and European dishes. Excellent value. Alcohol available.

$ Himalaya Bakery, SDV Rd. Large range of sweet and savoury pastries, and other snacks, to take out or eat in at the tiny seating area.

$ Hot Kitchen, Mullakal Main Rd.
Good for *iddli, dosa, vadai*, etc.
$ Indian Coffee House, Mullakal Main Rd.
Good value, tasty non-vegetarian snacks.
$ Komala, **Komala Hotel**, Zilla Court
Ward. Excellent South Indian *thalis*
and Chinese.
$ SAS, Jetty Rd. Good South Indian
vegetarian and Chinese.
$ Saurashtra, Cullan Rd. Vegetarian, ample
helpings on banana leaf, locally popular.

Kottayam and Kumarakom *p214*
The following are in Kottayam. For
options in Kumarakom, see hotels in
Where to stay.
$$ Aida, MC Rd. Large, uninspired menu.
Pleasantly cool 'chilled' drinks may arrive
slightly warm.
$$ Green Park, Kurian Uthup Rd.
International menu. Reasonable but
slow service. Dinner in mosquito-ridden
garden (or in own room for guests).
Alcohol available.

Near the state bus station
$ Black Stone, T B Rd. Good vegetarian.
$ Milkshake Bar, T B Rd, opposite
Blackstone Hotel. 20 flavours.

⊛ Festivals

Kollam (Quilon) *p210*
19 Jan Kerala Tourism Boat Race.
Apr Colourful 10-day **Vishnu festival**
in Asram Temple with procession
and fireworks.
Aug-Sep Avadayattukotta Temple
celebrates a 5-day **Ashtami Rohani**
festival. **Muharram** too is observed
with processions at the town mosque.

Alappuzha (Alleppey) and around
p213, maps p211 and p213
For details see www.keralatourism.org.

9-12 Jan Cheruppu is celebrated in the
Mullakkal Devi Temple with a procession
of elephants, music and fireworks.
17-19 Jan Tourism Boat Race.
Jul/Aug DTPC Boat Race (3rd Sat) in the
backwaters. **Champakulam Boat Race**,
Kerala's oldest, takes place 16-km ferry
ride away on 'Moolam' day. The Nehru
Trophy, inaugurated in 1952, is the largest
Snake Boat Race in the state. As many
as 40 highly decorated 'snake boats' are
rowed by several dozen oarsmen before
huge crowds. Naval helicopters do mock
rescue operations and stunt flying. Entry
by ticket; Rs 125 (Rs 60/75 tickets allow
access in to overcrowded and dangerous
areas). There are other snake boat races
held throughout the year.

⊙ What to do

Kollam (Quilon) *p210*
Tour operators
As well as houseboat trips on traditional
kettuvallams, there are also the much
cheaper options of Kollam–Alappuzha
cruises and shorter canal journeys to
Munroe Island. The gentle pace and
tranquil waterways make these tours
very worthwhile, but the heat and
humidity may sometimes make overnight
stays on houseboats uncomfortable.
DTPC, boat jetty, T0474-275 0170,
www.dtpckollam.com. Daily 8-hr
backwater cruise from Kollam to
Alappuzha; depart 1030 (Rs 300). You can
be dropped off halfway at Alumkadavu
(Rs 200) or at Vallikkavu for the Ashram
(Rs 150). The only stops are for meals;
some travellers find the trip a little too
long and samey. A good alternative is
a canal trip to Munroe Island village;
depart 0900, 1300 (6 hrs return, Rs 300).
  A more expensive option is to hire
a *kettuvallam*. For a 1-bed houseboat

prices start at Rs 5000 for 8 hrs day trip, Rs 6500 for overnight, to Rs 12,300 for 2 days and 1 night, inclusive of all meals. There are also cruise packages which combine a day cruise with an overnight stay at a backwater resort (Rs 3500).

Southern Backwaters Tour Operators, opposite KRSTC Bus Station, Jetty Rd, Kollam, T(0)9495-976037, www.southern backwaters.com. Independent operators. A/c deluxe and standard houseboats for 1- to 3-night packages. Also motorboat cruises and Munroe Island tours.

Alappuzha (Alleppey) and around
p213, maps p211 and p213
Tour operators

Alappuzha is the starting point of backwater boat trips to Kollam, Changanacherry, Kottayam and Kochi, and everybody you meet seems to have a houseboat to rent. Some find cruising the backwaters of Lake Vembanad utterly idyllic and restful, while for others the sluggish pace of the houseboats – combined with the heavy crowding of the waterways close to Alappuzha – a form of slow torture. Most first-time visitors go for an overnight tour, which is in some ways the worst of all worlds: you're often moored alongside a raft of other boats, you get trotted through the standard tourist 'village' visits (ie shopping trips), and you simply don't have time to get away from the crowds. If you can spare an extra night or more, longer cruises let you get away into the deeper reaches of the backwaters where canal life still continues more or less unmolested by tourism. On the other hand, if you just want a taste of the scenery, a day cruise – or even one of the cheap ferries that ply the lakes and canals – might satisfy you at a fraction of the price of a night on a houseboat.

It's always worth booking in advance during high season, when the theoretical government-set rates (which are printed and displayed in the DTPC booking office at the jetty in Alappuzha) go out the window, and houseboat owners jack the prices up by 50-80%. Houseboats vary widely depending on the number of bedrooms, facilities (some come with a/c, flatscreen TVs and DVD players), quality of food and the crew's level of English. Booking ahead gives you some degree of certainty over the level of luxury you will find; it also allows you to circumvent the persistent dockside touts, whose commissions mean that any discount you can negotiate comes at the cost of corners cut on the trip. If you're coming outside peak season, and don't mind spending a morning scouting around, making a booking on the spot gives you a chance to inspect a number of boats before agreeing on a price.

The following companies are generally at the top end of the market, but offer reliably good (in some cases superb) service.

CGH Earth, T0484-301 1711, Kochi, www.cghearth.com. Runs 'spice boat' cruises in modified *kettuvallams*, which are idyllic if not luxurious: shaded sit-outs, modern facilities including solar panels for electricity, 2 double rooms, limited menu. US$325.

Discovery 1, **Malabar House**, Fort Kochi, see page 230. **Malabar Escapes**' take on the houseboat is silent and pollutant free. Because it's nimble and trips are for a minimum of 3 nights, it's guaranteed to take you far from the wider watery motorways bigger rice boats ply. 1 bedroom, large bathroom and sitting room plus sun deck. Food is to Malabar House's high standard.

DTPC, Jetty Rd, T0477-225 1796, www.dtpcalappuzha.com. Runs the same 8-hr backwater cruises as its sister office in Kollam, except going the other way. Departs 1030 from Alappuzha ferry jetty (Rs 400). There is also a shorter round-trip to Kumarakom (4 hrs, Rs 200), and canoe trips through local waterways (Rs 200 per hr).

Lakes and Lagoons Tour Co, Punnamada, T0477-226 6842, www.lakes lagoons.com. Solar-powered 2-bed boats. Consistently recommended operator.

Rainbow Cruises, VCNB Rd, opposite jetty, Alappuzha, T0477-226 1375, www.rainbowcruises.in. Solar powered with high safety standards and emergency speedboat support (houseboats have been known to sink).

⊖ Transport

Kollam (Quilon) *p210*
Local auto-rickshaws are plentiful and bikes are available for hire.

Bus Local buses are plentiful. Long distance buses run from the KSRTC station, T0474-275 2008. Buses every 30 mins from 0600 to **Kochi** (3½ hrs, Rs 87) via **Alappuzha** (2 hrs, Rs 55) and other towns on the coast. Buses run 24 hrs to **Thiruvananthapuram**, leaving every 10 mins in the day and every 30 mins during the night (2 hrs, Rs 44). Change at Thiruvananthapuram for **Kovalam**. It is difficult to get to **Varkala** by bus; take the train.

Car To **Alappuzha**, Rs 750, from the bus station.

Ferry Public ferries sail to **Ghuhandapuram** at 0730, 1100, 1330, 1545 and 1745 (1 hr, Rs 5) and then return to Kollam. It's an interesting journey with views of village life and Chinese fishing nets on the way. The 1745 departure lets you enjoy sunset over the waterways.

Train Junction railway station, T131, is about 3 km east of the boat jetty and bus station. There are several trains a day south to **Thiruvananthapuram** including the *Island Exp 16526*, 1335 (1¾ hrs), which continues to **Kanniyakumari** (4¼ hrs). All the trains stop at **Varkala** (½ hr).

An equal number of trains head north to **Ernakulam** (**Cochin**) and points beyond, including the *TVC Chennai Exp 12696* (continues to **Chennai**, 15 hrs); and the *Island Exp 16525* (continues to **Bengaluru**, 16 hrs).

Alappuzha (Alleppey) and around
p213, maps p211 and p213
It is only a 5-min walk between the ferry jetty and the KSRTC bus station despite what many local rickshaw drivers will tell you.

Bus From the KSRTC Bus Station, T0477-225 2501, there are frequent long-distance buses to **Kochi**, 0630-2330 (1½ hrs, Rs 37); **Thiruvananthapuram**, 0600-2000, (4 hrs, Rs 96) via **Kollam** (2 hrs, Rs 55); **Champakulam**, 0515-2000 (45 mins, Rs 10) and **Kottayam**, 0730-1800 (1½ hrs, Rs 30). There are several buses daily to **Coimbatore**, from 0600 (7 hrs, Rs 96).

Car A car with driver from Alappuzha to **Fort Kochi** (65 km) costs Rs 500-600.

Ferry Public ferries, T0477-225 2015, sail to **Kottayam**, 0730, 1000, 1130, 1300, 1430 and 1730 (3 hrs) and **Changanassery**, 1000, 1300 and 1730 (3 hrs). Also frequent services to **Nedumudi** (1 hr).

Train The train station, T0477-225 3965, is on the coastal route from **Trivandrum– Varkala–Kollam– Ernakulam**, 3 km from the jetty. Frequent trains in both directions.

Kottayam and Kumarakom *p214*
Bus The new **Private Bus Station** is near the railway station. Buses to Alappuzha only leave from the **KSRTC Bus Station**, 2 km away; local buses to to **Kumarakom Tourist Village** also run frequently from here. There are fast and frequent long-distance buses to **Alappuzha**, every 45 mins (2 hrs, Rs 30); **Thiruvananthapuram**, every 30 mins (4 hrs, Rs 90); **Kochi**, every 30 mins (1½ hrs, Rs 45) and **Kumily**, every hour (4½ hrs, Rs 68). There are 2 evening departures to **Madurai**, 2045 and 2145 (7 hrs, Rs 120) and 5 buses daily head to **Munnar**, 0600-1600 (5 hrs, Rs 100).

Car Car with driver to **Thekkady**, Rs 850, 4 hrs.

Ferry Ferries leave from the **Kodimatha Jetty** except during the monsoons, when you should head to the **Town Jetty** 3 km southwest of the train station. Ferries to **Alappuzha**, 0730, 0930, 1130, 1430,1730 (3 hrs). This is an interesting trip but gets very busy in peak season. Other departures include **Champakulam**, 1530 (4 hrs) and **Mannar**, 1430 (3 hrs).

Train Trains run throughout the day, south to **Thiruvananthapuram** via **Kollam** and **Varkala**, and north to Ernakulam and beyond. No trains to Alappuzha, which is on the parallel coastal line.

ⓘ Directory

Kollam (Quilon) *p210*
Medical services District Hospital, T0474-279 3409. **Post** Head Post Office, Parameswara Nagar. Mon-Sat until 2000, Sun until 1800.

Alappuzha (Alleppey) and around
p213, maps p211 and p213
Banks Catholic Syria Bank, Jetty Rd, and State Bank of India, Cullan Rd. Both have ATMs. **Internet** Several places on Mullakal Rd. **Net Café**, opposite Kidangamparampu Temple, charges Rs 20 per hr. **Medical services** District Hospital, T0477-225 3324. **Post** Off Mullakal Rd.

Kottayam and Kumarakom *p214*
Banks In Kottayam: Banks are clustered around Ghandi Sq on TB and MC Rds including **Bank of India**, MC Rd and **Ing Bank**, TB Rd. Both have ATMs. **Internet** Many places around Ghandi Sq. **Medical services** District Hospital, T0481-256 3651. **Post** MC Rd, 0800-2000, 1400-1730 on holidays.

Fort Kochi and Ernakulam

Charming Fort Kochi (Cochin) is a true one-off in modern Kerala: a layer cake of colonial India, where British parade grounds overlay Portuguese forts, where Dutch palaces slowly crumble into the soil alongside synagogues, where every turn takes you down some romantically fossilized narrow winding street. Despite a tourist invasion that's flooded the lanes with antique shops, internet cafés and shops flogging fisherman trousers, parts of the ramshackle island still feel frozen back in the 15th and 16th centuries, and the huge trees here are so old that their parasitic aphids are as tall as trees themselves. In the southern quarter of Mattancherry, row upon row of wood-fronted doors give glimpses of rice and spice merchants sitting sifting their produce into small 'tasting' bowls. The iconic batwing Chinese fishing nets, first used in the 14th century, stand on the shores of the north fort area, silhouetted against the lapping waters of one of the world's finest natural harbours: a wide bay interrupted by narrow spits of land and coconut-covered islands.

Before arriving in Fort Kochi, however, you have to negotiate the city's modern centre of gravity – grubby, dynamic Ernakulam, a Rs 5 ferry ride and half a world away across the harbour. While Fort Kochi languishes dreamily in the past, its ambitious sibling is expanding outwards and upwards at breakneck pace, propelled by the vast new container terminal on Vallarpadam Island. The first port in India capable of handling the huge container ships that until now have had to berth in Colombo or Singapore, Kochi stands poised to transform India's logistical landscape, and over the next decade this hitherto sleepy southern city will undoubtedly assume a front-and-centre seat in the future of the Indian economy.

Arriving in Fort Kochi and Ernakulam → *Phone code: 0484.*
Population: 1.15 million (Kochi 596,500, Ernakulam 558,000).

Getting there

Kochi's mellow little international airport is at Nedumbassery, 36 km northeast of the city centre. The smoothest way into town is to arrange a pick-up from your hotel (Rs 900-1500 depending on type of car and what your hosts feel the market will support). Alternatively, hire a prepaid taxi from the booth after Customs; a transfer to Fort Kochi costs around Rs 800, a little less to downtown Ernakulam. Air-conditioned buses leave the airport for Fort Kochi bus stand, right in the centre next to the Chinese fishing nets, between 0500 and 1900, taking 90 minutes.

Most trains pull into Ernakulam Junction station in the busy city centre. State-run long distance buses arrive at the Central Bus Stand, 500 m north of Ernakulam Junction, while private buses pull in to the terminal at Kaloor Junction about 2 km further north. Local buses, taxis and auto-rickshaws connect the various transport hubs. A rickshaw from either to the main jetty, for Fort Kochi, costs approximately Rs 25. ▸▸ *See Transport, page 236.*

Getting around

Fort Kochi has all the sights and a huge number of hotels, and many visitors never leave its cosy bubble. The quiet roads are easy to explore on foot or by bicycle, with an occasional cameo from an auto-rickshaw. If you need to get across to Ernakulam there are two routes: a circuitous trip by bus, taxi or auto-rickshaw (Rs 250-500), or one of the cheap and cheerful ferries that chug across the harbour to Ernakulam's Main Jetty – an enjoyably breezy 30-minute trip that's most atmospheric around sunset (ferries run 0600 to 2130). From the jetty you can catch a rickshaw to the railway station or bus stand for around Rs 40. Leave plenty of spare time if you need to travel during peak hours. After 2130 public transport begins to grind to a halt and you'll need to take a rickshaw or taxi to get around.

Tourist information

Kerala Tourism Development Corporation (KTDC) ① *Shanmugham Rd, Ernakulam, T0484-235 3234, 0800-1800.* Tourist Desk ① *Main Boat Jetty, Ernakulam, T0484-237 1761, and on Tower Rd in Fort Kochi, T0484-221 6129, www.touristdesk.in, 0900-1800.* This travel agent, with good maps and local information, runs daily backwater tours, has information on more than 2000 temple festivals in Kerala, and runs **Costa Malabari** guesthouse (see page 269).

Background

"If China is where you make your money," declared Italian traveller Nicolas Conti in the Middle Ages, "then Kochi surely is the place to spend it." Kochi has acted as a trading port since at least Roman times, and was a link in the main trade route between Europe and China. From 1795 until India's Independence the long outer sand spit, with its narrow beach leading to the wide bay inland, was under British political control. The inner harbour was in Kochi State, while most of the hinterland was in the separate state of Travancore. The division of political authority delayed development of the harbour facilities until 1920-1923, when the approach channel was dredged so ships that could get through the Suez Canal could dock here, opening the harbour to modern shipping.

Places in Fort Kochi and Ernakulam → *For listings, see pages 230-237.*

If you land at the Customs Jetty, a plaque in nearby Vasco da Gama Square commemorates the landing of Vasco da Gama in 1500. Next to it is the **Stromberg Bastion**, "one of the seven bastions of Fort Emanuel built in 1767", named after the Portuguese king. Little is left of the 1503 Portuguese fort except ruins. Along the seafront, between the Fort Kochi Bus Stand, the boat jetty and the Dutch cemetery, run the cantilevered Chinese fishing nets. These are not unique to Kochi, but are perhaps uniquely accessible to the short-stay visitor.

Mattancherry Palace and **Parikshith Thampuran Museum** ① *Mattancherry, daily 1000-1700 except Fri and national holidays, Rs 2, photography not allowed*, was first built by the Portuguese around 1557 as a sweetener for the Raja Veera Kerala Varma of Kochi bestowing them trading rights. In 1663, it was largely rebuilt by the new trading power, the Dutch. The layout follows the traditional Kerala pattern known as *nalukettus*, meaning four buildings, which are set around a quadrangle with a temple. There are display cases of the Rajas of Kochi's clothes, palanquins, etc, but these are no match for the amazing murals. The royal bedroom's low wooden walls squeezes the whole narrative of the *Ramayana* into about 45 late 16th-century panels. Every inch is covered with rich red, yellow, black and white. To the south of the Coronation Hall, the *kovinithilam* (staircase room) has six large 18th-century murals including the coronation of Rama. Vishnu is in a room to the north. Two of the women's bedrooms downstairs have 19th-century murals with greater detail. They relate Kalidasa's *Kumarasambava* and themes from the *Puranas*. This stuff is triple x-rated. If you are of a sensitive disposition avert your eyes from panel 27 and 29, whose deer, birds and other animals are captioned as giving themselves up to 'merry enjoyment', a coy way of describing the furious copulation and multiple penetration in plain view. Krishna, meanwhile, finally works out why he was given so many limbs, much to the evident satisfaction of the gopis who are looking on.

The **synagogue** ① *Mattancherry, Sun-Fri 1000-1200, 1500-1700, no video cameras, shoes must be removed*, dating from 1568 (rebuilt in 1662), is near Mattancherry Palace at the heart of what is known as Jew Town, which is a fascinating mixture of shops (some selling antiques), warehouses and spice auction rooms. Stepping inside the synagogue is an extraordinary experience of light and airiness, partly due to the 18th-century blue Cantonese ceramic tiles, hand painted and each one different, covering the floor. There are original glass oil lamps. For several centuries there were two Jewish communities. The earlier group (often referred to as 'black' Jews), according to one source, settled here as early as 587 BC. The earliest evidence

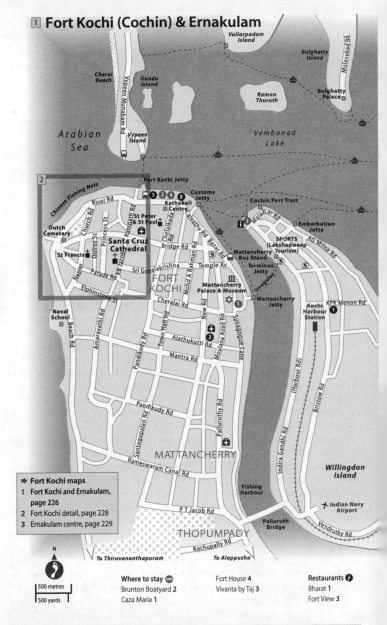

1 Fort Kochi (Cochin) & Ernakulam

Vallarpadam Island

Balghatty Island

Mulavukad Rd

Cheral Beach

Gundu Island

Vypeen Munakam Rd

Bolghatty Palace

Arabian Sea

Raman Thuruth

Vembanad Lake

Vypeen Island

2

Chinese Fishing Nets

Fort Kochi Jetty

Customs Jetty

Cochin Port Trust

River Rd

Ramath Rd

3 2 4 8

Kathakali Centre

Embarkation Jetty

Malabar Rd

Church Rd

Princess St

St Peter & St Paul

Calvathy Rd

SPORTS (Lakshadweep Tourism)

AG Mline Rd

Dutch Cemetery

Ouros St

Chelakada

Bridge Rd

Bazar Rd

Mattancherry Bus Stand

Santa Cruz Cathedral

St Francis

Napier

Parade Rd

Sri Gopalakrishna

Mohd R Rahman Rd

Temple Av

Terminus Jetty

Mattancherry Jetty

Elphinstone St

FORT KOCHI

Mattancherry Palace & Museum

Kochi Harbour Station

KPK Menon Rd

Naval School

Cheralai Rd

Town Hall Rd

New Rd

Beach Rd

Amaravathi Rd

Alathukutti Rd

2

Moulana Azad Rd

Syagogue Lane

Harbour Rd

Bistow Rd

Mantra Rd

Pandikudy Rd

Pandikudy Rd

MATTANCHERRY

Indira Gandhi Rd

Willingdon Island

Santogopalan Rd

Palluruthy Rd

Rameswaram Canal Rd

Fishing Harbour

Indian Navy Airport

→ **Fort Kochi maps**
1 Fort Kochi and Ernakulam, page 226
2 Fort Kochi detail, page 228
3 Ernakulam centre, page 229

P T Jacob Rd

Palluruth Bridge

Vendruthy Rd

THOPUMPADY

Kochupally Rd

To Thiruvananthapuram

To Alappuzha

N

500 metres
500 yards

Where to stay 🛏
Brunton Boatyard 2
Caza Maria 1

Fort House 4
Vivanta by Taj 3

Restaurants 🍴
Bharat 1
Fort View 3

Kayikkas 2
Seagull 8

of their presence is a copper inscription dated AD 388 by the Prince of Malabar. Those referred to as 'white' Jews came much later, when, with Dutch and then British patronage, they played a major role as trading agents. Speaking fluent Malayalam, they made excellent go-betweens for foreigners seeking to establish contacts. The community has shrunk to six families, with many now settled at Moshav Nevatim in Israel's Negev desert. The second Jewish synagogue (in Ernakulam) is deserted.

St Francis' Church ⓘ *Fort Kochi, Mon-Sat 0930-1730, Sun afternoon, Sun services in English 0800 (except for the 3rd Sun of each month)*, was originally dedicated to Santo Antonio, the patron saint of Portugal and is the first church to reflect the new and European-influenced tradition. The original wooden structure (circa 1510) was replaced by the present stone building (there is no authority for the widely quoted date of 1546). Vasco da Gama died on the site in 1524 and was originally buried in the cemetery. Some 14 years later his body was removed to Portugal. The church was renamed St Francis in 1663, and the Dutch both converted it to a Protestant church and substantially modified it. They retained control until 1795, adding the impressive gable façade at the entrance. In 1804, it became an Anglican church. In 1949 the congregation joined the Church of South India. Note the old string-pulled *punkahs* (fans) and the Dutch and Portuguese gravestones that now line the walls.

Santa Cruz Cathedral, near St Francis' Church, originally built in 1557 by the Portuguese, and used as a warehouse by the British in the 18th century, was rebuilt in the early 20th century. It has lovely carved wooden panels and pulpit, and an interesting graveyard.

Museum of Kerala History ① *Ernakulam, 1000-1200 and 1400-1600 except Mon and national holidays*, starts with Neolithic man through St Thomas and Vasco da Gama. Historical personalities of Kerala are represented with sound and light.

Around Fort Kochi and Ernakulam

Bolghatty Island has the 'palace' (circa 1745), set in large gardens and converted into a hotel. It was originally built by the Dutch and then became the home of the British Resident at the court of the Raja of Kochi after 1799. There is still some atmosphere of colonial decay which haunted the old building in its pre-modernized form and gave it much of its charm.

Vypeen Island lies on the northwestern fringe of the harbour. There are quiet beaches here, along with the Portuguese Azhikotta Fort, built around 1503. You can see cannon holes on the walls of the octagonal fort, which was garrisoned by 20 soldiers when it guarded the entrance to the backwaters. Vehicle ferries make the crossing from Fort Kochi.

② Fort Kochi detail

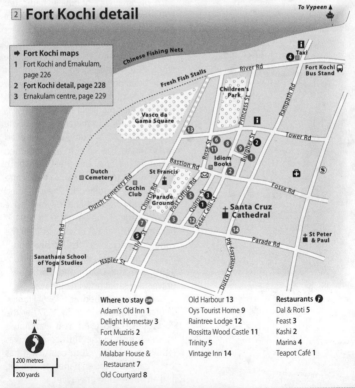

➡ Fort Kochi maps
1 Fort Kochi and Ernakulam, page 226
2 Fort Kochi detail, page 228
3 Ernakulam centre, page 229

Where to stay	Old Harbour **13**	Restaurants
Adam's Old Inn **1**	Oys Tourist Home **9**	Dal & Roti **5**
Delight Homestay **3**	Raintree Lodge **12**	Feast **3**
Fort Muziris **2**	Rossitta Wood Castle **11**	Kashi **2**
Koder House **6**	Trinity **5**	Marina **4**
Malabar House & Restaurant **7**	Vintage Inn **14**	Teapot Café **1**
Old Courtyard **8**		

200 metres
200 yards

Our Lady's Convent ⓘ *Palluruthy, Thoppampady, 14 km south, by appointment, T0484-223 0508,* specializes in high-quality needlework lace and embroidery. The sisters are very welcoming and it is an interesting tour with items for sale.

③ Ernakulam centre

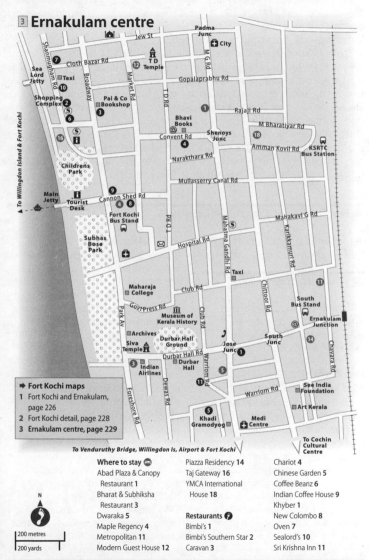

→ Fort Kochi maps
1 Fort Kochi and Ernakulam, page 226
2 Fort Kochi detail, page 228
3 Ernakulam centre, page 229

N

200 metres
200 yards

Where to stay 🛏
Abad Plaza & Canopy Restaurant 1
Bharat & Subhiksha Restaurant 3
Dwaraka 5
Maple Regency 4
Metropolitan 11
Modern Guest House 12
Piazza Residency 14
Taj Gateway 16
YMCA International House 18

Restaurants 🍴
Bimbi's 1
Bimbi's Southern Star 2
Caravan 3
Chariot 4
Chinese Garden 5
Coffee Beanz 6
Indian Coffee House 9
Khyber 1
New Colombo 8
Oven 7
Sealord's 10
Sri Krishna Inn 11

Raksha ① *Yasmin Manzil, VII/370 Darragh-es-Salaam Rd, Kochangadi, T0484-222 7707*, works with children with physical and mental disabilities. Interested volunteers should contact the principal.

Hill Palace Archaeological Museum ① *Thirpunithura, 12 km east of Ernakulam, Tue-Sun 0900-1230, 1400-1700, Rs 11*, has a huge number of historical records and artefacts of the old royal state of Cochin, with portraits, ornaments, porcelain, palm leaf records and ancient musical instruments.

Some 45 km northeast of Kochi is the town of **Kalady**, on the bank of the Periyar River. This popular pilgrimage site was the birthplace of one of India's most influential philosophers, **Sankaracharya**, who lived in the eighth century. He founded the school of *advaita* philosophy, which spread widely across South India. The **Adi Sankara Kirti Stambha Mandapam** ① *0700-1900, small entry fee*, is a nine-storied octagonal tower, 46 m high, and details Sri Sankara's life and works and the Shan Maths, or six ways to worship. Inside the **Shankara Temple** (Hindus only), are two shrines, one dedicated to Sankaracharya and the other to the goddess Sarada. The management of the shrines is in the hands of the Math at Sringeri in Karnataka. Kalady can easily be visited in an afternoon from Kochi.

⊕ Fort Kochi and Ernakulam listings

For hotel and restaurant price codes and other relevant information, see pages 13-17.

● Where to stay

Fort Kochi has bags more character than the busy commercial centre of Ernakulam; book well in advance for the Christmas period.

Fort Kochi *p223, maps p226 and p228*
$$$$ Koder House, Tower Rd, T0484-221 8485, www.koderhouse.com. Boutique hotel in a striking heritage town house formerly owned by prominent Jewish family, and sometime home to ambassadors and heads of state. Luxury suites have huge bedrooms, sitting room, bathroom and jacuzzi. Tiny plunge pool in the back courtyard, spa with massage and facials, plus valet, business centre, superb home-cooked food.

$$$$ Malabar House, 1/268 Parade Rd, near St Francis' Church, T0484-221 6666, www.malabarhouse.com. Fort Kochi's original boutique hotel, and still one of its best. Big and beautiful high-ceilinged rooms in a sensitively restored 18th-century mansion, set around a flagstoned courtyard with an excellent restaurant and small swimming pool. Helpful staff, reliable airport pick-ups and a funky bar make this a perfect if pricey first place to hang your hat.
$$$$ Old Harbour, Tower Rd, T0484-221 8006, www.oldharbourhotel.com. Impeccably restored, 300-year-old Portuguese and Dutch building slap on the harbour front. Rooms have private balconies, some with harbour views. Large garden plus swimming pool, Wi-Fi, Ayurveda, jacuzzi.
$$$$ Trinity, 1/658 Ridsdale Rd, Parade Ground, T0484-221 6669, www.malabar house.com. Ultra-modern, minimalist and modish 3-bedroom apartment

with airy bathrooms, spacious sitting/ dining room, mezzanine, tiny swimming pool. Service is immaculate, food is at **Malabar House** on the other side of the parade ground.

$$$$ Vivanta by Taj, Willingdon Island, T0484-664 3000, www.vivantabytaj.com. Large, swish hotel overlooking the harbour, with beautifully renovated rooms, the usual superb Taj service. Pool, spa, gym and 5 bars and restaurants.

$$$$-$$$ Brunton Boatyard, Calvathy Rd, T0484-301 1711, www.cghearth.com. Easily the best address in Fort Kochi, adjacent to the Chinese fishing nets on the edge of the Arabian Sea. 18 characterful rooms and 4 deluxe suites, each of which overlooks the harbour in an elegantly restored original boatyard and merchant's house built around a courtyard with a giant rain-tree. Generous swimming pool. Discounts Apr-Sep.

$$$ Fort House, 2/6A Calvathy Rd, T0484-221 7103, www.hotelforthouse. com. Tidy bungalows set in a quiet walled courtyard with its own little jetty. Some rooms charmingly old fashioned, others made from bamboo. Newer, more expensive rooms have modern baths, but they're pretty spartan for the price. Good restaurant overlooking the water.

$$$ Old Courtyard, 1/371 Princess St, T0484-221 6302, www.oldcourtyard.com. Beautiful, comfortable rooms, superbly styled with old wooden furniture, overlooking large, breezy courtyard of pretty pot plants and sit-outs. The suite is easily the most romantic with a 4-poster bed and white cotton. Attentive liveried staff, breakfast included, average food but excellent cakes and Turkish coffee, and lovely calm atmosphere. Recommended.

$$$-$$ Rossitta Wood Castle, Rose St, T0484-221 5671, www.rossittawood

castle.com. 300-year-old Dutch mansion. Rooms, with quirky features and lots of wood-panelling, set around an open-air restaurant courtyard. Breakfast included. Art gallery, library internet café, spa, hot water, yoga.

$$ Caza Maria Hotel, 6/125 Jew Town Rd, Mattancherry, T0484-395 8837, cazamaria@ rediffmail.com. Just 2 huge and wonderful rooms in beautiful converted house, with tiled floors, wooden furniture and antiques: isolated (the only hotel in Jew Town), romantic and shabbily elegant. Fan only. Breakfast is included, at French/Indian restaurant of same name (on the opposite side of the street). Highly recommended.

$$ Raintree Lodge, Petercelli St, T0484-325 1489, www.fortcochin.com. Friendly little lodge in quiet location. Large clean rooms all with hot water and a/c. Pretty roof terrace to relax on.

$$-$ Delight Homestay, Parade Ground, Ridsdale Rd, T0484-221 7658. This lovingly restored Portuguese provides a welcoming peaceful haven. Airy, spotlessly clean rooms open onto a wide terrace, budget rooms are great value. The garden is a riot of colourful blooms. Breakfast is served at the family table. A home away from home. Highly recommended.

$$-$ Fort Muziris, 1/415 Burgar St, T0484-221 5057, www.fortmuziris.com. Friendly backpacker refuge in the centre of things. The pick of the rooms are the upstairs suites with kitchen and shared terrace.

$ Adam's Old Inn, CC1/430 Burgher St, T0484-221 7595. Popular budget-traveller haunt in restored old building. Dorm beds are available for Rs 150. Helpful manager.

$ Oy's Tourist Home, Burgher St, T099-4759 4903. Decent rooms in lovely lamp-lit old building, with lots of plants. Can be noisy.

$ Vintage Inn, Ridsdale Branch Rd, near Jaliparambu Junction, T0484-221 5064, www.vintageresorts.in. Wonderful, homely guesthouse with a cheerful owner. Airy modern rooms with huge baths in a quiet corner of town. Excellent value. Recommended.

Ernakulam *p223, maps p226 and p229*
$$$$ Taj Gateway, Marine Dr, T0484-667 3300, www.thegatewayhotels.com. Immaculate rooms with commanding views over bay. Good restaurants, gym, bar, all business facilities and friendly service.
$$$ Abad Plaza, MG Rd, T0484-238 1122, www.abadhotels.com. A veteran of many monsoons, with large but slightly moth-eaten rooms all with a/c, fridge and cable TV. Rooms on street side can be noisy, quieter rooms on 5th floor. Breakfast included. Restaurants, gym, Ayurveda clinic, rooftop pool.
$$ Metropolitan, Chavara Rd, near Junction Station, T0484-237 6931, www.metropolitan cochin.com. Bright, spotlessly clean modern a/c rooms, excellent restaurants and service, superb value. "Best railway station hotel in South India". Recommended.
$$-$ Bharat, Gandhi Sq, Durbar Hall Rd, T0484-235 3501, www.bharathotel.com. Popular business hotel. Clean spacious rooms, some a/c, best sea-facing. Restaurant with excellent lunch *thalis* (South and North Indian). Great service, good value.
$$-$ Dwaraka, MG Rd, T0484-238 3236, dwaraka_hotel@rediffmail.com. Centrally located, family-run hotel. Good-sized, rather noisy rooms with TV, some with balcony. Only moderately clean. Adequate.

$$-$ YMCA International House, Chittoor Rd, 100 m from Central Bus Station, T0484-235 3479, www. ymcaernakulam.org. Simple rooms (some a/c), restaurant, welcoming.
$ Maple Regency, Cannon Shed Rd, T0484-235 5156. Large clean rooms, all with TV, in a great location right beside the boat jetty.
$ Modern Guest House, Market Rd, T0848-235 2130. Busy, clean hotel with helpful staff. Well-maintained rooms with bath.
$ Piazza Residency, Kalathiparambu Rd, near south railway station, T0484-237 6408. Slightly dank and musty rooms in quiet location. Good-value singles. Friendly staff.

🍴 Restaurants

Fort Kochi *p223, maps p226 and p228*
For a really fresh seafood meal, buy your own fish from the fishmonger stalls along the shorefront and take it to one of the nearby 'you buy, we cook' stalls, such as **Marina** or **Fort View**, where they'll be grilled or masala-fried with chips.
$$$ Malabar House Residency, (see Where to stay), Parade Rd. Excellent seafood platter and chef's salad, the latter of huge dimensions. Authentic Mediterranean and local dishes.
$$ Caza Maria (opposite hotel, see Where to stay), Jew Town Rd. Open 1200-2130. 2 large rooms with wooden chairs, frescoes and old framed prints on the wall. Small menu includes fish *moilee* and lime rice, *palak paneer* and *chapatti* and apple pie and ice cream. Great atmosphere.
$$ Feast, Peter Celli St. 1700-2100. With a menu focused on Keralite specialities, lovely staff that are passionate about their food and an ambient dining

room, this place is a great for trying out authentic local dishes.

$ Dal Roti, 1/293 Lilly St, T0484-221 7655. Firmly established favourite for pukka North Indian food – delicious *khati* rolls, huge stuffed *parathas* – served up by the affable Ramesh and his family. Don't arrive starving as queues often stretch out the door.

$ Kashi, Burgher St, Kochi, T0484-221 5769, www.kashiartgallery.com. If you've been away a while, **Kashi** is the type of place you'll fall on in wonder. The first 2 rooms are the art gallery, the rest is a restaurant where you can drink coffee fresh from your own cafetière, or indulge in a perfect cappuccino. There's a handful of excellently made sweets and 1-2 dishes they make for breakfast or lunch.

$ Kayikka's, **Rahmathulla Hotel**, Kayees, New Rd, near Aanavaadal, Fort Kochi, T0484-222 6080, kayees@sify.com. Open 1200-1430, 1830-2030. This family concern is the busiest biryani restaurant in Kochi and a local institution. Great mutton and chicken biryanis all week with fish biryanis on Fri and prawn on Tue. Arrive early to avoid disappointment.

$ Seagull, Calvathy Rd. Good value (Rs 80 buffet lunch), pleasant veranda for drinks and dining overlooking harbour.

$ Teapot Café , Peter Celli St, T0484-221 8035, tpleaz@hotmail.com. Bare terracotta roof tiles dangle with teapots and fans, tables are tea crates and walls are hung with antique tea-related paraphernalia. Stop in for a brew of Darjeeling, Assam, Nilgiris or mint-flavoured teas, an iced coffee, or milkshake. There's a delicious selection of cakes and desserts, tasty toasted sandwiches and more substantial meals

like prawn *moilee*, and mustard fish. With loads of newspapers and magazines left out for customers to read, it's a lovely place to while away a couple of hours.

Ernakulam *p223, maps p226 and p229*

$$ Bimbi's Southern Star, Shanmugam Rd. Generous portions of tasty Indian food.

$$ Khyber, Durbar Hall Rd. North Indian meals upstairs.

$$ Sealord's, Shanmugam Rd. Rooftop setting with good fish and Chinese dishes.

$$ Sri Krishna Inn, Warriom Rd, next to Chinmaya Vidya Peeth, T0484-236 6664. One of the best pure-veg places in a city of seafood, with great North and South Indian options.

$$ Subhiksha, **Bharat Hotel**, Durbar Hall Rd. Excellent value buffet lunch.

$ Bharat, Willingdon Island. Very good vegetarian *thalis* and Indian specialities in clean surroundings.

$ Chinese Garden, Warriom Rd. Good variety of decent Chinese meals. Alcohol available.

$ Indian Coffee House, Cannon Shed Rd. Tasty North and South Indian dishes.

$ New Colombo, Canon Shed Rd. Good snacks, fruit juices.

Cafés

Bimbi's, Durbar Hall Rd. Good fast food.

Caravan, Broadway (south). For ice creams and shakes.

Chariot, Convent Rd. Good café-style meals.

Coffee Beanz, Shanmugan Rd. Daily 0900-2300. Cold coffees, *appam*, *dosa*, popular, poky a/c coffee bar with just 6 tables.

Oven, Shanmugham Rd. Good pizzas and snacks (savoury and sweet).

🎭 Entertainment

Fort Kochi and Ernakulam *p223,
maps p226, p228 and p229*
There are daily *Kathakali* performances.
Arrive early to watch the extraordinary
make-up being applied.
Cochin Cultural Centre, Manikath
Rd, off Ravipuram Rd, Ernakulam,
T0484-235 7153. A/c 'theatre', authentic
performance with English explanations;
1830-1930, make-up 1730, Rs 125.
ENS Kalari, Nettoor, Fort Kochi, T0484-
280 9810. *Kalarippayattu* performances,
0400-0700 and 1700-2000.
Kerala Kathakali Centre, River Rd,
Fort Kochi, T0484-222 1827. Rustic
surroundings but lively performance,
enjoyable; 1830-1930 (make-up 1700) but
check timing, Rs 100.
See India Foundation, Kalathil Parampil
Lane (enter Chittoor Rd south) near
Junction station, Ernakulam, T0484-
236 9471. Dr Devan's 'interpreted'
taste of *Kathakali* with esoteric English
commentary; 1845-2000 (make-up from
1800), Rs 125.

🎪 Festivals

Fort Kochi and Ernakulam *p223,
maps p226, p228 and p229*
Jan/Feb Ulsavam at the Siva Temple
in Ernakulam for 8 days and at
Tripunithura Temple in **Nov/Dec**.
Elephant processions each day, folk
dance and music performances.
Aug/Sep Onam.

🛍 Shopping

Fort Kochi and Ernakulam *p223,
maps p226, p228 and p229*
Coir products (eg mats), carvings on
rosewood and buffalo horn and antiques

may catch your eye here. Several narrow
streets in **Jew Town**, towards the
synagogue, have become popular for
'antique' hunters in the last 25 years. All
these shops sport a similar range of old
(some faux) and new curios.
There are several government emporia
on MG Rd, Ernakulam, including **National
Textiles** (another in Banerji Rd). Other
shopping areas are in Broadway, Super
Bazar, Anand Bazar, Prince St and New Rd.
Cinnamon, Stuba Hall, 1/658 Ridsdale
Rd, Parade Ground, Fort Kochi, T0484-
221 7124. Posh clothing, fabrics and
interiors shop.
Dhamdhere, Pandithan Temple Rd,
Mattanchery, T0484-222 4481. Interesting
perfume manufacturers who confess
many are synthetic (Rs 12), but the
sandalwood oil is the real McCoy (Rs 100).
Idiom Books, branches on VI/183
Synagogue Lane, Jew Town and Bastion
Rd, Fort Kochi, T0484-221 7075. Very
good range on India, travel, fiction,
religion, philosophy, etc.
Indian Industries, Princess St, Fort Kochi,
T0484-221 6448. One of Fort Kochi's oldest
antique dealers. Lovely family-run store
with fixed prices and no-hassle browsing.

⚑ What to do

Fort Kochi and Ernakulam *p223,
maps p226, p228 and p229*
Body and soul
Be Beautiful, Princess St, Fort Kochi,
T0484-221 5398. Open 0900-2030.
Good, cheap beauty salon with massage,
hairdressers, pedicure and manicure in
new premises.
Sanathana School of Yoga Studies,
XV/2188-D Beach Rd Junction, T0484-
229 4155, www.sanathanayoga.com.
Daily classes 0730-0930 and 1630-1830,
pranayama and *asanas* plus 28-day

teacher training programmes in a pretty residence in downtown Fort Kochi.

Tour operators

Hi! Tours, Jomer Arcade, South Junction, Chittoor Road, Ernakulam, T0484-237 7415. Efficient and well-connected inbound travel agent, who can hook you up with homestays, authentic Ayurveda retreats and responsible tour operators throughout Kerala. Helpful and highly recommended.

KTDC, Shanmugham Rd, Ernakulam, T0484-235 3234. Full- and half-day backwater tours on *kettuvallams*. Full-day tour 0830-1830 (includes lunch), half-day tour 0830-1300 and 1400-1830. Tours include visits to coir factory, spice garden, canoe ride and toddy tapping demonstration. Also daily half-day Kochi sightseeing boat cruises, 0900-1230 and 1400-1730, which cover Bolgatty Island, Chinese fishing nets, St Francis Church and Mattancherry Palace. Tour departs from Sealord Jetty.

Malabar Escapes, **Malabar House** (see Where to stay), 1/268-1/1269 Parade Rd, Fort Kochi, T0484-221 6666, www.malabarhouse.com.

Olympus, south end of MG Rd, Ernakulam, T0484-236 9544. Very competent and helpful.

Pepper Tours, House No 127, Subash Chandra Bose Rd, Jawahar Nagar, Kadavanthara, PO Cochin 682020, T0484-405 8886, www.peppertours. com. Memorable journeys in Kerala, Rajasthan and Goa.

Pioneer Personalized Holidays, Pioneer House, 5th Cross, Willingdon Island, T0484-266 6148, www.pioneertravels. com. Fleet of cars with tailor-made tour packages from a well-established and highly competent tour company. Efficient and knowledgeable, with unusual homestay and guesthouse options.

Sundale Vacations, 39/5955 Atlantis Junction, MG Rd, Ernakulam, T0484-235 9127, www.sundale.com. Surface and hotel arrangements in Kerala, specializes in homestays catering to 'foreign independent tourists', promoting insight into Kerala's customs. Programmes from US$467.

Tourist Desk, Main Boat Jetty, Ernakulam, T0484-237 1761, www.tourist desk.in. One of the best budget tour operators. Daily backwater tours, 0800-1700, Rs 550, using both *kettuvalloms* and canoe. Tour includes visits to see coir making, spice garden, local village and lunch. Also 2- to 3-day tours to Wayanad and Kannur. Highly recommended.

Viceregal Travels and Resorts, S17/18 GCDA Shopping Complex, Marine Dr, Ernakulam, T0484-237 2644, www. viceregal travels.com. Runs a 9-day homestay package to charming properties, including a/c Ambassador cab, from Kochi to Peermade, Cherthala for the backwaters and Kovalam for Kanniyakumari. Rs 21,000 per person.

Visit India North Janatha Rd, T0484-233 9045, www.visitindiatravel.com. Half-day backwater tours in a dugout, punted and engineless, through very peaceful shady waterways passing unspoilt villages with toddy tappers, coir making, fishing, etc; led by an excellent guide. Rs 450 for 4 hrs, depart 0830, 1430. Highly recommended. Also offers trips in traditional *kettuvallams*; Rs 5000 (for couple) or Rs 8000 (2 bedroom); for 24 hrs, includes all meals.

⊖ Transport

Fort Kochi and Ernakulam *p223, maps p226, p228 and p229*

Air New international airport, 36 km northeast, T0484-261 0115. Prepaid taxis to Ernakulam Rs 600-800. A/c buses leave from outside the International Terminal for Fort Kochi (Rs 80) via Vytilla Junction (Rs 60), 3 km west of Ernakulam centre.

Daily domestic flights to: **Bengaluru, Chennai, Mumbai, Delhi** via **Goa, Thiruvananthapuram**; and several flights per week to **Coimbatore, Hyderabad, Kozhikode** and **Tiruchirapalli**.

International flights to: **Doha** (Qatar), **Dubai, Kuala Lumpur, Kuwait, Muscat** (Oman), **Sharjah** (UAE) and **Singapore**.

Airline offices All are on MG Rd unless stated otherwise. **Air India**, Durbar Hall Rd, T0484-235 1260, airport T0484-261 0070. **Emirates**, opposite Wyte Fort Hotel, NH47, T0484-337 7337. **Etihad**, Swapnil Enclave, High Court Junction, Marine Drive, T1800-223901. **Go Air**, Airport, T0484-261 0697. **Jet Airways**, BAB Chambers, Atlantis Junction, T0484-235 9212, airport T0484-261 0037. **Singapore Airlines**, c/o Aviation Travels, T0484-236 7911. **Spice Jet**, Airport, T0484-261 1750. **Sri Lankan Airlines**, T0484-236 1666.

Bus Local: Buses journey between Ernakulam, Willingdon and Fort Kochi frequently during the day. There are no local buses after 2100.
Long distance: Buses run from the **KSRTC Bus Station**, Chavara Rd, T0484-237 2033. There are frequent services to **Alappuzha**, every 20 mins (1½ hrs); **Kottayam**, every 30 mins (1½ hrs); **Kozhikode**, every 30 mins (5 hrs) and **Thiruvananthapuram**, every 30 mins (5 hrs). There are 7 departures daily to **Kumily** (6 hrs) or take a bus to

Kottayam and change there. There is an 0630 departure to **Munnar** (4 hrs), and departures to **Kannur** at 1445 and 2345 (7 hrs). Interstate services include: 9 daily to **Bengaluru** (14 hrs) via **Kozhikode** (5 hrs) and **Mysore** (10 hrs); **Kanniyakumari**, at 1430 (7½ hrs); and **Chennai** at 1400 (15 hrs) via **Coimbatore** (5 hrs).

Private operators from **Kalloor** and **Ernakulam South bus stands** including **Indira Travels**, DH Rd, T0484-236 0693; **SB Travels**, String Dew Building, Tripunithura, T0484-277 7949; and **Princy Tours**, opposite Sealord Hotel, T0484-237 3109. Overnight coaches to **Bengaluru** (12 hrs), and **Mysore** (10 hrs). Departures every 30 mins to **Kottayam** (2 hrs), and **Munnar**, (4 hrs). Also to **Chennai** and **Coimbatore**.

Ferry Regular ferry services connect Ernakulam with Fort Kochi and are the fastest and easiest form of transport. Ferry tickets cost Rs 2.50. Most ferries take bikes and motorbikes. It's also possible to hire a motor boat for up to 20, from Sea Lord jetty in Ernakulam through the KTDC office.

Ernakulam Main Boat Jetty, Cannon Shed Rd. Ferries depart approximately every 30 mins to Fort Kochi 'Customs' jetty 0555-2130. There are also regular ferries to the Fort Kochi Mattancherry jetty (last departure to Mattencherry is 1845), and to Willingdon Island's 'Embarkation' Jetty from here. Ferries to Bolghatty depart from the High Court Jetty off Shanmugham Rd approximately every 20 mins Mon-Sat 0600-2100.

Fort Kochi The main 'Customs' jetty links Fort Kochi with Ernakulam with regular departures between 0620-2150. The last ferry leaves for Ernakulam from the Mattencherry jetty at 1930.

From the northern Vypeen Jetty there are services every 30 mins to Vypeen Island between 0600-2130.

Willingdon Island There are 2 jetties: 'Embarkation' (north) and 'Terminus' (west). Ferries run every 30 mins to Ernakulam from 'Embarkation' from 0600-2110. From the 'Terminus' jetty there are irregular services to Mattencherry on Fort Kochi.

Rickshaw Auto-rickshaw drivers have a reasonably good reputation here. But, if you are likely to arrive late at night, insist on being taken directly to your hotel. A rickshaw between Fort Kochi and Ernakulam should cost around Rs 120. Fares within Fort Kochi or Ernakulam: Rs 20-40.

Taxi Ernakulam Junction to Fort Kochi, Rs 170. To airport, Rs 350-400. On MG Rd, Ernakulam: **Corp Taxi Stand**, T0484-236 1444.

Train Ernakulam/Kochi is on the broad gauge line joining Thiruvananthapuram to Mangalore, Bengaluru and Chennai. Most trains from major cities stop at Ernakulam Junction (the main station, booking code: ERS) although a few stop at Ernakulam Town (ERN), T0484-239 0920. Enquiries: Ernakulam Junction, T131 or T0484-237 5131.

Bengaluru: *Bangalore Intercity Exp 12678*, 0910 (from ERS), 11 hrs; *Island Exp 16525*, 1755 (from ERN), 13 hrs; both via Thrissur, Palakkad and Coimbatore.

Chennai: *Chennai Mail 12624*, 1915 (from ERN), 12 hrs. **Mangalore**: *Parasuram Exp 16650*, 1110 (from ERN), 9½ hrs); *Malabar Exp 16629*, 2350 (ERN), 10 hrs; both via Thrissur, Kozhikode and Kannur. **Thiruvananthapuram**: more than 20 trains a day, all via Kollam and Varkala.

Directory

Fort Kochi and Ernakulam *p223, maps p226, p228 and p229*
Banks In Ernakulam most banks congregate on MG Rd, including **ING Bank** and **Federal Bank**, and on Shanmugham Rd, including **State Bank of India**. All have ATMs. Most banks open till 1500. There are also several banks with ATMs in Fort Kochi including **ICICI** and **Federal Bank**, both on Chelaikada Rd. **Thomas Cook**, Palal Towers, 1st floor, MG Rd, T0484-236 8164 (Mon-Sat 0930-1800), changes TCs and currency. In Fort Kochi there are several foreign exchange offices on Princess St and Bastion St. **Medical services** General Hospital, Hospital Rd, Ernakulam, T0484-238 1768. Govt Hospital, Fort Kochi, T0484-222 4444. On MG Rd: **City**, T0484-236 1809, and **Medical Trust Hospital**, T0484-235 8001, have 24-hr pharmacies. **City Dental Clinic**, T0484-236 8164. **Useful contacts** Tourist Police: T0484-266 6076, help with information of all kinds. **Visa extension:** City Police Commissioner, High Court Ferry Station, Ernakulam, T0484-236 0700. **Foreigners' Regional Registration Office**, T0484-235 2454.

Munnar and Idukki's high ranges

Inland from the plains around Kottayam and Kochi lie the foothills of the Western Ghats, swathed in tropical evergreen forests and an ever-creeping tide of monoculture rubber plantations. As you climb higher these give way to pepper and cardamom, until finally you reach the rolling tea plantations and rarefied air of landlocked Idukki District. To the south sits Thekkady and the unmissable Periyar National Park, home to tiger, wild elephant, and an innovative project that is steadily turning yesterday's poachers into tomorrow's tour guides. Overnight treks into the park's hinterland offer an unmatched opportunity to see big animals up close and on foot, but even on a day visit Periyar can show you some impressive nature: wild boar foraging along the lakeside, butterflies as big as bats bouncing beneath the canopies of prehistoric jack trees, and the thud-thwack-holler as unruly gangs of Nilgiri Langur swoop through the high branches of giant figs.

Munnar, meanwhile, five hours uphill from Kochi, is *chai* central: a surreal rippling mosaic of yellow-green tea bushes and red dust roads stretching from valley deep to mountain high, with dark granite peaks pointing like fingers toward the bald grassy dome of South India's highest mountain, Anaimudi. At 1600 m, Munnar is much higher than Thekkady and gets genuinely cold, a fact that made it a favourite summer bolthole for the raj. Wildlife tourists flock to the nearby Eravikulam National Park for a glimpse of the endangered but semi-tame Nilgiri thar, a variety of ibex, while further to the north are the forests and deeply etched ravines of magnificent, rarely visited Chinnar Wildlife Sanctuary.

Arriving in Munnar and Idukki's high ranges

Getting there and around
The nearest transport hub for Munnar is Kochi-Ernakulam; Thekkady (Periyar Reserve/Kumily town) is best accessed from Kottayam. There are no train links to the high ranges; buses take a minimum of four hours to climb the hills to both hill stations, and roads linking the two take the same length of time. ▸▸ *See Transport, page 251.*

Tourist information
District tourism offices are at **Kumily** ① *T0486-922 2620*, and **Old Munnar** ① *T04865-253 1516*.

The Midlands (Kottayam to Thekkady) → *For listings, see pages 246-251.*

An interesting drive to the hills, this route follows the Ghat road, which has superb views down the east side of the Ghats onto the Tamil Nadu plains. You may meet herds of Zebu cattle, buffalo and donkeys being driven from Tamil Nadu to market in Kerala. Above 1000 m the air freshens and it can be cold. Be prepared for a rapid change in temperature.

Pala, off the Kottayam–Thekkady road, is a town famous for its learned citizens – graduates of the European-style Gothic university, which was built, along with the Gothic church, by one of its affluent sons. Nehru visited in the 1950s and said that Pala was full of "people of vision". The town was the most literate place in India long before Kerala achieved 100% literacy, and Meenachil Taluka has the highest proportion of educated women in the country. It is also famous for its tamarind and pepper as well as the rubber estates belonging to the Dominic family, who serve hot Syrian-Catholic lunches in their 100-year-old plantation bungalow and 50-year-old estate mansion. Plantation tours to watch latex collection and packing can be arranged through **CGH Earth**, see page 220.

Further east lies **Erattupetta**, whose grey St George's Church holds naïve wood-painted doves and disembodied cherubims, and which hosts the **High Range Festival** every April. Carry on for **Vagamon**, a village set on a chain of three hills: Thangal, Murugal and Kurisumala. A dairy farm here is managed by Kurisumala monks.

Some 25 km south from Vagamon is **Peermade**, named after Peer Mohammed, a Sufi saint and crony of the royal family of Travancore. It is surrounded by tea, rubber and cardamom plantations, including **Abraham's Spice Garden**, where a member of the family gives excellent spice tours for Rs 50. Buses between Kottayam and Kumily can drop you here.

Many Hindu pilgrims make the journey to the forest shrine dedicated to Sri Aiyappan at **Sabarimala**, 191 km north of Thiruvananthapuram (see box, page 241). Aiyappan is a particularly favoured deity in Kerala and there are growing numbers of devotees. The shrine is only open on specific occasions: **Mandalam**, mid-November to the end of December; **Makaravilakku**, mid-January; **Vishu**, mid-April; **Prathistha** one day in May-June; and during the **Onam** festival in August-September.

Covering 930 sq km of montane forest and grassland and centred on an attractive lake, the **Periyar National Park,** 115 km east of Kottayam, may not throw up many tiger sightings nowadays, but still attracts more than 300,000 visitors a year for its beautiful setting and unique range of soft adventure activities. Elephants, *gaur* and wild boar, though by no means guaranteed, are regularly spotted from the lake cruise boats, while sloth bear, porcupine and Malabar giant squirrel also haunt the woods.

The sanctuary was established by the old Travancore State government in 1934 and brought under the umbrella of Project Tiger in 1973, but Periyar's finest hour came in 1998 when the Kerala Forest Department, in partnership with the World Bank and the Thekkady Wildlife Society (a local NGO), set up a project to deploy a band of reformed cinnamon poachers from the surrounding villages as tour leaders and forest rangers in remote parts of the park. The camo-clad members of the **Ex-Vayana Bark Collectors Eco Development Committee** now earn a steady income from tourism, not to mention new-found respect within their communities, and their hard-won knowledge of the terrain and sharp instincts for animal behaviour makes them skilled, if not exactly chatty, forest guides. Trekking with them for a day represents your best chance of getting up close with elephants.

The centre of activities in the park is the boat jetty on pretty **Lake Periyar**, 3 km down a beautiful forest road from the tourist village of **Kumily**, which was created in 1895 by a dam that inundated 55 sq km of rich forest. A 180-m-long tunnel now leads the water eastward into the Suruli and Vaigai rivers, irrigating extensive areas of Ramanathapuram and Madurai districts in Tamil Nadu.

Periyar National Park

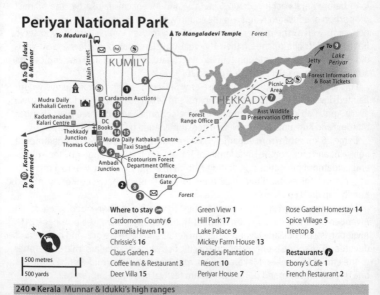

Where to stay 🛏	Green View **1**	Rose Garden Homestay **14**
Cardomom County **6**	Hill Park **17**	Spice Village **5**
Carmelia Haven **11**	Lake Palace **9**	Treetop **8**
Chrissie's **16**	Mickey Farm House **13**	
Claus Garden **2**	Paradisa Plantation	**Restaurants** 🍴
Coffee Inn & Restaurant **3**	Resort **10**	Ebony's Cafe **1**
Deer Villa **15**	Periyar House **7**	French Restaurant **2**

A modern mass pilgrimage

Sabarimala pilgrims are readily visible in many parts of South India as they wear black *dhotis* as a symbol of the penance they must undergo for 41 days before they make the pilgrimage. In addition to the black dress, pilgrims must take two baths daily and only eat food at home during this period. The pilgrimage, which begins at Deepavali, is only for males and prepubescent and post-menstrual females, to avoid the defilement believed to be associated with menstruation.

The pilgrimage in January is deliberately hard, writes Vaidyanathan, because "the pilgrimage to the shrine symbolizes the struggle of the individual soul in its onward journey to the abode of bliss and beatitude. The path of the spiritual aspirant is always long, arduous and hazardous. And so is the pilgrimage to Sabarimala, what with the observance of severe austerities and trekking up forested mountains, risking attacks from wild animals".

Hidden away in the hills to the south is **Sabarimala**, the focus of what some say is the world's biggest annual pilgrimage: 55 million pilgrims a year, almost all men, trek through the forest to the shrine, which is where the god Ayyappan is believed to have meditated after slaying a demoness.

Arriving in Thekkady (Periyar National Park, Kumily Town)

Getting there and around With the exception of a couple of government-run hotels down by the lakeside, everything that happens in Periyar happens in the busy little tourist trap of Kumily. The bus stand is at the north end of the main street, a 10-minute walk from most hotels. Buses run down to the lake jetty, or you can hire a bike (a tough ride back up the hill without gears), take an auto-rickshaw, share a jeep, or take the pleasant walk through the woods. ➤➤ *See Transport, page 251.*

Tourist information Entry to the park costs Rs 300 per day, Rs 150 for children; Indians pay Rs 25/Rs 5. The best time to visit is December to April, when dry weather brings animals closer to the lake. Dawn and dusk are best for wildlife, so stay overnight (winter nights can get quite cold). Avoid weekends and holidays, and especially the Makaravilakku festival in mid-January, which brings pilgrims by their millions to the Sabarimala shrine (see box, above). **Eco Tourism Office** ⓘ *Ambady Junction, Kumily, T0486-922 4571, www.periyartigerreserve.org*, has information and books tickets for all treks and tours in the park. **District Tourism Information Office** ⓘ *T0486-922 2620*, runs plantation tours to Abraham's Spice Garden (4 km) and Vandiperiyar (18 km).

Activities

The standard way to see Periyar is to take a trip across the lake on a **motor launch** ⓘ *depart 0730, 0930, 1115, 1345 and 1530, Rs 150; tickets on sale 90 mins before departure, no advance reservation required.* You can get good wildlife sightings on the first trip of the morning – elephants, gaur, wild boar, sambar and Barking deer are regularly spotted browsing on the banks, and packs of dhole (wild dog) very occasionally seen. However, noisy boats (and their occupants) and the heat soon drive animals away from the shore. Jeeps begin queueing at the park entrance gate from 0500 to get on the first launch of the morning, and there's a mad sprint to the ticket office once you reach the lake's edge.

From the same office you can book a three-hour **forest trek** ① *maximum 5 people, depart 0700, 0730, 1000, 1030, 1400, 1430, Rs 300, no advance reservations so get to office early to queue; carry water and beware of leeches*. There are good chances of seeing Malabar giant squirrel and Nilgiri langur, but much depends on your guide and not everybody comes face to face with a herd of elephants; some return very disappointed. Guides may also offer to arrange unofficial private walking tours in the park periphery in the afternoon (not the best time for spotting wildlife); try to assess the guide before signing up.

A more rewarding option is to sign up for one of the longer adventures into the park offered by the **Ex-Vayana Bark Collectors Eco Development Committee**. If you only have a day to spend in the park, spend it on the **bamboo rafting trip** ① *Rs 2000*, a full-day odyssey on land and water, trekking through a mosaic of grasslands, dense forest and rocky lakeshore, and navigating a long stretch of the lake on rickety rafts. Bird sightings are fabulous, with Malabar giant hornbill a real possibility, and the ex-poacher guides have been known to change the route to pursue – in a strictly non-violent sense – herds of elephant. A rifleman accompanies every group to ward off the threat of a charge.

If you've got longer, the **Tiger Trail** covers much the same ground but offers a chance to trek deeper into the forest, camping out for one or two nights (Rs 5000/7000 per person, maximum of six guests). Other activities include the **Jungle Patrol** (an exciting three-hour night trek, where you might spotlight porcupine and nightjars); the full-day **Border Hiking Trail** to a peak overlooking the Kambam Valley; and **bullock cart rides** to a traditional farming village.

Around Thekkady

There are a number of attractions within easy reach of Thekkady. These include the traditional Keralite-style **Mangaladevi Temple**, set amongst dense woodland on the peak of a 1337 m hill, 15 km northeast of Thekkady. Permission to visit the area must be obtained from the Wildlife Warden in Thekkady, though the temple itself is only open during the **Chithra Pounami** holiday. Other picturesque spots around Thekkady include **Pandikuzhi** (5 km) and **Chellarkovil** (15 km).

Munnar → *For listings, see pages 246-251. Phone code: 04865. Altitude: 1520 m.*

A major centre of Kerala's tea industry, Munnar sits in the lee of Anaimudi, South India's highest peak at 2695 m, and is the nearest Kerala comes to a genuine hill station. The landscape is European Alpine, minus the snow, plus tea bushes – inestimable millions of them. The town is surrounded by about 30 tea estates, among them the highest in the world at Kolukkumalai, yet despite the increasingly

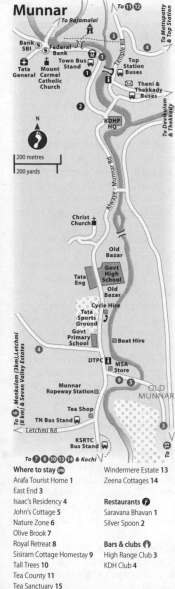

Munnar

To Rajamalai
To Matupatty & Top Station

Bank SBI
Federal Bank
Tata General
Mount Carmel Catholic Church
Town Bus Stand
Top Station Buses
Temple Rd
Theni & Thekkady Buses
KDHP HQ
To Devikulam & Thekkady

N
200 metres
200 yards

Christ Church
Old Bazar
Govt High School
Tata Eng
Old Bazar
Cycle Hire
Tata Sports Ground
Govt Primary School
Boat Hire
DTPC
MSA Store
Munnar Ropeway Station
OLD MUNNAR
Tea Shop
TN Bus Stand
Letchmi Rd
KSRTC Bus Stand

To Munkulam (3km), Letchmi (8 km) & Seven Valley Estates
To Kochi
Alwaye – Munnar Rd

Where to stay
Arafa Tourist Home 1
East End 3
Isaac's Residency 4
John's Cottage 5
Nature Zone 6
Olive Brook 7
Royal Retreat 8
Sisiram Cottage Homestay 9
Tall Trees 10
Tea County 11
Tea Sanctuary 15
Theresian Cottages 12
Windermere Estate 13
Zeena Cottages 14

Restaurants
Saravana Bhavan 1
Silver Spoon 2

Bars & clubs
High Range Club 3
KDH Club 4

commercial use of the hills you can still find forests that are rich in wildlife, including the endangered Nilgiri tahr. The workers on the tea estates are mostly Tamilians who moved here eight or nine generations ago. The surrounding hills are also home to the rare Neelakurunji orchid (*Strobilanthes*), which covers the hills in colour for a month once every 12 years (next due 2018). During the monsoon cotton wool swabs of cloud shift and eddy across hillsides sodden as a sponge with fresh rains, and springs burst their banks and surge across the pathways where villagers, dark-skinned tribals in ski jackets and woollen noddy hats, swing past on Enfields on their way home from a day on the tea plantations.

Arriving in Munnar

Getting there and around The easiest access is by bus or taxi from Kochi. There are also daily buses to Kumily and major towns in Kerala and Tamil Nadu. The town is small and pleasant for exploring on foot, although there are autos. It is worth hiring a bike or a jeep for trips out of town. » *See Transport, page 251.*

Tourist information DTPC ① *T04865-231516, www.munnar.com*, runs tours of plantations and rents cycles. Try also the free Tourist Information Service in the Main Bazar opposite the bus stop, run by Joseph Iype, a veritable mine of information. For trekking information, Senthil Kumar of local eco-guiding outfit **Kestrel Adventures** (see page 250) is hard to beat .

Places in Munnar

Tata Tea Museum ① *Nullatanni Estate, T04865-230561, www.keralatourism.org, open 1000-1600, Rs 50*, has a heap of artefacts, curios and photographs to help conjure something of the lives of the men who opened up the High Ranges to tea. The crop has grown here for over a century so relics include a rudimentary tea roller from 1905 and a wheel from the Kundale Valley Light Railway that used to transport men and materials between Munnar and Top Station. The museum has descriptions of the fully automated technology of today from the tea factory at Madupatty. The museum can also arrange a visit to this factory, watching tea pickers at work and processing.

In the centre of Old Munnar, set on a hill immediately above the road in the centre of town, is **Christ Church**. Built to serve tea estate managers and workers of the High Ranges, the last English-language service was held in 1981; it is now shared between protestant Tamil and Malayalam worshippers. The exterior is un-pre posessing: rather squat and now blackened by weathering, but inside it is a charming small church, and still contains its original 14 rows of wooden pews. Ask to see the diminutive record of births and deaths of the town's founders, the British planters. Immediately behind the church a zigzag path up the hill leads to the small pioneer cemetery that was established long before the church itself as the chosen burial ground of Mrs Eleanor Knight, General Manager Knight's 24-year-old bride who caught cholera after arriving in the High Range in 1894.

Mount Carmel Roman Catholic Church, the first Catholic church in the High Ranges, is in Old Munnar on the road up to the Tata General Hospital. The first chapel on the site was founded in 1898 by Friar Alphonse who arrived in Munnar from Spain in 1854. The present church was built by the then Bishop of Vijayapuram in 1938.

High Range Club ① *T04865-230253*, is a private members' club more relaxed than the famously 'Snooty' Ooty Club. A tradition allowed members to hang their hats on the wall of the bar after 30 years of belonging to the club – the last was hung in 1989 to make 51 hats in all. Saturday is strictly jacket and tie only and backpackers will need to scrub up well to get in any day of the week. "We like scholars and researchers, professionals and club people," says the club secretary, "they know how to move in a club." It's a wonderful place with teak floors, squash courts, library and fascinating planters to chat to if you're interested in the planters' social history.

Around Munnar

There are some excellent **cycle rides** around Munnar, not all of them steep. One ride goes up a gentle slope through a beautiful valley 8 km to the **Letchmi Estate**. There is a *chai* stall at the estate and the road continues to the head of the valley for views down to the forest. A second ride (or walk) leaves Munnar by the south road for 3 km, turning left at the Head Works Dam, then takes a right turn past Copper Castle, then left to a tea stall, viewpoint, tea and cardamom plantations, again with superb views. Continue to the next tea pickers' village for a tea stall. A shorter option for this route is to cross the dam and turn left, taking the quiet road north to the **High Range Club** and Munnar.

Mattupetty Lake **①** *13 km from Munnar, T04865-230389, visits between 0900-1100, 1400-1530, Rs 5*, at an altitude of 1700 m, is flanked by steep hills and woods. It was created by the small hydroelectricity dam. To its south is the Kerala Livestock Development Board's research and cattle breeding centre, formerly the Indo-Swiss dairy project. In a beautiful semi-Alpine setting surrounded for much of the year by lush green fields, the centre offers interesting insights into the practical realities and achievements of cattle breeding in India today.

Top Station, 34 km from Munnar on the Tamil Nadu border, at an altitude of 2100 m, has some of the highest tea estates in India. It is an idyllic spot, with superb views over the Tamil Nadu plains and the edge of the Western Ghats. Stalls serve tea and soft drinks. Top Station took its name from a ropeway that connected it via Middle Station to Lower Station at the valley bottom. The small town of **Bodinayakkanur**, which can be reached on the Devikulam road, lies in the valley. Buses leave from the shelter north of Munnar post office at 0715, 0915 and 1115 bound for Kovilor, passing Mattupetty Lake and Kundala Dam. Get off at Top Station, return bus after about one hour.

Across the valley from Top Station, and around 40 km east of Munnar, the small plantation of **Kolukkumalai** officially claims to pick the highest tea leaves in the world. The drive to the ridgetop at 2175 m takes two hours (the last section on a plantation road so bad it might be quicker to get out and walk) but the effort is repaid by astonishing views across misty valleys and distant peaks. It's worth being here for sunrise; set off by 0400 and wrap up warm for the journey. A path through the tea bushes leads down to the 1930s factory, where you can sample the local product and watch the antique processing equipment in action. As the plantation is privately owned you need to join a tour to get in; **Kestrel Adventures** (see What to do, page 250) is the main operator.

Eravikulam/Rajamalai National Park ① *21 km northeast of Munnar, www. eravikulam.org, closed Feb-Mar and during the monsoons, Rs 200, camera Rs 25, video Rs 200*, was set up in 1978 to preserve the endangered Nilgiri tahr (*Nilgiri ibex*). The conservation programme has resulted in the park now supporting the largest population of the species in the world, of nearly 2000. The sure-footed wild goats live in herds on the steep black rocky slopes of the Anaimudi mountains. They are brownish, have short, flat horns with the male carrying a thick mane, and can be easily seen around the park entrance. There are also elephants, sambars, gaurs, macaques and the occasional leopard and tiger. The scenery is magnificent, though the walks into the forest are steep and strenuous. There is an easier paved path from the park entrance following the road immediately below the bare granite outcrop of the Naikundi Hill to the Rajamalai Gap. The Forest Department issues a limited number of permits to trek through the park on the **Goldsbury Track**.

Adjoining Eravikulam to the north, and spreading down the eastern slope of the ghats into Tamil Nadu, the rarely visited **Chinnar Wildlife Sanctuary** ① *contact the Forest Information Office in Munnar, T04865-231587*, offers near-guaranteed sightings of elephant and bison, and has treehouses and log huts to stay in.

The road to Kochi

The route from Kochi to Munnar is one of South India's most attractive ghat roads. The one sight of note is the is the 25-sq-km **Salim Ali Bird Sanctuary** ① *Thattekad, 70 km east of Kochi on a side road heading north out of Kothamangalam; contact Assistant Wildlife Warden, Thattekad, T0485-258 8302*. A tropical evergreen and semi-evergreen forest with teak and rosewood plantations, the sanctuary is surrounded by the Periyar River, which remains shallow most of the year. It attracts water birds and the indigenous Malabar grey hornbill, rose and blue-winged parakeet, egret, heron and mynah, while rarer birds like the Ceylon frog-mouth and rose-billed rollers are also sometimes seen here.

◉ Munnar and Idukki's high ranges listings

For hotel and restaurant price codes and other relevant information, see pages 13-17.

● Where to stay

The Midlands (Kottayam to Thekkady) p239

$$$$ Kottukapally Nazarani Tharavad, Palai, T04822-212438, www.nazarani tharavad.com. An opportunity to stay with the Kottukapally family (Kerala political royalty). There are grand Byzantine icons, Persian carpets and Travancore brass lamps. The roomy 250-year-old Kerala/Dutch/Spanish-style house of teak, rosewood and Basel tiles has 3 roomy doubles. Book in advance.

$$$$ Serenity Kanam, at Kanam Estate, 25 km east of Kottayam off Kumily Rd, T0481-245 6353, www.malabarhouse.com. This wonderful villa hotel has just 6 huge rooms, decorated with quality art and sculpture, set in a gently restored 1920s bungalow surrounded by rubber plantations and spice gardens. There's a big pool, spa and excellent food, and you can spend a morning exploring the quiet lanes from the back of Lakshmi, the estate elephant. Far from any sights, but it's worth building in an extra night or 2 just to stay here.

$$$ The Pimenta, Haritha Farms, The Pimenta, Kadalikad Post, T0485-226 0216, www.harithafarms.com. An eco-tourism concern in a pepper-growing region. Guest numbers are limited to minimize impact on the village. 4 newly built simple cottages close to the family farmhouse. The family are advocates of the return to traditional methods of agriculture, Haritha grows bio-organic spices, medicinal herbs and tropical fruit and re-plants crops lost to monoculture tea and rubber plantations. All meals included.

$$$ Vanilla County, Mavady Estate, Teekoy, Vagamon, T0482-228 1225, www.vanillacounty.in. At the source of the Meenachil River. A charming, family-friendly place with 3 rooms within 60-year-old estate house that you share with your hosts. Coffee is from the plantation around you and you can swim in nearby natural ponds. Internet access. Price includes all meals.

Thekkady p240, map p240

Check www.thekkady.com for information.
$$$$ Cardomom County, Thekkady Rd, T0486-922 4501, www.cardamomcounty. com. Spacious, comfortable cottages, good restaurant, nice pool, friendly (request off-season discount). Recommended.

$$$$ Lake Palace, Lake Periyar, T0486-922 3887, www.lakepalacethekkady.com. 6 rooms in interesting building inside the reserve. Idyllic island setting with superb views and wildlife spotting. Access by free ferry (20 mins) from jetty (last trip 1600). Relaxed and informal.

$$$$ Paradisa Plantation Retreat, Murinjapuzha, Kottayam–Kumily Rd, T0469-270 1311, www.paradisaretreat.

com. 10 traditionally built new cottages with beautiful antique granite pillars and room furnishings, on an organic plantation estate with stunning valley views and a pool. Yoga recommended but booking essential.

$$$$ Spice Village (CGH Earth), Thekkady– Kumily Rd, T0486-922 2314, www.cghearth.com. Cottages with elephant grass thatch (cool and dark with wide eaves), spice garden, badminton, tennis, good pool, yoga centre. Excellent restaurant, lunch and dinner buffets (Rs 500), chilled beer. Good cookery demonstrations, great Ayurvedic massage and forest walks to see smaller wildlife. Luxurious, quiet, restful, friendly, with superb service. Discounts Apr-Sep.

$$$$-$$$ Carmelia Haven, Vandanmedu (20 km north on Puliyanmala Rd), on a tea, spice and coconut plantation, T0486-827 0272, www.carmeliahaven.com. Exclusive and private, with a tree house 6 m above ground, a cave house 3 m below, and a few discreetly spaced cottages in a local style using lots of thatch. An excellent open-air restaurant serves delicious Malabari food. Tours of tea factory, cardamom plantations, treks and boating. Tea and cardamom for sale.

$$$$-$$$ Hotel Treetop, Thekkady Rd, T0486-922 3286, www.hoteltreetop. com. Clean and efficient resort of gabled cottages with all mod cons and private balconies, just on the fringes of the Periyar National Park. Family bungalow has a kitchen and living area. Library, restaurant, Ayurveda massages available.

$$$-$$ Chrissie's, Thekkady Bypass Rd, T0486-922 4155, www.chrissies.in. Modern minimalist rooms all with balcony. Lush, peaceful garden with shady seating areas to relax in. Restaurant, yoga studio.

$$$-$$ Periyar House (KTDC), 5 mins' walk from the lake, T0486-222 2026, www.periyarhousethekkady.com. Pleasant, clean and comfortable rooms. Buffet meals and strong Goan beer available. Good service.

$$-$ Claus Garden, Rosapukandam, 10 mins' uphill from bus stand behind PO, 3rd turn right, T0486-922 2320, claus.hoppe@web.de. Spacious rooms in a peaceful house surrounded by jungle. Funky communal area, book exchange, friendly chilled-out vibe.

$ Coffee Inn, Thekkady Rd, 5-mins' walk from entrance gate, T0486-922 2763, coffeeinn@satyam.net.in. Wide variety of rooms, cheaper huts in quiet garden annex 100 m down the road. Popular budget traveller hang-out. Restaurant, book exchange, friendly. No reservations – rooms are allocated on a first come first served basis.

$ Deer Villa, Thekkady Bypass Rd, T0486-922 3568, www.deervilla.com. Friendly family home boasting clean, airy rooms with balcony, fan and hot water. Breakfast included. Internet café downstairs.

$ Green View, Hotel Ambadi Junction, Thekkady Bypass Rd, T0486-922 4617, www.sureshgreenview.com. Suresh and Sulekha run a welcoming 'home away from home' in a rambling house surrounded by mango trees. Hammocks are slung out in the garden. All 16 spotlessly clean rooms have large bathrooms (towels, loo roll and soap provided). Standard and deluxe rooms have cable TV and balcony. Suresh is an ex-tour guide and can provide maps for mountain treks and walks in the area. Meals available on request, cookery classes, breakfast included. Friendly and helpful. Recommended.

$ Hill Park, Main St, T0486-268 5509, hillpark@aol.in. 17 moderately clean and basic rooms all with bath and fan. Friendly staff.

$ Mickey Farm House, Thekkady Bypass Rd, T0486-922 3196, www.mickeyhomestay.com. Pleasant airy rooms in pretty garden, all with balcony. Cheaper rooms with outside bath. Mickey runs 4- to 7-day treks to Kottayam/Alappuzha (advance notice required). Friendly family, excellent value Recommended.

$ Rose Garden Homestay, Hotel Ambadi Junction, Thekkady Bypass Rd, T0486-922 3146, rosegardenhomestay@ yahoo.co.in. Sathi has 6 simply furnished rooms, all with TV, in the back garden of her flowered house. Lots of hanging wicker chairs on porches, Lovely family provide traditional Keralite breakfasts and suppers. Discounts for long stays.

Munnar *p242, map p243*
Hotel prices throughout Munnar are high for what you get, particularly in the summer high season. Cheaper places can be found around the bazar and bus stand, where touts will greet you brandishing the cards of 25-room concrete block 'cottages'.

$$$$ Tall Trees, Bison Valley Rd (3 km south of town), T04865-230641, www.ttr. in. A drastic price hike means the rather musty cottages here offer dubious value, but the location, beneath a canopy of ancient rainforest, is undeniably magic.

$$$$-$$$ Windermere Estate, Pothamedu, T04865-230512, www.windermeremunnar. com. Standalone cottages and an alpine farmhouse with 5 rooms and an elegant and utterly comfortable planters' bungalow with 3 rooms. The whole complex is set around an enormous granite boulder, that offers sweeping views of cloud-draped mountains, and there's a fantastically

light and airy reading room done out with rustic timber furniture and vaulted ceilings. Pricey but recommended.

$$$ Nature Zone, Pullipara, 5 km up dirt track off Letchmi Rd, west of TN Bus Stand, bookings on T0484-649 3301, www.thenaturezone.org. Arriving here is like stepping into Jurassic Park – you have to get out of the car and unhook the elephant-repelling electric fence. A leading outward-bound training centre with stunning valley views, the drawcards here are the jungly remoteness and the 2 rustic-chic treehouses, with branches growing right through the room. The safari tents down at ground level are OK but get pretty musty. On-site canteen serves good food.

$$$ Olive Brook, Bison Valley Rd, Pothamedu, 3 km south of Munnar, T04865-230588, www.olivebrookmunnar. com. 5 well-appointed double rooms in beautiful lush location on a cardamom farm, excellent alfresco barbecues on request. Price includes meals, trekking and cookery classes.

$$$ Tea County (KTDC), 1 km north of town, T04865-230460, www.ktdc.com. 43 immaculately kept rooms set in 3 ha of neat garden, good facilities, beautiful views, great walking, own transport essential.

$$$ The Tea Sanctuary, KDHP House, T04865-230141, www.theteasanctuary. com. 6 quaint old-fashioned bungalows on the working Kanan Devan tea estate, pukka colonial-style atmosphere plus activities like mountain biking, trekking, horse riding, golf and angling, and everything clubbable at the **High Range** and **Kundale** clubs.

$$$-$$ Royal Retreat, 500 m south of KSRTC Bus Stand, T04865-230240, www.royalretreat.co.in. Agreeable standard doubles with TV and hot water, plus excellent newly renovated garden rooms and suites with fluffy quilts and DVD players.

$$ East End, Temple Rd, T04865-230452. 18 pleasant rooms and some cottages (solar heated water), good but pricey restaurant, attractively designed, quiet garden location.

$$ Isaac's Residency, Top Station Rd, T04865-230501. Excellent quality, 32 lovely rooms with contemporary furnishings, Executive rooms with great views, 2 restaurants, bar. Recommended.

$$ John's Cottage, MSA Rd, near Munnar Supply Association, T04865-231823. Small bungalow home in a well-tended lawn running down to the river, with 8 clean rooms. Indian/Chinese food or use of kitchen.

$ Arafa Tourist Home, Upper Bazar, T04865-230302. 14 rooms with TV, phone in riverside lodge, handy for late-night bus arrivals. Noise travels, but the rooms are clean and good value.

$ Sisiram Cottage Homestay, IX/18A MSA Rd, T04865-231908, www.sisiram. com. 2-storey cottage on the riverbank, with large, nicely furnished rooms upstairs and a 3-bed apartment (**$$$**) downstairs.

$ Theresian Cottages, north of town before Tea County, T04865-230351. 3 rooms open off the shared living room of this sweet little 1930s house, and though sizes vary, each has a fireplace, chaise longue and clean bathroom.

$ Zeena Cottages, near **Hill View Hotel** in Tata tea plantation, T04865-230560, www.hillviewhotel.com. Basic and slightly gloomy rooms in a colonial house, but the owners are friendly and the plantation views spectacular. Ask at the **Tourist Information Service** in the bazar (see page 243).

The road to Kochi *p245*

$$$ Periyar River Lodge, Anakkayam, Kothamanagalam, T0485-258 8315, www.periyarriverlodge.com. 2-bedroom cottage in a rubber plantation on the banks of Periyar River right next to Thattekad Bird Sanctuary. Bamboo rafting, fishing, forest treks, jeep safaris to 30-m-high waterfalls for swimming, boat and bike tours. Lounge, en suite, river views. Keralite food.

$$$ Plantation Homestay, Mundackal Estate, Pindimana, Kothamangalam Junction, T0485-257 0717, www. mundackalhomestay.com. 3 rooms in a homestay that lies deep inside a rubber, pepper and coconut plantations. Daisy is a mean cook and offers lessons (US$20), while George arranges boat trips to the bird sanctuary.

❼ Restaurants

Thekkady *p240, map p240*

$$$ Spice Village, Thekkady Rd (see Where to stay). International, excellent food and service, rustic decor, fresh garden vegetables and chef's cooking show nightly.

$$ Coffee Inn, Thekkady Rd (see Where to stay). 0/00-2200. International dishes served at tables outside under the palms, bonfire in the evening, relaxed and peaceful. Friendly but very slow service.

$ Ebony's Café, Thekkady Bypass Rd. Rooftop restaurant with huge range of Indian and international dishes.

$ Edassery's Farm Yard, NH 49 Chattupara Adimali Idukki, T04864-224210. 0600-2200. Makes a good break on the Kottayam–Kumily road with tasty soups and meals, *dosa* and vegetable stews.

$ French Restaurant , Thekkady Rd. Good bread, muesli, snacks and coffee.

$ Our Place, next to **Jungle View Homestay**, Rosappukandam. Run by a British-Indian couple, this cosy café serves comfort food from back home alongside excellent Indian vegetarian options.

Munnar *p242, map p243*
$$ The Greens, East End (see Where to stay). Pleasant, glassed-in veranda serving good food, or go for the cheap simple meals in the eatery below.
$$ Royal Retreat (see Where to stay). International. Very pleasant, wide choice.
$ Saravana Bhavan, MG Rd. Clean, cheap and friendly place serving great *dosas* and huge Kerala-style *thalis* on banana leaves.
$ Silver Spoon, near **Munnar Inn**. For good breakfast choices.

⊕ Bars and clubs

Munnar *p242, map p243*
High Range Club, T04865-230253. Charming colonial-style planters' club, members only (or with reciprocal arrangements), visit by asking a planter to introduce you.
KDH Club, on side road opposite DTPC office. For Tata staff, old-world, visit with permission, excellent pool table.

⊕ Entertainment

Thekkady *p240, map p240*
Kadathanadan Kalari Centre, Thekkady Rd, Kumily, T0486-922 2988, www.thekkady tours.in. 1-hr demonstration of Kerala's traditional martial art, *Kalarippayattu*. Show time 1800, Rs 200, video charge Rs 250.
Mudra Daily Kathakali Centre, Thekkady Rd, Kumily, T(0)9447-157636, www.mudra Kathakali.com. Classical dance theatre show by performers from

Kalamandalam school of dance. Make-up 1600 and 1830, show times 1630 and 1900. Rs125, video charge Rs 200.

⊙ Shopping

Munnar *p242, map p243*
Good for tea, cardamom and pepper.
Munnar Supply Assoc (MSA), next to tourist information. Established 1900, a bit of the old world, where you can get everything. Tailors in the bazar can copy your garments in 24 hrs. The newer Main Bazar is to the north.
Uravu, near Ambady Junction, Idukki, T(0)9387-469369, www.uravu.org. Fair trade outfit supporting local producers of agrihorticultural products, bamboo products, processed foods, handicrafts, forest honey, spices tea and coffee.

⊕ What to do

Thekkady *p240, map p240*
Eco Tourism Information Centre, Hotel Ambadi Junction, Thekkady Bypass Rd, Kumily, T0486-922 4571, www. periyartigerreserve.com. Organizes a full range of tours within the park: bamboo rafting, tiger trails with 1 or 2 nights' camping, evening jungle patrols, border hiking and treks to tribal settlements.
Forest Information Centre, near boat jetty, Thekkady. Cruise times: 0730, 0930, 1115, 1345 and 1530 (Rs 150). Nature trek: 0700, 0730, 1000, 1030, 1400, 1430 (Rs 300). No advance bookings, arrive early and queue at office.

Munnar *p242, map p243*
DTPC, Old Munnar Bazar. Runs tours to: Tea Valley, 1000-1800, Rs 250; Sandal Valley and Wildlife, 0900-1900, Rs 300.
Kestrel Adventures, PB No 44, KTDC Rd, T(0)9447-031040, www.kestreladventures.

com. Senthil Kumar leads a team of 9 specialist guides, some expert in birds, others in tea growing and history. Highly recommended for camping and trekking, wildlife spotting in Chinnar Wildlife Sanctuary, and the only company in town that can get you into Kolukkumalai for sunrise. Also offers rock climbing, mountain bike tours/hire and jeep safaris.

⊖ Transport

Thekkady *p240, map p240*
Beware of 3-wheelers and guides at the bus station, who are working on commission from guesthouses. Nearly all hotels in Kumily are within a 10-min walk of the bus station.

Bus Local: Minibuses hourly from Kumily go down to **Aranya Nivas** on the lakeside, Rs 2. At Kumily jeep drivers will tell you there is no bus to Thekkady and charge Rs 50 for the trip; autos charge Rs 25 plus.
Long distance: From Kumily: frequent services to **Kottayam**, every 20 mins from 0600 (4½ hrs). Regular buses to **Kochi/Ernakulam**, 6 per day, 1st at 0600 (6½ hrs); **Alappuzha**, 6 per day, 1st at 0600 (6 hrs); **Thiruvananthapuram**, 3 per day, 1st at 0830 (8 hrs); **Munnar**, 5 per day, 1st at 0600 (4½ hrs). Daily bus to **Kodaikkanal** (cancelled occasionally), 0630 (5½ hrs), or go to **Vathalakundu** and change. Buses also go from Thekkady itself (behind *Aranya Nivas*): frequent departures to **Madurai**, every 20 mins, from 0600 (4 hrs).

Munnar *p242, map p243*
Bike hire From tourist information office, Rs 50 per day. **Kestrel Adventures** (see What to do) has 18-speed mountain bikes.

Bus State buses start and terminate at 2 separate stands south of town, but also call at the **Town Bus Stand** near the market. Enquiries, T04865-230201. Frequent services to **Mattupetty** (30 mins), **Devikulam** (30 mins), **Adimali** (1 hr) and **Top Station** (1 hr). Daily to **Coimbatore** (6 hrs); **Ernakulam/ Kochi** (4½ hrs); **Kodaikkanal** 0700 via Udumalpettai, change for Palani and Kodai. If the Palani–Kodai Rd is closed a further bus goes to Vatalakundu and then Kodai; **Kottayam** (5 hrs); **Madurai** via **Theni** (5 hrs); **Thekkady** (4½ hrs), leaves from stop next to the post office; **Thiruvananthapuram** (9 hrs), **Thrissur** via **Perumbavoor** (5 hrs).

Jeeps/taxis Shared jeeps and minibus taxis for **Eravikulam** and **Mattupetty Lake** wait around the post office.

⊕ Directory

Thekkady *p240, map p240*
Banks Federal Bank, Thekkady Junction, **State Bank of India**, Main St. Both have ATM. **Thomas Cook**, Thekkady Rd. **Medical services** Kumily Central Hospital, open 0900-1300 and 1630-2000, 24-hr call out for emergencies. **Post** Main St, next to bus station.

Munnar *p242, map p243*
Banks State Bank of Travancore ATM, in the centre near KDHP headquarters. **Federal Bank**, near Tata Hospital Rd, very helpful; **State Bank of India**, 1000-1400, Sat 1000-1200. **Medical services** Excellent **Tata General Hospital**, T04865-230270, on the north edge of town on the Rajamalai Rd. **Post** New Town centre.

Thrissur, Palakkad and the River Nila

The blue thread of the River Nila, Kerala's equivalent of the Ganges and the crucible of much of the state's rich cultural heritage, stitches together a collection of fascinating sights and experiences in the rarely explored central belt of Kerala between Kochi and Kozhikode. Busy Thrissur, the state's cultural capital, is unmissable in April and May when it holds its annual Pooram festival and millions pack into the city's central square, sardine-style, to watch the elephant procession and fireworks display. Coastal Guruvayur, meanwhile, is among Kerala's most sacred Hindu pilgrimage spots; it is home to one of India's wealthiest temples as well as an elephant yard where huge tuskers and their mahouts relax before they hit the road for the next festival. Inland, the Palakkad Gap cuts a broad trench through the Western Ghats, the only natural break in the mountain chain, providing a ready conduit for roads, railway lines, innumerable waves of historical migrants, and blasts of scorching air from the roasted plains of Tamil Nadu. Palakkad itself is now known as Kerala's granary, and makes a good stopover point on the route to or from Tamil Nadu.

Arriving in Thrissur, Palakkad and the River Nila

Getting there
Trains on the main north–south line stop in Thrissur and Shoranur Junction, a handy jumping-off point for the River Nila. Trains from Kerala to Coimbatore and Chennai call at Palakkad. There are bus connections from these towns to the smaller centres, though to properly explore the cultural and historical riches of the area it's much more efficient to hire a guide and driver. ➤➤ *See Transport, page 261.*

Tourist Information
Thrissur ① *Palace Rd, T0487-232 0800, www.dtpcthrissur.com.* **Guruvayur** ① *Vyjayanti Building, East Nada, Guruvayur, T0487-255 0400.* **Palakkad DTPC** ① *West Fort Rd, Palakkad, T0491-253 8996, www.dtpcpalakkad.com.*

Thrissur sits at the west end of the Palakkad Gap, which runs through the low pass between the Nilgiri and the Palani hills. The route through the ghats is not scenic but it has been the most important link to the peninsula interior since Roman times. Thrissur is built round a hill on which stand the Vadakkunnathan Temple and an open green, which form the centre of the earth-shaking festivities. The town's bearings are given in cardinal directions from this raised 'Round'.

The **Vadakkunnathan Temple** ① *0400-1030, 1700-2030, non-Hindus not permitted inside except during the Pooram festival*, a predominantly Siva temple, is also known as the Rishabhadri or Thenkailasam ('Kailash of the South'). At the shrine to the Jain Tirthankara Vrishabha, worshippers offer a thread from their clothing, symbolically to cover the saint's nakedness. The shrine to Sankara Narayana has superb murals depicting stories from the *Mahabharata*. It is a classic example of the Kerala style of architecture with its special pagoda-like roof richly decorated with fine wood carving.

The temple plays a pivotal role in the **Pooram** celebrations, held during April and May. This magnificent eight-day cacophony of a festival is marked by colourful processions joined by people of all religious groups irrespective of caste. Platoons of elephants decked out in gold, palm leaves and lamps march to the Vadakkunnathan Temple carrying priests and idols, to the accompaniment of dozens of drums, cymbals and pipes. On the final day temple teams meet on the Tekkinkadu maidan for a showdown of drumming and *Kudumattam* (the name roughly translates as 'umbrella swapping' – one of Kerala's more surreal spectator sports) before a huge fireworks display brings proceedings to a close. In September and October, there are live performances of *Chakyarkothu*, a classical art form. There is a small elephant compound attached to the temple.

The **Town Hall** is a striking building housing an art gallery with murals from other parts of the state. In the **Archaeological Museum** ① *Town Hall Rd, Tue-Sun 0900-1500*, ask to see the royal chariot. Next door, the **Art Museum** has woodcarvings, sculptures, an excellent collection of traditional lamps and old jewellery. Nearby, **Thrissur Zoo** ① *Tue-Sun 1000-1700, small fee*, is known for its snake collection. The impressive **Lourdes Church** has an interesting underground shrine.

Guruvayur → *For listings, see pages 257-261.*

As one of the holiest sites in Kerala, Guruvayur, 29 km west of Trichur, is a heaving pilgrimage centre, filled with stalls and thronged from 0300 to 2200 with people wanting to take *darshan* of Guruvayurappan.

Some 4 km outside the town, the 16th-century **Sri Krishna Temple** is one of the richest in India, and there is a waiting list for the auspicious duty of lighting its oil lamps that stretches to 2025. On well-augured marriage days there is a scrum in which couples are literally shunted from the podium by new pairs urgently pressing behind them in the queue, and the whole town is geared towards the wedding industry. The temple has an outer enclosure where there is a tall gold-plated flagpost and a pillar of lamps. The sanctum sanctorum is in the two-storeyed srikoil, with the image of the four-armed Krishna garlanded with pearls and marigolds. Photography of the tank is not allowed. Non-Hindus are not allowed inside and are not made to feel welcome.

The temple's inner sanctum is off limits to non-Hindus, but you can visit the **Guruvayur Devaswom Institute of Mural Painting** ① *Mon-Fri 1000-1600*, a tiny educational institute where you can meet and buy finished works from the next generation of mural painters. As with *Kathakali*, the age-old decorative arts of temple culture steadily declined during the 20th century under the weakening structure of feudalism and opposition to the caste system. When the temple lost three walls to a fire in 1970 there were hardly any artists left to carry out renovation, prompting authorities to build the school in 1989. Today the small institute runs a five-year course on a scholarship basis for just 10 students. Paintings sell for Rs 500-15,000 depending on size, canvas, wood, etc.

Punnathur Kotta Elephant Yard ① *0900-1700, bathing 0900-0930, Rs 25, take care as elephants can be dangerous, buses from Thrissur (45 mins)*, is situated within a fort 4 km out of town. Temple elephants (68 at the last count) are looked after here and wild ones are trained. There are some interesting insights into traditional animal training but this is not everyone's cup of tea. Though captive, the elephants are dedicated to Krishna and appear to be well cared for by their attendants. The elephants are donated by pious Hindus but religious virtue doesn't come cheap: the elephants cost Rs 500,000 each.

Kodungallur and around → *For listings, see pages 257-261.*

At one time **Kodungallur**, 50 km southwest of Trichur on the border of Ernakulam District, was the west coast's major port, and the capital of the Chera king Cheraman Perumal. Nearby **Kottapuram** is where St Thomas is believed to have landed in AD 52. The commemorative shrine was built in 1952. Kodungallur is also associated by tradition with the arrival of the first Muslims to reach India by sea. Malik-ibn-Dinar is reputed to have built India's first Juma Masjid, 2 km from town. Tiruvanchikulam Temple and the Portuguese fort are worth visiting. The Syrian orthodox church in **Azikode** blends early Christian architecture in Kerala with surrounding Hindu traditions. Thus the images of Peter and Paul are placed where the *dvarapalas* (doorkeepers) of Hindu temples would be found, and the portico in front of the church is for pilgrims.

Along the River Nila → *For listings, see pages 257-261.*

North of Thrissur the road and railway cut through lush countryside of paddy fields, quiet villages and craggy red hills mantled with coconut and rubber plantations, before crossing the wide sandy bed of the Bharatapuzha River at Shoranur. Known to the people who populate its banks as Nila, this is Kerala's longest river, rising on the eastern side of the Palakkad Gap and winding lazily through 209 km to spill into the Arabian Sea at the bustling fishing port of Ponnani. Though its flow is severely depleted by irrigation dams and its bed gouged by sand miners, the importance of the river to Kerala's cultural development is hard to overstate: Ayurveda, *Kathakali* and the martial art *Kalaripayattu* were all nurtured along the banks of the Nila, not to mention the cacophonous classical music that soundtracks festive blow-outs like the Thrissur **Pooram**. Folk tradition too is vibrantly represented: elaborately adorned devotees carry colourful effigies to temple festivals, snake worshippers roam house to house performing ancient rituals to seek blessing from the serpent gods, and village musicians sing songs of the paddy field mother goddess, passed down from generation to generation.

Despite all this, the Nila thus far remains refreshingly untouched by Kerala's tourism boom, and few travellers see more of it than the glimpses afforded by the beautiful train ride between Shoranur and Kozhikode. This is in part because there's little tourist infrastructure, few genuine 'sights', and no easy way for a travellers to hook into the cultural scene. Traditional potters and brass-smiths labour in humble workshops behind unmarked houses, while performers (singers and dancers by night, coolies, plumbers and snack sellers by day) only get together for certain events. With your own transport you can search out any number of beautiful riverside temples, but unless you join one of the superb storytelling tours run by local guiding outfit **The Blue Yonder** (see page 261), Kerala Kalamandalam (see below) might be the only direct contact you have with the Nila's rich heritage.

The residential school of **Kerala Kalamandalam** ① *3 km south of river, Cheruthuruthy, south of Shoranur Junction, T04884-262305, www.kalamandalam. org, Mon-Fri 0930-1300, closed public holidays and Apr-May*, is dedicated to preserving the state's unique forms of performance art. Founded in 1930, after the provincial rulers' patronage for the arts dwindled in line with their plummeting wealth and influence, the Kalamandalam spear-headed a revival of *Kathakali* dancing, along with *ottam thullal* and the all-female drama *mohiniyattam*. The school and the state tourism department run a fascinating three-hour tour of the campus, 'A Day With the Masters' (US$25), with in-depth explanations of the significance and background of the art forms, the academy and its architecture, taking you through the various open air *kalaris* (classrooms) to watch training sessions. There are all-night *Kathakali* performances on 26 January, 15 August, and 9 November. *Koodiyattam*, the oldest surviving form of Sanskrit theatre, is enshrined by UNESCO as an 'oral and intangible heritage of humanity'. Frequent private buses from Thrissur's northern bus stand (ask for Vadakkancheri Bus Stand) go straight to Kalamandalam, taking about one hour.

In the bustling port town of **Ponnani** at the mouth of the Nila, the **Ponnani Juma Masjid** ① *42 km northwest of Thrissur, nearest train station 21 km away at Kuttipuram; admission to non-Muslims not assured, dress conservatively, women should wear a headscarf*, was built in the mid-15th century by the spiritual leader Zainudhin Ibn Ali Ibn Ahmed Ma'bari, who employed a Hindu carpenter to design the exterior. Ignorant of traditional Islamic architecture, the carpenter carved the elaborate teak-wood facade to resemble a Hindu temple incorporating many intricate Hindu designs. The carpenter was killed by a fall from the roof as he finished construction and lies buried inside the mosque. The nearby fishing docks are a hive of activity, but prepare for plenty of attention from local boys.

Palakkad (Palghat) → *For listings, see pages 257-261. Phone code: 0491.*
Population: 130,700.

Kerala's rice cellar, prosperous Palakkad has long been of strategic importance for its gap – the only break in the mountain ranges that otherwise block the state from Tamil Nadu and the rest of India. Whereas once this brought military incursions, today the gap bears tourist buses from Chennai and tractors for the rich agricultural fields here that few educated modern Keralites care to plough using the old bullock carts (although the tradition is kept alive through *kaalapoottu*, a series of races between yoked oxen held in mud-churned paddy fields every January). The whole of Palakkad is like a thick paddy forest, its iridescent old blue mansions, many ruined by the Land Reform Act, crumbling into paddy ponds. There are village idylls like a Constable painting. Harvest hands loll idly on pillows of straw during lunch hours, chewing ruminatively on chapattis.

The annual festival of **Chinakathoor Pooram** (late February to early March) held at the Sri Chinakathoor Bhagavathy Temple, Palappuram, features a 33-tusker procession, plus remarkable evening puppet shows. Bejewelled tuskers can also be seen at the 20-day **Nenmara-Vallangi Vela**, held at the Sri Nellikulangara Bhagavathy Temple in Kodakara (early April): an amazing festival with grander firework displays than Trichur's **Pooram** but set in fields rather than across the city.

The region is filled with old architecture of *illams* and *tharavadus* belonging to wealthy landowners making a visit worthwhile in itself – but chief among the actual sights is **Palakkad Fort**, a granite structure in Palakkad town itself, built by Haider Ali in 1766, and taken over by the British in 1790. It now has a Hanuman temple inside. Ask directions locally to the 500-year-old Jain temple of **Jainimedu** in the town's western suburbs, a 10-m-long granite temple with Jain *Thirthankaras* and *Yakshinis* built for the Jain sage Chandranathaswami. Only one Jain family is left in the region, but the area around this temple is one of the only places in Kerala where remnants of the religion have survived.

Also well worth visiting in the region are the many traditional Brahmin villages: **Kalpathy**, 10 km outside Palakkad, holds the oldest Siva temple in Malabar, dating from AD 1425 and built by Kombi Achan, then Raja of Palakkad. But the village itself, an 800-year-old settlement by a self-contained Tamil community, is full of beautiful houses with wooden shutters and metal grills and is now a World Heritage Site that gives you a glimpse of village life that has been held half-frozen in time for nearly 1000 years. The temple here is called **Kasiyil Pakuthi Kalpathy** meaning Half Banares because its situation on the river is reminiscent of the Banares temple on the Ganges. A 10-day **car festival** in November centres on this temple and features teak chariots tugged by people and pushed by elephants.

Another unique feature of Palakkad is the *Ramassery Iddli* made at the **Sarswathy tea stall** ① *daily 0500-1830, iddli Rs 1.50, chai Rs 2.50*. If you spend any time on the street in South India, your morning meal will inevitably feature many of these tasty steamed fermented rice cakes. Palakkad is home to a peculiar take on the dumpling, one that has been developed to last for days rather than having to be cooked from fresh. The four families in this poky teashop churn out 5000 *iddlis* a day. Originally settlers from somewhere near Coimbatore, in Tamil Nadu, over 100 years ago, they turned to making this variety of *iddli* when there wasn't enough weaving work to sustain their families. They started out selling them door to door, but pretty soon started to get orders for weddings. The *iddlis* are known to have travelled as far afield as Delhi, by plane in a shipment of 300. Manufacturers have started to arrive in order to buy the secret recipe.

Nelliyampathy, 56 km from Palakkad town, is a hill station with a tiny community of planters. It is famous for its oranges, but there are also orchids, bison, elephant and butterflies in abundance. The view across the Keralite plains from Seethakundu stunning; a third of the district lies spread out under you. The area has good trekking, too.

Megalith trail: Guruvayur to Kunnamkulam

The Palakkad Gap has been one of the few relatively easy routes through the ghats for 3000 years and this area is noted for its megalithic monuments. Megalithic cultures spread from the Tamil Nadu plains down into Kerala, but developed local forms. The small villages of Eyyal, Chovvanur, Kakkad, Porkalam, Kattakampala and Kadamsseri, between Guruvayur and Kunnamkulam, have hoodstones, hatstones, dolmens, burial urns and *menhirs*.

◉ Thrissur, Palakkad and the River Nila listings

For hotel and restaurant price codes and other relevant information, see pages 13-17.

▣ Where to stay

Thrissur (Trichur) *p253*
Reserve ahead for **Pooram**, when prices rocket.
$$$$-$$$ Kadappuram Beach Resort, Nattika Beach, southwest of Thrissur, T0487-239 4988, www.kadappuram beachresorts.com. Self-contained complex of bungalows and cottages in traditional Kerala design, but the emphasis here is on the Ayurveda and most come for the 14-day *panchakarma*. The Ayurveda centre is functional and not luxurious, but massage and medical

attention are excellent. After treatments, cross the pretty river to a huge garden of coconut trees and hammocks that separates the hotel from the sea.
$$ Surya Ayurvedics, Kaipily Rd, Arimpur, T0487-231 2240, www.ayurvedaresorts. com. 10 rooms (some a/c) in impressive old buildings, vegetarian meals, Ayurvedic treatments, yoga, exchange.
$$-$ Luciya Palace, Marar Rd, T0487-242 4731, luciyapalace@hotmail.com. 35 rooms, 15 a/c, 2 suites, Large, clean and quiet rooms, TV, garden restaurant, internet next door, good service, very pleasant hotel.
$ Bini Tourist Home, Round North, T0487-233 5703. 24 rooms, TV, shower, 10 a/c, basic but clean and spacious rooms, restaurant, bar.

$ Railway Retiring Rooms. Well looked after and very good value.

Guruvayur p253
$$$-$$ Krishna Inn, East Nada, T0487-255 0777, www.krishnainn.com. Glossy hotel with white marble floors and spacious. 24-hr coffee shop, vegetarian, multi-cuisine **Thulasi** restaurant.
$$-$ Mayura Residency, West Nada, T0487-255 7174, www.mayuraresidency. com. 65 good-value, well-appointed rooms in high-rise hotel with excellent views from its rooftop. 24-hr coffee shop, **Amrutham** vegetarian (continental, South or North Indian) restaurant.
$$-$ Sree Hari Guest House, Samuham Rd, West Nada, T0487-255 6837. 8 big rooms, some a/c, with hot water, draped with purple crushed velvet in guesthouse stuffed with Krishnas and 1960s-style curtains.
$ Hotel Vanamala, Kusumam South Nada, T0487-255 5213. Popular with domestic tourists, 2-star hotel, very clean rooms with big beds and TV, telephone and hot water. A/c, vegetarian restaurant (Keralite food, 0600-2300), laundry.

Along the River Nila p254
If you're in search of Ayurvedic healing at its most authentic and traditional, the River Nila and Palakkad regions, far inland from the pore-clogging salt air coming off the Arabian Sea, are the best places in Kerala to find it. But don't come here expecting 5-star spa masseurs who'll tiptoe around your Western foibles about comfort and bodily privacy. These treatments are administered to you in the almost-raw, on hard wooden beds amid buckets of oil – and when your treatment is over your torturer may accompany you to the shower to make sure you thoroughly degrease.

$$$$-$$$ River Retreat, Palace Rd, Cheruthuruthy, T0488-426 2244, www.riverreatreat.in. Heritage hotel and Ayurvedic resort in the former (and much-extended) home of the maharajas of Kochi. Spacious rooms have a/c, TV and modern baths, great views onto large tree-filled garden that backs onto the Nila. Period furniture adds a nice touch to the airy communal areas. Tours of the local area, restaurant, bar, pool, Wi-Fi.
$$$ Ayurveda Mana, Peringode, via Kootanadu, T0466-237 0660, www. ayurvedamana.com. Authentic Ayurveda centre set in a fascinating 600-year-old *illam*, with treatments following the traditional methods of Poomully Aram Thampuran, a renowned expert in the discipline. Quiet airy rooms (all with TV) open onto shady veranda and peaceful manicured grounds. Full range of health care treatments available and specialized therapies for arthritis, sports injuries, infertility, etc. All treatments include individually assessed diet, massage and medicine.
$$$ Maranat Mana, Old Ooty–Mysore Rd, Pandikkad (an hour's drive north of Pattambi), T0493-128 6252, www. maranatmana.com. Special homestay in a traditional *namboodhiri* (Kerala Brahmin) household. Hosts Praveen and Vidya have sensitively converted the 160-year-old guesthouse attached to their ancestral home into 3 cool and airy rooms, all with fans and modern baths. You can visit the sprawling main family residence, one of the last surviving examples of Keralite *pathinaru kettu* ('four courtyards') architecture, which contains a Ganesh shrine to which devotees flock from far and wide. Delicious vegetarian meals included, and local tours, Ayurvedic treatments, yoga classes, cultural activities can be arranged. Fascinating and highly recommended, reservations essential.

Palakkad (Palghat) *p256*

$$$$ Kalari Kovilakom, Kollengode, T0492-326 3155, www.kalarikovilakom. com. Ayurveda for purists. Far from the Ayurveda tourist traps, the Maharani of Palakkad's 1890 palace has been restored to make this very elite retreat. It's extremely disciplined yet very luxurious: the indulgence of a palace meets the austerity of an ashram. Treatments include anti-ageing, weight loss, stress management and ailment healing. Lessons include yoga, meditation, Ayurvedic cookery. Strictly no exertion (no sunbathing or swimming). No mod cons (TV, etc), bar, internet. US$414 per day all-inclusive. Minimum stay of 14, 21 or 28 days.

$$$ Kairali Ayurvedic Health Resort, Kodumbu, T0492-322 2553, www.kairali.com. Excellent resort, beautifully landscaped grounds, own dairy and farm, pool, tennis, extensive choice of treatments (packages of Ayurveda, trekking, astrology, golf, pilgrimage), competent and helpful staff. Recommended.

$$$ Kandath Tharavad, Thenkurussi, T0492-228 4124, www.tharavad.info. A magical place tucked away in Palakkad's fields, 6 rooms in a 200-year-old mud and teak ancestral home with natural dyed floor tiles of ochre, terracotta and blue. Nadumuttams open out onto the stars and doors are thick wedges of teak and brass. Bagwaldas, your gracious host, will guide you through local customs and culture as engagingly as he steers you through the physical landscape.

$$$ Olappamanna Mana, Vellinezhi, T0466-228 5797, www.olappamanna mana.com. Majestic manor house, in rosewood, teak and jackfruit trees, to the highest Keralite Hindu caste of *namboodris*, parts of which date back

3 centuries. Pure vegetarian cuisine, no alcohol, 6 bedrooms, with bathroom and fan, no a/c.

$$ Garden House (KTDC), Malampuzha, T0491-281 5217. 17 somewhat chintzy rooms in a 1-star government restaurant on hilltop overlooking the Malampuzha Dam, a popular picnic spot. Mostly non-a/c rooms, pleasant.

$$-$ Fort Palace, West Fort Rd, T0491-253 4621. 19 rooms, groovy old-style hotel some good a/c, restaurant, brash mock turrets. Satellite TV and hot water. Continental/Indian food in restaurant, and bar, both gloomy and packed (lawn service). Nice shared sit-out on 1st floor, spotless, large double beds. Chandeliers, wood panelling.

$$-$ Indraprastha, English Church Rd, T0491-253 4641, www.hotelindraprastha. com. Kitsch and cool: 30 rooms in 1960s block, dark wood, leather banquettes and bronze lettering. Dark bar permanently packed, lawn service, 24-hr vegetarian coffee shop, exchange, internet, bookshop. Multi-cuisine restaurant.

Restaurants

Thrissur (Trichur) *p253*

Most **$** hotels have good restaurants, particularly **Siddhartha Regency's Golden Fork**, on Veliyannur Rd near the station. In general, though, eating out is still somewhat frowned on by the traditional Brahmin families of Kerala, so most eating options are down-at-heel *dhabas*.

$$ City Centre, next to **Priya Tourist Home**. Western snacks, bakery and good supermarket.

$$ Navaratna, Naduvilal, Round West, T0487-242 1994. 1000-2300. Pure vegetarian North Indian restaurant divided into booths.

$ Elite Bharat, Chembottil Lane. Good honest Keralan and South Indian food – *dosas*, *puttu*, *thalis* – served without ceremony to huge crowds of locals.
$ Sapphire, Railway Station Rd. 0630-2200. Excellent lime green and stone eatery dishing up *thalis* and the best chicken biryanis in town.

Palakkad (Palghat) *p256*
$ Ashok Bhavan, GB Rd. Modest vegetarian South Indian snacks.
$ Hotel Noor Jehan, GB Rd, T0491-252 2717. Non-vegetarian a/c restaurant that specializes in *moplah biryani* and *pathiri*, rice chappatis.
$ KR Bakes. 0900-2300. Puffs, ice creams, *halva* plus juice bar and savoury meals after 1600.

⊛ Festivals

Thrissur (Trichur) *p253*
Jan-Feb Several temple festivals involving elephants are held in the surrounding villages which can be as rewarding as **Pooram** (eg **Koorkancherry Thaippoya Mahotsavam**, or **Thaipooya Kavadiyattam**, held at Sri Maheswara Temple, Koorkancherry, 2 km from Thrissur). Also held at the end of Feb is the **Uthralikavu Pooram**, at its most colourful at the Sri Ruthura Mahakalikavu Temple, Parithipra, Vodakancherry, en route to Shornur Junction.
End Mar 7-day **Arratupuzha Festival** at the Ayappa Temple, 14 km from Thrissur. On the 5th day the deity parades with 9 decorated elephants, while on the 6th day **Pooram** is celebrated on a grand scale with 61 elephants in the temple grounds.
Apr-May The magnificent 8-day **Pooram**, a grand festival with elephants, parasols, drums and fireworks, should

not be missed. Several temples in town participate but particularly the Thiruvambady and Paramekkavu. It is marked by very noisy, colourful processions, joined by people from all religious groups, irrespective of caste. The festivities are held 1300-1700 and again at night from around 2000. Elaborately bedecked elephants (each temple allowed up to 15) specially decorated with lamps and palm leaves, march to the Vadakkunnathan Temple carrying priests and deities to the accompaniment of extraordinary drumming. On the final day temple teams meet on the Tekkinkadu *maidan* for the drumming and *Kudumattam* competition; the festival terminates with a huge display of fireworks.
Aug/Sep **Kamdassamkadavu Boat Races** at *Onam*. Also performances of **Pulikali**, unique to Thrissur, when mimers dressed as tigers dance to drumbeats.

Guruvayur *p253*
Punnathur Kotta
Feb/Mar **Utsavam**, 10 days of festivities start with an elephant race and continue with colourful elephant processions and performances of *Krishnanattom* dances. Details from Kerala tourist offices.
Nov-Dec 5-day **Ekadasi** with performances of *Krishnanattom*, a forerunner of *Kathakali* – an 8-day drama cycle.

⊘ What to do

Along the River Nila *p254*
Body and soul
Arya Vaidya Sala, Kottakal town, T0483-274 2216, www.aryavaidyasala.com. One of the biggest and best Ayurvedic centres in India, with a fully equipped hospital offering 4-week *panchkarma*

treatments as well as on-site medicine factory and research department.
The Blue Yonder, 23-24 Sri Guru Nivas, Bengaluru, Karnataka, T080-4115 2218, www.theblueyonder.com. Award-winning responsible travel tour operator, focused on conserving local culture and traditions. Tours are carried out in a way that allows travellers to become fully immersed in the region's way of life, and travelling here can feel like being in an episode of the Arabian Nights, as the knowledgeable guides unfold local folk tales and fables. Flexible, individual itineraries can include homestays, cultural performances, monsoon rafting in self-built bamboo-and-inner-tube rafts, backwater *thoni* (country boat) cruises, legend and heritage trails and wildlife safaris. Unique in India, and heartily recommended.

⊖ Transport

Thrissur (Trichur) *p253*
Bus There are yellow-top local buses available. For long distance, there are 3 bus stands. **KSRTC**, near railway station, T0487-242 1842, southwest of 'Round' including several to **Alappuzha** (3½ hrs), **Bengaluru** (10 hrs), **Coimbatore** (3 hrs), **Guruvayur** (1 hr), **Kochi** (2 hrs), **Kozhikode**, **Chennai** (13 hrs), **Palakkad**, **Thiruvananthapuram** (7 hrs). **North (Priyadarshini)**, just north of 'Round', buses to **Cheruthuruthy**, **Ottapalam**, **Palakkad**. Sakthan Thampuran, 2 km south of 'Round', for frequent private buses to **Guruvayur**, **Kannur**, **Kozhikode**.

Train Enquiries, T0487-242 3150. All trains connecting Kochi with points north stop in Thrissur. **Ernakulam**: more than 20 trains a day; *Kannur Ernakulam Intercity Exp 16306*, 1843, 1¼ hrs.
Chennai (MC): *Chennai Mail 12624*, 2040, 10½ hrs. **Bengaluru**: *Bangalore Intercity Exp 12678*,1020, 9½ hrs. **Mangalore**: *Parasuram Exp 16650*, 1240, 7½ hrs (via Kozhikode, 3 hrs).

Palakkad (Palghat) *p256*
Bus KSRTC, buses run from the **Municipal Bus Stand**, T0491-252 7298, to **Coimbatore**, **Kozhikode**, **Mannarghat** (Silent Valley), **Pollachi**.

Train The main **Junction station**, T0491-255 5231, is 5 km northeast of town. Some passenger trains also stop at the more central **Town station**.
Coimbatore: frequent trains all day, 1-1½ hrs, including *Bangalore Intercity Exp 12678*, 1145, continues to **Bengaluru** (8 hrs), and *Mangalore Chennai Exp 16108*, 1435, continues to **Chennai** (15 hrs). **Ernakulam (Kochi)**: many trains, including *Ernakulam Intercity Exp 12677*, 1420, 2½ hrs; all go via Thrissur, 1-2 hrs.
Mangalore: *Chennai Mangalore Exp 16107*, 1300, 9 hrs, via Kozhikode, 4 hrs.

❶ Directory

Thrissur (Trichur) *p253*
Banks ATMs are everywhere, including at the railway station. **State Bank of India**, Town Hall Rd, Round East, near Paramekkavu Temple; **State Bank of Travancore** (upstairs), opposite.
Internet Sruthy, north of temple ring. Good connections, Rs 30 per hr.
Medical services Amala Cancer Hospital, Amalanagar (9 km, along the Guruvayur Rd), T0487-221 1950. Recommended for medicine, surgery.

Malabar coast

The Malabar region is the unsung jewel of Kerala: the combination of the state's political administration in the south plus the pious Muslim community and orthodoxy of the Hindu population have made it more resistant to tourist development than the more easy-going Catholic-influenced stretch south from Kochi. Any cohesion between north and south Kerala is political, not cultural: Malabar was under the Madras Presidency before Independence, lumped together with the Travancore south only in 1956. The atmosphere couldn't be more different. The coastal towns of Kozhikode (formerly Calicut), Thalassery and Kannur are strongholds of the Muslim Moplah community, whose long-standing trading links with the Middle East have bred a deep cultural affinity that's reflected in the lime-green houses lining the roads and the increasing number of women seen in purdah. At the same time, Malabar is one of the best places to see Kerala's Hindu religious and cultural traditions in their proper context: *Theyyam* (the ritual temple dance that spawned *Kathakali*) and *Kalaripayattu* (the stunning martial art), are both practised here. Inland from Kozhikode, the glorious hilltop district of Wayanad experiences some of the heaviest levels of rainfall in the world, and its familiar stubble of tea plantations is interspersed with some of the most stunning and accessible rainforest in the state.

Kozhikode (Calicut) → For listings see pages 268-272. Phone code: 0495.
Population: 436,500

Kozhikode is a major commercial centre for northern Kerala and the centre for Kerala's timber industry; it is also dependent on the petro-dollar, as testified by the scores of direct flights to the Gulf each day. Around 1.2 million Keralites work in the Gulf, generating revenue of about US$12 billion for Kerala. The city itself is engaged in mostly small-scale retail. Off the brash and crowded main boulevard, tiny lanes thread between high laterite walls with everything happening on the street. Remnants of the spice trade remain and the markets are great. Court Road is home to pepper, the black gold that lured Vasco, as well as copra and coconut oil. There are beautiful wooden mosques built like Hindu temples, and in nearby Beypore, where the Chaliyar river meets the Arabian Sea, you still have half a chance of watching the birth of an *uru* – the massive deep-sea hauler-sized wooden boats

Kozhikode (Calicut)

Where to stay		Restaurants
Alakapuri Guest House 1	Hyson Heritage 4	Dakshin 1
Arora Tourist Home 2	Malabar Palace 5	Sagar 2
Asma Tower 3	Metro Tourist Home 6	Zain's 3

that have been built by Muslim Khalasi shipbuilders with few technological changes since Cheraman Perumal ordered one for a trip to Arabia in the sixth century.

Arriving in Kozhikode (Calicut)
Getting there and around Karipur airport, 25 km south, has connections with the Middle East as well as several major Indian cities. The station and main bus stand are on opposite sides of the town centre, both within easy reach of several hotels. Autos are widely available and surprisingly cheap. ▶ *See Transport, page 272.*

Tourist information Kerala Tourism ⓘ *Malabar Mansion hotel, SM Rd, T0495-272 1395*, has limited information about the town. The branch at the railway station hands out brochures on North Kerala and can help with hotel bookings.

Places in Kozhikode (Calicut)
The Sunni Muslim quarter of **Kuttichera**, behind the railway station to the west of town, holds several fascinating multi-tiered wooden mosques, set around a huge green pond to which flocks of white-capped elders gather in the late afternoon. Legend has it that a ghost within the pond seizes a human sacrifice each year, releasing the body after three days. The mosques date from the 15th century and bear a puzzlingly close resemblance to Hindu temple structures. **Mishkal Masjid** is one of the oldest, and was named for the wealthy trader who built it, but also look for **Jami Masjid** and **Munchunthi Palli**. The latter has a 13th-century *vattezhuthu* (inscribed slab of stone) that proclaims the donation of the land to the mosque by a Zamorin. Women should cover their head, shoulders and limbs in this area.

Note the size of the houses around here, which are known to accommodate more than 150 family members each. The *puyappala* tradition (literally translates as 'fresh husband') means that each marrying daughter takes the husband back into her parents' home. One house is supposed to have 300 people living under the same roof: each building has an average of three kitchens. From here you can walk along Beach Road, where crumbling old buildings that were once trading centres are now being busily demolished. The beach itself is more of a town latrine than a place for swimming.

Pazhassiraja Museum ⓘ *5 km north of the centre on East Hill, Tue-Sun 0900-1630, Rs 10*, has copies of original murals plus bronzes, old coins and models of the some of the area's megalithic monuments. Next door is the **art gallery**, with an excellent collection of paintings by Indian artists as well as wood and ivory carvings, and the **Krishna Menon Museum** ⓘ *Mon, Wed only, 1000-1230, 1430-1700, free*, dedicated to the Keralite politician who became a leading left-wing figure in India's post-Independence Congress government.

Around Kozhikode
Kappad, 16 km north, and now the site of a poor, mainly Muslim fishing village, is where Vasco da Gama and his 170 sailors landed on 27th May 1498. There is an old plaque by the approach road to the beach commemorating the event. Although it is a pleasant spot, the sea is unsuitable for swimming since pollution from Kozhikode filters down this far and the beach itself is used as a toilet by the fishermen.

Beypore, half an hour south of Calicut, was once a significant port, but is now famous only for its boatyard, where families of Khalasis have used traditional methods to make *urus* (huge wooden vessels) for 1500 years. The wiry Khalasis craft the ships using memorized plans and ancient construction techniques, now mainly for the benefit of wealthy Arab clients who deploy them as luxury yachts or floating restaurants.

Mahé → *For listings, see pages 268-272.*

The borders of the 9 sq km that make up French Kerala are marked not by baguette bakeries or pavement cafés, but by shops screaming 'Foreign Liquor'. By night, the 35,000 residents of this outpost of Pondicherry disappear to make way for the truckers who rush through to stock up on half-price whiskies and brandies, taking advantage of the colony's special tax status. By day, however, Mahé is pretty enough: policemen wear French hats and the town is beautifully positioned on a slight hill overlooking the river. It was named after Mahé de Labourdonnais, who captured it for the French in 1725. Many people here still speak French and the very French **Church of St Theresa** celebrates its feast day on 14-15 October. The beaches to the south and north of town are dirty and are not safe for swimming due to undercurrents.

Thalassery (Tellicherry) → *For listings, see pages 268-272. Phone code: 0490.*

Like everywhere along the Malabar's increasingly gold coast, banks here have queues for gold loans where your branch manager doubles as a pawnbroker. Despite an obsession with wealth, at the wide, tree-covered street level you'll find a town that's friendly, brilliantly walkable and lined with 19th-century shops complete with original wooden cupboards and cobwebs. Author Herman Hesse's mother was born here.

Thalassery was set up by the British East India Company in 1683 to export pepper and cardamom. In 1708 they obtained permission to build a **fort** which, having survived a siege laid by Haidar Ali, is still standing today on a rocky promontory about 15 m above sea level. Its proud little gateway, raised on a flight of steps, is flanked by colourful mustachioed figures. There are some attractive old buildings. The Armenian church is rather shabby now but the Catholic church still thrives though the population is largely *Moplah* (Kerala Muslims). The **Odathil Mosque**, believed to be 400 years old, is in the traditional Kerala style with a gabled roof and copper sheeting.

Mambally's Royal Biscuit Factory ⓘ *near the Old Police Station, T0490-232 1207, 0900-2030,* established in 1880, claims to be where cake was first baked in Kerala. Nowadays you'll find jam rolls, ketchup, Nestlé milky bars and lime pickle along with the fresh bakes. The downstairs of the double-decker shops is crowded with hessian sacks full of cinnamon from China, cloves from Madagascar, raisins from Afghanistan and star anise from China and Vietnam. Some of the owners are third generation traders.

The **fish market** ⓘ *0600-1800,* is one of the liveliest in Kerala. Men with cleavers stand tall over barracudas and manta, while stacks of clams, mussels, shrimp and mackerel are constantly replenished with new loads. Fish are then sped along the state highway to reach markets in Kochin and Mangalore.

Thalassery is also a centre for training in gymnastics and circus acts, so street performers and acrobats are not uncommon; 90% of India's circus companies originate here. You can see martial arts in local *kalaris*: one of the best being the tricky-to-find *kalari* of **K Viswanathan Gurukkal** ① *MKG Kalari Sangham, Kuzhippangad, PO Chirakkara, T0490-237110, call in advance.*

Muzhapilangad Beach, 8 km from Thalassery, is nicknamed 'Drive In Beach'. It is an unspoilt, beautifully picturesque 4-km-long stretch of golden sand edged by palm trees at the northern end. Amazingly empty most of the time, it earned its nickname from the local custom of ragging trucks and Ambassadors up and down its firm sands.

Kannur (Cannanore) → *For listings, see pages 268-272. Phone code: 0497.*

Standing on raised ground with cliffs at the sea face, this town boasts a coconut-fringed coastline with some attractive beaches. Weavers' co-operatives and *beedi* factories provide employment but this is also a good place to watch *Theyyam* dances. DTPC ① *at the railway station, T0497-270 3121, www.dtpckannur.com.*

The centre of the Moplah community (a group of Arab descent), Kannur was also the capital of the North Kolathiri Rajas for several hundred years. **Fort St Angelo** ① *0900-1800* was built out of laterite blocks by the Portuguese in 1505 and taken over by the British in 1790 as their most important military base in the south. The picturesque **Moplah town** is round the bay to the south of the fort. The attractive **Payyambalam Beach** is 2 km away.

Handloom weavers produce silk and cotton saris, shirts, *lungis* and soft furnishings sold through local cooperatives. **Kanhirode Weavers' Cooperative Society** ① *Koodali Kannur, T0497-285 7259, 0900-1700, free*, was founded in 1952 on Gandhian principle, has a yearly turnover of Rs 150 million (US$3.7 million) and exports 95% of its pure handloom fabric to the UK for the Futon Bed Company. Spun cotton is shipped in from Coimbatore, and dyed in huge vats after which the cooperative's 450 staff are expected to feed bobbins through the high wooden looms fast enough to make 42 m within 3½ days for women, or three for men. While some weave, others feed the raw heaps of cotton from wire frames onto wheels to make thread – in the silk section they use bicycle wheels. The daily wage is Rs 100 (US$2.45), and apparently the co-op is having trouble recruiting more of the caste, who, as caste rules relax, are going for higher paid jobs elsewhere. A visit here is well worth the journey.

Bekal and Kasaragod → *For listings, see pages 268-272. Phone code: 04994.*

Bekal, 16 km south of Kasaragod, has an ancient **fort** on the sea, the largest and best preserved in Kerala, which gives superb views of the coastline. Originally built by the Kadamba kings, the fort passed under the control of Vijayanagar and of Tipu Sultan before being brought into the hands of the East India Company. Excavations have exposed some interesting structures. Just outside the fort is the **Sri Mukhyaprana Temple**. North and south of the fort stretch long, largely unspoiled beaches, whose sands the Kerala tourism authorities visualize as a future Kovalam; so far there are just a couple of outlandish and isolated resorts. En route to Bekal the road passes **Ezhimala**, with a beach and a hill famous for its Ayurvedic herbs.

Kasaragod is the northernmost town in Kerala. From the bus stand, the walk to the sea through a sprawling residential area – mainly Moplah – takes about 30 minutes. The beach is magnificent and deserted. You can walk a long way before scrambling back to the main road, crossing paddy fields, backwaters, and the Konkan railway line. For *Theyyam* and *Yakshagana* performances contact the Kasaragod DTPC ① *Vidya Nagar, T04994-256450, www.dtpckasaragod.com.*

Wayanad → *For listings, see pages 268-272. Phone code 04936.*

The forest-shrouded shoulders of Chembra Peak stand guard over Wayanad ('land of paddy fields'), a beguiling highland district of spice farms, tea plantations, waterfalls and weird upwellings of volcanic rock, inland from Kozhikode on the picturesque road to Mysore. An easy weekend break from either city, Wayanad so far remains delightfully unspoiled, and its cool misty mornings make a refreshing contrast with the sultry coastal plains. It's also prime wildlife spotting territory: elephants patrol the woodlands of Muthanga and Tholpetty sanctuaries, while the dense *shola* forests around Vythiri are home to whistling thrushes, leaping frogs and giant squirrels. Many of the plantation bungalows have thrown open their doors as luxurious, atmospheric homestays, and the vogue for building treehouses makes this the best place in India if you want to wake up among the branches of a fig tree looking out over virgin forest.

Arriving in Wayanad
Getting there and around The main transport hubs are Kalpetta and Sultan Bathery, with buses from both to Kozhikode and Mysore, and from Sultan Bathery south to Ooty. Local buses connect these towns to the smaller villages, with jeeps and auto-rickshaws available for local transfers. However, hiring a car can save a lot of time and hassle.

Tourist information DTPC ① *north Kalpetta, T04936-202134, www.dtpcwayanad. com*, is run by the efficient and knowledgeable Dinesh, who is a good source of information on trekking and wildlife.

Places in Wayanad
The road from Kozhikode to Wayanad corkscrews steeply up the Western Ghats, topping out after 65 km at **Vythiri**, a popular but low-key weekend getaway set amid stunning forests, with kayaking and nature walks available at **Pookot Lake**. At Chundale (5 km from Vythiri) the road divides: the main route continues to busy **Kalpetta**, which offers plenty of hotels and banks but little in the way of charm, while the more appealing Ooty road leads east to **Meppadi**, the starting point for treks up wild and rugged **Chembra Peak** (2100 m) ① *Forest Range Office, Kalpetta*

Rd, Meppadi, T04936-282001, trekking Rs 1000 per group including guide; call ahead to check the track is open, on whose summit lies a heart-shaped lake. Beyond Meppadi the road continues through the rolling teascapes of Ripon Estate, then through cardamom, coffee, pepper tree and vanilla plantations to reach **Vaduvanchal** (18 km). Six kilometres south of here, **Meenmutty Falls** ① Rs 600 per group including guide (ask for Anoop, who speaks English and knows the forest intimately), are Wayanad's most spectacular waterfalls, tumbling almost 300 m in three stages. An adventurous forest track leads down to a pool at the base of the second fall; take your swimming things.

Sulthan Bathery (Sultan's Battery), the main town of western Wayanad, was formerly known as Ganapathivattom, or 'the fields of Ganapathi'. In the 18th century Tipu Sultan built a fort here, but not much of it remains. Some 12 km southwest of the town are the **Edakkal Caves**, a natural deep crevice set high on a granite hill on which engravings dating back to the Neolithic era have been discovered. Around 30 km to the east is **Muthanga Wildlife Sanctuary** ① 0700-0900 and 1500-1830 (last entry 1700), Rs 100, Indians Rs 10, guide fee Rs 100 per group, jeep entry Rs 50; jeeps can be hired for Rs 300 per safari, the least developed section of a giant reserve that also includes Karnataka's Bandipur and Tamil Nadu's Mudumalai National Parks. Jeep rides in the sanctuary, noted for its elephants, leave from the entrance gate.

◉ Malabar coast listings

For hotel and restaurant price codes and other relevant information, see pages 13-17.

◐ Where to stay

Kozhikode (Calicut) p263, map p263
$$$ Harivihar Ayurvedic Heritage Home, Bilathikulam, T0495-276 5865, www.harivihar. com. In Calicut's pretty Brahminical suburbs, this immaculate former royal home is surrounded by lawns with giant mango and jackfruit trees and a beautiful green water tank where you can undertake pukka Ayurveda or study Indian philosophy, Sanskrit, vasthu and yoga in a small guesthouse setting run by conventional medics. You can also stay on a B&B basis, in one of 5 doubles and 3 singles. Gentle Sivananda yoga, Ayurveda from Coimbatore Arya Vaidya Pharmacy, no alcohol.
$$$ Tasara, Calicut–Beypore Rd, Beypore, T0495-241 4832, www.tasara

india.com. A weaving centre amid a garden of mango and jackfruit trees. Rooms with fan and basic bath. Vasudevan, Balakrishnan and their sisters have been running textile workshops here since 1979, and guests come to take courses in weaving, block-printing, batik, silkscreen and natural dyeing. Price includes all meals, tuition and activities. Good discounts for monthly stays, reservations essential.
$$ Hotel Asma Tower, Mavoor Rd, T0495-272 3560, www.asmatower.com. 44 a/c and non-a/c rooms in gleaming new tower. Inside, expect 2-tone mint green decor, frosty a/c system, perfumed air, muzak and TV and telephone in every room. Good value.
$$ Malabar Palace, GH Rd, Manuelsons' Junction, T0495-272 1511, www.malabar palacecalicut.com. 52 a/c rooms, excellent a/c restaurant, bar, very helpful reception.

$$-$ Hyson Heritage, 114 Bank Rd, T0495-276 6423, www.hysonheritage. com. A breezy, efficient and well-maintained business hotel, with 89 spotless, smallish rooms with phone, cable TV, bath, 47 a/c, set around a large courtyard. Ayurvedic treatments available.

$ Alakapuri Guest House, Moulana Mohammed Ali Rd, T0495-272 3451. 40 rooms set around a charming garden brimming with plants and trees and lotus pond. Simple, spacious, with old furniture, phone, tubs and TV. Dates from 1958, and easily Calicut's most characterful mid-range option. Bar 1000-2200, dining hall 0700-2200.

$ Arora Tourist Home, Railway Station Rd, T0495-230 6889. Not as ship-shape as the outside and ground floor suggest, but the huge rooms here are clean enough if you just want to dump your bags after a train ride. Street noise dies down overnight, but mosquitoes don't rest.

$ Metro Tourist Home, Mavoor Rd Junction, T0495-276 6029. 42 pleasing rooms in bustling hotel, some with TV, a bit noisy, South Indian restaurant. Gloomy with grubby paintwork but clean sheets, big mirrors and good fans.

$ Railway Retiring Rooms. Very spacious, clean, good service.

Thalassery (Tellicherry) *p265*
$$$$ Ayisha Manzil, Court Rd, T0490-234 1590, www.ayishamanzil. uniquehomestays.com. A delightful mid-19th century, colonial-style heritage home overlooking the sea. 6 huge a/c rooms with carved teak and rosewood furniture, massive baths, lots of British and Malabari memorabilia, amazing fresh seafood and cookery courses, temple pond pool, superb panoramic views, excursions.
$$-$ Hotel Pranam, AVK Nair Rd, Narangapuram, T0490-222 0634.

14 cleanish rooms with bath – 4 with a/c, a little grubby. The a/c deluxe room has an extraordinary green carpeted sitting room attached.

$ Paris Presidency, New Paris Complex, Logan's Rd, T0490-234 2666, www.paris presidency.com. 24 clean and comfortable rooms with baths, TV, phone, restaurant, wood furniture, bright white walls in busy shopping area. Multi-cuisine restaurant.

Kannur (Cannanore) *p266*
$$ Costa Malabari, near Adykadalaya Temple, 6 km south of town (by bus, ask to get out at Thazhe Chowwa), T0484-237 1761, www.costamalabari.com. An unpretentious guesthouse converted from a warehouse with 5 rooms off a main hall. The owners have authored a book on Kerala's festivals and have encyclopaedic knowledge of the local *Theyyam* scene. Difficult to get to and far from the centre, but there are 5 idyllic, wholly empty beaches within walking distance. Meals included.

$$-$ Mascot Beach Resort, near Baby Beach, Burnassery, 2 km from centre, T0497-270 8445, www.mascotresort.com. Good rooms in high-rise business hotel overlooking the sea, residents-only pool, located in the quiet cantonment area (Ayurvedic centre attached).

$$-$ Royal Omars Thavakkara Kannur, very close to the railway station and colourful market area, T0497-276 9091. Spanking new, with spacious standard non-a/c doubles at bargain rates. 65 rooms, TV, credit cards.

$ Hotel Savoy, Beach Rd, T0497-276 0074. Bags of character in this super-clean, old-fashioned complex of bungalow cottages set around a lawn. A/c cottages are wonderfully spacious and cool. Bar attached.

Wayanad *p267*

Wayanad is Kerala's treehouse capital, and has superb homestay options, but offers relatively little joy at the budget end. Cheaper places are generally restricted to Kalpetta and Sulthan Bathery.

$$$$-$$$ Vythiri Resort, 6 km up dirt road east of highway, T04936-255366, www.vythiriresort.com. Beautiful resort hidden beside a tumbling forest stream, with a choice of cute *paadi* rooms (low beds and secluded courtyards with outdoor shower), high-ceilinged cottages, or a pair of superb new treehouses in the branches of fig trees, one of which involves being hand-winched up and down. Leisure facilities include spa, pool (swimming and 8-ball), badminton and yoga, and there's a good outdoor restaurant (buffet meals included in price) where you can watch monkeys trying to make away with the leftovers.

$$$ Aranyakam, Valathur (south of Ripon off Meppadi–Vaduvanchal Rd), T04936-280261, T(0)9388-388203, www.aranyakam.com. Atmospheric homestay in Rajesh and Nima's 70-year-old bungalow, set amid a sea of coffee bushes and avocado trees. Huge rooms in the elegant main house come with raked bare-tile ceilings and balconies, or opt for the valley-facing treehouses where you can look out for deer and sloth bear while watching sunset over Chembra Peak. Nima serves genuine home-style Kerala food in the thatched, open sided dining room.

$$$ Edakkal Hermitage, on road before Edakkal Caves, T04936-260123, www.edakkal. com. A sustainable tourism initiative with 5 comfortable cottages and a sweet, simple treehouse, built in, around and on top of a series of huge boulders. Tree frogs inhabit the bamboo-fringed pond, and the sunset views over

paddy fields and mountain ranges are magic. The highlight, though, is dinner, served in a natural grotto that's lit with hundreds of candles. Price includes meals.

$$$-$$ Green Gates, TB Rd, North Kalpetta, T04936-202001, www.green gateshotel.com. Modern if slightly scuffed and musty rooms with a/c, TV and hot showers, within walking distance of Kalpetta's shops. There's a pool and Ayurvedic spa, and a helpful travel desk arranges trips to caves, wildlife sanctuaries and tribal colonies of Wayanad.

$$$-$ Haritagiri, Padmaprabha Rd, T04936-203145, www.hotelharitagiri. com. A modern building in the heart of Kalpetta just off the highway, some a/c rooms, clean and comfortable, restaurant 'reasonable', good value but rather noisy.

$$-$ Regency, on the main road in Sulthan Bathery, T04936-220512. Good range of neat and tidy rooms, better value at the cheaper end.

$ Dwaraka, on the main road in Sulthan Bathery, T04936-220512. Far from sparkling, but offers the cheapest rooms in town.

$ PPS Tourist Home, just off highway at south end of Kalpetta, T04936-203431. Reasonable rooms, good cheap restaurant.

$ YMCA Camp, off the highway in Vythiri, T(0)9895-544609. There's just one simple room in this peaceful encampment, but it's big, cool and exceptional value.

❶ Restaurants

Kozhikode (Calicut) *p263, map p263*
$$ Malabar Palace (see Where to stay). International, a/c, excellent food and service.
$ Dakshin, 17/43 Mavoor Rd, T0495-272 2648. 0630-2230. Dead cheap place for *dosa*, pizza, cutlet and curd rice (meals from Rs 15).

$ Hotel Sagar, 5/3305 Mavoor Rd,
T0495-272 5058. 0530 onwards.
So popular they've launched their
own hotel, and another restaurant
(the original is already multistorey).
Sagar is famous for its biriyanis, and
also does superb breakfasts of *dahl* and
parotta. Upstairs is for families and a/c
rooms; downstairs is the cattle class.
$ Zain's Hotel, Convent Cross Rd, T0495-
276 1482. A simple place run by a Muslim
husband and wife. Mussels, biriyanis for
Rs 30 and fish curries for Rs 15.

Thalassery (Tellicherry) *p265*
$$ Ayisha Manzil, Court Rd, T0490-234
1590. Peerless homestay, serving food
unlike you'll get anywhere outside a
home. Phone for meals in advance.
$ Royal Visitors' Family Restaurant,
Pranam Tourist Home, T0490-234 4292.
0630-2300. Grilled mussels, etc.

Kannur (Cannanore) *p266*
$$ Chakara Drive in Restaurant,
Cliff Exotel International, Payyabalam,
T0497-271 2197. Specials are sizzlers
plus spicy fried *kallumakais* mussels
and Malabar biriyani.
$ Indian Coffee House, Fort Rd.
For snacks.
$ Mascot Beach Resort's Restaurants,
near Baby Beach, Burnasseri, T0497-270
8445, www.mascotresort.com. Some of
the best top-end eating in town.
$ MVK Restaurant, SM Rd, T0497-276
7192. 1000-2200. A local institution which
has been packed from its opening 50
years ago, thanks to its commitment to
fresh, home-ground spice mixes for its
biriyanis, their rice grains steeped in ghee.
Serves beautiful, potent lime tea too.
$ Regency Snacks and Fast Food,
opposite Sangeetha Theatre, SN Park Rd,
T0497-276 8676. Popular café with locals.

$ Your Choice Restaurant, Fort Rd.
Authentic Malabari food.

⏏ Entertainment

Kannur (Cannanore) *p266*
Theyyam dance
At **Parssinikadavu Temple**, 20 km north
of Kannur, reached by bus. Performances
(Dec-Mar) of ritual dance theatre at
dawn (taxi essential) and often late
afternoon to dusk. Pilgrims sometimes
seek blessing from the principal dancer
who may go into a trance after taking on
the role of Mutthapan, a manifestation of
Siva as Hunter.

⏾ What to do

Kannur (Cannanore) *p266*
**PVA Ayurvedic Multi Speciality
Nursing Home**, Onden Rd, T0497-
276 0609, www.pvaayurvedic.com.
The down-at-heel PVA provides
training courses in Ayurveda as well
as rejuvenation, purification packages
and direct treatments for ailments like
disc prolapse, psoriasis and obesity. The
3 doctors here are highly regarded.

Bekal *p266*
**Bekal Resorts Development
Corporation**, T0467-227 2007,
www.bekal.org. The tourism-
starved north wants a piece of the
houseboat action. Happily it has
amazingly pristine mangroves.

Wayanad *p267*
The Blue Yonder (see page 261) can
arrange excellent, forest-savvy guides.

⊖ Transport

Kozhikode (Calicut) *p263, map p263*
Air Airport, T0495-271 1314 (Domestic), T0495-271 0517 (International). Transport to town: prepaid taxi Rs 300. **Air India**, Eroth Centre, Bank Rd, T0495-276 7401; airport, T0495-271 3700, flies to **Mumbai**, **Coimbatore**, **Goa**, **Chennai**, **Tiruchirapalli**. Jet Airways, Arayedathupalam, near BM Hospital, T0495-274 0052, to **Mumbai**.

International flights to **Abu Dhabi** (UAE), **Bahrain**, **Doha** (Qatar), **Jeddah** (Saudi Arabia), **Kuwait**, **Muscat** (Oman), **Ras-Al-Khaimah** (UAE) and **Sharjah** (UAE).

Bus KSRTC, T0495-272 2771, from bus stand Mavoor Rd (near Bank Rd junction) to **Bengaluru**, **Thiruvananthapuram** (via Thrissur, Ernakulam, Alappuzha, Kollam), 0630-2200 (10 hrs), **Ooty** (see Wayanad, below). The **New Bus Stand**, T0495-272 2823, is further east on Mavoor Rd for private buses to the north including **Kannur**. Local buses operate from **Palayam Bus Stand** on Kallai Rd, T0495-272 0397.

Train Enquiries, T0495-270 1234. Trains to **Chennai**, **Coimbatore**, **Ernakulam** (4½ hrs) via **Shoranur** and **Thrissur**, **Goa**, **Mangalore** (5 hrs), **Mumbai**, **Thiruvananthapuram** (9½-10 hrs).

Kannur (Cannanore) *p266*
Bus Enquiries: T0497-270 7777. To **Kozhikode** (2½ hrs), **Mangalore** (4½ hrs), **Mercara** (6 hrs), **Mysore** (6 hrs).

Train Enquiries: T0497-270 5555. To **Mangalore**: *Chennai Mangalore Mail 12601*, 0940, 2¾ hrs; *Parasuram Exp 16650*, 1740, 2½ hrs. **Palakkad**: *Kannur Yesvantpur Exp 16528*, 1745, 5 hrs, continues to **Bengaluru** (YPR), add 9 hrs; *Mangalore*

Chennai Mail 12602, 1550, 5 hrs, continues to **Chennai**, add 10 hrs. **Ernakulam** (**Kochi**): *Kannur Ernakulam Intercity Exp 16306*, 1430, 5½ hrs.

Wayanad *p267*
Bus From **Kalpetta** Bus Stand, T04936-203040, to **Kozhikode**, 3½ hrs, via **Vythiri**; **Mysore** via **Sulthan Bathery**. From **Sulthan Bathery**, T04936-220217, to **Ambalavayal** (for Edakkal Caves), **Vaduvanchal** and **Ooty**.

❶ Directory

Kozhikode (Calicut) *p263, map p263*
Banks ATMs on Kallai Rd and at station. Exchange at **SBI**, Bank Rd. Good rates, no commission, friendly. Also **Thomas Cook**. **Internet** Nidhi, near New Bus Stand or behind **Malabar Mansion**, SM St. Fast, Rs 30 per hr. **Sreeram Travels**, shop 3, opposite district hospital. **Medical services** Government Hospital, T0495-236 5367. Medical College Hospital, T0495-235 6531.

Thalassery (Tellicherry) *p265*
Banks Federal Bank, MM Rd, 1000-1530 (Sat 1000-1230 Sun closed) for speedy transactions. **Internet** Telynet Internet Café, Masjid Building near Municipal Office, MG Rd, telynet@ rediffmail.com. 0900-2100.

Kannur (Cannanore) *p266*
Internet Search World, near Railway Station, MA Rd. Fast connection, Rs 30 per hr.

Wayanad *p267*
Banks ATMs in Kalpetta and Sulthan Bathery. For exchange, try **UAExchange**, on the main road in Kalpetta.
Internet Several places in Kalpetta and Sulthan Bathery.

Lakshadweep, Minicoy and Amindivi Islands

The islands, which make up the Lakshadweep ('100,000 islands'), have superb beaches and beautiful lagoons. There are, despite the name, only 11 inhabited and 11 uninhabited islands making up the group. Minicoy, the southernmost island, is 183 km from Kalpeni, its nearest neighbour. Geologically they are the northernmost extensions of the chain of coral islands that extends from the far south of the Maldives. The atolls are formed of belts of coral rocks almost surrounding semi-circular lagoons, with none more than 4 m above sea level. They are rich in guano, deposits of centuries of bird droppings. The wealth of coral formations (including black coral) attracts a variety of tropical fish including angel, clown, butterfly, surgeon, sweetlip, snappers and groupers. There are also manta and sting rays, harmless sharks and green and hawksbill turtles. At the right time of the year you may be able to watch turtles laying their eggs. Arriving on the beach at night, each lays 100-200 eggs in holes they make in the sand.

Arriving in Lakshadweep, Minicoy and Amindivi Islands

You can only visit the islands on a package tour – individuals may not book independently. Lakshadweep Tourism's Society for Promotion of Recreational Tourism and Sports (SPORTS) and other tour operators organize package tours. Everyone needs a permit, for which you need to provide details of the place and date of birth, passport number, date and place of issue, expiry date and four photos; apply two months ahead. If you plan to dive, get a doctor's certificate. Foreign tourists may only visit Bangaram and Kadmat Islands; Indians can also visit Kadmat, Kavaratti, Kalpeni and Minicoy. Thinakkara and Cheriyam are being developed.
➤➤ *See What to do and Transport, pages 275-276.*

The islands → *For listings see pages 275-276. Population: 60,600. 225-450 km west of Kerala. Total land area: 32 sq km.*

Kavaratti, the administrative capital, is in the centre of the archipelago. The Ajjara and Jamath mosques have the best woodcarvings and the former has a particularly good ceiling carved out of driftwood; a well nearby is believed to have medicinal water. The aquarium with tropical fish and corals, the lake nearby and the tombs are the other sights. The woodcarving in the Ajjara is by superb local craftsmen and masons. Kayaks and windsurfers are available for rent, there's a dive centre, plus a bank and a few *dhabas* selling local food.

Some of the other islands in this group are **Andratti**, one of the largest which was first to be converted to Islam, and **Agatti**, which has Lakshadweep's only airport, a beautiful lagoon and a palm-shaded resort.

Barren, desolate and tiny, **Pitti Island** comprises a square reef and sand bank at its south end. It is a crucially important nesting place for terns and has now been listed as a wildlife sanctuary. Conservation groups are pressing for a ban on the planting of trees and the mining of coral, but the main risk to the birds is from local fishermen who collect shells and the terns' eggs for food. Nearby **Cheriam** and **Kalpeni** have suffered most from storm damage.

Bangaram is an uninhabited island where CGH Earth runs the Bangaram Island Resort (see Where to stay, below).

Kalpeni, with its group of three smaller uninhabited satellite islands, is surrounded by a lagoon rich in corals, which offers excellent snorkelling and diving. The raised coral banks on the southeast and eastern shores are remains of a violent storm in 1847; the Moidin Mosque to the south has walls made of coral. The islands are reputedly free from crime; the women dress in wrap-around *lungis* (sarongs), wearing heavy gold ornaments here without any fear. Villagers entertain tourists with traditional dances, *Kolkali* and *Parichakkali*, illustrating themes drawn from folk and religious legends and accompanied by music and singing.

Minicoy (Maliku), the southernmost and largest island, is interesting because of its unique Maldivian character, having become a part of the archipelago more recently. Most people speak *Mahl* (similar to *Dhivehi*; the script is written right to left) and follow many of their customs. The ancient seafaring people have been sailing long distances for centuries and the consequential dominance by women may have led Marco Polo to call this a 'female island'. Each of the nine closely knit matrilineal communities lives in an *athir* (village) and is headed by a *Moopan*. The village houses are colourfully furnished with carved wooden furniture. Tuna fishing is a major activity and the island has a cannery and ice storage. The superb lagoon of the palm-fringed crescent-shaped island is enclosed by coral reefs. Good views from the top of the 50-m lighthouse built by the British. You can stay at the **Tourist Huts**.

The **Amindivi** group consists of the northern islands of **Chetlat**, **Bitra** (the smallest, heavily populated by birds, for a long time a rich source of birds' eggs), **Kiltan** where ships from Aden called en route to Colombo, **Kadmat** and the densely populated **Amini**, rich in coconut palms, which was occupied by the Portuguese. **Kadmat**, an inhabited island 9 km long and only 200 m wide, has a beach and lagoon to the east and west, ideal for swimming and diving. The **Tourist Huts** shaded by palms are away from the local village. The Water Sports Institute has experienced, qualified instructors. There are 10 executive and **Tourist Cottages** and a **Youth Hostel** with a dorm for 40.

◉ Lakshadweep, Minicoy and Amindivi Islands listings

For hotel and restaurant price codes and other relevant information, see pages 13-17.

🛏 Where to stay

Lakshadweep, Minicoy and Amindivi Islands *p273*
Kavaratti and Kadmat have basic tourist cottages resembling local huts. Each hut has 1-2 bedrooms, mosquito nets, fans and attached baths; electricity is wind or diesel. Meals are served on the beach and are similar to Keralite cuisine, with plenty of coconut. Breakfast might be iddlis or *puris* with vegetables. Lunch and dinner might be rice and vegetable curry, sambhar, meat or fish curry. Vegetarian meals available on request. Alcohol is available on board ship and on Bangaram Island (tourists requested not to carry it though).
$$$$ Bangaram Island Resort,
T0484-301 1711, www.cghearth.com.
26 standard huts on the beach with fan, fridge and bathrooms or 3 deluxe beach

huts which sleep 4. Activities include scuba-diving, snorkelling, deep-sea fishing and kayaking. International cuisine served.

⏱ What to do

Lakshadweep, Minicoy and Amindivi Islands *p273*
Tourism is still in its infancy and facilities on the islands are limited. Package tours (the only way to visit) are relatively expensive. Tours operate Oct-May; most are late Jan to mid-May. **Schedules** may change, so allow for extra days when booking onward travel.
CGH Earth, Kochi, see page 220.
For the resort only, US$250-350 (for 2), US$500-700 for 4, US$70 extra person (discounts Apr-Sep). On Bangaram, kayaks, catamarans and sailing boats are free. For an extra charge each time: scuba diving (equipment for hire); deep-sea big-game fishing 1 Oct-15 May – only minimal fishing equipment and

boat crew; excursion to 3 neighbouring islands or snorkelling at shipwreck (for 8); glass-bottomed boat. Snorkelling in the lagoon can be disappointing due to poor visibility and dead corals. Kadmat Island scuba-diving US$800, 1-star CMAS Certificate US$30; certified diver US$25 per dive; adult US$350, child (under 10) US$165. Travel by ship from Kochi (deck class) included; return air from Kochi or Goa to Agatti, US$300; return helicopter (Agatti-Kadmat), 15 mins, US$60, or local pablo boat.

SPORTS (Lakshadweep Tourism), Indira Gandhi Rd, Willingdon Island, Kochi, T0484-266 8387, T0484-266 6789. 3 packages costing Rs 6000-10,000 per person (student discounts), including transport from Kochi. Coral Reef: 5 days to Kavaratti, Kalpeni and Minicoy Islands. Kadmat Water Sports: 6 days (including 2-day sailing, stay in Kadmat Cottages or hostel). Paradise Island Huts: 6 days to Kavaratti.

Tour operators
For a full list of authorized tour operators, see www.lakshadweep tourism.com/agents.html.

Watersports
Activities include windsurfing, scuba-diving (Poseidon Neptune School), parasailing, waterskiing and snorkelling.

Deep-sea fishing (barracuda, sailfish, yellow-fin, trevally) is possible on local boats with crew; serious anglers should bring their own equipment; no diving or deep-sea fishing Apr-Sep.

⊖ Transport

Lakshadweep, Minicoy and Amindivi Islands *p273*
Air Agatti has a basic airport. **Indian Airlines** and **Kingfisher** fly to/from Kochi, daily except Tue and Sun.

Ferry *MV Tipu Sultan* sails from Kochi. 26 passengers in 1st and executive class have 2- and 4-berth a/c cabins with washbasins, shared toilets, Rs 5000; 120 passengers in 2nd class in reclining seats in a/c halls, Rs 3500. Ship anchors 30-45 mins away from each island; passengers are ferried from there. Total travel time from Kochi can take up to 30 hrs.

Inter-island transfers are by helicopter (when available) during monsoons, 15 May-15 Sep (return US$60), or by pablo boats for 8.

ⓘ Directory

Lakshadweep, Minicoy and Amindivi Islands *p273*
Agatti has a medical centre; emergencies on the islands have helicopter back-up.

Contents

Footprint features

Karnataka

At a glance

◉ **Getting around** The Konkan railway, local buses or chartered taxi, especially for the more remote ruins around the Deccan.

⟳ **Time required** A weekend in Bangalore, 2 days in Mysore, minimum 4 days to see Hampi and its environs justice, 2-3 days for the Western Plateau temples, a week to walk in Coorg.

❀ **Weather** Hot all year round.

✖ **When not to go** Oppressively hot in Apr and May.

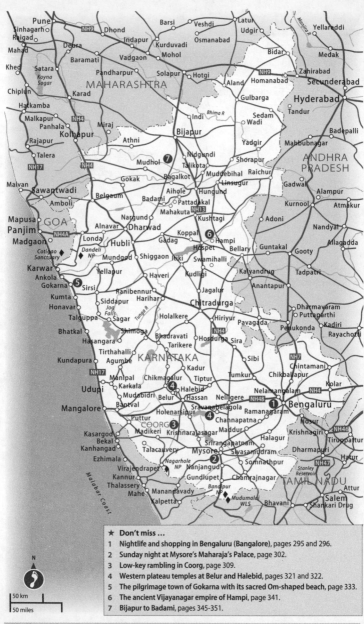

★ **Don't miss ...**
1 Nightlife and shopping in Bengaluru (Bangalore), pages 295 and 296.
2 Sunday night at Mysore's Maharaja's Palace, page 302.
3 Low-key rambling in Coorg, page 309.
4 Western plateau temples at Belur and Halebid, pages 321 and 322.
5 The pilgrimage town of Gokarna with its sacred Om-shaped beach, page 333.
6 The ancient Vijayanagar empire of Hampi, page 341.
7 Bijapur to Badami, pages 345-351.

The chasm between the values, outlook and prosperity of rural Karnataka – the source matter for novelist R K Narayan's Malgudi Tales – and the cosmopolitan high-tech metropolis of Bengaluru (Bangalore), is at times shockingly wide. While the city takes huge strides on the global software and biotechnology stages, switchboards hum with outsourced call centre traffic, world-class medics perform miracle heart and brain surgeries, and roads grind to a halt in rush-hour traffic, much of Karnataka remains as if frozen: its red and black earth rocky and covered with scrub, its villagers' concerns wholly agrarian.

Wealth has always come and gone here: the state's interior, home to some of the earliest settlements in peninsular India, bears chastening witness to the ravages of time. The state has been seat to a roll-call of dynasties, both alien and home-grown – Hindu, Muslim, Jain, British – whose once-great cities and civilizations now stand largely in dusty ruins. As a result, it is brimming with architectural and archaeological riches: the still-emerging Vijayanagara kingdom capital of Hampi in the north; Chalukyan and Hoysala temples throughout Pattadakal, Belur and Halebid; the Islamic palaces of Tipu Sultan in the south; the onion-dome tombs of his Turkish and Persian antecedents in the far northeast; the British boulevards of Bengaluru; and the wondrous palaces of the Hindu maharajas at Mysore.

Karnataka's three great rivers – the Kaveri, Tungabhadra and Krishna – originate in the beautiful, forested hill country of the Western Ghats, the state's natural and hugely biodiverse border. Here awesome waterfalls – Jog Falls being one of the world's highest – stud the Malnad's wildlife parks. The little-visited coastline is emerald lush with river estuaries feeding unique mangrove swamps that rival Kerala's famous backwaters.

The land
Geography The Western Ghats, called the Malnad or hill country, have beautiful forests with waterfalls and wildlife parks. To the east stretches the Mysore Plateau. Parts of northern Karnataka are barren, rocky and covered with scrub, but the state in other places is richly fertile (particularly around the 'sugar bowl' region of Mandya) and it has a lush coastline. From Coondapur to Karwar, the estuaries of the short fast-running rivers flowing west from the ghats still have mangroves, some in uniquely good condition, although commercial exploitation seriously threatens their survival.

Climate The whole of the west coast is extremely wet from June to September, with 1500 mm falling in June and July alone. However, immediately to the east of the Western Ghats rainfall decreases dramatically. Temperatures rise to the low 30°C between February and June but fall slightly during and after the monsoon. On the plateaux of the south, especially around Bengaluru (Bangalore) and Mysore, temperatures are moderated somewhat by the altitude (generally around 1000 m), and nights are pleasantly cool most of the year. The central and northern parts of the state get considerably hotter in April and May, often exceeding 40°C for days at a time.

History
The region between the Tungabhadra and the Krishna rivers was home to some of the earliest settlements in peninsular India, dating back more than 500,000 years. By the Middle Stone Age there was already a regional division appearing between the black cotton soil area of the north and the granite-quartzite plateau of the south. In the north hunters used pebbles of jasper taken from riverbeds while quartz tools were developed to the south. The first agricultural communities of the peninsula have been identified from what is now northern Karnataka. Radiocarbon dating puts the earliest of these settlements at about 3000 BC; millets and gram were already widely grown by the first millennium BC. They have remained staple crops ever since.

Karnataka has borne witness to an alarming array of dynasties, and their ruins. Legend has it that India's first emperor, Chandragupta Maurya, became a Jain and renounced all worldly possessions, retiring to Sravanabelagola to meditate. The Western Gangas, from the third to 11th centuries, and the Banas, from fourth to ninth centuries, controlled large parts of the region. The Chalukyas of central Karnataka took some of the lands between the Tungabhadra and Krishna rivers in the sixth century and built great temples in Badami. They and the Rashtrakutas tried to unite the plateau and the coastal areas while there were Tamil incursions in the south and east. The break-up of the Tamil Chola Empire created a power vacuum in their former fiefdoms. In Karnataka the Hoysalas (11th-14th centuries) seized their chance, and left magnificent temples at their old capitals at Belur, Halebid and Somnathpur, exquisite symbols of their power and their religious authority. Then came the Sangama and Tuluva kings of the Vijayanagar Empire, which reached its peak in the mid-16th century with Hampi as its capital.

Karnataka was repeatedly in the frontline in the power struggle between Hindu and Muslim rulers. **Muhammad bin Tughlaq** attacked northern Karnataka in the 13th century, and during the Vijayanagar period the **Muslim sultanates** to the north continued to extend their influence. The Bidar period (1422-1526) of Bahmani rule was marked by wars with Gujarat and Malwa, continued campaigns against Vijayanagar, and expeditions against Orissa. **Mahmud Gawan**, the Wazir of the Bahmani sultanate, seized Karnataka between 1466 and 1481, and also took Goa, formerly guarded by Vijayanagar kings. By 1530 the kingdom had split into five independent sultanates. At times they came together to defend common interests, and in 1565 they co-operated to oust the Vijayanagar Raja. But two of the sultanates, Bijapur and Golconda, gathered the lion's share of the spoils until the Mughals and British supplanted them.

South Karnataka saw a different succession of powers. While the Mughals were preoccupied fighting off the Marathas, the Hindu **Wodeyar** rulers of Mysore took Srirangapatnam and then Bengaluru (Bangalore). They lost control to **Haidar Ali** in 1761, the opportunist commander-in-chief who joined forces with the French to extend his control west to make Srirangapatnam his capital. The fierce Mysore Wars followed and with Haidar Ali's and then his son Tipu Sultan's death, the **British** restored the Wodeyars' rule in 1799. The Hindu royal family was still administering Mysore up to the reorganization of the states in the 1950s when the maharaja was appointed state governor.

Culture

A fault line runs through mainstream Kannada culture and politics, cleaving society into the northern Karnataka peasant caste, the **Lingayats,** and the **Vokkaligas** of the south. Lingayats follow the egalitarian and keen educationalist 12th-century saint Basavanna. The name Vokkaligas comes from 'okkalu', meaning to thresh, and these people are mostly farmers. The Kodavas from the southwest are a culture apart, physically fair and tall, worshippers of the goddess Cauvery and Lord Iguthappa. Karnataka has its share of tribal people. The nomadic Lambanis in the north and west are among several tribal peoples in the hill regions. The coastal region of Uttara Kannada is home to the Siddis, brought as slaves from Southeast Africa, who retain the practice of ancestor worship, and the Navayats, from Saudi Arabia and Persia. The state has a significant Muslim minority of nearly seven million, and Mangalore particularly has a notable Catholic community.

Cuisine The Kannada temple town of Udupi has spawned its own fabled brand of pure vegetarian food – the *idli* and *dosa* that you'll find in cheap and cheerful cafes in every decent-sized town in India. They are traditionally served on a plantain leaf or stainless steel plate. Another distinctive food of Karnataka is *ragi* (finger millet), the highly nutritious staple grain of villagers throughout the state, most often served as *ragi mudde* – a moist brown cricket ball of baked millet dough that is broken into bite-size chunks and dipped into spicy *sambhar*.

Indian tiger

The economic transformation of India has been one of the greatest business stories of modern times. Now acknowledged as major player in the fields of IT and pharmaceuticals, in the past five years the economy has been growing at close to 9% a year, largely thanks to an investment boom, and as stifling regulations have been lifted entrepreneurship has flourished.

So powerful has the economy become that, 67 years after independence, the colonized have turned colonizers. The global ambitions of 'India Inc' have become evident in a series of high-profile buyouts, none more symbolic than the Tata Corporation's US$13.2 billion acquisition of Anglo-Dutch steel giant Corus, a company whose ancestry can be traced to many of the companies that once symbolized Britain's industrial pre-eminence. Chairman

Ratan Tata proudly boasted that the takeover was "the first step in showing that Indian industry can step outside its shores into an international market place as a global player". Tata has also snapped up such emblems of Englishness as Jaguar and Tetley Tea and, not content with taking over the world, has set itself to cultivating the ambitions of India's rapidly growing middle class. The Nano car, launched in 2009 with a price tag of less than US$1000, together with the Shubh Griha project in suburban Mumbai which sells new apartments for just US$10,000, has made the house-and-car lifestyle a realistic aspiration for millions of Indians.

How big a dent the global recession might put in India's plans for growth remains to be seen. The IT industry, dependent on outsourcing dollars from the hard-hit US market, has

Language Most people speak the Dravidian language *Kannada* (Kanarese), although this has fused to form Indo-Aryan dialects in the north. Kannada has the second oldest Dravidian literary tradition. The earliest known classic is the ninth-century *Kavirajamarga*.

Art and architecture Karnataka's role as a border territory was illustrated in the magnificent architecture of the Chalukyan Dynasty from AD 450 to 650. Here, notably in Aihole, were the first stirrings of *Brahman* temple design. Relics show the parallel development of Dravidian and North Indian temple architecture: in Pattadakal alone there are four temples built on North Indian *Nagari* principles and six built on South Indian *Dravida* lines. Belur, Halebid and Somnathpur's star-shaped bases, bell-towered shrines and exquisite carvings represent a distinctive combination of both traditions. The Vijayanagara kings advanced temple architecture to blend in with the rocky, boulder-ridden landscape at Hampi. Bijapur has some of the finest Muslim monuments on the Deccan from the austere style of the Turkish rulers to the refinement in some of the pavilions and the world's second largest dome at the Gol Gumbaz.

suffered a profit slowdown and been forced to send workers on year-long sabbaticals. However, with most of the major banks being publicly owned, the country has been shielded from the worst excesses of the credit crunch, and the relatively low importance of exports – 22% of the economy, compared to China's 37% – puts India in a good position to survive comparatively unscathed.

A bigger issue for India is how to reduce poverty. Arundhati Roy, a notorious fly in the ointment of Indian triumphalism, wrote (in the days before Tata takeovers) that India, having nowhere else to colonize, has made its fortune by colonizing itself. Rich Indians, disconnected from the reality of where their money comes from, pay little regard to the plight of eight-year-old workers hammering fist-sized lumps of rock into powder in Karnataka's iron ore mines, or the villagers whose lands are repossessed so companies can build cars on the cheap. While the media trumpets the nation's new-found power to put men into space, Infosys executives into mansions and millions of rupees into cricketers' pockets, government reports suggest that 75% of people in India survive on less than Rs 20 per day. As much as 40% of the country still exists below the official poverty line, and statistics on child malnourishment (India has the third highest rate in the world, after Timor-L'Este and Yemen), infant mortality (2.1 million children die every year) and corruption (bribes worth Rs 9 billion a year are hoovered up from below-poverty-line households for basic public services such as policing and schooling) show that for all its progress, the economy still has an awful lot of growing up to do.

Dance, drama and music Open-air folk theatre or *Bayalata* grew from religious ritual and is performed in honour of the local deity. Actors improvise their plays on an informal stage. Performances usually start at night and often last into the early hours. The famous *Yakshagana* or *Parijata* tends to have just one narrator while other forms have four or five, assisted by a jester. The plots of the *Dasarata* which enacts several stories and *Sannata* which elaborates one theme, are drawn from mythology but sometimes highlight real-life incidents. The *Doddata* is less refined than the *Yakshagana* but they have much in common, beginning with a prayer to the god Ganesh, using verse, and drawing from the stories of the epics *Ramayana* and *Mahabharata*. The costumes are elaborate with fantastic stage effects, loud noises and war cries and vigorous dances.

Modern Karnataka

Government The 19 districts are grouped into four divisions: Bengaluru (Bangalore), Mysore, Belgaum and Gulbarga. Caste rivalry between Vokkaligas and Lingayats remains a powerful factor and faction fighting within parties is a recurrent theme. In 2004, Congress suffered a swingeing backlash against its liberal economic policies that had fuelled Bengaluru's rise to become the darling of the IT and biotechnology industries. The BJP became the largest single party in the Assembly, though it was initially prevented from forming a government by a short-lived coalition between Congress and the secular Janata Dal party.

The BJP finally took power in its own right in 2008 under Lingayat leader BS Yeddyurappa. The party's reign was tarred with accusations of corruption and nepotism – several senior ministers served jail time for scams, including Yeddyurappa himself – and its woes were compounded by three leadership coups in five years. In 2013, to a background of unease about the BJP's push towards "saffronization" of public life in the state, Karnataka's voters overwhelmingly reinstalled the Congress party under the leadership of avowed atheist Siddaramaiah.

Economy Karnataka is one of India's most rapidly modernizing states, and an undisputed leader in IT skills, biotech and industrial activity. Based on its early development of aeronautics and high precision machine tools, Bengaluru has become a world centre for the computer industry, receiving a much-quoted seal of approval from Bill Gates. Outside the cities agriculture and forestry remain important. Demand for irrigation is growing rapidly against a backdrop of frequent droughts. The water issue is the cause of escalating tension with neighbouring Tamil Nadu, a conflict that plays out at the top political level, with a verdict reached by the Indian Supreme Court to allocate resources in 2007, and as a trigger for mass demonstrations, rallies have led to violent clashes against Tamilian interests, property and people within Karnataka's borders.

Bengaluru (Bangalore)

IT capital Bengaluru (Bangalore), the subcontinent's fastest-growing major city, is the poster boy of India's economic ascendance. Its buoyant economy has cost the so-called 'garden city' and 'pensioner's paradise' its famously cool climate and sedate pace. In their place are streets throttled with gridlocked traffic, a cosmopolitan café culture, a lively music scene and dynamic, liberal-minded people, which combine to make the city a vibrant and forward-thinking metropolis, one whose view of the world is as much attuned to San Francisco as to the red baked earth of the surrounding state of Karnataka.

And there's more to Bengaluru than Wipro, Infosys and call centres: Bengaluru rivals Kancheepuram for silk; it's the site of India's aeronautical defence industry's headquarters; it boasts a mammoth monolithic Nandi Bull temple; has boulevards shaded by rain and flame trees and the great green lungs of Lal Bagh Gardens and Cubbon Park; and holds a number of fine administrative buildings left over from the British. For all its outward-looking globalism, if you walk around the jumbles of rope and silk shops, tailors, temples and mosques in the ramshackle and unruly bazars of Gandhi Nagar, Sivaji Nagar, Chickpet and City Market, you can almost forget the computer chip had ever been invented.

Arriving in Bengaluru → *Colour map 3, A4. Phone code: 080. Population: 9.6 million.*
Getting there The new **Bengaluru International Airport** (BLR), 25 km north of the city in Devanahalli, has direct flights from London, Frankfurt, the Middle and Far East, Sri Lanka and Nepal, as well as all major Indian cities. There are metered taxis (generally better value than the overpriced prepaid taxi booths in the Arrivals terminal), and fast airport buses serve a range of destinations in the city including **Kempegowda Bus Station** (the main long-distance bus station, also handy for the City railway station and the seedy 'Majestic' area, home to many cheap hotels) and the MG Road/Brigade Road area, where more upscale hotels are located. Trains arrive at one of three main stations: **City**, in Gandhi Nagar next to the main bus stand; **Cantonment**, a few kilometres to the northwest, most convenient for MG Road; and **Yeswantpur** in the inner northern suburbs. Virtually all long-distance buses, both state-run and private, will leave you at or near the bus stand. ▸▸ *See Transport, page 298.*

Getting around Bengaluru is very spread out and you need transport to get around. You also need to allow plenty of time: despite a new Metro and highway flyovers being in place, infrastructure has completely failed to keep pace with the city's population explosion. Traffic is so bad that road travel on weekdays is best avoided, and even weekends can see the streets descend into something approaching gridlock. The Metro, touted as the city's salvation, is at the "good start" stage: trains currently run along two short and as-yet unconnected stretches, one running eastward from MG Road, the other northward from Sampige Road (a few hundred metres north of Majestic) via Yesvantpur station. Trains run between 0600-2200. City buses run a frequent and inexpensive service throughout the city. Taxis and auto-rickshaws are available for trips around town and should readily use their meters; they charge 50% extra after 2200. There are prepaid rickshaw booths at each of the stations. If you're planning on covering a lot of sights in a day it can work out cheaper to hire a car and driver, though you'll need a good book.

Tourist information Karnataka State Tourism Development Corporation (KSTDC) ① *head office, No 49, Khanija Bhavan, West Entrance, Race Course Rd, T080-2235 2901, www.kstdc.net, Mon-Sat 1000-1730, closed every 2nd Sat; booking counter, for tours and hotels at Badami House, NR Square, T080-4334 4334*, has counters at the airport and City railway station. **Karnataka Tourism House** ① *8 Papanna La, St Mark's Rd, T080-4346 4351*, is a one-stop shop for bookings and information. **India Tourism** ① *KSFC Building, 48 Church St, T080-2558 5417; Mon-Fri 0930-1800, Sat 0900-1300*, is very helpful. For events, pick up the fortnightly *Time Out* magazine (www.timeoutbengaluru.net), and the bimonthly *City Info* (www.explocity.com). An excellent online resource is http://bangalore.burrp.com/events.

Background
The 16th-century Magadi chieftain Kempe Gowda built a mud fort and four watchtowers in 1537 and named it Bengalaru (you can see his statue in front of the City Corporation buildings). Muslim king Haidar Ali strengthened those

Bengaluru: India's high-tech centre

The contemporary high-tech and biotech blossoming in Bengaluru (Bangalore) has deep roots: the city was consciously developed into India's research capital after Independence, with public sector units in electronics, aeronautical industry and telecoms established in the city, and educational institutions to match. National programmes of space research and aircraft design continue to be concentrated here, and it is home to the Indian Institute of Science.

fortifications before his death at the hands of the British, leaving his son Tipu Sultan to pick up where he left off. When the British gained control after 1799 they installed the Wodeyar of Mysore as the ruler and the rajas developed it into a major city. In 1831 the British took over the administration for a period of 50 years, making it a spacious garrison town, planting impressive avenues and creating parks, building comfortable bungalows surrounded by beautiful lawns with tennis courts, as well as churches and museums.

Places in Bengaluru

The 1200 ha of **Cubbon Park** in the Cantonment area was named after the 19th-century British representative in Bangalore. The leafy grounds with bandstand, fountains and statues are also home to the Greco-Colonial High Court, State Library and museums, now overshadowed by the post-Independence granite of Vidhana Soudha, the state's legislature and secretariat buildings across the street.

Government Museum ⓘ *Kasturba Rd, Cubbon Park, T080-2286 4483, Tue-Sun 1000-1700, Rs 4*, is idiosyncratic and slightly dog eared; opened in 1886, it is one of the oldest in the country. There are 18 galleries: downstairs teems with sculptures, huge-breasted Durga and a 12th-century figure of Ganesh from Halebid sit alongside intricate relief carvings of Rama giving his ring to Hanuman, and there are Buddhas from as far afield as Bihar. An upstairs gallery holds beautiful miniatures in both Mysore and Deccan styles, including a painting of Krishnaraj Wodeyar looking wonderfully surly. There are also Neolithic finds from the Chandravalli excavations, and from the Indus Valley, especially Mohenjo Daro antiquities. In the same complex, the **K Venkatappa Art Gallery** ⓘ *Kasturba Rd, Cubbon Park, T080-2286 4483, Tue-Sun 1000-1700, Rs 4*, shows a small cross-section of work by the late painter (born 1887). His paintings of the southern hill stations give an insight into the Indian fetishization of all things pastoral, woody and above all cold. There is also the story and blueprints of his truncated design for the Amba Vilas Durbar Hall in Mysore and miniatures by revered painter Abanindranath Tajore (1871-1951), alongside a second portrait of Krishnaraj Wodeyar.

Visveswaraya Industrial and Technological Museum ⓘ *Kasturba Rd, next to the Government Museum, Tue-Sun 1000-1800, Rs 15*, will please engineering enthusiasts, especially the basement, which includes a 1917 steam wagon and India's oldest compact aircraft. Others might be left cold by exhibits on the 'hydrostatic paradox' or

Bengaluru

To ISKCON Temple (2 km), Tumkur, NH 4 & Hesarghatta (26 km)

To Guntakal (NH 7) & Nandi Hills

To Bangalore Palace

SRIRAMPURAM

5th Cross Rd

Sampige Rd

Sheshadri Puram Main Rd

Kumara Park West

Kumarakupa Rd

Crescent Rd

Sankey Rd

Palace Rd

Miller's Rd

Miller's Rd

Cantonment Station

Queen's Rd

Cunningham Rd

SHIVAJI

Ali Asker Rd

Infantry Rd

Cricket Stadium

HIGH GROUND

Club House

Race Course Rd

Race Course

Anand Rao

Gandhi Gardens

Palace Rd

Dr Ambedkar Rd

Vidhan Soudha

Queen Victoria Statue

Mahatma Gandhi Statue

Sheshadri Rd

GANDHI NAGAR

Magadhi Rd

City Station

Subedar

Chatham Rd

Bhashyam Rd

Agrahara Rd

BINNYPETE GARDENS

City Central (KSRTC)

Kempe Gowda Rd

Chikpete Rd

Janata Market

Gandhinagar Rd

KG Post Office Rd

KR Circle

Cubbon Park

Museums

Kasturba Gandhi Rd

Grant Rd

MACIVER TOWN

St Mark's Rd

Mallya Hospital

KG Circle

Jami Masjid

City Market

Avenue Rd

CUBBON PETE

SULTANPETE

DODPETE

Nrupathunga Rd

SAMPANGIRAM NAGAR

Kasturba Gandhi Rd

Raja Rammohan Roy Rd

Richmond Circle

Residency Rd

Lal Bagh Rd

ANJANAPPA GARDENS

Police Rd

Fort

S J Park Rd

Narasimharaja Rd

Unity Building

Town Hall

Mission Rd

SHANTI NAGAR

Langford Rd

LANGFORD

To Mysore

Mysore Rd

Brand Circle

CHAMRAJPET

Tipu's Summer Palace

KALASIPALYAM

P Chetty Rd

Kempe Gowda

Bull Temple Rd

Krishnarajendra Rd

Kalasipalya Main Rd

Jayachamaraja Wodeyar Rd

Lal Bagh

MAVALLI

Kengal Hanumanthaiah Rd

Lal Bagh Fort Rd

Kempambudhi Tank

To Soap Factory

GANDHI BAZAR

Vanivilas Rd

Indian Institute of World Culture

4th Main Rd

Lal Bagh Gardens

Kempe Gowda Tower

SIDDAPURA

Hosur Rd

Bugle Rock Rd

Bugle Park

To Bull Temple

To Archaeological Survey of India

To Bannerghatta (21 km) & Muthyala Maduvu (45 km)

N

600 metres
600 yards

Where to stay

Ajantha 1
Green Path Serviced Apartments 3
Ivory Tower 18
Kamat Yatrinivas 2
Keys 17

Mahaveer 4
New Central Lodge 5
New Rainbow 16
Oberoi 6
Park 10
Railway Retiring Rooms 7
St Mark's 8

Taj West End 9
Vellara 11
Villa Pottipati 12
Vybhav 13
Woodlands 14
YMCA Guest House 15

1 G Road area

Restaurants 🍴
Benjarong **12**
Chalukya **2**
Coconut Grove **7**
Halli Mane **3**
Indian Coffee House **11**
Karavalli **4**

Koshy's **8**
MTR **5**
Nilgiri's Upper Crust **9**
Palmgrove **10**
Sukh Sagar **6**
Tandoor **1**
Vidyarthi Bhavan **13**

'the invention of the hook and eye and zip fastener technology'. Upstairs is a wing devoted to educating the inhabitants of Bengaluru on genetic engineering. You might find the debate a little one-sided: "agricultural biotechnology is a process … for the benefit of mankind," it states in capital letters. A small corner (next to the placard thanking AstraZeneca, Novo Nordisk Education Foundation, Novozymes and Glaxo-SmithKline), is dubbed 'Concerns', but you can see how cloning and genetically strengthened 'golden' rice might seem more attractive when put in the context of the growling Indian belly.

To the southwest lies the summer palace that Tipu Sultan, the perennial thorn in the side of the British, boasted was "the envy of heaven". **Tipu's Summer Palace** ① *City Fort, 0800-1730, foreigners Rs 100, Indians Rs 5, video camera Rs 25*, was begun by his father Haidar Ali and was completed by Tipu in 1789. Based on the Daria Daulat Bagh in Srirangapatnam, the understated two-storey structure is largely made of teak with walls and ceilings painted in brilliant colours with beautiful carvings. A room downstairs is given over to documenting Haidar and Tipu's reigns and struggles against the British.

Lal Bagh Gardens ① *southeast of the Summer Palace, 0900-1830, Rs 7*, were laid out across 97 ha by Haidar Ali in 1760 and are second only to Kolkatta's in size. Tipu added a wealth of plants and trees from many countries (there are over 1800 species of tropical, subtropical and medicinal plants) and the British brought a bandstand. Sadly, the Indian affection for botanical beauty means that the rose gardens are kept behind bars. At dusk, Lal Bagh is popular with businessmen speed-walking off their paunches, and

Health tourism

For decades, Western travel to India was synonymous with emaciated hippies, and backpackers' conversations invariably veered towards the scatological as everyone, at some stage, was sure to catch the dread 'Delhi belly'. It's a sign of the times that, although the British National Health Service failed to award India its whole back-up project in 2004, the country has become a very real alternative to private health care, representing huge cost reductions on surgery.

The centrepiece for this emerging industry is arguably Bengaluru, which has the largest number of systems of medicine approved by the World Health Organization in a single city: cardiac, neurology, cancer care and dentistry are just a few of the areas of specialization, and clients include the NHS and America's largest insurance company. Open-heart surgery will set you back US$4500 in Bengaluru, for example, as opposed to US$18,000 abroad. And afterwards, of course, you can recuperate at an Ayurveda resort. Lately Bengaluru has knitted its medical specialists with its IT cred to pioneer virtual medicine too, whereby cardiac experts in the city hold teleconferences with outposts up and down the subcontinent to treat emergencies, examine and monitor patients via phone, text and video, a method specialists at Narayana Hrudayalaya confidently predict will one day become the norm.

courting couples and newlyweds who sit on the banks of the lotus pond eating ice cream. The rocky knoll around the Kempe Gowda tower has great city views, and is popular at sunset. There are fortnightly Sunday evening performances of Kannada folk theatre, song and dance; go on for supper at MTR (see Restaurants, page 295) for a pukka Bengaluru evening. The **Glass House**, with echoes of London's Crystal Palace and Kew Gardens, holds flower shows in January and August to mark Republic and Independence days.

Further south, the hefty **Nandi Bull at Bull Temple** ① *Bull Temple Rd, Basavanagudi, 0600-1300, 1600-2100*, was carved at the behest of Kempe Gowda, making it one of the city's oldest temples. The monolithic Nandi was believed to be growing unstoppably until a trident was slammed into his forehead: he now towers nearly 5 m high and is 6 m in length. His huge proportions, draped imperiously in jasmine garlands, are made of grey granite polished with a mixture of groundnut oil and charcoal. Under his hooves you can make out the *veena* or south Indian sitar on which he's resting. Behind him is a yonilingam. Just outside the temple are two bodhi trees, with serpent statues draped with sacred strands in offering for children. To your right as you exit the temple lies Bugle Park, a pretty little patch of wood whose trees are packed with fruit bats. It also holds one of Kempe Gowda's four 16th-century watchtowers. You can walk past the old fort under the subway to reach the atmospheric City Market, and from there to the busy market area of the Old Town around Avenue Road and Chikpet.

For those interested in ancient Indian astrological practices, the **Palm Leaf Library** ① *33 V Main Rd, Chamarajpet*, is supposed to be the repository for everyone's special leaf, which gives accurate details of character, past, present and future. Locating each leaf is not guaranteed.

Sri Gavi Gangadhareshwara Temple is most remarkable for its two quirks of architecture. First, the 'open window' to the left of the temple, which only once a year (on **Makara Sankrati Day**, 14/15 January) allows a shaft of light to shine between the horns of the stone Nandi bull in the courtyard and to then fall on the Siva lingam in the inner sanctum. The second quirk can only be seen by bending double to crouch around the back of the cave shrine. The Dravida-style **Venkataramanasvami Temple** is where the Wodeyar Maharaja chose to worship first, when his dynasty's rule was reinstated at the end of the 18th century, before entering the palace.

The grand, Tudor-style **Bangalore Palace** ⓘ *north of Cubbon Park, T080-2336 0818, 1000-1800, foreigners Rs 200, Indians Rs 100, camera Rs 500, video Rs 1000; frequent buses from Majestic/Sivaji Nagar,* built by Chamaraja Wodeyar in 1887, was incongruously inspired by Windsor Castle. The entry price buys you a tour of the Mysore mahahrajas' collection of art and family portraits.

The sprawling modern **International Society for Krishna Conscious temple complex (ISKCON)** ⓘ *Hare Krishna Hill, 1R Block, Chord Rd, Rajaji Nagar, northwest of the centre, 0700-1300, 1615-2030,* holds five shrines, a multimedia cinema showing films on the Hare Krishna movement, lofty *gopurams* and the world's tallest *kalash shikara*. Around 9000 visitors make the pilgrimage every day; *bhajans* (religious songs) are sung daily.

Around Bengaluru

Whitefield, 16 km east of Bengaluru, is the centre of the city's ongoing industrial revolution, and the fastest growing suburb in all Asia. Once best known for the **Sai Baba Ashram** at Brindavan, if you venture out here now it's almost certain to be on business: Whitefield is home to innumerable industrial estates, IT parks and hospitals, not to mention the hotels, international schools and malls that service their employees.

To the north of Bengaluru, 10 km from Chikballapur, lies **Nandidurg**, Tipu's fortified summer retreat in the Nandi Hills, set on top of a granite hill with sheer cliffs on three sides. Literally 'the fort of Nandi', the place, today a minor hill resort with great views from the 60-m-high 'Tipu's drop', was named after Siva's bull. The ninth-century **Bhoganandisvara Temple** at the foot of the hill is a good example of the Nolamba style; its walls are quite plain but the stone windows feature carvings of Nataraja and Durga. The 16th century brought typical Vijayanagar period extensions such as the *gopuram* at the entrance. To get there, take a bus from the Central Bus Stand (ask for the Nandi Hill bus, not Nandidurga); they leave at 0730, 0830, 0930, returning at 1400, 1630, 1830.

Nrityagram ⓘ *30 km north of Bengaluru, T080-2846 6313, Tue-Sat 1000-1730,* is a dance village where young dancers learn all disciplines of traditional Indian dance. It was founded by the late Odissi dancer Protima Gauri. Guided tours include lunch, dance demonstrations and a short lecture.

Bannerghatta Bio Park ⓘ *22 km south of the city, T080-2782 8540, Wed-Mon 0900-1300, 1400-1700, Rs 200, Indians Rs 60, includes safari; guide fee Rs 200, video* *camera Rs 150*, covers more than 100 sq km of dry deciduous forest, and is home to wild populations of elephant, bison, boar, deer and the occasional leopard. A portion has been fenced, and the Forest Department run a range of minibus safaris to see tigers, bears and Asiatic lions at close range in almost-natural surroundings; many of the animals here have been rescued from circuses. The park also contains a butterfly garden and an unappealing zoo.

⦿ Bengaluru (Bangalore) listings

For hotel and restaurant price codes and other relevant information, see pages 13-17.

● Where to stay

Bengaluru *p285, map p288*
Cheap hotels share the streets of the ill-named Majestic district, northeast of the bus stand around SC (Subedar Chatram) Rd, with seedy bars and cinemas; a daunting prospect at night. MG Rd offers a more sanitized environment, and has rooms for every budget from backpacker to super-luxury. Top end hotels can add 25% in taxes.

$$$$ Oberoi, 39 MG Rd, T080-2558 5858, www.oberoihotels.com. 160 superb rooms and suites with private sit-outs, all of which have views across the lush tropical gardens. Decent-sized pool. Good restaurants, bar, spa and fitness centre, beauty salon.

$$$$ The Park, 14/7 MG Rd, T080-2559 4666, www.theparkhotels.com. Global minimalist chic, 109 plush rooms in an achingly hip business hotel. Each room has a balcony, there's a lovely long pool surrounded by gazebos. Cool black and white photographs on the walls, DVDs, library, Wi-Fi and 24-hr room service. Some suites have jacuzzi.

$$$$ Taj West End, 23 Race Course Rd, near railway, T080-6660 5660, www.tajhotels.com. Charming 1887 colonial property set in beautiful gardens;

much more than a business hotel. 117 immaculately appointed suites and rooms with balconies and verandas, Wi-Fi, flatscreen TV. There's also a splendidly restored Heritage Wing, dating from 1907. **Blue Ginger**, one of Bengaluru's most romantic garden restaurants, serves authentic Vietnamese food in low-lit jungly surroundings.

$$$$-$$$ St Mark's Hotel, 4/1 St Mark's Rd, T080-4001 9000, www.stmarkshotel.com. Nice carpeted rooms in very quiet and capable business hotel. All rooms have Wi-Fi and bath. Good views, questionable decorative taste. Price includes breakfast.

$$$ Green Path Serviced Apartments, 32/2 New BEL Rd, Seenappa Layout (north of centre near Hebbal flyover), T080-4266 4777, www.thegreenpath.in. Comfortable and spacious if slightly anonymous 1- to 3-bedroom (**$$$$**) apartments, built and run on eco principles: rainwater harvesting, solar hot water, renewable materials. There's the obligatory Wi-Fi lifeline, plus bikes to ride to the local shops, and the price includes an organic breakfast spread.

$$$ Ivory Tower, Penthouse (12th) floor of Barton Centre, 84 MG Rd, T080-4178 3333, www.hotelivorytower.com. 22 comfortable, spacious rooms (huge beds) in slightly ragged venue, stunning views over city, old fashioned but spotless, good value, friendly. Wi-Fi, a/c, fridge, phone. Good terrace bar and restaurant onsite.

$$$ Keys Hotel, Hosur Main Rd (opposite the Volkswagen showroom), T080-3944 1000, www.keyshotels.com. Ultra-modern hotel near Electronic City with free Wi-Fi, pool and all mod cons. Also opening soon is **Keys Hotel and Apartments**, Plot 6 Kundalahalli Main Rd, Whitefield, 16 km east of Bengaluru.

$$$ Villa Pottipati, 142 8th Cross, 4th Main Rd, Mallesaram, T080-2336 0777, www.neemranahotels.com. 8 rooms in historic townhouse furnished with rosewood 4-posters and sepia Indian portrait photography. Set in garden in the charming quiet tree-lined avenues of Bengaluru's Brahminical suburbs. A/c and internet facilities, small plunge pool. Atmospheric, but a bit lacklustre. Thin mattresses.

$$$-$$ New Rainbow, 93 Residency Rd, T080-2559 4788, www.rainbow hotel.in. Decent-value place offering slightly poky rooms in a handy location close to MG Rd.

$$$-$$ Woodlands Hotel, 5 Raja Ram Mohan Roy Rd, T080-2222 5111, info@ woodlands.in. Large but charming old-fashioned hotel with 240 rooms, some a/c and cottages, with attached baths and fridge, good a/c restaurant, bar, coffee shop, exchange, safe, good location but calm, good value. Phone, satellite TV, lockers.

$$ Kamat Yatrinivas, 1st Cross, Gandhinagar, T080-4124 1114, www. kamatyatri.in. 57 decent rooms set around a central courtyard. Thin mattress spring beds, but it's clean and well maintained. 2 dining rooms, North Karnatakan and South Indian meals. Satellite TV, direct-dial phone, lockers.

$$ YMCA Guest House (City), Nrupathunga Rd, near Cubbon Park,

T080-2221 1848, www.ymcablr.net. One of the best budget deals in the city. The location is wonderfully peaceful, just across the fence from Cubbon Park, and many of the rooms open on to an indoor sports hall where you can sit like Caesar watching badminton or karate championships. Afternoon cricket matches, excellent café.

$$-$ Ajantha, 22A MG Rd, T080-2558 4321. 62 basic 'deluxe' rooms and much better value cottages with sitting areas and campbed-style beds, set in a calm compound filled with bougainvillea and pot plants. South Indian veg restaurant, helpful management.

$$-$ Vellara, 126 Brigade Rd, T080-2536 9116, www.hotelvellara.com. A grim exterior conceals one of the MG Rd area's best deals. 36 spacious and well-kept rooms, which get better the higher up you go. TV and phone in each room, and the value and location are excellent. Recommended.

$ Mahaveer, 8/9 Tank Bund Rd, opposite bus station, near City railway station, T080-3271 0384. Basic and decaying place on a noisy road, but just about OK if you want to drop your bags after a long bus ride. The larger (**$$**) deluxe rooms at the back are quieter.

$ New Central Lodge, 56 Infantry Rd, at the Central St end, T080-2559 2395. 35 simple, rooms, clean enough, some with bath, hot water (0500-1000).

$ Railway Retiring Rooms, City Station. 23 rooms and cheaper dorm for passengers in transit.

$ Vybhav, 60 SC Rd, down passageway opposite Movieland Talkies, T080-2287 3997. As basic as they come, and pretty grimy, but the rooms are relatively big and airy and some open on to a shared terrace where pot-bellied Brahmins hang out and chat to each other. Good value.

Around Bengaluru *p291*

$$$$ Shreyas Bangalore, 35 km northwest of town in Nelamangala, T080-2773 7102, www.shreyasretreat. com. The place for peace and yoga in 5-star luxury, with twice-daily classes and silent meditations, Vedanta consultants and life coaching. Pampering includes Balinese massage and exotic fruit body scrubs, and the vegetarian cuisine is exceptional. Alcohol is forbidden, but there's a gym, book and DVD library, and in case you forgot you were in Bangalore, Wi-Fi throughout the property. 3- to 6-night packages start at around US$1500.

$$$$ Soukya International Holistic Health Centre, Whitefield, 17 km east of Bengaluru, T080-2801 7000, www. soukya.com. This healing centre offers restorative, personalized programmes: detox, de-stress and weight loss, or relax with naturopathy and Ayurveda suited to asthma, diabetes, hypertension and addictions. Accommodation is in individual cottages around lawns, flowers and trees. Programmes cost from US$200-500 a day.

❼ Restaurants

Look out for Grover wine, which is the product of the first French grape grown in Indian soil, sown 40 km from Bengaluru at the foot of the Nandi hills. Veuve Clicquot has a stake in the company, which is now exporting to France.

Bengaluru *p285, map p288*
For excellent fresh, cheap, South Indian staples like *iddli*, *dosa* and *vada* look for branches of **Darshini**, **Shiv Sagar**, **Shanthi Sagar**, **Sukh Sagar** and **Kamat**, all of which are hygienic and efficient. At the other end of the price scale, the

Taj West End hotel has the Vietnamese restaurant **Blue Ginger** and The Park has the Italian **i-t.ALIA**, both of which are pricey but excellent if you yearn for non-Indian fare. The Sunday all you-can-eat brunch at the Leela is popular with expats and the city's business elite. If you're missing international fast food head for Brigade and MG Rd and the food court at the Forum shopping mall. Chains of **Barista** and **Cafe Coffee Day** are ubiquitous.

$$$ Ebony Restaurant, Ivory Tower (see Where to stay), T080-6134 4880. Open 1230-1500 and 1900-2300. Serves Parsee dishes like mutton *dhansak* and curry *chawal*, along with Muglai, Tandoori and French food, but come for the views from this penthouse terrace restaurant, which are the best in Bengaluru.

$$$ Karavalli, at the Taj Gateway, 166 Residency Rd, T080-6660 4519. The best high-end Indian restaurant in the city, offering upscale Karnataka coastal food.

$$ Benjarong, 1/3 Ulsoor Rd, T080-3221 7201. If you're craving Thai, this is the place. Expect charming service and authentic red curry, dished up with lots of free extras.

$$ Coconut Grove, 86 Spencer Building, Church St, T080-2559 6262. Good varied Southern Indian menu, beers, buzzing place with sit-outs under shades.

$$ Koshy's, 39 St Mark's Rd, T080-2221 3793. Open 0900-2330. Pleasant, old fashioned, atmospheric, licensed. Good grills and roasts, Syrian Christian fish curries and Sunday South Indian brunch. Also does Western breakfasts like baked beans on toast, cutlets, eggy bread or eggs any way you like. A local institution.

$$ Tandoor, MG Rd, T080-2558 4620. Open 1230-1500 and 1900-2330. Possibly the city's best North Indian restaurant, serving Punjabi, Mughlai and Tandoori.

$ Chalukya, Race Course Rd, by the **Taj West End Hotel**. Excellent vegetarian.
$ Halli Mane, 12 Sampige Rd, Malleswaram. Fun and buzzing vegetarian canteen decked out like a village house: order at the counter, present your ticket at the relevant counter and elbow yourself a bit of table space. A good place to try Karnataka specials like *ragi roti*.
$ Indian Coffee House, 19 Church St. Open 0800-2030. The South Indian filter coffee is some of the best in the city, but it's worth coming just to sample one of the last vestiges of old Bangalore: waiters in turbans and old men at formica tables arguing about politics.
$ MTR (Mavalli Tiffin Rooms), 11 Lalbagh Rd, T080-222 0022. Tiffin 0600-1100 and 1530-1930, lunch 1230-1430 and 2000-2100. Closed Mon lunch. The quintessential Bengaluru restaurant: a classic Kannadiga Brahmin vegetarian oozing 1920s atmosphere, full of Bengaluru elders, at the edge of Lalbagh gardens. A 14-course lunch lasts 2 hrs, but you'll be lucky to get a table; if you're in a hurry it does parcels. The simple vegetarian food is superb and the interiors and people watching is half the fun.
$ Palmgrove, Ballal Residence Hotel, 74/3 III Cross, Residency Rd, T080-2559 7277. Atmospheric place for Kannada Brahmin food, a/c, serves excellent giant lunch *thalis*, Rs 75.
$ Vidyarthi Bhavan, 32 Gandhi Bazar, T080-2667 7588. Sat-Thu 0630-1130 and 1400-2000. Unassuming vegetarian joint in the Basavanagudi district (near Nandi Bull and Gandhi Bazar) whose 'Mysore Masala Dosa' is justly famous, served with a side order of butter, coconut chutney and potato and onion curry. Open since 1938.

Cafés, bakeries and ice cream
Nilgiri's Upper Crust Café, Brigade Rd. Primarily a supermarket.
Sweet Chariot Bakery, 15/2 Residency Rd and branches all across the city. Open 1030-2030. Excellent cakes and pastries.

❶ Bars and clubs

Bengaluru *p285, map p288*
Bengaluru is trying hard to reclaim its role as India's coolest party town: the 2330 curfew that for years threw a wet blanket over the hard-rocking bars along Brigade Rd, Residency Rd and Church St has been pushed back, allowing the beer and cocktails to flow and rock, and hip-hop and house to ring out until a more urbane 0100. Hotel bars are exempt from any curfew, and tend to offer a more refined atmosphere: those at the Taj West End have a particular raj-esque elegance, while the Park Hotel's **i-bar** is sleek and pared down. New venues spring up all the time, while others fall out of fashion or change names, so ask around for the latest hotspot. Note that most of the better places have a hefty cover charge and a couples-only policy to prevent an oversupply of slavering stags.
13th Floor, Hotel Ivory Tower, 84 MG Rd, T080-4178 3355. The least pretentious bar, with the best view of the city.
Hard Rock Cafe, St Mark's Rd, T080-4124 2222. Brand-phobics beware: this spanking-new venue is one of the hottest tickets in town, with a variety of drinking and dining spaces carved out of a lovely old library building.
Pecos, Rest House Rd, off Brigade Rd. Connoisseurs of dinge should head directly here for cheap beer and hard-rockin' tunes.

O Shopping

Bengaluru *p285, map p288*
Bengaluru is a byword for shopping in India. **Commercial St**, **MG Rd** and **Brigade Rd** remain favourite hangouts for the city's youth.

Unless you want Western goods, though, the best shopping is to be had at the **City Market** (officially known as the KR Market) in Chickpet, where you can get silver, gold and silk saris; it's supposed to be the country's biggest silk wholesale/retail district and makes for some seriously fun people watching when it comes alive at dusk. **Russel Market**, in Shivajinagar, is stuffed with vegetables, meat and antiques.

Shops and markets open early and close late (about 2000) but close 1300-1600.

Books
Gangarams, 72 MG Rd. Has a wide-ranging and expanding collection.
Premier, 46/1 Church St (and Museum Rd). Small, with a good selection of specialist and academic books (as well as an impressive PG Wodehouse collection), helpful owner.
Sankar's, 394 First D Main Rd, Domlur Layout (east of town towards old HAL airport, T080-25357899. A bit of a trip from the centre, but worth it for one of the best selections in the city.

Crafts and gifts
Karnataka is best known for silks, especially saris, and sandalwood products, from oils and incense to intricate carvings. Other local products include Mysore paintings (characterized by gold leaf and bright colours from vegetable and mineral dyes), *dhurries* (carpets incorporating floral and natural motifs, traditionally made from wool

though cotton is now more widely used), inlaid woodwork and wooden toys and Channaptna dolls. Bidriware, a form of metalwork whereby silver and gold is inlaid or engraved onto copper and polished with zinc, originates from Bidar in the state's far northeast, but is produced throughout the state.
Cauvery Crafts Emporium, 49 MG Rd.
Central Cottage Industries Emporium, 144 MG Rd.
Desi, 27 Patalamma St, near South End Circle.
Kala Madhyam, 77/8 Nandidurg Rd (Benson Cross Rd Corner), Benson Town, T080-2353 7358, www.kalamadhyam.org. NGO-run store showcasing metalwork, pottery, clothing and jewellery made by folk artists and tribal craftspeople throughout India. High quality.
Khadi Gramudyog, Silver Jubilee Park Rd, near City Market. For homespun cotton.
Mota Shopping Complex, Brigade Rd.
Raga, A-13, Devatha Plaza, 131 Residency Rd. For attractive gifts.
UP Handlooms, 8 Mahaveer Shopping Complex, Kempe Gowda Rd.

Jewellery
Most gold and jewellery is, logically enough, on Jewellers St, but also look along MG Rd, Brigade Rd, Residency Rd and Commercial St.

Silk and saris
Silk is, to many, what shopping in Bengaluru is really all about. There's a vast range at the following places.
Deepam, MG Rd. Fixed prices, excellent service, 24 hrs from placing an order to making up your designs.
Janardhana, Unity Building, JC Rd.
Karnataka Silks Industries, Jubilee Showroom, 44/45 Leo Complex,

MG Rd. Specializing in traditional Mysore Crepe designs.

Vijayalakshmi, 20/61 Blumoon Complex, Residency Rd. Will also make shirts.

◑ What to do

Bengaluru *p285, map p288*
Golf
Bangalore Golf Club, Sankey Rd, T080-2228 7980. Foreign visitors pay US$30.
KGA Golf Club, Golf Av, Kodihalli, Airport Rd, T080-4009 0000. Rs 2000.

Horse racing
Bengaluru is famous for racing and stud farms.
Bangalore Turf Club, Race Course Rd, T080-2226 2391, www.bangaloreraces.com. Season May-Jul and Nov-Mar.

Swimming
Of late, the top hotels have become reluctant to let non-residents use their pools. However, there are great municipal pools, with swimming times segregated by gender. Try **Kensington Park Rd**, near Ulsoor Lake, or **Sankey Tank**, Sadhiv Nagar, Jayanagar 3rd Block. Rs 40, closes at 1600.

Tour operators
The Blue Yonder, 23-24 Sri Guru Nivas, Amarjyoti Layout, Sanjay Nagar, T080-4115 2218, www.theblueyonder.com. Superb responsible tourism packages in Kerala, Karnataka and elsewhere, and also offer reliable ticketing and hotel bookings.
Clipper Holidays, 4 Magrath Rd, T080-2559 9032, www.clipperholidays.com. Tours, treks (everything provided), Kerala backwaters, etc. Very helpful and efficient.
Golden Chariot, Tourism House, Pappanna Lane, St Marks Rd, T080-

4346 4342, www.goldenchariot.org. A southern counterpart to Rajasthan's famous Palace on Wheels, offering absolutely luxurious train journeys through Karnataka, Kerala and Tamil Nadu.
Hammock Leisure Holidays, Indiranagar, T080-2521 9000, www.hammockholidays.com.
Karnataka State Tourism Development Corporation (KSTDC), Badami House, opposite Corporation Office, NR Sq, T080-4334 4334, www.karnatakaholidays.net.
Bangalore city sightseeing half-day tours, covering Tipu's Palace, Bull Temple, Lal Bagh, Ulsoor Lake, Vidhan Soudha, Gava Gangadhareshwara Temple, museums, at 0730-1400 and 1400-1930. Rs 230, admissions extra, recommended. Full-day tour to Rajarajeshwari Temple, HAL Museum, Bannerghatta Bio Park, ISKCON temple and more, 0715-2000, Rs 385-485, long and exhausting. Also runs Mysore and Srirangapatnam day tour, 0630-2330, Rs 650-850.
ITDC, departing from Swiss Complex, No 33 Race Course Rd, T080-2238 6114, same schedule as half-day tour but lasts from 0900-1700 and includes ISKCON, Rs 250. **Mysore** daily, 0715-2300, Rs 600-700 including meals.
Sita, Queens Rd, T080-2286 9161, www.sita.in
Thomas Cook, 55 MG Rd, T080-2558 1337 (foreign exchange and TCs), and 70 MG Rd (all services), T080-2558 8028.

Trekking and adventure sports
Getoff Ur Ass, 858 1D Main Rd, Girinagar, T089-7408 6709, www.getoffurass.com. The shop has camping and outdoor gear for sale and hire, while the owner organizes a variety of trekking and rafting trips in the Nilgiris and Western Ghats, plus kayaking and paragliding courses,

photography workshops and camping weekends in private forest areas.

Walking tours
Bangalore Walks, T(0)9845-523660, www.bangalorewalks.com. Excellent guided tours of the city's cultural and historic landmarks, Rs 495 including brunch.

⊖ Transport

Bengaluru *p285, map p288*
Air Opened in 2008, **Bengaluru International Airport (BLR)**, T080-6678 2251, www.bengaluruairport.com, is the bold new face of Indian airports: it's gleaming, expensive and the taxi touts in Arrivals greet you in suits. The domestic and international terminals are in the same building, around 35 km northeast of the city by a fast new road. Prepaid taxis in the terminal quote upwards of Rs 1000 to deliver you to the city centre, but metered taxis queue outside Arrivals and work out at roughly half the price. Airport buses run every 20-30 mins on 9 fixed routes to and from various parts of the city: Route 9 to Kempegowda Bus Station (Majestic) and Route 4 to Jeevan Bhima Nagar (via Cubbon Rd, parallel to MG Rd) are the most useful for hotels.
Note Departing domestic passengers must pay a Rs 260 'User Development Fee' at a counter outside the terminal; allow 10 mins to queue, and show the receipt to gain entry.

Bengaluru is becoming an increasingly important international hub, with direct flights to London, Frankfurt and Paris, as well as Singapore, Kuala Lumpur and many Gulf cities.

Daily domestic flights serve **Chennai, Coimbatore, Delhi, Goa, Guwahati, Hubli, Hyderabad, Jaipur, Kochi, Kolkata, Mangalore, Mumbai, Pune** and **Thiruvananthapuram**. The best network is with **Air India (Indian Airlines)**, Unity Building, JC Rd, T080-2297 8427, airport T080-6678 5168, Reservations T141. **Indigo**, T080-2221 9810. **Jet Airways**, 1-4 M Block, Unity Building, JC Rd, T080-3989 3333. **Spicejet**, T080-2522 9792.
International Airline offices Air India, Unity Building, JC Rd, T080-2297 8447. **Air France** and **KLM/Northwest**, Sunrise Chambers, 22 Ulsoor Rd, T080-2555 9364, airport T080-6678 3109. **British Airways**, airport T080-6678 3160. **Cathay Pacific**, Taj West End, Race Course Rd, T080-4008 8400. **Emirates**, 3 Vittal Mallya Rd, T080-6629 4444. Etihad, Level 15 UB City, Vittal Mallya Rd, T1800-223901; **Gulf Air**, T080-2522 3106. **Interglobe Air Tansport (Air Mauritius, China Eastern, Delta, SAS, United Airlines**, 17-20 Richmond Towers, 12 Richmond Rd, T080-2224 4621. **Kuwait**, T080-2558 9841. **Lufthansa**, 44/42 Dickenson Rd, 080-2506 0800. **Nepal Airlines**, 205 Barton Center, MG Rd, T080-2559 7878. Qatar Airways, 307-310 Prestige Meridian, MG Rd, T080-4000 5333; **Singapore Airlines**, T080-2286 7870. **Sri Lankan**, Cears Plaza, Residency Rd, T080-4112 5207. Thai Airways, airport T080-4030 0396.

Bus City Bus Station, opposite the City Railway Station, is the very busy but well-organized departure point for services within the city.

Just to the south, the **Central Bus Station** handles long-distance buses run by the governments of **Karnataka (KSRTC)**, T080-2287 3377; **Andhra Pradesh (APSRTC)**, T080-2287 3915; **Kerala**, T080-2226 9508; and **Tamil Nadu (SETC)**, T080-2287 6975.

Computerized reservations from the booking counter are available on many services. There are efficient, frequent and inexpensive services to all major cities in South and Central India. Frequent service to **Mysore** (3 hrs); several to **Hassan** (4 hrs), **Hyderabad**, **Madikeri** (6 hrs), **Madurai** (9 hrs), **Mangalore** (9 hrs), **Ooty** (7 hrs), **Puttaparthi** (4-5 hrs, Rs 65), **Tirupati** (6½ hrs). 'Deluxe' or 'ordinary' coaches run by private operators are usually more comfortable though a bit more expensive. They operate from opposite the **Central** and **Kalasipalyam** bus stations.

Car Firms for city and out-of-town sightseeing include **Classic City Cabs**, T080-2238 6999; **Safe Wheels**, T080-2343 1333; **KSTDC** (see page 286); Angel City Cabs, T091-6486 7774, driven by women and for female passengers only. Rs 1000-2000 for 8 hrs or 80 km; extra kilometre Rs 10-25 depending on the type of car. Rates for overnight or extended sightseeing will be higher, with additions for driver overnight charges and hill driving.

Taxi and auto-rickshaw There are prepaid taxi booths at the airport and all 3 railway stations; prices should be clearly marked, and will be a little higher than the meter fare. Minimum charge in a meter taxi is Rs 125, which covers up to 5 km; Rs 10 per extra kilometre. There are severable reputable radio taxi companies with clean a/c vehicles and digital meters, including **EasyCabs**, T080-4343 4343, callcenter@easycabs.com.

Auto-rickshaws should also operate on a meter system: Rs 25 for the first 2 km, Rs 13 per extra kilometre. In practice it can be hard to persuade drivers to use the meter, especially during rush hour.

Both taxi and rickshaw fares increase by half between 2300 and 0500.

Train Bangalore City Junction (still known by the old spelling) is the main departure point; enquiries T131, reservations T139. Computerized advance reservations are in the newer building on left of the entrance; No 14 is the 'Foreigners' Counter'. The Chief Reservations Officer is on the ground floor. Many trains also stop at **Cantonment Station**, T135. A few begin at **Yesvantpur Junction**, 10 km north of the city. Unless stated departure times are from City.

Arsikere (for **Belur** and **Halebid** temples): *Siddhaganga Exp 12725*, 1300, 2½ hrs; **Chennai**: *Shatabdi Exp, 12008*, daily except Tue, 1625, 5 hrs; *Lalbagh Exp 12608*, 0630, 5½ hrs; *Brindavan Exp 12640*, 1510, 5¼ hrs. **Goa** (Londa): *Ranichennamma Express 16589*, 2115, 11 hrs. **Hospet**: *Hampi Exp 16592*, 2200, 10 hrs. **Madurai**: *Tuticorin Exp 16236*, 2120, 10 hrs. **Mumbai** (CST): *Udyan Exp 11302*, 2000, 24 hrs. **Maddur** and **Mysore**: *Chamundi Exp 16216*, 1815, 2½ hrs; *Tipu Express 12614*, 1500, 2½ hrs; *Shatabdi Exp 12007*, daily except Wed, 1100, 2 hrs. **Secunderabad**: *Hazrat Nizamuddin Rajdhani Exp 22691/22693*, 2020, 11½ hrs. **Thiruvananthapuram**: *Island Exp 16526*, 2140, 17 hrs, via Kochi (12½ hrs).

❶ Directory

Bengaluru *p285, map p288*
Banks Usually open Mon-Fri 1000-1400. There are hundreds of 24-hr ATMs that are compatible with cards bearing the MasterCard, Visa, Maestro, Cirrus or Plus logos. **Citibank**, **Canara Bank**, **HSBC**, **HDFC** are reliable. For counter services: **Citibank**, MG Rd, T080-2559 6363; **HDFC**, Kasturba Rd, T080-2227 4600; **Standard Chartered**, MG Rd, T080-3940 4444; **State Bank of India**,

St Mark's Rd, T080-2594 3120. For foreign exchange: **Thomas Cook**, 55 MG Rd, T080-2558 1337, and **Weizmann Forex**, Residency Rd, T080-2559 5379, are quicker than banks for TCs. **Cultural centres Alliance Française**, Millers Tank Bund Rd, off Thimmaiah Rd, opposite station, T080-4123 1340. **British Library**, St Mark's Rd/Church St corner (Koshy's Building), 1030-1830, Tue-Sat. **Goethe Institut**, 716 CMH RD, Indranagar, T080-2520 5305. **Medical services** Ambulance: T102. **Bowring and Lady Curzon Hospital**, Hospital Rd, T080-2559 1362, north of Cubbon Park. **Mallya Hospital**, Vittal Mallya Rd, south of Cubbon Park, T080-2227 7997, one of the best. There are chemists at hospitals and **Cure**, 137 GF2, Business Point, Brigade Rd T080-2227 4246. For dentists contact **Grace**, 1 Dinnur Main Rd, RT Nagar, T080-2333 4638; excellent. **Post GPO**, Cubbon Rd near Raj Bhawan, 1000-1800. Poste Restante, Mon-Sat, 1030-1600, T080-2286 6772. **DHL**, Jubilee Building, 43 Museum Rd, T080-25588855. **UPS**, 4 1st Cross 10th Main Indiranagar, T080-2525 3445. **Telephone** Mobile **Store**, Devatha Plaza, 131/14 Residency Rd, and branches all over town, www.mobilestore.in. For reliable mobile connections and handsets.

Useful contacts Visa extensions: Commissioner of Police, Infantry Rd. **Police** T100. **Fire** T101. **Chief Wildlife Warden**, Aranya Bhavan, 18th Cross, Malleswaram, T080-2334 1993.

Mysore and Southern Maidan

The charming, unruly city of Mysore, the former capital of the princely state, does a brisk trade in its eponymous shimmering silks, sandalwood and jasmine against a backdrop of its stunning, borderline gaudy Indo-Saracenic palace. On the outskirts of the city is the empty ruin of Srirangapatnam, the island fortress of Britain's nemesis Tipu Sultan, and the bird-crammed Ranganathittu Sanctuary.

Further on is the Chennakesava Temple of Somnathpur, a spellbinding example of Hoysala architecture. Leopards and tigers stalk the two parklands, Bandipur and Nagarhole, that spill over Karnataka's borders with neighbouring Tamil Nadu and Kerala, and closer to the coast you can climb the Ghats to the tiny Kodagu district for forests of wild elephants and coffee plantations nursed by a warrior people. Also in Kodagu lies Sera, the university at the centre of one of India's biggest Tibetan Buddhist refugee settlements.

Mysore → *For listings, see pages 312-320. Colour map 3, B3.*

Mysore centre is a crowded jumble presided over by the gaudy, wondrous kitsch of the Maharaja's Palace, a profusion of turquoise-pink and layered with mirrors. But for some Mysore's world renown is centred less on the palace, its silk production or sandalwood than on the person of Sri Pattabhi Jois and his Mysore-style ashtanga yoga practice (see box, page 318). This all happens outside the chaotic centre, in the city's beautiful Brahmin suburbs, where wide boulevard-like streets are overhung with bougainvillea.

Arriving in Mysore → *Phone code: 0821. Population: 742,300.*
Getting there The railway station is about 1 km to the northwest of the town centre while the three bus stands are all in the centre, within easy reach of the hotels. → *See Transport, page 319.*

Getting around Karnataka's second biggest town, Mysore is still comfortably compact enough to walk around, though there are plenty of autos and buses.

Tourist information Department of Tourism ① *Old Exhibition Building, Irwin Rd, T0821-242 2096, www.mysore.nic.in, 1000-1730.* See also www.karnataka.com/

tourism/mysore. There are information counters at the train station and bus stand. **Karnataka State Tourism Development Corporation (KSTDC)** ① *Yatri Nivas, 2 JLB Rd, T0821-242 3652*, is efficient.

Places in Mysore

The **Maharaja's Palace** ① *enter by south gate, T0821-243 4425, 1000-1730, Rs 200 includes audio guide, cameras must be left in lockers (free, you take the key), allow 2 hrs if you wish to see everything, guidebook Rs 10; go early to avoid the crowds; downstairs is fairly accessible for the disabled,* or 'City Palace' (Amba Vilas) was designed by Henry Irwin and built in 1897 after a fire burnt down the old wooden incarnation. It is in the Indo-Saracenic style in grand proportions, with domes, arches and colonnades of carved pillars and shiny marble floors. The stained glass, wall paintings, ivory inlaid

Mysore

Where to stay ⌂
Bombay Tiffany's 1
Green Hotel 10
Greens' Boarding &
 Lodging 2
Indus Valley 5
Lalith Mahal Palace 6
Mayura Hoysala 11
Mysore Dasaprakash 7
Park Lane 9
Ritz 4
Royal Orchid Metropole 8
Siddharta 3

Restaurants ⑦
Anu's Bamboo
 Hut 2
Ganesh 1
Jewel Rock 7
King's Kourt Hotel 3
Mylari 11
Penguin Ice-cream
 Parlour 4
Raghu Niwas 5
RRR 6
Samrat 12
Shilpashri 8
Sri Rama Veg & Ashok
 Books 9
SR Plantain Leaf 10

Medieval pageantry at Mysore

The brilliantly colourful festival of Dasara is celebrated with medieval pageantry for 10 days. Although the Dasara festival can be traced back to the Puranas and is widely observed across India, in the south it achieved its special prominence under the Vijayanagar kings. As the Mahanavami festival, it has been celebrated every year since it was sponsored by Raja Wodeyar in September 1610 at Srirangapatnam. It symbolizes the victory of goddess Chamundeswari (Durga) over the demon Mahishasura. On the last day a bedecked elephant with a golden *howdah* carrying the statue of the goddess processes from the palace through the city to Banni Mantap, about 5 km away, where the Banni tree is worshipped. The temple float festival takes place at a tank at the foot of Chamundi Hill and a car festival on top. In the evening there is a torchlight parade by the mounted guards who demonstrate their keen horsemanship and the night ends with a display of fireworks and all the public buildings are ablaze with fairy lights.

doors and the ornate golden throne (now displayed during Dasara) are remarkable. The fabulous collection of jewels is seldom displayed. Try to visit on a Sunday night, public holiday or festival when the palace is lit up with 50,000 fairy lights.

On the ground floor, visitors are led through the 'Car Passage' with cannons and carriages to the *Gombe thotti* (Dolls' Pavilion). This originally displayed dolls during Dasara and today houses a model of the old palace, European marble statues and the golden *howdah* (the maharaja used the battery-operated red and green bulbs on top of the canopy as stop and go signals to the *mahout*). The last is still used during Dasara but goddess Chamundeshwari rides on the elephant. The octagonal *Kalyana Mandap* (Marriage Hall), or Peacock Pavilion, south of the courtyard, has a beautiful stained glass ceiling and excellent paintings of scenes from Dasara and other festivities on 26 canvas panels. Note the exquisite details, especially of No 19. The Portrait Gallery and the Period Furniture Room lead off this pavilion.

On the first floor, a marble staircase leads to the magnificent Durbar Hall, a grand colonnaded hall measuring 47 m by 13 m with lavishly framed paintings by famous Indian artists. The asbestos-lined ceiling has paintings of Vishnu incarnations. A passage takes you past the beautifully ivory-on-wood inlaid door of the Ganesh Temple, to the Amba Vilas where private audiences (*Diwan-i-Khas*) were held. This exquisitely decorated hall has three doors. The central silver door depicts Vishnu's 10 incarnations and the eight *dikpalas* (directional guardians), with Krishna figures on the reverse (see the tiny Krishna on a leaf, kissing his toes), all done in *repoussé* on teak and rosewood. The room sports art nouveau style, possibly Belgian stained glass, cast iron pillars from Glasgow, carved wood ceiling, chandeliers, etched glass windows and the *pietra dura* on the floors.

The jewel-encrusted Golden Throne with its ornate steps, which some like to attribute to ancient Vedic times, was originally made of figwood decorated with ivory before it was padded out with gold, silver and jewels. Others trace its history to 1336 when the Vijayanagar kings 'found' it before passing it on to the Wodeyars who continue to use it during Dasara.

The **Maharaja's Residence** ① *1000-1730, Rs 20, no photography*, is a slightly underwhelming museum. The ground floor, with a courtyard, displays children's toys, musical instruments, costumes and several portraits. The upper floor has a small weapon collection.

A block west of the palace, housed in the smaller Jagan Mohan Palace, is the **Jaya-chamarajendra Art Gallery** (1861) ① *0800-1700, Rs 25, no photography*, which holds a priceless collection of artworks from Mysore's erstwhile rulers, including Indian miniature paintings and works by Raja Ravi Varma and Nicholas Roerich. There's also an exhibition of ceramics, stone, ivory, sandalwood, antique furniture and old musical instruments. Sadly, there are no descriptions or guidebooks and many items are randomly displayed.

North of KR Circle is the **Devaraja market**, one of India's most atmospheric: visit at noon when it's injected with fresh pickings of marigolds and jasmines. The bigger flowers are stitched onto a thread and wrapped into rolls which arrived heaped in hessian sacks stacked on the heads of farmers.

Immediately to the southeast of the town is **Chamundi Hill** ① *temple 0600-1400, 1530-1800, 1915-2100; vehicle toll Rs 30, City Bus No 185*, with a temple to Durga (Chamundeswari), guardian deity to the Wodeyars, celebrating her victory over the buffalo god. There are lovely views, and a giant Nandi, carved in 1659, on the road down. Walk to it along the trail from the top and be picked up by a car later or catch a return bus from the road. If you continue along the trail you will end up having to get a rickshaw back, instead of a bus.

The **Sandalwood Oil Factory** ① *T0821-248 3651, Mon-Sat 0900-1100, 1400-1600 (prior permission required), no photography inside*, is where the oil is extracted and incense is made. The shop sells soap, incense sticks and other sandalwood items.

At the **Silk Factory** ① *Manathavadi Rd, T0821-248 1803, Mon-Sat 0930-1630, no photography*, weavers produce Mysore silk saris, often with gold *zari* work. Staff will often show you the process from thread winding to jacquard weaving, but they speak little English. The shop sells saris from Rs 3000. Good walks are possible in the Government House if the guard at the gate allows you in.

Sri Mahalingeshwara Temple ① *12 km from Mysore, 1 km off the Bhogadi road (right turn after K Hemmanahalli, beyond Mysore University Campus), taxi or auto-rickshaw*, is an 800-year-old Hoysala Temple that has been carefully restored by local villagers under the supervision of the Archaeological Survey of India. The structure is an authentic replica of the old temple: here, too, the low ceiling encourages humility by forcing the worshipper to bow before the shrine. The surrounding garden has been planted with herbs and saplings, including some rare medicinal trees, and provides a tranquil spot away from the city.

Srirangapatnam → *Colour map 3, B3. Phone code: 08236. Population: 21,900. See map, page 306.*

ⓘ *The island is over 3 km long and 1 km wide so it's best to hire a cycle from a shop on the main road to get around.*

Srirangapatnam, 12 km from Mysore, has played a crucial role in the region since its origins in the 10th century. Occupying an easily fortified island site in the Kaveri River, it has been home to religious reformers and military conquerors. It makes a fascinating day trip from Mysore; Daria Daulat Bagh and the Gumbaz are wonderful.

The name Srirangapatnam comes from the **temple of Sri Ranganathaswamy**, which stands aloof at the heart of the fortress, containing a highly humanistic idol of Lord Vishnu reclining on the back of a serpent. Dating from AD 894, it is far older than the fort and town, and was subsequently added to by the Hoysala and Vijayanagar kings. The latter built the fort in 1454, and occupied the site for some 150 years until the last Vijayanagar ruler handed over authority to the Hindu Wodeyars of Mysore, who made it their capital. In the second half of the 18th century it became the capital of Haidar Ali, who defended it against the Marathas in 1759, laying the foundations of his expanding power. He was succeeded by his son Tipu Sultan, who also used the town as his headquarters until Colonel Wellesley, the future Duke of Wellington, established his military reputation by defeating the Tiger of Mysore in battle on 4 May 1799 (see page 516). Tipu died in exceptionally fierce fighting near the north gate of the fort; the place is marked by a simple monument.

The fort had triple fortifications, but the British destroyed most of it. The **Jama Masjid** ⓘ *0800-1300, 1600-2000*, which Tipu had built, has delicate minarets, and there are two Hindu **temples**, to Narasimha (17th century) and Gangadharesvara (16th century). The **Daria Daulat Bagh** (Splendour of the Sea) ⓘ *1 km east of the fort, Sat-Thu 0900-1700, foreigners Rs 100, Indians Rs 5*, is Tipu's beautiful summer palace, built in 1784 and set in a lovely garden. This social historical jewel has colourful frescoes of battle scenes between the French, British and Mysore armies, ornamental arches and gilded paintings on the teak walls and ceilings crammed with interesting detail. The west wall shows Haidar Ali and Tipu Sultan leading their elephant forces at the battle of Polilur (1780), inflicting a massive defeat on the British. As a result of the battle Colonel Baillie, the defeated British commander, was held prisoner in Srirangapatnam for many years. The murals on the east walls show Tipu offering hospitality to neighbouring princes at various palace durbars. The small museum upstairs has 19th-century European paintings and Tipu's belongings.

Three kilometres east, the **Gumbaz** ⓘ *Sat-Thu 0800-1830, donation collected*, is the family mausoleum, approached through an avenue of cypresses. Built by Tipu in memory of his father, the ornate white dome protects beautiful ivory-on-wood inlay and Tipu's tiger-stripe emblem, some swords and shields. Haider Ali's tomb is in the centre, his wife to the east and Tipu's own to the west.

On the banks of the Cauvery just north of the Lal Bagh Palace is a jetty where six-seater *coracles* are available for river rides.

Ranganathittu Bird Sanctuary

ⓘ *5 km upstream of Srirangapatnam, 0700-1800, foreigners Rs 300, Indians Rs 50, camera Rs 25, video Rs 250. Boats (0830-1330, 1430-1830), foreigners Rs 300, Indians Rs 50. Jun-Oct is the best time to visit. Mysore City Bus 126, or auto-rickshaw from Srirangapatnam.*

The riverine site of this sanctuary was established in 1975. Several islands, some bare and rocky, others larger and well wooded, provide an excellent habitat for waterbirds, including the black-crowned night heron, Eurasian spoonbill and cormorants. Fourteen species of waterbirds use the sanctuary as a breeding ground from June onwards. There is a large colony of fruit bats in trees on the edge of the river and a number of marsh crocodiles between the small islands. Guided boat trips from the jetty last 15-20 minutes.

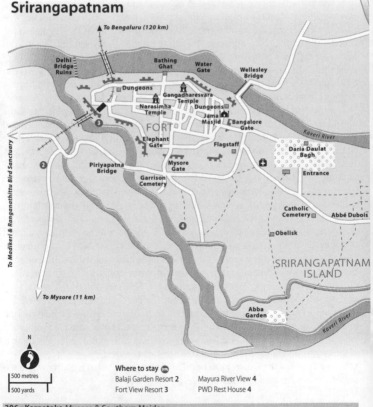

Srirangapatnam

Where to stay 🏠
Balaji Garden Resort **2**   Mayura River View **4**
Fort View Resort **3**   PWD Rest House **4**

Somnathpur → *Phone code: 08227.*

This tiny village boasts the only complete Hoysala temple in the Mysore region. The drive east from Srirangapatnam via Bannur is particularly lovely, passing a couple of lakes through beautiful country and pretty, clean villages. The small but exquisite **Kesava Temple** (1268) ① *0900-1700, foreigners Rs 100, Indians Rs 5, allow 1 hr, canteen, buses from Mysore take 1-1½ hrs; via Bannur (25 km, 45 mins) then to Somnathpur (3 km, 15 mins by bus, or lovely walk or bike ride through countryside)*, is one of the best preserved of 80 Hoysala temples in this area. Excellent ceilings show the distinctive features of the late Hoysala style, and here the roof is intact where other famous temples have lost theirs. The temple has three sanctuaries with the *trikutachala* (triple roof) and stands in the middle of its rectangular courtyard (70 m long, 55 m wide) with cloisters containing 64 cells around it. From the east gateway is a superb view of the temple with an ambulatory standing on its raised platform, in the form of a 16-pointed star. The pillared hall in the centre with the three shrines to the west give it the form of a cross in plan. Walk around the temple to see the fine bands of sculptured figures. The lowest of the six shows a line of elephants, symbolizing strength and stability, then horsemen for speed, followed by a floral scroll. The next band of beautifully carved figures (at eye level) is the most fascinating and tells stories from the epics. Above is the *yali* frieze, the monsters and foliage possibly depicting the river Ganga and uppermost is a line of *hamsa*, the legendary geese.

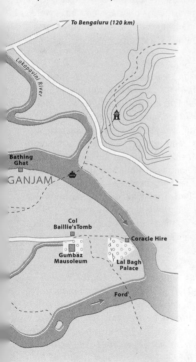

Sivasamudram

Here, the Kaveri plunges over 100 m into a series of wild and inaccessible gorges. At the top of the falls the river divides around the island of Sivasamudram, the Barachukki channel on the east and the Gaganchukki on the west. The hydro-electricity project was completed in 1902, the first HEP scheme of any size in India. It's best visited during the wet season, when the falls are an impressive sight, as water cascades over a wide area in a series of leaps.

Biligiri Rangaswamy Wildlife Sanctuary → *Altitude: 1000-1600 m.*
① *80 km south of Mysore, open 0600-0900, 1600-1830, foreigners Rs 1000,*

Passage to Mysore

The southern route to Mysore through Kanakapura and Malvalli is longer than the more northerly rail and road route. This way crosses the open parkland of the Maidan, rising to over 1200 m. The ancient rocks of some of the oldest granites in India which give reddish or brown soils, often with extraordinary hilly outcrops and boulders, provided David Lean and Richard Goodwin with the ideal filming location to capture the atmosphere of EM Forster's Barabar Cave for their film of *A Passage to India* without the hazards of working in Bihar. The lower cave sequences were filmed at Savandurga. To get there, take the BTS bus from Bengaluru City Bus Stand at 0700, 0900, or take a bus to Magadi, then an auto-rickshaw, Rs 50; ask at the Lakshmi store for directions or a guide. It's a stunning climb up Kempi Gowda hill.

There is also a small Forest Park and the upper caves at Rama Dhavara, 2 km from Ramanagaram. The caves are visible from the road and easy to find, though only false entrances were made for the film, with interior shots filmed in a studio.

Indians Rs 200, shared safari Rs 200 per person, trekking Rs 75, guide fee for private safaris Rs 250, camera free, video Rs 1000. From Mysore, access is via Nanjangud (23 km) and Chamarajanagar, where there's a Forest Check Post. For information, contact Deputy Conservator of Forests, Sultan Sheriff Circle, Chamarajanagar, T08226-222059. A hilly area with moist deciduous and semi-evergreen forests interspersed with grassland, the Biligiri Rangaswamy hills represent a biodiversity crossroads between the eastern and western sides of the Ghats. Some of the largest elephant populations east of the divide occur here, along with sloth bear (better sightings here than at other southern sanctuaries), panther, elephant, deer, gaur and the occasional tiger, as well as 270 species of bird. The local Forest Department has recently begun offering treks through the sanctuary, guided by members of the tribal community. The best time for wildlife sighting is November to May. The local Soliga hill tribes pay special respect to an ancient champak tree (*Doddasampige mara*) believed to be 1000 years old and the abode of Vishnu.

Bandipur National Park → *Colour map 3, B3. Altitude: 780-1455 m. Area: 874 sq km.*
① *96 km southwest of Mysore. Open 0600-0900, 1530-1830, reception centre 0900-1630; Mysore–Ooty buses stop at the main entrance. Except for jeep safaris run by local lodges, the only access is by the Forest Department's uninspiring 1-hr bus safari: Rs 100, plus entry fees of Rs 1000, Indians Rs 60, video Rs 150. 30-min elephant 'joy rides', Rs 65. Best times to visit are Nov-Feb to avoid the hot, dry months. For information, contact the Deputy Conservator of Forests, T08229-236043, Mysore T0821-248 0901, dcfbandipur@yahoo.co.in.*
Bandipur was set up by the Mysore maharaja in 1931, and now forms part of the Nilgiri Biosphere Reserve, sharing borders with Mudumalai National Park in Tamil Nadu and Kerala's Wayanad Wildlife Sanctuary. It has a mixture of subtropical moist

and dry deciduous forests (principally teak and anogeissus) and scrubland in the Nilgiri foothills. The wetter areas support rosewood, silk cotton, sandalwood and *jamun*. You may spot gaur, chital (spotted deer), elephant, sambar, flying squirrel and four-horned antelope, but tigers and leopards are rare. There's also a good variety of birdlife including crested hawk, serpent eagles and tiny-eared owls.

Coorg (Kodagu) → *For listings, see pages 312-320.*

Coorg, once a proud warrior kingdom, then a state, has now shrunk to become the smallest district in Karnataka. It is a beautiful anomaly in South India in that it has, so far, retained its original forests. Ancient rosewoods jut out of the Western Ghat hills to shade the squat coffee shrubs which the British introduced as the region's chief commodity. Like clockwork, 10 days after the rains come, these trees across whole valleys burst as one into white blossom drenching the moist air with their thick perfume, a hybrid of honeysuckle and jasmine. Although the climate is not as cool as other hill stations, Coorg's proximity by road to the rest of Karnataka makes it a popular weekend bolt hole for inhabitants of Bengaluru (Bangalore). The capital of Coorg District, Madikeri, is an attractive small town in a beautiful hilly setting surrounded by the forested slopes of the Western Ghats and has become a popular trekking destination.

Arriving in Coorg
Getting there At present Coorg is only accessible by road, although an airport and railway station are planned. Frequent local and express buses arrive at Madikeri's bus stand from the west coast after a journey through beautiful wooded hills passing small towns and a wildlife sanctuary. From Mysore and Coimbatore an equally pleasant route traverses the Maidan. In winter there is often hill fog at night, making driving after dark dangerous.

Getting around Madikeri is ideal for walking though you may need to hire an auto on arrival to reach the better hotels. ▶▶ *See Transport, page 320.*

Tourist information There's a small tourist office ① *Mysore Rd south of the Thinmaya statue, T08272-228580.* Coorg Wildlife Society ① *2 km further out on Mysore Rd, T08272-223505*, can help with trekking advice and permits for catch-and-release mahseer fishing on the Kaveri River.

Background
Although there were references to the Kodaga people in the Tamil Sangam literature of the second century AD, the earliest Kodaga inscriptions date from the eighth century. After the Vjiayanagar Empire was defeated in 1565, many of their courtiers moved south, establishing regional kingdoms. One of these groups were the Haleri Rajas, members of the Lingayat caste whose leader Virarajendra set up the first Kodaga dynasty at Haleri, 10 km from the present district capital of Madikeri.

The later Kodagu rajas were noted for some bizarre behaviour. Dodda Vira (1780-1809) was reputed to have put most of his relatives to death, a pattern followed by the last king, Vira Raja, before he was forced to abdicate by the British in 1834. In 1852 the last Lingayat ruler of Kodagu, Chikkavirarajendra Wodeyar, became the first Indian prince to sail to England, and the economic character of the state was quickly transformed. Coffee was introduced, becoming the staple crop of the region.

The forests of Kodagu are still home to wild elephants, who often crash into plantations on jackfruit raids, and other wildlife. The Kodaga, a tall, fair and proud landowning people who flourished under the British, are renowned for their martial prowess; almost every family has one member in the military. They also make incredibly warm and generous hosts – a characteristic you can discover thanks to the number of plantation homestays in inaccessible estates of dramatic beauty pioneered here following the crash in coffee prices. Kodagu also has a highly distinctive cuisine, in which *pandi* curry (pork curry) and *kadumbuttu* (rice dumplings) are particular favourites.

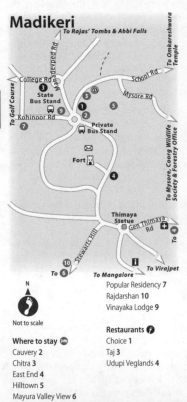

Madikeri

Where to stay 🛏
Cauvery 2
Chitra 3
East End 4
Hilltown 5
Mayura Valley View 6
Popular Residency 7
Rajdarshan 10
Vinayaka Lodge 9

Restaurants 🍴
Choice 1
Taj 3
Udupi Veglands 4

Madikeri (Mercara) → *Colour map 3, B2. Phone code: 08272. Population: 32,300. Altitude: 1150 m.*

The **Omkareshwara Temple**, dedicated to both Vishnu and Siva, was built in 1820. The tiled roofs are typical of Kerala Hindu architecture, while the domes show Muslim influence. On high ground dominating the town is the **fort** with its three stone gateways, built between 1812-1814 by Lingarajendra Wodeyar II. It has a small **museum** ① *Tue-Sun 0900-1700, closed holidays,* in St Mark's Church as well as the town prison, a temple and a chapel while the palace houses government offices. The **Rajas' Tombs** (*Gaddige*), built in 1820 to the north of the town, are the memorials of Virarajendra and his wife and of Lingarajendra. Although the rajas were Hindu, their commemorative monuments are Muslim in style; Kodagas both bury and cremate their dead. The **Friday market** near the bus stand is very colourful as all the local tribal people come to town to sell their produce. It is known locally as Shandy, a British bastardization of the Coorg word *shante*, meaning market. On Mahadevped Road, which leads to the

Rajas' tombs, is a 250-year-old **Siva temple** which has an interesting stone façade. Madikeri also has an attractive nine-hole golf course.

Around Madikeri

Madikeri and the surrounding area makes for beautiful walking but if you want to venture further you'll need to take a guide as paths can soon become indistinct and confusing. **Abbi Falls** is a 30-minute rickshaw ride (9 km, Rs 150 round-trip) through forests and coffee plantations. It is also an enjoyable walk along a fairly quiet road. The falls themselves are beautiful and well worth the visit. You can do a beautiful short trek down the valley and then up and around above the falls before rejoining the main road. Do not attempt it alone since there are no trails and you must depend on your sense of direction along forest paths. **Honey Valley Estate** (see page 315) has a book of walks around the guesthouse.

At **Bhagamandala** ① *36 km southwest, half-hourly service from Madikeri's private bus stand from 0630-2000, Rama Motors tour bus departs 0830, with 30-min stop*, the Triveni bathing ghat can be visited at the confluence of the three rivers: Kaveri, Kanike and Suiyothi. Among many small shrines the **Bhandeshwara Temple**, standing in a large stone courtyard surrounded by Keralan-style buildings on all four sides, is particularly striking. You can stay at the temple for a very small charge.

Kakkabe ① *35 km south of Madikeri, bus from Madikeri to Kakkabe at 0630, jeep 1 hr*, is a small town, giving access to the highest peak in Coorg, **Thandiandamole** (1800 m). Nearby, **Padi Iggutappa** is the most important temple in Coorg.

Cauvery Nisargadhama ① *0900-1800, Rs 150, still camera Rs 10*, is a small island reserve in the Kaveri River, 2 km from Kushalnagar, accessed over a hanging bridge. Virtually untouched by tourism, it consists mostly of bamboo thickets and trees, including sandalwood, and is very good for seeing parakeets, bee eaters, woodpeckers and a variety of butterflies. There is a deer park, pedalo boating, a resident elephant and tall bamboo tree houses for wildlife viewing.

Nagarhole (Rajiv Gandhi) National Park → *Colour map 3, B2.*

① *Open 0600-0800, 1500-1700. Foreigners Rs 1000, Indians Rs 200, video Rs 1000. The main entrance is near Hunsur on the northern side of the park where the Deputy Conservator of Forests may grant permission for private jeep safaris (Rs 1000, plus guide fee of Rs 500) and forest treks; enquire in advance on T08222-252064, dcfhunsur@ rediffmail.com. The southern entrance, with better accommodation, is at Karapur, 5 km from Kabini River Lodge. Arrive during daylight as elephant activity means the roads are closed after dusk.*

Nagarhole (meaning 'snake streams') was once the maharajas' reserved forest and became a national park in 1955. Covering gentle hills bordering Kerala, it includes swampland, streams, moist deciduous forest, stands of bamboo and valuable timber in teak and rosewood trees. The Kabini River, which is a tributary of the Kaveri, flows through the forest where the upper canopy reaches 30 m. The park is accessible both by road and river. A number of tribesmen, particularly Kurumbas (honey gatherers) who still practise ancient skills, live amongst, and care for, the elephants.

In addition to elephants, the park also has gaur (Indian bison), dhole (Indian wild dogs), wild cats, four-horned antelopes, flying squirrels, sloth bears, monkeys and sambar deer ("better sightings than at Mudumalai"). Tigers and leopards are sighted very rarely. Many varieties of birds include the rare Malabar trogon, great black woodpecker, Indian pitta, pied hornbill, whistling thrush, green imperial pigeon and also waterfowl and reptiles.

The edge of the dam is the best place to view wildlife, particularly during the dry period from March to June. The Forest Department runs 45-minute bus tours (Rs 100 per person) during the morning and evening opening hours; there's a one-hour tour at 1715 with viewing from *machans* near the waterholes. You can also visit the government's Elephant Training Camp at Haballa, and take a 30-minute ride (Rs 75).

◉ Mysore and Southern Maidan listings

For hotel and restaurant price codes and other relevant information, see pages 13-17.

◉ Where to stay

Mysore *p301, map p302*
May is the most important wedding month and so hotels get booked in advance. In the expensive hotels sales tax on food, luxury tax on rooms and a service charge can increase the bill significantly. The Gandhi Square area has some Indian-style hotels which are clean and good value. Note that JLB Rd is Jhansi Lakshmi Bai Rd and B-N Rd is Bengaluru-Nilgiri Rd.
$$$$-$$$ Green Hotel,
Chittaranjan Palace, 2270 Vinoba Rd, Jayalakshmipuram (near Mysore University), T0821-251 2536, www.green hotelindia.com. Princess's beautiful palace lovingly converted with strong sustainable tourism ethos: hot water from solar panels, profits to charity and staff recruited from less advantaged groups. The best of the 31 rooms are in the palace but if you stay in the cheaper, newer block you can still loll about in the huge upper lounges: excellent library, chess tables and day beds. Unique, but beyond walking distance from Mysore centre.

$$$$-$$$ Lalitha Mahal Palace (ITDC), Narasipur Rd, Siddartha Nagar T0821-252 6100. 54 rooms (**$$$**) and suites in the palace built in 1931 for the maharaja's non-vegetarian, foreign guests. Regal setting near Chamundi Hill, old fashioned (some original baths with extraordinary spraying system); for nostalgia stay in the old wing. Attractive pool, but avoid the below par restaurant.
$$$$-$$$ Royal Orchid Metropole, 5 JLB Rd, T0821-425 5566, www.royal orchidhotels.com. After languishing in disrepair for years, the Karnataka government has resuscitated the glorious colonial Metropole building. Airy, high-ceilinged rooms, massage and yoga classes plus a small pool and excellent restaurant.
$$$ Sandesh the Prince, 3 Nazarbad Main Rd, T0821-243 6777, www.sandesh theprince.com. 4-star centrally located hotel with a restaurant, bars, pool, spa and gym.
$$$-$$ Indus Valley, near **Lalith Mahal** (see above), T0821-247 3437, www.ayurindus.com. Health resort in a splendid location, halfway up a hill, 22 rooms (in main building or in cottage), hot showers and Western toilets, TV in

lounge, Ayurvedic massages, pleasant walks, vegetarian Ayurvedic restaurant, herbal wines, friendly staff, family-run.

$$$-$$ Mayura Hoysala (KSTDC), 2 JLB Rd, T0821-242 6160. 20 rooms in lovely, ochre-painted, ramshackle Raj-style hotel: full of chintzy soft furnishings, overspilling with plant pots, en suite bathrooms have both Western and squat loos, tiny whitewashed cane stools are propped up on terracing along with mismatched 1970s furniture. 3 restaurants, bar, tourist desk.

$$$-$$ Siddharta, 73/1 Guest House Rd, Nazarabad, T0821-428 0999, www.hotelsiddharta.com. 105 rooms, some a/c, huge with baths, good restaurant (Indian vegetarian), exchange, immaculate, well run.

$$ Park Lane, 2720 Sri Harsha Rd, T0821-400 3500, www.parklanemysore.com. Freshly renovated, with a price hike to match, but the folk-art-rustic rooms are clean and good value. The noise, including nightly classical Indian performances, from popular downstairs restaurant (open 1030-2330) does travel.

$$-$$ Bombay Tiffany's, 313 Sayyaji Rao Rd, T0821-243 5255, bombaytiffanys@ yahoo.com. Affable owner in hotel with 60 clean rooms (12 a/c in new hotel). The regular rooms are spartan, but the deluxe and a/c ones are very good value.

$$-$$ Mysore Dasaprakash, Gandhi Sq, T0821-244 2444, www.mysore dasaprakash group.com. 144 rooms in this labyrinthine blue-white complex set around an attractive, large courtyard. Milk coffee-coloured rooms are stocked with wood furniture and scrupulously clean white sheets. Peaceful and quiet despite being slap bang in the centre.

$ Greens' Boarding and Lodging, 2722/2 Curzon Park Rd, T0821-242 2415. Dark hallways give onto these green gloss-painted rooms with dark wood furniture. Cool, spacious, central and darn cheap, but bathrooms are not the best.

$ Hotel Ritz, Bengaluru–Nilgiri Rd near Central Bus Station, T0821-242 2668, www. hotelritzmysore.com. Bags of character in this 60-year-old house and garden set back from the busy road. 4 rooms with wooden furniture off cool communal area with TV, dining table and chairs. Pleasant open shaded courtyard. Legendary amongst backpackers so book ahead.

Srirangapatnam *p305, map p306*
$$$-$$ Fort View Resort, T08236-252577. 12 upmarket rooms (4 with corner tub), Rajasthani architecture, huge

beds, shady landscaped gardens, gloomy and pricey restaurant, organic kitchen garden, pool, boating, fishing, efficient.
$$ Mayura River View, Mysore Rd, T08236-217454. Beautifully situated on the croc-filled river with 8 comfortable rooms, sit-outs, 2 a/c, good vegetarian restaurant (Indian, Chinese), most relaxing, really quiet.
$$-$ Balaji Garden Resort, Mysore Rd (1 km from Piriyapatna Bridge), T08236-217355. 12 good-value cottages and 28 smallish rooms built with some style around a central courtyard, well furnished, tiled and comfy, cottages are good value, pool, restaurant.
$ PWD Rest House. Book ahead at PWD office near Ranganathaswami Temple, T08236-252051. Charming former residence of George Harris. Basic rooms, but clean and quiet.

Biligiri Rangaswamy Wildlife Sanctuary *p307*
As in most Karnataka wildlife parks, the lodges and forest rest houses here charge foreigners double the rate Indians pay.
$$$ K Gudi Camp, Kyathadevara, book via **Jungle Lodges**, T080-4055 4055, www.junglelodges.com. 8 twin-bedded quality tents with modern toilets, simple meals in the open air or 4 rooms with 4 beds at royal hunting lodge, elephant rides, birding, trekking, comfortable experience despite remoteness.

Bandipur National Park *p308*
Reserve rooms in advance; avoid weekends.
$$$ Bandipur Safari Lodge, at Melkamanahalli nearby, T080-4055 4055, www.junglelodges.com. Simple rooms in cottages and restaurant under shady trees; rates include nature walks, park safaris and entry fees.

$$$ Dhole's Den, Kaniyanapura village, T08229-236062, www.dholesden.com. Lovely small resort, with 2 rooms, a spacious suite and 2 large cottages, in modern minimalist style with a low-impact ethic: there's no TV or a/c, most electricity is wind or solar generated, and you can pick-your-own veg from the organic garden for dinner.
$ Venu Vihar Lodge, 20 km from park reception. Book in advance through Forest Department, Woodyard, Mysore, T0821-248 0110. Set in the beautiful Gopalaswamy Hills. Meals available but take provisions.

Madikeri *p310, map p310*
Power cuts are common. Carry a torch, keep candles handy. Book early during holidays.
$$$$ Orange County, Karadigodu Post, Siddapur, T08274-258481, www.orange county.in. The poshest place for miles around, with beautiful red-brick cottages set among 120 ha of coffee plantation. Good bird guides, coracle rides on the river and great food.
$$$-$$ Capitol Village, 5 km southeast of town on Siddapur Rd, T08272-225929. 13 large, airy rooms, dorm (Rs 150), traditional Keralan building (tiled roof, wooden beams) set in a coffee, cardamom and pepper estate, very quiet, outdoor eating under shady trees (Rs 75-150), rickshaw from centre Rs 40.
$$ Rajdarshan,116/2 MG Rd, T08272-229142, hotelrajdarshan.net. 25 well laid-out, clean rooms (need renovating), excellent restaurant, friendly staff, modern, with views over town.
$$-$ Chitra, School Rd, near bus stand, T08272-225372, www.hotelchitra.com. 54 nondescript rooms with Western toilets, hot shower, simple but clean, North Indian vegetarian restaurant, bar,

helpful and knowledgeable English-speaking trekking guide (Mr Muktar).
$$-$ East End, Gen Thimaya Rd, T08272-229996. Darkish rooms but good restaurant, serves excellent *dosas*.
$ Cauvery, School Rd, T08272-225492. 26 clean, pleasant but basic rooms with fans, Indian meals, bar, away from main road. Helpful management, information on trekking (stores luggage).
$ Hilltown, Daswal Rd, T08272-223801, hilltown@rediffmail.com. 38 modern, pleasant and airy rooms with TV in newish hotel, marble-floored throughout, restaurant, great value. Recommended.
$ Popular Residency, Kohinoor Rd, T08272-221644. 10 clean and pleasant rooms, well fitted out, North Indian vegetarian restaurant, good value.
$ Vinayaka Lodge, 25 m from bus stand, T08272-229830. Good value 50 rooms with bath, hot water buckets, friendly staff, clean, quiet (bus stand can be noisy early morning).

Around Madikeri *p311*
$$-$ Forest Rest House, Cauvery Nisargadhama, contact Forestry Office, Madikeri, T08272-228305, dfo_madikeri@yahoo.com. 11 simple cottages built largely of bamboo and teak, some with balconies on stilts over the water, electricity (no fan), hot water, peaceful (despite nocturnal rats), but poor food.
$$-$ Honey Valley Estate, Yavakapadi, Kakkabe, 3 km up a track only a jeep can manage, T08272-238339, www.honeyvalleyindia.in. This place has less stunning views than **Palace Estate** (the house is screened by tall trees) but equally good access by foot to trekking trails. Facilities are mostly better and it can fit over 30 guests, charming host family too. Also has a hut 2 km into the forest for those wanting more isolation.

$$-$ Palace Estate, 2 km south of Kakkabe (Rs 35 in a rickshaw) along Palace Rd, T08272-238446, www.palaceestate.co.in. A small traditional farm growing coffee, pepper, cardamom and bananas lying just above the late 18th-century Nalnad Palace, a summer hunting lodge of the kings of Coorg. 6 basic rooms with shared veranda looking across forested hills all the way to Madikeri. Isolated and an excellent base for walking; Coorg's highest peak is 6 km from the homestay. Home-cooked local food, English-speaking guide Rs 150.

Nagarhole National Park *p311*
Safari lodges within Nagarhole are uniformly very expensive, though rates generally include jeep safaris. More affordable rooms are available in homestays around Kutta on the western fringe of the park. A 2-tier pricing structure operates in many lodges and hotels; prices quoted are for foreigners.
$$$$ Kabini River Lodge, at Karapur on reservoir bank, T080-4055 4055, www.junglelodges.com. 14 rooms in Mysore Maharajas' 18th-century hunting lodge and bungalow, 6 newer cabins overlooking lake, 5 tents, simple but acceptable, good restaurant, bar, exchange, package includes meals, sailing, rides in buffalo-hide coracles on the Kaveri, jeep/minibus at Nagarhole and Murkal complex, park tour with naturalist, very friendly and well run.
$$$ Waterwoods, 500 m from Kabini River Lodge, surrounded by the Kabini river, T08228-264421. Exquisitely furnished ranch-style house, 6 luxury rooms with sit-outs, beautiful gardens on water's edge, delicious home cooking, solar power, friendly staff, boating, jeep, Ayurvedic massage, gym, swimming, walking, charming,

informal atmosphere, peaceful, secluded. Highly recommended.

$$$-$ Forest Department Rest Houses, at various locations within the park, book at least 15 days in advance via the Deputy Conservator of Forests, Hunsur, T08222-252401. Facilities range from **$** dorm beds to simple cottages with attached bath and hot water.

🍴 Restaurants

Mysore *p301, map p302*
$$$ Green Hotel (see Where to stay). Atmospheric, with food served in the palace itself, on a veranda, or under the stars in the hotel's immaculate garden. But not the best food.

$$$ Om Shanti, Siddharta (see Where to stay). Pure vegetarian either with/ without a/c, thronged with domestic tourists, which is a fair reflection of its culinary prowess.

$$ Park Lane (see Where to stay). Red lights hang from the creeper-covered trellis over this courtyard restaurant: turn them on for service. Superb classical music played every evening 1900-2130, good food, including barbecue nights. Popular, lively and idiosyncratic.

$$ Shilpashri, Gandhi Sq. Comfortable rooftop, reasonably priced, tourist orientated, chilled beers, friendly but service can be slow.

$ Anu's Bamboo Hut, 367 2nd Main, 3rd Stage, Gokulam, T0821-428 9492. Friendly little rooftop cafe in the midst of the Western yogi ghetto of Gokulam. The vegetarian buffet (daily except Thu, 1300-1500) is packed with salads and bean dishes, and always sells out quickly; Anu also does good smoothies and lassies from 1700-1900, and offers vegetarian cooking classes. Call ahead.

$ Jewel Rock, **Maurya Residency**, Sri Harsha Rd. Dark interior, great chicken tikka, spicy cashew nut chicken, go early to avoid queues.

$ Mylari, Nazarbad Main Rd (ask rickshaw driver). The best *dosas* in town served on a banana leaf, mornings until 1100, basic surroundings, may have to queue. Biriyanis also legendary.

$ Mysore Dasaprakash (see Where to stay). Good breakfast, huge southern *thali* (Rs 25).

$ RRR, Gandhi Sq. Part a/c, tasty non-vegetarian on plantain leaves, good for lunch.

$ Samrat, next to Indra Bhavan, Dhanvantri Rd. Range of tasty North Indian vegetarian.

$ SR Plantain Leaf (Chalukya's), Rajkamal Talkies Rd. Decent vegetarian *thalis* on banana leaf; also tandoori chicken.

Cafés and snacks
Bombay Tiffany's, Devraja Market Building. Try the 'Mysore pak', a ghee-laden sweet.

Indra Café, Sayaji Rd, on fringes of market. Excellent *bhel puri*, *sev puri*, *channa puri*.

Penguin Ice-cream Parlour. Sofas shared with local teens listening to Hindi pop.

Raghu Niwas, B-N Rd, opposite **Ritz**. Does very good breakfasts.

Sri Rama Veg, 397 Dhanvantri Rd. Serves fast food, good juices.

Madikeri *p310, map p310*
$ Capitol, near Private Bus Stand. Despite its exterior, serves excellent vegetarian fare.
$ Choice, School Rd. Wide menu, good food, choice of ground floor or rooftop.
$ Taj, College Rd. 'Cheap and best', clean and friendly.
$ Udupi Veglands, opposite fort. Lovely, clean, spacious wooden eatery, delicious and cheap vegetarian *thalis*.

🌓 Bars and clubs

Mysore *p301, map p302*
The best bars are in hotels: try the expensive but elegant Lalitha Mahal Palace, or the funky lounge at the **Adhi Manor**, Chandragupta Rd.

✦ Festivals

Mysore *p301, map p302*
Mar-Apr **Temple car festival** with a 15-day fair, at the picturesque town of Nanjangud, 23 km south (Erode road); **Vairamudi** festival which lasts 6 days when deities are adorned with 3 diamond crowns, at Melkote Temple, 52 km.
11 Aug **Feast of St Philomena**, 0800-1800, the statue of the saint is taken out in procession through the city streets ending with a service at the Gothic, stained-glass-laden cathedral.
End Sep to early Oct **Dasara**, see box, page 303.

◯ Shopping

Mysore *p301, map p302*
Books
Ashok, Dhanvantri Rd, T0821-243 5533. Excellent selection.

Clothing
For silks at good prices, try Sayaji Rao Rd.
Badshah's, 20 Devraj Urs Rd, T0821-242 9799. Beautifully finished *salwar kameez*. Mr Yasin speaks good English.
Craft Emporium, middle part of Vinoba Rd. Good selection and quality but beware those pretending to be government emporia. Also sells cloth.
Karnataka Silk Industry, Mananthody Rd, T0821-248 1803. Mon-Sat 1030-1200, 1500-1630. Watch machine weaving at the factory shop.

Handicrafts
Superb carved figures, sandalwood and rosewood items, silks, incense sticks, handicrafts. The main shopping area is Sayaji Rao Rd.
Cauvery Arts & Crafts Emporium, for sandalwood and rosewood items, closed Thu (non-receipt of parcel reported by traveller).
Devaraja Market, lanes of stalls selling spices, perfumes and much more; good 'antique' shop (fixed price) has excellent sandalwood and rosewood items. Worth visiting.
Ganesh, 532 Dhanvantri Rd.
Shankar, 12 Dhanvantri Rd.
Sri Lakshmi Fine Arts & Crafts (opposite the zoo); also has a factory shop at 2226 Sawday Rd, Mandi Mohalla.

🕐 What to do

Mysore *p301, map p302*
Body and soul
Jois Ashtanga Yoga Research Institute, www.kpjayi.org. Not for novice yogis at Rs 8000 a month, the minimum period offered.
Sri Patanjali Yogashala, Parakala Mutt, next to Jaganmohan Palace. Ashtanga Vinyasa yoga; daily instruction in English from BNS Iyengar, 0600-0900, 1600-1900, US$100 per month: some say the conditions here are slapdash, although teaching is good.

Swimming
Mysore University, Olympic-sized pool, hourly sessions 0630-0830 then 1500-1600, women only 1600-1700.
Southern Star Mysore, 13-14 Vinoba Rd, T0821-242 1689, www.ushalexus hotels.com. More of a pool to relax by and sunbathe.

Power yoga

If you know the primary series, speak fluent *ujayyi* breath and know about the *mulla bandha* odds are that you have heard the name of Sri Pattabhi Jois, too. His is the version of yoga that has most percolated contemporary Western practice (it's competitive enough for the type-A modern societies we live in, some argue), and although for most of the years of his teaching he had just a handful of students, things have certainly changed.

Though the Guru left his body in May 2009, a steady flow of international students still make the pilgrimage to his Ashtanga Yoga Nilayam in Mysore, where his daughter Saraswathi and grandson Sharath Rangaswamy continue the lineage.

Saraswathi's classes are deemed suitable for Ashtanga novices, but studying with Sharath is not for dilettante yogis; the Westerners here are extremely ardent about their practice – mostly teachers themselves – and there is a strict pecking order which first-timers could find alienating. Classes start from first light at 0400, and the day's teaching is over by 0700, leaving you free for the rest of the day. The schooling costs US$500 a month.

There's no rule that says you must know the series, but it might be better, and cheaper, to dip a toe in somewhere a bit less hardcore and far-flung, such as Purple Valley in Goa (see page 441).

In a curious side note, the prevalence of foreigners running under-the-table yoga businesses in Mysore has led the local police to institute what may be the world's only city-specific visa. Prospective students heading for Mysore must now apply for a Yoga Visa, essentially a student visa which requires admission papers from a recognized yoga school. Teachers risk a fine if they so much as demonstrate a Surya Namaskar without checking your papers.

Kerala police have been pushing for a similar rule, but as yet, yoga centres outside Mysore seem unaffected by the new rule.

For details and Sharath's teaching schedule, see www.kpjayi.com.

Tour operators

KSTDC, **Yatri Nivas** hotel, 2 JLB Rd, T0821-242 3492. **Mysore**, daily 0715-2030, Rs 155, tours of local sights and Chamundi Hill, Kukkara Halli Lake, Somanathapura, Srirangapatnam and Brindavan Gardens. Tours also run to **Belur**, **Halebid**, and **Sravanabelagola** if there are 10 or more guests: a long and tiring day, but worth it if you are not travelling to Hassan. **Seagull Travels**, 8 Hotel Ramanashree Complex, BN Rd, T0821-426 0054. Good for cars, drivers, flights, wildlife tours, etc.

Skyway International Travels, No 370/4, Jansi Laxmibai Rd, T0821-244 4444, www.skywaytour.com.
TCI, Gandhi Sq, T0821-526 0294. Very pleasant and helpful.

Madikeri *p310, map p310*
Fishing
Coorg Wildlife Society (see page 309). Arranges licences for fishing on the Kaveri river (Rs 500 per day, Rs 1000 weekend). The highlight is the prospect of pulling in a *mahseer*, up to 45 kg in weight; all

fish must be returned to the river. Fishing takes place at Trust Land Estate, Valnoor, near Kushalnagar, where there is a lodge; you'll need to bring your own food.

Trekking
Friends' Tours and Travel, below **Bank of India**, College Rd, T08272-229974. Recommended for their knowledge and enthusiasm. Tailor-made treks Rs 275 per person per day including guide, food and accommodation in temples, schools, etc. A base camp is at Thalathmane, 4 km from Madikeri, which people can also stay at even if not trekking. Basic huts and blankets for Rs 50 each, home cooking nearby at little extra cost. **Hotel Cauvery** (see page 315). Also arranges treks.

⊖ Transport

Mysore *p301, map p302*
Bus Local City bus station, southeast of KR Circle, T0821-242 5819. To **Silk Weaving Centre**, Nos 1, 2, 4 and 8; **Brindavan Gardens**, No 303; **Chamundi Hill**, No 201; **Srirangapatnam**, No 313. **Central Bus Station**, T0821-2529853. **Bandipur**, Platform 9, **Ooty** etc, Platform 11.

Long distance There are 2 bus stations. **Central**, T0821-252 0853, is mainly used by long-distance **SRTC** companies of Karnataka, Tamil Nadu and Kerala, all of which run regular daily services between Mysore and other major cities. The bus station has a list of buses with reserved places. To **Bengaluru (Bangalore)**: every 15 mins from non-stop platform. Also frequent services to **Hassan**, 3 hrs; **Mangalore** (7 hrs); and **Ooty** (5 hrs) via **Bandipur** (2 hrs). Daily services to **Coimbatore**; **Gokarna** (12 hrs); **Hospet**: 1930 (10 hrs), very tiring; **Kochi**, 10 hrs; **Kozhikode** via **Wayanad**; **Salem** (7 hrs);

Thiruvananthapuram (Super deluxe, 14 hrs). Several to **Satyamangalam** where you can connect with buses to Tamil Nadu. The journey is through wilderness and forests with spectacular scenery as the road finally plunges from the plateau down to the plains.

The **Suburban** and **Private bus stands**, T0821-244 3490, serves nearby destinations including **Somnathpur**, around 1 hr direct, or longer via Bannur or via Narasipur. Many private companies near Gandhi Sq operate overnight sleepers and interstate buses which may be faster and marginally less uncomfortable. Book ahead for busy routes.

Car Travel companies and **KSTDC** charge about Rs 700 (4 hrs/40 km) for city sightseeing; Rs 1100 to include Srirangapatnam and Brindavan.

Train Advance Computerized Reservations in separate section; ask for 'foreigners' counter'. T131. Enquiries T0821-252 0103, 0800-2000 (closed 1330-1400); Sun 0800-1400. Left luggage 0600-2200, Rs 3-6 per day. Tourist information, telephone and toilets on Platform 1. Taxi counter at entrance. To **Bengaluru (Bangalore)** (non-stop): *Tipu Exp, 16205*, 1120, 2½ hrs; *Shatabdi Exp 12008*, daily except Wed, 1415, 2 hrs (continues to **Chennai**, another 5 hrs). **Bengaluru** via **Srirangapatnam, Mandya** and **Maddur**: *Chamundi Exp 16215*, 0645, 3 hrs; *Kaveri Chennai Exp 16221*, 2015, 2¾ hrs. **Chennai**: *Chennai Exp 16221*, 2015, 10½ hrs; *Shatabdi Exp, 12008*, not Wed, 1415, 7 hrs. **Madurai**: change at Bengaluru. **Mumbai**: *Sharavathi Exp, 11036*, Sun only, 0630, 24 hrs.

Srirangapatnam *p305, map p306*
Trains and buses between **Bengaluru (Bangalore)** and **Mysore** stop here but

arrival can be tiresome with hassle from rickshaw drivers, traders and beggars. Buses 313 and 316 from Mysore **City Bus Stand** (half-hourly) take 50 mins.

Bandipur National Park *p308*
Bus Bandipur and the neighbouring Mudumalai NP in Tamil Nadu are both on the Mysore to Ooty bus route, about 2½ hrs south from Mysore and 2½ hrs from Ooty. Buses go to and from **Mysore** (80 km) between 0615-1530.

Madikeri *p310, map p310*
Auto-rickshaw From **Hotel Chitra** to **Abbi Falls**, Rs 150 including 1 hr wait there.

Bus From KSRTC Bus Stand, T08272-229134, frequent express buses to **Bengaluru** (**Bangalore**), Plat 4, from 0615 (6 hrs); **Chikmagalur**; **Hassan** (3½ hrs); **Kannur**; **Mangalore**, Plat 2, 0530-2400 (3½ hrs); **Mysore** Plat 3, half-hourly 0600-2300 (3 hrs) via **Kushalnagar** (for Tibetan settlements), very crowded during the rush hour; **Thalassery**. Daily to **Coimbatore**, **Madurai**, **Mumbai**, **Ooty**, **Virajpet**.
   Private Bus Stand: Kamadenu Travels, above bus stand, T08272-225524, for **Purnima Travels** bus to **Bengaluru**. Shakti Motor Service to **Nagarhole** (4½ hrs).

Train The closest stations are Mysore (120 km), Hassan (130 km) and Mangalore (135 km). Computerized reservations office on Main Rd, T08272-225002, Mon-Sat 1000-1700, Sun 1000-1400.

Around Madikeri *p311*
The bus from Madikeri to **Nisargadhama** passes park gates 2 km before Kushalnagar. A rickshaw from Kushalnagar Rs 10.

Nagarhole *p311*
Bus From **Mysore**, *Exp*, 3 hrs, Rs 35; **Madikeri**, 4½ hrs. **Bengaluru** (**Bangalore**), 6 hrs. For **Kabini River Lodge** and **Water Woods**, be sure to get the KSRTC bus to **Karapur**, not Nagarhole. **Jungle Lodges**, T080-2559 7021, www.junglelodges.com, buses leave Bengaluru at 0730, stop in Mysore (around 0930), reaching Kabini around 1230; return bus departs 1315.

Train The nearest station is Mysore (96 km).

ⓘ Directory

Mysore *p301, map p302*
Banks Many ATMs accepting international cards on Ashoka Rd and DD Urs Rd. **State Bank of Mysore**, corner of Sayaji Rao Rd and Sardar Patel Rd and opposite GPO in city centre. **LKP Forex**, near clock tower. **Thomas Cook**, Ashoka Rd, T0821-242 6157. **Medical services** KR Hospital, T0821-242 3300; **Medical College**, corner of Irwin and Sayaji Rao Rd; **Mission Hospital** (Mary Holdsworth), Tilaknagar, T0821-244 6644, in a striking building dating from 1906. **Post** GPO, on corner of Ashoka and Irwin roads. T0821-241 7326, has Poste Restante. **Useful contacts** Deputy Conservator of Forests, T0821-248 3853.

Madikeri *p310, map p310*
Banks Canara Bank, Main Rd, has an ATM and accepts some TCs. **Internet** Cyber Zone, next to Chitra Hotel. Rs 30 per hr, excellent. **Post** Behind Private Bus Stand. **Useful contacts** Community Centre, south of Fort, Main Rd, holds occasional shows. **Forestry Office**, Aranya Bhavan, Mysore Rd, 3 km from town, T08272-225708.

Western Plateau

The world's tallest monolith – that of the Jain saint Gommateshwara – has stood majestic, 'skyclad' and lost in meditation high on Sravanabelagola's Indragiri hill since the 10th century. It is a profoundly spiritual spot, encircled by long sweeps of paddy and sugar cane plains, and is one of the most popular pilgrimage points for practitioners of the austere Jain religion. Some male Jain followers of the Digambar or skyclad sect of the faith climb the rock naked to denote their freedom from material bonds. Nearby lie the 11th- and 12th-century capital cities of Halebid and Belur, the apex of Hoysala temple architecture whose walls are cut into friezes of the most intricate soapstone. These villages of the Central Maidan sit in the path of one of the main routes for trade and military movement for centuries.

Western Plateau temples → *For listings, see pages 325-328.*

Sravanabelagola, Belur and Halebid can all be seen in a very long day from Bengaluru, but it's far better to stay overnight near the sights themselves. Hotels in the temple villages tend to be very basic; for more comfortable options look at the relaxed coffee-growing hill station of Chikmagalur, or **Hassan**, a pleasant, busy and fast-developing little city with direct buses from Mysore and Bengaluru.

Belur → *Colour map 3, A2. Phone code: 08177.*
ⓘ *Daily 0600-2000, but some temples close 1300-1600; free; carry a torch, ASI-trained guides on-site (often excellent), Rs 200 for 4 visitors, though official rate is higher.*
Belur, on the banks of the Yagachi River, was the Hoysala dynasty's first capital and continues to be a significant town that is fascinating to explore. The gloriously elaborate Krishna Chennakesavara temple was built over the course of a century from 1116 as a fitting celebration of the victory over the Cholas at Talakad.

At first glance **Chennakesava Temple** (see also Somnathpur, page 307) appears unimpressive because the super-structure has been lost. However, the walls are covered with exquisite friezes. A line of 644 elephants (each different) surrounds the base, with rows of figures and foliage above. The detail of the 38 female figures is perfect. Look at the young musicians and dancers on either side of the main door and the unusual perforated screens between the columns. Ten have typical bold geometrical patterns while the other 10 depict scenes from the *Puranas* in their tracery. Inside superb carving decorates the hand lathe-turned pillars and the bracket-

Temples of Belur and Halebid

The Hoysalas, whose kingdom stretched between the Krishna and Kaveri rivers, encouraged competition among their artisans; their works even bear 12th-century autographs. Steatite meant that sculptors could fashion doily-like detail from solid rock since it is relatively soft when fresh from the quarry but hardens on exposure to air. The temples, built as prayers for victory in battle, are small but superb.

figures on the ceiling. Each stunning filigree pillar is startlingly different in design, a symptom of the intensely competitive climate the sculptors of the day were working in. The **Narasimha pillar** at the centre of the hall is particularly fine and originally could be rotated. The detail is astounding. The jewellery on the figures is hollow and movable and the droplets of water seem to hang at the ends of the dancer's wet hair on a bracket above you. On the platform in front of the shrine is Santalesvara dancing in homage to Lord Krishna. The shrine holds a 3-m-high black polished deity, occasionally opened for *darshan*. The annual **Car Festival** is held March-April. To the west is the **Viranarayana Temple** with some fine sculpture and smaller shrines around it. The complex is walled with an ambulatory. The entrance is guarded by the winged figure of Garuda, Vishnu's carrier, who faces the temple with joined palms.

Halebid

ⓘ *Daily 0700-1730, free.*

The ancient capital of the Hoysala Empire was founded in the early 11th century. It was destroyed by the armies of the Delhi sultanate in 1311 and 1327. The great Hoysalesvara Temple, still incomplete after the best part of a century's toil, survived but the capital lay deserted and came to be called Halebid (ruined village), a name it continues to live up to.

Detour 1 km south to walk around the Basthalli garden filled with remarkably simple 12th-century Jain Bastis. These have lathe-turned and multi-faceted columns, dark interiors and carved ceilings. The smaller **Kedaresvara Temple** with some highly polished columns is on a road going south. There are cycles for hourly hire to visit these quieter sites.

The **Hoysalesvara Temple** set in lawns has two shrines dedicated to Siva with a Nandi bull facing each. The largest of the Hoysala temples, it was started in 1121 but remains unfinished. It is similar in structure to Belur's, but its superstructure was never completed. Belur's real treats are in its interiors, while Halebid's are found on the outside reliefs. Six bands circle the star-shaped temple, elephants, lions, horsemen, a floral scroll and stories from the epics and the Bhagavata Purana. This frieze relates incidents from the *Ramayana* and *Mahabharata*; among them Krishna lifting Mount Govardhana and Rama defeating the demon god Ravana. The friezes above show *yalis* and *hamsa* or geese. There are exceptional half life-size deities with minute details at intervals. Of the original 84 female figures (like the ones at Belur) only 14 remain; thieves have made off with 70 down the centuries.

The **Archaeological Museum** ① *Sat-Thu 1000-1700, Rs 5, no photography*, is on the lawn near the south entrance, with a gallery of 12th- to 13th-century sculptures, wood carvings, idols, coins and inscriptions. Some sculptures are displayed outside. To the west is a small lake.

Sravanabelagola (Shravanabelgola) → *Phone code: 08176*

The ancient Jain statue of Gommateshwara stands on Vindhyagiri Hill (sometimes known as Indrabetta or Indragiri), 150 m above the plain; Chandragiri to the north (also known as Chikka Betta) is just under half that height. The 17-m-high Gommateshwara statue, erected somewhere between AD 980 and 983, is of the enlightened prince Bahubali, son of the first Tirthankara (or holy Jain teacher). The prince won a fierce war of succession over his brother, Bharata, only to surrender his rights to the kingdom to take up a life of meditation.

You'll have to clamber barefoot up over 700 hot steep granite steps that carve up the hill to reach the statue from the village tank (socks, sold on-site, offer protection from the hot stone; take water), or charter a *dhooli* (a cane chair tied between two poles and carried), to let four bearers do the work for you. The small, intricately carved shrines you pass on the way up are the **Odeagal Basti**, the **Brahmadeva Mandapa**, the **Akhanda Bagilu** and the **Siddhara Basti**, all 12th-century except the Brahmadeva Mandapa which is 200 years older.

The carved statue is nude (possibly as he is a *Digambara* or 'sky-clad' Jain) and captures the tranquillity typical of Buddhist and Jain art. The depth of the saint's meditation and withdrawal from the world is suggested by the spiralling creepers shown growing up his legs and arms, and by the ant hills and snakes at his feet. Although the features are finely carved, the overall proportions are odd: he has huge shoulders and elongated arms but stumpy legs.

The 'magnificent anointment' (or *Mastakabhisheka*) falls every 12th year when Jain pilgrims flock from across India to bid for 1008 *kalashas* (pots) of holy water that are left overnight at the saint's feet. The next morning their contents, followed with ghee, milk, coconut water, turmeric paste, honey, vermilion powder and a dusting of gold, are poured over the saint's head from specially erected scaffolding. Unusually for India, the thousands of devotees watching the event do so in complete silence. The next celebration is in 2017.

In the town itself is the **Bhandari basti** (1159, with later additions), about 200 m to the left from the path leading up to the Gommateshwara statue. Inside are 24 images of Tirthankaras in a spacious sanctuary. There are 500 rock-cut steps to the top of the hill that take half an hour to climb. It is safe to leave luggage at the tourist office branch at the entrance, which closes 1300-1415. The main **tourist office** ① *Vartha Bhavan, BM Rd, T08172-268862*, is very helpful. There are 14 shrines on Chandragiri and the Mauryan emperor Chandragupta, who is believed by some to have become a Jain and left his empire to fast and meditate, is buried here. The temples are all in the Dravidian style, the **Chamundaraya Basti**, built in AD 982 being one of the most remarkable. There is a good example of a free-standing pillar or *mana-stambha* in front of the Parsvanathasvami Basti. These pillars, sometimes as high as 15 m, were placed at the temple entrance. Here, the stepped base with a square cross section transforms to a circular section and the column is then topped by a capital.

Chikmagalur
Situated northeast of Belur, Chikmagalur sits at the centre of one of the country's most important coffee growing areas. Coffee was first smuggled from Mocha to India in 1670 by the Sufi saint Baba Budan, after whom the surrounding Baba Budangiri Hills are named, and the Central Coffee Research Institute was set up here in 1925. Chikmagalur is now a popular weekend destination from Bengaluru, with scores of plantation homestays. There are excellent views from the top of Mulayanagiri (1930 m), reached by a motorable road. Chikmagalur town has the Hoysala-style Kodandarama Temple, a number of mosques and a moated fort.

Jog Falls → *Colour map 3, A2.*
These falls, the highest in India, are not the untamed spectacle they once were, but still make a stunning sight if you visit at the end of the wet season; the best times are from late November to early January. Come any earlier and you'll be grappling with leeches and thick mist; any later, and the falls will be more a trickle than a roar, thanks to the 50-km-long **Hirebhasgar Reservoir**, which regulates the flow of the Sharavati River in order to generate hydroelectricity. The Mysore Power Corporation releases water to the falls every second Sunday from 1000 to 1800, but even on a low-flow day the scenery and the rugged walk to the base of the falls make a visit worthwhile.

There are four falls. The highest is the **Raja**, with a fall of 250 m and a pool below 40 m deep. Next is the **Roarer**, while a short distance to the south is the **Rocket**, which shoots great gouts of water into the air. Finally comes the **Rani** (once called the White Lady), which froths elegantly over rocks. A walk to the top (not possible in the monsoons) offers breathtaking views of the cascading river and the valley. Less ambitiously, you can get another excellent view from the Inspection Bungalow on the north side of the river gorge.

Central Maidan → *For listings, see pages 325-328. Colour map 3, A3.*

Chitradurga → *Colour map 3, A3.*
At the foot of a group of granite hills rising to 1175 m in the south, is Chitradurga, 202 km northwest of Bengaluru (Bangalore). The **Fort of Seven Rounds** ① *2 km from the bus stand, 4 km from the railway station, open sunrise to sunset, closed public holidays, Rs 100, allow 2 hrs*, was built in the 17th century by Nayak Poligars, semi-independent landlords who fled south after the collapse of the Vijayanagar Empire in 1565. They were crushed by Haidar Ali in 1779 who replaced the Nayaka's mud fort with stone and Tipu Sultan built a palace, mosque, granaries and oil pits in it. There are four secret entrances in addition to the 19 gateways and ingenious water tanks which collected rainwater. There are also 14 temples, including a cave temple to the west of the wall. They are placed in an extraordinary jumble of granite outcrops, a

similar setting to that of Hampi 300 km to the north. The Hidimbeshwara temple is the oldest temple on the site.

Belgaum → *Colour map 1, C4. Phone code: 0831. Population: 399,600.*
An important border town, Belgaum makes an interesting stop on the Mumbai–Bengaluru (Bangalore) road or as a trip from Goa. The crowded market in the centre gives a glimpse of India untouched by tourism. With its strategic position in the Deccan plateau, the town had been ruled by many dynasties including the Chalukyas, Rattas, Vijaynagaras, Bahmanis and the Marathas. Most of the monuments date from the early 13th century. The **fort**, immediately east of the town centre, though originally pre-Muslim, was rebuilt by Yusuf Adil Shah, the Sultan of Bijapur, in 1481. Inside the **Masjid-i-Sata** (1519), the best of the numerous mosques in Belgaum, was built by a captain in the Bijapur army, Azad Khan. Belgaum is also noted for its Jain architecture and sculpture. The late Chalukyan **Kamala Basti**, with typical beautifully lathe-turned pillars and a black stone Neminatha sculpture, stands within the fort walls. To the south of the fort and about 800 m north of the **Hotel Sanman** on the Mumbai-Bengaluru bypass, is a beautifully sculpted Jain temple which, according to an inscription, was built by Malikaryuna.

⊚ Western Plateau listings

For hotel and restaurant price codes and other relevant information, see pages 13-17.

⊜ Where to stay

Hotels in Belur, Halebid and Sravanabelagola have only basic facilities, but allow you to see these rural towns and villages before or after the tour groups. Due to the climb, Sravanabelagola particularly benefits from an early start. Hassan and Chikmagalur are more comfortable.

Western Plateau temples *p321*
Hassan
$$$$ Hoysala Village Resort, Belur Rd, 6 km from Hassan T08172-256764, www.trailsindia.com. 33 big cottage rooms with hot water, TV, tea and coffee maker and fan spread out across landscaped, bird-filled resort. Rustic, with small handicraft shops, good

restaurant, very attentive service, good swimming pool.
$$$$-$$$ The Ashhok Hassan (ITDC), BM Rd, 500 m from bus stand, T08172-268731, www.hassanashok.com.
A dramatic renovation has created 36 lovely rooms in this immaculate, soundproofed central hotel. Clean lines, with modern art and all mod cons from a/c to Wi-Fi. Charming suites have big rattan armchairs, and the Hoysaleshara suite has its own dining room, bar and steam bath (**$$$$**). Excellent service and tidy garden grounds with pool.
$$$ Hotel Southern Star, BM Rd, T08172-251816, www.ushalexus hotels.com. Large modern hotel with 48 excellent a/c rooms, hot water, phone, satellite TV, great views across town and countryside, excellent service.
$$-$ Hotel Sri Krishna, BM Rd, T08172-263240. 40 rooms with hot water 0600-1000, TV, some with a/c, also double

bedded twin suites for 4 and a dorm for 10. Busy South Indian restaurant with plantain leaf service, car hire. Good value. **$$-$ Hotel Suvarna Regency**, 97 BM Rd, 500 m south of bus stand, T08172-264006. 70 clean, big rooms, some with bath, a/c a bit musty but deluxe and suite rooms are nice, good vegetarian restaurant, car hire. Very helpful. Also has 6 bed, 4 bed and triples.

Belur *p321*
$$-$ Mayura Velapuri (KSTDC), Temple Rd, T08177-222209. Reasonably clean and spacious 6 doubles, 4 triples and 2 dorms sleeping 20, hot water, with fan, TV and sitting areas. Friendly staff. Good South Indian meals in restaurant.
$$-$ Vishnu Regency, Main Rd, T08177-223011, vishnuregency_belur@yahoo. co.in. 20 clean rooms opening onto a courtyard, some with TV, fan, hot water in the morning. Welcoming hotel with shop and good veg restaurant serving tandoor, curries and *thalis*.

Halebid *p322*
$$-$ Mayura Shantala (KSTDC), T08177-273224. Inspection Bungalow compound in nice garden overlooking temple. 4 twin-bed tiled rooms with fan, nets and bath, kitchen.

Sravanabelagola *p323*
The temple Management Committee (SDJMI), T08176-257258, can help organize accommodation in basic pilgrim hostels. Check in the **SP Guest House** by the bus stand.
$ Raghu, near base of stairs up to Indragiri, T08176-257238. Small and utterly basic but clean rooms above a decent veg restaurant.
$ Vidyananda Nilaya Dharamshala, closest to the bus stand, reserve through

SDJMI. Rooms with toilet and fan, bucket baths, blanket but no sheets, courtyard, good value.

Chikmagalur *p324*
$$$$ The Serai, 7 km from town on Kadur–Mangalore Rd, T08262-224903, www.theserai.in. Fabulously deluxe new resort owned by the **Coffee Day** café chain, with beautiful and very private villas cascading down the hill among coffee and pepper bushes. Everything's designed on clean lines, the villas come with private pools, and service is discreet and efficient. There's a spa, billiard room, and daily plantation tours. Popular with visiting cricketers and movie stars.
$$$ Gateway, KM Rd, T08262-660660, www.thegateway hotels.com. 29 luxury a/c rooms lined along the pool, superb staff and food, a good base for visiting Belur and Halebid (40 km).

Jog Falls *p324*
Hotels are very basic and there are very limited eating facilities at night. Local families take in guests. Stalls near the falls serve reasonable breakfast and meals during the day.
$ Mayura Gerusoppa (KSTDC), Sagar Taluk, T08186-244732. Decaying concrete hotel overlooking the falls; 22 rooms and a 10-bed dorm.
$ PWD Inspection Bungalow, west of the falls, T08186-244333. Just a handful of neat a/c rooms, preferable to the various KSTDC options, but a challenge to book.
$ Youth Hostel, Shimoga Rd, T08186-244251. Utterly basic dorms with mattresses on the floor.

Chitradurga *p324*
$$ Amogha International, Santhe Honda Rd, T08194-220763. Clean,

spacious, modern rooms, some a/c suites, 2 restaurants, good vegetarian but service slow. Best in town.
$ Maurya, Santhe Bagilu (within city walls), T08194-224448. 26 acceptable rooms, some with a/c and TV, bit noisy.

Belgaum *p325*
Hotels are mostly on College and PB roads.
$$-$ Adarsha Palace, College Rd, T0831-243 5777, www.hoteladarshapalace.com. Small, modern and personal, some a/c rooms, excellent **Angaan** vegetarian restaurant (rooftop non-vegetarian), good value, pleasant atmosphere, friendly staff. Recommended.
$$-$ Milan, Club Rd (4 km railway), T0831-242 5555. 45 rooms with bath (hot shower), some a/c, vegetarian restaurant, good value.
$$-$ Sanman Deluxe, College St, T0831-243 0777, www.hotelsanman.org. Similar to **Adarsha Palace**, in a new building (much cheaper in old **Sanman**), 2 restaurants.
$ Keerthi, Pune–Bengaluru Rd, short walk from Central Bus Stand, T0831-246 6999. Large modern hotel, some a/c rooms, restaurant.
$ Mayura Malaprabha (KSTDC), Ashok Nagar, T0831-247 0781. 6 simple clean rooms in modern cottages, dorm (Rs 40), restaurant, bar, tourist office.
$ Sheetal, Khade Bazar near bus station, T0831-242 9222. Clean-ish rooms with bath, vegetarian restaurant, Indian style, noisy hotel in busy and quite entertaining bazar street.

❶ Restaurants

Western Plateau temples *p321*
Hassan
The veg restaurant and multi-cuisine **Suvarna Gate** at **Hotel Suvarna Regency**
are the best in town, but the restaurant at **Hotel Sri Krisha** is popular, while the restaurants attached to **Hassan Ashhok**, **Hoysala Village** and **Southern Star** are best for those worried about hygiene.
$ GRR, opposite bus stand. For non-vegetarian food and friendly staff.

Belur *p321*
This sizeable town has numerous tea shops and vegetarian stands. **Vishnu Hotel** has the best tourist restaurant.

Belgaum *p325*
$ Gangaprabha, Kirloskar Rd. Recommended for pure veg food.
$ Zuber Biryaniwala, Kaktives Rd. For creamy biryanis and good non-vegetarian curries.

❷ Transport

Western Plateau temples *p321*
Hassan
Bus For local buses, T08172-268418. Long-distance buses at least hourly to **Belur** from about 0700 (35 km, 1 hr) and **Halebid** from about 0800 (31 km, 1 hr); very crowded. Few direct to **Sravanabelagola** in the morning (1 hr); alternatively, travel to **Channarayapatna** and change to bus for Sravanabelagola. Also to **Bengaluru** about every 30 mins (4½ hrs), **Goa** (14 hrs), **Mangalore** (5 hrs), **Mysore** hourly (3 hrs). If heading for Hampi, you can reserve seats for the 0730 bus to **Hospet** (9 hrs).

Taxi Taxis charge around Rs 1000 for a day tour to **Halebid** and **Belur**, and the same for a trip to **Sravanabelagola**. Drivers park up along AVK College Rd near the bus stand.

Train The railway station is 2 km east of centre, T08172-268222, with connections to **Bengaluru**, **Mysore** and **Mangalore**.

Belur *p321*
Bus Bus stand is about 1 km from the temples. Half-hourly to **Hassan** (1 hr; last at 2030) and **Halebid** (30 mins). Also to **Shimoga**, where you can change for **Hampi** and **Jog Falls** (4 hrs); and to **Mysore** (1½ hrs).

Halebid *p322*
Bus The bus stand, where you can get good meals, is near the temples. KSRTC buses run half-hourly to **Hassan** (45 mins) and from there to **Bengaluru** (**Bangalore**), **Mangalore**, **Mysore**. Also direct to **Belur** (12 km, 30 mins).

Sravanabelagola *p323*
Bus Direct buses to/from **Mysore** and **Bengaluru** run in the morning; in the afternoon, change at **Channarayapatna**. The morning express buses to/from Mysore serve small villages travelling over dusty but interesting roads up to Krishnarajapet, then very few stops between there and Mysore.

Jog Falls *p324*
Bus Daily buses connect Jog Falls with **Honnavar** (2½ hrs) and **Karwar**, both on the Konkan railway line; some Honnavar buses continue to **Kumta** (3 hrs), which has frequent services to **Gokarna**. Direct buses also go daily to **Mangalore** (7hrs), **Bengaluru** (9 hrs) and **Panaji**. Hourly buses to **Shimoga** (4 hrs) for connections to **Belur**, **Hassan** and **Hospet** (7 hrs from Shimoga). For a wider choice of departures get a local bus to **Sagar**, 30 km southeast on NH-206.

Taxi To **Panaji**, Rs 1500 (6 hrs).

Train Jog Falls is 16 km from the railway at **Talguppa**. Trains from **Bengaluru** (**Bangalore**) involve a change in **Shimoga** town.

Chitradurga *p324*
Bus Buses to/from **Bengaluru**, **Davangere**, **Hospet**, **Hubli** and **Mysore**. Train from **Arsikere**, **Bengaluru**, **Guntakal**, **Hubli**.

Belgaum *p325*
Bus Long-distance buses leave from the **Central Bus Stand**, T0831-246 7932, to **Panaji** (0600-1715), **Margao** (0545-1500), **Mapusa** (0715-1715). The train station is near the bus stand, 4 km south of the centre; autos available **Bengaluru**: *Ranichennamma Exp 6590*, 1810, 13 hrs. **Mumbai** (**CST**) and **Pune**: change at Pune for Mumbai *Chalukya/Sharavathi Exp 1018/1036*, Mon, Tue, Fri, Sat, 1805, 14 hrs. **Goa via Londa** 8 trains daily, 0135-2030, 1 hr.

ⓘ Directory

Western Plateau temples *p321*
Hassan
Banks State Bank of Mysore and State Bank of India, Narasimharaja Circle, have ATMs and change currency and TCs. **Medical services** General Hospital, Hospital Rd. **Mission Hospital**, Race Course Rd. **Internet** next to Suvarna and Vaishnavi hotels. **Post** 100 m from bus stand.

West coast

Despite being sandwiched between the holiday honeypots of Goa and south Kerala and despite having been given a glittering new name by the tourist board, Karnataka's 'Sapphire Coast' has thus far been slow to attract tourists. Yet the landscapes here are dreamy, riven by broad mangrove-lined creeks and carpeted with neon green paddy fields, and the beaches retain a wild beauty, almost entirely innocent of the joys and perils of banana pancakes, necklace hawkers and satellite TV.

The hilly port town of Mangalore makes a pleasant, relaxing stop between Goa and Kerala, but the jewel in the Sapphire Coast's crown thus far is undoubtedly Gokarna: a hippy stronghold, mass pilgrimage site and tremendously sacred Hindu centre. It's little more than one narrow street lined with traditional wooden houses and temples, but it is packed with pilgrims and has been adopted, along with Hampi, by the Goa overspill: people lured by spirituality and the beautiful, auspiciously shaped Om beach. The no-frills hammock and beach hut joints of yore have now been joined by the snazzy, eco-conscious CGH Earth's well-regarded boutique yoga hotel, SwaSwara, based on the Bihar school.

Set on the banks of the Netravathi and Gurupur Rivers, the friendly capital of South Kanara District is rarely explored by Western tourists, but Mangalore offers some interesting churches and temples and makes a worthy stopping point on your way between beaches. An important shipbuilding centre during Haider Ali's time, it is now a major port exporting coffee, spices and cashew nuts.

Arriving in Mangalore → *Phone code: 0824. Population: 328,700.*
Getting there Bajpe airport is 22 km north of town, with flights from Mumbai, Bengaluru, Chennai and Dubai. The Konkan railway carries trains from Goa and Mumbai while the broad gauge line goes down the coast to Kozhikode and then inland to Coimbatore.

The old Mangalore City railway station is just south of the busy Hampankatta junction which marks the town centre, but only trains that start and finish in Mangalore use it; trains on the Mumbai–Kerala line stop at the newer Kankanadi station, 10 km east of the city.

The KSRTC bus station is 3 km north of the centre. To get to the town centre and railway, leave the bus station, turn left for 50 m to the private bus shelter and take bus Nos 19 or 33. Long-distance private buses use a more convenient stand a few minutes southwest of Hampankatta.

Getting around The centre is compact enough to be covered on foot but auto-rickshaws are handy for longer journeys. Most refuse to use their meters. Local buses roar around town from the City Bus Stand, opposite the Private Bus Stand. ▶ *See Transport, page 338.*

Tourist information Main **tourist office** ① *City Corporation Building, Lalbagh, just west of the State Bus Stand, T0824-245 3926, 1000-1730.*

Places in Mangalore
St Aloysius College Chapel ① *Lighthouse Hill, 0830-1300, 1600-2000,* has remarkable 19th-century frescoes painted by the Italian-trained Jesuit priest Moscheni, which cover the walls and ceilings in a profusion of scenes. The town has a sizeable Roman Catholic population (about 20%). The nearby **Old Lighthouse** in Tagore Park was built by Haider Ali.

The tile-roofed low structure of the 10th-century **Mangaladevi Temple** ① *south of the train station, bus 27 or 27A, 1600-1200, 1600-2000,* is named after a Malabar Princess, Mangala Devi, who may have given her name to Mangalore. The 11th-century **Sri Manjunatha Temple** ① *4 km northeast of the centre in the Kadri hills, 0600-1300, 1600-2000, Rs 30-40 by auto,* has a rough lingam; its central image is a superb bronze Lokeshwara made in AD 968, said to be one of the finest in South India. **Sreemanthi Bai Memorial Museum** ① *just north of the KSRTC Bus Station, 0900-1700, free,* has a collection including archaeology, ethnology, porcelain and woodcarvings.

South of the Netravathi River lies **Ullal**, which has a pleasant beach and the *dargah* of **Sayyed Mohammed Shareefulla Madani**, a Sufi saint who sailed here from Medina in the 16th century. The *dargah* itself was built in the 19th century, and is credited with healing powers: You can take a trip out to the sand bar at the river mouth to watch fascinating boat building and river traffic on the Netravathi River.

Mangalore

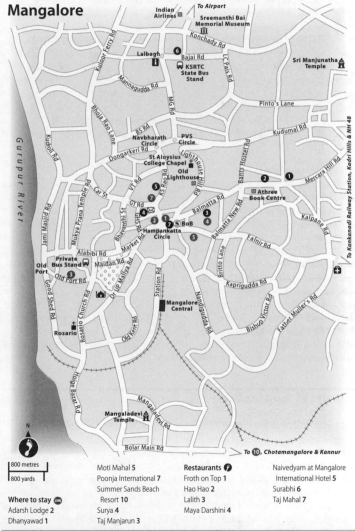

800 metres
800 yards

Where to stay 🛏
Adarsh Lodge **2**
Dhanyawad **1**
Moti Mahal **5**
Poonja International **7**
Summer Sands Beach
 Resort **10**
Surya **4**
Taj Manjarun **3**

Restaurants 🍴
Froth on Top **1**
Hao Hao **2**
Lalith **3**
Maya Darshini **4**
Naivedyam at Mangalore
 International Hotel **5**
Surabhi **6**
Taj Mahal **7**

Vegetarian victuals

The name of Udupi is associated across South India with authentic Brahmin cooking, which means vegetarian food at its best. But what is authentic Udupi cuisine? Pamela Philipose, writing in the *Indian Express*, suggests that strictly it is food prepared for temple use by Shivali Brahmins at the Krishna temple. It is therefore not only wholly vegetarian, but it also never uses onions or garlic.

Pumpkins and gourds are the essential ingredients, while *sambar*, which must also contain ground coconut and coconut oil, is its base. The spicy pepper water, *rasam*, is compulsory, as are the ingredients jackfruit, heart-shaped colocasia leaves, raw green bananas, mango pickle, red chilli and salt. *Adyes* (dumplings), *ajadinas* (dry curries) and chutneys, including one made of the skin of the ridge gourd, are specialities. Favourite dishes are *kosambiri* with pickle, coconut chutney and *appalam*. At least two vegetables will be served, including runner beans, and rice. Sweets include *payasa* and *holige*.

Around Mangalore

The forested hills of the Western Ghats are home to some wonderful examples of Jain and Hindu sculpture and architecture, easily visited on a long day's excursion from Mangalore or as a break on the journey to Belur and Halebid (see pages 321 and 322). The temples are often centres of pilgrimage, such as the **Subrahmanya Temple** at Sullia and the Shaivite **Manjunatha Temple** at Dharmasthala; the latter, 70 km inland, receives thousands of pilgrims every day. From here you can head north through **Venur**, with a 12-m monolith of Bahubali built in 1605, to **Karkala**, where the Bahubali statue is second in height only to that of Sravanabelagola (see page 323); the Mastabhisheka ceremony is performed here every 12 years (next scheduled for 2014). Further northeast is the small town of **Sringeri**, near the source of the Tunga River, which is associated with the Hindu philosopher Sankaracharya. South of Karkala lies **Mudabidri**, the 'Jain Varanasi', with a collection of superbly carved *basti*. In Jain tradition, no two columns are alike, and many are elaborately carved with graceful figures and floral and knot patterns.

Karnataka's Sapphire Coast → *For listings, see pages 335-340. Colour map 3, A2.*

Udupi (Udipi) and around → *Phone code: 0820. Population: 113,000.*

One of Karnataka's most important pilgrimage sites, Udupi is the birthplace of the 12th-century saint Madhva, who set up eight sannyasi *maths* (monasteries) in the town, see page 535. Almost as well known today as the home of a family of Kanarese Brahmins who have established a chain of coffee houses and hotels across South India, it is a pleasant town, rarely visited by foreigners.

According to one legend the statue of Krishna once turned to give a low caste devotee *darshan*. The **Sri Krishna Math**, on Car Street in the heart of the town, is set around a large tank, the *Madhva Sarovar*, into which devotees believe that the Ganga flows every 10 years. There are some attractive *math* buildings with colonnades and arches fronting the temple square, as well as huge wooden temple chariots. This Hindu temple, like many others, is of far greater religious than architectural importance, and receives a succession of highly placed political leaders. Visitors are 'blessed' by the temple elephant. In the biennial **Paraya Mahotsava**, on 17/18 January of even-numbered years, the temple management changes hands (the priest-in-charge heads each of the eight *maths* in turn). The **Seven-Day Festival**, 9-15 January, is marked by an extravagant opening ceremony complete with firecrackers, dancing elephants, brass band and eccentric re-enactments of mythical scenes, while towering wooden temple cars, illuminated by strip lights followed by noisy portable generators, totter around the square, pulled by dozens of pilgrims. **Sri Ananthasana Temple**, where Madhva is believed to have dematerialized while teaching his followers, is in the centre of the temple square. The eight important *maths* are around Car Street: Sode, Puthige and Adamar (south); Pejawar and Palamar (west); Krishna and Shirur (north); and Kaniyur (east).

Some 5 km inland from Udupi, **Manipal** is a university town famous throughout Karnataka as the centre of *Yakshagana* dance drama, which like *Kathakali* in Kerala is an all-night spectacle. **Rashtrakavi Govind Pai Museum** ① *MGM College*, has a collection of sculpture, bronze, inscriptions and coins.

There are good beaches north and south of Udupi, so far with little in the way of accommodation or infrastructure. The closest is at **Malpe**, 5 km west of Udupi, but it's none too appealing: the fishing village at one end of the beach and the fish market on the docks are very smelly, and the beach itself is used as a public toilet in places. If you are prepared for a walk or cycle ride you can reach a deserted sandy beach. Across the bay is the island of Darya Bahadurgarh and 5 km to the southwest is tiny **St Mary's Isle**, which is composed of dramatic hexagonal basalt; Vasco da Gama landed here in 1498 and set up a cross. Boats leave Malpe for the island from 1030; the last one returns at 1700, Rs 70 return.

One of the many bullock cart tracks that used to be the chief means of access over the Western Ghats started from **Bhatkal**, a stop on the Konkan Railway. Now only a small town with a mainly Muslim population, in the 16th century it was the main port of the *Vijayanagar* Empire. It also has two interesting small temples. From the north, the 17th-century Jain *Chandranatha Basti* with two buildings linked by a porch, is approached first. The use of stone tiling is a particularly striking reflection of local climatic conditions, and is a feature of the Hindu temple to its south, a 17th-century Vijayanagar temple with typical animal carvings. In the old cemetery of the church is the tomb of George Wye (1637), possibly the oldest British memorial in India.

Gokarna → *Colour map 3, A1. Phone code: 08386.*

Shaivite pilgrims have long been drawn to Gokarna by its temples and the prospect of a holy dip in the Arabian Sea, but it's the latter half of the equation that lures backpackers. The long, broad expanses of beach stretching along the coast, of which the graceful double curve of **Om Beach** is the most famous, provide an appealing alternative hideaway to Goa, and the busy little town centre plays host to some fascinating cultural inversions: pilgrims wade in the surf in full *salwar kameez* while hippy castaways in bikinis sashay past the temple. And whilst the unspoiled beaches south of town remain the preserve of bodysurfers, *djembe* players and frisbee throwers, the recent rise in incidences of rape (by outsiders, the locals hasten to point out) should serve to remind that travellers would do well to respect local sensitivities.

Gokarna's name, meaning 'cow's ear', possibly comes from the legend in which Siva emerged from the ear of a cow but also perhaps from the ear-shaped confluence of the two rivers here. Ganesh is believed to have tricked Ravana into putting down the famous Atmalinga on the spot now sanctified in the **Mahabalesvara Temple**. As Ravana was unable to lift the lingam up again, it is called *Mahabala* ('the strong one'). The **Tambraparni Teertha** stream is considered a particularly sacred spot for casting the ashes of the dead.

Most travellers head for the beaches to the south. The path from town passing **Kudle Beach** (pronounced *Koodlee*) is easy enough to follow but quite rugged, especially south of **Om Beach** (about 3 km), and should not be attempted with a full backpack during the middle of the day. Stretches of the track are also quite isolated, and even during the day it's advisable for single women to walk with a companion, especially on weekends when large groups of Indian men descend on the beaches with bottles of rum. Both Om and Kudle beaches can get extremely busy in season, when the combination of too many people, a shortage of fresh water and poor hygiene can result in dirty beaches. **Half Moon** and **Paradise Beaches**, popular with long-stayers, can be reached by continuing to walk over the headlands and are another 2 km or so apart.

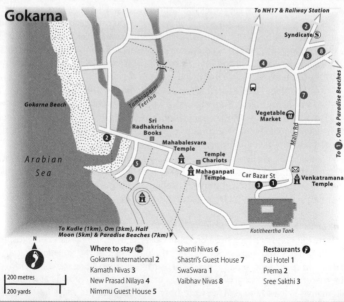

Gokarna

Where to stay
Gokarna International 2
Kamath Nivas 3
New Prasad Nilaya 4
Nimmu Guest House 5

Shanti Nivas 6
Shastri's Guest House 7
SwaSwara 1
Vaibhav Nivas 8

Restaurants
Pai Hotel 1
Prema 2
Sree Sakthi 3

Project Seabird, Karwar and Anjedives → *Colour map 3, A1.*

Karwar, on the banks of the Kalinadi River, is the administrative headquarters of North Kanara District. **Devbagh Beach**, off the coast, has a deep-water naval port protected by five islands. One of these was 'Anjedive' of old, known to seafarers centuries before Vasco da Gama called at the island in 1498, and the Portuguese built a fort there. It was later used as a Goan penal colony. From 1638 to 1752 there was an English settlement here, surviving on the pepper trade. The Portuguese held it for the next 50 years until the old town was destroyed in 1801. Today Karwar, strung out between the port and the estuary, has an unpleasant beach. However, the beaches a little to the south rival those of Goa but are still deserted. Of interest is the hill fort, an octagonal church, and a 300-year-old temple.

India's Western Naval Command, which controls the 'sword arm' of the subcontinent's powerful Western fleet, has since the 1960s planned to move here from Mumbai – a principally commercial port and one that is worryingly close to Pakistani missiles – but work on the immense **Project Seabird** only began in October 1999. When complete it will become the largest naval base this side of the Suez Canal and will hold 140 plus warships, aircraft and repair dockyards, while the hillsides will be put to use concealing submarines. Karwar, crucially, is 900 nautical miles from Karachi versus Mumbai's 580. Since the area is under the control of the Navy it is off-limits to foreigners but driving past it gives a striking portrait of the subcontinent's military might and ambition.

◉ West coast listings

For hotel and restaurant price codes and other relevant information, see pages 13-17.

● Where to stay

Mangalore *p330, map p331*
$$$ Gateway (Taj), Old Port Rd, T0824-666 0420, www.tajhotels.com. 87 excellent rooms and 6 spacious suites, some with sea/river view, restaurant, all facilities, pool, friendly service.
$$$ Summer Sands Beach Resort, Ullal Beach, 10 km south of town, T0824-246 7690, www.summer-sands. com. 85 rooms, 30 a/c, in simple but comfortable local-style bungalows, superb Konkani meals, bar, good pool, Ayurvedic treatments, yoga, local trips.
$$$-$$ Moti Mahal, Falnir Rd, T0824-244 1411, www.motimahalmangalore.com.

Tired-looking on the outside, but the 90 rooms and suites are comfortable and fresh. Excellent pool and health club (non-residents Rs 120), decent Chinese and Indian restaurants and a poolside BBQ.
$$ Poonja International, KS Rao Rd, T0824-244 0171, www.hotelpoonja international.com. 154 rooms, central a/c, wide range of facilities including exchange, spotlessly clean, excellent complimentary buffet breakfast, great value.
$$-$ Dhanyawad, Hampankatta Circle, T0824-244 0066. With 44 spacious rooms, not the quietest location but the non-a/c doubles are huge for the price.
$ Adarsh Lodge, Market Rd, T0824-244 0878. 60 basic rooms with bath, some with TV, well kept and friendly, excellent service, good value especially for singles.

$ Surya, Greens Compound, Balmatta Rd, T0824-242 5736. 3 floors of uninspiring but adequate rooms with bath in a popular backpacker hotel, set back from road in a tranquil tree-shaded compound. Friendly and helpful management.

Udupi and around p332
$$$ Valley View International, on campus, Manipal, T0820-257 1101. Has 70 good a/c rooms with upmarket facilities, pool. Recommended.
$$-$ Green Park, Manipal, T0820-257 0562. 38 rooms, some a/c, has a restaurant.
$$-$ Silver Sands, Thottam Beach, 1 km north of Malpe, T0820-253 7223. 8 pleasant cottages, limited menu restaurant, friendly. Recommended.
$$-$ Srirama Residency, opposite post office, Udupi, T0820-253 0761. Top-quality newish hotel with 30 excellent rooms, bar, 2 restaurants, travel desk, good service.
$$-$ Swadesh Heritage, MV Rd, Udupi, T0820-252 9605, www.hotelswadesh. com. 34 spotlessly clean rooms, 14 a/c rooms (even basic ones are very good value), bar, 2 restaurants. Highly recommended.
$$-$ Udupi Residency, near Service Bus Stand, Udupi, T0820-253 0005. Newish hotel with 33 excellent rooms, 11 a/c, clean, well maintained, restaurant. Highly recommended.
$ Tourist Home, halfway to Thotham Beach, Malpe. 4 pleasant, seaside rooms. Indian breakfast at the top of the road.

Gokarna p333, map p334
$$-$ Gokarna International, Main Rd, T08386-256848. From the outside this looks like Gokarna's smartest hotel, but

the decaying lift and gritty, musty rooms are a huge letdown. OK in a pinch.
$ Kamath Nivas, Main Rd, T08386-256035. Newish, plain and simple rooms, some with TVs and balconies overlooking the road.
$ New Prasad Nilaya, behind **Om Hotel** near bus stand, T08386-257133. Spacious but dusty and fairly run-down rooms with shower, some with balconies, friendly staff.
$ Nimmu Guest House, near Temple, Mani Bhadra Rd, T08386-256730, nimmuhouse@yahoo.com. Small but decent rooms spread over 2 separate wings, the 5 newest rooms are better value as they are big, bright and catch the breeze, limited roof space for overspill, garden, laid-back and friendly, safe luggage storage. Recommended.
$ Shanti Nivas, Gayatri Rd (behind **Nimmu**'s), T08386-256983. Set in a coconut grove just inland from the south end of Gokarna Beach. Choose from clean simple rooms in the main house, apartments in the annexe, or a couple of solid hexagonal huts with mosquito nets and mattresses.
$ Shastri's Guest House, Main Rd near the bus stand, T08386-256220. 24 rooms with bath, some have up to 4 beds, set back from road, a bit gritty but quiet and decent value. Luggage storage.
$ Vaibhav Nivas, Ganjigadde off Main Rd (5 mins' walk from bazar), T08386-256714. Family-run guesthouse with small rooms, annexe with 10 rooms, some with bath (Indian and Western WC), meals, luggage storage.

Beaches
The cafés along **Gokarna**, **Kudle**, **Om** and **Paradise** beaches let out mud and palm leaf huts with shared facilities (often just one squat toilet and a palm-

screened shower) for Rs 50-150 a night during season; many are closed from Apr-Oct. The more expensive huts come with thin mattresses, fans and mosquito nets, but little in the way of security. The guesthouses in town offer to store luggage for a small charge. The options listed below are secure.

$$$$ SwaSwara, Om Beach, 15 mins from town, T08386-257131, www. swaswara.com. Elite retreat with 'yoga for the soul' on 12-ha complex on the curve of gorgeous Om Beach. Classes taught by Indian *swamis*: ashtanga, hasya, kundalini, yoga nidra (psychic sleep) and meditation. From the hilltop the thatched Konkan stone villas look like an Ewok village, with private gardens and a pool; beds are strewn with flowers in the day and philosophical quotes in the evening. But despite its size and expense the resort has virtually no visual impact on the beach, and fishermen can still shelter under the mangroves out front. Also offers Ayurveda, archery, kayaking, trekking, butterfly and birdwatching, and jungle walks.

$$ Gokarna International Resort, Kudle Beach, T08386-257843. The smartest rooms on Kudle beach, some with sea-facing balconies. Ayurvedic massages on site.

$ Namaste Café, Om Beach, T08386-257141. Open all year. The hub of Om's traveller scene has adequate rooms with en suite, some with beach views, and a cute but not mosquito-proof bamboo cottage up in the woods. Travel agent, internet, OK food.

$ Nirvana Café, Om Beach, T08386-329851. Pleasant complex under coconut trees, with a choice of basic huts and solid concrete-and-tile cottages.

⊘ Restaurants

Mangalore *p330, map p331*
$$ Froth on Top, Balmatta Rd. Convivial pub, serving a good range of beers and beer-friendly snacks.
$ Hao Hao, Bridge Rd, Balmatta. Fun old-school Chinese restaurant dishing out mountain-sized bowls of fried noodles.
$ Lalith, Balmatta Rd. Basement restaurant with excellent non-veg and seafood, cold beer and friendly service.
$ Maya Darshini, GHS Rd. Succulent veg biryanis and great north Indian fare, plus interesting local breakfasts – rice balls and *goli baje* (fried dough balls with chutney).
$ Naivedyam, Mangalore International (see Where to stay), KS Rao Rd. Smart, superb value place for pure veg cooking, with a/c and non-a/c sections.
$ Surabhi, opposite State Bus Stand, Lalbagh. Tandoori and cold beer, handy if waiting for a night bus.
$ Taj Mahal, Hampankatta Circle. Dingy ancient joint serving superb chilli-laden *upma*, crispy *dosa* and good cheap juices.

Udupi and around *p332*
$ Dwarike, Car St, facing Temple Sq, Udupi. Immaculately clean, modern, good service, comfortable, Western and South Indian food, excellent snacks, ice creams.
$ Gokul, opposite **Swadesh Heritage** (see Where to stay), Udupi. Excellent vegetarian, good value.
$ JJ's Fast Food, Hotel Bhavani, Parkala Rd, Manipal. For Western snacks.
$ Mitra Samaj, Car St. Full of pilgrims from the nearby Krishna temple, this humble place churns out endless plates of *idli*, *vada* and dozens of variety of *dosa*.

Gokarna *p333*, map *p334*
Cheap vegetarian *thalis* are available near the bus stand and along Main St while places towards the town beach serve up the usual array of pancakes, falafel, spaghetti and burgers. Standards are improving on the southern beaches, with Nepali-run kitchens dishing out traveller food, often of excellent quality. If you don't want to add to the mounds of plastic bottles littering the beaches, ask around for cafés that will let you fill your bottle from their cooler – it should cost a little less than the price of a new bottle.
$ Dragon Café, Kudle Beach. Good *thalis* and *pakora*, excellent pizza and, perhaps, the best mashed potatoes in Gokarna.
$ Old La Pizzeria, Kudle. Popular hangout joint, with laundry and internet facilities as well as good Western food.
$ Pai Hotel, near Venkatramana Temple in Main St. Good *masala dosa*.
$ Prema, by the car park at Gokarna Beach. Serves great fruit salads, the best *gudbad* in town and its own delicious soft garlic cheese, but popularity has resulted in slow and surly service.
$ Sree Sakthi, near Venkatramana Temple. Superb ice cream and Indian food, comfort snacks (try the home-made oil-free peanut butter on toast). Basic but clean and well run.

Karwar *p335*
$$ Fish Restaurant, in the **Sidvha Hotel**. Excellent bistro-type place.

O Shopping

Mangalore *p330*, map *p331*
Athree Book Centre, Sharavasthi Building (below **Quality Hotel**), Balmatta Rd, T0824-242 5161. Excellent selection of English-language novels and non-fiction.

Gokarna *p333*, map *p334*
Sri Radhakrishna Books, on main road near beach. Tiny bookshop with an astonishingly good range of beach reads.

☼ What to do

Mangalore *p330*, map *p331*
The pool at **Moti Mahal hotel** (see Where to stay) is open to non-residents for Rs 120 per hr.

Gokarna *p333*, map *p334*
You can hire canoes from a small office on the northern part of Om Beach: Rs 200 per hr.

☻ Transport

Mangalore *p330*, map *p331*
Air Mangalore's Bajpe Airport is 22 km out of town, with services to **Bengaluru**, **Hyderabad**, **Chennai**, **Mumbai**, **Delhi**, and several cities in the Gulf. Transport from town: taxi Rs 400; shared Rs 100 each; coach from **Indian Airlines**, Hathill Complex, Lalbag, T0824-245 1045, airport, T0824-225 4253. **Jet Airways**: Ram Bhavan Complex, Kodialbail, T0824-244 1181, airport, T0824-225 2709.

Bus Numerous private long-distance bus companies around Taj Mahal Restaurant, Falnir Rd (and a few opposite KSRTC) serve **Bengaluru** (**Bangalore**), **Bijapur**, **Goa**, **Ernakulam**, **Hampi**, **Gokarna**, **Kochi**, **Mumbai**, **Udupi**, etc.
KSRTC State Bus Stand, Bajjai Rd, is well organized. Booking hall at entrance has a computer printout of timetable in English; main indicator board shows different bus categories: **red** – ordinary; **blue** – semi-deluxe; **green** – super-deluxe. (*Exp* buses may be reserved 7 days ahead). **Mysore** and

Bengaluru (Bangalore): 296 km, 7 hrs and 405 km, 9 hrs, every 30 mins from 0600 (route via Madikeri is the best); trains take 20 hrs. **Chennai** 717 km; **Madurai** 691 km, 16 hrs. **Panaji**, 10 hrs.

Rickshaw Minimum charge Rs 10, though if arriving at the train station or bus stand at night you'll be charged extra. Rs 100 to **Kankanadi** station from centre.

Train Central Station has a computerized booking office, T0824-242 3137. **Bengaluru**: *Yesvantpur Exp 16518/16524*, 2055, 11½ hrs, via Hassan (6 hrs).**Chennai**: *Mangalore Mail 12602* (AC/II), 1315, 16 hrs; *West Coast Exp 16628*, 2200, 18 hrs. Both via **Kozhikode**, 4 hrs, and Palakkad, 8 hrs. **Gokarna Rd**: *Matsyagandha Exp 12620* 1435, 4 hrs; *Mangalore Madgaon Pass 56640*, 0630, 4 hrs. **Madgaon (Margao)**: *Matsyagandha Exp 12620*, 1435, 6 hrs (on to Thane and Lokmanya Tilak for Mumbai). **Thiruvananthapuram** (17 hrs) via Kochi (9 hrs) and **Kollam** (15 hrs): *Malabar Express 16630*, 1820; *Ernad Exp 16605*, 0720.

From Mangalore Jn (**Kankanadi**) Station, T0824-243 7824: **Mumbai** (Lokmanya Tilak) via Madgaon: *Nethravati Exp 16346*, 2330, 17½ hrs.

Udupi and around *p332*
Bus Udupi's **State** and **Private bus stands** are next to each other in the central square. From Udupi, frequent service to **Mangalore** (1½ hrs). Mornings and evenings to **Bengaluru** (**Bangalore**) and **Mysore** from 0600; **Hubli** from 0900; **Dharmasthala**, from 0600-0945, 1400-1830; **Mumbai** at 1120, 1520, 1700, 1920.

Train The station is 5 km from the town centre; auto Rs 90. All express and passenger trains between Mangalore and Madgaon stop here.

Gokarna *p333, map p334*
Boat Boatmen on Om Beach quote Rs 300-500 for a drop-off to either **Gokarna** or **Paradise Beach**, or Rs 50-100 per person if there's a group. Return trips to Paradise Beach may only give you 30 mins on land.

Bus KSRTC buses provide a good service: **Chaudi** 2 hrs; **Karwar** (via Ankola) frequent (1 hr); **Hospet** 1430 (10 hrs); **Margao**, 0815 (4 hrs); **Mangalore** via **Udupi** 0645 (7 hrs); **Panaji** 0800 (5 hrs). Private sleeper buses to **Bengaluru** (**Bangalore**) and **Hampi** can be booked from agents in the bazar; most depart from Kumta or Ankola.

Taxi Most hotels and lodges offer to organize taxis, but often quote excessive prices; no destination seems to be less than 100 km away. To **Gokarna Rd**, bargain for Rs 120; to Ankola, around Rs 550.

Train Gokarna Road Station is 10 km from town, 2 km from the NH17; most trains are met by auto-rickshaws and minibus taxis: Rs 125 to Gokarna Bus Stand, Rs 200 to Om Beach. State buses to/from Kumta pass the end of the station road, a 1-km walk from the station. **Madgaon** (**Margao**): *Matsyagandha Exp 12620*, 1840, 2 hrs; *Mangalore-Madgaon Pass 56640*, 1023, 2¼ hrs. **Mangalore** (**Central**): *Madgaon-Mangalore Pass 56641*, 1528, 5 hrs.

Karwar *p335*
Bus To **Jog Falls**, 0730 and 1500 (6 hrs).
Frequent buses to **Palolem**, **Margao**
(Madgaon) and **Panaji**, also direct buses
to **Colva**. Buses often full; you may have
to fight to get on. The road crosses
the Kali River (car toll Rs 5) then reaches
the Goa border and checkpoint post
(8 km north).

✪ Directory

Mangalore *p330, map p331*
Banks Several ATMs on Balmatta Rd
and near Hampankatta Circle. **Canara**
Bank, Balmatta Rd, cash against credit
cards. **Trade Wings**, Lighthouse Hill Rd,
T0824-242 6225, good service for TCs,
plus flight bookings.

Gokarna *p333, map p334*
Banks Foreign exchange at: **Pai STD**,
opposite **Ramdev Lodge**, and **Kiran's**
Internet, change money. The Karnataka
Bank ATM on Bus Stand Rd accepts
Visa cards.

Northern Karnataka

Down the centuries, northeast Karnataka has been host to a profusion of Deccani rulers. Hampi, site of the capital city of the Vijayanagar Hindu empire that rose to conquer the entire south in the 14th century, is the region's most famous, and is an extraordinary site of desolate temples, compounds, stables and pleasure baths, surrounded by a stunning boulder-strewn landscape. The cluster of temple relics in the villages of Aihole, Pattadakal and Badami dates from the sixth century, when the Chalukyans first started experimenting with what went on to become the distinct Indian temple design. Nearby are the Islamic relics of Bijapur and Bidar, sudden plots of calm tomb domes with their Persian inscriptions ghosted into lime, and archways into empty harems; all the more striking for being less visited.

Hampi-Vijayanagar → *For listings, see pages 359-364. Colour map 1, C5.*

Climb any boulder-toppled mountain around the ruins of the Vijayanagar Empire and you can see the dizzying scale of the Hindu conquerors' glory; Hampi was the capital of a kingdom that covered the whole of southern India. Little of the kingdom's riches remain; now the mud huts of gypsies squat under the boulders where noblemen once stood, while the double decker shopfronts of the old Hampi Bazar, where diamonds were once traded by the kilo, have transformed into a more prosaic marketplace geared to profiting from Western tourists and domestic pilgrims. Yet away from the hubbub and hassle of the bazar – somewhat reduced since 2012 when the Archaeological Survey of India sent in bulldozers to knock down many of the 'unauthorized' houses and shops – Hampi possesses a romantic, hypnotic desolation that's without parallel in South India. You'll need at least a full day to get a flavour of the place, but for many visitors the chilled-out vibe has a magnetic attraction, and some end up staying for weeks.

Arriving in Hampi-Vijayanagar → *Phone code: 08394.*
Getting there and around Apart from the hugely expensive five-seater aircraft, buses and trains arrive in Hospet, from where it is a 30-minute rickshaw (around Rs 200) or bus ride to Hampi. The site is spread out, so hiring a bicycle is a good idea though some paths are too rough to ride on. You enter the area from the west at Hampi Bazar or from the south at Kamalapuram. ▶ *See Transport, page 362.*

Tourist information Tourist office ⓘ *on the approach to Virupaksha Temple, T08394-241339, 0800-1230, 1500-1830.* A four-hour guided tour of the site (without going into the few temples that charge admission) costs around Rs 250.

Background

Hampi was founded on the banks of the Tungabhadra River in 1336 by two brothers, Harihara and Bukka, and rose to become the seat of the mighty Vijayanagar Empire and a major centre of Hindu rule and civilization for 200 years. The city, which held a monopoly on the trade of spices and cotton, was enormously wealthy – some say greater than Rome – and the now-sorry bazar was packed with diamonds and pearls, the crumbled palaces plated with gold. Although it was well fortified and defended by a large army, the city fell to a coalition of northern Muslim rulers, the Deccan Sultans, at Talikota in 1565. The invading armies didn't crave the city for themselves, and instead sacked it, smiting symbolic blows to Hindu deities and taking huge chunks out of many of the remaining white granite carvings. Today, the craggy 26-sq-km site holds the ghost of a capital complete with aqueducts, elephant stables and baths as big as palaces. The dry arable land is slowly being peeled back by archaeologists to expose more and more of the kingdom's ruins.

The site for the capital was chosen for strategic reasons, but the craftsmen adopted an ingenious style to blend in their architectural masterpieces with the barren and rocky landscape. Most of the site is early 16th century, built during the 20-year reign of Krishna Deva Raya (1509-1529) with the citadel standing on the bank of the river.

Sacred Centre

The road from the west comes over Hemakuta Hill, overlooking the sacred centre of Vijayanagar (the 'Town of Victory'), with the Virupaksha Temple and the Tungabhadra River to its north. On the hill are two large monolithic Ganesh sculptures and some small temples. The road runs down to the village and the once world-famous market place. You can now only see the wide pathway running east from the towering **Virupaksha** (*Pampapati*) **Temple** with its nine-storey *gopuram*, to where the bazar once hummed with activity. The temple is still in use; note the interesting paintings on the *mandapam* ceiling.

Riverside

You can walk along the river bank (1500 m) to the famous Vitthala Temple. The path is easy and passes several interesting ruins including small 'cave' temples – worthwhile with a guide. Alternatively, a road skirts the Royal Enclosure to the south and goes all the way to the Vitthala Temple. On the way back (especially if it's at sunset) it's worth stopping to see **Raghunatha Temple**, on a hilltop, with its Dravidian style, quiet atmosphere and excellent view of the countryside from the rocks above.

After passing **Achyuta Bazar**, which leads to the Tiruvengalanatha Temple 400 m to the south, the riverside path goes near **Sugriva's Cave**, where it is said that Sita's jewels, dropped as she was abducted by the demon Ravana, were hidden by

Sugriva. There are good views of the ancient ruined bridge to the east, and nearby the path continues past the only early period Vaishnavite shrine, the 14th-century **Narasimha Temple**. The **King's Balance** is at the end of the path as it approaches the Vitthala Temple. It is said that the rulers were weighed against gold, jewels and food, which were then distributed to Brahmins.

Hampi-Vijayanagar

To Anegondi & Gangawati

Ruined Bridge

Vitthala Temple

Talarighat   Coracles

King's Balance

Coracles
Tungabhadra River

Sugriva's Cave

Siva Temple

Narasimha Temple

Virupaksha Temple

Kodanda Rama Temple

Achyuta Bazar

HAMPI BAZAR

To Hospet (12 km)

Ganesh

SACRED CENTRE   Matanga Parvata

Tiruvengalanatha Temple

Hemakuta Hill

Krishna Temple

Dharamsalas

Lakshmi Narasimha Statue

KRISHNAPURA

Veerabhadra Temple

Malayavanta

ZENANA ENCLOSURE   Elephant Stables   VIJAYNAGARA

Raghunatha Temple

To Kampili

Nobleman's Palace

Lotus Mahal

Hazara Rama Temple

ROYAL ENCLOSURE

Prasanna Virupaksha Temple

Mahanavami Dibba

DURBAR ENCLOSURE

Aqueduct

Queen's Bath

Jaina Temple

Bhima's Gate

To Daroji Bear Sanctuary &

Archaeological Survey Office

KAMALAPURAM   Dharamsalas

Archaeological Museum

Pattabhi Rama Temple

Nageshwara Temple

To Hospet

N

500 metres
500 yards

Where to stay
Archana **2**
Gopu **4**
Mayura Bhuvaneswari **1**

Mowgli Guest House **5**
Padma Guest House **2**
Ranjana Guest House **2**
Shambhu **3**

Shanthi Guest House **6**
Sloth Bear Resort **7**
Vicky **4**

Restaurants
Mango Tree **1**

Vitthala Temple ① *0830-1700, US$5/Rs 250, allows entry to Lotus Mahal on the same day*, a UNESCO World Heritage Monument, is dedicated to Vishnu. It stands in a rectangular courtyard enclosed within high walls. Probably built in the mid-15th century, it is one of the oldest and most intricately carved temples, with its *gopurams* and *mandapas*. The *Dolotsava mandapa* has 56 superbly sculpted slender pillars which can be struck to produce different musical notes. It has elephants on the balustrades and horses at the entrance. The other two ceremonial *mandapas*, though less finely carved, nonetheless depict some interesting scenes, such as Krishna hiding in a tree from the *gopis* and a woman using a serpent twisted around a stick to churn a pot of buttermilk. In the courtyard is a superb chariot carved out of granite, the wheels raised off the ground so that they could be revolved!

Krishnapura

On the road between the Virupaksha Bazar and the Citadel you pass Krishnapura, Hampi's earliest Vaishnava township with a Chariot Street 50 m wide and 600 m long, which is now a cultivated field. **Krishna temple** has a very impressive gateway to the east. Just southwest of the Krishna temple is the colossal monolithic **statue of Lakshmi Narasimha** in the form of a four-armed man-lion with fearsome bulging eyes sheltered under a seven-headed serpent, Ananta. It is over 6 m high but sadly damaged.

The road south, from the Sacred Centre towards the Royal Enclosure, passes the excavated **Prasanna Virupaksha** (misleadingly named 'underground') **Temple** and interesting watchtowers.

Royal Enclosure

At the heart of the metropolis is the small **Hazara Rama Temple**, the Vaishanava 'chapel royal'. The outer enclosure wall to the north has five rows of carved friezes while the outer walls of the *mandapa* has three. The episodes from the epic *Ramayana* are told in great detail, starting with the bottom row of the north end of the west *mandapa* wall. The two-storey **Lotus Mahal** ① *0600-1800, US$5/Rs250, allows entry to Vitthala Temple on the same day*, is in the **Zenana** or ladies' quarter, screened off by its high walls. The watchtower is in ruins but you can see the domed **stables** for 10 elephants with a pavilion in the centre and the guardhouse. Each stable had a wooden beamed ceiling from which chains were attached to the elephants' backs and necks. In the **Durbar Enclosure** is the specially built decorated platform of the **Mahanavami Dibba**, from which the royal family watched the pageants and tournaments during the nine nights of *navaratri* festivities. The 8-m-high square platform originally had a covering of bricks, timber and metal but what remains still shows superb carvings of hunting and battle scenes, as well as dancers and musicians.

The exceptional skill of water engineering is displayed in the excavated system of aqueducts, tanks, sluices and canals, which could function today. The attractive **Pushkarini** is the 22-sq-m stepped tank at the centre of the enclosure. The road towards Kamalapuram passes the **Queen's Bath**, in the open air, surrounded by a narrow moat, where scented water filled the bath from lotus-shaped fountains. It measures about 15 m by 2 m and has interesting stucco work around it.

Daroji Bear Sanctuary

① *15 km from Hampi Bazar, daily 0600-1800.*

The relatively new Daroji sanctuary protects 55 sq km of boulder-strewn scrubland, which is home to around 120 sloth bears. The bears have become accustomed to regular treats of honey, courtesy of the park rangers, and a handful of them come regularly to a particular rock to feed. A watchtower placed high above the spot makes this perhaps the best place in India to observe the species in the wild. The sanctuary also has leopard, wolf, jackal, Eurasian horned owl, and good populations of the beautiful painted sa.

Hospet → *Colour map 1, C5. Phone code: 08394. Population: 163,300.*

The transport hub for Hampi, Hospet is famous for its sugar cane; the town exports sugar across India, villagers boil the milk to make *jaggery* and a frothing freshly wrung cup costs you just Rs 4. Other industries include iron ore, biscuit making and the brewing of Royal Standard rum. The main bazar, with its characterful old houses, is interesting to walk around. **Tungabhadra Dam** ① *6 km west, Rs 5, local bus takes 15 mins,* is 49 m high and offers panoramic views. One of India's largest masonry dams, it was completed in 1953 to provide electricity for surrounding districts.

Muharram, the Muslim festival that marks the death of Mohammed's grandson Imam Hussein, is celebrated with a violent vigour both here and in the surrounding villages by both the area's significant Muslim population and Hindus. Ten days of fasting is broken with fierce drum pounding, drink and frequent arguments, sometimes accompanied by physical violence. Each village clusters around icons of Hussein, whose decapitation is represented by a golden crown on top of a face covered with long strings of jasmine flowers held aloft on wooden sticks. Come evening, fires are lit. When the embers are dying villagers race through the ashes, a custom that may predate Islam's arrival. The beginnings or ends of livestock migrations to seasonal feeding grounds are marked with huge bonfires. Cattle are driven through the fires to protect them from disease. Some archaeologists suggest that Neolithic ash mounds around Hospet were the result of similar celebrations over 5000 years ago.

Bijapur → *For listings, see pages 359-364. Colour map 1, C5.*

Mohammed Adil Shah was not a man to be ignored; the tomb he built from the first day of his rule in anticipation of his own death hovers with dark magnificence over Bijapur and is so large it can be seen from 20 km. His brooding macabre legacy threw down the gauntlet to his immediate successor. Ali Adil Shah II, who took over from Mohammed in 1656, began his own tomb, which would surely have been double in size and architectural wonder had he not died too soon, 26 years into his reign, with only archways complete. His Bara Kamaan is nearby, while to the north of the city lies Begum's equally thwarted attempt to match Mohammed's strength in death.

With its mausoleums, palaces and some of the finest mosques in the Deccan, Bijapur has the air of a northern Muslim city and retains real character. The *chowk* between the bus station and MG Road is quite atmospheric in the evening.

Arriving in Bijapur → *Phone code: 08352. Population: 245,900.*

Getting there Bijapur is connected by train with Bangalore (Bengaluru), Hyderabad and Mumbai. The railway station is just outside the east wall of the fort less than 1 km from the Gol Gumbaz. Long-distance buses draw in just west of the citadel. Both arrival points are close enough to several hotels.

Getting around It is easy to walk or cycle round the town. There are also autos and *tongas*; negotiate for the 'eight-sight tour price'. ⟫ *See Transport, page 363.*

Tourist information There's a tourist office ① *opposite the stadium, T08352-250359, Mon-Sat 1030-1330 and 1415-1730*, but it's not very useful.

Background

The Chalukyas who ruled over Bijapur were overthrown in the late 12th century. In the early years of the 14th century the Delhi Sultans took it for a time until the Bahmanis, with their capital in Gulbarga, ruled through a governor in Bijapur who declared Independence in 1489 and founded the Adil Shahi Dynasty. Of Turkish origin, they held power until 1686.

The 55-ton cannon was employed against Vijayanagar. Ali Adil Shah I, whose war it was, was somewhat chastened at the destruction his marauding Muslim armies had wreaked on the Hindu empire at Hampi. By way of atonement, and in a show of the inordinate riches that had fallen into his lap by supplanting Vijayanagar, he did his communal civic duty and built the exquisite Jama Masjid. It was his nephew Mohammed, he of the giant Gol Gumbaz, who later commissioned the Quranic calligraphy that so sumptuously gilds the western wall.

Places in Bijapur

Hulking in the background wherever you look in Bijapur, the **Gol Gumbaz** ① *0630-1730, foreigners Rs 100, Indians Rs 5, video camera Rs 25, some choose to just view it from the gate*, is the vast whitewashed tomb of Mohammad Adil Shah, buried here with his wife, daughter and favourite court dancer, underneath the world's second largest dome (unsupported by pillars) – and one of its least attractive. Its extraordinary whispering gallery carries a message across 38 m which is repeated 11 times. However, noisy crowds make hearing a whisper quite impossible; it's quietest in the early morning. Numerous narrow steps in one of the corner towers lead to the 3-m-wide gallery. The plaster here was made out of eggs, cow dung, grass and jaggery. There is an excellent view of the city from the base of the dome. The Nakkar Khana, or gatehouse, is now a **museum** ① *1000-1700, Rs 2*, housing an excellent collection of Chinese porcelain, parchments, paintings, armoury, miniatures, stone sculpture and old Bijapur carpets.

To the south is the **Jama Masjid**, one of the finest in the Deccan, with a large shallow, onion-shaped dome and arcaded court. Built by Ali Adil Shah I (ruled 1557-1579) during Bijapur's rise to power it displays a classic restraint. The Emperor Aurangzeb added a grand entrance to the mosque and also had a square painted for each of the 2250 worshippers that it can accommodate. West of here is the Mehtar

Mahal (1620), whose delicate minarets and carved stone trellises were supposedly built for the palace sweepers.

Bijapur's Citadel, encircled by its own wall, now has few of its grand buildings intact. One is the Durbar Hall, Gagan Mahal (Sky Palace), open to the north so that the citizens outside were not excluded. It had royal residential quarters on either side with screened balconies for the women to remain unseen while they watched the court below. Another worth visiting is the Jal Manzil, or the water pavilion, a cool sanctuary. Just to the east is the Asar Mahal (circa 1646), once used as a court house with teak pillars and interesting frescoes in the upper floor.

The Bara Kaman was possibly a 17th-century construction by Adil Shah III. Planned as a huge 12-storey building with the shadow of the uppermost storey designed to fall onto the tomb of the Gol Gumbaz, construction was ended after two storeys with the death of the ruler. An impressive series of arches on a raised platform is all that remains.

The western gateway to the walled city, Sherza Burj (Lion Gate), has the enormous 55-tonne, 4.3-m-long, 1.5-m-diameter cannon Malik-i-Maidan (Ruler of the Plains).

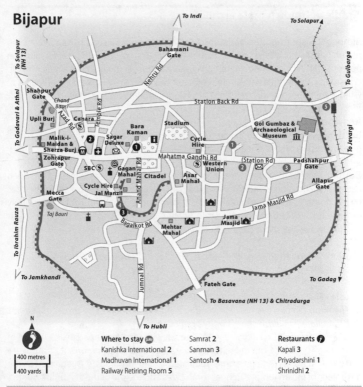

Bijapur

Where to stay		Restaurants
Kanishka International **2**	Samrat **2**	Kapali **3**
Madhuvan International **1**	Sanman **3**	Priyadarshini **1**
Railway Retiring Room **5**	Santosh **4**	Shrinidhi **2**

400 metres
400 yards

Cast in the mid-16th century in Ahmadnagar, it was brought back as a prize of war pulled by "400 bullocks, 10 elephants and hundreds of soldiers". The muzzle, a lion's head with open jaws, has an elephant being crushed to death inside, and the gun's roar was said to be so loud that the gunner used to dive into the tank off the platform to avoid being deafened. Inside the city wall nearby is Upli Burj, a 24-m-high watchtower with long guns and water tanks.

West of the city centre is the **Ibrahim Rauza** ① *0600-1800, Rs 100, Indians Rs 5, video camera Rs 25, visit early morning to avoid crowds*, the palatial 17th-century tomb and mosque built by Ibrahim Adil Shah. Rais during the dynasty's most prosperous period (after the sacking of Vijayanagar) when the arts and culture flourished, the corners of both buildings are decorated with slender minarets and decorative panels carved with lotus, wheel and cross patterns as well as bold Arabic calligraphy, bearing witness to the tolerance of the Adil Shahi Dynasty towards other religions. Near the Rauza is a huge tank, the Taj Bauri, built by Ibrahim II in memory of his wife. The approach is through a giant gateway flanked by two octagonal towers.

Cradle of Hindu temple architecture → *For listings, see pages 359-364.*

Although Bijapur became an important Muslim regional capital, its surrounding region has several villages which, nearly 1500 years ago, were centres of Chalukyan power and the heart of new traditions in Indian temple building. At a major Indian crossroads, the temples at Aihole represent the first finely worked experiments in what were to become distinct North and South Indian temple styles.

Arriving in the area
Getting there Trains from Bijapur to Gadag stop at Badami, which makes a useful hub for visiting other sights. Buses operate from Hubli, Hospet and Kolhapur.

Getting around If you're travelling by bus it's best to visit Badami first, then Pattadakal and Aihole, but since it takes half a day to see Badami, visiting the sites by bus doesn't allow time for Mahakuta. If you want to see all the sights comfortably in a day it is well worth hiring a car in Bijapur, going to Aihole first and ending at Badami.▸▸ *See Transport, page 363.*

Tourist information Tourist office ① *next to Mayura Chalukya, Badami, T08357-220414.*

Aihole → *Colour map 1, C5. Phone code: 0831.*
① *The main temples are now enclosed in a park, open sunrise to sunset, foreigners Rs 100, Indians Rs 5, flash photography prohibited.*
Aihole was the first Chalukyan capital, but the site was developed over a period of more than 600 years from the sixth century AD and includes important Rashtrakuta and late Chalukyan temples, some dedicated to Jain divinities. It is regarded as the birthplace of Indian temple architectural styles and the site of the first built temples,

as distinct from those carved out of solid rock. Most of the temples were dedicated to Vishnu, though a number were subsequently converted into Shaivite shrines.

There are about 140 temples – half within the fort walls – illustrating a range of developing styles from Hoysala, Dravida, Jain, Buddhist, Nagara and Rekhanagara. There is little else. All the roads entering Aihole pass numerous temple ruins, but the road into the village from Pattadakal and Bagalkot passes the most important group of temples which would be the normal starting point for a visit. Some prefer to wander around the dozens of deserted (free) temples around town instead of joining the crowds in the park.

Durgigudi Temple is named not after the Goddess Durga but because it is close to the *durga* (fort). Dating from the late seventh century, it has an early *gopuram* structure and semi-circular apse which imitates early Buddhist *chaitya* halls. It has numerous superb sculptures, a series contained in niches around the ambulatory: walking clockwise they represent Siva and Nandi, Narasimha, Vishnu with Garuda, Varaha, Durga and Harihara.

According to recent research **Lad Khan Temple** has been dated from around AD 700, not from AD 450 as suggested by the first Archaeological Survey of India reports in 1907. This is indicated by the similarity of some of its sculptures to those of the Jambulinga Temple at Badami, which has been dated precisely at AD 699. Originally an assembly hall and *kalyana mandapa* (marriage hall), it was named after Lad Khan, a pious Muslim who stayed in the temple at the end of the 19th century. A stone ladder through the roof leads to a shrine with damaged images of Surya, Vishnu and Siva carved on its walls. It bears a striking resemblance to the megalithic caves that were still being excavated in this part of the Deccan at the beginning of the period. The roof gives an excellent view of the village.

Gaudar Gudi Temple, near the Lad Khan temple, is a small, rectangular Hindu temple, probably dating from the seventh century. It has a rectangular columned *mandapa*, surrounded on three sides by a corridor for circumambulation. Its roof of stone slabs is an excellent example of North Indian architecture. Beyond the Gaudar Gudi Temple is a small temple decorated with a frieze of pots, followed by a deep well. There are others in various states of repair. To see the most important of the remaining temples you leave the main park. Excavations are in progress, and the boundaries of the park may sometimes be fenced. Turning right out of the main park, the Bagalkot road leads to the **Chikki Temple**. Similar in plan to the Gaudar Gudi, this temple has particularly fine carved pillars. The beams which support the platform are also well worth seeing.

Ravan Phadi Cave Temple is reached from the main park entrance on the left, about 300 m from the village. The cave itself (formerly known as the Brahman) is artificial, and the sixth-century temple has a variety of carvings of Siva both outside and inside. One is in the *Ardhanarisvara* form (half Siva, half Parvati), another depicts Parvati and Ganesh dancing. There is a huge lotus carved in the centre of the hall platform; and two small eighth-century temples at the entrance, the one to the northwest dedicated to Vishnu and that to the south, badly weathered, may have been based on an older Dravidian-style temple.

The **Buddhist Temple** is a plain two-storey Buddhist temple on a hill beyond the end of the village on the way to the Meguti Temple. It has a serene smiling Buddha with the Bodhi Tree emerging from his head, on the ceiling of the upper floor. Further uphill is the **Jain temple**, a plain structure lacking the decorations on the plinth, columns and *gopuram* of many Hindu temples. It has a statue of Mahavira in the shrine within. Climb up through the roof for a good view of Aihole.

The **Meguti Temple** (AD 634) is reached from the Buddhist Temple down a path leading to a terrace. A left-hand route takes you to the foot of some stairs leading to the top of a hill which overlooks the town. This is the site of what is almost certainly the oldest building in Aihole and one of the oldest dated temples in India. Its 634 date is indicated by an inscription by the court poet to the king Ravikirtti. A Dravidian-style temple, it is richly decorated on the outside, and although it has elements which suggest Shaivite origins, it has an extremely impressive seated Jain figure, possibly Neminath, in the sanctuary which comprises a hall of 16 pillars.

The **Kunti Group** is a group of four Hindu temples (dating from seventh to ninth centuries). To find them you have to return down to the village. The oldest is in the southeast. The external columns of its *mandapa* are decorated with *mithuna*, or erotic couples. The temple to the northwest has beautifully carved ceiling panels of Siva and Parvati, Vishnu and Brahma. The other two date from the Rashtrakuta period.

Beyond these temples is the **Hucchappayya Math**, seventh century, which has sculptures of amorous couples and their servants, while the beams inside are beautifully decorated. There is a tourist resthouse close to the temples should you wish to stay.

Pattadakal

On the banks of the Malaprabha River, Pattadakal, a UNESCO World Heritage Site, was the second capital of the Chalukyan kings between the seventh and eighth centuries and the city where the kings were crowned. Ptolemy referred to it as 'Petrigal' in the first century AD. Two of their queens imported sculptors from Kanchipuram. Most of the **temples** ① *open sunrise to sunset, foreigners Rs 250, Indians Rs 10*, cluster at the foot of a hill, built out of the pink-tinged gold sandstone, and display a succession of styles of the southern Dravida temple architecture of the Pallavas (even miniature scaled-down models) as well as the North Indian Nagara style, vividly illustrating the region's position at the crossroads of North and South Indian traditions. With one exception the temples are dedicated to Siva. Most of the site is included in the archaeological park. Megalithic monuments dating from the third to fourth centuries BC have also been found in the area.

Immediately inside the entrance are the small eighth-century **Jambulinga** and **Kadasiddheshvara Temples**. Now partly ruined, the curved towers survive and the shrine of the Jambulinga Temple houses a figure of the dancing Siva next to Parvati. The gateways are guarded by *dvarapalas*.

Just to the east is the eighth-century **Galaganatha Temple**, again partly damaged, though its curved tower characteristic of North Indian temples is well preserved, including its *amalaka* on top. A relief of Siva killing the demon Andhaka is on the south wall in one of three original porches.

The **Sangamesvara Temple** dating from the reign of Vijayaditya (AD 696-733) is the earliest temple. Although it was never completed it has all the hallmarks of a purely Dravidian style. Beautifully proportioned, the mouldings on the basement and pilasters divide the wall. The main shrine, into which barely any light is allowed to pass, has a corridor for circumambulation and a *lingam* inside. Above the sanctuary is a superbly proportioned tower of several storeys.

To the southwest is the late eighth-century North Indian-style **Kashi Vishveshvara Temple**, readily distinguishable by the *Nandi* in front of the porch. The interior of the pillared hall is richly sculpted, particularly with scenes of Krishna.

The largest temples, the **Virupaksha** (AD 740-744) with its three-storey *vimana* and the **Mallikarjuna** (745), typify the Dravida style, and were built in celebration of the victory of the Chalukyan king Vikramaditya II over the Pallavas at Kanchipuram by his wife, Queen Trailokyamahadevi. The king's death probably accounted for the fact that the Mallikarjuna temple was unfinished, and you can only mark out some of the sculptures. However, the king's victory over the Pallavas enabled him to express his admiration for Pallava architecture by bringing back to Pattadakal one of the chief Pallava architects. The Virupaksha, a Shaivite temple, has a sanctuary surrounded by passageways and houses a black polished stone Siva *lingam*. A further Shaivite symbol is the huge 2.6-m-high chlorite stone *Nandi* at the entrance, contrasting with the pinkish sandstone surrounding it. The three-storey tower rises strikingly above the shrine, the outside walls of which, particularly those on the south side, are richly carved. Many show different forms of Vishnu and Siva, including some particularly striking panels which show Siva appearing out of a *lingam*. Note also the beautifully carved columns inside. They are very delicate, depicting episodes from the *Ramayana*, *Mahabharata* and the *Puranas*, as well as giving an insight into the social life of the Chalukyas. Note the ingenuity of the sculptor in making an elephant appear as a buffalo when viewed from a different side.

In the ninth century the Rashtrakutas arrived and built a Jain temple with its two stone elephants a short distance from the centre. The carvings on the temples, particularly on the **Papanatha** near the village which has interesting sculpture on the ceiling and pillars, synthesizes North and South Indian architectural styles.

Badami → *Colour map 1, C5. Phone code: 08357. Population: 25,900.*

Badami occupies a dramatic site squeezed in a gorge between two high red sandstone hills. Once called Vatapi, after a demon, Badami was the Chalukyan capital from AD 543-757. The ancient city has several Hindu and Jain temples and a Buddhist cave and remains peaceful and charming. The transcendent beauty of the Hindu cave temples in their spectacular setting warrants a visit. The village with its busy bazar and a large lake has whitewashed houses clustered together along narrow winding lanes up the hillside. There are also scattered remains of 18 stone inscriptions (dating from the sixth to the 16th century). The sites are best visited early in the morning. They are very popular with monkeys, which can be aggressive, especially if they see food. End the day by watching the sun set from the eastern end of the tank. The area is well worth exploring by bicycle.

The **South Fort** ① *foreigners Rs 100, Indians Rs 5*, is famous for its cave temples, four of which were cut out of the hillside in the second half of the sixth century. There are 40 steps to **Cave 1**, the oldest. There are several sculpted figures, including

Harihara, Siva and Parvati, and Siva as Nataraja with 18 arms seen in 81 dancing poses. **Cave 2**, a little higher than Cave 1, is guarded by *dvarapalas* (door keepers). Reliefs of Varaha and Vamana decorate the porch. **Cave 3**, higher still, is dedicated to Vishnu. According to a Kannada inscription (unique in Badami) it was excavated in AD 578. It has numerous sculptures including Narasimha (man-lion), Hari-Hara (Siva-Vishnu), a huge seated Vishnu and interesting friezes. Frescoes executed in the tempera technique are similar to that used in the Ajanta paintings, and so are the carved ceilings and brackets. **Cave 4**, probably about 100 years later than the three earlier caves, is the only Jain cave. It has a statue of the seated Parsvanatha with two *dvarapalas* at the entrance. The fort itself above the caves is closed to the public.

The **Buddhist Temple** is in the natural cave close to the ancient artificial Bhutanatha Lake (Agasthya Lake), where the mossy green water is considered to cure illnesses. The Yellamma Temple has a female deity, while one of the two Shaivite temples is to Bhutanatha (God of souls); in this form, Siva appears angry in the dark inner sanctuary.

The seventh-century **Mallegitti Sivalaya Temple**, which is one of the finest examples of the early Southern style, has a small porch, a *mandapa* (hall) and a narrower *vimana*

Badami

To ② & Railway Station (5 km)

To Mahakuta (5 km)

Upper Sivalaya Temple

North Fort

Mallegitti Sivalaya Temple

Lower Sivalaya Temple

Medieval Sculpture Gallery

Bhutanatha Group

Station Rd

Taxis & Tongas

Bhutanatha Temple Rd

Jambulinga Temple

Bhutanatha Lake

Yellamma Temple

(Main Rd)

Cave Temples

South Fort

Ramdurg Rd

Archaeological Survey of India

To Belgaum

N

| 100 metres |
| 100 yards |

To Pattadakal (15 km) & Banashankari

Where to stay 🛏
Badami Court **2**

Shree Laxmi Vilas & Restaurant **1**

Restaurants 🍴
Sanman **1**

(shrine), which Harle points out is typical of all early Western Chalukya temples. The slim pilasters on the outer walls are reminders of the period when wooden pillars were essential features of the construction. Statues of Vishnu and Siva decorate the outer walls, while animal friezes appear along the plinth and above the eaves. These are marked by a moulding with a series of ornamental small solid pavilions.

Jambulinga Temple is an early temple in the centre of the town near the rickshaw stand. Dating from AD 699 as attested by an inscription and now almost hidden by houses, the visible brick tower is a late addition from the Vijayanagar period. Its three chapels, dedicated to Brahma, Vishnu and Siva, contain some fine carving, although the deities are missing and according to Harle the ceiling decoration already shows signs of deteriorating style. The carvings here, especially that of the Nagaraja in the outside porch, have helped to accurately date the Lad Khan Temple in Aihole (see page 349). Opposite the Jambulinga temple is the 10th-century Virupaksha Temple.

The mainly seventh-century **North Fort temples** ① *Rs 2, carry water*, provide an insight into Badami's history. Steep steps, almost 1 m high, take you to 'gun point' at the top of the fort which has remains of large granaries, a treasury and a watchtower. The **Upper Sivalaya Temple**, though damaged, still has some friezes and sculptures depicting Krishna legends. The North Fort was taken in a day by Colonel Munro in 1918, when he broke in through the east side.

An ancient **dolmen** site can be reached by an easy hike through interesting countryside; allow 3½ hours. A local English-speaking guide, Dilawar Badesha, at Tipu Nagar, charges about Rs 2.

The Archaeological Survey's **Medieval Sculpture Gallery** ① *Sat-Thu 1000-1700, free*, north of the tank, has fine specimens from Badami, Aihole and Pattadakal and a model of the natural bridge at Sidilinapadi, 5 km away.

Mahakuta

Once reached by early pilgrims over rocky hills from Badami, 5 km away, Mahakuta is a beautiful complex of Chalukyan temples dating from the late seventh century and worth a detour. The superstructures reflect influences from both North and South India and one has an Orissan *deul*.

The restored temple complex of two dozen shrines dedicated to Siva is built around a large spring-fed tank within an enclosure wall. The old gateway to the southeast has fasting figures of Bhairava and Chamunda. On entering the complex, you pass the *Nandi* in front of the older **Mahakutesvara Temple** which has fine scrollwork and figures from the epics carved on the base. Larger Siva figures appear in wall niches, including an *Ardhanarisvara*. The temple is significant in tracing the development of the super-structure which began to externally identify the position of the shrine in Dravidian temples. Here the tower is dome-like and octagonal, the tiers supported by tiny 'shrines'. The **Mallikarjuna Temple** on the other side of the tank is similar in structure with fine carvings at the entrance and on the ceiling of the columned *mandapa* inside, depicting Hindu deities and *mithuna* couples. The enclosure has many smaller shrines, some carrying fine wall carvings. Also worth visiting is the **Naganatha Temple**, 2 km away.

The dry and undulating plains from Hospet to Bidar are broken by rocky outcrops providing superb sites for commanding fortresses, such as the one that sits in ruins overlooking Gulbarga. From 1347 to 1525 Gulbarga served as the first capital of the Bahmanis, but it is also widely known among South Indian Muslims as the home of Saiyid Muhammad Gesu Daraz Chisti (1320-1422) who was instrumental in spreading pious Islamic faith in the Deccan. The annual **Urs festival** in his memory can attract up to 100,000 people.

Places in Gulbarga

The town's sights and hotels are quite spread out so it is worth hiring an auto for half a day. The most striking remains in the town are the fort, with its citadel and mosque, the Jami Masjid, and the great tombs in its eastern quarter – massive, fortress-like buildings with their distinctive domes over 30 m high.

The **fort** is just 1 km west of the centre of the present town. Originally built by Ala-ud-din Bahmani in the 14th century, most of the outer structures and many of the buildings are in ruins. The outer door of the west gate and the *bala hissar* (citadel), a massive structure, however, remain almost intact although the whole place is very overgrown. A flight of ruined steps leads up to the entrance in the north wall; beware of dogs. It's easy to see why the Bahamis were so keen to upgrade their fortress. The fat fort walls at Gulbarga – romantically named as the 'bouquet of lovers' – may sit proud above the more modern artificial lake, and the *bala hissar* itself stands high with its plump rotund columns, but the whole is all too pregnable and modest. And there's no commanding hilltop to provide the impenetrability that the plateaux around Bidar bequeathed the dynasty's subsequent rulers.

All that remains of the palace structures are solitary walls stamped with arches, but the **Jami Masjid**, with its incongruous, uncanny likeness to the mosque at Córdoba in southern Spain, is both active and well maintained (similarities with the mosque at Córdoba have contributed to the legend that it was designed by a North African architect from the Moorish court). Beautiful geometrical angles of archways form as you walk under the 75 small roof domes zagging between the four corner domes. The whole area of 3500 sq m is covered by a dome over the *mihrab*, four corner domes and 75 minor domes, making it unique among Indian mosques. It was built by Firoz Shah Bahmani (1397-1432).

The **tombs** of the Bahmani sultans are in two groups. One lies 600 m to the west of the fort, the other on the east of the town. The latter have no remaining exterior decoration though the interiors show some evidence of ornamentation. The Dargah of the Chisti saint, **Hazrat Gesu Nawaz** – also known as Khwaja Bande Nawaz – who came to Gulbarga in 1413 during the reign of Firoz Shah Tughlaq, is open to visitors. The two-storey tomb with a highly decorated painted dome had a mother-of-pearl canopy added over the grave. Note that women are not allowed to enter the tombs. The **Dargah library**, which has 10,000 books in Urdu, Persian and Arabic, is open to visitors.

The most striking of all the tombs near **Haft Gumbaz**, the eastern group, is that of **Taj-ud-Din Firuz** (1422). Unlike the other tombs it is highly ornate, with geometrical patterns developed in the masonry.

Bidar → *For listings, see pages 359-364. Colour map 1, B6. Phone code: 08357. Population: 172,300.*

The scruffy bungalow town that is modern-day Bidar spreads out in a thin layer of buildings both within and without the imposing rust-red walls of the 15th-century fort that once played capital to two Deccan-ruling Muslim dynasties. The buildings may be new but there's still something of a medieval undercurrent to life here. Islam still grows sturdily: apart from the storehouses of government-subsidized industries to counter 'backwardness', the outskirts are littered with long white prayer walls to mop up the overspill from over-burdened mosques during Id. A few lone tiles, tucked into high corners, still cling to the laterite brick structures that stand in for the succession of immaculately made palaces which must once have glowed incandescent with bright blue, green and yellow designs. Elsewhere you can only see the outline of the designs. The old fort commands grand vistas across the empty cultivated land below. Each successive palace was ruined by invasions then built anew a little further east.

Background

The walled fort town, on a red laterite plateau in North Karnataka, once the capital of the **Bahmanis** and the **Barid Shahis**, remained an important centre until it fell to Aurangzeb in 1656. The Bahmani Empire fragmented into four kingdoms, and the ninth Bahmani ruler, **Ahmad Shah I**, shifted his capital from Gulbarga to Bidar in 1424, rebuilding the old Hindu fort to withstand cannon attacks, and enriching the town with beautiful palaces and gardens. With the decline of the Bahmanis, the Barid Shahi Dynasty founded here ruled from 1487 until Bidar was annexed to Bijapur in 1619.

Places in Bidar

The intermingling of Hindu and Islamic architectural styles in the town has been ascribed to the use of Hindu craftsmen, skilled in temple carving in stone (particularly hornblende), who would have been employed by the succeeding Muslim rulers. They transferred their skill to Muslim monuments, no longer carving human figures, forbidden by Islam, but using the same technique to decorate with geometric patterns, arabesques and calligraphy, wall friezes, niches and borders. The pillars, often of wood, were intricately carved and then painted and burnished with gold to harmonize with the encaustic tiles.

The **Inner Fort** built by Muhammad Shah out of the red laterite and dark trapstone was later embellished by Ali Barid. The steep hill to the north and east provided natural defence. It was protected to the south and west by a triple moat (now filled in). A series of gates and a drawbridge over the moat to the south formed the main entrance from the town. The second gate, the **Sharaza Darwaza** (1503) has tigers carved in bas relief on either side (Shia symbols of Ali as protector), the tile decorations on the walls and the *Nakkar Khana* (Drum gallery) above. Beyond this is a large fortified area which brings you to the third gate, the huge **Gumbad Darwaza**, probably built by Ahmad Shah Wali in the 1420s, which shows Persian influence. Note the decorated *gumbad* (dome).

You will see the triple moat to the right and after passing through the gateway, to your left are steps leading to the **Rangin Mahal** (Coloured Palace) where Muhammad Shah moved to, after finding the nearby Shah Burj a safe refuge in 1487 when the Abyssinians attacked. This small palace (an indication of the Bahmanis'

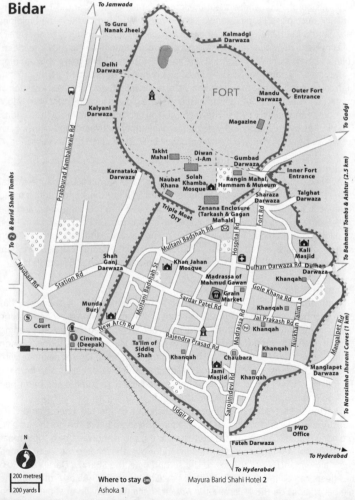

Bidar

To Jamwada
To Guru Nanak Jheel
Kalmadgi Darwaza
Delhi Darwaza
FORT
Mandu Darwaza
Outer Fort Entrance
Kalyani Darwaza
To Gadgi
Magazine
Takht Mahal
Diwan-I-Am
Gumbad Darwaza
Karnataka Darwaza
Naubat Khana
Solah Khamba Mosque
Rangin Mahal, Hammam & Museum
Inner Fort Entrance
To Bahmani Tombs & Ashtur (2.5 km)
Sharaza Darwaza
Talghat Darwaza
To ② & Barid Shahi Tombs
Triple Moat -Dry
Zenana Enclosure (Tarkash & Gagan Mahals)
Prabuard Kambliwale Rd
Hospital Rd
Fort Rd
Multani Badshah Rd
Kali Masjid
Shah Ganj Darwaza
Khan Jahan Mosque
Dulhan Darwaza Rd
Dulhan Darwaza
Khanqah
To ② Naubad Rd
Station Rd
Multani Badshah St
Madrassa of Mahmud Gawan
Gole Khana Rd
Munda Burj
Sardar Patel Rd
Grain Market
Khanqah
Madrassa Rd
Nurkhan Talim
Mangalbel Rd (1 km)
Court
New Arch Rd
Jai Prakash Rd
Khanqah
Cinema (Deepak)
Rajendra Prasad Rd
Ta'lim of Siddiq Shah
Khanqah
Chaubara
Khanqah
Sarojinidevi Rd
Jami Masjid
Khanqah
Manglapet Darwaza
To Narasimha Jharani Caves (1 km)
Udgir Rd
PWD Office
N
Fateh Darwaza
To Hyderabad
200 metres
200 yards
Where to stay 🛏
Ashoka **1**
Mayura Barid Shahi Hotel **2**

declining years) was built by him, elaborately decorated with coloured tiles, later enhanced by Ali Barid with mother-of-pearl inlay on polished black granite walls as well as intricate wood carvings. If locked, ask at the museum (see below) for a key.

The old banyan tree and the **Shahi Matbak** (once a palace, but served as the Royal Kitchens) are to the west, with the **Shahi Hammam** (Royal Baths) next to it, which now houses a small **museum** ① *0800-1700*. Exhibits include Hindu religious sculptures, Stone Age implements and cannon balls filled with bits of iron.

The **Lal Bagh**, where remains of water channels and a fountain witness to its former glory, and the *zenana*, are opposite the hammam. The **Sola Khamba** (16 columns) or **Zanani Mosque** is to the west (1423). The adjacent **Tarkash Mahal** (possibly refurbished by the Barid Shahis for the harem), to the south of Lal Bagh, is in ruins but still retains some tilework. From behind the mosque you can get to the **Gagan Mahal** (Heavenly Palace) that once carried fine decorations and is believed to have allowed the women to watch animal fights in the moat below from the back of the double hall. There's a good view from the roof. The **Diwan-i-Am** (Hall of Public Audience) is to the northwest of the *Zenana* which once held the *Takht-i-Firoza* (turquoise throne). To the north stands the **Takht Mahal** with royal apartments, audience hall and swimming baths. The steep staircase will take you down to underground chambers.

South of the Royal Apartments is the well that supplied water to the fort palaces through clay pipes. Of the so-called **Hazar** ('thousand') **Kothri** ① *cycling is a good way of exploring the site, free,* you can only see a few underground rooms and passages which enabled a quick escape to the moat when necessary. Further south, the **Naubat Khana** probably housed the fort commander and the musicians. The road west from the Royal Apartments leads to the encircling Fort Wall (about 10 km) with bastions carrying vast cannons, the one to the northwest being the most impressive. You can see the ammunition magazine inside the **Mandu Darwaza** to the east before returning to the main fort entrance.

As you walk south from the fort you can see the ruins of the **Madrassa of Mahmud Gawan** (1472). It is a fine example of his native Persian architecture and still bears signs of the once-brilliant green, white and yellow tiles which covered the whole façade with swirls of floral patterns and bold calligraphy.

The **Chaubara** is a 23-m circular watchtower at the crossroads, south of the town centre (good views from the top). South of this is the **Jami Masjid** (1430) which bears the Barid Shahis' typical chain and pendant motif. The **Kali Masjid** (1694), south of the Talghat Darwaza, is made of black trapstone. It has fine plaster decorations on the vaulted ceiling. There are also a number of **khanqahs** (monasteries).

The road east from the Dulhan Darwaza, opposite the General Hospital, leads to the eight **Bahmani tombs** ① *Ashtur, 0800-1700, free, carry your own torch*. These are best seen in the morning when the light is better for viewing the interiors.

The square tombs, with arched arcades all round, have bulbous domes. The exteriors have stone carvings and superb coloured tile decoration showing strong Persian influence, while the interiors have coloured paintings with gilding. The tomb of **Ahmad Shah I**, the ninth Bahmani ruler, is impressive with a dome rising to nearly 35 m, and has a particularly fine interior with coloured decorations and calligraphy in the Persian style, highlighted with white borders. To the east and south are minor tombs of his wife and son. The tomb of **Alauddin Shah II** (1458) is possibly the finest. Similar in size to his father's, this has lost its fine painting inside but enough remains of the outer tilework to give an impression of its original magnificence.

On the way back is the **Chaukhandi of Hazrat Khalil-Ullah** which is approached by a flight of steps. Most of the tilework has disappeared but you can see the fine carvings at the entrance and on the granite pillars.

The **Barid Shahi tombs**, each of which once stood in its own garden, are on the Nanded Road to the west of the old town. That of **Ali Barid** is the most impressive, with the dome rising to over 25 m, with granite carvings, decorative plasterwork and calligraphy and floral patterns on the coloured tiles, which sadly can no longer be seen on the exterior. Here, abandoning the customary *mihrab* on the west wall, Ali Barid chose to have his tomb left open to the elements. It includes a prayer hall, music rooms, a combined tomb for his concubines and a pool fed by an aqueduct are nearby. There are fine carvings on the incomplete tomb to his son **Ibrahim Barid**, to the west. You can also see two sets of granite *ranakhambas* (lit battleposts) which may have been boundary markers. Other tombs show the typical arched niches employed to lighten the heavy walls which have decorative parapets.

The road north from Ali Barid's tomb descends to **Nanak Jhera**, where a *gurdwara* marks the holy place where Sikhs believe a miracle was performed by Guru Nanak (see page 553) and the *jhera* (spring) rose.

Raichur → *For listings, see pages 359-364. Colour map 1, C6. Phone code: 08532. Population: 205,600.*

The main road from Hospet to Hyderabad passes through the important medieval centre of Raichur, once dominant in the Tungabhadra-Krishna *doab*, now an important but dusty market town, in the middle of a cotton-growing area.

The site of the fort's **citadel** at Raichur gives magnificent views over the vast open spaces of the Deccan plateau nearly 100 m below. Built in the mid-14th century Raichur became the first capital of the Bijapur Kingdom when it broke away from the Bahmani Sultans in 1489. Much of the fort itself is now in ruins, but there are some interesting remains. The north gate is flanked by towers, a carved elephant standing about 40 m away. On the inner walls are some carvings, and a tunnel reputedly built to enable soldiers access to barricade the gate in emergency. Near the west gate is the old palace. The climb to the citadel begins from near the north gate. In the citadel is a shrine with a row of cells with the Jami Masjid in the east. Its eastern gateway has three domes. The top of the citadel is barely 20 sq m.

There are some other interesting buildings in the fort below the hill, including the **Daftar ki Masjid** (Office Mosque), built around 1510 out of masonry removed from Hindu temples. It is one of the earliest mosques in the Deccan to be built in this way, with the bizarre result of producing flat ceilings with pillars carved for Chalukyan temples. The **Ek Minar ki Masjid** ('one-minaret mosque') is in the southeast corner of the courtyard. It has a distinctively Bahmani-style dome.

For hotel and restaurant price codes and other relevant information, see pages 13-17.

● Where to stay

Hampi-Vijayanagar *p341, map p343*
Some use Hospet as a base for visiting Hampi; it has plusher accommodation and the nearest railway station. However, it means a 30-min commute to Hampi. Hampi is quieter, more basic and infinitely more atmospheric, though note that the ASI still has notional plans to bulldoze the entire village of Hampi Bazar, so ring in advance. Across the river (by *coracle*, Rs 15) you can reach the hamlet of Virupapur Gaddi, a beautiful paddy planted village with budget guesthouses, coco-huts and cottages to stay in. Power cuts are common both sides of the river – a supply of candles and a torch are essential – and mosquitoes can be a real menace. A small selection from many guesthouses are listed here. All are similar and many are **$**; prices rise 30% at the height of the season, Nov-Jan.
$$$$ Sloth Bear Resort, near Kannada University, Kamalapur, bookings T080-4055 4055, www.junglelodges.com. Excellent newish nature resort, with tribal-style stone-and-thatch cottages set amid scrub a 20-min drive from Hampi Bazar. Good birding safaris, visits to Daroji bear sanctuary and a sunrise trip to Hampi are included. Great food and attentive service.
$$$ Mayura Bhuvaneswari, 2 km from site, Kamalapuram, T08394-241574. Government-run place that feels by turns weird and worn out; the budget rooms are overpriced, grimy and falling apart, while the newer suites have bizarre ultraviolet tube lights that lend the feel of sleeping in an abandoned nightclub.

Decent food and chilled beer, but service is stretched.
$$ Gopi, Janata Plot, T08394-241695, kirangopi2002@yahoo.com. Clean rooms hot water, older wing has Indian toilets.
$$ Ranjana Guest House, behind Government school, T08394-241330. A friendly guesthouse with 5 rooms, plus hot water, cheaper rooms have a cooler, rather than a/c.
$$-$ Mowgli Guest House, 1.5 km from ferry in Virupapur Gaddi, T08533-287033, www.mowglihampi.com. A wide selection of rooms, from basic cells with shared bath to cute circular huts and lovely bright a/c rooms on the second floor with expansive views over stunningly green paddy fields terracing down to the river. Hot water a few hours a day, international restaurant and pool table. Mellow without being over the top.
$$-$ Shanthi Guest House, next to Mowgli, Virupapur Gaddi, T08394-325352, shanthi.hampi@gmail.com. More chilled-out than its neighbour, with atmospheric mud huts and a lovely covered lounge gazing out over the swaying rice. Great for absorbing the sunset, good service, hot water by the bucket.
$ Archana, Janata Plot, T08394-241547, addihampi@yahoo.com. The pick of the Hampi Bazar hotels, with 9 clean, quiet rooms (some a/c), good atmosphere and great views from the roof.
$ Padma Guest House, T08394-241331. Family guesthouse, 4 doubles, exchange.
$ Shambhu, Janata Plot, T08394-241383, rameshhampi@yahoo.com. 5 rooms with bath and nets, plenty of plants, rooftop restaurants (egg dishes), friendly.
$ Vicky, 200 m north of main road (turn off at tourist office), T08394-241694, vickyhampi@yahoo.co.in. 7 rooms

(4 with bath), bucket hot water, Indian toilet, good rooftop restaurant, internet.

Hospet *p345*

Station Rd has been renamed Mahatma Gandhi Rd (MG Rd).

$$$$-$$$ Malligi, 6/143 Jambunatha Rd, T08394-228101, www.malligihotels. com. 188 a/c rooms and large **$$$** suites, restaurant and bar by pool (non-residents pay Rs 25 per hour), health club, exchange, travel (good Hampi tour), creakingly slow internet and overpriced STD/ISD service, but generally pleasant.

$$ Karthik, 252 Sardar Patel Rd, T08394-220038. 40 good-sized, clean rooms, 10 a/c in quiet, modern hotel, garden dining, friendly and good value.

$$ The Shine, near Bus Stand, Station Rd, T08394-694233, www.sainakshatra. com. Sparkly newish business hotel, with functional but pleasant and clean rooms, hot water and lift. Excellent value.

$$-$ Nagarjuna Residency, Sardar Patel Rd, opposite **Karthik**, T08394-229009. Spotless, modern, excellent value rooms, some a/c, extra bed Rs 30-50, very helpful.

$$-$ Shanbhag Towers, College Rd, T08394-225910, shanbhagtowers@ yahoo.com. 64 spacious rooms, 32 a/c with tub, TV, fridge, in new hotel, breathtaking Hampi theme, restaurants (one rooftop with great views), bar.

$$-$ SLV Yatri Nivas, Station Rd, T08394-221525. 15 bright, airy rooms and dorm in clean, well-run hotel. Good vegetarian restaurant and bar.

$ Shivananda, next to bus stand, T08394-220700. 23 rooms, 4 a/c, simple but clean, and complete with resident astrologer!

$ Viswa, MG Rd, opposite bus station, away from the road, T08394-227171. 42 basic rooms (some 4-bed) with bath, adjacent **Shanthi** restaurant. No frills but good value.

Bijapur *p345, map p347*

There has been a sudden spurt in decent hotels and restaurants.

$$$-$$ Madhuvan International, off Station Rd, T08352-255571. 35 rooms, 10 a/c, very pleasant, good vegetarian garden restaurant and rooftop terrace, beer in rooms only, travel desk, but a bit overpriced. Quite noisy till 2330 because of restaurant.

$$-$ Hotel Kanishka International, Station Rd, T08352-223788, kanishka_ bjp@rediffmail.com. 24 rooms (10 a/c) with decidedly garish decor (giant mirrors) also has cable TV, telephone, en suite, laundry, and excellent **Kamat Restaurant** downstairs.

$$-$ Hotel Pearl, opposite Gol Gumbaz, Station Rd, T08352-256002, www.hotel pearlbijapur.com. 32 rooms (17 a/c) in a modern, 3-storey, scrupulously clean, modest, mint pastel-coloured hotel set round a central courtyard with vegetarian basement restaurant (booze and non-vegetarian food through room service). Telephones, cable TV in all rooms, laundry and parking.

$$-$ Godavari, Athani Rd, T08352-270828. 48 good rooms, friendly staff, good vegetarian and non-vegetarian food.

$$-$ Santosh, T08352-252179. 70 good, clean rooms including some **$$** a/c, quieter at back, convenient, good value.

$ Hotel Navaratna International, Station Rd, T08352-222771. The grand colonnaded drive belies the modest price tag of the 34 rooms here (12 a/c). Communal areas scream with huge modernist paintings and rooms are done up with colour-coded care. TV, phone and smaller rooms have sit-outs. Very popular non-vegetarian courtyard restaurant, bar and pure vegetarian restaurant. Also rooms and baths for drivers; a giant leap in the humane direction for an Indian hotel.

$ Railway Retiring Room and dorm. Very clean, contact ticket collector on duty.
$ Samrat, Station Rd, T08352-250512. 30 basic rooms, 6 with a/c are passable, but the rest are battered. Good vegetarian garden restaurant but beware of the mosquitoes.
$ Sanman, opposite Gol Gumbaz, Station Rd, T08352-251866. 24 clean, pleasant rooms with shower, nets, 6 a/c. Very good value. Separate vegetarian and non-vegetarian restaurant with bar.

Badami *p351, map p352*
There is no formal money exchange but the **Mukambika** hotel, opposite the bus stand, may change small denominations of TCs.
$$$ Badami Court, Station Rd, 2 km from town, T08357-720207. Pleasant stroll or frequent buses. 26 clean, modern, though cramped rooms (with bath), some a/c, good restaurant, pool (but small and only knee-deep; non-residents Rs 80 per hr), gym, garden. Rates sometimes negotiable, only accepts rupees, has a near-monopoly on accommodation and service; maintenance reflects the absence of competition.
$$ Heritage Resort, Station Rd, T08357-220250, www.theheritage.co.in. Smart and spacious rooms in handsome stone cottages, each with its own sit-out opening on to a green lawn. Vegetarian restaurant, and transport and guides arranged.
$ Shree Laxmi Vilas, Main Rd, T08357-220077. Simple rooms, 3 with balconies with great views back to the temples. Right in the thick of it, so it's interesting but noisy.

Gulbarga *p354*
$$ Santosh, University Rd (east of town), T08472-247991. Some a/c rooms, good non-veg restaurant (beer). Best in town.

$$-$ Aditya, Humnabad Rd, T08472-224040. Reasonable rooms, some a/c with bath, clean veg restaurant, good value.
$$-$ Pariwar, Humnabad Rd, near station, T08472-221421, hotelpariwar@yahoo.com. Some a/c rooms, some cleaner and better value than others. Old but tidy, friendly staff and tasty vegetarian meals (no beer).

Bidar *p355, map p356*
Several very basic hotels near Old Bus Station. A roadside Punjabi *dhaba* near the junction of NH9 and the Bidar Rd serves very good meals, clean (including toilet at back).
$ Ashoka, off Udgir Rd, near Deepak Cinema, T08482-223931. A bit of a dive, but the best on offer, friendly, with 21 clean, good-sized rooms, hot water, some a/c. The 'restaurant' is more of a drinking den.
$ Mayura Barid Shahi (KSTDC), opposite New Bus Stand, T08482-228142. Small but well-kept rooms, and some larger suites, with a good restaurant downstairs. A good deal for the price.

Raichur *p358*
$ Laxmi Lodge, Koppal.
$ Railway Retiring Rooms. Also has a dorm.

⚙ Restaurants

Hampi-Vijayanagar *p341, map p343*
All restaurants are vegetarian, eggs are sometimes available.
$ Gopi (see Where to stay). Good cheap *thalis*.
$ Mango Tree, south of the bus stand but quite quiet. Relaxed and pleasant, slightly expensive restaurant that's popular with backpackers.
$ Mayura Bhuvaneswari, Kamalapuram (see Where to stay). Cheap adequate meals.

$ New Shanti, opposite **Shanthi Guest House**, between Virupaksha Temple and the river. Good carrot/apple/banana/chocolate cakes to order.

Hospet *p345*
The hotels serve chilled beer.
$$ Waves, **Malligi**. By pool. Multi-cuisine. Good food, bar.
$ Iceland, Station Rd, behind the bus station. Good South Indian meals.
$ Shanbhag, near bus station. Good South Indian cuisine.

Bijapur *p345, map p347*
Most good places to eat are north of Sation Rd.
$ Kapali, opposite bus stand. Decent South Indian food.
$ Priyadarshini, MG Rd, opposite Gagan Mahal. Vegetarian snacks.
$ Shrinidhi, Gandhi Chowk. Quality vegetarian meals.

Badami *p351, map p352*
$ Dhabas near the Tonga Stand sells snacks.
$ Laxmi Vilas, near taxi stand (see Where to stay). Veg meals.
$ Parimala and **Geeta Darshini**. South Indian.
$ Sanman, near bus stand. Non-vegetarian.

✹ Festivals

Hampi-Vijayanagar *p341, map p343*
Jan-Feb Virupaksha Temple Car festival. **3-5 Nov** Hampi Music festival at Vitthala Temple when hotels get packed.

Bijapur *p345, map p347*
Jan Siddhesvara Temple festival. Music festival accompanied by Craft Mela.

Pattadakal *p350*
Jan Nrutytsava draws many famous dancers and is accompanied by a Craft Mela. **Mar-Apr** Temple car festivals at Virupaksha and Mallikarjuna temples.

○ Shopping

Bidar *p355, map p356*
Shops sell excellent *bidriwork* (see page 369), particularly near the Ta'lim of Siddiq Shah. Craftsmen can be seen in the narrow lanes.

◐ What to do

Hospet *p345*
Tour operators
Tours from **KSTDC**, T08394-221008; **KSRTC**, T08394-228537; and **SRK Tours and Travels** at Malligi Hotel, T08394-224188. All run day tours to Hampi, some also including Tungabhadra Dam; Rs 100-150 per person. Day trips also go to Aihole, Badami and Pattadakal, 0830-1930, Rs 350 per person, but it's a very long day. Local sightseeing by taxi Rs 800 per day. Bijapur 1-day trip by bus Rs 175, taxi Rs 2100. English-speaking guide but rather rushed.

⊖ Transport

Hampi-Vijayanagar *p341, map p343*
Air The closest airport to Hampi is at Hubli, 3 hrs' drive to the west, with flights to **Bengaluru**, **Chennai** and **Mumbai**.

Bicycle hire Any guesthouse in Hampi Bazar can help you organize bike or scooter hire (bikes Rs 30-40 per day; scooters Rs 200 plus fuel).

Bus Buses to/from Hospet run every 30 mins from the bazar. A few KSRTC long-distance buses also go to **Bengaluru**

(**Bangalore**) and **Goa**. Agents in the bazar sell train tickets and seats on overnight sleeper buses to Goa and **Gokarna**, most of which leave from Hospet.

Coracles and ferries Take passengers across the river from the jetty west of the Virupaksha Temple, Rs 5 (Rs 10 with luggage). Services stop early in the evening so check the time of the last boat.

Hospet *p345*
Bus Frequent buses to **Hampi**'s 2 entry points (Kamalapuram and Hampi Bazar, both taking around 30 mins), from 0530; last return around 2000. The Kamalapuram road is better, especially in the rainy season when the slower road to Hampi Bazar is barely passable.
From the busy bus stand, T08394-228802, express buses run to/from **Bengaluru** (**Bangalore**) (10 hrs) and **Mysore** (10½ hrs). Several daily services to other sites, eg **Badami** (6 hrs), **Bijapur** (6 hrs), **Chitradurga** (3 hrs). More comfortable **Karnataka Tourism** luxury coaches run overnight to various towns. A few buses go direct to **Panaji** (**Goa**) – *Luxury*, 0630 (10½ hrs), State bus, 0830 (reserve a seat in advance); others involve a change in **Hubli** (4½ hrs). **Paulo Travels Luxury Sleeper** coach from Hotel Priyadarshini, at 1845, Rs 350, daily; **West Coast Sleeper**, from Hotel Shanbhag, 1830, Rs 350; daily (Oct-Mar only); strangers may be expected to share a bunk. It's better to take a train to **Londa** (under 5 hrs) and get a bus to **Madgaon** or **Panaji** (3 hrs).

Rickshaw From train station to bus stand should cost about Rs 30. To **Hampi**, Rs 150-200.

Taxi KSTDC, T08394-21008, T08394-28537 or from Malligi Hotel; about Rs 700 per day.

Train Bengaluru (**Bangalore**), *Hampi Exp 16591*, 2045 (via Guntakal, 2½ hrs) 10½ hrs. For **Belur/Halebid**: *Amaravati Exp 17225*, 0635 to **Hubli**; then *Hubli-Arsikere Pass 56274* (**S**), 1530. To **Badami**: via **Gadag**, 4 hrs. **Hyderabad (via Guntakal)**: *Amaravati Exp 17226*, 1450, 14 hrs. **Madgaon**, *Amaravati Exp 18047*, Mon, Wed, Thu, Sat 0630, 7 hrs.
From nearby **Gadag**, train to **Bijapur**: *Hubli-Solapur Exp 11424*, 1620, 4½ hrs.

Bijapur *p345, map p347*
Bus A service runs between the station and the west end of town. Horse-drawn carriages ply up and down MG Rd; bargain hard.
From the bus stand, T08352-251344, frequent services to **Bidar**, **Hubli**, **Belgaum** and **Solapur** (2-2½ hrs). Buses to **Badami** 3½ hrs. For **Hospet**, travel via Gadag or Ikal. Reservations can be made on the following daily services to **Aurangabad**: 0600, 1830, **Hospet**, **Bengaluru** (**Bangalore**): 1700, 1800, 1930, 2130 (12 hrs), Ultra fast at 1900, 2000; **Belgaum**: 0630, **Hubli**: 0900, 1400, 1600, **Hyderabad**: 0600, 1800; Deluxe at 2130, **Mumbai** (**CT**): 0800, 1600, 1700, 2030, **Mumbai** (**Kurla**): 1900, 2000, 2100, **Mysore**: 1700, **Panaji**: 1900 and **Vasco de Gama**: 0715. Several private agents also run services to **Bengaluru** (**Bangalore**), **Mangalore**, **Mumbai** and **Pune** (7 hrs).

Train Computerized Reservation Office open 0800-2000, Sun 0800-1400. **Solapur**: 0945, 1635 (2½ hrs). **Gadag**: 5 trains daily for long distance connections. Buses more convenient.

Badami *p351, map p352*
Bicycle Bike hire from stalls along the main road, Rs 5 per hr; pleasant to visit Banashankari, Mahakuta and Pattadakal.

Bus Few daily to **Hospet** (6 hrs), very slow and crowded but quite a pleasant journey with lots of stops; **Belgaum** via **Bagalkot**, 4 hrs; **Bijapur**, 0645-0930 (4 hrs). Several to **Pattadakal** and **Aihole** from 0730. **Aihole** (2 hrs), from there to **Pattadakal** (1600). Last return bus from Aihole 1715, via Pattadakal.

Car Hire from Badami with driver for Mahakuta, Aihole and Pattadakal, about Rs 650.

Train The station is 5 km north on the **Bijapur–Gadag** line, with 6 trains daily in each direction (enquire about schedules); frequent buses to town.

Gulbarga *p354*
Bus There are bus connections to **Hyderabad** (190 km) and **Solapur**.

Train Mumbai (CST): 8 trains daily, 13 hrs. **Bengaluru**: *Udayan Exp 6529*, 1900, 13½ hrs; *Lokmanya Tilak 1013*, 0905, 13 hrs. **Chennai (MC)**: *Chennai Exp 6011* (AC/II), 0130, 15 hrs; *Mumbai Chennai Mail 6009*, 1140, 18 hrs; *Dadar Chennai Exp1063*, 0605, 14 hrs. **Hyderabad**: *Mumbai-Hyderabad Exp 7031* (AC/II), 0020, 5¾ hrs; *Hussainsagar Exp 7001*, 0740, 5 hrs.

Bidar *p355, map p356*
Auto-rickshaw Easily available, Rs 15 being the going rate for most short hops across town.

Bicycle Cycling is the best way to get around and see the sights. 'Cycle taxis' can be hired for Rs 20 per day from several outlets all over town and near the **New Bus Station**. You may have to ask a few before you find a shop that will rent to you, but persevere.

Don't waste time with Ganesh Cycle Taxi near the New Bus Station.

Bus Services from **New Bus Station**, 1 km west of centre, to most regional destinations, but check timings since the last bus is often quite early. From **Hyderabad** or **Gulbarga** (under 4 hrs), or **Bijapur** (8 hrs). Private buses to **Mumbai**: 1700, 5 hrs, Rs 260. **Pune**: 1530, 3½ hrs, Rs 220. Taxi to **Gulbarga** Rs 800.

Train Bidar is on a branch line from Vikarabad to Parbhani Junction. Too slow to be of much use. **Aurangabad**: *Kacheguda-Manmad Exp 7664*, 2140, 8½ hrs. **Bengaluru**: *Hampi Link Exp 6593*, 1237, 18 hrs. **Secunderabad**: *Manmad-Kacheguda Exp 7663*, 0352, 5 hrs.

ⓘ Directory

Hampi-Vijayanagar *p341, map p343*
Banks Several money changers on main street. **Modi Enterprises**, main road, near tourist office, changes TCs and cash. Also **Neha Travels**. **Internet** Some lodges (eg **Shanti**, **Sree Rama**), also offer money exchange and internet, Rs 60 per hr (frequent power cuts).

Hospet *p345*
Banks State Bank of India, next to tourist office, with ATM; only changes cash (US$ and £). **Monica Travel**, near bus station, changes TCs (3% charge). **Internet** Cybernet, College Rd, next to Shivananda. **Post** Opposite veg market.

Bijapur *p345, map p347*
Banks State Bank of India in the citadel, **Canara Bank**, north of market, best for exchange. **Internet** Cyber Park, 1st floor, Royal Complex, opposite GPO, 0930-2300 fast connection.

Contents

Telangana & Andhra Pradesh

At a glance

⊖ **Getting around** As sites are
spread out, local bus, Ambassador
cabs or internal flights advised;
reach Tirumalai from Chennai.
↻ **Time required** Allow 3 days
for Hyderabad.
🌀 **Weather** Either bakingly hot or
hit by NW monsoon (with cyclones
in Nov and Dec) for much of the year;
the window is Jan-Mar.
✖ **When not to go** Apr and
May, when temperatures of up
to 45°C make travel intolerable.
In Hyderabad, aim for a weekend
to avoid city congestion.

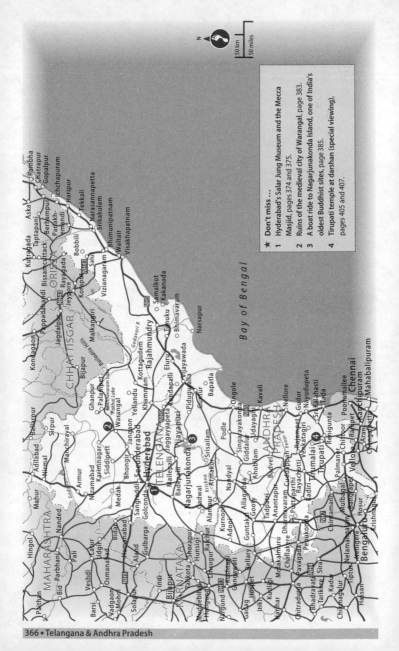

Bay of Bengal

★ Don't miss ...
1 Hyderabad's Salar Jung Museum and the Mecca Masjid, pages 374 and 375.
2 Ruins of the medieval city of Warangal, page 383.
3 A boat ride to Nagarjunakonda Island, one of India's oldest Buddhist sites, page 385.
4 Tirupati temple at darshan (special viewing), pages 405 and 407.

N

50 km
50 miles

The red soil plains of Telangana, carved from the erstwhile state of Andhra Pradesh in 2014, have long been the stage for some of the world's wealthiest men. The Deccani sultans – whose fetish for jewels was sated with the diamonds quarried from rich local seams – left a landscape dotted with their courtly pleasure gardens and palaces, and though the India's largest Muslim-ruled princely state was integrated into the Indian union when the army quashed its claims for independence, much of the splendour of its architecture remains, particularly in Hyderabad and its nearby fortress city of Golconda. And the city's fortunes have revived along with the success of the software industries who have their headquarters at the glass-and-chrome satellite town of 'Cyberabad'.

Yet away from the capital, Telangana ranks among the nation's most underdeveloped corners, providing a backdrop to a meagre bullock-and-cart paddy economy.

The catchments of Andhra Pradesh's great rivers, the Krishna and Godavari, are second in size only to the Ganges and are vital in supporting the lush paddy fields of coastal Andhra Pradesh. Rural Andhra holds the ancient Buddhist centres of Nagarjunakonda and Amaravati and one of India's most important modern Hindu pilgrimage centres, Tirumala.

The land
Geography For much of the year the interior looks dry and desolate although the great delta of the Krishna and Godavari rivers retains its lush greenness by virtue of their irrigation water. Water is the state's lifeblood, and the great peninsular rivers have a sanctity that reflects their importance. The Godavari, rising less than 200 km north of Mumbai, is the largest of the peninsular rivers. The Krishna rises near Mahabaleshwar at an altitude of 1360 m. After the Ganga these two rivers have the largest watersheds in India, and between them irrigate nearly six million ha of farmland.

Climate Andhra and Telangana are hot throughout the year, and getting hotter: the record-breaking heatwave in 2014 saw temperatures in Hyderabad climb above 45°C. The interior is in the rain shadow of the Western Ghats and receives less rainfall than much of the coast. The heaviest rainfall is between June and October, but the south gets the benefit of the retreating monsoon between October and December. Cyclones sweeping across the Bay of Bengal can wreak havoc in the flat coastal districts in November and December.

History
The first evidence of a people called the Andhras came from Emperor Asoka. The first known Andhra power, the **Satavahanas** encouraged various religious groups including Buddhists. Their capital at Amaravati shows evidence of the great skill of early Andhra artists and builders. Around AD 150 there was also a fine university at Nagarjunakonda. In 1323 Warangal, to the northeast of the present city of Hyderabad, was captured by the armies of Muhammad bin Tughlaq. Muslim expansion further south was prevented for two centuries by the rise of the **Vijayanagar Empire**, itself crushed at the Battle of Talikota in 1565 by a short-lived federation of Muslim States; the cultural life it supported had to seek fresh soil.

From then on Muslim rulers dominated the politics of the drylands of modern Telangana. The Bahmani kingdoms in the region around modern Hyderabad controlled central Telangana in the 16th century, even managing to hold the Mughals at bay until Aurangzeb finally forced them into submission in the late 17th century. Hyderabad, founded in 1591 by **Mohammad Quli Qutb Shah**, became the most important centre of Muslim power in Central and South India from the 17th to the 19th centuries. Through his successors Hyderabad became the capital of a Princely State the size of France, ruled by a succession of Muslim Nizams from 1724 till after India's Independence in 1947.

During the 18th century British and French traders spread their influence up the coast. Increasingly they came into conflict and looked for alliances with regional powers. At the end of the 18th century the British reached an agreement with the **Nizam of Hyderabad** in which he accepted British support in exchange for recognition of British rights to trade and political control of the coastal districts. Thus Hyderabad retained a measure of independence until 1947 while accepting British suzerainty.

There was doubt as to whether the Princely State would accede to India after Partition. The Nizam of Hyderabad would have liked to join fellow Muslims in the newly created Muslim State of Pakistan. However, political disturbances in 1949 gave the Indian government the pretext to take direct control, and the state was incorporated into the Indian Union.

Culture

Most of Andhra Pradesh's 78 million people are Dravidians. Over 85% of the population speaks Telugu. However, there are important minorities. Tamil is widely spoken in the extreme south, and on the border of Karnataka there are pockets of Kannada speakers. In Hyderabad there are large numbers of Urdu speakers who make up 7% of the state's population.

Hyderabad was the seat of government of the Muslim Nizams. Under their rule many Muslims came to work in the court, from North India and abroad. The Nizam's capital was a highly cosmopolitan centre, drawing extensively on Islamic contacts in North India and in west Asia, notably Persia.

Andhra **food** stands out as distinct because of its northern influence and large number of non-vegetarians. The rule of the Muslim Nawabs for centuries is reflected in the rich, spicy local dishes, especially in the area around the capital. Try *haleem* (spiced pounded wheat with mutton), *paya* (soup) or *baghara baigan* (stuffed aubergines). Rice and meat *biryani, nahari, kulcha,* egg *paratha,* and *kababs* have a lot in common with the northern Mughlai cuisine. The abundance of locally grown hot chillies has led to a fiery traditional cuisine, for which 'Andhra-style' is a byword. Also grown locally, good quality grapes (especially *anab-e-shahi*) or *khobani* (puréed apricots) provide a welcome neutralizing effect.

Craft industries

Andhra's **bidriware** uses dark matte gunmetal (a zinc and copper alloy) with silver damascening in beautiful flowing floral and arabesque patterns and illustrates the Persian influence on Indian motifs. The articles vary from large vases and boxes, jewellery and plates to tiny buttons and cuff links. The name is derived from Bidar in Karnataka and dates back to the Bahmani rulers.

Miniature wooden figures, animals, fruit, vegetables and birds are common subjects of *Kondapalli* **toys** which are known for their bright colours. *Nirmal* toys look more natural and are finished with a herbal extract which gives them a golden sheen, *Tirupati* toys are in a red wood while *Ethikoppaka* toys are finished in coloured lacquer. Andhra also produces fine figurines of deities in sandalwood.

Hyderabadi **jewellers** work in gold and precious stones which are often uncut. The craftspeople can often be seen working in the lanes around the Char Minar – shops selling the typical local bangles set with glass lie to the west. Hyderabadi cultured pearls and silver filigree ware from Karimnagar are another speciality.

The state is famous for **himru shawls** and **fabrics** produced in cotton/silk mixes with rich woven patterns on a special handloom. Silver or gold threads produce an even richer brocade cloth. A boy often sits with the weavers 'calling out' the intricate pattern.

The All India Handicrafts Board has revived the art of weaving special **ikat** fabrics. Pochampally, a village about 60 km east of Hyderabad, is synonymous with its *ikat* fabric in cotton and silk. The world-famous textile has been awarded IPR (Intellectual Property Rights) protection to safeguard it from imitation and competition. Interestingly, oil is used in the process of dyeing the warp and weft threads before weaving in to produce a pattern, hence the fabric's name *teli rumal* (literally oil kerchief).

Kalahasti, in Andhra's south, and Pedana, in coastal Andhra, produce distinctive **Kalamkari cloth paintings** (*kalam* refers to the pen used); the dyes come from indigo, turmeric and pomegranate. The blues stand out from the otherwise dullish ochre colours. Designed from mythology tales (*Mahabharata* and *Ramayana*), they make excellent wall hangings.

Modern Andhra Pradesh

Government Andhra State was created in 1953 from the Telugu-speaking areas of the erstwhile Madras State. This was not enough for those who were demanding statehood for a united Telugu-speaking region – one political leader, Potti Sreeramulu, starved himself to death in protest at the government's refusal to grant the demand – and in 1956 Andhra was merged with Telangana (itself carved from the Telugu parts of the old Hyderabad State) to create the state of Andhra Pradesh. Yet movements to separate the two regions began soon after, spurred by a sense that the interests of dusty, underdeveloped Telangana were being neglected in favour of the fertile coastal districts.

Andhra Pradesh was regarded as a stronghold of the Congress Party until 1983 when a regional party, the Telugu Desam Party (TDP), founded by the film star NT Rama Rao, won a crushing victory in the State Assembly elections. The Assembly elections on 5 October 1999 saw a repeat performance, with the highly regarded modernizing Chief Minister N Chandrababu Naidu being swept back to power with nearly a two-thirds majority. Allied with the BJP in the governing coalition in New Delhi, the Telugu Desam had a reputation for pushing ahead with rapid economic modernization, particularly visible in Hyderabad, but Naidu, who borrowed heavily from the World Bank and took China, Singapore and Malaysia as his business models, won only 47 of the 295 seats in the State Assembly elections in 2004. The Congress and its newly formed regional party ally, the Telangana Rashtra Samiti, with 226 seats, reclaimed power.

The Congress Chief Minister YS Rajasekhara Reddy (known as YSR) took charge of a state with high debts to the World Bank, where rural poverty was endemic and where suicide had become a major problem among poor farmers. YSR charmed the rural poor with a series of social welfare initiatives, including low-interest loans to women entrepreneurs and free medical treatments for people living below the poverty line. He became one of the most popular leaders in recent Indian history, making serious inroads into Andhra's hitherto intractable Naxalite problem, and he led the Congress Party to a rare absolute majority victory in the May 2009 elections. His death in a helicopter crash over Naxalite-controlled jungle in September 2009 has left a power vacuum in the state that has yet to be convincingly filled.

In June 2014 the Telangana movement finally won its long campaign, for separate statehood. The new state, India's 29th, retains Hyderabad as its capital (the city will also remain capital of Andhra Pradesh for the next decade), but faces severe challenges: outside of the tech hub, it ranks among the most underdeveloped regions of India, and its far-flung rural areas have been a breeding ground for Naxalism. Meanwhile, battle lines have already emerged with the remaining parts of Andhra Pradesh over rights to water and power, with Telangana refusing to release water from the Nagarjunasagar Dam to the heavily irrigated Krishna delta, and Andhra countering with threats to withhold electricity supplies to the new state.

Hyderabad and Telangana

Hyderabad, one of the poster boys for India's biotech and software boom, has emerged as a great place to soak up the atmosphere of the New India. It's also a city that heaves with history, with its splendid markets, mosques, architecture and museums and pearl bazars. On the outskirts of the city are film-set theme parks, the grand medieval fortress of Golconda and a collection of 17th-century tombs of old rulers lying in gardens of frilly bougainvillea. A day's drive to the southeast lies Nagarjunakonds, where the relocated ruins of one of India's richest Buddhist civilizations rise from the middle of an artificial lake.

Hyderabad and Secunderabad → *For listings, see pages 387-393. Colour map 6, B1.*

The Twin Cities of Hyderabad and Secunderabad, founded by the rulers of two separate Muslim dynasties, have long since bled into one conglomerate metropolis. The southern half, **Hyderabad**, holds the dusty and congested Old City; here you will find the beautiful but faded palaces of Islamic architecture, while the atmospheric lanes around the Char Minar throb with a contemporary Muslim mania. **Secunderabad**, which served as a prominent British army base prior to independence and remains the biggest military cantonment in the country, is separated from Hyderabad by the Hussain Sagar lake.

N Chandrababu Naidu, Andhra's chief minister from the late 1990s until 2004, had development dreams as lofty as the legendarily eccentric Nizam. The result is a city with town planning unequalled in India, including huge theme resorts where you can stand at minus temperatures (a tribute to the famous heat of Andhra), and Hitech City (brilliantly named 'Cyberabad'; a rival to Silicon Valley and home to Microsoft's first overseas base). The success of these high-tech and biotech industries has spawned a new elite to keep the old pearl peddlers in business since trade from the jewel-draped Nizams dried up.

Arriving in Hyderabad and Secunderabad → *Phone code: 040. Population: 5.5 million.*
Getting there Hyderabad's new **Rajiv Gandhi International Airport**, 25 km south of the city, equipped with world-class amenities, has ambitions to take over as India's aviation hub. Meter taxis from outside Arrivals charge Rs 15 per kilometre, while air-conditioned Pushpak buses run a round-the-clock service to various locations in the twin cities for Rs 200 per person. **Secunderabad station**, with trains to major cities, is in the Cantonment area, while the **Hyderabad City station** at Nampally is close to the Abids shopping district, with the majority of budget accommodation. The large

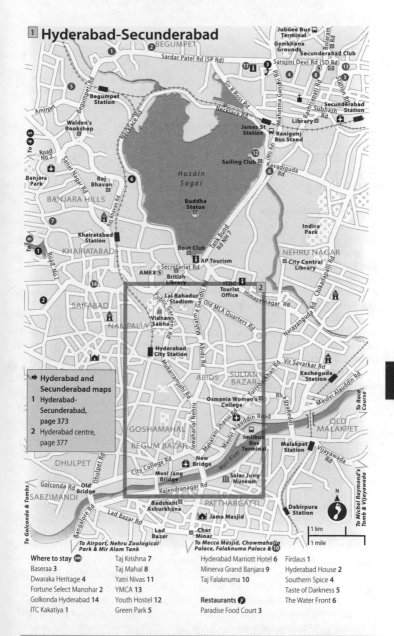

Hyderabad-Secunderabad

Where to stay
Baseraa 3
Dwaraka Heritage 4
Fortune Select Manohar 2
Golkonda Hyderabad 14
ITC Kakatiya 1
Taj Krishna 7
Taj Mahal 8
Yatri Nivas 11
YMCA 13
Youth Hostel 12
Green Park 5
Hyderabad Marriott Hotel 6
Minerva Grand Banjara 9
Taj Falaknuma 10

Restaurants
Paradise Food Court 3

Firdaus 1
Hyderabad House 2
Southern Spice 4
Taste of Darkness 5
The Water Front 6

Imlibun Bus terminal for long-distance buses is south of Abids on an island in the Musi River. The Jubilee Bus Terminal is in Secunderabad.

Getting around Autos or taxis are the best means of getting about the city north of the Musi and in Secunderabad, but in the congested old quarter you are best off walking, though there are cycle-rickshaws. ►► *See Transport, page 391.*

Tourist information Government of Andhra Pradesh ① *Yatri Nivas, SP Rd, Secunderabad, T040-6457 7598, www.aptdc.gov.in; Tank Bund Rd, near Secretariat, T040-6558 1555.* Andhra Pradesh Tourism Development Corporation (APTDC) ① *Tourism House, Himayatnagar, T040-2326 2151.* India Tourism ① *Netaji Bhavan, Himayatnagar, T040-2326 1360,* runs an excellent walking tour of the old city.

Old City and Char Minar

To celebrate the founding of Hyderabad, Sultan Mohammed Quli Qutb Shah built the lofty archway of **Char Minar** ① *0900-1730, Rs 5,* at the entrance to his palace complex. Capped with four soaring minarets (*char minar* means 'four towers') and holding the city's original mosque on its roof, it has been the showpiece of the city since construction was finished in 1612. Today it stands at the centre of a busy crossroads, surrounded by the Old City's sprawling bazar of pearl, perfume and jewellery shops. The monument is lit up every evening from 1900-2100.

Immediately to the southwest is the vast **Mecca Masjid**, so named because of the red clay bricks from Mecca embedded in its impressive outer walls. The second largest mosque in India and among the seven biggest in the world, construction of the building began in 1614 under the sixth Sultan Abdulla Qutb Shah and was completed by Aurangzeb when he annexed Golconda in 1692. Comprising huge slabs of black granite quarried nearby, the mosque was designed to hold 10,000 people at prayer times. The tombs of the Asaf Jahi rulers, the Nizams of Hyderabad, are in an enclosure with a roof, to the left of the courtyard.

Towards the river is the **Jama Masjid**, the second mosque built in the old city at the end of the 16th century, beyond which on Sadar Patel Road are the four arches of **Charkaman**. The eastern Black Arch was for the drums, the western arch led to the palaces, the northern was the Fish Arch, and the southern arch was for the Char Minar.

Lad Bazar area The heart of the Muslim part of the city, the area around the Mecca Masjid and the Char Minar is a fascinating hive of bazars, made up of beautiful wooden buildings with stone carvings and pink elephant gates, packed with people. You arrive at the **chowk** which has a mosque and a Victorian clock tower.

Southeast of the Lad Bazar is the enormous complex of palaces which were built by the different Nizams, including the grand **Chowmahalla Palace** ① *1100-1700, closed holidays, Rs 150; T040-2452 2032,* a facsimile of the Shah's Palace in Tehran. The stuccoed, domed Durbar Hall, courtyards and gardens have been carefully restored at the behest of Princess Esra, the eighth Nizam's wife. In the Durbar Hall is a platform of pure marble on which the *Takht-e-Nishan* (royal seat) was placed.

Nizam Salabhat Jung began the splendid palace complex in 1750, but it was only completed more than a century later by Nizam Afzar-ud-Dawla Bahadur. Refreshed and sparkling after a thorough restoration, the four (*chow*) palaces (*mahal*) of the complex's name – the Afzal Mahal, Mahtab Mahal, Tahniyat Mahal and Aftab Mahal – now play host to a museum packed with artefacts from the Nizam's reign, while the central Khilawat Mubarak (Durbar Hall) has been brought back to its original glory, complete with 19 Belgian crystal chandeliers.

The modern **Salar Jung Museum** ① *Salar Jung Marg, T040-2452 3211, Sat-Thu 1030-1700, closed public holidays, allow 1½ hrs, Rs 150, cameras and bags must be left at counter, tape recorded guides at ticket office*, houses the collection of Sir Yusuf Ali Salar Jung III, the *wazir* (prime minister) to the Nizam between 1899-1949. The fact that it is one of only three national museums in India is a telling indication of the extant of the riches he amassed. Originally housed on the edge of the city in one of the palaces, it was rehoused in this purpose-built museum in 1968. Exhibits are described in English, Urdu, Hindi and Telugu. The collection includes Indian textiles, bronzes, paintings and fine ivory art pieces, armoury, Far Eastern porcelain and entertaining curiosities. The Indian miniatures are stunning.

The **High Court**, built on the new roads laid out along the Musi's embankments after the great flood, is a splendid Mughal-style building in the old Qutb Shahi gardens **Amin Bagh**, near Afzal Ganj Bridge. This was Vincent Esch's most striking work. It was built in 1916 from local pink granite, with red sandstone carved panels and columns, a large archway and domes. These days it is painted pink. A further change is the enclosure of the verandas. The detail is Mughal, but some argue that the structure and internal form are Western.

Next door to the High Court is Esch's **City College** (1917-1920), originally the City High School for boys. Built largely of undressed granite, there are some distinctive Indian decorative features including some marble *jalis*. Esch deliberately incorporated Gothic features, calling his style Perpendicular Mogul Saracenic.

In the opposite direction along the riverbank from the Salar Jung Museum is one of the oldest *imambaras* in the country, the **Badshahi Ashurkhana** (House of Mourning), built in the Qutb Shahi style in the late 16th century. It has excellent tile mosaics and wooden columns in the outer chamber, both later additions.

Over the river is the **Osmania Women's College**, the former British residency built by James Achilles Kirkpatrick – the central character of William Dalrymple's history, *White Mughals* – in 1803. This imposing colonial structure, whose grounds run down to the river bank, was the first symbol of British presence in the city. It was deliberately built to the same proportions as the Char Minar in order to be the only equal to its minarets on the city skyline. After decades of decline, the World Monuments Fund is carrying out structural conservation as well as fundraising for further restoration, while it continues to function as an educational institute for 4000 girl students (whose modesty visitors are urged to respect). The ornate palace Kirkpatrick built for his Muslim bride was razed in 1861 as a symbol of his perceived immorality. Dalrymple's book was launched from the stately, ochre-painted stately building's Durbar Hall. This is a room of giant chandeliers, French windows, mirrors shipped in from Brighton palaces, tatty fans and glorious floral tracings on its ceiling. The Palladian-villa style central complex, the entrance porch with Corinthian columns, the Durbar Hall, oval offices, billiard rooms and bedrooms were initially independent of the flanking wings, separated by drawbridges, whose pulleys are still in place. Outlying buildings hold printing presses dating from the 1900s. Turn out of the King's Gate then left down a pathway towards the pigeon rookery to see the model of the Residency that Kirkpatrick had made so his Hyderabadi princess Khairunnissa could see the main house without breaking her *purda*.

Hyderabad Centre: New City

The **Osmania General Hospital** (1918-1921) is the third of Vincent Esch's impressive buildings in Hyderabad. It stands across the river, opposite the High Court. The 200-m-long building was one of the largest and best equipped hospitals in the world when it opened. To its east, also on the river, is the imposing **Asafia State Central Library** (1929-1934) with its priceless collection of Arabic, Persian and Urdu books and manuscripts.

The **Public Gardens** ① *closed public holidays,* in Nampally, north of Hyderabad Station, contain some important buildings including the Archaeological Museum and Art Galleries and the State Legislative Assembly (Vidhan Sabha).

Andhra Pradesh State Museum ① *near the Lal Bahadur Shastri Stadium, 10 mins by car from Banjara Hills area, 1030-1700, closed public holidays, nominal entrance fee, photography Rs 10, guidebook Rs 15,* is a small museum with a crowd-drawing 4000-year-old Egyptian mummy. Behind the museum in Ajanta Pavilion are life-size copies of frescoes from the Ajanta Caves while the Nizam's collection of rare artefacts is housed in the Jubilee Hall.

The **City Railway Station** (1914) was intended by Esch to be pure Mughal in style but built entirely of the most modern material then available: pre-cast, reinforced concrete. It has a wide range of distinctively Indian features including the *chhattris* of royalty, wide *chajjas* (eaves) and onion domes.

Naubat Pahad (Kala Pahad or Neeladri) are two hills situated north of the Public Gardens. The Qutb Shahis are believed to have had their proclamations read from the hill tops accompanied by drums. In 1940 pavilions were built and a hanging garden was laid out on top of one; it's now occupied by the **Birla Planetarium** ① *Fri-Wed at 1130, 1600 and 1800, Rs 20,* and **Science Centre** ① *1030-2000, Rs 20.*

The nearby **Venkatesvara Temple** (Birla Mandir) ① *reached by a stall-lined path opposite Thomas Cook on Secretariat Rd, 0700-1200, 1400-2100, photography of inner sanctum prohibited,* is a modern, stunning white marble temple with an intricately carved ceiling which overlooks Husain Sagar. It was built by the Birlas, the Marwari business family who were responsible for building important new Hindu temples in several major cities, including Laxmi Narayan Temple in New Delhi. Completed in 1976, the images of the deities are South Indian, although the building itself drew craftsmen from the north as well, among them some who claimed to have ancestors who built the Taj Mahal.

The massive State Legislative Assembly building, **Vidhan Sabha**, originally the Town Hall, was built by the Public Works Department (PWD) in 1922. Although Esch had nothing to do with its design, he reportedly admired it for its lightness and coolness,

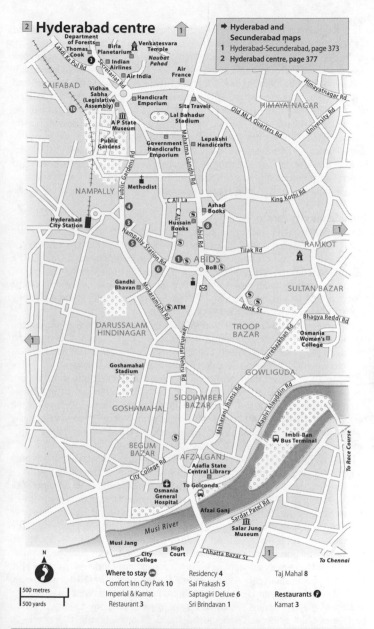

➡ **Hyderabad and Secunderabad maps**
1 Hyderabad-Secunderabad, page 373
2 Hyderabad centre, page 377

Department of Forests
Thomas Cook
Birla Planetarium
Venkatesvara Temple
Indian Airlines
Naubat Pahad
Air India
Air France
SAIFABAD
Secretariat Rd
Lakdi Ka Pul Rd
Vidhan Sabha (Legislative Assembly)
Handicraft Emporium
Sita Travels
Lal Bahadur Stadium
HIMAYATNAGAR
Himayatnagar Rd
A P State Museum
Old MLA Quarters Rd
University Rd
Public Gardens
Government Handicrafts Emporium
Lepakshi Handicrafts
Methodist
NAMPALLY
Public Gardens Rd
Mahatma Gandhi Rd
C Ali La
King Kothi Rd
Ashad Books
Hyderabad City Station
Hussain Books
Abid Rd
Tilak Rd
RAMKOT
Nampally Station Rd
ABIDS
BoB
Gandhi Bhavan
Mukarramjahi Rd
SULTAN BAZAR
ATM
Bank St
Bhagya Reddi Rd
DARUSSALAM HINDINAGAR
Maharani Nehru Rd
TROOP BAZAR
Turebazkhan Rd
Osmania Women's College
Goshamahal Stadium
GOWLIGUDA
SIDDIAMBER BAZAR
GOSHAMAHAL
Mahatma Jhansi Rd
BEGUM BAZAR
AFZALGANJ
Maulvi Alauddin Rd
Imbli-Ban Bus Terminal
To Race Course
City College Rd
Asafia State Central Library
Osmania General Hospital
To Golconda
Afzal Ganj
Sardar Patel Rd
Salar Jung Museum
Musi River
Musi Jang
City College
High Court
Chhatta Bazar St
To Chennai

N
500 metres
500 yards

Where to stay 🛏
Comfort Inn City Park **10**
Imperial & Kamat Restaurant **3**

Residency **4**
Sai Prakash **5**
Saptagiri Deluxe **6**
Sri Brindavan **1**

Taj Mahal **8**

Restaurants 🍴
Kamat **3**

which the building maintained even on the hottest day. **Jubilee Hall** (1936), behind the Vidhan Sabha, is another remarkable PWD building, with clear simple lines.

The deep **Husain Sagar Lake** ① *boat trips organized by APTDC leave from Lumbini Park, near the APTDC office on Secretariat Rd, T040-2345 3315,* was created in the mid-16th century by building the *bund* that links Hyderabad and Secunderabad, and was named to mark the gratitude of Ibrahim Quli Qutb Shah to Hussain Shah Wali, who helped him recover from an illness. The *bund* is a favourite evening promenade for the city dwellers. At the far end of the lake is the **Nizamia Observatory**. The 17.5-m-high, 350-tonne granite **statue of Buddha** was erected in the lake after years of successive disasters and finally inaugurated by the Dalai Lama in 1993. The tank, fed by streams originating from the Musi River, supplies drinking water to Hyderabad. Although it supports a rich birdlife and is used for fish culturing it also receives huge amounts of industrial effluent, agricultural waste and town sewage.

Outside the city centre

Originally a rich nobleman's house, **Falaknuma Palace** was built in 1873 in a mixture of classical and Mughal styles. Bought by the Nizam in 1897, it has a superb interior (particularly the state reception room) with marble, chandeliers and paintings. The palace houses Eastern and European treasures, including a collection of jade, crystal and precious stones and a superb library. Currently operating as one of India's most luxurious hotels – a high bar to jump – it's particularly atmospheric in the evening, when the lights of Hyderabad twinkle at your feet.

Osmania University ① *T040-2709 6048,* built by the Nizam in 1939, is just outside the city towards the east. Inaugurated in 1917 in temporary buildings, its sprawling campus with its black granite Arts College combines Moorish and Hindu Kakatiya architectural styles. There is a botanical garden and the State Archives.

The **tomb of Michel Raymond** is off the Vijayawada Road, about 3 km from the Oliphant Bridge. The Frenchman joined the second Nizam's army in 1786 as a common soldier and rose to command 15,000 troops. His popularity with the people earned him the combined Muslim-Hindu name Moosa Ram, and even today they remember him by holding a commemorative Urs fair at his grey granite tomb, which is 7 m high and bears the initials JR.

Mir Alam Tank, to the southwest of the old city, is a large artificial lake. It was built by French engineers under instructions of the grandfather of Salar Jung III and is a popular picnic spot. It is now part of the **Nehru Zoological Park** ① *Apr-Jun 0800-1730, Jul-Mar 0830-1700, closed Mon, Rs 20 (extra charges for nocturnal house, safari ride, etc), camera Rs 20, video Rs 100, bus 7Z from Secunderabad Station and Public Garden Rd,* which occupies a remarkable 13-ha site studded with huge boulders. The hilly grounds offer a welcome relief from the bustle of the city, and birdwatching here provides a good introduction to Indian avifauna, but this is also one of India's best zoos (the animals are kept in natural surroundings) and well worth a visit. There's also a lion safari park and a nocturnal house. The **Natural History Museum**, **Ancient Life Museum** and **Prehistoric Animals Park** are here as well.

West of the city centre lies **Hitec City**, a major technology township set up by former Chief Minister Chandrababu Naidu to promote the IT industry in

Andhra Pradesh. In a distinctly more low-tech vein, nearby Madhapur is home to **Shilparamam** ① *1100-2300*, a crafts village spread over 12 ha, where you can interact with artisans and craftsman from all over the country.

Ramoji Film City ① *25 km southeast of Hyderabad on the Vijayawada road, T08415-246555, www.ramojifilmcity.com, 0900-1800, Rs 700 (children under 12 Rs 600), includes guided tour and various shows, take bus 204, 205, 206 or 207 from Hyderabad (Women's College stop, Koti), or 290 from Secunderabad's Uppal bus stop*, is a sherbet-dipped shrine to the many uses of plaster of Paris. Bus tours take visitors around the 'city', and though they're conducted mainly in Hindi, you'll still gather that everywhere from Mumbai's Chor Bazar to Mysore's Brindavan Gardens have been recreated since media baron Ramoji Rao founded his film lot in 1991. Over 3000 films have been shot here since then. It's oddly compelling to see an audience sit in rapt thrall to a show of aspiring film dancers gyrating in spandex hot pants, while their male opposite numbers inexplicably morris dance; this is only for the committed Indian film buff. It doesn't have the diversionary value of a Universal Studios, but there is a theme park, **Fundustan**, for kids. **AP Tourism** runs daily bus services from Hyderabad.

Golconda → *For listings, see pages 387-393. Colour map 1, B6.*

Golconda, one of the most accessible of great medieval fortresses in India, was the capital of the Qutb Shahi kings who ruled over the area from 1507 to 1687. Nizam-ul-Mulk repossessed it in 1724 and restored it to its former glory for a time. Modern day restorations are being carried out by the Archaeological Survey of India.

Arriving in Golconda
Golconda is 11 km west of Hyderabad. Buses 119 or 142M from Nampally or 66G from Char Minar, take one hour to the fort. Buses 123 and 142S go direct from Char Minar to the Qutb Shahi Tombs, Rs 10. Autos take 30 minutes, Rs 150. Cycling in the early morning is a good option as it's an easy journey. Both the fort and the tombs are popular sites and get crowded and very noisy after 1000; if you arrive early it's worth asking to be allowed in.

The fort → *The numbers in brackets below refer to the map.*
① *T040-2351 2401, 0700-2000, Rs 100, Indians Rs 10. Official guides wait at the entrance (Rs 250), unofficial ones greet you under the Fateh Darwaza. Allow 2-3 hrs. There is an excellent 1-hr son et lumière show in English (Mar-Oct 1800, Nov-Feb 1900; Rs 50/100); tickets go on sale at Golconda 1 hr before the start, Rs 25. Some people buy buy their 'sound and light' ticket as soon as the office opens and take a quick tour (45 mins) of the fort before sunset in time for the show.*
Originally built of mud in the 12th century by the Hindu Kakatiyas, the fort was reinforced by masonry by the Bahmanis who occupied it from 1363. The massive fort, built on a granite hill, was surrounded by three walls. One encircled the town, another the hill on which the citadel stood and the last joined huge boulders on the

high ridge with parts of masonry wall. The citadel's 5-km double wall had 87 bastions with cannons and eight huge gates with outer and inner doors and guardrooms between. Some of the guns of the Qutb Shahis are still there with fortifications at various levels on the way up. Another of India's supposed underground tunnels is believed by some to run for about 8 km from a corner of the summit to Gosha Mahal. The fort had an ingenious system of laminated clay pipes and huge Persian Wheels to carry water to cool the palace chambers up to the height of 61 m where there were hanging gardens. The famous diamond vault once held the *Koh-i-noor* and *Hope* diamonds. The fort fell to Emperor Aurangzeb after two attempts, an eight-month siege and the help of a Qutb general-turned-traitor. English traveller Walter Hamilton described it as being almost deserted in 1820: "the dungeons being used by the Nizam of Hyderabad as a prison for his worst enemies, among whom were several of his sons and two of his wives".

The Fateh Darwaza or Victory Gate at the **Grand Portico (1)** entrance, made of teak, with a Hindu deity engraved, is studded with iron spikes as a defence against war elephants. The superb acoustics enabled a drum beat, bugle call or even a clap under the canopy of this gate to be heard by someone at the very top of the palace;

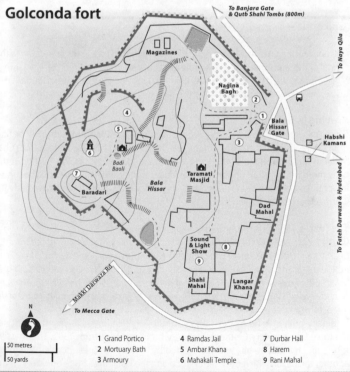

Golconda fort

To Banjara Gate
& Qutb Shahi Tombs (800m)

To Naya Qila

Magazines

Nagina Bagh

Bala Hissar Gate

Habshi Kamans

To Fateh Darwaza & Hyderabad

Badi Baoli

Taramati Masjid

Bala Hissar

Dad Mahal

Baradari

Sound & Light Show

Shahi Mahal

Langar Khana

Rani Mahal

Makki Darwaza Rd

To Mecca Gate

N

50 metres
50 yards

1 Grand Portico	4 Ramdas Jail	7 Durbar Hall
2 Mortuary Bath	5 Ambar Khana	8 Harem
3 Armoury	6 Mahakali Temple	9 Rani Mahal

it is put to the test by the visiting crowds today. A couple of glass cases display a map and some excavated finds.

Beyond the gate the **Mortuary Bath (2)** on the right has beautiful arches and a crypt-like ceiling; you see the remains of the three-storey **armoury (3)** and the women's palaces on the left. About halfway up is a large water tank or well and to the north is what was once the most densely populated part of the city. Nearby, the domed storehouse turned into the **Ramdas Jail (4)** and has steps inside that lead up to a platform where there are relief sculptures of deities on the wall, dominated by Hanuman. The **Ambar Khana (5)** (granary) has a Persian inscription on black basalt stating that it was built between 1626 and 1672. The steps turn around an enormous boulder with a bastion and lead to the top passing the Hindu **Mahakali Temple (6)** on the way. The breezy **Durbar Hall (7)** is on the summit. It is well worth climbing the stairs to the roof here for good views. The path down is clearly signposted to take you on a circular route through the **harem (8)** and **Rani Mahal (9)** with its royal baths, back to the main gate. A welcome chilled drink and snack is available at several cafés opposite the gate.

Qutb Shahi tombs → *The numbers in brackets below refer to the map.*
ⓘ *Sat-Thu 0930-1830, Rs 100, Indians Rs 10, camera Rs 10, car Rs 20, bicycle Rs 5. Allow 2 hrs, or half a day for a leisurely exploration. Inexpensive guidebook available.*

Qutb Shahi tombs

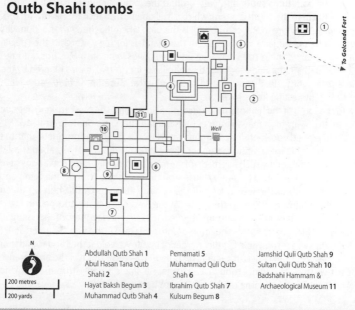

N

200 metres
200 yards

Abdullah Qutb Shah **1**	Pemamati **5**	Jamshid Quli Qutb Shah **9**
Abul Hasan Tana Qutb Shahi **2**	Muhammad Quli Qutb Shah **6**	Sultan Quli Qutb Shah **10**
Hayat Baksh Begum **3**	Ibrahim Qutb Shah **7**	Badshahi Hammam & Archaeological Museum **11**
Muhammad Qutb Shah **4**	Kulsum Begum **8**	

About 800 m north-northwest of Golconda fort on a low plateau (a road leaves the fort through the Banjara Gate) are the Qutb Shahi Tombs. Each tomb of black granite or greenstone with plaster decoration is built on a square or octagonal base with a large onion dome and arches with fine sculptures, inscriptions and remains of glazed decoration. The larger tombs have their own mosque attached which usually comprises an eastward opening hall with a *mihrab* to the west. The sides have inscriptions in beautiful Naksh script, and remnants of the glazed tiles that used to cover them can still be seen in places. The tombs of the rulers were built under their own supervision but fell into disrepair and the gardens ran wild until the end of the 19th century when Sir Salar Jang restored them and replanted the gardens. It is now managed and kept in an excellent state of repair by the Archaeological Survey of India. The gardens are being further improved.

The road north from Golconda fort passes the tomb of **Abdullah Qutb Shah (1)** (1626-1672) as it approaches the entrance to the tombs, which is at the east gate of the compound. On the left side of the road just outside the compound is the tomb of **Abul Hasan Tana Qutb Shahi (2)** (ruled 1672-1687). He was the last of the kings to be buried here as the final king in the line of the Qutb Shahi Dynasty, Abul Hasan, died in the fort at Daulatabad in 1704. To the right of the entrance are the tomb of Princess **Hayat Baksh Begum (3)** (died 1677), the daughter of Ibrahim Qutb Shah, and a smaller mosque, while about 100 m directly ahead is the granite tomb of **Muhammad Qutb Shah (4)** (ruled 1612-1626). Tucked away due north of this tomb is that of **Pemamati (5)**, one of the mistresses of Muhammad Qutb Shah, dating from 1663. The path turns south and west around the tomb of Muhammad Qutb Shah. About 100 m to the south is a tank which is still open. The **Badshahi Hammam (11)**, the oldest structure in the compound, is the bath where the body of the king was washed before burial. You can still see the channels for the water and the special platforms for washing the body. The Badshahi kings were Shi'a Muslims, and the 12 small baths in the Hammam stand symbolically for the two *imams* revered by the Shi'a community. Next door, a small **Archaeological Museum** ① *1000-1300, 1400-1630,* has interesting items in glass cases.

To the south of the hammam is a series of major tombs. The most striking lies due south, the 54-m-high mausoleum of **Muhammad Quli Qutb Shah (6)** (ruled 1581-1612), the poet king founder of Baghnagar (Hyderabad). It is appropriate that the man responsible for creating a number of beautiful buildings in Hyderabad should be commemorated by such a remarkable tomb. The underground excavations here have been turned into a Summer House. You can walk right through the tomb and on to the tomb of the fourth king of the dynasty, **Ibrahim Qutb Shah (7)** (ruled 1550-1580), another 100 m to the south. At the west edge of the compound is the octagonal tomb of **Kulsum Begum (8)** (died 1608), granddaughter of Mohammad Quli Qutb Shah. To its east is the tomb of **Jamshid Quli Qutb Shah (9)** (ruled 1543-1550), who was responsible for the murder of his 90-year-old father and founder of the dynasty, **Sultan Quli Qutb Shah (10)** (ruled 1518-1543). This has the appearance of a two-storey building though it is in fact a single-storey structure with no inscription. There are some other small tombs here.

The capital of the Kakatiya Empire in the 12th and 13th centuries, Warangal's name is derived from the Orugallu (one stone) Hill, a massive boulder with ancient religious significance that stands where the modern town is situated.

Arriving in Warangal → *Phone code: 0870. Population: 528,600.*

Warangal is 156 km northeast of Hyderabad and most express trains between Chennai and Delhi stop here. **Warangal Tourist Office** ① *1st floor, Talwar Hyndai Show Room, Chaitanyapuri, opposite REC Petrol Pump, Kazipet, T0870-244 6606.*

Background

The city was probably laid out during the reigns of King Ganapatideva (1199-1262) and his daughter Rudrammadevi (until 1294). Warangal was captured by armies from Delhi in 1323, enforcing the payment of tribute. Control of Warangal fluctuated between Hindus and Muslims but between the 14th and 15th centuries it remained in Bahmani hands. Thereafter it repeatedly changed hands, and some argue that although the military fortifications were repeatedly strengthened, the religious buildings were largely destroyed, including the great Siva temple in the middle of the city. Marco Polo was highly impressed by Warangal's riches, and it is still famous for the remains of its temples, its lakes and wildlife, and for its three circuits of fortifications. The modern town itself, however, is not very interesting.

Places in Warangal

At the centre of the 'fort' ① *0600-1800, US$2,* is a circular area about 1.2 km in diameter. Most of it is now farmland with houses along the road. Near the centre are the ruins of the original Siva temple. Remains include the large beautifully carved stone entrance gateways, replicas of which adorn many of the government offices, hotels and even private residences in the city. The gateways lead to the almost square enclosure, aligned along the cardinal directions and beyond are overturned slabs, smashed columns, brackets and ceiling panels.

Nearby Siva temples are still in use, and to the west is the **Khush Mahal**, a massive royal hall used by the Muslim Shitab Khan in the early 16th century for state functions. It may well have been built on the site of earlier palaces, near its geometric centre, while some structures in the central area may have been granaries.

From the centre, four routes radiate along the cardinal directions, passing through gateways in the three successive rings of fortification. The innermost ring is made of massive granite blocks, and is up to 6 m high with bastions regularly spaced along the wall. The middle wall is of unfaced packed earth, now eroded, while the outermost circuit, up to 5 m high, is also of earth. The four main roads pass through massive gateways in the inner wall, and there are also incomplete gateways in the second ring of fortifications. Some of the original roads that crossed the city have disappeared.

Some suggest that the plan of Warangal conforms to early Hindu principles of town planning. **'Swastika towns'**, especially suited to royalty, followed the pattern of concentric circles and swastika of the *yantras* and *mandalas*. They were a miniature representation of the universe, the power of god and king recognized symbolically, and in reality, at the centre.

The Chalukya-style '1000-pillar' **Siva Rudresvar temple** ⓘ *0500-1200, 1600-2000*, on the slopes of the Hanamakonda Hill, 4 km to the north, has beautiful carvings. It is a low, compact temple, built on several stepped platforms with subsidiary shrines to Vishnu and Surya, rock-cut elephants, a large superbly carved *Nandi* in the courtyard and an ancient well where villagers have drawn water for 800 years.

Around Warangal → *For listings, see pages 387-393. Colour map 2, B1.*

Pakhal, Ethurnagaram and Lakhnavaram
ⓘ *Warangal Bus Station to Narsampet. Regular bus service from Narsampet to Pakhal Lake or take a taxi.*

The great artificial lakes 40 km northeast of Warangal – from the south, Pakhal, Lakhnavaram, Ramappa and Ghanpur – were created as part of the Kakatiya rulers' water management and irrigation schemes in the 12th and 13th centuries and are still in use. The lakes are fringed with an emerging marsh vegetation and surrounded by extensive grasslands, tropical deciduous forests and evergreens. The park was set up in 1952 and has problems of the grazing of domestic livestock and illegal burning.

This is the richest area for wildlife in the state, with tiger, panther, hyena, wild dogs, wild boars, gaur, foxes, spotted deer, jackals, sloth bears and pythons. There are also otters and alligators and a variety of waterbirds and fish in the lakes. Pakhal Lake is especially important as an undisturbed site well within the sanctuary; Laknavaram Lake is 20 km to the north. They are superb for birdwatching (numerous migratory birds in winter) and occasional crocodile spottings. Tigers and panthers live deep in the forest but are rarely seen. Forest rangers might show you plaster casts of tiger pug marks.

Palampet → *Colour map 2, B2.*

Palampet lies close to the Ramappa Lake. The **Ramappa Temple**, dedicated to Siva as Rudreswara, was built in 1234 and is one of the finest medieval Deccan temples. The black basalt sculpture is excellent (even richer than that at the 1000-pillar temple) with famous Mandakini figures of female dancers which appear on brackets at the four entrances. The base of the temple has the typical bands of sculpture, the lowest of elephants, the second, a lotus scroll, the third which is the most interesting depicting figures opening a window on the life of the times and finally another floral scroll. There are more fine sculptures inside, some displaying a subtle sense of humour in common with some of the figures outside, and paintings of scenes from the epics on the ceiling. Note that no bottled water is available.

Some 150 km southeast of Hyderabad is one of India's richest Buddhist sites, now almost entirely under the lake created by the Nagarjunasagar Dam, completed in 1960. The remains of a highly cultured Buddhist civilization had remained almost undisturbed for 1600 years until their discovery by AR Saraswati in March 1926. The reconstructed buildings are on a comparatively small scale, in a peaceful setting on top of the hilltop fort, now an island planted with low trees.

Arriving in Nagarjunakonda → *Phone code: 08680.*
Buses from Hyderabad arrive at Vijayapuri, which is 7 km from the boat jetty for Nagarjunakonda. Boats leave for the island roughly every hour from 0930; prepare for a chaotic scrum to get on board. The last ferry leaves the island at 1600. Enquiries T08642-243457. Other ferries are reserved for APTDC tours, which can be organized locally or from Hyderabad. **AP State Tourist Office** ⓘ *Project House, Hill Colony, T08680-277364/276540*. A guide is available through this office; others can be arranged from the APTDC in Hyderabad.

Background
Rising from the middle of the artificial lake is the Nagarjuna Hill which was once nearly 200 m above the floor of the secluded valley in the northern ranges of the Nallamalais (black hills) which surround the lake on three sides. On the fourth side was the great river Krishna, superimposed on the hills as it flows towards the Bay of Bengal.

Early archaeological work showed the remnants of Buddhist monasteries, many limestone sculptures and other remains. The Archaeological Survey carried out a full excavation of the sites before they were covered by the rising waters of the lake. More than 100 distinct sites ranging from the prehistoric early Stone Age period to the late medieval were discovered. Some of the most important remains have been moved and reconstructed on the hilltop fort. These include nine monuments, rebuilt in their original form, and 14 large replicas of the ruins.

The Ikshvakus made Nagarjunakonda the centre of extraordinary artistic activity from the third century AD. In the mid-fourth century AD the Pallavas pushed north from Tamil Nadu and eclipsed the Ikshvaku Kingdom, reducing Nagarjunakonda to a deserted village. However, during the Chalukya period a Saiva centre was built at Yellaswaram, on the other bank of the Krishna. In the 15th and 16th centuries the hill became a fortress in the contest for supremacy between the Vijayanagar, Bahmani and Gajapati kings. After the fall of the Vijayanagar Empire both the hill and the valley below lost all importance.

Places in Nagarjunakonda
The Ikshvaku's capital was a planned city on the right bank of the Krishna – **Vijayapuri** (city of victory). The citadel had rampart walls on three sides with the river on the fourth. The buildings inside including houses, barracks, baths and wells were probably destroyed by a great fire. The nine **temples** show the earliest

developments of Brahmanical temple architecture in South India. The Vishnu temple (AD 278) had two beautifully carved pillars which were recovered from its site. Five temples were dedicated to Siva or Karttikeya. The river bank was dotted with Brahmanical shrines.

Nagarjunakonda excavations also revealed some of India's finest early sculptures and memorial pillars. Over 20 pillars were raised in the memory not just of rulers and nobles but also of artisans and religious leaders. The sculptures represent the final phase of artistic development begun at Amaravati in the second century BC.

The **hill fort** (early 14th-century) has remnants of the Vijayanagar culture though the present layout of the fort probably dates from as recently as 1565. The main entrance was from the northeast, near where the ferry now lands on the island. In places the walls are still over 6 m high, with regular bastions and six gateways. There are two temples in the east, where the museum now stands.

The **museum** ① *Sat-Thu 0900-1600*, has a collection of coins and ornaments, but most importantly sculptures (including a 3-m-high standing Buddha). There are also prehistoric and protohistoric remains and several panels and friezes depicting Buddhist scenes.

Srisailam Wildlife Sanctuary → *Colour map 2, C1. Altitude: 200-900 m.*
① *Information from AP Dept of Forests (see Useful contacts, page 393). Cars are not permitted in the reserve 2100-0600. Temperature: 12-42°C. Rainfall: 1500 mm. Best to visit Oct-Mar.*
The largest of the state's wildlife sanctuaries is at Srisailam, a popular pilgrimage town on the banks of the Krishna near Nagarjunasagar. The park is India's largest tiger reserve, covering 3560 sq km of the Nallamalai Hills in an area deeply incised by gorges, with deciduous and bamboo forest and semi-desert scrubland. Besides tigers, there are leopards, Indian pangolins, panthers, wild dogs, civets, hyenas, jackals, wolves, giant squirrels, crocodiles, lizards, pythons, vipers, kraits and over 150 species of bird. There is a nature trail signposted 1 km short of Srisailam, or you can walk the access road and explore from there; a guide is available. Unfortunately the sanctuary is frequently disturbed by Naxalite activity and can be very difficult to get permission to visit. Check the latest position with the Forest Officer.

Srisailam also attracts Shaivite pilgrims, who come for the 14th century **Mallikarjuna Temple**, containing one of India's 12 *jyotirlingas*. Some 300 m long, the outer face has often been attacked and damaged, but is richly decorated with carved scenes from the Hindu epics and a portrait of Krishna Deva Raya, the Vijayanagar Emperor who visited the site in 1514. Non-Hindus are allowed into the inner sanctuary to witness the daily *puja*. Arrive early to avoid queuing in the middle of the day; the first prayers are at 0545. The **Mahasivaratri festival** draws large crowds. The ancient **Mahakali Temple** on a hill in the Nallamalai forest contains a rare *lingam* attracting large crowds of pilgrims, especially during **Sivaratri**.

For hotel and restaurant price codes and other relevant information, see pages 13-17.

🛏 Where to stay

Secunderabad is closer to the interstate train station and business district, but Hyderabad is better placed for sightseeing. High demand from business travellers has meant soaring room rates at middle and top end. Power cuts are routine. Larger hotels have generators, but a/c, lifts and other electricity-dependent facilities in smaller hotels can fail.

Hyderabad *p372, maps p373 and p377*
$$$$ The Golkonda Hyderabad, Masab Tank, Mahavir Marg, T040-6611 0101, www.the golkondahyderabad.com. Completely renovated with minimalist decor and 5-star status, the **Golkonda** has 150 rooms, a/c, phone, TV, excellent showers. Breakfast included. Complimentary airport transfers.
$$$$ ITC Kakatiya, Begumpet, T040-2340 0132, www.itcwelcomegroup.in. 188 exquisitely furnished guest rooms and suites for business and leisure travellers. There's a 24-hr coffee shop and speciality Indian restaurants, and an unusual pool built around a natural rock.
$$$$ Taj Falaknuma, Engine Bowli, Falaknuma, T040-6629 8585, www.tajhotels.com. The most opulent palace ever built by the Hyderabadi Nizams has been restored to its original condition and now plays host to one of India's most extraordinary hotels. The pick of the 60 rooms are the Historical and Royal suites, fitted out with Edwardian antiques and Italian marble floors, with sweeping views over the city or carefully tended lawns. Public areas are similarly exquisite, with cavernous ballrooms and dining tables that stretch for miles, and the overall feeling is akin to being a private guest in a stately home.
$$$$ Taj Krishna, Road No 1, Banjara Hills, T040-6666 2323, www.tajhotels.com. The flagship luxury Taj hotel in the city's elite district has 2 restaurants (Indian, Chinese), 260 rooms, 24-hr gym, the city's best pool and nightclub, **Ahala**, beautiful gardens and immaculate service. The Presidential suite has its own private pool.
$$$ Minerva Grand Banjara, Road No 11, Banjara Hills, T040-6612 7373, www.minervagrand.com. A boutique hotel with 44 designer rooms and suites in the upmarket Banjara Hills, close to the main commercial, retail and entertainment centres. Breakfast included.
$$$-$$ Residency (Quality Inn), Public Garden Rd, T040-3061 6161, www.qualityinnresidency.com. Efficient business hotel, 95 a/c rooms, polite service, popular with Indians, good vegetarian restaurant and basement pub, **One Flight Down**.
$$ City Park, Chirag Ali Rd, T040-6610 5510, www.cityparkhyd.com. 54 bright prefab rooms with phone, en suite and writing tables, car park, internet, but stale a/c smell. Well placed just at the edge of Abid shopping district. Breakfast included. Rooftop multi-cuisine restaurant **Degh** has panoramic views over city.
$$ Taj Mahal, 4-1-999 Abid Rd, T040-2475 8250, www.hoteltajmahalindia.com. 20 good-sized simple a/c rooms in 1940s building. Busy South Indian vegetarian restaurant, meals, laundry, good value, friendly and the most characterful of the budget options. Recommended.

$ Imperial, corner of Nampally Station and Public Gardens roads (5 mins from Hyderabad station), T040-2320 2220. Large hotel with 48 clean rooms, some with bath, avoid roadside rooms, bucket hot water, helpful, excellent service. Not recommended for lone women travellers.

$ Sai Prakash, Nampally Station Rd, T040-2461 1726, www.hotelsaiprakash.com. Business hotel with 102 clean, comfortable a/c rooms and a good restaurant.

$ Saptagiri Deluxe, off Nampally Station Rd, T040-2461 0333. Peaceful hotel in interesting area with 36 scrupulously clean rooms. Choice of a/c and non-a/c. Western toilet, shower. Gets busy so book in advance.

$ Sri Brindavan, Nampally Station Rd, near the Circle, T040-2320 3970. 70 clean rooms in a custard-coloured compound set back from road. Mostly male guests; unsuitable for lone female travellers. Otherwise decent value, good restaurants, good budget choice.

Secunderabad *p372, map p373*
$$$$ Fortune Select Manohar, adjacent to old airport in Begumpet, T040-6654 3456, www.fortunehotels.in. A full-service business-class hotel with 132 well-appointed rooms and suites, club lounge overlooking pool, health club. Check for discounts.

$$$$ Hyderabad Marriot Hotel, Tank Bund Rd, T040-2752 2999, www.marriott.com. Plush business hotel with charming pool and spa, set on the shores of Hussain Sagar Lake. Rates fluctuate according to city conference schedule; it's worth phoning. Low categories exclude breakfast.

$$$ Green Park, Begumpet, T040-6651 5151, www.hotelgreenpark.com. A sedate and large Indian business and family hotel with 146 rooms. Rooms come with bath, a/c and TV. Free Wi-Fi.

$$$ Hotel Baseraa, 9-1, 167/168 SD Rd, T040-2770 3200, www.baseraa.com. 75 tatty but comfortable a/c rooms in busy friendly, family hotel with great service and good restaurants.

$$$-$$ Yatri Nivas, SP Rd, T040-2346 1855. Clean, airy, well kept, 32 rooms, mostly a/c, 3 restaurants, bar.

$$-$ Dwaraka Heritage, Chenoy Trade Centre, Parklane, SD Road, T040-2789 5111. In the heart of the business district with 40 clean and comfortable rooms.

$$-$ Taj Mahal, 88 SD Rd, T040-2781 2171. Characterful 40-year-old building with 20 faded but good rooms (a/c suite, a/c double, non-a/c double and non-a/c single). Popular South Indian vegetarian restaurant.

$ Retiring Rooms, at railway station.

$ YMCA, SD Rd, T040-2780 5408. This place has 15 rooms (mostly singles, but big enough to take an extra bed), shared bath, clean, roomy, friendly, 'treated as family', Extra charge for temporary membership.

Warangal *p383*
Though it is possible to visit Warangal in a long day from Hyderabad, it's worth staying a night to soak in the old-world atmosphere.

$$ Ashoka, Hanamkonda, near Chowrashta city bus station, T0870-6692220. One of the oldest hotels in the city, with spacious but poorly maintained rooms. Safe for women travellers.

$$ Suprabha, Nakkalagutta, Hanamkonda, T0870-2573888. New hotel near railway station, 52 clean airy rooms (a/c and non a/c), excellent service, internet, breakfast included.

Nagarjunakonda *p385*

$$ Vijay Vihar (APTDC), Nagarjuna Sagar, T08680-277362. The most luxurious and picturesque accommodation, with lake-facing rooms and suites (all a/c), bar and restaurant.

$$-$ Nagarjuna Resort, near the jetty, T08642-242471. Clean comfortable rooms (a/c and non a/c) and garden, but no views.

Srisailam Wildlife Sanctuary *p386*

At the time of writing, the Forest Rest Houses in Srisailam Sanctuary were not accepting bookings. Most accommodation in town is managed by the Temple Management Committee, T08524-288883.

$$ Haritha Hotel (APTDC), 1 km south of Mallikarjuna Temple, T08524-288311. Clean a/c and non a/c rooms, garden, veg restaurant.

$ Ganga Sadan, 1 km south of temple, T08524-288888. Clean spacious rooms and excellent view. Recommended.

🍴 Restaurants

Hyderabad *p372, maps p373 and p377*

To foodies, the city is synonymous with one dish: the Hyderabadi biryani. Succulent mounds of rice, piled high with meat and spices and served with emergency bowls of yoghurt to counter the blistering heat, emerge from the kitchens of grubby and basic cafés along Pathergatti Rd, in the old city near the Char Minar. **Hotel Shaadab** is one of the most famous purveyors. While you're in the area, sample another Hyderabad institution – a cup of extra-sweet and extra-milky Irani chai.

If your tastes run more to the familiar, you'll find many international fast food chains are in the city, as well as the pure

vegetarian chain **Kamat**. The shopping malls **Lifestyle** and **Hyderabad Central** have good food courts.

$$$ Taste of Darkness, Inorbit Mall, Hitech City, T040-6460 3341. A unique concept that's part restaurant, part social commentary. Blind waiters lead you through the pitch black dining room, and you 'see' your meal – a simple curry-rice-roti set menu of 1-4 courses – through the eyes of a blind person. A fascinating insight, that only heightens your senses of smell and taste.

$$$ The Water Front, Eat St, Necklace Rd, T040-2330 8899. Lunch and dinner. When Hyderabadis need to impress, they go to this open-air restaurant right on Hussain Sagar Lake. The food is coastal Indian and Asian, the bill hefty, the atmosphere stylish and romantic.

$$$-$$ Firdaus, Taj Krishna hotel (see Where to stay), T040-6666 2323. Excellent Mughlai cuisine and one of the only places in the city where you can get the special Hyderabadi treat, *haleem*. Meaning 'patience', this meat, wholewheat and gram dish is slow-cooked and is traditionally made to break the Ramadan fast.

$$ Hyderabad House, opposite JNTU College, Masab Tank, T040-2332 7861; also opposite Mosque Rd, No 3, Banjara Hills, T040-2355 4747. Very good biryanis and *lukhmis*. Parcel service available.

$$ Southern Spice, 8-2-350/3/2, Road No 3, Banjara Hills, T040-2335 3802. Breakfast, lunch and dinner. Good Andhra, Chettinad, tandoori and Chinese cuisine.

$$-$ Paradise Food Court, 38 Sarojini Devi Rd/MG Rd. T040-6631 3721. Open 1100-2400. Utterly synonymous with biryani, and such an institution that the surrounding area is now named 'Paradise'. You can get parcels from downstairs, eat standing up at the fast food section, or go upmarket at **Persis Gold**.

🍸 Bars and clubs

Hyderabad-Secunderabad *p372, maps p373 and p377*
Mostly in the top-end hotels; night life doesn't compare to Bengaluru. **Kismet**, at the Park hotel, is the most modish; **One Flight Down**, opposite Hyderabad Railway Station, Public Garden Rd (1100-2300) is a modern, British-style pub, snooker tables and TV. Dark but popular.

🎭 Entertainment

Hyderabad-Secunderabad *p372, maps p373 and p377*
Cinema
Some cinemas show English-language films.
Lalit Kala Thoranam, Public Gardens. Hosts art exhibitions and free film shows daily.
Ravindra Bharati, Public Garden Rd, Saifabad, T040-2323 1245. Regularly stages dance, theatre and music programmes, a/c.

Sound and light show
Golconda fort (page 379). Spectacularly voiced over by Bollywood legend Amitabh Bhachan.

🛍 Shopping

Hyderabad-Secunderabad *p372, maps p373 and p377*
Most shops open 1000-1900. Some close on Fri. Every other shop sells pearls; look for shape, smoothness and shine to determine quality. Size is the last criteria in deciding a pearl's price. Bargain for at least 10% off asking prices. Also look out

for *bidri* ware, crochetwork, Kalamkari paintings, *himroo* and silk saris. **Lad Bazar**, around the Char Minar, is great for bangles. For more on Andhra Pradesh's craft tradition, see page 369.

Antiques
Govind Mukandas, Bank St.
Humayana, Taj Banjara hotel.

Books
Akshara, 8-2-273 Pavani Estates, Road No 2, Banjara Hills, T040-2354 3906. Excellent collection on all aspects of India in English.
Haziq and Mohi, Lal Chowk. Good antiquarian bookshop, especially for Arabic and Persian.

Handicrafts
Government emporia include: **Nirmal Industries**, Raj Bhavan Rd; **Lepakshi**, and **Coircraft**, Mayur Complex, Gun Foundry; and **Co-optex**. There are several others in Abids. Non-government shops may charge a bit more but may have more attractive items.
Bidri Crafts, Abids.
Fancy Cloth Store, 21-2-28 Pathergatti, Hyderabad, T040-2452 3983. For silk. Exports cloth to Selfridges in the UK.
Khadi, Sultan Bazar and Municipal Complex, Rashtrapati Rd, Secunderabad.
Kalanjali, Hill Fort Rd, opposite Public Gardens. Large selection of regional crafts.
In Secunderabad try: **Baba Handicrafts**, MG Rd; and **Jewelbox**, SD Rd.

Pearls
Mangatrai Pearl and Jewellers, 6-3-883 Punjagutta, T040-2341 1816, www.manga trai.com. For quality pearls. Jewellers to Indian nobility, with everything from Basra pearls to black Tahitian pearls.

☼ What to do

Hyderabad-Secunderabad *p372, maps p373 and p377*
Swimming
BV Gurumoorthy Pool, Sardar Patel Rd.

Tour operators
APTDC, T040-2326 2151, offers the following tours: **City sightseeing**: full day, 0915-1745, from offices at Yatri Nivas and Secretariat Rd, Rs 500; unsatisfactory as it allows only 1 hr at the fort and includes unimportant sights. **Night tour**: including Golconda sound and light show, Qutb Shahi tombs, boat ride and dinner 1700-2200, Rs 500.
Nagarjunasagar: Sat and Sun only to Dam, Nagarjunakonda Museum, Right Canal and Ethipothala Falls, 0730-2200, Rs 500. **Ramoji Film City**: 0745-1800, Rs 1020 (entry fee included). Allows 4-5 hrs at the studios, plus Sanghi Temple and shopping time.
Sita, 3-5-874, Sita House, Hyderguda, T040-4009 4444.
TCI, 102 Regency House, Greenland Rd, Somajiguda, T040-2340 2722.
Thomas Cook, 5-9-100, Doyen Trade House, Public Garden Rd, T(0)9849-258491; also at Cyber Tower, Madhapur, T040-6666 1100.

Nagarjunakonda *p385*
Tour operators
APTDC, runs a day trip from Hyderabad; tiring (with 4 hrs on a coach each way) but convenient and cheap. 0645-2145, Rs 500 (transport only). Nagarjunasagar is the village beside the dam from which boats ferry visitors to the temples and museum on the island (at 0800, 1200, 1500, trip takes 1 hr). If you take the 2nd boat you still have time to visit the sights and return on the next boat. You can leave your luggage for a few hours at this pier provided someone is on duty.

☼ Transport

Hyderabad-Secunderabad *p372, maps p373 and p377*
Air
Rajiv Gandhi International Airport is 25 km south of the city, T040-6676 4000, www.hyderabad.aero. Transport to town: pre-paid taxis cost Rs 450-500; there are no auto-rickshaws. A/c **Pushpak buses**, T1800 200 4599, www.apsrtc.gov. in, run on fixed routes to various parts of the city, including Secunderabad (Rs 250) and Hi-Tech City (Rs 200).

Daily domestic flights to **Ahmedabad, Bengaluru, Chennai, Coimbatore, Delhi, Goa, Jaipur, Kochi, Kolkata, Kozhikode, Mumbai, Pune, Tirupati, Vijayawada, Visakhapatnam**.

International connections with: **Abu Dhabi, Bangkok, Doha, Dubai, Frankfurt, Hong Kong, Kuala Lumpur, London, Muscat, Sharjah** and **Singapore**.

Bicycle
Hire is readily available (ask for the 'bicycle taxi' shop near Nampally Railway station), Rs 50 per day, but may ask for a large deposit. Good for visiting Golconda, but the city is only for cyclists who are experienced with heavy, fast-flowing traffic.

Bus
Local City buses are crowded in rush hour. Useful routes: No 119 (Nampally to Golconda); 87 (Nampally to Char Minar); 2/2V (Charminar to Secunderabad Station).
Long distance The vast **Imlibun Bus Station**, T040-2461 4406, (also **APSRTC**, T040-2343 4269, www.apsrtc. gov.in), has long-distance state-run

buses to all destinations in Telangana/ Andhra Pradesh and neighbouring states. Advance reservations available. Private deluxe coaches depart from opposite Hyderabad Railway Station to **Aurangabad**, **Bengaluru** (**Bangalore**), **Mumbai**, **Chennai** and **Tirupati**; reservations from **Royal Lodge**, at the entrance to the station.

Secunderabad has the **Jubilee Bus Station**, T040-2780 2203, with services to major destinations. From Nampally: buses to **Golconda**. **Venus Travel**, opposite Residency Hotel, runs a bus to **Gulbarga**, 0730, 5 hrs.

Car

Tourist taxis and luxury cars from **AP Tourism**, Tank Bund Rd, T040-2345 3036, **Ashok Travels**, ground floor, Mukhram Jha Rd T040-2326 1360. **Travel Express**, 58 Nagarjuna Hills, Punjagutta, T040-2335 8855. Rs 1500 per 8 hrs or 80 km, Rs 900 per 4 hrs.

Rickshaw and taxis

Auto-rickshaws charge Rs 20 for the first kilometre, Rs 11 per kilometre thereafter; will use meter after mild insistence. Cycle rickshaws are cheaper. Local taxis charge Rs 40 for the first 2 km, then Rs 21 per kilometre; reliable radio taxi companies include **Easy Cabs**, T040-4343 4343, and **Meru Cabs**, T040-4422 4422.

Train

Trains listed below arrive and depart at 2 main stations: **Hyderabad** (**H**), also known as Nampally; **Secunderabad** (**S**); and Kacheguda (**K**). South-Central Enquiries: T139. Reservations: T134. Online reservations at www.irctc.co.in. Buses 20V and 49 link the 2 stations, Rs 10.

Trains to: **Aurangabad**: *Devagiri Exp 17058*, 1330, 9½ hrs. **Bengaluru** (Bangalore): *Bangalore Exp 12785*, 1905, 11½ hrs (K); *Rajdhani Exp 12430*, 1910 (Tue, Wed, Thu, Sun) (S), 12 hrs. **Chennai** (MC): *Charminar Exp 12760* (AC/II), 1830 (H), 1930 (S), 14½ hrs; *Hyderabad Chennai Exp 12604*, 1655 (S), 14½ hrs. **Delhi** (HN): *Rajdhani Exp 12429*, 0750 (Mon, Tue, Thu, Fri) (S), 22½ hrs. **Delhi** (ND): *New Delhi AP Exp 12723*, 0625 (H), 0700 (S), 26 hrs. All Delhi trains go via Nagpur and Bhopal. **Guntakal**: (for Hospet and Hampi), *KCG-YPR Exp 17603*, 2100, 6½ hrs (K). **Kolkata** (Howrah): *E Coast Exp 18646*, 1000, 32½ hrs (H). **Mumbai** (CST): *Hyderabad-Mumbai Exp 17032*, 2040, 17 hrs; *Hussainsagar Exp 12702*, 1445 (H), 15¾ hrs; *Konark Exp 11020*, 1145 (S), 17½ hrs. **Tirupati**: *Krishna Exp 17406*, 0600 (S), *Venkatadri Exp 12797*, 2005, 11½ hrs (K); *Narayanadri Exp 12734*, 1805 (S), 13½ hrs.

Warangal *p383*

Bus Frequent buses to **Hyderabad** (3½ hrs) and **Vijayawada** (7 hrs).

Train Many Express trains stop here. **Chennai** (MC): *Tamil Nadu Exp 12622*, 2101, 10 hrs. **Delhi** (ND): *Tamil Nadu Exp 12621*, 0724, 24 hrs; **Nagpur**: Several daily 7½-8½ hrs. **Secunderabad**: *Konark Exp 11020*, 0735, 3½ hrs; *Golconda Exp 17201*, 1012, 3½ hrs; *Krishna Exp 17405*, 1704, 3½ hrs. **Vijayawada**: *Secunderabad-Guntur Exp 12706*, 1000, 3½ hrs.

Nagarjunakonda *p385*

Buses from Hyderabad to Macherla stop at Nagarjuna Sagar (4 hrs), and buses also go to Vijayawada. It's easier, if rushed, to visit on an APTDC day tour (see What to do).

Srisailam Wildlife Sanctuary *p386*
Srisailam can be reached from Kurnool,
170 km away on the Hyderabad–
Bengaluru highway and railway line.
From Hyderabad it's a 200-km drive
across the wide open Telangana Plateau;
buses take about 6 hrs. The nearest train
station is Macherla (13 km).

● Directory

Hyderabad-Secunderabad *p372,
maps p373 and p377*
Banks Mon-Fri 1000-1400, Sat 1000-
1200. In Hyderabad, several banks with
ATMs on Bank St, Mahipatram Rd and
Mukaramjahi Market; in Secunderabad
look on Rashtrapati Rd. **Amex**, Samrat
Complex, 5-9-12, Saifabad, T040-2323
4591. **Thomas Cook**, Nasir Arcade,
6-1-57, Saifabad, T040-259 6521. **Travel
Club Forex**, next door, carries Western
Union transfers. **Cultural centres
and libraries** Alliance Française,
near Planetrium, Naubat Pahad, T040-
2770 0731. **British Library**, Secretariat
Rd, T040-2323 0774, Tue-Sat 1100-1900.
Goethe Centre, Hill Fort Rd, T040-2324
1791. **Bharatiya Vidya Bhavan**, King
Kothi Rd, T040-223 7825. **Medical
services** Outpatients usually from
0900-1400. Casualty 24 hrs. **General
Hospital** in Nampally, T040-223 4344.
Newcity (Secunderabad), T040-2780
5961. **Post** In Hyderabad: **GPO** (with
Poste Restante) and **CTO**, Abids. In
Secunderabad: **Head PO** in RP Rd and
CTO on MG Rd. **Useful contacts
AP Dept of Forests**, ARANYA BHAVAN,
SAIFABAD, T040-2323 1686. Excellent
advice, may help with arrangements
to visit wildlife reserves. The Chief
Conservator of Forests T(0)9440-810001
is very helpful. **Foreigners' Regional
Registration Office**: Commissioner of
Police, Purani Haveli, Hyderabad, T040-
2452 1041, www.hyderabadpolice.gov.in.

Krishna-Godavari Delta

The rice-growing delta of the Krishna and Godavari rivers is one of Andhra Pradesh's most prosperous and densely populated regions, and the core region of Andhra culture. The flat coastal plains are fringed with palmyra palms and occasional coconut palms, rice and tobacco. Inland, barely 40% of the land is cultivated. About 120 km to the west of the road south to Chennai run the Vellikonda Ranges, only visible in very clear weather. To the north the ranges of the Eastern Ghats can often be clearly seen.

Vijayawada → *Colour map 2, C2. Phone code: 0866. Population: 1,048,000.*
At the head of the Krishna delta, 70 km from the sea, the city of Vijayawada has been in existence for over 2000 years, and derives its name from the goddess Kanakdurga or Vijaya, the presiding deity of the city; there is an important temple to her on a hill beside the river. The city is surrounded by bare granite hills, which radiate heat during the searing summer: temperatures of over 45°C are not uncommon in April and May, though in winter they drop to a positively fresh 20°C. The Qutb Shahi rulers made Vijayawada an important inland port. It is still a major commercial town and has capitalized on its position as the link between the interior and the main north–south route between Chennai and Kolkata. It is also the operational centre of the Krishna delta canal scheme, one of the earliest major irrigation developments in South India (completed in 1855), which irrigates nearly one million hectares of land, banishing famine from the delta and converting it into one of the richest granaries in the country. The **Prakasam Barrage**, over 1 km long, carries the road and railway lines across the water.

There are several sites with caves and temples with inscriptions from the first century AD. The **Kanakdurga Temple**, on a hill to the east of town, is the most atmospheric of the temples. **Mogalarajapuram Temple** has an Ardhanarisvara statue which is thought to be the earliest in South India. There are two 1000-year-old Jain temples and the **Hazratbal Mosque**, which has a relic of the Prophet Mohammed. **Victoria Jubilee Museum** ① *MG Rd, Sat-Thu 1030-1700, free, camera Rs 5*, has sculpture and paintings.

AP Tourist Office ① *MG Rd, T0886-2157 1539, 0600-2000*, also has counters at the bus stand on Machilipatnam Road, and the train station.

Amaravati

Located 30 km west of Vijaywada, Amaravati was the capital of the medieval Reddi kings of Andhra, but some 1500 years before they wielded power Amaravati was a great Mahayana Buddhist centre (see page 550). Initially built in the third and second centuries BC, the shrine was dedicated to the Hinayana sect, but under

Nagarjuna was changed into a Mahayana sanctuary where the Buddha was revered as Amareswara. Very little remains *in situ*, most of the magnificent sculpted friezes, medallions and railings having been removed to museums in Chennai, Kolkata and London's British Museum. The onsite **Archaeological Museum** ⓘ *Sat-Thu 0900-1700, free, buses via Guntur or by ferry from Krishneveni Hotel*, contains some exquisitely carved sculptures of the Bodhi Tree alongside a collection of broken panels, *chakras* and caskets holding relics.

Guntur → *Colour map 6, C2.*

From Vijayawada the NH5 southwest crosses the barrage (giving magnificent views over the Krishna at sunset) to Guntur, a major town dealing in rice, cotton and tobacco where the ancient charnockite rocks of the peninsula meet the alluvium of the coastal plain. In the 18th century it was capital of the region Northern Circars and was under Muslim rule from 1766 under the Nizam of Hyderabad. The Archaeological Museum in Amaravati exhibits local finds including fourth-century Buddhist stone sculptures. Some 40 km to the south, the unspoiled golden sands of **Suryalanka Beach** see very little tourist traffic; there is a newly built AP Tourism resort right on the beach.

Machilipatnam and around

The once-flourishing sea port of Machilipatnam ('fish town'), 60 km southeast of Vijayawada, derived its name from the old city gateways, one of which still stands, decorated with painted fish eyes. A one-time port of the kingdom of Golconda, it was one of the earliest British settlements in India, existent as early as 1611. It is also well known for its Kalamkari painting (see page 370) widely prevalent in the neighbouring village of Pedana, the art having been fostered by the Qutub Shahis. The beach at Manginapudi, 10 km from Machilipatnam, has black clay sand. This area is battered by frequent cyclones; one in 1864 is said to have taken 30,000 lives.

Rajahmundry and the Konaseema Backwaters → *Colour map 2, C3.*
Phone code: 0883.

Set on the banks of the Godavari, Rajahmundry was the scene of a bitter 300-year tug-of-war between the Chalukya, Vengi and Orissan kingdoms and the Deccan Muslims, until the French annexed the city in 1753. It is remembered for the poet Nannayya who wrote the first Telugu classic *Andhra Mahabharathamu*, and is also noted for its carpets and sandalwood products. Every 12 years the **Pushkaram** celebration (next in 2015) draws thousands of pilgrims to the river banks.

Rajahmundry makes a convenient base from which to visit both the Eastern Ghats and the coastal districts. Some 80 km northwest of the town, the Godavari cuts through a gorge in the Papi hills, creating a succession of stunningly beautiful lakes, reminiscent of Scottish lochs, where you can take boat trips. Another appealing side trip is to the **Konaseema Delta**, 70 km south of Rajahmundry, a verdant cocktail of coconut groves, mango orchards and paddy fields encircled by the waters of the Godavari and the Bay of Bengal. AP Tourism operates **houseboat trips** on the Godavari, and a 24-hour trip from Dindi (departs 1000 from the Coconut

County resort, bookings T08862-227993, T(0)9848-780524), sailing up past quaint little villages and islands, offers the kind of peace and solitude that have long been missing from the Kerala backwaters. Houseboats have two well-furnished air-conditioned bedrooms; meals and drinks are served on board.

◉ Krishna-Godavari Delta listings

For hotel and restaurant price codes and other relevant information, see pages 13-17.

◉ Where to stay

Vijayawada *p394*
There are some **$** hotels on MG Rd near the bus stand and around the railway station.
$$$ Fortune Murali Park, MG Rd, Labbipet, T0866-398 8008. The smartest rooms in town by a long chalk, plus a host of extra services including babysitting.
$$$-$ Ilapuram, Besant Rd, T0866-257 1282. 81 large clean rooms, some a/c, restaurants.
$$-$ Berm Park (AP Tourism), on the banks of Krishna river T0866-241 8057. 30 clean rooms (most a/c), restaurant, tourist office, car hire, boat trips to nearby Bhavani Island.
$$-$ Santhi, Near Apsara Theatre Governorpet, T0866-257 7355. Clean rooms with bath (hot water), good vegetarian restaurant.
$ Kandhari International, MG Rd, Labbipet, T0866-249 7797. Some a/c in the 73 rooms, some a/c, also restaurants with a/c.
$ Mamata, Eluru Rd, 1 km from centre, T0866-257 1251. Standard Indian cheapie, with reasonably well-kept rooms (most a/c with bath), good restaurants and friendly staff.
$ Railway Retiring Rooms. Large and well-maintained rooms, an excellent budget option.

Guntur *p395*
$$ Haritha Beach Resort, Suryalanka, Bapatla Mandal, Guntur, T08643-224616. 13 beach-facing a/c cottages, garden, multi-cuisine restaurant.
$$ Vijayakrishna International, Collectorate Rd, Nagarampalem, T0863-222 2221. The best place in town and often frequented by Telugu cinestars, several of whom hail from Guntur. 42 good rooms, some a/c, and a popular restaurant.
$ Annapurna Lodge, opposite APSRTC Bus Stand, T0866-222 2979. A/c and non-a/c rooms, quality meals, helpful and obliging.
$ Sudarsan, Kothapet, Main Rd, T0863-222 2681. 28 rooms, some a/c, good vegetarian restaurant.

Machilipatnam and around *p395*
$ Swarnandhra Resort, Manginapudi Beach, T08672-242070. Sea-facing cottages (a/c and non a/c) set in landscaped gardens, food available.

Rajahmundry *p395*
$$$ Anand Regency, 26-3-7, Jampet, T0883-246 1201, www.hotelanand regency.co.in. Business hotel but with great ambience, good service, 3 restaurants, arranges sightseeing and boating trips.
$$$ River Bay Hotel, Near Gowthami Ghat, T0883-244 7000, www.riverbay.co.in. Decent rooms with excellent river views, complimentary breakfast.

$$ Coconut Country Resort, Dindi (starting point of houseboat cruise), T08862-227991. 32 well-furnished a/c rooms overlooking the river, swimming pool, garden.

$ Dwaraka Hotel, Kandakam Rd, Fort Gate, T(0)9848-484349. Budget hotel in city centre, decent rooms, good service.

🍴 Restaurants

Vijayawada *p394*
The restaurants in the **Kandhari** and **Mamata** hotel are recommended.
$ Aromas, DV Manor Hotel, MG Rd. Slick hotel restaurant offering good Punjabi curries.
$ Greenlands, Bhavani Gardens, Labbipet. Food served in 7 huts on the garden lawns.

⭕ Shopping

Vijayawada *p394*
Some shops close 1300-1600. Local Kondapalli toys and Machilipatnam Kalamkari paintings are popular.

The emporia are in MG Rd, Eluru Rd, and Governorpet. Recommended are: **Apco**, Besant Rd; **Ashok**, opposite Maris Stella College, T0866-247 6966; **Handicrafts Shop**, Krishnaveni Motel; **Lepakshi**, Gandhi Nagar.

🕐 What to do

Vijayawada *p394*
KL Rao Vihara Kendram, Bhavani Island on Prakasham Barrage Lake. Offers rowing, canoeing, water scooters, pedal boats.

Rajahmundry *p395*
Maruthi Mini Travels, T0883-242 4577. Booking agent for Konaseema backwater cruises, and also conducts daily boat trips to Papi Hills from Rajahmundry, 0630-2100, Rs 500 per person.

🚌 Transport

Vijayawada *p394*
Bus
Good local network in city but buses get very crowded. Long-distance buses to destinations in AP and neighbouring states including **Chennai** (9 hrs) operate from the **New Bus Stand** on MG Rd near the river; enquiries T0866-247 3333.

Car hire
From **AP Tourist Office**, see page 394.

Ferry
To **Bhavani Islands**, 0930-1730. Also services between Krishnaveni Hotel and **Amaravati**. Daily 0800. Rs 50 return. Book at hotel or at bus station.

Rickshaw and taxi
Very few metered yellow-top taxis. *Tongas*, auto- and cycle-rickshaws are available.

Train
Vijayawada is an important junction, with trains to **Chennai** (MC): *Pinakini Exp 12711*, 0600, 7 hrs; *Coromandel Exp 12841* (AC/II), 1045, 6¾ hrs. **Delhi** (HN): *GT Exp 12615*, 0205, 30 hrs; *Link Daksin Exp 12861*, 2130, 31 hrs. **Hyderabad**: *Godavari Exp 12727*, 2355, 7 hrs. **Hospet**: *Amaravati Exp 18047*, 1855, 13 hrs. **Kolkata** (H): *Coromandel Exp 12842* (AC/II), 1525, 22 hrs, via Bhubaneswar, 11½ hrs. **Secunderabad**: *Satavahana Exp 12713*, 0610, 5½ hrs; *Krishna Exp 17405*, 1330, 7 hrs.

Guntur *p395*
Bus
The **APSRTC Bus Stand** is well organized and clean. Buses every 30 mins to **Vijayawada** (0600-2300) and **Bapatla** (0600-2000), from where shared auto-rickshaws can get you to **Surylanka**.

Train
Kolkata: *Falaknuma Exp 12704*, 2035, 21 hrs. **Chennai**: *Hyderabad Chennai Exp 17054*, 2200, 8 hrs. **Hospet**: *Amravati Exp 12604*, 2225, 12 hrs. **Secunderabad**: *Palnadu Exp 12747*, 0545, 5 hrs; *Golconda Exp 17201*, 0530, 8 hrs.

Rajahmundry *p395*
Trains to **Kolkata** (H): *Coromandel Exp 12842* (AC/II),1830, 19½ hrs. **Vijayawada**: *Coromandel Exp 12841*, 0733, 2¾ hrs; *Chennai Mail 12839*, 1730, 3½ hrs; *Ratnachal Exp12717*, 1530, 3 hrs. **Visakhapatnam**: *Coromandel Exp 12842*, 1830, 3¾ hrs; *Chennai Howrah Mail 12840*, 0909, 4 hrs; *Ratnachal Exp 12718*, 0829, 3½ hrs.

❶ Directory

Vijayawada *p394*
Banks State Bank of India, Babu Rajendra Prasad Rd. ATMs at the bus stand and on Atchutaramaiah St.
Post Kaleswara Rao Rd.

Northeastern Andhra Pradesh

From Rajahmundry the NH5 travels north over the narrowing coastal plain, the beautiful hills of the Eastern Ghats rising sharply inland. The pattern of life here contrasts sharply with that further south. Higher rainfall and a longer wet season, alongside the greater fertility of the alluvial soils, contribute to an air of prosperity; they also mean you should check weather forecasts before setting out on a journey. Village houses, with their thatched roofed cottages and white painted walls, are quite different and distinctive, as are the bullock carts.

Background

The area was brought under Muslim rule by the Golconda kings of the Bahmani Dynasty in 1575 and ceded to the French in 1753. In 1765 the Mughal emperor granted the whole area to the East India Company, its first major territorial acquisition in India. The region is also the most urbanized part of Andhra Pradesh, with a dozen towns of more than 100,000 people. Most are commercial and administrative centres with neither the functions nor the appearance of industrial cities, but they serve as important regional centres for trade, especially in agricultural commodities, and they are the homes of some of Andhra's wealthiest and most powerful families.

Although the building of dams on both the Krishna and the Godavari rivers has eliminated the catastrophic flooding common until the mid-19th century, the totally flat delta, lying virtually at sea level, is still prone to cyclones; in 1864 one claimed over 34,000 lives. The area was completely engulfed by a tidal wave in 1883 when the volcano of Mount Krakatoa blew up 5000 km away, and further catastrophic cyclones in 1977 and 1996, not to mention the 2004 tsunami, caused massive damage and loss of life. You may notice the increasing number of small concrete buildings on raised platforms along the roadside designed to provide temporary shelter to villagers during cyclones.

Visakhapatnam → For listings, see pages 401-403. Colour map 2, B4.

Set in a bay with rocky promontories, Visakhapatnam (Vizag) commands a spectacular position between the thickly wooded Eastern Ghats and the sea. It has become one of the country's most rapidly growing cities. Already India's fourth largest port, it has developed ship building, oil refining, fertilizer, petrochemical, sugar refinery and jute industries, as well as one of India's newest and largest steel mills. This is also the Navy's Eastern Fleet's home base. On the Dolphin's Nose, a cliff rising 174 m from the sea, is a lighthouse whose beam can be seen 64 km out to sea.

Its twin town of **Waltair** to the north used to be thought of as a health resort with fine beaches, though increasing atmospheric pollution is a problem. **Ramakrishna**

Beach, along the 8 km Lawson's Bay and below the 300 m Mount Kailasa, 6 km away, is best. Don't swim at the harbour end of the beach.

Arriving in Visakhapatnam → *Phone code: 0891. Population: 1,730,320.*
AP Tourism ① *RTC Complex, T0891-278 8820, 1000-1700, closed Sun and 2nd Sat of the month.* Also at the railway station, T0891-278 8821.

Places in Visakhapatnam
Andhra University was founded in 1926 in the Uplands area of Waltair. The red stone buildings are built like a fortress and sit on a large campus. The country's major **Ship Building Yard** at Gandhigram makes all types of ocean-going vessels: passenger liners, cargo vessels as well as naval ships. The **zoo** to the northeast is

Visakhapatnam

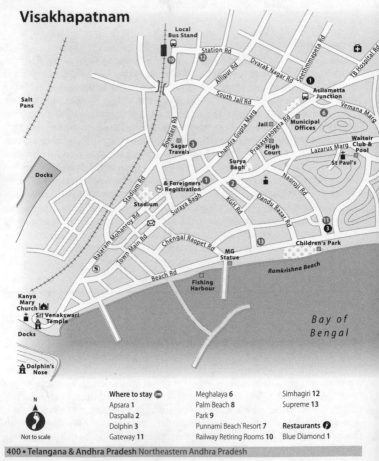

N

Not to scale

Where to stay		
Apsara **1**	Meghalaya **6**	Simhagiri **12**
Daspalla **2**	Palm Beach **8**	Supreme **13**
Dolphin **3**	Park **9**	
Gateway **11**	Punnami Beach Resort **7**	**Restaurants**
	Railway Retiring Rooms **10**	Blue Diamond **1**

large and attempts to avoid cages, keeping its animals in enclosures which are close to their natural habitat.

The **Venkateswara Temple** on the Venkateswa Konda was built in 1866 by the European Captain Blackmoor. The Muslims have a **mausoleum** of the saint Baba Ishaq Madina on the Darga Konda, while the highest Ross Hill has a **Roman Catholic Church**. A Buddhist relic was discovered at Dhanipura nearby.

Simhachalam, 16 km northwest, is noted for its 13th-century Varaha Narasimha Temple, set in the Kailasa Hills, which has some well-known hot springs.

Araku Valley

The Araku Valley, nestling amid the Anantagiri Hills 110 km inland from Vishakhapatnam, lies at the end of one of India's most scenic train rides. The four-

hour journey through dense forests is liberally spiced with waterfalls, lush green paddy fields, views of distant blue hills and no less than 48 tunnels, the longest measuring 1.2 km. The valley itself is home to over 17 tribal groups, and in April plays host to the fascinating but strictly non-vegetarian **Itika Pongal**, a hunting festival. The **Tribal Museum** ⓘ *near AP Tourism's Mayuri Resort, 000-1700, Rs 15,* has a small but worthwhile collection of artefacts and exhibits related to tribal life. If you return to Visakhapatnam by road you can stop off at the million-year-old **Borra Caves** and coffee plantations in Ananthagiri; **AP Tourism** runs this trip as a one- or two-day tour.

ⓦ Northeastern Andhra Pradesh listings

For hotel and restaurant price codes and other relevant information, see pages 13-17.

🛏 Where to stay

Visakhapatnam *p399, map p400*
Late night arrivals are quoted high prices by auto-rickshaws to go to the beach. Stay overnight at a simple hotel near the bus station (walk right from railway station) and move next morning.

Delight **2**
Infinity **3**
Jaya G Spuds **4**

$$$ Gateway Hotel, Beach Rd (2 km from centre), T0891-662 3670, www. thegateway hotels.com. 93 narrow sea-facing rooms, restaurant (pricey but generous), best in town, access to an unremarkable public beach across road.
$$$ Park, Beach Rd, T0891-275 4488, www.theparkhotels.com. 64 rooms, pricey suites, spa with gym, clean pool, well-kept gardens, slick management, best for direct beach access (beware of rocks when swimming), popular with German and Czech expats.
$$$-$$ Dolphin, Daba Gardens, T0891-256 7000, www.dolphinhotelsvizag.com. Family-run hotel with 147 rooms, popular restaurants, rooftop has good views, live band, health club, exchange and pool. Excellent service. Highly recommended but reserve ahead.
$$ Punnami Beach Resort (AP Tourism), Bhimili Beach Rd, Rushikonda Beach (15 km north), T0891-2788826. Great location, superb sea view, but poor maintenance. Ask for rooms in the new block.
$$ Supreme, Beach Rd near Coastal Battery, T0891-278 2472 www.hotel supremevizag.com. 54 sea-view rooms (a/c and non a/c) with running hot and cold water, TV, multi-cuisine restaurant. Great location, friendly staff. Good value.
$$-$ Palm Beach, Beach Rd (next to **Park** hotel), Waltair, T0891-255 4026, www. hotelpalmbeachvizag.com. Pleasant hotel set in a shady palm grove. 55 rooms, 30 a/c, restaurant, beer garden, pool.
$ Apsara, 12-1-17 Waltair Main Rd, T0891-276 4861. Central a/c, 130 rooms, restaurants, bar, exchange, very helpful and friendly staff.
$ Daspalla, Surya Bagh, T0891-256 4825. 102 rooms, **$$** suites, central a/c, 2 good restaurants (continental and *thalis*), exchange bar, set back from road, no late-night check-in.

$ Meghalaya, Asilametta Junction (5-min walk from bus, short rickshaw ride from station), T0891-255 5141. Popular with Indian tourists, good value, dull vegetarian restaurant (non-veg available from room service), pleasant roof garden, friendly and helpful.
$ Railway Retiring Rooms. Decent rooms (a/c and non a/c), men's dorm.
$ Simhagiri, Main Rd 500 m from railway station, T0891-250 5795, www.hotelsimha giri.com. 35 clean, spacious rooms (a/c and non a/c), a budget traveller favourite.

Araku Valley *p401*
$$$-$$ Mayuri and Valley Resort (AP Tourism), next to Tribal Museum, T08936-249201. 115 rooms and suites, pool, barbeque area, playground, bar, restaurant. Spacious and well maintained. Prior reservation mandatory.
$ Krishnatara Comforts, Padmapuram junction, T08936-249330. Rooms are good value for money and have great view, friendly staff. Recommended.
$ Rajadhani, Padmapuram junction, T08936-249745. Clean rooms, restaurant serves great Indian and Chinese food.

❶ Restaurants

Visakhapatnam *p399, map p400*
Most eateries serve alcohol. Apart from hotels, there are restaurants on Station Rd.
$$$ Infinity, Novotel, Beach Rd, T0891-282 2222. Elegant rooftop place, glass walls with fabulous views of the Bay of Bengal. Come here at sunset for sizzlers and cold beer. Also in the hotel is **Zaffran**, with exquisite Northwest Frontier cuisine.
$ Blue Diamond, opposite RTC, Dabagardens.
$ Delight, 7-1-43 Kirlampudi, Beach Rd.
$ Jaya G Spuds, Beach Rd. Multi-cuisine restaurant serves good succulent *kababs*.

✷ Festivals

Visakhapatnam *p399, map p400*
Dec Navy Mela and **Navy Day Parade**
along Beach Rd.

ⓞ What to do

Visakhapatnam *p399, map p400*
Swimming
Pools at **Park** and **Palm Beach** hotels
are open to non-residents. **Waltair Club**
has a pool.

Tour operators
Boat rides from Rushikonda, T(0)9848-
235793, 0900-1700, run for 30 mins
and go 2-3 km out to sea where there's
a good chance of seeing dolphins.
Rs 150 per person.
AP Tourism, RTC Complex, T0891-
278820. Local sightseeing day trip,
0830-1700, Rs 300. Araku Valley rail/road
tour, departs 0700: 1 day Rs 650, 2 days
Rs 1500-2200 including accommodation.

ⓞ Transport

Visakhapatnam *p399, map p400*
Air
Airport is 16 km from city centre; taxi
(Rs 650) or auto-rickshaw. Flights to
Hyderabad, **Bengaluru**, **Bhubaneswar**,
Kolkata, **Chennai** and Mumbai.

Bus
Aseelmetta Junction Bus Station is
well organized. APSRTC run services
to main towns in the state. Enquiries,
T0891-274 6400, reservations 0600-2000.
Araku Valley, **Guntur** (0930, 1545, 2045),
Hyderabad (638 km, 1630), **Kakinda**,
Puri (0700), **Rajahmundry**, **Srikakulam**,
Vijayawada (1945, 2015), **Vizianagram**
(57 km, 0610-2130).

Ferry
Operates 0800-1700 between the
Harbour and **Yarada Hills**.

Rickshaw
Auto-rickshaws are common. Minimum
fare Rs 15; night fares exorbitant. Only
cycle rickshaws in the centre.

Taxi
At airport, train station or from hotels:
5 hrs/50 km, Rs 500; 10 hrs/100 km, Rs 1000.

Train
Enquiries, T0891-256 9421. Reservations
T0891-254 6234. 0900-1700. Advance
Reservations, left of building (facing
it). Computer bookings close 2100, Sun
1400. Counter system avoids crush at
ticket window. City Railway Extension
Counter at Turner's Chowltry for
Reservations. Taxi from centre, Rs 50.
    Chennai: *Howrah-Chennai Mail 12839*,
1355, 16 hrs. **Kolkata** (H): *Coromandel Exp
12842*, 2210, 15 hrs; *Chennai Howrah Mail
12840*, 1320, 17¼ hrs; **Secunderabad**:
Godavari Exp 12727, 1725, 13¾ hrs; *VSKP
Garib Rath 12739*, 2030, 12 hrs; *East Coast
Exp 18645*, 0410, 14 hrs; *Falaknuma Exp
12703*, Tue 2135, 12 hrs. **Tirupati**: *Tirumala
Exp 17488*, 1350, 16 hrs. For **Araku Valley**,
take *Kirandul Pass 58501*, 0650, 5 hrs. Sit
on the right for the best views.

ⓞ Directory

Visakhapatnam *p399, map p400*
Banks Several on Surya Bagh, with
ATMs. **State Bank of India** is at Old
Post Office. **Hospital** King George,
Hospital Rd, Maharani Peta, T0891-256
4891. **Useful contacts** Foreigners'
Regional Registration Office, SP Police,
T0891-256 2709.

Southern Andhra Pradesh and Tamil borders

Southern Andhra plays host to one of India's most astounding religious spectacles, the 10th-century Sri Venkatesvara Temple of Tirupati, to which devotees flock in their tens of thousands for a second's glimpse of the bejewelled deity of Lord Vishnu.

Tirupati and Tirumala → *For listings, see pages 410-412. Colour map 3, A5.*

The Tirumala Hills provide a picture-book setting for the Sri Venkatesvara Temple, possibly the most famous and most revered temple in all India. So important is the shrine that Bollywood royal Amitabh Bachchan made a special journey here to seek Lord Venkateshwara's blessings prior to his son Abhishek's wedding to Aishwarya Rai. Thankfully for the wedding snaps, but no doubt to the regret of the temple's accountants, Aishwarya didn't actually take part in the ritual for which Tirupati is renowned: a ceremonial head-shave, with the fallen locks being sold off to the wig-making trade (see box, page 406). The main town of Tirupati lies at the bottom of the hill where there are several other temples, some pilgrimage centres in their own right. The seven hills are compared to the seven-headed Serpent God Adisesha who protects the sleeping Vishnu under his hood.

Arriving in Tirupati and Tirumala → *Phone code: 0877. Population: 245,500.*
Getting there Flights from Chennai and Hyderabad arrive at the airport 15 km from Tirupati. The railway station in the town centre has several fast trains from Chennai and other southern towns while the main (central) bus stand is 500 m east of it, with frequent express buses to Chennai, Bengaluru (Bangalore) and Hyderabad. Private buses arrive from an incredible array of destinations all across India. To save time and hassle on arrival, try to buy a through Link ticket to Tirumala. **→ *See Transport, page 411.***

Getting around Buses for Tirumala leave from stands near the station every half hour, but there are also share taxis available. Some choose to join pilgrims for a four- to five-hour walk uphill, starting before dawn to avoid the heat, though the path is shaded most of the way. Luggage is transported free from the toll gate at the start of the 15-km path and may be collected from the reception office at Tirumala.

Tourist information AP State tourist office ⓘ *Srinivasam Complex, T0877-228 9129.* APTDC ⓘ *Sridevi Complex, Tilak Rd, T0877-225 5385.* **Karnataka Tourism** ⓘ *Hotel Mayura (see page 410).* **Tirumala Tirupati Devasthanam (TTD)** ⓘ *TTD Administrative Building, KT Rd , T0877-223 3333, www.tirumala.org; also has counters at the airport and railway station,* is an independent trust that manages the Tirumala Venkateswara Temple.

Places in Tirupati and Tirumala

In Tirupati itself the **Govindarajasvami Temple** (16th to 17th centuries), is the most widely visited. Built by the Nayakas, the successors to the Vijayanagar Empire, the temple has an impressive outer *gopuram*. Of the three *gopurams* the innermost is also the earliest, dating from the 14th to 15th centuries. The main sanctuaries are dedicated to Vishnu and Krishna. Another temple worth seeing is **Kapilesvarasvami**, in a beautiful setting with a sacred waterfall, **Kapila Theertham**.

About 1 km away are strange **rock formations** in a natural arch, resembling a hood of a serpent, a conch and a discus, thought to have been the source of the idol in the temple. There is a sacred waterfall **Akasa Ganga**, 3 km south of the temple. The **Papa Vinasanam Dam** is 5 km north.

Sri Venkatesvara Temple

Dating from the 10th century, this temple is believed to have been dedicated by the Vaishnava saint Ramanuja and is known as *Balaji* in the north and *Srinivasa Perumalai* in the south. Of all India's temples, this draws the largest number of pilgrims: even on a slow day the grounds swarm with a crowd of 10,000 people, while on festival days the number can be closer to 150,000. The town of Tirupati at the base of the hill was established in approximately AD 1131 under the orders of Ramanuja that the temple functionaries who served in the sacred shrines must live nearby. Although a road runs all the way up the hill to a bus stand at the top, most pilgrims choose to walk up the wooded slope through mango groves and sandalwood forest, chanting

Where to stay
Bhimas Deluxe 2
Bhimas Paradise 9
Quality Inn Bliss 10
Ramee Guestline Days 8
Sri Kumara Lodge 4

Sri Oorvasi
International 3
Vasantham Lodge 6
Vishnupriya & Indian
Airlines 7

Restaurants
Dwarka 1
Laxmi Narayan Bhawan 1

Tirupati haircuts

Sri Venkatesvara Temple, architecturally unremarkable, is probably the wealthiest in India, and the *devasthanam* (or temple trust) now sponsors a huge range of activities, from the Sri Venkatesvara University in Tirupati to hospitals, orphanages and schools. Its wealth comes largely from its pilgrims, numbering on average over 10,000 a day. All pilgrims make gifts, and the *hundi* (offering) box in front of the shrine is stuffed full with notes, gold ornaments and other offerings.

Another important source of income is the hair-cutting service. Many pilgrims come to Tirupati to seek a special favour (eg to seek a suitable wife or husband, to have a child or to recover from illness) and it is regarded as auspicious to grow the hair long and then cut it as a sacrifice. You may see many pilgrims fully shaven at the temple when appearing before the deity. Lines of barbers await the arriving pilgrims. Free numbered ticket and a razor blade can be collected from the public bath hall, which pilgrims take to the barber with the same number to claim a free haircut. The hair is collected, washed and softened before being exported to the American and Japanese markets for wig making.

"*Om namo Venkatesaya*" or "*Govinda, Govinda*" as they walk. Order is maintained by providing 'Q sheds' under which pilgrims assemble.

Theoretically the inner shrines of the Tirumala temple are open only to Hindus. However, foreigners are usually welcome. They are sometimes invited to sign a form to show they sympathize with Hindu beliefs. According to the tourist information leaflet: "The only criterion for admission is faith in God and respect for the temple's conventions and rituals".

The atmosphere inside is unlike any other temple in India. Turnstiles control the never-ending flow of pilgrims into the main **temple complex**, which is through an intricately carved *gopuram* on the east wall. There are three enclosures. The first, where there are portrait sculptures of the Vijayanagar patrons, include Krishnadeva Raya and his queen and a gold-covered pillar. The outer colonnades are in the Vijayanagar style; the gateway leading to the inner enclosure may be of Chola origin. The second enclosure has more shrines, a sacred well, and the temple kitchen, where cooks prepare the holy *prasadam* (consecrated sweet) given to pilgrims after their *darshan*; the kitchen gets through an estimated 4.5 tonnes of ghee a day, supplied direct by pipeline from the dairy. The main temple and shrine is on the west side of the inner enclosure. The **sanctuary** (ninth to 10th centuries), known as *Ananda Nilayam*, has a domed *vimana* entirely covered with gold plate, and gold covered gates. Inside, dimly lit by oil lamps, stands the image for which people queue for hours to see: a 2-m-high statue of Vishnu (Sri Venkatesvara) carved of black stone, standing on a lotus and richly ornamented with gold and jewels. Two of his four arms carry a conch shell and a *chakra* or discus and he wears a diamond crown which is said to be the most precious single ornament in the world. The idol is flanked by *Sridevi* and *Bhudevi*, Vishnu's consorts.

There is a small **museum** ① *0800-2000*, of temple art in the temple compound, with a collection of stone, metal and wooden images.

Every day is festival day with shops selling holy souvenirs remaining open 24 hours. The image of Sri Venkatesvara is widely seen across South India, in private homes, cars, taxis and in public places, and is instantly recognizable from his black face and covered eyes, shielded so that the deity's piercing gaze may not blind any who look directly at him. In the temple the deity's body is anointed with camphor, saffron and musk.

Visiting the temple ① *The temple is at Tirumala, 22 km by road or a tough 4-hr climb on foot from central Tirupati.* No electronic items are allowed in the temple. There are two types of queue: for *darshan*, or viewing. Sarvadarsan is open to all, and it can take between two and five claustrophobic hours to reach the idol (Mondays and Tuesdays tend to be quieter). Those who pay for 'special' *darshan* (Rs 40 and up) enter by a separate entrance and join a shorter queue. The actual *darshan* (0600-1100) itself lasts a precious 1½ seconds, even though the 'day' at the temple may last 21 hours: from *Suprabhatham* (awakening of the deity) at 0330 to *Ekantha seva* at 2330.

The Sudarsanam token system has been introduced to minimize the waiting time for Sarvadarsanam, 'special' *darshan* and other paid *darshan/sevas*; pilgrims can enter the Vaikuntam Queue Complex at Tirumala at the time indicated on the tokens. The tokens are available free of cost at the First Choultry (opposite the Tirupati Railway Station), Second Choultry (behind the Railway Station), Alipiri Bus Stand, Vaikuntam Queue Complex, Pilgrim Amenities Centre (Near CRO) and near the Rambagicha Guest House in Tirumala. TTD has also started the E-Darshan, which makes it possible to book special *darshans* and accommodation at Tirumala in advance through www.ttdonline.com.

Sri Venkatesvara Temple

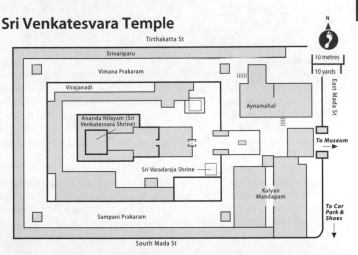

Around Tirupati

Chandragiri, 11 km southwest, became the capital of the Vijayanagaras in 1600, after their defeat at the battle of Talikota 35 years earlier. The **fort** ① *1930-2015, Rs 30, children Rs 20,* was built on a 180-m-high rock. You can still see the well-preserved defences and some of the palaces and temples, including the Rani Mahal and Raja Mahal with a pretty lily pond and a small museum (closed Friday) containing Chola and Vijayanagar bronzes. A visit to the fort would be incomplete without witnessing the **sound and light show** organized everyday by the APTDC. The Palace of Sri Ranga Raya, built in 1639, witnessed the signing by Sri Ranga Raya of the original land grant entitling the East India Company to build Fort St George, the starting point of modern-day Chennai.

Srikalahasti (Kalahasti) ① *state buses run the 36 km northeast from Tirupati*, is sited on the banks of the Svarnamukhi River at the foot of the Kailasa Hills, the southernmost limit of the Vellikonda Ranges. The town and temple, built in the 16th and 17th centuries, developed largely as a result of the patronage of the Vijayanagar kings and their successors, the Nayakas. The **Kalahastisvara Temple** dominates the town and, like the temple at Tirumala, is built in the Dravida style, set within high walls with a single entrance to the south, with a strong Nayaka influence typified by the columns carved into the shape of rearing animals. The temple is particularly revered for the white stone Siva *lingam* in the western shrine, believed to be worshipped by *sri* (spider), *kala* (king cobra) and *hasti* (elephant). The detached *gopuram* facing the river was built by the Vijayanagar emperor Krishnadeva Raya. The bathing ghats of the Swarnamukhi (golden) River and the temple attract a steady flow of pilgrims.

In addition to its function as a pilgrim centre, the town is known for its *kalamkaris*, colourful **hand-painted textiles** used as temple decoration. You can find pieces for sale in the BP Agraharam area, 1 km west of the temple, but they may come as a disappointment if you've seen the fine examples in Hyderabad's Salar Jung Museum (see page 375).

South Andhra Coast

Pulicat Lake, on the coast 48 km east of Srikalahasti and 50 km north of Chennai, is the second largest saltwater lagoon in India and one of the most important wetlands for migratory shorebirds on the eastern seaboard of India. The northern area near the islands of Vendadu and Irukkam has large concentrations of greater flamingos. There are also many birds of prey. About 20 km north of Suluru is the **Neelapattu Lake**, which was given protected status in 1976 to conserve a large breeding colony of spotbilled pelicans.

Some 80 km north of Pulicat Lake, the town of **Nellore** derives its name from the sweet-smelling nelli rice, grown in abundance in the area. It is also reputed to produce the best shrimp on the east coast. **Mypadu Beach**, 20 km away, offers golden sands, surf and, outside the weekend rush, a slice of solitude. AP Tourism runs a guesthouse on the beach.

Horsley Hills

Popularly known as 'the Ooty of Andhra', this small hill station is located about 114 km west of Tirupati in the Nallamala Range. Nestling at an elevation of 1265 m, the resort is named after WD Horsley, the Collector of Cuddapah District, who chose the spot for his summer residence. It remains more popular with weekending public servants than anybody else, but the hills are thickly forested and home to a wide variety of wildlife, and can make a relaxing break from the roasting Andhra plains. **Madanapalle**, the nearest town 30 km to the south, is the birthplace of the famous 20th-century philosopher J Krishnamurti.

Lepakshi

This tiny village, close to the Karnataka border and 130 km from Bengaluru (Bangalore), houses a massive sculpture of Siva's bull *Nandi*, 5 m high and 8 m long, carved out of a single red granite boulder. Nearby, set on an outcrop of gneiss, is the remarkable **Virabhadra Temple**, built in 1538 under the Vijayanagar emperor Achutyadeva Raya. It has well-preserved sculptures, including a towering 6-m-high *nagalingam* and a life-size Virabhadra, decked with skulls and carrying weapons and apparently bent on revenge, while the roof of the shrine is decorated with what is claimed to be the largest mural in Asia.

Rural Development Trust FVF ⓘ *Bangalore Highway, T08554-31503, fvfatp@ hd2.dot. net.in*, an NGO working in over 1500 villages, was started by a former Spanish Jesuit, Vincente Ferrer, more than 30 years ago. The project covers health, education, housing, among other areas. Visitors interested in seeing the work can be accommodated for up to four days.

Puttaparthi → *Colour map 3, A4.*

Puttaparthi, a remote village 150 km from Bengaluru, is now famous as the birthplace of **Bhagawan Sri Sathya Sai Baba**, a tremendously popular figure revered by millions as a reincarnation of the Maharashtrian saint Sai Baba of Shirdi. The current Sai Baba's predilection for spectacle (celebrations at his imposing **Prasanthi Nilayam** ashram typically involve stunt shows with massed ranks of motorcycle riders) have led some to dismiss him as a charlatan, and there have been allegations of sexual misconduct by a handful of former devotees. Nevertheless, the ashram provides free schooling and medical care to all comers, and fosters a peaceful atmosphere that attracts people from all around the world.

For hotel and restaurant price codes and other relevant information, see pages 13-17.

🛏 Where to stay

Tirupati *p404, map p405*
$$ Bhimas Deluxe, 34-38 Govindaraja Car St, T0877-222 5521, www.thirupathibhimashotels.com. 60 rooms, 40 a/c, restaurant (Indian, a/c), exchange.
$$ Bliss, Renigunta Rd, T0877-223 7773. 72 modern clean a/c rooms, restaurants.
$$ Ramee Guestline Days, 14-37 Karakambadi Rd, 3 km from town, T0877-228 0800. 140 rooms, central a/c, restaurants (including non-veg), bar, pool.
$$-$ Bhimas Paradise, 33-37 Renigunta Rd, T0877-222 5744, www.hotelbhimas.com. 90 rooms, some a/c, pool, garden, good restaurant.
$$-$ Sri Oorvasi International, Renigunta Rd, 1 km from railway station, T0877-222 0202. 78 rooms, some a/c, veg restaurant.
$ Mayura, 209 TP Area, T0877-222 5925. 65 rooms, half a/c, veg restaurant, exchange. More expensive than others in this price category.
$ Sri Kumara Lodge, near railway station. Decent rooms.
$ Vasantham Lodge, 141 G Car St, T0877-222 0460. Reasonable rooms with bath.
$ Vishnupriya, T0877-225 8401. 134 rooms, some a/c, restaurants, exchange, **Air India** office.

Tirumala *p404*
The Temple Trust's *choultries* in Tirumala can accommodate about 20,000 pilgrims. They vary from luxury suites and well-furnished cottages to dorms and unfurnished rooms (some

free). Contact T0877-223 3333, www.tirumala.org. Accommodation can also be booked at www.ttdsevaonline.com. If you arrive without a reservation, go to the Central Reception Office in Tirumala, T0877-226 3883.

South Andhra Coast *p408*
$$ DR Uthama, near Madras Bus Stand, Nellore, T0861-231 7777. Best hotel in town, with 51 rooms, pool, health club.
$ Beach Resort, Mypadu, T0861-234 1877. 6 rooms, right on the beach, restaurant.
$ Murali Krishna, beside Leela Mahal, Nellore, T0861-230 9030. Well-reputed hotel with 22 spacious, clean rooms and a restaurant serving authentic Andhra fare.

Horsley Hills *p409*
All accommodation here (except Forest Rest House which can be booked from Madanapalle, T08571-222436) is owned by **AP Tourism**.
$$ Haritha Resort, T08571-279324. Cottages and rooms (a/c and non a/c) on hill top, Governor's Bungalow recommended.

Puttaparthi *p409*
Good **$** accommodation in rooms and dorms at the ashram, T08555-287164, www.srisathyasai.org.in. No advance bookings.

🍴 Restaurants

Tirupati and Tirumala *p404, map p405*
Tirupathi-Tirumala Devasthanam Trust (TTD) provides free veg meals at its guesthouses. Outside hotels, veg restaurants include:
Laxmi Narayan Bhawan ($$) and **Dwarka**, opposite APSRTC Bus Stand;
Indian Coffee House, TTD Canteen

and the APSRTC Bus Stand. **Konark**, Railway Station Rd; **New Triveni**, 139 TP Area; **Woodlands**, TP Area. **Tea Board Restaurant**, near the Indian Coffee House (all **$**).

South Andhra Coast *p408*
$$ Komala Vilas Hotel, Trunk Rd, Nellore. Andhra lunch (prawn curry and *chepala pulusu* (murrel fish cooked in tamarind gravy), eaten with aromatic *nelli* rice. Highly recommended.

⊛ Festivals

Tirupati and Tirumala *p404, map p405*
May/Jun Govind Brahmotsavam.
Sep-Oct Brahmotsavam is the most important festival, especially grand every 3rd year when it is called **Navarathri Brahmotsavam**. On the 3rd day the Temple Car Festival **Rathotsavam** is particularly popular. **Rayalseema Food and Dance** follows later in the month.

O Shopping

Tirupati and Tirumala *p404, map p405*
Copper and brass idols, produced at Perumallapalli village, 8 km away, and wooden toys are sold locally. Try **Poompuhar** on Gandhi Rd and **Lepakshi** in the TP Area.

⟳ What to do

Tirupati and Tirumala *p404, map p405*
AP Tourism, Room 15, Srinivasa Choultry, T0877-2289123. Local sightseeing tour starts at the **APSRTC** Central Bus Stand, 0915-1730. Rs 340. Tirupati (not Venkatesvara), Kalahasti, Tiruchanur, Chandragiri and Srinivasamangapuram. From Chennai to Tirumala, Rs 1350.

⊖ Transport

Tirupati and Tirumala *p404, map p405*
Air Transport to town by APSRTC coach to **Tirupati** (Rs 50) and **Tirumala** (Rs 80); taxis Rs 250. **Indian Airlines** fly to **Hyderabad and Delhi.**

Bus Local service between Tirupati and Tirumala every 3 mins, 0330-2200.
  In Tirupati: **Sri Venkatesvara Bus Stand**, opposite railway station for passengers with through tickets to Tirumala; Enquiries: 3rd Choultry, T0877-222 5203. **Padmavati Bus Stand** in TP Area, T0877-220203; queues for buses but buying a return ticket from Tirupati (past the railway footbridge) saves queuing.
  In Tirumala: **Kesavanagar Bus Stand**, 500 m southeast of temple; walk past canteen and shop. Depart from **Rose Garden Bus Stand**, east of the temple.
  Long distance to **Chennai**, 4 hrs, **Kanchipuram**, 3 hrs, **Vellore**, 2½ hrs. Enquiries, T0877-228 9900. 24-hr left luggage.

South Andhra Coast *p408*
Train Tirupati–Hyderabad trains stop at Nellore.

Horsley Hills *p409*
Bus A direct bus leaves the **Central Bus Station** in Tirupati at 1300. Easier to go via **Madanapalle**, from where buses for the hills leave every 2 hrs till 1700.

Taxi Tourist taxis through **AP Tourism** from the bus stand and railway station to **Tirumala**, Rs 800 return, for 5½ hrs. Share taxi between Tirupati and Tirumala, about Rs 75 per person. **Balaji Travels**, 149 TP Area, T0877-2224894.

Train Trains are often delayed. Phone the station, T0877-227 5227, in advance if catching a night train as it could be delayed until next morning. **Chennai** (C): *Intercity Exp 16204*, 0620, 3¼ hrs; *Saptagiri Exp 16058*, 1720, 3¼ hrs. **Mumbai** (CST): bus to Renigunta (10 km) for *Chennai-Mumbai Exp 11042*, 1445, 24 hrs; or direct: *Cape Mumbai Exp 16382*, 0345, 25 hrs. **Guntakal**: *Rayalaseema Exp 17430* (AC/II), 1600, 6½ hrs. *Hyderabad: Narayanadri Exp 12733*, 1825, 13¾ hrs (for Secunderabad).

⊙ Directory

Tirupati and Tirumala *p404, map p405*
Banks Most are on Gandhi St.
State Bank of India, opposite APSRTC.
Useful contacts Foreigners' Regional Registration Office: 499 Reddy Colony, T0877-222 0503

Contents

Footprint features

At a glance

⊗ **Getting around** Goa is rickshaw free. Local buses, chartered minibuses, taxis and motorbike taxis are all the norm. Hiring your own Honda or Enfield is a popular option.

⟲ **Time required** Allow 1 day for Old Goa, 1 day for the palaces of the south; and 3 days' round-trip for Hampi (in Karnataka). Then factor in beach time: some tire of Goa's beaches after 1-2 days, some spend a fortnight, some never leave.

◈ **Weather** Chilly evenings in Dec and Jan, best Oct-Feb. Humidity rises from Mar.

⊗ **When not to go** Avoid monsoon and peak season (Christmas and New Year) when prices sky rocket as the state opens up for the domestic Indian tourist's equivalent of 'Spring Break'.

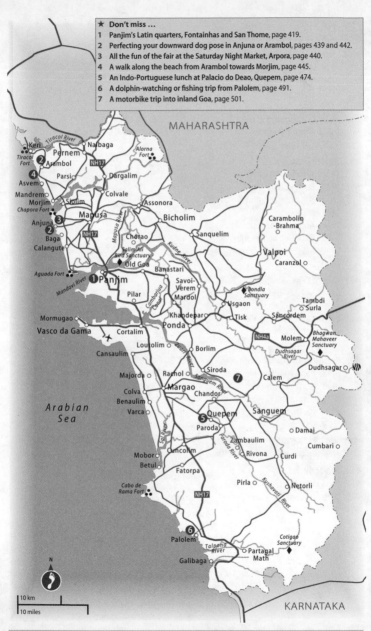

★ **Don't miss ...**
1 Panjim's Latin quarters, Fontainhas and San Thome, page 419.
2 Perfecting your downward dog pose in Anjuna or Arambol, pages 439 and 442.
3 All the fun of the fair at the Saturday Night Market, Arpora, page 440.
4 A walk along the beach from Arambol towards Morjim, page 445.
5 An Indo-Portuguese lunch at Palacio do Deao, Quepem, page 474.
6 A dolphin-watching or fishing trip from Palolem, page 491.
7 A motorbike trip into inland Goa, page 501.

MAHARASHTRA

Tiracol River
Keri
Tiracol Fort
Narbaga
Pernem
2 Arambol
Alorna Fort
4
NH17
Parsi
Dargalim
Asvem
Colvale
Mandrem
Siolim
Assonora
Morjim
Chapora Fort
Mapusa
Bicholim
Caramboli-Brahma
Anjuna 3
Chotao
Sanquelim
Valpoi
Baga
Salim Ali Bird Sanctuary
NH17
Mapusa River
Caranzol
Calangute
Kudne River
Old Goa
Banastari
Aguada Fort
1 Panjim
Savoi-Verem
Bondla Sanctuary
Pilar
Mardol
Usgaon
Tambdi Surla
Mandovi River
Cumbarjua Canal
Khandepar
Tisk
Sancordem
Mormugao
Ponda
NH4a
Bhagwan Mahaveer Sanctuary
Vasco da Gama
Cortalim
Loutolim
Borlim
Molem
Cansaulim
Zuari River
Dudhsagar River
Dudhsagar
Majorda
Rachol
Siroda
Calem
Margao
Sanguem River
Colva
Chandor
7
Arabian Sea
Benaulim
Quepem 5
Sanguem
Varca
Paroda
Damai
Paroda River
Zambaulim
Cumbari
Mobor
Cuncolim
Rivona
Curdi
Betul
Fatorpa
Pirla
Netorli
Cabo de Rama Fort
NH17
Kushavati River
Palolem 6
Cotigao Sanctuary
Talpona River
Partagal Math
Galibaga

N
10 km
10 miles

KARNATAKA

Head north to the beaches of Anjuna and Arambol for yoga, meditation and a whole smorgasbord of complementary therapies, as well as a thriving live music scene. Central Goa, around Baga and Calangute and further south around Colva and Majorda, appeals more to the package tourists, but there are some great restaurants and sparkly shops. Southern Goa has more beautiful beaches, particularly Agonda and the busy strip of Palolem and Patnem. Benaulim too has an alternative arty scene. Inland Goa is often overlooked but, just a short drive from the beach resorts, there are cashew and spice plantations, rolling hills, beautiful waterfalls and interesting wildlife; it's a little like walking back in time when you happen upon and the fading Portuguese-style mansions in villages such as Loutolim and Quepem. So if it's beach life and sundowners, meditation and navel gazing, or paragliding and kitesurfing, Goa has it all. There is a laid-back beauty that is inviting and intoxicating. And we didn't discover it. The Goans have had a word for it all along – *susegad* –a relaxed attitude and enjoyment of life to the fullest.

Panjim (Panaji) and Old Goa

Sleepy, dusty Panjim was adopted as the Portuguese capital when the European empire was already on the wane, and the colonizers left little in the way of lofty architecture. A tiny city with a Riviera-style promenade along the Mandovi, it's also splendidly uncommercial: the biggest business seems to be in the sale of *kaju* (cashews), gentlemen-shaves in the *barbieris* and *feni*-quaffing in the booths of pokey bars – and city folk still insist on sloping off for a siesta at lunch. The 18th- and 19th-century bungalows clustered in the neighbouring quarters of San Thome and Fontainhas stand as the victims of elegant architectural neglect. Further upriver, a thick swathe of jungle – wide fanning raintrees, the twists of banyan branches and coconut palms – has drawn a heavy, dusty blanket over the relics of the doomed Portuguese capital of Old Goa, a ghost town of splendid rococo and baroque ecclesiastical edifices.

Arriving in Panjim and Old Goa

Getting there Panjim is the transport hub of Central Goa. Pre-paid taxis or buses run the short distance from Dabolim airport across Mormugao Bay to Panjim. The closest station on the Konkan Railway is at Karmali, 10 km east, with trains from Mumbai to the north and coastal Karnataka and Kerala to the south; taxis and buses run from Karmali to Panjim. The state-run Kadamba buses and private coach terminals are in Patto to the east of town. From there it is a 10-minute walk across the footbridge over the Ourem Creek to reach the city's guesthouses. ▶ *See Transport, page 431.*

Getting around Panjim is laid out on a grid and the main roads run parallel with the seafront. The area is very easy to negotiate on foot, but autos are readily available. Motorcycle rickshaws are cheaper but slightly more risky. Local buses run along the waterfront from the City Bus Stand past the market and on to Miramar.

Tourist information Goa Tourism Development Corporation (GTDC) ① *east bank of the Ourem Creek, beside the bus stand at Patto, T0832-243 8750, www.goa-tourism. com, Mon-Sat 0900-1130, 1330-1700, Sun 0930-1400*. Also has an information counter at Dabolim airport, and runs a moderately helpful information line, T0832-241 2121. **India Tourism** ① *Church Sq, T0832-222 3412, www.incredibleindia.com*.

There are some great themed walks around Panjim with **Cholta Cholta** ① *www. choltacholta.com* (which means 'whilst walking' in Konkani) and their popular tours

Goa ins and outs

Vasco da Gama is the passenger railway terminus of the Central Goa branch line, and is the capital of the industrial heart of modern Goa. Dabolim Airport is 3 km away and was developed by the Navy. It is currently shared between the needs of the military and the escalating demands of tourism. Vasco is 30 km from Panjim, the main arrival point for long-distance buses. Trains via Londa bring visitors from the north and east (Delhi and Agra, Hospet and Bengaluru) while trains from Mumbai, Kerala and coastal points in between arrive via the Konkan Railway, which offers several jumping-off points in Goa besides the main station at Margao (Madgaon). For rail reservations, call T0832-251 2833.

Charter companies fly direct to Dabolim Airport between October and April from the UK, the Netherlands, Switzerland and Russia. There are several flights daily from various cities in India (including Mumbai, Thiruvananthapuram, Bengaluru, Delhi and Chennai) with Air India, Indian Airlines, Indigo and Spice Jet. Package tour companies and luxury hotels usually arrange courtesy buses for hotel transfer, but even if you're coming independently the Arrivals terminal is relatively relaxed. A pre-paid taxi counter immediately outside has rates clearly displayed (such as Panjim Rs 700, 40 minutes; north Goa beaches from Rs 700; Tiracol Rs 1600; Arambol Rs 1400; south Goa beaches from Rs 500; Palolem Rs 1200). State your destination at the counter, pay and obtain a receipt that will give the registration number of your taxi. Keep hold of this receipt until you reach your destination. The public bus stop on the far side of the roundabout outside the airport gates has buses to Vasco da Gama, from where there are connections to all the major destinations in Goa.

A popular way to get around is by hiring a scooter, available in all towns and villages. However, make sure the bike has yellow and black number plates, which signal that the vehicle is for hire; plain black-and-white plates could result in a fine from the police.

See also pages 4-13.

offer real insight into the city and its history. Many of the walks focus on the areas of San Thome and Fontainhas and their beautiful architecture.

Panaji is the official spelling of the capital city, replacing the older Portuguese spelling Panjim. It is still most commonly referred to as Panjim, so we have followed usage.

Background

The Portuguese first settled Panjim as a suburb of Old Goa, the original Indian capital of the sea-faring *conquistadores*, but its position on the left bank of the Mandovi River had already attracted Bijapur's Muslim king Yusuf Adil Shah in 1500, shortly before the Europeans arrived. He built and fortified what the Portuguese later renamed the Idalcao Palace, now the oldest and most impressive of downtown Panjim's official buildings. The palace's service to the sultan was short-lived: Alfonso de Albuquerque seized it, and Old Goa upstream – which the Islamic rulers had been using as both a trading port and their main starting point for pilgrimages to Mecca – in March 1510. Albuquerque, like his Muslim predecessors, built his headquarters in Old Goa, and proceeded to station a garrison at Panjim and made it the customs clearing point for all traffic entering the Mandovi.

The town remained little more than a military outpost and a staging post for incoming and outgoing viceroys on their way to Old Goa. The first Portuguese buildings, after the construction of a church on the site of the present Church of Our Lady of Immaculate Conception in 1541, were noblemen's houses built on the flat land bordering the sea. Panjim had to wait over two centuries – when the Portuguese Viceroy decided to move from Old Goa in 1759 – for settlement to begin in earnest. It then took the best part of a century for enough numbers to relocate from Old Goa to make Panjim the biggest settlement in the colony and to warrant its status as official capital in 1833.

Places in Panjim → For listings, see pages 427-432.

The waterfront
The leafy boulevard of Devanand Bandodkar (DB) Marg runs along the Mandovi from near the New Patto Bridge in the east to the Campal to the southwest. When Panjim's transport and communication system depended on boats, this was its busiest highway and it still holds the city's main administrative buildings and its colourful market.

Walking from the east, you first hit **Idalcao Palace** ① *behind the main boat terminal, DB Marg*. Once the castle of the Adil Shahs, the palace was seized by the Portuguese when they first toppled the Muslim kings in 1510 and was rebuilt in 1615 to serve as the Europeans' Viceregal Palace. It was the official residence to Viceroys from 1759 right up until 1918 when the governor-general (the viceroy's 20th-century title) decided to move to the Cabo headland to the southwest – today's Cabo Raj Niwas – leaving the old palace to become government offices. After Independence it became Goa's secretariat building (the seat of the then Union Territory's parliament) until that in turn shifted across the river to Porvorim. It now houses the bureaucracy of the state passport office. Next to it is a striking dark statue of the **Abbé Faria** (1756-1819) looming over the prone figure of a woman. José Custodio de Faria, who went on to become a worldwide authority on hypnotism, was born into a Colvale Brahmin family in Candolim. The character in Dumas' Count of Monte Cristo may have been based on this Abbé.

Further west, on Malacca Road, almost opposite the wharf, are the central library and public rooms of the **Braganza Institute** ① *Mon-Fri 0930-1300, 1400-1745*. It was established as the Instituto Vasco da Gama in 1871 (the anniversary of the date that the Portuguese explorer da Gama sailed round the Cape of Good Hope), to stimulate an interest in culture, science and the arts. It was renamed for Luis Menezes de

Braganza (1878-1938), an outstanding figure of social and political reform in early 20th-century Goa. The blue tile frieze in the entrance, hand painted by Jorge Colaco in 1935, is a mythical representation of the Portuguese colonization of Goa. An art gallery upstairs has paintings by European artists of the late 19th and early 20th centuries and Goan artists of the 20th century. The **central library** ⓘ *0930-1300, 1200-1700*, dating from 1832, has a rare collection of religious and other texts.

City centre

The giant whitewashed 16th-century **Church of the Immaculate Conception** ⓘ *Church Sq, Emidio Gracia Rd, Mon-Sat 0900-1230, 1530-1730, Sun 1100-1230, 1530-1700, free, English Mass Mon-Fri 0800, Sun 0830*, looms pristine and large up a broad sweep of steps off the main square, Largo Da Igreja, blue and white flags fluttering at its fringes. Its dimensions were unwarranted for the population of what was at the time of its construction in 1541, in Panjim, little more than a marshy fishing village; its tall, Portuguese baroque twin towers were instead built both to act as a landmark for and to tend to the spiritual needs of arriving Portuguese sailors, for whom the customs post just below the hill at Panjim marked their first step on Indian soil. The church was enlarged in 1600 to reflect its status as parish church of the capital and in 1619 was rebuilt to its present design. Inside is an ornate jewel in Goan Catholicism's trademark blue, white and gold, wood carved into gilt corkscrews, heavy chandeliers and chintz. The classic baroque main altar *reredos* (screens) are sandwiched between altars to Jesus the Crucified and to Our Lady of the Rosary, in turn flanked by marble statues of St Peter and St Paul. The panels in the Chapel of St Francis, in the south transept, came from the chapel in the Idalcao Palace in 1918. Parishioners bought the statue of Our Lady of Fatima her crown of gold and diamonds in 1950 (candlelight procession every 13 October). The church's feast day is on 8 December.

The Hindu **Mahalaxmi Temple** ⓘ *Dr Dada Vaidya Rd, free* (originally 1818, but rebuilt and enlarged in 1983) is now hidden behind a newer building. It was the first Hindu place of worship to be allowed in the Old Conquests after the close of the Inquisition. The **Boca de Vaca** ('Cow's Mouth') spring is nearby.

San Thome and Fontainhas

On Panjim's eastern promontory, at the foot of the Altinho and on the left bank of the Ourem Creek, sit first the San Thome and then, further south, Fontainhas districts filled with modest 18th- and 19th-century houses. The cumulative prettiness of the well-preserved buildings' colour-washed walls, trimmed with white borders, sloping tiled roofs and decorative wrought-iron balconies make it an ideal area to explore on foot. You can reach the area via any of the narrow lanes that riddle San Thome or take the footbridge across the Ourem Creek from the New Bus Stand and tourist office that feeds you straight into the heart of the district. A narrow road that runs east past the Church of the Immaculate Conception and main town square also ends up here. But probably the best way in is over the Altinho from the Mahalaxmi Temple: this route gives great views over the estuary from the steep eastern flank of the hill, a vantage point that was once used for defensive purposes. A footpath drops down between the Altinho's 19th- and 20th-century buildings just south of San Sebastian Chapel to leave you slap bang in middle of Fontainhas.

The chief landmark here is the small **San Sebastian Chapel** ① *St Sebastian Rd, open only during Mass held in Konkani Mon-Tue, Thu-Sat 0715-0800, Wed 1800-1900, Sun 0645-0730, English Mass Sun 0830-0930, free* (built 1818, rebuilt 1888) which houses the large wooden crucifix that until 1812 stood in the Palace of the Inquisition in Old Goa where the eyes of Christ watched over the proceedings of the tribunal. Before being moved here, it was in Idalcao Palace's chapel in Panjim for 100 years.

The **Goa State Museum** ① *Patto, 0930-1730, free, head south of Kadamba Bus Stand, across the Ourem Creek footbridge, right across the waste ground and past the State Bank staff training building*, is an impressive building that contains a disappointingly small collection of religious art and antiquities. Most interesting are

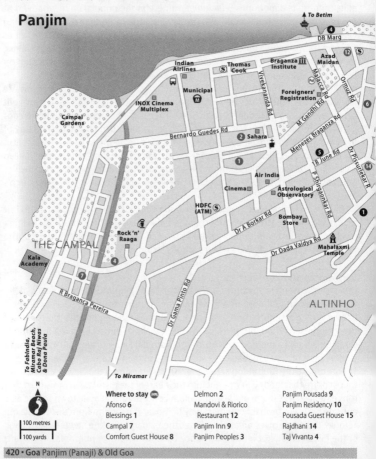

Panjim

Where to stay 🛏
Afonso **6**
Blessings **1**
Campal **7**
Comfort Guest House **8**

Delmon **2**
Mandovi & Riorico
  Restaurant **12**
Panjim Inn **9**
Panjim Peoples **3**

Panjim Pousada **9**
Panjim Residency **10**
Pousada Guest House **15**
Rajdhani **14**
Taj Vivanta **4**

the original Provedoria lottery machines built in Lisbon that are on the first floor landing. A few old photos show how the machines were used.

Old Goa and around → *For listings, see pages 427-432.*

The white spires of Old Goa's glorious ecclesiastical buildings burst into the Indian sky from the depths of overgrown jungle that has sprawled where admirals and administrators of the Portuguese Empire once tended the oriental interests of their 16th-century King Manuel. The canopies of a hundred raintrees cast their shade across the desolate streets, adding to the romantic melancholy beauty of the deserted capital. Tourists and pilgrims continue to flock to the remains of St Francis

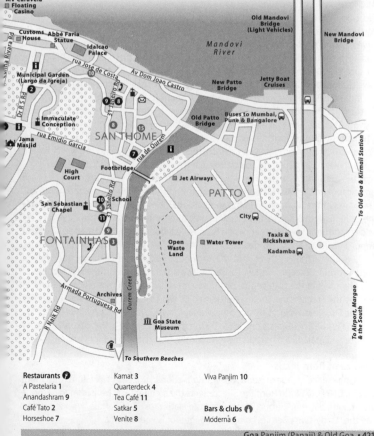

Restaurants

A Pastelaria **1**
Anandashram **9**
Café Tato **2**
Horseshoe **7**

Kamat **3**
Quarterdeck **4**
Tea Café **11**
Satkar **5**
Venite **8**

Viva Panjim **10**

Bars & clubs

Modernà **6**

Xavier in the giddying baroque Basilica of Bom Jesus, where hawkers thrust spindly votive candles into their hands and compete to slake thirsts with fresh coconut, lime or sugarcane juice.

Arriving in Old Goa
Getting there Old Goa lies on the south bank of the Mandovi on the crest of a low hill 8 km from Panjim. The frequent bus service takes 15-20 minutes. Buses drop you off opposite the Basilica of Bom Jesus; pick up the return bus near the police station. Karmali station on the Konkan Railway, just east of the centre, has taxis for transfers.

Getting around The major monuments are within easy walking distance of the bus stop. All monuments are open daily year-round 0830-1730.

Background
Old Goa is to Christians the spiritual heart of the territory. It owes its origin as a Portuguese capital to Afonso de Albuquerque and some of its early ecclesiastical development to St Francis Xavier who was here, albeit for only five months, in the mid-16th century. Before the Portuguese arrived it was the second capital of the Muslim Bijapur Kingdom. Today, all the mosques and fortifications of that period have disappeared and only a fragment of the Sultan's palace walls remain.

Under the Portuguese, Old Goa was grand enough to be dubbed the 'Rome of the East', but it was a flourishing port with an enviable trade even before the Portuguese arrived. The bustling walled city was peopled by merchants of many nationalities who came to buy and sell horses from Arabia and Hormuz, to trade silk, muslin, calico, rice, spices and areca nuts from the interior and other ports along the west coast. It was a centre of shipbuilding and boasted fine residences and public buildings.

After the arrival of the Portuguese, Old Goa swelled still further in size and significance. In the west lay barracks, mint, foundry and arsenal, hospital and prison. The banks of the Mandovi held the shipyards of Ribeira des Gales and next door lay the administrative and commercial centre. Streets and areas of the city were set aside for different activities and merchandise, each with its own character. The most important, Rua Direita ou dos Leiloes (Straight Street), was lined with jewellers, bankers and artisans. It was also the venue for auctions of precious goods, held every morning except Sunday. To the east was the market and the old fortress of Adil Shah, while the true centre of the town was filled with magnificent churches built by the Franciscans, themselves joined by waves of successive religious orders: first the Dominicans in 1548, the Augustinians from 1572, the Carmelites from 1612 and finally the Theatines from 1655. By the mid-17th century, the city, plagued by cholera and malaria and crippled economically, was abandoned for Panjim.

Basilica of Bom Jesus
The Renaissance façade of Goa's most famous church, the Basilica of Bom (the Good) Jesus, a UNESCO World Heritage Site, reflects the architectural transition to baroque then taking place in Europe. Apart from the elaborate gilded altars, wooden pulpit and the candy-twist Bernini columns, the interior is very simple.

The church has held the treasured remains of **St Francis Xavier**, a former pupil of soldier-turned-saint Ignatius Loyola, the founder of the Order of Jesuits since the 17th century. Francis's canonization was in 1622.

The tomb, which lies to the right of the main chancel (1698), was the gift of one of the last of the Medicis, Cosimo III, Grand Duke of Tuscany, and took the Florentine sculptor Giovanni Batista Foggini 10 years to complete. It is made of three tiers of marble and jasper; the upper tier holds scenes from the saint's life. The casket is silver and has three locks, the keys being held by the Governor, the Archbishop and the Convent Administrator. You can look down on to the tomb from a small window in the art gallery next to the church.

After his canonization, St Francis's body was shown on each anniversary of his death until 1707, when it was restricted to a few special private expositions. In 1752, the cadaver was again paraded to quash rumours that the Jesuits had removed it. The exhibition now happens every 10 to 12 years (the last exposition was in 2005), when the relics are taken to the Sé Cathedral. Feast Day is 3 December.

Sé Cathedral

Across the square sits the Sé Cathedral, dedicated to St Catherine on whose day (25 November) Goa was recaptured by Albuquerque. Certainly the largest church in Old Goa, it could even be the biggest in Asia and was built on the ruins of a mosque by the Dominicans between 1562 and 1623. The building is Tuscan outside and Corinthian inside, with a barrel-vaulted ceiling and east-facing main façade. One of the characteristic twin towers collapsed in 1776 when it was struck by lightning. The remaining tower holds five bells including the Golden Bell (cast in Cuncolim in 1652).

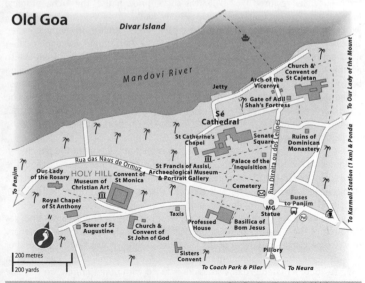

The vast interior, divided into the barrel-vaulted nave with clerestory and two side aisles, has a granite baptismal font. On each side of the church are four chapels along the aisles; on the right, these are dedicated to St Anthony, St Bernard, the Cross of Miracles and the Holy Spirit, and on the left, starting at the entrance, to Our Lady of Virtues, St Sebastian, the Blessed Sacrament and Our Lady of Life. The clerestory windows are protected by a shield crowned by a balustrade to keep out the sun. The main altar is superbly gilded and painted, with six further altars in the transept. The marble-top table in front of the main altar is where, since 1955, St Francis Xavier's remains have been held during their exposition. The main *reredos* has four panels illustrating the life of St Catherine. There is also an **art gallery** ⓘ *Mon-Thu, Sat 0900-1230, Sun 0900-1030, closed during services, Rs 5.*

Around the cathedral

Southwest of the cathedral's front door are the ruins of the **Palace of the Inquisition**, where over 16,000 cases were heard between 1561 and 1774. The Inquisition was finally suppressed in 1814. Beneath the hall were dungeons. In Old Goa's heyday this was the town centre.

There are two churches and a museum in the same complex as the Cathedral. The **Church and Convent of St Francis of Assisi** is a broad vault of a church with two octagonal towers. The floor is paved with tombstones and on either side of the baroque high altar are paintings on wood depicting scenes from St Francis' life while the walls above have frescoes with floral designs. The original **Holy Spirit Church** in the Portuguese Gothic (manueline) style was begun by Franciscan friars in 1517; everything except the old doorway was replaced by the larger present structure in the 1660s (itself restored 1762-1765). The convent now houses the **Archaeological Museum and Portrait Gallery** ⓘ *T0832-228 6133, 1000-1230, 1500-1830 (closed Fri), Rs 5,* with sculptures pre-dating the Portuguese, many from the 12th-13th centuries when Goa was ruled by the Kadamba Dynasty. There are 'hero stones' commemorating naval battles, and 'sati stones' marking the practice of widow burning. There is also a rather fine collection of portraits of Portuguese governors upstairs that is revealing both for its charting of the evolution of court dress as well as the physical robustness of the governors inside. Some governors were remarkable for their sickly pallor, others for the sheer brevity of their tenure of office, which must have set the portrait painters something of a challenge. (The ASI booklet on the monuments, *Old Goa*, by S Rajagopalan, is available from the museum, Rs 10.)

To the west is **St Catherine's Chapel**. It was built at the gate of the old city on the orders of Albuquerque as an act of gratitude after the Portuguese defeat of the forces of Bijapur in 1510. The original mud and thatch church was soon replaced by a stone chapel which in 1534 became the cathedral (considerably renovated in 1952), remaining so until Sé Cathedral was built.

On the road towards the Mandovi, northeast from the cathedral compound, lies the **Arch of the Viceroys** (**Ribeira dos Viceroys**), commemorating the centenary of Vasco da Gama's discovery of the sea route to India. It was built at the end of the 16th century by his great-grandson, Francisco da Gama, Goa's Viceroy from 1597 to 1600. Its laterite block structure is faced with green granite on the side approached from the river. This was the main gateway to the seat of power: on arrival by ship each new Viceroy would be handed the keys and enter through this ceremonial archway before taking office. The statue of Vasco da Gama above the arch was originally surmounted by a gilded statue of St Catherine, the patron saint of the city. Walking east towards the convent from the arch you pass the **Gate of the Fortress of the Adil Shahs**, probably built by Sabaji, the Maratha ruler of Goa before the Muslim conquest of 1471. The now-ruined palace was home to the Adil Shahi sultans of Bijapur who occupied Goa before the arrival of the Portuguese. It was the Palace of the Viceroys until 1554 after which it served as both the hall of trials for the Inquisition and to house prisoners.

A little further still stands the splendid, domed baroque **Convent and Church of St Cajetan** (**Caetano**). Pope Urban III dispatched a band of Italian friars of the Theatine order to spread the Gospel to the Deccani Muslim city of Golconda near Hyderabad but they got a frosty reception so headed back west to settle in Goa. They acquired land around 1661 to build this church, which is shaped like a Greek cross and is partly modelled on St Peter's in Rome. It is the last domed church in Goa.

The crypt below the main altar, where the Italian friars were buried, has some sealed lead caskets that are supposed to contain the embalmed bodies of senior Portuguese officials who never returned home. Next door is the beautiful former convent building which is now a pastoral foundation (closed to the public).

On a hill a good way further east is the modest **Chapel of Our Lady of the Mount**, dating from 1510, which gives you a good idea of how the other churches here must originally have looked. It is a peaceful spot with excellent panoramic views across Old Goa, evocative of the turbulent past when Albuquerque and Adil Shah vied for control of the surrounding area. The altar gilding inside has been beautifully restored. In front of the main altar lies the body of architect Antonio Pereira whose burial slab requests the visitor to say an Ave Maria for his soul.

Holy Hill

Between the domineering central monuments of Old Goa's broad tree-lined centre and Panjim stand the cluster of churches of Holy Hill. The first building you reach (on your left) as you leave the central plaza is the **Church and Convent of St John of God**, built in 1685 and abandoned in 1835. The **Museum of Christian Art** ⓘ *everyday 0930-1700, Rs 5*, is to the right, with 150 items gathered from Goa's churches, convents and Christian homes to give a rich cross section of Indo-Portuguese sacred craft in wood, ivory, silver and gold. There is a little outdoor café too.

Next door sits the **Convent of St Monica** (1607-1627), the first nunnery in India and the largest in Asia. A huge three-storey square building, with the church in the southern part, it was built around a sunken central courtyard containing a formal garden. At one time it was a royal monastery, but in 1964 it became a theological institute, the Mater Dei Institute for Nuns. It was here in 1936 that Bishop Dom Frei Miguel Rangel is believed to have had a vision of the Christ figure on the Miraculous Cross opening his eyes, his stigmata bleeding and his lips quivering as if to speak. The vision was repeated later that year in the presence of the Bishop, the Viceroy Dom Pedro de Silva and a large congregation.

It is well worth the effort of the hike, taking the left fork of the road, to reach the **Royal Chapel of St Anthony** (1543) – dedicated to Portugal's national saint and restored by its government in 1961 – and, opposite, the **Tower of St Augustine**. The Augustinians came to Goa in 1572; the church they immediately began, bar the belfry, now lies in ruins. It once boasted eight chapels, a convent and an excellent library and was enlarged to become one of the finest in the kingdom. It was finally abandoned in 1835 because of religious persecution. The vault collapsed in 1842, burying the image; the façade and main tower followed in 1931 and 1938. Only one of the original four towers survives. The large bell now hangs in Panjim's Church of the Immaculate Conception. The Archaeological Survey of India is spearheading extensive repairs.

Behind is the **Chapel of Our Lady of the Rosary** (1526). Belonging to the earliest period of church building, it is called Manueline after Manuel I, the Portuguese king who oversaw a period of great prosperity that coincided with the country's conquest of Goa. The use of Hindu and Muslim craftsmen in building the chapel led to an architectural style that borrowed from Iberian decoration but also absorbed both local naturalistic motifs and Islamic elements (seen on the marble cenotaph). The church here has a two-storey entrance, a single tower and low flanking turrets. It was from here that Albuquerque directed the battle against the Adil Shahi forces in 1510.

Around Panjim → For listings, see pages 427-432.

Gaspar Dias Fortress was finished around 1606. The Panjim–Ribandar causeway, built in 1634, gave it direct land access to the capital at Old Goa and its significance grew accordingly. The walls, likely laterite blocks 1.5 m thick and 5 m high, made space for 16 cannons. These saw repeated action against the Dutch until the middle of the 17th century, but the fortress' importance waned after the Maratha onslaught and it fell into disrepair under 15 years of occupation by a British garrison in the early 19th century. It was made new but the Portuguese army finally abandoned it in 1870 as a result of further damage sustained during the mutiny against the Prefect of 1835. For a while the military still stationed soldiers here to convalesce but by the 20th century it had crumbled beyond recognition. All that is left is one cannon at the Miramar circle that marks the possible site of the fort. **Miramar Beach** is a bit grubby but it's a pleasant drive with good views over the sea and, if you've got a little time to kill, it offers the best quick escape from the city.

The nearby fort **Cabo Raj Niwas** has fared little better: six cannons and some bits of wall crumbling in the gardens of Raj Bhavan, or the State Governor's House, are all that remain. It is closed to the public but you can get passes for Sunday Mass at 0930 on the gate. The first small **Our Lady of Cabo shrine** was built in 1541. Documents from 1633 refer to both the chapel and a fort with four guns. A British troops garrison stationed here from 1799 during the Napoleonic Wars explains the overgrown graves in the nearby **British Cemetery**. Around 1844, after the religious orders were abolished, the Archbishop of Goa was given the convent, which he converted into an impressive residence. It was the official address of the governor-general of Goa in 1918. Its grand interior was left intact after the Portuguese left in

1961. The viewing platform near the entrance gives superb views over the sweep of the coastline across the Mandovi estuary to Fort Aguada.

Some 5 km north of Panjim, in Bardez, you will find a fascinating museum **Houses of Goa** ① www.archgoa.org, created by architect Gerard da Cunha on a traffic island. It's a beautiful building shaped like a ship that follows traditional Goan architecture and style. Inside is a collection of doors, tiles, altars, lamps and rare postcards. It offers a unique insight into Goa's heritage.

◉ Panjim (Panaji) and Old Goa listings

For hotel and restaurant price codes and other relevant information, see pages 13-17.

● Where to stay

Panjim has a wide choice of accommodation, Old Goa none. There are upmarket options south of Panjim in the beach resorts of Miramar and Dona Paula, but for character it's best to book into one of the guesthouses in the atmospheric Fontainhas district. If you don't want to stay overnight you can pack the best of Panjim and Old Goa into a day. Guesthouses have early checkout to make way for new arrivals coming off the trains and buses and many do not take advance bookings – it's first come first served.

Panjim *p418, map p420*
$$$$-$$$ Taj Vivanta, www.vivanta bytaj.com. The **Taj Vivanta** opened in Panjim in 2009 and is a smart upmarket option centrally located. Common areas and restaurants are beautiful (the restaurants are highly recommended). Rooms are a little on the boutique-side, ie small and with glass-walled bathrooms where you have to shut the blinds each time if you are sharing the room. Overall everything you would expect from the Taj group.
$$$-$$ Mandovi, D B Marg, T0832-242 6270, www.hotelmandovigoa.com.

Old building with hints of art deco, relaxing but lacks great character. 66 large a/c rooms (river-facing more expensive); rates include breakfast. 1st floor **Riorico** restaurant, popular pastry shop, terrace bar, exchange.
$$ Delmon, C de Albuquerque Rd, T0832-222 6846, www.alcongoa.com. 50 clean rooms, TV, desk, some a/c, breakfast included. Modern, comfortable hotel, popular restaurant.
$ Blessings, MG Rd, behind Bhatkar House, T0832-222 4770, hotelblessings@yahoo. com. 18 ordinary rooms, TV (extra Rs 50), 2 have huge terraces instead of balconies, restaurant, quiet tree-filled backyard.
$ Hotel Campal, opposite Kala Academy, Campal, T0832-222 4533. Clean rooms with TV and a/c possible, hidden in beautiful location in Campal area, near Kala Academy, Inox cinemas and the river. Being renovated at time of writing. Recommended.
$ Panjim Residency (GTDC), overlooking the river, T0832-242 4001. Best views from top floor, 40 good-sized rooms with balcony, some a/c (overpriced), good open-air restaurant, often full, can organize tours and boat trips.
$ Rajdhani, Dr Atmaram Borkar Rd, T0832-222 5362. Modern business hotel with 35 smallish clean rooms with bath, some a/c (Rs 100 extra), pure vegetarian restaurant.

Fontainhas *p419, map p420*

$$$ The Panjim Peoples, opposite **Panjim Inn**, www.panjiminn.com. The latest heritage project from the Sukhija family, this one is genuinely top end with just 4 rooms, antique 4-poster beds and bathtubs, plus internet access. Changing art exhibitions on the ground floor.

$$ Panjim Inn, E212, 31 Janeiro Rd, T0832-222 6523, www.panjiminn.com. Goa's first heritage hotel is idiosyncratic, even in the context of the historic Fontainhas district. 14 rooms of varying size all fitted with 4-poster beds, a/c for an extra Rs 250.

$$ Panjim Pousada, up the road from **Panjim Inn**. Slightly cheaper sister hotel to the **Panjim Inn** with double rooms set around a permanent art gallery in a courtyard. It is an evocative, attractive renovation. Best rooms at the back overlook another courtyard. Recommended.

$$-$ Afonso, near San Sebastian Chapel, Fontainhas, T0832-222 2359. Atmospheric family-run guesthouse, obliging and friendly, 8 clean rooms with bath, shaded roof terrace for breakfast. It's first come first served, though, as the owners don't take advance bookings. Recommended.

$ Comfort Guest House, 31 Janeiro Rd, T0832-222 8145. Good location, some rooms with TV, but often full and you can't book ahead. The cheaper of its 12 basic rooms have shared bath.

$ Pousada Guest House, Luis de Menezes Rd, T0832-561 8308. Pousada's basic rooms are higgledy-piggledy but have a/c, TV and fridge and attached bath. Will take advance bookings.

Around Panjim *p426*
Miramar Beach

$$$ Goa Marriott Resort, Mandovi River, T0832-246 3333, www.marriott.com.

153 large rooms, good facilities, pool, close to public beach, best hotel in area. Weekend buffet lunches popular with Panjim locals.

$$ Swimsea Beach Resort, T0832-246 4481, swimsea@satyam.net.in. 28 a/c rooms with small balconies, pretty underwhelming, sea-facing best, pool, if you want a quality beach experience better to stay elsewhere.

🍴 Restaurants

Panjim *p418, map p420*

$$ Horseshoe, Rua de Ourem, T0832-243 1788. Mon-Sat 1200-1430, 1900-1030. Portuguese/Goan restaurant set in 2 high-ceilinged rooms with exceptionally good service. Most meals excellent value (Rs 60-80) but daily fish specials are far more costly (from Rs 300). The house pudding, a cashew cake, *Bolo San Rival* (Rs 50), trumps all the great main courses.

$$ Quarterdeck, next to Betim ferry jetty, T0832-243 2905. Goan, Indian, Chinese. Riverside location is the best in Panjim, very pleasant in the evening when brightly lit cruise boats glide gaudily by. Live music.

$$ Venite, 31 Janeiro Rd, T0832-222 5537. Mon-Sat 0800-2200, closes in the afternoon. The most charming of Panjim's eateries has 1st-floor balconies overlooking the Sao Thome street life and good music. Specializing in fish, this place has a great atmosphere.

$$ Viva Panjim, house No 178, signposted from 31 Janeiro Rd, T0832-242 2405. This family-run joint in the atmospheric Fontainhas quarter spills out of the restaurant and out into a courtyard, and dishes up Goan specials like *xacuti* and *cafreal* along with seafood, plus takeaway parcels of Indian, Chinese and continental.

$ Anandashram, opposite **Venite**
31 Janeiro Rd. Serving up platters of
fish and veg *thali*, this is a great place to
break *pao* (local bread) with the locals.
Recommended.
$ Café Tato, off east side of Church Sq.
Closed evenings. Something of a local
institution, tiny little **Tato** is packed at
lunchtime when office workers descend
for its limited range of Goan vegetarian
food. Expect tiny platters of chickpea,
tomato or mushroom bhaji served with
fresh puffed *puris* or soft bread rolls, or
vegetarian cutlets and *thalis*. Upstairs is a/c.
$ Kamat, south end of Municipal Gardens.
Pure vegetarian canteen, huge servings of
thalis, excellent paper *dosas* and *puri bhajis*.
Very popular large central dining hall.
$ Satkar, 18 June Rd, opposite Bombay
Bazaar. **Satkar** serves up fantastic pure
veg food that runs the gamut from South
Indian *idlis* and *thalis* to north Indian *sabzi*
and tandoor dishes, and the best Punjabi
samosas in India. Recommended.

Bakeries, cafés and snacks
$$ A Pastelaria, Dr Dada Vaidya Rd.
Good choice of cakes, pastries and
breads. **Mandovi Hotel** has a branch
too (side entrance).
$$-$ Tea Cafe, house No 5/218, 31
Janerio Rd. In the heart of Fontainhas,
this is a cosy little café serving up cakes
and sandwiches. A nice place to rest
before exploring more of Panjim.

🍷 Bars and clubs

Panjim *p418, map p420*
You can't go 20 paces in Panjim without
finding a bar: pokey little rooms with
a handful of formica tables and chairs
and some snacks being fried up in
the corner. Many are clustered around
Fontainhas. The *feni* (Goa's cashew- or

coconut-extracted moonshine) comes
delivered in jerry cans, making it cheaper
than restaurants. Try **Café Moderna**,
near Cine National, food none too good,
claustrophobic upstairs dining area, but
quality atmosphere.

🎭 Entertainment

Panjim *p418, map p420*
Read the 'today's events' columns
in the local papers for concerts
and performances.
Astronomical Observatory, 7th floor,
Junta House, 18 June Rd (entrance in
Vivekananda Rd). Open 14 Nov-31 May,
1900-2100, in clear weather. Rooftop
6-inch Newtonian reflector telescope and
binoculars. Worth a visit on a moonless
night, and for views over Panjim at sunset.
Inox, Campal, near Kala Academy, www.
inoxmovies.com. Fantastic state-of-the-art
glass-fronted cinema – like going to the
movies in California. You can catch the
latest Bolly- and Hollywood blockbusters
here, and they try to show the Oscar-
nominated Best Movies every year.
Kala Academy, D B Marg, Campal, T0832-
222 3288. This modern and architecturally
impressive centre designed by Charles
Correa was set up to preserve and
promote the cultural heritage of Goa.
There are exhibition galleries, a library
and comfortable indoor and outdoor
auditoria. Art exhibitions, theatre and
music programmes (from contemporary
pop and jazz to Indian classical) are held,
mostly during the winter months. There
are also music and dance courses.
MV Caravela, Fisheries dept building,
D B Marg, Panjim, www.casinocity.com/
in/panjim/caravela. India's first floating
casino is docked on the Mandovi,
66 m of high-rupee-rolling catamaran
casino, all plush wall-to-wall carpets,

chandeliers and sari-bedecked croupiers. The boat accommodates 300 people, has a sun deck, swimming pool and restaurant and the Rs 1200 entrance includes short eats and dinner and booze from 1730 till the morning.

⊛ Festivals

Panjim *p418, map p420*
Feb/Mar In addition to the major festivals in Feb, the **Mardi Gras Carnival** (3 days preceding Lent in Feb/Mar) is a Mediterranean-style riot of merrymaking, marked by feasting, colourful processions and floats down streets: it kicks off near the Secretariat at midday. One of the best bits is the red-and-black dance held in the cordoned-off square outside the old world Clube Nacional on the evening of the last day: everyone dresses up (some cross-dressing), almost everyone knows each other, and there's lots of old-fashioned slow-dancing to curiously Country and Western-infused live music. The red and black theme is strictly enforced.
Mar-Apr Shigmotsav is a spring festival held at full moon (celebrated as **Holi** elsewhere in India); colourful float processions through the streets often display mythological scenes accompanied by plenty of music on drums and cymbals.
1st Sun after Easter Feast of Jesus of Nazareth. Procession of All Saints in Goa Velha, on the Mon of Holy Week.
Dec/Jan Fontainhas Festival of Arts. Timed to coincide with the film festival (see below), 30 heritage homes open up as temporary art and artefact galleries in an event organized by Fundacao Oriente, Goa Heritage Action Group and the Entertainment Society of Goa.
International Film Festival of India, www.iffigoa.org. India's answer to Cannes: a 10-day film mart packed with

screenings for the industry and general public alike, with its headquarters based around the Kala Academy and the Inox building on the banks of the Mandovi. Held in Goa since 2004.
Food and Culture Festival at Miramar Beach.
8 Dec Feast of Our Lady of the Immaculate Conception. A big fair is held in the streets around Church Sq and a firework display is put on in front of the church each night of the week before the feast (at 1930). After morning Mass on the Sun, the Virgin is carried in a procession through the town centre.
24 Dec Christmas Eve. This is celebrated with midnight Mass at 140 churches in the state, but some of the best attended are the Church of the Immaculate Conception and Dom Bosco Church in Panjim and the Basilica of Bom Jesus in Old Goa.

O Shopping

Panjim *p418, map p420*
Books and music
Broadway Books, next to Rock and Raaga off 18 June Rd, T0832-664 7038. Largest bookshop in Goa with good range.
Mandovi Hotel (see Where to stay, page 427). The hotel bookshop has a small range of books and magazines, including American news magazines.
Pedro Fernandes & Co, Rua Jose de Costa, near Head Post Office, T0832-222 6642. If you have a hankering to pick up a sitar or learn to play tabla, this small store has a great selection of musical instruments.
Varsha, near Azad Maidan. Holds a large stock in tiny premises, and is especially good for books on Goa. Obscure titles are not displayed but ask the knowledgeable staff.

Clothes and textiles

Government handicrafts shops are at the tourist hotels and the Interstate Terminus. There are other emporia on RS Rd.

Bombay Store, Casa Mendes, SV Rd, opposite Old Passport Office. A new branch of the lifestyle retail store has arrived in Goa close to the main shopping road 18 June Rd, with good selection of fabrics and clothes, as well as cards, stationery and homewares.

Fab India, Braganza Bungalow, opposite Indoor Stadium, Campal, T0832-246 3096. This is a particularly lovely branch of the great chain which sells handblock print clothes, textiles, home furnishings and furniture. They have an extensive collection.

Government Emporia, RS Rd. Good value for fixed-rate clothes, fabric and handicrafts.

Khadi Showroom, Municipal (Communidade) Building, Church Sq, good value for fixed-rate clothes, fabric and handicrafts. Nehru jackets, plus perishables such as honey and pickles.

Sacha's Shop, Casa Mendes, next to **Bombay Store**, T0832-222 2035. Dubbed a 'curious little space' by the owner, the eponymous **Sacha**, it is a collection of clothes, flea market finds, designer frocks, organic soaps and textiles.

Velha Goa Galeria, 4/191 Rua De Ourem, Fontainhas, T0832-242 6628. Hand-painted ceramics, wall hangings and tabletops of tiles.

Wendell Rodricks Design Space, 158 near Luis Gomes Garden, Altinho, T0832-223 8177, www.wendellrodricks. com. Goa's own fashion designer, brought up in the small village of Colvale, has a beautiful shop in the Altinho district of Panjim. Beautiful fabrics and stylish cuts.

⏱ What to do

Panjim *p418, map p420*
Cruises
Lots of evening cruises go along the Mandovi River, but as all boats seem to sport loud sound systems it's hardly a peaceful cruise.

Music lessons
Manab Das plays regularly at the **Kala Academy** and the **Kerkar** in Calangute (see page 435). He and his wife, Dr Rupasree Das, offer sitar and singing lessons to more long-term visitors. To arrange lessons T0832-242 1086 or email manabrupasreegoa@yahoo.in.

Tour operators
Alpha Holidays, 407-409 Dempo Tower, 4th floor, 16 EDC Patto Plaza, T0832-243 7450, www.alphagoa.com.
Goa Eco Tourism, Rua de Ourem, T0832 2443551. Some interesting tours including the **Jungle Book Tour** staying a night at Bhagwan Mahaveer Sanctuary.
Pepper Tours, 127 Subash Chandra Bose Rd, Jawahar Nagar, Kadavanthara, PO Cochin 682020, T484-405 8886, T(0)9847-322802 (mob), www.peppertours.com.

➔ Transport

Panjim *p418, map p420*
Air The airport is at Dabolim. 29 km via the Zuari Bridge from Panjim. Pre-paid taxis charge Rs 700 to Panjim.
Airline offices Air India, 18 June Rd, T0832-243 1101. **Indian Airlines and Alliance Air**, Dempo House, D B Marg, T0832-223 7821, reservations 1000-1300, 1400-1600, airport T0832-254 0788.**British Airways**, 2 Excelsior Chambers, opposite Mangaldeep, MG Rd, T0832-222 4573.
Jet Airways, Sesa Ghor, 7-9 Patto Plaza,

T0832-243 1472, airport T0832-251 0354. **Qatar Airways**, 001/003 Dempo Trade Center, Patto Plaza, T079 3061 6000. For more information on domestic flights and expected prices see page 6.

Auto-rickshaw Easily available but agree a price beforehand (often Rs 50 minimum); more expensive after dark. Motorcycle taxis and private taxis are a little cheaper.

Bus **Local**: Crowded **Kadamba** (**KTC**) buses and private buses operate from the bus stand in Patto to the east of town, across the Ourem Creek, T0832-243 8035. Booking 0800-1100, 1400-1630. The timetable is not strictly observed; buses leave when full. Frequent service to **Calangute** 35 mins; **Mapusa** 15 mins (try to catch a direct one, you will hear someone calling out what sounds like "durry, durry, durry"!). Via Cortalim (Zuari bridge) to **Margao** 1 hr; **Vasco** 1 hr. To **Old Goa** (every 10 mins) 20 mins, continues to **Ponda** 1 hr. Fares are between Rs 8-20 for these local services.

Long distance: 'Luxury' buses and 'Sleepers' (bunks are shared). Prices double at Diwali, Christmas and New Year, and during the May school holidays. Private operators include **Paulo Travels**, Cardozo Bld, near Kadamba Bus stand, T0832 6637777, www.phmgoa.com, and charge between Rs 450 and 800 for Panjim to **Mumbai**, for example (15 hrs); similar for Bangalore and Pune.

State buses are run by **Kadamba TC**, **Karnataka RTC**, **Maharashtra RTC**. Check times and book in advance at Kadamba Bus Stand. Unlicensed operators use poorly maintained, overcrowded buses; check before travelling. Fares are cheaper than with private operators, but it's not so easy to book or as comfortable. Expect to pay

Rs 350-600 for Panjim to **Mumbai** (15 hrs), similar pricing for **Bangalore** and **Pune**; between Rs 150-400 for Hampi (10 hrs).

Car hire Hertz, T0832-222 3998; **Joey's**, Office No 6, Panjim Park, near Ferry Wharf, T0832-222 8989. **Goa Wheels Unlimited**, T0832-222 4304, is close by in Calangute, www.goawheelsunlimited.com or **Wheels Rental**, airport, T0832-251 2138.

Ferry Flat-bottomed ferries charge a nominal fee to take passengers (and usually vehicles) when rivers are not bridged. **Panjim–Betim** (the Nehru bridge over the Mandovi supplements the ferry); **Old Goa–Diwar Island**; **Ribandar–Chorao** for Salim Ali Bird Sanctuary.

Taxi Tourist taxis are white; hire from your hotel or contact **Goa Tourism**, Trionora Apts, T0832-242 4001. Shared-taxis run on certain routes; available near the the ferry wharves, main hotels and market places (up to 5). **Mapusa** from Panjim, around Rs 10 each.

Train Most trains stop at Thivim and Madgaon, some **Konkan Railway** trains stop at **Karmali**, T0832-228 6398, near Old Goa (20 mins by taxi). **Rail Bookings**, Kadamba Bus Station, 1st floor, T0832-243 5054, 0930-1300 and 1430-1700. **South Central Railway** serves the Vasco–Londa/Belgaum line; for details see page 504, and Margao (Madgaon), page 493.

ⓘ Directory

Panjim p418, map p420
Medical services Goa Medical College, Av PC Lopez, west end of town, T0832-222 3026, is very busy; newer College at Bambolim; **CMM Poly Clinic**, Altinho, T0832-222 5918.

North Goa

While Baga and Calangute, the fishing villages first settled by the 'freaks', now stand as cautionary tales to all that's bad about mass tourism, Anjuna, a place synonymous with psychedelia, drugs and Goa trance parties, has managed to retain a village feel. Despite the existence of its unquestionably shady underbelly, it's a more tranquil place to be now that a 2200 music curfew has put a stop to outdoor parties. The weekly flea market is a brilliant bazar – like Camden or Portobello but with sacred cows, sadhus, fakirs and snake charmers – and makes it onto every holidaymaker's itinerary. But if you stick around you'll find that the little stretch of shoreline from the northern end of Anjuna Beach to the Chapora River is beautifully desolate: rust-coloured rugged cliffs covered with scrub interrupt scrappy bays strewn with laterite boulders. Pretty cliff-backed Vagator stands just south of the romantic ruins of Chapora Fort, with its busy fishing jetty, where trawler landings are met by a welcoming committee of kites, gulls and herons wheeling hungrily on high. Further upstream, around the pretty village of Siolim, young men wade through mangrove swamps to sift the muds for clams, mussels and oysters. Over the Chapora lies Arambol, a warm, hippy backpacker hamlet, and its beach satellites of Mandrem, Asvem and Keri and the wonderful little Catholic enclave clustered around the ancient Tiracol Fort.

Arriving in North Goa

Getting there
The NH17 acts as the main arterial road between all of Goa's coastal belt. From Panjim, the highway crosses the Mandovi Bridge to the area's main hub, Calangute (16 km from Panjim, 10 km from Mapusa). Buses from Mapusa (20 minutes) and Panjim (35 minutes) arrive at Calangute Bus Stand near the market; a few continue to Baga to the north from the crossroads. You can charter tourist minivans from places such as Panjim and Dabolim. The closest stop on the Konkan Railway route between Mumbai and Mangalore is Tivim near Mapusa. On market days there are boats between Baga and Anjuna. There are buses from Mapusa and Panjim to Calangute, Anjuna, Chapora and Arambol.

Getting around
There are 9 km of uninterrupted beach between Fort Aguada and the bridge over Baga river in the north, which takes you to Anjuna. These are split into four beaches, south to north: Sinquerim, Candolim, Calangute and Baga. Each has its own stab at a high street, Calangute's being the most built up. There are taxis, motorcycle taxis, tourist vans and old Ambassador cabs, or cheap but slow public buses. Roads are fairly good for motorbikes and scooters; watch out for speed bumps. Accidents happen with grim regularity, but bikes give you the independence to zip between beaches.

Background

The name Bardez may have come from the term *bara desh* (12 'divisions of land'), which refers to the 12 Brahmin villages that once dominated the region. Another explanation is that it refers to 12 *zagors* celebrated to ward off evil. Or it could be *bahir des*, meaning 'outside land' – ie, the land beyond the Mandovi River. It was occupied by the Portuguese as part of their original conquest, and bears the greatest direct imprint of their Christianizing influence.

Baga to Candolim → For listings, see pages 446-470.

The faultless fawn shoreline of Bardez *taluka*, particularly Calangute, until 40 years ago was a string of fishing villages. Now it acts as sandpit to the bulk of Goa's travel trade. Chock full of accommodation, eateries, travel agents, money changers, beggars and under-dressed, over-sunned charter tourists, the roads snarl up with minivans, buses and bikes, and unchecked development has made for a largely concrete conurbation of breezeblock hotels and mini markets. For all that, if you squint hard or come in monsoon you can still see what once made it such a hippy magnet: wonderful coconut-fringed sands backed by plump dunes occasionally broken by rocky headlands and coves. The main reason to head this way is for business, banks, or posh food and nightlife. To get out again, you can paddle in the waters of the Arabian Sea all the way between the forts of Aguada and Vagator.

Baga

Baga is basically Calangute North: there's continuity in congestion, shops, shacks and sun loungers. Here though, there are also paddy marshes, water tanks and salt pans, the beach is still clean, and the river that divides this commercial strip of sand from Anjuna in the north also brings fishermen pulling in their catch at dawn, and casting their nets at dusk. The north bank, or **Baga River**, is all thick woods, mangroves and birdlife; it has quite a different, more villagey feel, with a few classy European restaurants looking out across the river. You can take an hour to wade across the river at low tide, then walk over the crest of the hill and down into Anjuna South, or detour inland to reach the bridge.

Baga

To Anjuna (2 km)
To Anjuna (500m)
St Ann's
Salt Lake
Salt Pans
Baga River
Baga Bridge
Football Pitch
Arabian Sea
BAGA
Lady of Candelaria
Natural Health Centre
Tito's Rd
Bike Hire
To Calangute

N
200 metres
200 yards

Where to stay
Alidia Beach Cottages 1
Cavala 6
Nani's & Rani's 8
Riverside 3

Restaurants
Baba Au Rhum 2
Britto's 15
Casa Portuguesa 12
Fiesta 1
J&A's Italiano House 6
Lila's Café 9

Bars & clubs
Mambo's 13
Tito's 16

Calangute

More than 25 years of package tourism has guaranteed that there is little left to draw you to Calangute apart from ATMs, some decent restaurants and a quirky hexagonal *barbeiria* (barber's shop) at the northern roundabout. In the 1960s, the village was short-hand for the alternative life, but the main feature of the streets today is their messy Indian take on beach commercialism. Shops peddle everything from cheap ethnic tat to extravagant precious gemstones. The shacks on the beach serve good food and cheap beer and most fly the St George's Cross in tribute to Calangute's charter coin. Between the busy beachfront and the grubby main road, coconut trees give shade to village houses, some of which rent out private rooms.

Away from the town centre, the striking gold and white **Church of St Alex** is a good example of rococo decoration in Goa, while the false dome of the central façade is an 18th-century architectural development. The pulpit and the *reredos* are particularly fine. **Kerkar Art Complex** ⓘ *Gaurawaddo, T0832-227 6017, www. subodhkerkar.com*, is a beautiful art space showcasing Subodh Kerkar's paintings and installation work. Inspired by the ocean, nature is both the theme and medium of his work, using shells, light and water to create static waves or, in his recent installations, using fishermen standing on the beach to create the shapes and forms of fishing boats – all captured in stunning black and white photography.

Calangute

Candolim and Sinquerim beaches

The wide unsheltered stretch of beach here, backed by scrub-covered dunes, offers unusual visual stimulus courtesy of the unlovely rusting wreck of the *Sea Princess* tanker, an eyesore and environmental nightmare (the currents eddying around its bows are playing havoc with coastal sand deposition) which has been resting offshore for years waiting for someone to muster the will to remove it. Nevertheless, the beach still attracts a fair crowd: more staid than Baga and Calangute to the north, chiefly because its restaurants and hotels are pricier and the average holidaymaker more senior. The road from Calangute to Fort Aguada is lined with shiny glass-fronted shops, while the sands at the foot of the Taj complex offers the full gamut of watersports – jet skis, windsurfers, catamaran and dinghies are all for hire – making it a favourite of India's fun-loving domestic tourists.

Fort Aguada

The Portuguese colonizer's strongest coastal fort was built on this northern tip of the Mandovi estuary in 1612 with one goal: to stay the Dutch navy. Two hundred guns were stationed here along with two magazines, four barracks, several residences for officers and two prisons. It was against the Marathas, though, rather than the Dutch, that Aguada saw repeated action – Goans fleeing the onslaught at Bardez took refuge here – and its ramparts proved time and again impregnable. The main fortifications (laterite walls nearly 5 m

Where to stay 🛏
Coco Banana **4**
Kerkar Retreat **3**
Martin's Guest Rooms **13**
The Park **10**
Pousada Tauma **17**
Saahil **1**
Villa Goesa **20**

Restaurants 🍴
A Reverie **3**
Bomras **1**
Café Ciocolatti **6**
Fisherman's Cove **9**
Infanteria **2**
Plantain Leaf **7**
Souza Lobo **8**
Tibetan Kitchen **5**

high and 1.3 m thick) are still intact, and the buildings at sea level now house Goa's Central Jail, whose 142 male and 25 female inmates are incarcerated in what must be one of the world's prettiest lock-ups.

Reis Magos, the Nerul River and Coco Beach

The position of **Reis Magos**, across the Mandovi River from Panjim, made it imperative for Albuquerque to station troops on this shoulder of headland from day one of Portuguese rule – today, come for the views to the capital, and for the crumbling **Royal Fort** whose angular 16th-century architecture is now overrun with jungle. Its canons served as the second line of defence against the Dutch after Aguada. The next door **church** is where the village gets its name – this was where the first Mass on Goan soil was celebrated in 1550, and the Hindu temple was promptly turned over into a church to the three Magi Kings – Gaspar, Melchior and Balthazar – whose stories are told on the inside *reredos*. Fort Aguada and Fort Reis Magos are divided by the Nerul River: stop off at Nerul's **Coco Beach** for lunch and a swim. The temple in the village dates from 1910 and the Church of Our Lady of Remedies from 1569.

Mapusa → *For listings, see pages 446-470.*

Standing in the nape of one of Goa's east–west ridges lies Bardez's administrative headquarters: a buzzy, unruly market town filled with 1960s low-rise buildings set on former marshland on the banks of the Mapusa River; (Maha apsa' means 'great swamps, a reference to Mapusa's watery past). Mapusa town won't find its way onto many tourist postcards, but it's friendly, small and messy, is an important transport hub and has an excellent daily **municipal market**, worth journeying inland for, especially on its busiest day, Friday. Open from early morning Monday to Saturday, it peters out 1200-1500, then gathers steam again till night, and has giant rings of *chourica* sausage, tumbles of spices and rows of squatting fruit and vegetable hawkers.

Walk east for the small 16th-century **St Jerome's Church**, or 'Milagres', Our Lady of Miracles (1594), rebuilt first in 1674 then again in 1839 after a candle sparked a devastating fire. In 1961 the roof was badly damaged when the Portuguese blew up a nearby bridge in their struggle with the liberating Indian army. The church has a scrolled gable, balconied windows in the façade, a belfry at the rear and an interesting slatted wood ceiling. The main altar is to Our Lady, and on either side are St John and St Jerome: the *retables* (shelves behind the altar) were brought from Daugim. The church is sacred to Hindus as well as Catholics, not only because it stands near the site of the Shanteri Temple but also because 'Our Lady of Miracles' was one of seven Hindu sisters converted to Christianity. Her lotus pattern gold necklace (kept under lock and key) may also have been taken from a Hindu deity who preceded her.

The **Maruti Temple** ① *west of the market opposite taxi stand*, was built on the site of a firecracker shop where Rama followers in the 1840s would gather in clandestine

The trance dance experience

The 'freaks' (beatniks with super-nomadic genes, giant drug habits and names like Eight Finger Eddie) first shipped into Goa shortly after the Portuguese left. Some brought guitars on which, after soaking up a bit of Hindu spirituality on the way, they were charged with playing devotional songs at beach campfire parties.

By the end of the 1960s, thousands of freaks were swarming into Goa, often spilling down from Kathmandu, and word got back to proper paid-up acid rock musicians about the scene. Some more substantial entertainment was called for.

The first music to run through the speakers was rock and reggae. Led Zeppelin, The Who and George Harrison rocked up and played live, but the freaks' entertainment was mostly recorded: Santana, Rolling Stones and Bob Marley. Kraftwerk and synth had filtered in by the late 1970s but the shift to electronica only really came in the early 1980s when musicians got bored of the lyrics and blanked out all the words on albums of industrial noise, rock and disco, using the fully lo-fi production method of taping between two cassette decks. Depeche Mode and New Order albums were stripped down for their drum and synth layers. Some of the rock faithful were angry with the change in the soundtrack to their lives; at those early 1980s parties, when the psychedelic-meets-machine-drum sound that still defines Goa trance was first being pumped out, legend has it that the decks had to be flanked by bouncers.

The music, developing in tandem to German nosebleed techno and UK acid house, locked into a worldwide worship of first a picture, then a silver image, of monkey god Hanuman after the Portuguese destroyed the local Hindu temples.

Barely 5 km east of Mapusa lies **Moira**, deep in the belly of a rich agricultural district that was once the scene of Portuguese mass baptisms. The town is ancient – some say it was the site of a sixth or seventh century AD Mauryan settlement – and until the arrival of the Portuguese it must have been a Brahmin village. A total of seven important temples were destroyed during the Inquisition and six idols moved to Mulgaon in Bicholim district (immediately east).

Today the village is dominated by the unusual **Church of Our Lady of the Immaculate Conception**. Originally built of mud and thatch in 1619, it was rebuilt during the 19th century with square towers close to the false dome. The balustrades at the top of the first and second floors run the length of the building and the central doorways of the ground and first floors have Islamic-looking trefoil arches that contrast with the Romanesque flanking arches. There is an interesting exterior pulpit. Inside, the image of the crucifixion is unusual in having its feet nailed apart instead of together. A Siva *lingam* recycled here as the base of the font after its temple was razed is now in the Archaeological Museum at Old Goa. Moira's famous long red bananas (grown nearby) are not eaten raw but come cooked with sugar and coconuts as the cavity-speeding sweet *figada*.

tapestry of druggy drumscapes, but the Goan climate created its own sound. As records would warp in India's high temperatures, music had to be put down on DATS rather than vinyl which in turn meant tracks were played out in full, unmixed. A track had to be interesting enough then, self-contained, so it could be played uninterrupted in full; producers had to pay more attention to intros, middles and outros – in short, the music had to have a story. It also meant there was less art to a set by a trance DJ in Goa than DJs in Manchester, Detroit and Paris, who could splice records together to make their own new hybrid sounds.

Many of the original makers of this music had absorbed a fair whack of psychedelia and had added the inevitable layer of sadhu thinking to this – superficially measured in incense, *oms*, dreads and the swirling dayglo mandalas that unmistakeably mark out a Goa trance party. The music reflected this: sitars noodled alongside sequencer music to make the Goan signature sound.

By the 1990s, though, Ecstasy had arrived in Goa. The whole party scene opened right up, peopled by Spiral Tribe crusties as well as middle-class gap year lovelies and global party scenesters who came looking for an alternative to the more mainstream fare in Ibiza. Paul Oakenfold's Perfecto was a key label in fuelling the sound's popularity but there were more: Dragonfly, The Infinity Project, Return to the Source. Today trance is still a thriving part of the Goa circuit and, although much of it is from European or Japanese studios, there's also the odd home-grown label.

Anjuna and around → For listings, see pages 446-470.

When the freaks waded across the Baga River after the squares got hip to Calangute, Anjuna was where they washed up. The village still plays host to a large alternative community: some from that first generation of hippies, but the latest influx of spiritual Westerners has brought both an enterprising spirit and often young families, meaning there's fresh pasta, gnocci, marinated tofu or chocolate brownies to be had, cool threads to buy, great, creative childcare, amazing tattoo artists, alternative therapists and world-class yoga teachers. For the beautiful life lived cheap Anjuna is still hard to beat; the countryside here is hilly and lush and jungly, the beaches good for swimming and seldom crowded. A state crackdown has made for a hiatus in the parties for which Anjuna was once synonymous, but as you head south along the shore the beach shack soundtracks get progressively more hardcore, until **Curlies**, where you'll still find arm-pumping techno and trance.

The **Flea Market** ① *Dandovaddo, south Anjuna, Oct-Apr Wed 0800 till sunset, water taxis (from Baga) or shared taxis from anywhere in Goa*, is a brilliant hullabaloo with over 2000 stalls hawking everything from Gujarati wooden printing blocks to Bhutanese silver and even Burberry-check pashminas. The trade is so lucrative by the subcontinent's standards that for six months a year several thousand Rajasthani, Gujaratis, Karnatakans and Tibetans decamp from their home states to tout their wares. The flea had very different origins, and was once an intra-community car boot-style bric-a-brac sale for the freaks. Anjuna's links with trade pre-date the hippies though – the port was an important Arab trading post in the 10th and 12th centuries.

Saturday Night Bazar ① *Arpora Hill, 1630-2400*, is a more sanitized and less headlong version of the flea. There's no shortage of dazzling stall fronts draped with glittering saris and the beautiful Rajasthani fare, but while there are fewer stalls there's more variety here; expats who've crafted everything from organic yoga clothes and designer mosquito nets to handmade leather goods are more likely to pitch up here than at the Wednesday event. But there's no need to shop at all – the live music and huge range of food stalls make the Night Bazaar the weekly social

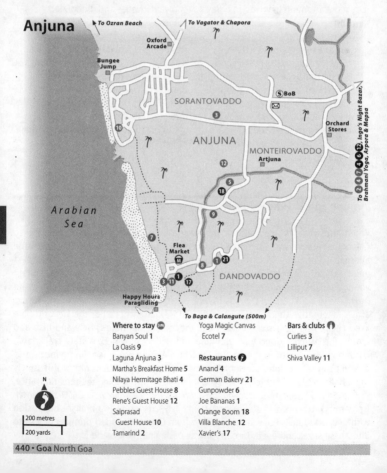

Anjuna

To Ozran Beach
To Vagator & Chapora
Oxford Arcade
Bungee Jump
ⓈBoB
SORANTOVADDO
❸
To Ingo's Night Bazaar,
Brahmani Yoga, Arpora & Mapsa
Orchard Stores
❷❹❼❻❷
ANJUNA
MONTEIROVADDO
❶❷
Artjuna
❺
❶❽
Arabian Sea
❾
❼
Flea Market
❽ ❶❷❶
❸❶❶ ❶❼
DANDOVADDO
Happy Hours Paragliding
To Baga & Calangute (500m)

N
200 metres
200 yards

Where to stay 🛏	Yoga Magic Canvas	Bars & clubs 🍸
Banyan Soul 1	Ecotel 7	Curlies 3
La Oasis 9		Lilliput 7
Laguna Anjuna 3	**Restaurants** 🍴	Shiva Valley 11
Martha's Breakfast Home 5	Anand 4	
Nilaya Hermitage Bhati 4	German Bakery 21	
Pebbles Guest House 8	Gunpowder 6	
Rene's Guest House 12	Joe Bananas 1	
Saiprasad	Orange Boom 18	
Guest House 10	Villa Blanche 12	
Tamarind 2	Xavier's 17	

event for tourist and long-stayer alike. You'll find most of North Goa out for the evening, and many businesses shut up shop for the night as a result of the bazar's magnetic appeal. Bring cash and an appetite.

The Anjuna area is also home to two of Goa's best contemporary yoga schools. **Brahmani** ⓘ *www.brahmaniyoga.com*, housed in in the grounds of **Tito's White House**, runs workshops and drop-in classes, from excellent *ashtanga*, Mysore-style, to more free-flowing movement like dance yoga, and *Scaravelli*. Packages with unlimited yoga are offered, but accommodation is not on site or specifically for yoga students. Ten minutes away in the neighbouring village of **Assagao**, the **Purple Valley Yoga Retreat** ⓘ *T0832-226 8364, www.yogagoa.com, offer retreat packages including yoga and meals (see box, page 465),* runs two-week *ashtanga* retreats with leading teachers like Sharath Rangaswamy, grandson of Sri K Pattabhi Jois, David Swenson and Nancy Gilgoff, two of the first to introduce *ashtanga* to the West in the 1970s. Lessons are held in a lovely *shala* in delightful gardens, food is vegetarian and the atmosphere collegiate.

Vagator

Vagator's beaches are possibly Goa's most dramatic: here, muddied sand bays upset by slabs of gray rock, quite different from the bubblings of porous laterite in Anjuna, fall at the bottom of terraced red cliffs planted with coconut trees that lean out towards the crashing waves, some of their trunks painted bright neon from past parties.

Big Vagator Beach is a long sweep of beach to the right of the main access road, behind which stands the profile of the wide outer rim of the ruined **Chapora Fort** against a stunning backdrop of India's western coastline, stretching beyond Goa's northern borders and into Maharashtra. The factory you can just pick out in the distance marks the border.

To your left, running inland, is **Little Vagator Beach**, its terracing lorded over by **Nine Bar**, a giant venue with an unswerving musical loyalty to trance (see box, page 438). Just out of sight is **Ozran Beach**, christened 'Spaghetti Beach' by English settlers for its Italian community. Though a bit scrappy and dogged by persistent sarong sellers, **Spaghetti** is more sheltered, more scenic and more remote than the other beaches, ending in tumbled rocks and jungle, with excellent swimming spots. To get straight to Spaghetti from Vagator follow the signposts to Leoney Resorts, then when you reach the headland turn off the tarmac road onto one of the gravel tracks following the sign for Shiva Place shack; coming from Anjuna, take the path that starts just inland from Zoori's and thread your way down the gravelly terracing.

Chapora Fort

Looming over the north end of Big Vagator Beach, there's little left of Chapora Fort but crumbling blocks of black rock overgrown with tawny grasses and a general air of tranquil ruination. Built by Adil Shah (hence the name, Shah pura), the remaining ramparts lead out to a jutting promontory that affords spectacular sunset views across the mouth of the Chapora River, where fishing boats edge slowly out of harbour and seabird flocks settle on the sand spits across from Morjim.

Chapora village itself may be too feral for some tastes. At dusk the smoke from domestic fires spreads a haze through the jungle canopy between which Portuguese houses stand worn and derelict. Down by the river's edge men lean to mend their fuzzy nets while village boys saunter out to bat on threshed fields, and Enfields and Hondas hum along the potholed roads bearing long-stayers and Goan village folk home – many of them toting fresh catch from the buzzing fish market (ignore the stern 'No Entry' signs and ride on in) held every sunset at the harbour. Along the village's main street the shady bars are decked with fairy lights and the internationals (who call Chapora both 'home' and, in an affectionate nod to its less savoury side, 'the Bronx') settle down to nurse their drinks.

The flat arc of the estuary here is perfect for cycling: the rim-side road will take you all the way out to the bridge at **Siolim** where you can loop back to take a look at the **Church of St Anthony**. Built in 1606, it replaced an earlier Franciscan church dating from 1568. Both Goa's Hindu and Catholic communities pray to St Anthony, Portugal's patron saint, in the hope of good fishing catches. The high, flat-ceilinged church has a narrow balustraded gallery and Belgian glass chandeliers, with statues of Jesus and St Anthony in the gabled west end.

Splendid Portuguese houses stand scattered about the village's shadows in varying degrees of disrepair; it's worth walking around to take in some of the facades. You can even stay in one which has been refurbished, the lovely Siolim House, see page 450. The ferry that once crossed the Chapora River at the northern end of the village no longer runs (there's a bridge instead) but it's worth heading up this way for the little daily fish market and the handful of food stalls selling fresh grilled catch. The village also has a basic bar, **Mandola**, on the coast road heading back towards Chapora, selling European snacks and cold beer.

Arambol, Keri, Morjim, Asvem and Mandrem → *For listings, see pages 446-470.*

The long bridge that spans the Chapora River joins Bardez to the last – and thus most heavily Hindu – of the new conquests, hilly Pernem *taluka*. This is the gateway to a series of pretty and quiet beaches that hug the coastal road in a nearly unbroken strip up to the Maharashtra border, where a tiny pocket of Catholicism squats in the shadow of the pretty pride of the district, Tiracol Church and Fort. Haphazard and hippy Arambol has a warm community feel and is rightly popular with open-minded travellers of all ages, who are drawn to its vibey scene, its live music, the dolphins that fin along its beaches and its famous saltwater lake. Sunset takes on the magnitude of a ritual in Arambol: people gather to sing, dance, juggle, do *capoeira* or find a silent spot for meditation and contemplation. To the south, Mandrem and Asvem are more chic and less busy, and will suit those less prepared to compromise on their accommodation. With construction of a new airport near Pernem and a large road bridge over the Tiracol to Maharashtra finally open, Northern Goa is becoming more accessible, and there will be increased development no doubt.

Arriving in Arambol, Keri, Morjim, Asvem and Mandrem

All of Pernem *taluka* is within easy reach of the hotels in Panjim or Calangute, but you'd be doing yourself a disservice to visit what are arguably North Goa's loveliest beaches just on a day trip. Better to set up camp in one and make it your base to explore the rest. If you are crossing the bridge at Siolim on a motorbike turn left off the new main road immediately after the bridge to use the smaller, more scenic coastal roads. There also regular buses to the villages from Mapusa and from Chopdem. Each beach is about 10 minutes apart.

Background

The Bhonsles of Sawantwadi in modern Maharashtra were the last to rule Pernem before being ousted by the Portuguese in 1788, and Maratha influences here remain strong.

Arambol (Harmal)

Arambol, which you reach when the plateau road noses down through paddy fields and cashew trees, is a beautiful long stretch of sand at the bottom of a bumpy dirt track that's fringed with stalls selling brightly coloured, heavily embroidered

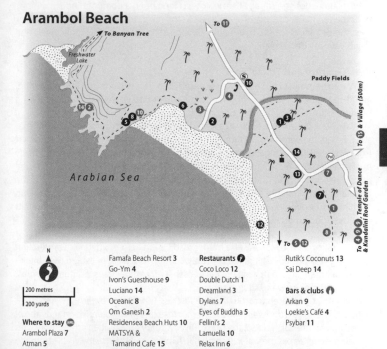

Arambol Beach

N

200 metres
200 yards

Where to stay
Arambol Plaza 7
Atman 5
Ave Maria 1

Famafa Beach Resort 3
Go-Ym 4
Ivon's Guesthouse 9
Luciano 14
Oceanic 8
Om Ganesh 2
Residensea Beach Huts 10
MATSYA &
  Tamarind Cafe 15
Whispering Lakes 12

Restaurants
Coco Loco 12
Double Dutch 1
Dreamland 3
Dylans 7
Eyes of Buddha 5
Fellini's 2
Lamuella 10
Relax Inn 6
Rice Bowl 8

Rutik's Coconuts 13
Sai Deep 14

Bars & clubs
Arkan 9
Loekie's Café 4
Psybar 11

clothes and pretty *lungis*. This is the creative and holistic hub of Goa – many Western designers, artists, performers, yogis and healers have been inspired to make the area home, and because people have put down roots here, the village is abuzz with industriousness. Flyers advertise *satsang* with smiling Western gurus: there's also *tabla* classes and drumming circles, yoga teacher training, reiki and belly dancing. Arrive at the right time of year and you might catch the International Juggling Convention in full swing, or stumble across a phenomenal fire-dancing show by performers who work their magic on the stages of Vegas. Arambol is also synonymous with live music, with everything from Indian classical to open mike, Sufi musicians and psychedelic metal bands playing in rotation at the beach bars. Inevitably, though, Arambol's ever-growing popularity means both long and short-term accommodation get more expensive by the year.

You have to skirt the beach's northern cliff and tiny basalt rocky bays by foot to reach the real lure: a second bay cut off from the roads and a natural 'sweet water' lake that collects at the base of a jungle spring. The lagoon collects just metres from the high tide line where the lush forest crawls down to the water's edge. You can walk up the spring's path to reach a belt of natural mineral clay: an idyllic spot for self-service mud baths. Further into the jungle is the famous banyan tree, its branches straddling 50 m, which has long been a point of Hindu and hippy pilgrimage. Or clamber over the boulders at the north to join the scrappy dirt track over the headland for the half-hour walk it takes to reach the achingly lovely and reliably empty Keri Beach.

Keri (Querim) and Tiracol Fort

Goa's northernmost beach is uniquely untouched. The drive towards Keri (Querim) along the banks of the Tiracol River from Pernem passes through some stunning rural areas untouched by any tourist development.

Walk across deep dunes to a casuarina thicket and out onto empty sand that stretches all the way from the mouth of the Tiracol river to the highland that splits it from Arambol. Querim gets busy on weekends with Indian tourists and occasionally hosts parties, but remains a lovely spot of sand. You can reach the beach from the north on foot from the Tiracol ferry terminal, or from the south by walking round the headland from Arambol. The Tiracol ferry runs every 30 minutes 0600-2130 taking 15 minutes, depending on the tides. The ferry is still charming, but more redundant now the bridge is open.

Tiracol (Terekhol), at the northernmost tip of Goa, is a tiny enclave of just 350 Catholics on the Maharashtra border just 3.5 km across where *feni* production is the biggest business. Its name probably comes from *tir-khol* ('steep river bank') and it's a jungly little patch of land full of cashew trees, banyans, orange blossoms, black-faced monkeys and squirrels.

The small but strategic fort ① *0900-1800, cross Tiracol river by ferry (every 30 mins 0600-2130) and walk the remaining 2 km; ferries take cars and motorbikes*, stands above the village on the north side of the Tiracol River estuary on a rugged promontory with amazing views across the water. Its high battlement walls are clearly visible from the Arambol headland. Built by the Maharaja Khem Sawant Bhonsle in the 17th century, it is protected from attacks from the sea, while the walls on the land side rise from a dry moat. It was captured in 1746 by the Portuguese Viceroy Dom Pedro Miguel de Almeida (Marques de Alorna), who renamed it Holy Trinity and had a chapel built inside (now St Anthony's). You can explore the fort's battlements and tiny circular turrets that scarcely seem fit for slaying the enemy. The views south are magnificent. Steps lead down to a terrace on the south side while the north has an open plateau.

St Anthony's Church ① *open on Wed and Sun for Mass at 1730*, inside the tiny fort, was built in the early 1750s soon after the Portuguese takeover. It has a classic Goan façade and is just large enough to cater for the small village. In the small courtyard, paved with laterite blocks, stands a modern statue of Christ. The **Festival of St Anthony** is held here at the beginning of May (usually on the second Tuesday) instead of on the conventional festival day of 13 June.

Morjim (Morji) to Asvem

Morjim, which stands on the opposite side of the estuary from Chapora, has two wide sweeping beaches that both sit at the bottom of separate dead end streets. This inaccessibility means that, development-wise, it has got away relatively unscathed. The southern, protected, turtle beach appears at the end of the narrow track that winds along the north bank of the Chapora rivermouth. Loungers, which are mostly empty, are strewn haphazardly north of the official-looking **Turtle Nesting Control Room**.

The wide shoreline with its gentle incline (the water is hip height for about 100 m) is washed by easy rolling breakers, making it one of North Goa's best swimming beaches. The northern beach, or **Little Morjim**, a left turn off the main coast road is, by comparison, an established tourist hamlet with guesthouses and beach huts.

The road from Morjim cuts inland over the low wooded hills running parallel to the coast. After a few kilometres the road drops down to the coast and runs along the edge of northeast tilting **Asvem Beach**. (Morjim faces Chapora to the south and west.) The northern end of this peaceful palm-fringed beach is divided by a small river. It's a great stretch of beach, which, alas, is gaining in popularity, with increasing development.

Mandrem

Mandrem creek forces the road to feed inland where it passes through a small commercial centre with a few shops and a bank. Mandrem village has the **Shri Bhumika Temple** housing an ancient image. In the **Shri Purchevo Ravalnatha Temple** there is a particularly striking medieval image of the half-eagle, half-human Garuda, who acts as the *vahana* (carrier) of Vishnu.

A little further on, a lane off to the left leads down towards the main beach and a secluded hamlet in a beautifully shaded setting. The **beach** is one of the least developed along this stretch of coast; for the moment it is managing to tread that fine line between having enough facilities for comfort and enough isolation to guarantee idyllic peace. Further north there is a lagoon fringed by palm trees and some simple rooms, virtually all with sea view.

North Goa listings

For hotel and restaurant price codes and other relevant information, see pages 13-17.

⊜ Where to stay

For more on places to stay in this area, see www.goatourism.org/accomodation/north.

Baga *p435, map p435*
Of the family guesthouses on the northern side of Baga River up towards Arpora, those to the left of the bridge (west or seaward) are quieter. You might be able to get a room in houses/cottages with good weekly or monthly rates. Standards vary so check room and security first. Try Wilson Fernandes at **Nani's & Rani's**.
$$$-$ Cavala, Sauntavaddo, top end of Baga village, T0832-227 6090, www.cavala. com. Sandwiched between Baga Rd and a big field stretching towards the mountains, **Cavala** is traditional but very well maintained, with friendly and attentive management, and set in lovely gardens. The 30 rooms are big, with giant fridges and huge bathrooms, although only shower. Some have TV. They have regular music nights in their popular restaurant and they also have a new villa for rent in neighbouring Anjuna. Recommended.
$$ Alidia Beach Cottages, behind the Church, Sauntavaddo, T0832-227 9014, alidia@rediffmail.com. Weave around the pot-plant covered yards to reach this charming hotel in a series of 2-storey cottages, run professionally but with the warmth of a guesthouse. Rooms are spotless and old fashioned, with features including handmade fitted wardrobes, and offer lots of privacy around the well-tended garden. One of the best of its kind so book ahead.

$$-$ Riverside, Baga River by the bridge, T0832-227 7337, www.hotelriversidegoa. com. Nice location overlooking the river. Clean modern rooms with good balconies. Some cottages with kitchens available near the pool. Has a tour group feel about the place, but lovely location.
$ Nani's & Rani's, T0832-227 7014, www.naniranigoa.com. 8 spartan rooms (shared or own bath), budget meals served in pleasant garden, bar, email, STD/ISD. One of the few local budget options with a sea view and a relaxing quiet location – attractive main building. Renowned healer Dr Patrick hosts sessions and workshops here on occasion. Short walk across Baga Bridge for nightlife.

Calangute *p435, map p436*
$$$$ The Park, Holiday St Calangute, www.theparkhotels.com. Boutique number offering up chic white rooms – 2 suites have sea views but to enjoy the beach at its best head to the bar and restaurant. There is a lovely pool as well and cute shop on site. Best doors ever with fantastic photography from Rohit Chawla adorning them.
$$$$ Pousada Tauma, Porbavaddo Calangute, T0832-227 9061, www.pousada-tauma.com. A shady little complex built of Goa's trademark laterite rock set around a beautiful pool. It's discreet but full of character, with old-fashioned yet understated service. Suites are spacious, but come with shower not bath. Classy without a modern 5-star swagger.
$$$ Kerkar Retreat, Gauravaddo, T0832-227 6017, www.subodhkerkar. com/retreat. Get inspired by staying above this beautiful art gallery (see page 435). **Subodh Kerkar** is a visionary artist and has created a beautiful oasis in

the midst of Calangute. Just 5 doubles with an overflowing library and an array of stunning artwork. A guesthouse feel that's ideal for families since it also has a kitchen you can use. Somewhat sedate by Calangute's standards – but that's a compliment. Highly recommended.
$$$-$$ Villa Goesa, Cobravaddo, off Baga Rd, T0832-227 7535, www.nivalink. com/vilagoesa. 57 clean rooms, some a/c, some very shaded, excellent restaurant, lovely gardens, pool, quiet, relaxing, very friendly owners, 300-m walk from the beach. Recommended.
$$-$ Coco Banana, 5/139A Umtavaddo, back from Calangute Beach, T0832-227 6478, www.cocobananagoa.com. In a nice neighbourhood in the backlanes of Calangute, this is one of the best local guesthouses and has 6 spotless en suite bungalows set in a leafy garden. All rooms come with nets and fridges, some have TV and a/c, and the place is airy, light and comfortable. The Swiss-German owners are caring and helpful. They also rent out 2 apartments in **Casa Leyla**, and have a whole house, **Soledad**, with all mod cons and maid service.
$ Martin's Guest Rooms, Baga Rd, T0832-227 7306, martins@goatelecom. com. 5 rooms in family house, attractive verandas, use of kitchen but on the busy main road and could do with a lick of paint.
$ Saahil, Cobravaddo, Baga Rd, T0832-227 6647. Lots of big, clean rooms within walking distance of all the action. Good value.

Candolim and Sinquerim beaches
p436

$$$$ Fort Aguada Beach Resort, Sinquerim, T0832-664 5858, www.taj hotels.com. The self-confessed sprawling Taj complex spreads over 36 ha. In descending order of cost, these are

17 hilltop family villas that make up the Aguada Hermitage, 130 rooms with sea views at the Fort Aguada Beach Resort, built in the fort's ruins, and scores of cottages for up to 8 on the beach in the newer and very beautifully kept **Taj Holiday Village**, about 2 km away – there is a shuttle bus between the 2 resorts. Between the 2 hotels there is a recommended spa, 2 freshwater pools, 9 restaurants, plus golf, tennis and a crèche. The **Banyan Tree Thai** restaurant is especially recommended.
$$$$-$$$ Aashyana Lakhanpal, Escrivao Vaddo, Candolim, T0832-248 9225, www.aashyanalakhanpal.com. One of the most stunning places in Goa – delightful gardens with great swathes of green lead right down to the beach. If you don't fancy the beach, there's a lovely pool. And the rooms and villas are beautifully decorated. This is a great place to hide away. Recommended.
$$$$-$$$ Lemon Tree Amarante Beach Resort, Vadi, Candolim, T0832-398 8188 (central reservations T0991-170 1701), www.lemontreehotels.com. Try to get one of the 6 heritage rooms here, housed inside a grand century-old Portuguese mansion but restored now, as the rest of the hotel, in mock 15th-century Portuguese style. The complex has Wi-Fi, a kids' centre, pool, 2 restaurants, a spa and all mod cons.
$$$$-$$$ The Sol, road opposite Bank of India, Nerul (directly inland 2 km from Calangute/Sinquerim), T0832-671 4141, www.thesol.in. Designed by fashion designer Tarun Tahiliani this is a nouveau heritage-style property where they strive to create an atmosphere that honours Goa as it once was. Tucked in lush foliage with views of Sinquerim river, the rooms are big, the beds are 4-postered.

$$$ Marbella Tourist Home, left off the road to Taj Fort Aguada Beach Resort, T0832-247 9551, www.marbellagoa.com. Splendid mock-Portuguese period mansion with 6 lovingly decorated rooms. Its owners have scavenged bona fide antiques and furnishings like mosaic tiles from old villas to create this elegant and unpretentious homestay in a forest at the end of a dirt track. Lovely garden sit-out for meals. All rooms have a/c and cable TV. Recommended.

$ Ludovici Tourist Home, Dando, Sinquerim, T0832-237 9684. Pretty family home set back off the main road with 4 modest en suite doubles, all with fan. It very much feels that you are one of the family. There's a bar and restaurant and a lovely porch with chairs that gives onto a spacious garden. Sedate and modest guesthouse with traditional charm.

Mapusa and inland *p437*
$$$$ Avanilaya, on the island of Corjuem, 9 km east of Mapusa, T0832-2484888, www.avanilaya.com. Just 4 elegant rooms in this stunning secluded house overlooking the Mapusa River, potentially by time of reading there will be more rooms available in neighbouring properties. Not much to do here except laze in bliss with Ayurvedic massages and facials, amazing food and mesmerizing views.
$$$ Presa di Goa, Arais Wado, Nagoa-Saligao, T0832-240 9067, www.presadigoa.com. Dubbed as a country house retreat, **Presa di Goa** is a beautifully decorated place with antique furniture, some with 4-poster beds. There's a relaxed vibe and a lovely swimming pool. And even though it's not close to the sea and there's not much going on around there, it's perfect for getting away from it all.

$$$ Wildernest, www.wildernestgoa. com. Amazing eco resort tucked into the border of Goa with Maharashtra and Karnataka – it's 1½ hrs from Mapusa. This eco-hotel sprung up as a protest – the land was to be sold to a big mining company and in order to save it **Wildernest** was created. So this place is the real deal, they are concerned with the local wildlife and there is a research centre on-site and for guests there are birdwatching tours and waterfall treks. The luxe log cabins hug the valley with amazing views of the ghats and there is an infinity swimming pool hanging just above the horizon. Working closely with 6 local villages from all 3 states, they offer up delicious home-cooked food. This is an alternative view of Goa. Wholeheartedly recommended.

Anjuna and around *p439, map p440*
At the budget end, the best options in Anjuna, Vagator and Chapora tend to be unofficial, privately owned residences. .
$$$$ Nilaya Hermitage Bhati, T0832-227 6793, www.nilayahermitage. com. A luxury retreat in topaz on a hilltop in Arpora overlooking Anjuna. Elite accommodation in 10 unique bungalows and 4 tents in lush gardens set around a beautiful plunge pool. Tennis, badminton, gym, yoga, jogging trail, DVD library and excellent restaurant, highly prized music room, but some have found fault with the warmth of service and food.

$$$ Laguna Anjuna, Sorantovaddo, T(0)9822-162111, www.lagunaanjuna. com. Atmospheric cottages spiralling off behind stunning swimming pool and lush gardens, some with amazing domed ceilings and divan daybeds. Beautiful bathrooms and comfy beds. It's good for a romantic getaway. This is a vibey place serving up great food from the popular restaurant by the frangipani-fringed pool. You can come and use the lovely pool for Rs 150.

$$$ La Oasis, Flea Market Rd, T0832-227 3181, www.theverda.com. New kid on the block offering up a 3-storey hotel with all mod cons in the heart of Anjuna. It's all quite typical fare but there is a lovely rooftop pool – you are literally up in the palm leaves.

$$ The Banyan Soul, behind German Bakery, off Flea Market Rd, T(0)9820-707283, sumityardi@thebanyansoul. com. Chic complex of rooms nestled under giant banyan tree. Funky modern rooms with beautiful artistic lighting and all mod cons, sexy showers, TVs and compact verandas. The only drawback is the rooms take up the whole site; there are smart gardens bordering the hotel, but it is a bit boxed in.

$$ The Tamarind, 3 km inland from Anjuna, behind St Michael's Church, Kumar Vaddo, Mapusa Rd, T0832-227 3074, www.the tamarindhotel.com. With a chic facelift and change in management, **The Tamarind** is offering up stylish accommodation in a quiet part of Anjuna. There is a pretty pool and new restaurant.

$$ Yogamagic Canvas Ecotel, 2 km from Anjuna beach, T0832-652 3796, www.yogamagic.net. With Maharani suites and Rajasthani hunting tents with added bamboo roofs, this is a luxe campsite surrounded by fields of paddy and palms. Beautifully landscaped, there is a naturally filtered pool, immaculate gardens of bougainvillea, lilies and lotus flowers, yoga and holistic therapies, delicious vegetarian South Indian food and everything has been built with a nod towards the environment. The yoga temple is very beautiful.

$$-$ Martha's Breakfast Home, House No 907, Monteiro Vaddo Anjuna, T0832-227 3365, mpd8650@hotmail.com. Set in the gardens of a house that give onto an orchard where pigs roam in the shade. 8 spic-and-span rooms, twin beds, small shower rooms (cold water) with nice little balconies. Better though are the 2 villas with 2 doubles, little lounges with telly, and kitchenettes with gas stove, sink and fridge. Ask for the Sunset Villa, which has incredible views. Basic but perfect.

$ Pebbles, Piqueno Peddem, Flea Market Rd, T(0)880-685 9992, www. anjunapebbles.com. Well located for market and beach – you could almost get away without getting your own transport which is a rarity for Anjuna. Basic rooms but great value, friendly owner. You might want to hide on Wed when the road will be busy outside.

$ Rene's Guest House, Monterio Waddo, opposite Artjuna, T0832-227 3405, renesguesthousegoa@yahoo.co.in. A gem: 14 rooms around a colourful garden run by a friendly family. Best are the 3 self-contained cottages, with 4-poster beds, good kitchens with gas stove, sinks and big fridges; these are meant for long lets (2 are designed for couples, the other sleeps 3). Individual rooms are decent too.

$ Saiprasad, north beach, T(0)9890-394839, saiprasadguesthouse@gmail. com. Uninspiring rooms some with a/c, but great location – right on the beach which is unusual for Anjuna. Pretty little gardens and beachside restaurant.

Vagator p441

$$$ Living Room, T(0)830-881 1640, www.livingroomhotel.in. Brand new shiny hotel in stark contrast to the rest of the Vagator abodes. Definitely a sign of the changing face of Goa, chic rooms with all the mod cons, nice courtyard pool, Arabian-themed restaurant.

$$$ Ozran Heights Beach Resort, Ozran Beach, T0832-227 4985, www. ozranheights.com. "We promise the best view in Goa", proclaims their website and for once they might just be right. This cliffside hangout is a bit pricey, but what a view. High-end cabins nicely decorated, there is also a small pool and on-site restaurant as well as being neighbours to the immensely popular Greek restaurant, **Thalassa**.

$$ Leoney Resort, 10-min walk from beach, T0832-227 3634, www.leoney resort.com. 13 rooms, 3 cottages, a/c extra Rs 400. Clean, modern, family-run, low-key, quiet, pool.

$$-$ Julie Jolly, **Jolly Jolly Lester**, **Jolly Jolly Roma**, T0832-227 3620, www.hotel jollygoa.com. With 3 different properties offering a whole range of a/c and non-a/c rooms with hot showers, TV and a pool.

$ Paradise Huts, Small Vagator, Ozran, T(0)9922-230041. Good selection of huts on the cliff, some with views, shared bathroom.

$ Santonio,Ozran Beach Rd, near Holy Cross Chapel, T09769-913217, www. santonio.in. Cluster of little garden sheds, sweet though with nice bathrooms.

$ Thalassa Huts, T(0)9850-033537, www. thalassagoa.com. Tucked behind popular atmospheric Greek restaurant, great huts with attached bathrooms and a couple have their own rooftop chill-out area. Short walk down the cliff to the beach. Although staying here might seriously affect your waistline. And there are 2 nice boutiques on site too – be warned.

Chapora Fort p441

Chapora Fort and Siolim caters mainly for long-term budget travellers.

$$$$-$$$ Casa Colvale, inland on the Chapora river, T0832-241 6737, www. casacolvale.com. Beautiful chic rooms and stunning river views make this an exceptional find. Perfect for getting away from it without actually having to go too far – that's the gift of inland Goa. Lovely pool on the river and another high level infinity pool. There's lots of fresh seafood and plenty of other dishes on offer.

$$$$-$$$ Riverside Shakti, Guddem Village on the Chapora river, www. riversideshaktiretreat.com. Beautiful new villa with inspired design, a spiral staircase takes you up to several bedrooms and a rooftop pyramid fit for yoga or chilling. There are lots of nice outdoor spaces with swing chairs and river views. This is a great space for families or small retreat groups as it sleeps up to 10. Great Goan food is available from the caretaker, and yoga, healing and massage can be arranged. Wholeheartedly recommended.

$$$$-$$$ Siolim House, opposite Vaddy Chapel, Siolim, T0832-227 2138, www. siolimhouse.com. Lovingly restored 300-year-old house. This is a stunning property once owned by the governor of Macau. 4-poster beds, epic bathrooms and fantastic large windows. Restored in 1999, it recently had a further facelift in 2009 and the pool is one of the most beautiful places you could find yourself. Great food, chilled atmosphere. There is a sister property with just 3 rooms away in another beautifully crafted house – **Little Siolim**. And further up on the Arpora Hill there is a new development for rent aimed at yoga groups. Highly recommended.

$ Noble Nest, opposite the Holy Cross Chapel, Chapora, T0832-227 4335. Basic but popular, 21 rooms, 2 with bath but ample facilities for sharing, exchange and internet.

Arambol *p443, map p443*

$$$-$$ Samata Holistic Retreat Centre,
Temple Rd, 10 mins from downtown
Arambol, www.samatagoa.com. Inspiring
new retreat centre in beautiful location
just outside of Arambol. Bringing hints
of Bali and using reclaimed wood from
Indonesia, this exceptional site has
accommodation for 40 people with a
beautiful pool surrounded by nature
and an organic farm. There is also a
drop-in space **MATSYA and Tamarind
Cafe** with 2 great restaurants on-site, a
beautiful swimming pool and drop-in
yoga, dance classes and workshops. It's
super family friendly with a kindergarten
and swimming lessons. Coming in 2014
there will also be another lovely retreat
space with huts in a cashew plantation
for those on a tighter budget. **Samata**
keeps on inspiring as its profits also go
to the **Dunagiri Foundation**, which
works to preserve Himalayan herbs and
Ayurvedic plants.

$$-$ Atman, Palm Grove Girkar waddo,
next to Surf Club, T(0)869-888 0135,
www.atmangoa. com. A lovely collection
of palm-fringed coco huts with good
use of sari drapes and chic decor, all
surrounding a pretty restaurant. There
is also a yoga space and it's all just steps
from the beach. Lots of pretty artwork.

$$-$ Residensea Beach Huts, north
end of Arambol Beach, close to **Arambol
Hammocks**, T0832-224 2276, www.
arambolresidensea.com. Pretty location
with basic bamboo shacks set back
from the beach, all have fans and secure
locker facilities. There are some rooms
with attached bathroom, but some huts
have shared facilities. German Shepherd
keeps watch.

$ Arambol Plaza, Beach Rd, T 0832-
2242052, www.hotelsarambol.com.
Very different to the usual Arambol fare

but lacking any design aesthetic, basic
modern rooms with swimming pool.

$ Ave Maria, inland, down track
opposite police post, Modhlowado,
T0832-224 7674, avemaria@satyam.net.
in. One of the originals, offering some
of the best accommodation. Simple
but nevertheless recommended. Very
popular but hard to reserve in advance.

$ Famafa Beach Resort, Beach
Rd, Khalchawada, T0832-224 2516,
famafa_in@yahoo.com. 25 rooms in an
unimaginative development on the right
of the stall-studded road down to the
beach. No a/c, but many pitch up for the
hot showers.

$ Go-Ym Beach Resort, Bag Dando,
south end of Arambol beach, T(0)9637-
376335, www.go-ym.com. Great little
cottages with swathes of coloured fabric
and views of the coconut grove. Just
moments from the beach, there is also
an on-site restaurant.

$ Ivon's Guest House, Girkarwada, near
Kundalini Yoga Roof Garden, T(0)9822-
127398. Popular rooms looking out on
to the coconut grove, from the top floor
you can just about see the sea. Basic
clean rooms with attached bathrooms.

$ Luciano Guest Rooms, Cliffside,
T(0)9822-180215. Family house with
toilet and shower. Cliffside rooms get
heavily booked up.

$ Oceanic, inland at south end,
T0832-224 2296. Secluded guesthouse
with simple rooms, all hidden behind
wall in mature gardens, popular.
Recommended.

$ Om Ganesh, Cliffside on way to Sweet
Lake, T0832-224 2957. Lots of rooms
clustered on the cliffside – great views
and lots of places to hang a hammock.
Rooms are basic, but with attached
bathroom. Ask at **Om Ganesh** restaurant
on cliff or in town at **Om Ganesh General**

Store. Now have rooms on high street above general store too. Recommended.
$ Whispering Lakes, Girkar Waddo, follow signs to Surf Club and Wooden Heritage, T(0)9823-484333. Simple huts hugging lake, each with it's own cushioned sit-out hanging over the lake. A bit pricey for what you get and noise can carry from the Surf Club, but a very pretty location – catch special sunsets from your lakeside podium.

Keri and Tiracol Fort *p444*
Keri is pretty out of the way and it helps to have your own transport. The beaches around here are dotted with typical budget beach shacks.
$$$$ Fort Tiracol Heritage Hotel, Tiracol, T0236-622 7631, www.fort tiracol.com. In 2003 the owners of **Nilaya** in Arpora, took over Fort Tiracol to create an outpost of isolated, personalized luxury with unbroken views of the Arabian Sea. Just 7 exquisite rooms, all with giant en suite, set in the fort walls that surround the Catholic Church which is still used by the 350 villagers of the wholly Christian Tiracol for their Mass. Goa's most romantic hotel. Prices include breakfast and delicious dinners. Highly recommended.
$ Dream House, Keri, off main road on way to beach, T(0)9604-800553. Large rooms with attached bathroom sandwiched between family house and **Coconut Inn** rooftop restaurant.
$ Raj Star, Keri, near New English High School, T(0)9881-654718, raj-star@ hotmail. co.uk. Pretty rooms in attractive guesthouse. Nice communal sitting areas.

Morjim to Asvem *p445*
This is a beautiful stretch of coastline which is becoming more and more happening and increasingly built up,

but there are some special places to stay dotted along the coast.
$$$ Ku, Asvem Beach, www.kugoa morjim.webs.com. In stark contrast to its naff neighbour in Asvem, **Marbela Beach Resort**, Ku is quite possibly one of the most beautiful places you can stay in India. With just two handbuilt Japanese-style wooden bungalows with sliding doors and true rustic elegance you will not want to leave. And sitting on the upper deck looking out at rice fields and palm trees or gazing down at the water feature that runs through Ku like an aorta, is pretty close to Nirvana. A change in management means that now food is Goan *thali* style rather than Mediterranean.
$$$ Sur La Mer, above Asvem Beach, T(0)9850-056742, www.surlamergoa. com. Beautiful rooms with 4-poster beds and super-stylish bathrooms around lovely pool. All have good views of the neighbouring fields and the beach; with special mention going to the stunning penthouse with almost 360° views of paradise. The food is also highly praised.
$$$ Yab Yum Eco Resort, Asvem Beach, T0832-651 0392, www.yabyumresorts. com. 10 deluxe 'eco-domes' made of local materials – blue painted lava rocks make up the bases, woven palm leaves and mango wood the roofs, spread across a huge shady expanse of coconut and banana grove tucked behind a row of trees from the sand dunes. The pods come in 2 sizes – family or single – but both have living areas, and en suite bathrooms. It's classy, discreet and bohemian. There are also some cottages on-site. There's a reading room over the sea, a yoga *shala*, swimming pool and a children's teepee crammed with toys. The price includes breakfast and papers. Also now new chic accommodation

at their villa, **Artists' House**, which is absolutely stunning.

$$$-$$ Leela Cottages, Asvem Beach, T(0)9823-400055, www.leelacottage. com. Close to the beach, these are posh wooden huts with antique doors from a palace in Andhra Pradesh and decorated with beautiful furniture. Very stylish. Alas their new neighbours are the lovely but noisy clubs of **Soma** and **Bardo** so bear that in mind, perfect if you want to party.

$$$-$$ Yoga Gypsys Asvem, close to **Yab Yum**, T(0)9326-130115, www. yogagypsys.com. 5 beautifully decorated terracotta bungalows, charming floppy-fringed bamboo huts and tipis in palm grove right on the beach and close to a Hindu temple. Yes certainly as the name suggests you can explore all things yogic here, but it's also simply a relaxed place to stay and meditate on the sound of the waves. You can check the website for forthcoming retreats and workshops. Wholeheartedly recommended.

$$-$ Montego Bay Beach Village, Vithaldas Wado, Morjim, T(0)9822-150847, www.montegobaygoa.com. Rajasthani-style luxury tents pitched in the shade past beach shrubs at the southern end of the beach, plus log cabins, a/c rooms and a beach villa.

$$-$ Palm Grove, Asvem towards Morjim, T(0)9657-063046, www.palm groveingoa.com. Quirky place with cottages and huts named 'Happy Hippie' and 'Rosie Slow' there are comfy beds and a sweet beach restaurant.

$$-$ Simply Special, House No 750, 759, Ashwem–Morjim road, T(0)9820-056920, www.simplyspecialinn.com. Great for families as some rooms have little kitchens, but if you don't want to cook there is a lovely rooftop restaurant. They also have some nice art events and fair-trade markets.

Mandrem *p445*

$$$$ Elsewhere's Beach House, T(0)9326-020701, www.aseascape.com. **Elsewhere** is 4 lovingly restored 19th-century houses, just a sigh from the beach. Some are closer to the sea while others have views of the saltwater creek. Facilities include maid service, day and nightwatchman, but you pay extra for a cook. Minimum rental period 1 week at US$2000-4000. There are also the beautiful **Otter Creek Tents** with 4-poster beds Rajasthani style close to the creek.

$$$ Ashiyana, Mandrem River, opposite **Villa River Cat** by footbridge, www. ashiyana-yoga-goa.com. Revamped in 2013, **Ashiyana** offers up a beautiful place for yoga holidays and detox retreats. Many rooms have river views and are stacked with Rajasthani furniture and heaps of character. It's a peaceful place on large grounds with 2 yoga shalas, spa and natural swimming pool. There are a couple of lovely rooms with domed ceilings as well as the stunning Lake View and Ashiyana Villas. The good onsite restaurant serves nourishing healthy food. Prices are per person and often rooms are shared.

$$$ Beach Street, T(0)9423-882600, www.beachstreet.in. Summer house of the Deshprabhu family built in the early 1920s, this interesting building has had many incarnations including a prawn hatchery and nightclub. Now the family have transformed it into a beautiful resort with a courtyard swimming pool, restaurant and chic beach cabanas. There is also a yoga space here with regular drop-in classes and workshops run by the highly recommended **Himalaya Yoga Valley** team.

$$$-$$ Mandala, next to **Ashiyana**, access from Asvem–Mandrem road, T(0)9657-898350, www.themandalagoa.com.

The highlights at Mandala are the chic 2-storey open-plan chalets – downstairs you will find a swing seat, up the stairs a tented bedroom with 2 loungers on the front deck. Murals by Danish artist Ulrik Schiodt decorate the walls. There are also stylish rooms in the main house and smaller huts and Maharajah tents. The large pretty gardens often host live music and an open-air film festival.

$$-$ O'Saiba, Junasvaddo, T(0)9552-997440/(0)8308 415655, sunnymehara@ yahoo.com. **O'Saiba** offers a range of coco huts, bungalows and nicely decorated rooms. It also has a good restaurant by the beach.

$$-$ Villa River Cat, Junasvaddo, T0832-224 7928, www.villarivercat. com. 13 rooms in a 3-tiered roundhouse overlooking the river and a wade over deep sand dunes from the beach. The whole place is ringed with a belt of shared balconies and comes with big central courtyards stuffed with swings, sofas, plantation chairs and daybeds. There's a mosaic spiral staircase and a cavalier approach to colour: it's downbeat creative and popular with musicians and actors – in the best possible way. Cat lovers preferred.

$ Oceanside, Junasvaddo, T(0)9421-40483. Great little sunny coloured huts and pretty cottages a short walk from the beach and with an excellent restaurant on site.

❼ Restaurants

Even Calangute's most ardent detractors will brave a trip for its restaurants, some of which are world class. While costly by Indian standards, a slap-up meal will cost you a fraction of its equivalent at European prices.

Baga *p435, map p435*

$$$ Casa Portuguesa, Baga Rd. An institution of a restaurant run by German/Goan couple with live music in the gloriously overgrown jungle of a garden. Strongly recommended.

$$$ Fiesta, Tito's Lane, T0832-227 9894. Open for dinner Wed-Mon. Stunning restaurant hidden behind the gaudy Tito's Lane. Beautifully decorated intimate restaurant with fabulous Italian-style food as well as great steaks, fish suppers and cocktails. Recommended.

$$$ J&A's Ristorante Italiano House, 560 Baga River, T0832-228 2364, italyingoa.com. Jamshed and Ayesha Madon's beautiful restaurant has earned them an evangelical following. Whether its authentic pastas or wood-fired pizzas, tender steaks or delicious desserts, it's all served passionately. They also have a beautiful homestay – **Capella**.

$$ Britto's Bar and Restaurant, Baga Beach, T0832-227 7331. Cajie Britto's puddings are an institution and his staff (of 50) boast that in high season you'll be pushed to find an inch of table space from the restaurant's inside right out to the seashore. Fantastic range of traditional Goan dishes such as *vindaloo* and *cafreal*. It's a great spot to watch India on the beach. Highly recommended.

$ Baba au Rhum, off the main road between Arpora and Baga. Serving up fantastic cappuccino, breads, croissants and salads in a laid-back vibe. Extraordinarily good desserts, coffee éclair or chocolate and passion fruit pie anyone?

$ Lila's Café, north bank of Baga River, T0832-227 9843, lilacafe@sify.com. Closed in the evenings. Slick German-run restaurant, good selection of European dishes, check blackboard for specials, smoked kingfish. Home-made cheeses and jams. Also serves beers. Shaded terrace overlooking the river.

Calangute and Candolim *p435, map p436*

$$$ A Reverie, next to **The Park**, Holiday St, T(0)9823-14927, areveriegoa@gmail.com. Award-winning restaurant offering a globally inspired menu in chic surrounds. You can try a Thai vegetable *thali* or opt for Australian John Dory. Although when there is so much local fish available do you need to have Norwegian salmon?

$$$ Bomras, Candolim towards Sinquerim, T(0)9822-106236, bawmra@yahoo.com. Mouth-watering Burmese and Asian fusion food, such as seared rare tuna, mussel curry and Nobu-esque blackened miso cod. Fantastic vegetarian dishes and curries too, washed down with quite possibly the best cocktail in the world spiced with lemongrass and ginger. Chic setting – amidst the bright lights of Candolim, you could almost blink and miss it. Highly recommended.

$$$-$$ Souza Lobo, on the beach. Somewhat of an institution, this place serves up excellent fresh seafood, lobster and sizzlers served on a shaded terrace, well-known restaurant that has managed to retain a good reputation for years.

$$ Café Ciocolatti, main road Candolim, T(0)9326-112006. Fantastic range of all things chocolate. Lovely daytime café. They also do salads to outweigh any potential guilt incurred by eating the orange marmalade brownie.

$$ Fisherman's Cove, main road Candolim, T0832-248 9538. Sometimes you just have to go on the busyness of a place – and this one is always packed to the rafters. They serve up good portions of traditional Goan fare such as *xacuti* and *sorpotel* and other Indian and Euro dishes.

$ Infanteria, Baga Rd, near beach roundabout. 'The breakfast place' to locals, Rs 125 set breakfast, eggs, coffee, juice, toast. Bakery and confectionery. Very atmospheric.

$ Plantain Leaf, near petrol pump, Almita III. T0832-227 6861. Mean *dosas*, jumbo *thalis*, sizzlers and a range of curries; unbeatable for your pukka pure vegetarian Indian.

$ The Tibetan Kitchen, at the bottom of a track leading off Calangute Beach Rd. This airy garden restaurant is part tent, part wicker awning, part open to the skies. Tibet's answer to ravioli – *momos* – are good here, but more adventurous starters such as prawns, mushrooms and tomatoes on wilting lettuce leaves are exceptional.

Mapusa *p437*

$ Ashok, opposite the market's entrance. Serves genuine South Indian breakfasts like *uttapam* and *dosa*.

$ Café on the Corner, in the middle of the market. A good pit-stop for refuelling during the market.

$ Navtara, on Calangute Rd. Excellent range of Goan, South and North Indian fare – great *dosas* and yummy mushroom *xacuti* with *puris* for breakfast.

Anjuna and around *p439, map p440*

$$$ Xavier's, Praias de San Miguel (follow signs from behind small chapel near Flea Market site, bring a torch at night), T0832-227 3402. One of the very first restaurants for foreigners has grown into a smart restaurant with 3 separate kitchens (Indian/Chinese/continental), excellent fresh seafood, tucked away under palm trees.

$$$-$$ Villa Blanche, Badem Church Rd (better known as International Animal Rescue Rd), Assagao, T(0)9822-155099. 10 mins' drive from downtown Anjuna, you will find this beautiful daytime retreat. Some of the firm favourites are German meatballs with potato salad, smoked salmon bagels with capers and home-made ice creams. They serve up an infamous Sunday brunch, which you must book a table in advance for.

$$ Anand, Siolim Rd, Anjuna. Roadside shack which looks like any other, except for the queue of people waiting for a table. This place has a devoted following from here to Mumbai and serves up the freshest seafood with every type of masala and all the Goan favourites.

$$ Gunpowder, Mapusa road, Assagao, T0832-226 8091, www.gunpowder.in. Inland from Anjuna you will find the delicious **Gunpowder** restaurant, which offers more unusual South Indian food and dishes from Andhra Pradesh. They have an acclaimed sister restaurant in Delhi and they stay open during the monsoon. Another Delhi institution, **People Tree**, is on site selling fair-trade clothes and recycled products.

$$ Joe Bananas, through the Flea Market behind **Curlies**, family-run place serving amazing fish *thalis* – the fish is seasoned to perfection or there is a great array of bhaji.

$$-$ German Bakery, south Anjuna, towards the Flea Market and **Curlies**. A little fiefdom of bohemian perfection: the bakery's sign is hung over a huge garden with an awning of thick tropical trees, where comfortable mattresses pad out the sides of low-slung booths. Huge salads with every healthy thing under the sun (including sprouts and avocado) plus good veggie burgers, Indian food and extreme juices. There is massage available on site and a small health food counter. This, ladies and gentlemen, is the original German Bakery, don't be put off by the copy cats that have taken over every baking tray around India.

$ Orange Boom, south Anjuna, Flea Market Rd. Daytime only. Efficient and spotlessly clean canteen. Food is hyper-hygienic and meticulously made, with a menu offering the usual breakfast fare plus 100 ways with eggs (from poached eggs to French toast), most served with mushrooms and grilled tomatoes. Baked beans can be masala or Heinz (proper ketchup on the tables), also croque madame and sautéed avocado on toast.

Vagator *p441*

$$$ Sakana, past petrol pump on Chapora Rd, T(0)9890-135502. Fantastic Japanese food, **Sakana** is packed out with the Westerners that call Goa home. They serve delicious tuna *teriyaki*, beef *yakinuki*, sushi and wakame salads. With the potential of green tea or *wasabi* ice cream (made by **Niko's** in Assagao). Remember to book a table in advance.

$$$ Thalassa, on the clifftop overlooking Ozran Beach, T(0)9850-033537. Beautiful restaurant perched on the cliff, amazing sunset views and great Greek food from *dolmades* and *souvlaki* and many varieties of lamb dishes and feta for the vegetarians. Booking essential. Great boutique on site too.

$$$-$$ Sri, close to **Thalassa**, T09822-383795. Having migrated from Anjuna's **Shore Bar** to Vagator, Richard has opened up **Sri** serving up his trademark salad platters and delicious Indian and seafood. There is often live music. Incidentally, the new-look **Shore Bar** is a real disappointment.

$$ The Alcove, on the cliff above Little Vagator. Smartish, ideal position, excellent food, pleasant ambience in the evening, sometimes live music.

$$ Bean Me Up, near the petrol pump, Vagator, T0832-227 3479. Closed all day Sat and daily 1600-1900. You can choose

from salad plates and delicious tempeh and tofu platters. There's massage offered on site, a useful noticeboard for mind-body-spirit stuff, kids' area and a few simple, clean rooms for rent. Under new management, so maybe in for a revamp.
$$ Mango Tree, in the village. Wide choice of continental favourites.

Chapora Fort *p441*
$$ Da Felice & Zeon, above **Babba's**. Open 1800-2400. Just a handful of tables dancing with fairy lights and psychedelic art at this rooftop restaurant run by the Italian brothers Felice and Zeon. Felice is an Italian chef in London over monsoon, Zeon makes trance music and trance art. Carbonara, lasagna, prosciutto, *spaghetti alle vongole* all feature, but meat is recommended.
$$ La Befa, Chapora Market road. Some people drive an hour for the roast beef sandwich here. Or there's parma ham or marinated aubergine – all on freshly baked French bread.
$ Jai Ganesh Juice Bar, the hub of Chapora. This is the only place to be seen in Chapora for every juice under the sun.

Arambol *p443, map p443*
There are beach cafés all along the main beach and around the headland to the north. The 2 German bakeries fall short of the lovely restaurant in Anjuna.
$$ Double Dutch, Beach Rd, T0832-652 5973, doubledutchgoa@yahoo.co.uk. Open 0700-2300. Lovely laid-back garden restaurant with sand underfoot and lots of leafy foliage and sculptures created by the owner around. Breakfasts are tip top here with home-made breads (such as carrot or watermelon) seed and also home-made jams – you can also get a full 'English', Goa style. Candlelit in the evening, there are lots of great salads as

well as Dutch dishes, Indonesian, Thai, pastas and the steaks come with the best recommendation. There is a lively Sun morning second-hand market. Recommended.
$$ Fellini's, Beach Rd, T0832-229 2278, arambolfellini95@yahoo.com. Thu-Tue 1000-2300, Wed 1800-2300. **Fellini's** is an institution serving up pizzas and calzone to the hungry masses.
$$ Lamuella, Main Rd, T0832-651 4563. Atmospheric restaurant in the heart of Arambol. Home-made mushroom or pak choi raviolis, great fish, tagines, salads and huge breakfast platters. This is a great spot to meet and greet. There's also a great shop specializing in clothes crafted by Westerners in Arambol. If you can't face the night market, see what Westerners get up to creatively here. Recommended.
$$ MATSYA, Temple Rd, www.samatagoa.com. This beautiful restaurant is inspired by the organic garden of **Samata Retreat** (see Where to stay, page 451) and the fresh seafood of Goa and fused with delights from Israeli chef Gome. Breakfasts are a lazy affair and dinners draw a crowd of Westerners that call north Goa home – take their word for it, the food is amazing. For lunches, there is another beautiful restaurant on site: **Tamarind Cafe** by the pool offers up healthy vibrant treats and lots of raw food specialities from Japanese chef Kaoru. If you get a chance ask to visit their organic farm. And you can always work off the calories by taking a drop-in yoga or dance class here too. Highly recommended.
$ Dreamland Crepes, main road, near **Double Dutch**. Blink-and-you-miss-it 2-tier coffee house serving up fabulous cappuccinos and healthy juices, as well as a wide range of crêpes and sandwiches. And Wi-Fi.

$ Dylans, coconut grove near **El Paso Guesthouse**. Coffee houses have sprung up in Arambol to fuel the creative types and designers that make Arambol their home. If you like your coffee strong, this Manali institution delivers, along with hot melty chocolate cookies and soups and sandwiches. Film nights and occasional live music.

$ Eyes Of Buddha, north end of Arambol Beach. Long on Arambol's catering scene, this place has you well looked after with scrupulously clean avocado salads, a wide range of fish and the best Indian food in town, all topped off with a great view of the beach. Highly recommended.

$ Relax Inn, north end of beach. The only beach shack with a good reputation, this is a firm favourite with the expats. Slow service but worth the wait for *spaghetti alle vongole*, grilled kingfish with ratatouille and a range of fresh pasta dishes. Exceptional, although you cannot book and in season it can be tough to get a table.

$ Rice Bowl, next door to **Eyes of Buddha**. Great views south across Arambol Beach, with a billiard table. Simple restaurant that has been serving reliably good Chinese for years. All the usual chop suey, wontons, noodles and sweet and sours of calamari, pork, beef or fish, plus Japanese dishes such as *gyoza*, *sukiyaki*, tempura and Tibetan *momos*.

$ Rutik's Coconuts, entrance to beach behind **Coco Loco**. Serving up *thalis* all day, this place is best visited for coconuts. It's a great place to hang-out, see and be seen.

$ Sai Deep, Beach Rd. A family-run *dhaba* offering amazing veg and fish plates at lunchtime, mountainous fruit plates and a good range of Indian and continental food. Great value.

Morjim to Asvem *p445*
Join the masses as they descend on La Plage every Sun. Restaurants in Morjim central cater mainly to Russians.

There are plenty of shacks catering to Asvem and Mandrem beaches. Some have free loungers, others charge up to Rs 100.

$$$ Bardo, Asvem-Morjim Beach. T(0)9890-167531. The Sunday brunch at newly opened **Bardo** has gained a great reputation. It's a pricey affair but has a good range of food and drinks. You can sit inside, but poolside is best. Come sunset time the DJs take over.

$$$ La Plage, Asvem, T(0)9822-121712. Hidden slightly from the beach, you can still feel the breeze in this lovely laid-back restaurant. The food is excellent and changes seasonally; you might discover seared rare tuna with *wasabi* mash, calamari risotto, great steaks or even a giant hamburger. Vegetarians well catered for too, try the sage butter ravioli. Most people daydream about the chocolate *thali* or the *île flottante*. There is a good selection of wines and cocktails, including a fabulous peppery Bloody Mary with mustard seeds and curry leaf. Also has rooms to let and an excellent shop featuring jewellery from expat designer Simona Bassi. Booking essential.

$$$ Sublime, Morjim Beach, T(0)9822-484051. Exceptional food is guaranteed at this Goa institution. Chris Saleem Agha Bee has opened up the latest incarnation of **Sublime** on Morjim beach and it's a chic spin on the beach shack offering punchy Asiatic beef, delicious rare tuna with anchovy sauce, the renowned mega organic salad and delicious melt-in-the-mouth pesto and mozzarella parcels, to name but a few. The cocktails go down very easily and it's a laid-back vibe – the perfect combination for balmy Goan nights. Booking essential.

$ Change Your Mind, Asvem Beach. This typical beach shack serves up great Indian food, tasty fried calamari and monumental fruit plates. You can get refreshing lemon and mint juices and strawberry shakes in season.

$ Pink Orange, Asvem Beach. Low-level seating overlooking the beach with chilled trance vibe. Menu serves up a great range of salads, tagines, sweet and savoury crêpes, juices, coffees and great chocolate brownies. Recommended.

Mandrem *p445*

$$$-$$ Café Nu, Junnaswaddo, Mandrem Beach, T(0)9850-658568. Another helping from **Sublime** guru Chris Saleem Agha Bee – great food in laid-back locale. Mustard-encrusted fish, the non-yogi burger (Mandrem does cater to a large yogi clientele), the phenomenal mega organic salad for the aforementioned yogis and the legendary chocolate bon-bons. People have been known to cry when there was a problem with the oven and the bon-bons were temporarily unavailable. Good food to linger over. Highly recommended.

$$$-$$ Lazy Dog, Beach St, Mandrem Beach, T(0)94238-82600, www.beach street.in. Great food served up at this consciously renovated summer palace. **Lazy Dog** is a manali institution, so this is their summer residence. There is an eclectic menu with some tasty Korean food and sushi, as well as the fabulous breakfast burrito (you might have worked up an appetite if you go to the great drop-in yoga class on site) and a good range of seafood and Indian dishes.

$$-$ Sunset, next to Beach St. For classic Indian food and tandoori dishes, you cannot do better than **Sunset**. Their fish and chicken tikkas are fantastic. They also have the usual selection of European and Chinese food, but all done well.

$ Well Garden Pizzeria, near O'Saiba, off main road. Sweet garden restaurant with great range of pizzas, broccoli and pesto pastas and an almost infamous warm chickoo cake. Service can be a bit hit or miss though.

♦ Bars and clubs

The new place to be seen is Asvem where there are now 6 clubs in 1 sq km – right on the beach. Elsewhere, perennial favourites are **Cubana** next to the Night Market and **Titos**, in Baga. The newest additions to the scene are **LPK** and **Sinq** in Candolim.

Baga *p435, map p435*

Many bars here have a happy hour 1700-1930 and show live Premier League football, in a bit of a home-from-home for many visitors. Along the beach, shacks also serve a wide range of drinks and cocktails to sip while watching the sunset.

Cavala, Sauntavaddo, top end of Baga village. A genuine bar, with friendly atmosphere, attentive staff, great cocktails, and occasional live music and 1960s evenings.

Tito's, Tito's Lane, T0832-227 5028, www. titosgoa.com. Tito's is an institution in Goa, and has adapted down the decades to reflect the state's changing tourist reality by going from down-at-heel hippie playground in the 1960s to swish international dance club. Now the focus seems to be more on food – are the dancing days of Goa really over? Further along Tito's Lane towards the beach is the **Tito's** spin-off, **Mambo's**. It's more laid back than the club and free to get in.

Calangute and Candolim *p435, map p436*

LPK, inland from Candolim on Nerul river, www.lpkwaterfronts.com. Billing itself as

India's first super club and "the world's most unique architectural construction", **LPK** have a little bit of ego and a little bit of media savvy. It certainly is an unusual place to party – dancing in a massive sculpture overlooking the river and Goa jungle, but what's the music like? They appeal to the masses. They are also offering themselves up as the ultimate wedding venue.

Saligao

Club WestEnd, near Porvorim, 3 km out of Calangute towards Panjim. This club gets away with hosting 3-day parties by being too remote to disturb anyone.

Anjuna *p439, map p440*

The days of all-night parties in North Goa are long gone, and politicians imposed a ban on loud music after 2200 for several seasons – they keep changing the rules so sometimes you might be lucky and find yourself dancing until dawn. Indoor venues like **Bardo** in Asvem and **West End** in Saligao stay open later. Wed and Fri tend to be the big nights especially at places like **Curlies** (see below) and Sunday Night at **Soma Project** in Asvem is the place to be seen but there is usually something going on each night over the Christmas and New Year period; just ask around (taxi drivers invariably know where).

Curlies, at the very far south of Anjuna. A kind of unofficial headquarters of the scene, playing techno and ambient music, although **Shiva Valley** next door has taken over in recent years.

Lilliput, a few hundred metres north of **Curlies**, www.cafelilliput.com. Lots of live music and fire-dancing performances at this beach shack – usually after the flea market on Wed and sometimes on Fri. Also has an a/c internet booth.

Vagator *p441*

Hilltop, Little Vagator Hill, above Vagator. Although it has suffered from the 2200 curfew, **Hilltop** just celebrated it's 30th birthday fully dressed up for the occasion in fluoro! It has been inventive with day parties Sun 1600-2200. They often host concerts too – in 2013, Talvin Singh played here and Prem Joshua plays each season.

Nine Bar, Ozran Beach. A booming mud-packed bar with huge gargoyle adornments and a manic neon man carved out of the fountain. Majestic sunset views.

Arambol *p443, map p443*

Live music and performances are the highlight of being in Arambol. **Ash**, **Surf Club**, **Coco Loco** and **Psybar** offer up both live music and DJ nights. **Arkan Bar** and **Loekie's** have open mic nights. Special mention goes to **Ash**, a stunning performance space with beautiful artwork hosting nights as diverse as mesmerizing bellydancing performances, Siberian shamanic singing or fantastic fire dancing. At dusk there's normally drumming, dancing and high spirits outside **Full Moon** on the beach to celebrate the sun going down on another day.

Morjim to Asvem *p445*

With pricey drinks and sometimes entry fees, the venues in Morjim and Asvem are mostly Russian affairs, but **Soma Project** is a fun and welcoming place. Check www.facebook.com/somaprojectgoa for listings – it has a chic seafront locale and great music know-how as they also run a renowned club in Moscow. Guest DJs from Europe and Russia feature on the playlist, but great coups have been Djuma Sounsystem,

Talvin Singh and DJ Cheb i Sabbah – open every night but Sun is the big night out here. You will also find **Bardo**, **Blue Waves** and **Marbella** in this Asvem club zone, all competing for the attention of the beautiful people.

Mandrem *p445*

There are frequent concerts and an open-air cinema festival at **Mandala** in Mandrem and live music and DJs often at **Beach Street**.

⊕ Entertainment

Calangute *p435, map p436*
Heritage Kathakali Theatre, **Hotel Sunflower**, opposite the football ground, Calangute Beach Rd, T0832-258 8059. Daily in season, 1800-2000. The breathtakingly elaborate mimes of 17th-century Keralan mime dance drama take over 12 hrs to perform in the southern state. Here, however, it comes abbreviated for tourist attention spans: watch the players apply their make-up, brief background of the dance, then a snatch of a classic dance-drama.

⊛ Festivals

Calangute *p435, map p436*
Mar Carnival is best celebrated in villages or in the main district towns but Calangute has brought the party to the tourists.
May (2nd week) The **Youth Fête** attracts Goa's leading musicians and dancers.

Mapusa *p437*
Mon of the 3rd week after Easter Feast of Our Lady of Miracles The *Nossa Senhora de Milagres* image is venerated by Christians as well as Hindus who join together to celebrate the feast day of the

Saibin. Holy oil is carried from the church to Shanteri temple and a huge fair and a market are held.

Mandrem *p445*
Jan International Juggling Convention, Gala performances, juggling workshops, firedancing, creative movement of a phenomenally high standard. This is an event not to be missed – check out www.injuco.org.

O Shopping

Do your homework before you buy: prices in tourist shops are massively inflated, and goods are often worth less than a 3rd of the asking price. 92.5 silver should be sold by weight; check the current value online, but be ready to pay a little more for elaborate workmanship. The bigger Kashmiri shops, particularly, are notorious both for refusing to sell by weight and for their commission tactic whereby rickshaw and taxi drivers get Rs 100 per tourist delivered to shops plus 10% commission on anything sold.

Calangute *p435, map p436*
Casa Goa, Cobravaddo, Baga Rd, T0832-228 1048, cezarpinto@hotmail.com. Cezar Pinto's shop is quite a razzy lifestyle store: beautifully restored reclining plantation chairs next to plates brought over by the Portuguese from Macau plus modern-day dress from local fashion designer Wendell Rodricks. Cool modern twists on old Goan shoes by local Edwin Pinto too.
Literati, off main road, Calangute, parallel to Holiday St, T0832-227 7740, www.literati-goa.com. Wonderful bookshop in beautiful old house – it's like stumbling into someone's library. The best selection of books, novels, non-fiction and poetry

you'll find in Goa. There are sometimes readings here, including an inaugural reading by William Dalrymple.

PlayClan, Shop No S-3, Ida Maria Resort, next to HDFC bank, Calangute, T(0)9372-280862, www.theplayclan.com. Fantastic shop selling all manner of clothes, notebooks, lighters and pictures with great colourful cartoon designs created by a collective of animators and designers – giving a more animated view of India's gods, goddesses, gurus and the faces of India **Purple Jungle** in same strip of shops sells similar kitsch India-centric gifts.

Candolim and Sinquerim beaches
p436

Supermarkets like **Delfinos** on Calangute Beach Rd or **Newtons** on Fort Aguada Rd sell staples, plus adaptor plugs, water heating filaments, quince jam, wine, cashew *feni* in plastic bottles to take home, full range of sun lotion factors and brands, tampons, etc and money change.

For silver, head for either of the Tibetan covered handicraft markets where you can buy by weight.

Fabindia, Sea Shell Arcade, opposite Canara Bank, Candolim. Branch of this great shop selling textiles, homewares and funky traditional Indian *kurtas* and clothes.

Rust, 409A Fort, Aguada Rd, Candolim, T0832-247 9340. Everything from wrought-iron furniture to clothes.

Sangolda, Chogm Rd, opposite Mac de Deus Chapel, Sangolda, T0832-240 9309, sangolda@sancharnet.in. Mon-Sat 1000-1930. Lifestyle gallery and café run by the owners of **Nilaya Hermitage** selling handcrafted metalware, glass, ethnic furniture, bed and table linen, lacquerware, wooden objects.

The Private Collection, 1255 Annavado, Candolim Beach Rd, T0832-248 9033. Ramona Galardi has a good eye and has

brought together a great collection of clothes and jewellery from designers based in Goa and also offers some of her own creations. She is also a healer and has a healing space on site.

Mapusa *p437*
Municipal Mapusa Bazaar, on south edge of the fruit and veg market. Fixed-price basic food supplies like rice, spice, lentils and cereals; useful if you're here long term.

Other India Bookstore, 1st floor, St Britto's Apartment, above Mapusa clinic, T0832-226 3306. Unconventional and excellent. Heavily eco-conscious. Has a large catalogue and will post worldwide.

Union Ayurveda, 1st floor, opposite the taxi and bus stand. Great one-stop shop for all things Ayurvedic, herbal and homeopathic – phenomenal range of products to keep you travelling healthy.

Anjuna *p439, map p440*
Artjuna, House No 972, Monteiro Vaddo, T0832-321 8468, www.artjuna.com. Beautiful collection of mainly jewellery and clothes, but with a few nice bits of home decor too. Stunning collection of gold jewellery, but also cheaper tribal trinkets from Nagaland. Owners Moshe and Anastasia showcase quite a few local designers here as well as offering up their own wares. You will also find art and photography on sale here. Stays open through monsoon. Recommended.

Flea Market, Wed. Attracts hordes of tourists from all over Goa. By mid-morning all approach roads are blocked with taxis, so arrive early.

Orchard Stores, Monteirovaddo. Amazing selection catering for Western cravings. Olive oil, pasta, fresh cheese, frozen meats, etc, as well as a good range of organic products from all over India and fresh produce from Ambrosia farms in Goa. Locally made soaps and organic supplements too.

Oxford Arcade, De Mellovaddo, next to **Munche's**. Good general store close to beach.

Chapora Fort *p441*

Narayan, Chapora. Book stall, local newspapers.

Arambol *p443, map p443*

Arambol Hammocks, north end of Arambol Beach, near **Eyes of Buddha**, www.arambol. com. The original and the best place for hammocks and their famous flying chair designs – these are no ordinairy hammocks and are extremely comfortable. And now they even have baby hammocks.

Lamuella. Serving up the best of the Western designers who make Arambol their home, as well as imported clothes and bikinis from Thailand and Europe. Stunning jewellery for little magpies too. Highly recommended.

Vishwa Book Shop, T(0)992-146 1107. Excellent bookshop on main road with good holiday reads and for all the yogi types he has a great range of holistic titles.

Morjim to Asvem *p445*

As well as having a great little boutique on site with lovely clothes and jewellery from Simona Bassi, **La Plage** has competition on its hands from a cluster of neighbouring chic beach shack boutiques including one little black number from Jade Jagger. But special mention goes to **Dust** which sells beautifully designed clothes in raw silk and hand-block prints from JonnyJade (www.jonnyjade.com) and also a handful of one-off pieces crafted by local Westerners.

◉ What to do

Baga *p435, map p435*
Boat trips and wildlife

Mikes Marine, **Fortune Travels**, Sauntavaddo, by the bus stand at the top end of Baga, T0832-227 9782. Covered boat, dolphin trips, river cruises and birdwatching.

Rahul Alvares, all over Goa, based in Parra, T(0)9881-961071, www.rahul alvares.com. Fancy getting eye-to-eye with a cobra? For an alternative day out in Goa, maybe you want to handle or at least see a wild snake. For the less wild at heart or snakeaphobic, there are also amazing birdwatching trips and jungle camping expeditions. You will be in expert hands with Rahul. He organizes trips all over Goa.

Body and soul

Ayurclinic Goa, Baga Creek, T(0)9822-312021, www.ayurvedagoa.com. Under the watchful eye of fantastic Dr Rohit Borkar, you can get a whole host of treatments, massages and *panchakarma* processes here. Has another branch in Mandrem.

Ayurvedic Natural Health Centre (ANHC), Baga–Calangute road, Villa 2, Beira Mar Complex, www. healthandayurveda.com; also in Saligao. The **ANHC** is not for the faint-hearted; the centre was originally built for the local community that it continues to serve and hasn't made many concessions to Western sensibilities. Those checking into the 2-week *panchakarma* can expect almost every cavity to be flushed. They do offer smaller, less daunting packages, such as 2½-hr rejuvenations (Rs 300), and have a herb garden where you can taste first-hand leaves that tingle your tongue (used to stop stuttering) or others that eliminate your sense of sweet taste.

Sun salutations

It's one of those funny ironies that yoga, now at the zenith of its international popularity, is given a resounding thumbs down by your average metropolitan Indian, who's much more likely to pull on lycra and go jogging or pump iron down the gym than pursue the perfect *trikonasana*. They look with curiosity at the swarms of foreign yogis yearning to pick up extreme postures from the various *guru-jis* scattered about the subcontinent.

There is business to be had in selling enlightenment it turns out. At one place you can pay US$2000 for your course – enlightenment guaranteed and a certificate to prove it. Naturally India has its fair share of spiritual wisdom and compassionate gurus, but there is also a percentage of dodgy dealers and predatory gurus. Be aware of the showmen. Some might baulk at seeking out a Western teacher in India, but often Western teachers have a better understanding of the needs of their students.

India remains one of the best places to study the ancient art, and many people who have embarked on yoga courses purely for its physical benefits also end up reaping some mental and emotional rewards. Yoga done with awareness can give you a taste of the bigger picture. Just keep asking around to find the right teacher.

The large alternative communities settled around Arambol and Anjuna make good starting points if you are looking for some ad hoc teaching, but if you are travelling to India specifically to practice it's worth doing your homework first. Here are some places that are recommended.

Going furthest north first, where there is more yoga than you can shake a yoga mat at, there are two places of special mention: Samata Holistic Retreat Centre (www.samatagoa.com), is 10 minutes inland from Arambol proper on a beautiful swathe of land. Bringing hints of Bali and using reclaimed wood from Indonesia, this exceptional place focuses on retreats and has accommodation for 40 people with a beautiful pool surrounded by nature and an organic farm. There is also a drop-in space MATSYA and Tamarind Café with two great restaurants, a beautiful swimming pool and drop-in yoga, dance classes and workshops. Samata keeps on inspiring as its profits also go to the Dunagiri Foundation (set up by the founder) which works to preserve Himalayan herbs and Ayurvedic plants. Another good option is Kundalini Yoga Rooftop Garden and Healing Centre (www.organickarma.co.uk), close to the beach on the way out of Arambol, is one of the few places in India where you can study Kundalini Yoga as taught by Yogi Bhajan. They have beautiful space for yoga, meditation, in-depth courses, therapeutic bodywork, and offer popular courses in Ayurvedic Yoga Massage.

Travelling south to Mandrem, you will find Ashiyana (www.ashiyana-yoga-goa.com) which has had a recent revamp and offers yoga holidays and detox retreats. Many rooms have river views and are stacked with Rajasthani furniture and heaps of character. It's a peaceful place on large grounds with two yoga shalas, spa and natural swimming pool. In the very peaceful beach area of Mandrem you will also find **Himalaya Yoga Valley** (www. yogagoaindia.com). They hold great drop-in classes (morning and late afternoon) at an elevated *shala* at **Beach Street** but the main focus here is the exceptional Yoga Teacher Training with talented team headed up by Lalit Kumar. They run regular trainings throughout the season just outside Mandrem and then head to Europe and Thailand for the summer months. If you want to take your practice to the next level, this place is inspirational. On Asvem beach, you have the lovely **Yoga Gypsys** (www. yogagypsys.com), which hosts yoga holidays, trainings and satsangs. There are terracotta bungalows, charming floppy-fringed bamboo huts and tipis in palm grove right on the beach and close to a Hindu temple.

In Anjuna, you will find excellent drop-in classes, workshops and their own brand teacher trainings at **Brahmani** (www.brahmaniyoga.com), there is Mysore-style self practice and excellent *ashtanga*, as well as a smattering of free-flowing movement yoga classes and and *Scaravelli*. Close by is **Yogamagic Canvas Ecotel** (www.yogamagic.net) who host a whole range of yoga classes and holidays in their beautiful yoga temple and you can stay like a Maharani in a suite or Rajasthani hunting tents – this is a very special place. Some 10 minutes away in the neighbouring village of Assagao you find the renowned **Purple Valley Yoga Retreat** (www.yogagoa.com) who host the heavy weights of the yoga world like Sharath Rangaswamy, grandson of Sri K Pattabhi Jois, David Swenson and Nancy Gilgoff. Lessons are held in a lovely *shala* in delightful gardens, food is vegetarian and the atmosphere collegiate. Travel a little further into inland Goa to find **Satsanga Retreat** (www.satsangaretreat.com), a beautiful space with two inspiring *shalas*, a lovely pool and great accommodation. This is often where Brahmani host their longer trainings.

Skipping to South Goa, you will find two inspiring centres in Patnem beach. **Harmonic Healing Centre** (www. harmonicingoa.com) have an enviable location high above the north end of the beach with superlative views so that you can perform your *asanas* while looking out to sea. There is drop-in yoga and holistic treats of all varieties. While **Lotus Yoga Retreats** (www.lotus-yoga-retreat.com) focuses on yoga holidays and retreats with guest teachers from Europe, including the fantastic Dynamic Yoga teacher Dina Cohen.

Seek out different schools in the four corners of India in Pune (BKS Iyengar), Mysore (Pattabhi Jois), Neyyar Dam (Sivananda), Anandapur Sahib (Yogi Bhajan – Kundalini Yoga) and Bihar (Paramahamsa Satyananda). There is also the International Yoga Festival in Rishikesh every year in February or March.

Good books include: BKS Iyengar's *Light On Yoga, Asana, Pranayama, Mudra, Bandha* from the Bihar school and anything by Georg Feuerstein.

Diving and snorkelling

Goa Dive Center, Tito's Lane, T0832-215 7094. Goa isn't really on the diving map, chiefly because it has only 2 dive sites, both of which have what's known as variable, ie less than great, visibility. However, this outfit offers inexpensive PADI courses. Options range from the half-day Discover Scuba programme (from aged 10 years, Rs 2700) to the 4-day Open Water Diver programme, Rs 14,500. Snorkelling tours also available.

Calangute p435, map p436
Body and soul

Cyril Yoga, Naikavaddo, T0832-249 7400, www.cyrilyoga.com. 4 classes daily, 0830, 1000, 1530 and 1630, Rs 300 a class. All abilities. Inner healing yoga meditation, juice bar, yoga camps and good karma-promoting volunteer activities.

River cruises

Floating Palace, book through **Kennedy's Adventure Tours and Travels**, T0832-227 6493, T(0)9823-276520, kennedy@goatelecom.com, opposite **Milky Way** in Cobravaddo. Try a Kerala-style backwater cruise by staying overnight in this 4-cabin bamboo, straw and coir houseboat. You sail from Mandovi in late afternoon, are fed a high tea then a continental dinner as you drift past the Chorao Island bird sanctuary. International standards of safety. Much pricier than a similar boat trip in Kerala.

Tour operators

Day Tripper, Gauravaddo, T0832-227 6726, www.daytrippergoa.com. Offers tours all over Goa, best deals in the region. Also runs trips to spice plantations, or short tours out of state, for birdwatching or empty beaches in Karnataka. Recommended.

Candolim and Sinquerim beaches p436
Body and soul

Amrita Kerala Ayurvedic, next to Lawande supermarket, Annavaddo, T0832-312 5668. Open 0730-2000. Set inside an old Goan villa, this massage centre is geared up for the foreign tourist. Westerners are on hand to explain the philosophy behind Indian life science. The centre also runs courses. A basic course takes 7 days. Courses in *panchakarma* last 6 months.

Dolphin watching

John's Boats, T0832-227 7780. Promises 'guaranteed' dolphin watching, morning trips start around 0900, Rs 550 (includes meal and hotel pickup). Also crocodile-spotting river trips with lunch.

Parasailing

Occasionally offered independently on Candolim Beach, Rs 600-850 for a 5-min flight.

Fort Aguada p436
Taj Sports Complex, Fort Aguada Beach Resort. Excellent facilities that are open to non-residents at the **Taj Holiday Village**, and a separate access between Aguada Beach Resort and the Holiday Village. Rs 450 per day for the complex, Rs 350 for the pool. Tennis (Rs 450 per hr); squash and badminton (Rs 150 for 30 mins); mini golf (Rs 200). Yoga classes, scuba diving, sailing/water skiing/windsurfing/rod fishing Rs 450-500 per hr; parasailing/jet ski Rs 900-950 per hr.

Anjuna p439, map p440
Body and soul

Some excellent yoga teachers teach in Goa during the season, many of whom gravitate towards Anjuna: check the noticeboards at the **German Bakery**, **Thalassa** and **Bean Me Up** (see page 456). You'll also stumble on practitioners of all sorts of alternative therapies: reiki healers, acupuncturists, chakra and even vortex cleansing.

Brahmani Yoga, at **Tito's White House**, night market road, Anjuna, www.brahmani yoga.com. Drop-in centre for all things yogic – flex your limbs Mysore style, or try *vinyasa* flow, hatha, *pranayama*. There are also 1-day workshops and regular *bhajans*. They also promote beach cleaning Karma Yoga. Deservedly popular.

Healing Here And Now, The Health Center, St Michael's Vaddo, T0832-227 3487, www.healinghereandnow.com. If you want an 'ultimate cleanse', sign up for a 5-day detox: fasting, detoxifying drinks and twice-daily enemas. Also offers parasite cleansing, kidney cleanse and wheat grass therapy.

Purple Valley Yoga Retreat (see pages 441 and 465). 2-week retreats with celebrities of the *ashtanga vinyasa* yoga circuit. Beautiful backdrop for downward dog poses.

Watsu, Assagao–Mapusa road, T(0)9326-127020, www.watsugoa.com. Utterly amazing treatment. Working one-on-one, you are in a heated pool and the practitioner takes you through a range of movements both above and below the water. Using the art of shiatsu, this is an underwater massage which takes relaxation to a whole new level. The underwater dance makes you feel that you are flying and can give you a total release – a bit like being reborn. Highly recommended.

Bungee jumping
Offered by a Mumbai-based firm with US-trained staff, at Rs 500 a go. Safety is a priority, with harnesses, carabinas and air bags employed. There are pool tables, a bar, an auditorium for slide/film shows and beach volleyball. 1000-1230 and 1730 until late.

Paragliding
Happy Hours Café, south Anjuna Beach. 1230-1400. Rs 500 (children welcome), or at the hill-top between Anjuna/Baga, or Arambol.

Arambol *p443, map p443*
Boat trips and dolphin watching
21 Coconuts Inn, 2nd restaurant on left after stepping on to the beach. Dolphin-watching trips or boats to Anjuna, Rs 150 for each.

Body and soul
You can practise every form of yoga here including *Kundalini* – a rarity in India – as well as learn massage of all styles, have your *chakras* balanced, receive Tibetan singing bowl healing, participate in *satsang*, capoeira on the beach at sunset, do firewalking and learn all styles of dance. There is an amazing group of internationally trained therapists here, along with lots of practitioners with zero qualifications, so ask around.

Balanced View, in the rice fields behind Double Dutch, www.balancedview.com. Arambol has become one of the hubs for Balanced View – guidance to living life in clarity and awareness. Has a great following – definitely worth checking out.

Himalaya Iyengar Yoga Centre, follow the many signs, T01892-221312, www.hiyogacentre.com. Established Iyengar centre in town, 5-day courses and teacher training.

Kundalini Yoga Rooftop Garden and Healing Centre, Girka Waddo, near Temple of Dance, www.organickarma.co.uk. One of the few places in India where you can study Kundalini yoga as taught by Yogi Bhajan. Beautiful space for yoga, meditation, in-depth courses, healing sessions, Ayurvedic yoga massage and therapeutic bodywork. Massage trainings also possible. Highly recommended.

T'ai Chi Garden, near **Sufi Woodstock**, www.pandayoga.net. Panda has been teaching T'ai Chi and chakra healing in Arambol for many years and has a great reputation. Most courses are 2 weeks.

Temple of Dance, off shortcut road towards **Ivons** and **Kundalini Rooftop Garden**, Girko Waddo. Beautiful location offering dance classes from Bollywood to Gypsy, Balinese to tribal fusion belly dance, as well as fire dancing, hula hooping and *poi*.

Bronze casting and sculpting
One-off classes and a 3-week course in bronze casting, held every Jan with Lucie from **Double Dutch** (see Restaurants, page 457), a woman of many talents. Ask at **Double Dutch** for details.

Jewellery making and silversmithing
Several places on Arambol high street offer jewellery-making courses; one of the best is with Krishna at **Golden Hand Designs**, on the Kinara junction before Arambol main road.

Paragliding and kitesurfing
Paragliding is synonymous with the hill between Arambol and Keri – ask for Andy at **Arambol Hammocks** on the cliff near **Eyes of Buddha** for tandem flights and the paragliding lowdown. Check

boards in **Double Dutch** or **Lamuella** for kitesurfing lessons.

Tour operators
SS Travels, Main Rd Arambol, near Om Ganesh General Store. Quality service on tours, tickets and money exchange. Also for **Western Union**. This is the place where all the local ex-pats go. Tried and trusted.

Morjim to Asvem *p445*
Body and soul
Raso Vai, S No 162/2-A, Morjim–Asvem road (towards Mandrem from Morjim), Mardi Wada, Morjim, T(0)9850-973458 and T(0)9623-556828, www.rasovai.com. Runs training courses in their signature treatments (Ayuryogic massage and Ayurbalancing), fusion massages encompassing traditional Ayurvedic techniques and yoga stretches as well as offering more traditional Ayurvedic treatments such as *panchakarma*, *swedan*, *pizhichil*, *shirodhara* and *snehapanam*, from a community oriented centre with meditation. Ayurvedic doctor on site. Highly recommended.

Surfing
Banana Surf School, at **Shanti** on the inlet in Asvem beach, www.goasurf.com.

Tour operators
Speedy, near post office, Mazalvaddo, T0832-227 3208. Open 0900-1830. Very helpful for all your onward travel arrangements; also changes money. Very helpful, comprehensive service.

Mandrem *p445*
Body and soul
Ashiyana (see Where to stay, page 453). Stunning yoga *shalas* in Balinese-style complex. There is drop-in yoga, meditation

and dance here as well as courses and retreats and a range of massage and healing options in their new spa.
Himalaya Yoga Valley www.yogagoa india.com. Great drop-in classes (morning and late afternoon) at beautiful elevated *shala* at **Beach St** but the main focus here is exceptional Yoga Teacher Training with talented team headed up by Lalit Kumar. They run regular trainings throughout the season just outside of Mandrem and then head to Europe and Thailand for the summer months. If you want to take your practice to the next level, this place is inspirational. Highly recommended.

⊖ Transport

Baga *p435, map p435*
Bicycle/scooter hire The only place in Baga to hire bikes is 200 m down a small lane past the Hacienda, on the left. Rs 40 per day, a little extra to keep it overnight. Almost every guesthouse owner or hotelier can rustle up a scooter at short notice – expect to pay Rs 150-350 for 1 day, discounts for longer periods. Those recycled water bottles of lurid orange liquid displayed at the side of the road are not Tizer but petrol often mixed with kerosene and therefore not good for the engine. Better to find a proper petrol station – dotted around in Baga, Vagator and Arambol. Petrol is Rs 55 per litre or 65/70 at the side of the road.

Mapusa *p437*
Bus To **Calangute** (every 20-30 mins), some continue on to **Aguada** and **Baga**, some go towards **Candolim**; check before boarding or change at Calangute. Non-stop minibuses to **Panjim**; buy tickets from booth at market entrance. Buses also go to **Vagator** and **Chapora** via **Anjuna** and towns near by. Buses to

Tivim for Konkan Railway and trains to **Mumbai** (allow 25 mins).
Long-distance buses line up opposite the taxi stand and offer near-identical routes and rates. Expect to pay between Rs 450 and 800 for Panjim to Mumbai for example (15 hrs); similar for Bangalore and Pune; between Rs 350 and 600 for Hampi with private operators like **Paolo Travels** or **Neeta Volvo**; you can book through any travel agent.

Car hire Pink Panther, T0832-226 3180.

Motorcycle hire Peter & Friends Classic Adventures, Casa Tres Amigos, Socol Vado 425, Parra, Assagao, 5 km east (off the Anjuna Rd), T0832-225 4467, www.classic-bike-india.com. To really get off the beaten track and see India in the raw, go on an enfield bike tour with **Peter & Friends**. Recommended for reliable bikes and tours of Southern India, Himachal and Nepal. Also has quality rooms and a lush swimming pool at his Casa. Many families rent out motorbikes and scooters – check the lights etc work before you commit.

Taxis Maximum capacity 4 people. Taxi fares have risen in Goa, just like the rest of the world. To **Panjim**, Rs 250; **Calangute/Baga**, Rs 300; **Arambol**, Rs 500. **Auto-rickshaws** are cheaper. **Motorcycle taxi** to **Anjuna** or **Calangute**, also available.

Train Thivim station, on the Konkan Railway, is convenient if you want to head straight to the **northern beaches** (Calangute, Baga, Anjuna and Vagator), avoiding Panjim and Margao. A local bus meets each train and usually runs as far as the Kadamba Bus Stand in Mapusa. From here you either continue on a local bus to the beach or share a tourist taxi (rates above). Enquiries and computerized tickets: T0832-229 8682. Bookings through a travel agent or if you have an Indian debit card, you can use it online at www.cleartrip.com. Rather than trying to work out **Trains at a Glance**, **Clear Trip** offers you an easy way of finding what trains are available, fares and timings. Timings do change, so double check.

To **Ernakulam** (for junction): *Mangalore Exp 12618*, 18 hrs. To **Jaipur** (from Ernakulam): *Exp 12977*, only Mon. To **Mumbai** (**CST**): *Mandovi Exp 10104*, 1038, 10 hrs; *Konkan Kanya Exp 10112*, 1856, 11 hrs. To **Thiruvananthapuram** (**Trivandrum**): *Netravati Exp 16345*, 2202, 19 hrs (via Margao and Canacona for Palolem beach).

Arambol *p443, map p443*
Bus There are regular buses from **Mapusa** and a frequent service from **Chopdem**, 12 km along the main road (1 hr); the attractive coastal detour via **Morjim** being slightly longer. It's a 2-hr walk north through Morjim and Mandrem by the coast. **SS Travels** and **Tara**, in the village, exchange cash and TCs, good for train tickets (Rs 100 service charge); also sells bus tickets.

Keri and Tiracol Fort *p444*
Bus Regular buses from **Mapusa** to Keri, then catch ferry to Tiracol Fort.

Mandrem *p445*
Bus Buses towards **Siolem** pass along the main road at about 0930 and 1345. Direct services also to **Mapusa** and **Panjim**.

❶ Directory

Calangute *p435, map p436*
Police T0832-227 8284.

Candolim and Sinquerim beaches *p436*
Medical services Health Centre, Main Rd; **Bosto Hospital**, Panjim Rd.

Mapusa *p437*
Medical services Ambulance: T0832-226 2372. **Vision Hospital**, T0832-225 6788. **Pharmacies** Including **Bardez Bazar**; **Drogaria**, near the Swiss Chapel, open 24 hrs; **Mapusa Clinic**, T0832-226 2350. **Police** T0832-226 2231. **Post** Opposite the police station.

Anjuna *p439, map p440*
Medical services St Michael's Pharmacy, Main Rd, Sorranto, open 24 hrs. **Police** T0832-227 3233.

Arambol *p443, map p443*
Medical services Best to travel to Mandrem (see below) **Police** T0832-229 7614. **Post** The small village post office is at the T-junction, 1.5 km from the beach.

Mandrem *p445*
Medical services Dr Fernandes clinic, T(0)94233-09338. Will also make house calls. Also **Goa Clinic 24/7**, T(0)98218-67459.

South Goa

The prosperous south is poster-paint green: lush coconut thickets that stretch along the coastline blend with broad swathes of iridescent paddy, broken by the piercingly bright white spears of splendid church steeples. Beneath the coastal coconut fronds sit the pretty villages of fishermen and agriculturalists: Salcete *taluka* is where the Portuguese were most deeply entrenched, and in the district's interior lie the beautiful remnants of centuries-old mansion estates built by the Goan colonial elite. Sprawling drawing rooms and ballrooms are stuffed with chandeliers and antiques and paved with splendid marble, every inch the fairytale doll's house.

Margao and coastal Salcete → *For listings, see pages 481-494.*

A wide belt of golden sand runs the length Salcete's coast in one glorious long lazy sweep, hemmed on the landward side by a ribbon of low-key beach shacks; tucked inland lie Goa's most imposing and deluxe hotels. The thrumming nightlife of North Goa is generally absent here, but some beaches, Cavelossim in particular, have been on the receiving end of a building boom kept afloat by Russian package tourists, while Colva has gone all out and built itself a line of Baywatch-style lifeguard shacks – buxom blonde lifesavers not included. Inland, in various states of decline, lie the stately mansions of Goa's landowning classes: worn-out cases of homes once fit for princes.

Arriving in Margao and coastal Salcete
Getting there and around The Konkan Railway connects Margao directly with Mumbai, Mangalore and Kerala. Madgaon/Margao station is 1.5 km southeast of the bus stands, municipal gardens and market area (where you'll find most of the hotels and restaurants). Rickshaws charge Rs 15 to transfer or walk the 800 m along the railway line. Interstate buses and those running between here and North Goa use the New Kadamba (State) Bus Stand 2 km north of town. City buses take you to the town bus stands for destinations south of Margao. Colva and Benaulim buses leave from the local bus stand east of the gardens. There are plenty of auto-rickshaws and eight-seater taxis for hire. ▸▸ *See Transport, page 492.*

Tourist information Goa Tourism Development Corporation (GTDC) ① *Margao Residency, south of the plaza, T0832-271 5204.* Also has a counter at the railway station, T0832-270 2298.

Margao (Madgaon)

Margao is a fetching, bustling market town which, as the capital of the state's historically richest and most fertile fertile *taluka*, Salcete, is a shop window for fans of grand old Portuguese domestic architecture and churches. Sadly, in their haste to get to the nearby beaches, few tourists take the time to explore this charming, busy provincial town.

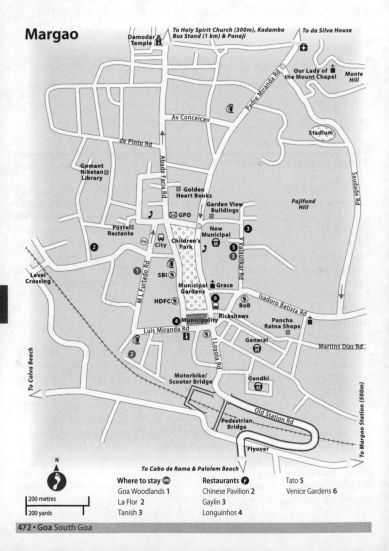

Margao

To Holy Spirit Church (300m), Kadamba Bus Stand (1 km) & Panaji

To da Silva House

Damodar Temple

Our Lady of the Mount Chapel

Monte Hill

Padre Miranda Rd

Av Conceicao

Stadium

de Pinto Rd

Saudade Rd

Gomant Niketan Library

Abade Faria Rd

Golden Heart Books

Garden View Buildings

Pajifond Hill

GPO

New Municipal

Poste Restante

City

Children's Park

Vhalvatkar Rd

Level Crossing

SBI

HDFC

Municipal Gardens

Grace

Isadoro Batista Rd

BoB

Rickshaws

Pancha Ratna Shops

M L Furtado Rd

Municipality

Luis Miranda Rd

Loyola Rd

General

Martins Dias Rd

Motorbike/ Scooter Bridge

Gandhi

To Colva Beach

Old Station Rd

To Margao Station (500m)

Pedestrian Bridge

Flyover

To Cabo de Rama & Palolem Beach

N

200 metres
200 yards

Where to stay 🛏
Goa Woodlands 1
La Flor 2
Tanish 3

Restaurants 🍴
Chinese Pavilion 2
Gaylin 3
Longuinhos 4

Tato 5
Venice Gardens 6

The impressive baroque **Church of the Holy Spirit** with its classic Goan façade dominates the Old Market square, the Largo de Igreja. Originally built in 1564, it was sacked by Muslims in 1589 and rebuilt in 1675. A remarkable pulpit on the north wall has carvings of the Apostles. There are also some glass cabinets in the north aisle containing statues of St Anthony and of the Blessed Joseph Vaz. Vaz was a home-grown Catholic missionary who smuggled himself to Sri Lanka dressed as a porter when the Dutch occupation challenged the island's faith. The church's feast day is in June.

The real gem of Margao is the glut of run-down 18th-century houses especially in and around Abade Faria Road, of which **da Silva House** ① *visits arranged via the GTDC*, is a splendid example. Built around 1790 when Inacio da Silva stepped up to become Secretary to the Viceroy, it has a long façade whose roof was once divided into seven separate cropped 'towers', hence its other name, 'Seven Shoulders'; only three of these have survived. The house's grandeur is also evident in its interiors, featuring lavishly carved dark rosewood furniture, gilded mirrors and fine chandeliers. Da Silva's descendants still live in a small wing of the house.

The **municipal market** (Mercado de Afonso de Albuquerque) is a labyrinthine treat of flower garlands, silks and agricultural yield.

Loutolim

By the late 18th century, an educated middle-class elite had emerged in the villages of the Old Conquests. With newly established rights to property, well-to-do Goans began to invest in large homes and very fine living. West of the Zuari River, the villages of Loutolim and Chandor are two of a number that saw the distinct development of estates and houses built on this grand scale. Their houses were stuffed with tokens of their European influence and affluence, mixed with traditions appropriated from their native ancestry, installing personal chapels instead of *devachem kuds*, or Hindu prayer rooms. One beautiful example is the **Figuerda Mansion** (Casa Museu Vicente Joao de Figueiredo) in Loutolim; if you are lucky you will get shown around by the lady of the house who is now in her 80s and has many a story to share about Goa. Ask for directions by the church in Loutolim as there are no signs.

Chandor

Despite being something of a backwater today, the once-grand village of Chandor nonetheless boasts several fine Portuguese mansions. Foremost among them is the enormous **Menezes Braganza family house** ① *13 km east of Margao, both wings usually open 1000-1730 but confirm by telephone; West Wing: T0832-278 4201, 1300-1400 or early evening after 1830; East Wing: T0832-278 4227; a donation of Rs 100 at the end of the tour is greatly appreciated*. Luis de Menezes Braganza was an influential journalist and politician (1878-1938) who not only campaigned for freedom from colonial rule but also became a champion of the less privileged sections of Goan society. The late 16th-century two-storey mansion he inherited (extended in the 18th and 19th centuries), still complete with much of the family furniture and effects, shows the sheer opulence of the life enjoyed by those old Goan families who established great plantation estates. The two wings are occupied separately by members of the Braganza family who have inherited the property.

The **West Wing**, which is better maintained and has finer antiques, is owned by Aida de Menezes Braganza. The guided tour by this elderly member of the family – when she resides here – is fascinating. She has managed to restore the teak ceiling of the 250-year-old library gallery to its original state; the old *mareta* wood floor survived better since this native Goan timber can withstand water. There is much carved and inlaid antique furniture and very fine imported china and porcelain, some specially ordered, and bearing the family crest.

The faded **East Wing**, occupied by Sr Alvaro de Perreira-Braganza, partly mirrors the West Wing. It also has some excellent carved and inlaid furniture and a similar large salon with fine chandeliers. The baroque family chapel at the back now has a prized relic added to its collection, the bejewelled nail of St Francis Xavier, which had, until recently, been kept guarded away from public view.

The guide from the East Wing of the Braganza House can also show you the **Fernandes House** ① *open daily, phone ahead T0832-278 4245, suggested donation Rs 100*, if he's not too busy. It's another example of a once-fine mansion just to the southeast of the village, on the Quepem road. This too has an impressive grand salon occupying the front of the house and a hidden inner courtyard. Recent excavations have unearthed an underground hiding place for when Christian families were under attack from Hindu raiders.

Back in Chandor village itself, the **Church of Our Lady of Bethlehem**, built in 1645, replaced the principal **Sapta Matrika** (Seven Mothers) **temple**, which was demolished in the previous century.

Chandor is closest to Margao but can also easily be visited from Panjim or the beaches in central Goa. It would be an arduous day trip from the northern beaches. Buses from Margao Kadamba Bus Stand (45 minutes) take you within walking distance of the sights but it is worth considering a taxi. Madgaon Railway Station, with connections to Mumbai and the Konkan coastal route as well as direct trains to Hospet, is close by.

Quepem

Heading south from Chandor you can have a tour of the **Palacio do Deao** (Priest's House) ① *T0832-266 4029, www.palaciododeao.com*, opposite Holy Cross Church in Quepem. This house has been lovingly restored by Ruben and Celia Vasco da Gama and has an interesting collection of old Goan stamps, coins and books. Time it so that you can have lunch here on their beautiful veranda – it's a multi-course affair with Indo-Portuguese food. Book in advance.

Colva (Colwa)

Although it's just 6 km from Margao and is the tourist hub of the southern beaches, sleepy Colva is a far cry from its overgrown northern equivalent, Calangute. The village itself is a bit scruffy, but the beach ticks all the right boxes: powdery white sand, gently swaying palms, shallow crystalline waters and lines of local fishermen drawing their nets in hand over fist, dumping pounds of mackerel which are left to dry out in glistening silver heaps.

Margao's parasol-twirling elite, in their search for *mudanca* or a change of air, were the first to succumb to Colva's charms. They would commandeer the homes of local fisher-folk, who had decamped to their shacks for months leading up to the monsoon. The shacks have now traded up for gaudy pink and turquoise guesthouses and the odd chi-chi resort, but Colva's holiday scene remains a mostly domestic affair, beloved of Indian fun-seekers who'll willingly shell out the cash to go parasailing for 90 seconds.

Out on the eastern edge of town, the large **Church of Our Lady of Mercy** (Nossa Senhora das Merces), dating from 1630 and rebuilt in the 18th century, has a relatively simple façade and a single tower on the south side that is so short as to be scarcely noticeable, and the strong horizontal lines normally given to Goan churches by three of four full storeys is broken by a narrow band of shallow semi-circular arches above the second floor. But the church is much less famous for its architecture than for the huge fair it hosts, thanks to its association with the miraculous **Menino Jesus**. Jesuit Father Bento Ferreira found the original image in the river Sena, Mozambique, en route to Goa, and brought it to Colva where he took up his position as rector in 1648. The image's miraculous healing powers secured it special veneration.

The **Fama of Menino Jesus festival** (Monday of 12-18 October) sees thousands of frantic devotees flock to kiss the statue in hope of a miracle. Near the church, specially blessed lengths of string are sold, as well as replicas of limbs, offered to the image in thanks for cures.

Betalbatim to Velsao
A short walk from Colva, **Betalbatim** is named after the main Hindu temple to Betall that stood here before the deity was moved to Queula in Ponda for safety. This is a pleasant stretch with a mix of coconut palms and casuarinas on the low dunes. At low tide, when the firm sand is exposed, you can cycle for miles along the beach in either direction.

The broad, flat open beaches to the north – **Velsao**, **Arossim**, **Utorda** and **Majorda** – are the emptiest: the odd fishing village or deluxe resort shelters under coconut thicket canopy.

Bogmalo is a small, palm-fringed and attractive beach that's exceptionally handy for the airport (only 4 km, and a 10-minute drive away). **Hollant Beach**, 2 km further on, is a small rocky cove that is fringed with coconut palms. From Bogmalo village you can get to **Santra Beach**, where fishermen will ferry you to two small islands for about Rs 350 per boat.

The quiet back lanes snaking between these drowsy villages make perfect bicycle terrain and Velsao boasts some particularly grand examples of old mansions.

Verna
The church at Verna (the 'place of fresh air'), inland from the northern Salcete beaches on the NH17, was initially built on the site of the Mahalsa Temple, which had housed the deity now in Mardol (see page 497) and featured exquisite carvings, but was destroyed and marked by the cross to prevent it being re-used for Hindu worship. As a sanctuary for widows who did not commit *sati*, it was dubbed the Temple of Nuns.

Verna was also picked to house the fifth century BC, 2.5-m-high **Mother Goddess figure** from Curdi in Sanguem, which was under threat of being submerged by the Selaulim Dam project in 1988. Two megalithic sites were found in the area. It is surrounded by seven healing springs. Just north towards Cortalim are the popular medicinal **Kersarval springs**.

Benaulim to Mobor

At Colva Beach's southern end lies tranquil **Benaulim**, which, according to the myth of Parasurama, is 'where the arrow fell' to make Goa. It is now a relaxed village set under palms, where business centres around toddy tapping and fishing. The hub of village activity is Maria Hall crossing, just over 1 km from the beach.

On a hill beyond the village is the diminutive **Church of St John the Baptist**, a fine piece of Goan Christian architecture rebuilt in 1596. Although the gable façade, with twin balustraded towers, is striking, the real treat is inside, in its sumptuous altar *reredos* and wonderful rococo pulpit with its depiction of the Lamb of the Apocalypse from the *Book of Revelation*.

The picturesque lane south from Benaulim runs through small villages and past white-painted churches. Paddy gives way to palm, and tracks empty onto small

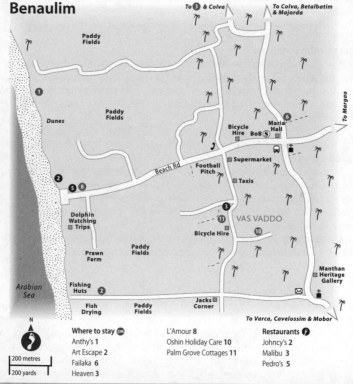

Benaulim

To **3** & Colva
To Colva, Betalbatim & Majorda
To Margao

Paddy Fields

Paddy Fields

1

Dunes

Bicycle Hire
BoB **$**
Maria Hall **6**

Beach Rd
Football Pitch
Supermarket

2 **5** **8**

Taxis

Dolphin Watching Trips

3
VAS VADDO

11

Bicycle Hire

10

Prawn Farm

Paddy Fields

Arabian Sea

Manthan Heritage Gallery

Fishing Huts **2**

Fish Drying
Paddy Fields
Jacks Corner

To Varca, Cavelossim & Mobor

N

200 metres
200 yards

Where to stay 🛏
Anthy's **1**
Art Escape **2**
Failaka **6**
Heaven **3**

L'Amour **8**
Oshin Holiday Care **10**
Palm Grove Cottages **11**

Restaurants 🍴
Johncy's **2**
Malibu **3**
Pedro's **5**

seaside settlements and deserted beaches. Benaulim has a more alternative vibe to its neighbouring beaches and has the **Goa Chitra Museum** ① *www.goachitra.com*, which is a beautifully created museum giving insight into the day-to-day living of rice farmers, toddy tappers and fishermen of not-so-yesteryear. They are creating another wing, **Goa Chakra**, focusing on transportation. Benaulim beach runs into **Varca**, and then **Fatrade**, before the main road finally hits the shoreline amid a sprouting of resorts and restaurants at **Cavelossim**. Furthest south, **Mobor**, about 6 km from Cavelossim, lies on the narrow peninsula where the river Sal joins the sea. The Sal is a busy fishing route, but doubles as a lovely spot for boat rides.

Varca to Betul

N

1 km
1 mile

Where to stay 🛏
Bamboo House **1**
Taj Exotica **13**

Restaurants 🍴
River View **4**

Bars & clubs 🍸
Aqua at Leela Palace
  Hotel **7**

Betul

Idyllic Betul, which overlooks Mobor from the opposite bank of the Sal in Quepem *taluka*, is an important fishing and coir village shaded by coconut palms and jackfruit, papaya and banana trees. A sand bar traps the estuary into a wide and protected lagoon and the cool breezes from the sea temper even the hottest Goan high noon. Just after the bridge, which crosses the mouth of a small river, a narrow road off to the right by the shops zigzags through the village along the south side of the Sal.

From Cavelossim the shortest route to Betul is by taking the ferry across the Sal (a signposted road leads southeast from a junction just north of Cavelossim) to Assolna; turn left off the ferry, then turn right in the village to join the main road towards Betul. From Margao, the NH17 forks right (6 km) towards Assolna at Chinchinim. After a further 6 km, there is a second turning in Cuncolim for Assolna. Buses from Margao to Betul can be very slow, but there is a fairly regular service stopping in all the settlements along the way (a couple of them continue as far as Cabo de Rama).

Cuncolim

The Jesuits razed Cuncolim's three principal Hindu temples (including the Shantadurga) and built churches and chapels in their stead.

Hindu 'rebels' killed five Jesuits and several converts in reprisal, triggering a manhunt which saw 15 men killed by the captain of Rachol Fort's soldiers. The relics of the Christian 'martyrs of Cuncolim' now lie in the Sé Cathedral in Old Goa (see page 423). The cathedral's golden bell, Goa's largest, was cast here in 1652.

Cabo de Rama, Palolem and the far south → For listings, see pages 481-494.

Palolem is the closest Goa gets to a picture-postcard perfect bay: a beautiful arc of palm-fringed golden sand that's topped and tailed with rocky outcrops. Under the canopy of the dense coconut forests lie numerous restaurants and coco-huts. To the north, a freshwater stream and a short swim or wade will get you to the jungle of the tiny Canacona Island.

Palolem's sheer prettiness has made it popular and perhaps less pretty than it once was, prompting some travellers to drift south to the tranquil beaches of neighbouring Colomb, Patnem and Galgibaga (beautiful Rajbag is ring-fenced by a five-star). Patnem, hemmed in by crags and river at either end, doesn't have the same rash of coconut trees that made Palolem so shadily alluring and has mopped up most of the overspill. Again to the north Agonda is also picking up some of the Palolem overspill, yet it retains its charm as a pretty fishing village strung out along a windswept casuarina-backed bay. There are more dramatic waves here than the calm waters of Palolem and Patnem. The dramatic ruined fort at Cabo de Rama yields some of Goa's most dramatic views from its ramparts and has empty coves tucked about at its shores.

Arriving in Cabo de Rama, Palolem and the far south

Getting there The nearest major transport junction for all these beaches is Canacona, also known as Chaudi, on the NH17 between Panjim and Karwar in Karnataka. Buses from here shuttle fairly continuously down to Palolem, and less frequently to Agonda, while there's a less frequent service from the beaches direct to Margao (37 km) which take about an hour. Canacona station on the Konkan railway is only 2 km from Palolem. Canacona's main square has the bus and auto-rickshaw stands; rickshaws cost Rs 50-150 to any of these bays.

Getting around The area between the beaches is small and wandering between them becomes a leisure pursuit in itself. The drive to Cabo de Rama, although riddled with hairpin bends, is particularly lovely, and going under your own steam means you can hunt out tucked away beaches nearby and stop over at the fishing dock at the estuary north of Agonda. Buses run along this route between the bays roughly hourly.

Cabo de Rama (Cape Rama)

Legend has it that the hero of the Hindu epic *Ramayana* lived in this desolate spot with his wife Sita during their exile from Ayodhya, and the fort predated the arrival of the Portuguese who seized it from its Hindu rulers in 1763. Its western edge, with its sheer drop to the Arabian Sea, gives you a stunning vista onto a secluded stretch of South Goa's coastline.

The main entrance to the **fort** seems far from impregnable, but the outer ramparts are excellently preserved with several cannons still scattered along their length. The gatehouse is only 20 m or so above the sea, and is also the source of the fort's water supply. A huge tank was excavated to a depth of about 10 m, which even today contains water right through the dry season. If a local herdsman is about ask him to direct you to the two springs, one of which gives out water through two spouts at different temperatures.

Agonda
Snake through forests and bright paddy south from Cabo De Rama towards Palolem to uncover artless Agonda, a windswept village backed by mountains of forestry full of acrobatic black-faced monkeys. Local political agitators thwarted plans for a five-star hotel and so have, temporarily at least, arrested the speed of their home's development as a tourist destination. However year on year, more restaurants and coco-huts open up along the length of the beach. There's no house music, little throttling of Enfield engines and you need to be happy to make your own entertainment to stay here for any serious length of time. Less photogenic than Palolem, Agonda Bay has pine-like casuarina trees lining the beach instead of coconuts and palms. The swimming is safe but the sea is livelier than in neighbouring Palolem. The northern end of the beach, close to the school and bus stop, has a small block of shops including the brilliantly chaotic and original **Fatima stores and restaurant** (Fatima Rodrigues, not one to be a jack of all trades, has limited her menu to just spaghetti and *thali*) and **St Annes bookstore**, a video library.

Hourly buses between Betul and Palolem call at Agonda (and Cabo de Rama). It's also easy to visit for the day by taxi, motorbike or bicycle from Palolem Beach. From Palolem/Chaudi Junction, auto-rickshaws charge Rs 120-150; turn off the road by the **Niki** bar and restaurant.

Palolem
For a short spell, when the police cracked down most severely on parties up north, Palolem looked like it might act as the Anjuna overflow. Today, **Neptune's Point** has permission to hold parties every Saturday, but so far, Palolem's villagers are resisting the move to make the beach a mini-party destination and authorities are even stumping up the cash to pay for litter pickers. The demographic here is chiefly late 20s and 30-something couples, travellers and students. The large church and high school of **St Tereza of Jesus** (1962) are on the northern edge of town.

Beaches further south
Over the rocky outcrops to the south you come to the sandy cove of **Colomb**. Wholly uncommercial, its trees are pocked with long-stayers' little picket fences and stabs at growing banana plants, their earthy homesteads cheek by jowl with fishermen's huts. The locals are currently holding firm against a controversial development planned by a Russian group, and for now the only sounds here are the rattle of

coconut fronds and bird song. Although just a bay away, you could almost be on a different planet to Palolem.

At the end of the track through Colomb, a collection of huts marks the start of the fine sweep of **Patnem Beach**. The 500 villagers here have both put a limit on the number of shacks and stopped outsiders from trading, and as a result the beach has conserved much of its unhurried charm. The deep sandbanks cushion volleyball players' falls and winds whip through kite flyers' sails: but fishing boats far outnumber sun loungers. A hit with old rockers, Israelis and long-stayers, there is no nightlife, no parties and, no coincidence, a healthy relationship between villagers and tourism. Hindu temples in Patnem have music most Fridays and Saturdays, with tabla, cymbals and harmonica.

Further south, wade across a stream (possible before the monsoon) to reach the dune- and casuarina-fringed **Rajbag Beach**, its southern waters a-bob with fishing boats. Although it's virtually unvisited and has perfect swimming, the luxury five-star that opened here in 2004 provoked a storm of protest; allegations against the hotel have included the limited access to the sea, the failure to meet local employment quotas, and the rebuilding of the ancient Shree Vita Rukmayee Temple, which villagers argue was tantamount to the hotel 'swallowing our God'. The isolated **Kindlebaga Beach** is east of Rajbag, 2 km from Canacona.

Galgibaga

Nip across the Talpona River by the ferry to reach a short strip of land jutting out to sea, where well-built houses lie among lucrative casuarina plantations. Like Morjim, **Galgibaga Beach** is a favourite stopover for Olive Ridley **turtles**, which travel vast distances to lay their eggs here each November. Shacks are mushrooming, to environmentalists' concern.

Partagali and Cotigao Wildlife Sanctuary

At a left turn-off the NH17, 7 km south of Canacona, to Partagali, a massive concrete gateway marks the way to the temple. If you go a little further, you reach a 2-km-long road that leads to the Cotigao Wildlife Sanctuary. Partagali's **Shri Sausthan Gokarn Partagali Jeevotam Math** is a centre for culture and learning on the banks of the river Kushavati. The *math* (religious establishment) was set up in AD 1475 at Margao when the followers, originally Saivites, were converted and became a Vaishnav sect. During the period of Portuguese Christianization (1560-1568), the foundation was moved south to Bhatkal (in northern Karnataka). The sixth Swami returned the *math* to Partagali, and built its Rama, Lakshman, Sita and Hunuman temple. An ancient *Vatavriksha* (banyan tree) 65 m by 75 m, which represents this Vaishnav spiritual movement, is a sacred meditation site known as *Bramhasthan*. The tree and its *Ishwarlinga* (the *lingam* of the Lord, ie Siva) have drawn pilgrims for more than a millennium. The temple, which also has a typical tall Garuda pillar, celebrates its festival in March/April.

Cotigao Wildlife Sanctuary ① *60 km south of Panjim, www.goaforest.com/wildlife mgmt/body_cotigao.htm, year-round 0730-1730 (but may not be worthwhile during the monsoon), Rs 5, 2-wheelers Rs 10, cars Rs 50, camera Rs 25, video Rs 100,* lies in one of the most densely forested areas of the state. The 86-sq-km sanctuary is hilly to the south and east and has the Talpona River flowing through it. There is a nature interpretation centre with a small reference library and map of the park roads at the entrance. The vegetation is mostly moist deciduous with some semi-evergreen and evergreen forest cover. You may be very lucky and spot gazelles, panther, sloth bear, porcupine and hyena, and several reptiles, but only really expect wild boar, the odd deer and gaur and many monkeys. Bird-spotting is more rewarding; rare birds include rufous woodpecker, Malabar crested lark and white-eyed eagle. You need your own vehicle to reach the treetop watchtowers and waterholes that are signposted, 3 km and 7 km off the main metalled road on a variable rough track. There are no guides available, but the forest paths are easy to follow – just make sure you have drinking water and petrol. The chances of seeing much wildlife, apart from monkeys, are slim, since by the opening time of 0730 animal activity has already died down to its daytime minimum.

The first tower by a waterhole is known as **Machan Vhutpal**, 400 m off the road, with great views of the forest canopy. The second tower is sturdier and the best place to spend a night (permission required).

Most visitors come for a day trip, but if you are keen on walking in the forest this is a great place to spend a day or two. You can either stay near the sanctuary office or spend a night in a watchtower deep in the forest. A short way beyond the sanctuary entrance the metalled road passes through a small hamlet where there is a kiosk for the villagers living within the reserve, which sells the usual array of basic provisions. If you are planning to spend a few days in the park it is best to bring your own fresh provisions and then let the staff prepare meals. Rudimentary facilities like snake-proof campsites, with canvas tents available from the forest office. You'll also need written permission to stay in the forest rest house or watchtower from the Deputy Conservator of Forests (third floor, Junta House, Panaji), as far in advance of a visit as possible.

The cheapest way to visit the park is to get a group together from Palolem. If you leave the beach just before 0700 you will be at the park gates when they open. Motorbikes are also allowed in the sanctuary.

◉ South Goa listings

For hotel and restaurant price codes and other relevant information, see pages 13-17.

◉ Where to stay

Margao *p472, map p472*
With Colva and other beaches little over 15 mins away, there is not much point staying in Margao itself.
$$ Goa Woodlands, ML Furtado Rd, opposite City Bus Stand, T0832-271 5522, www.goawoodlandshotel.com. This swish business hotel has 35 clean, spacious and anonymous rooms. Restaurant, bar, good value although reports have been mixed.
$ La Flor, E Carvalho St, T0832-273 1402, www.laflorhotelgoa.com. 35 rooms with bath, some a/c, restaurant, clean, away from bustle of town and very pleasant for the price.

$ Tanish, Reliance Trade Centre, V V Rd, T0832-273 5656. New place with smart, good-value rooms, sharing a business complex with cybercafés and mobile phone dealers. It's an OK-for-1-night kind of place. Several good restaurants nearby.

Loutolim p473
$$$ Casa Susegad, T0832-264 3477, www.casasusegad.com. This gem of a place tucked away in sleepy Loutolim village has just 5 rooms in a converted 300-year-old Portuguese house. There is a beautiful swimming pool, an enormous games room and delicious food cooked up, sometimes even home-smoked mackerel pâté or mango pie from the enormous mango trees dotted around the garden. Norman and Carole have done a remarkable job restoring this place and are very happy to share their little bit of paradise with you.

Chandor p473
$$$ The Big House, T0832-264 3477, www.ciarans.com. Ancestral Portuguese/Goan home of John Coutinho, owner of **Ciaran's Camp** in Palolem (see page 485). 2 bedrooms plus high-beamed ceilings, large sitting room, fully fitted kitchen, hot water, maid service, cable TV, DVD, phone and cooking available. Great for families, couples or groups of friends.

Colva p474
Most hotels are 6-8 km from Margao Railway Station. Prices rise on 1 Dec. Discounts are possible for stays of a week or more.
$$ C A Guest House, 470/2 4th Ward), T0832-278 0047. Cool and pleasant 2-bed apartments with balconies and basic kitchen in a huge, pastel-pink house.
$ Sea Pearl, 476/4 South Ward T0832-278 0176. Not particularly well maintained, but the big high-ceilinged rooms upstairs with private bath and balcony offer the best cheap deal in town. Good seafood restaurant downstairs.
$ Tourist Nest, 2 km from the sea, T0832-278 8624, touristnest@indiatimes. com. Crumbling old Portuguese house, 12 rooms in secure new block, fan, Rs 200 with bathroom, 2 small self-contained cottages, good restaurant. Old part of house recommended for long stay (Rs 8000 per month for 2 bedrooms), spacious dining area, large lounge, antique furniture, balcony, bathroom and cooking facilities.

Betalbatim to Velsao p475
$$$$ Alila Diwa Goa, Adao Waddo, Majorda, T0832-274 6800, www. aliladiwagoa.com. The latest of the lush hotels to open its doors in the Majorda area, it has already racked up a host of awards. Stunning lobby and beautiful infinity pool – beyond that the rooms are stylish and have lovely balconies. You can even get authentic home cooking; they have enlisted local Goan Edia Cotta to share her family recipes.
$$$$-$$$ Vivenda Dos Palhacos, Costa Vaddo, Majorda, T0832-322 1119, www.vivendagoa.com. One of the most charming places you can lay your hat in Goa. Stunning renovation of old Portuguese mansion – all rooms are different; Madras has a beautiful outdoor bathroom so you can shower under the stars, The Chummery is a lovely cottage with its own veranda, there is the Darjeeling with a mezzanine floor and you can stay in a huge luxe tent beyond the pretty swimming pool. Dinners are a fantastic communal affair although obviously you can opt out. Run by the hosts with the most Simon and Charlotte Hayward who come

from the lineage of Haywards 5000 and their bar is dedicated to the tipple. Wholeheartedly recommended.

$ Baptista, Beach Rd, Thonvaddo, Betalbatim, T0832-288 0048. 2 simple rooms with fan, 2 self-catering flats with gas stove, use of fridge and utensils (Rs 350), good for long stays – discounts, short walk from beach. Friendly family and friendly dog once he gets to know you.

$ Manuelina Tourist House, Thonvaddo, behind **Ray's**, T0832-880 1154. 5 spacious, clean rooms with bath, TV lounge, some food available, pleasant, secure, quiet with a lovely communal veranda next to the banyan tree.

Benaulim to Mobor *p476*, *maps p476 and p477*

Budget hotels and rooms in private houses can be found along Benaulim Beach Rd, in the coconut groves on either side, and along the beach south of **Johncy's**, but the rock bottom deals are drying up fast. Even simple beach guesthouses don't mind charging Rs 1000 a night for a room with bath.

$$$$ Taj Exotica, Calvaddo, towards Varca, T0832-658 3333, exoticabc.goa@ tajhotels.com. 23 ha of greenery and views of virgin beaches from each of its 138 luxurious rooms. Good restaurants, including Mediterranean, coffee shop, nightclub, excellent pool, golf course, floodlit tennis, kids' activities, jacuzzi, watersports, gym, jogging track, library and bike hire. Spa offers treatments such as Balinese massage, acupuncture and aromatherapy.

$$ Bamboo House Goa, Mobor Beach, Behind Leela Kempinski, T(0)976-664 9369, www.bamboohousegoa.com. This place packs real eco-credentials and works with **Green Goa Works** to reduce their carbon footprint including

composting and solar panels. They have also planted 80 varieties of plant around their grounds to prevent soil erosion. Beyond that, it's a pretty little place with 10 bamboo cottages and swanky bathrooms. Recommended.

$$ Palm Grove Cottages, Vas Vaddo, Benaulim, T0832-277 0059, www. palmgrovegoa.com. 20 clean, spacious but not stylish rooms. The newer blocks at rear with showers and balconies are better. Pleasant palm-shaded garden, good food, Ayurvedic treatments. Not on the beach but plenty of places to hire a bicycle just outside. Welcoming.

$$-$ Art Escape Vaddi beach, south Benaulim, T(0)989-228 6666, artescape. in. Lovely place to stay with wood and bamboo huts. There is lots of live music including a Qawalli Sufi music festival, art and holistic therapy workshops. It's a great place close to the beach to relax or be inspired.

$$-$ L'Amour, end of Beach Rd, Benaulim, T0832-277 0404, www.lamourbeachresort goa.com. Close to the sea, 20 cottage-style rooms amid pleasant gardens, in a well-established hotel run by same team as **Johncy's** beach shack. Good terrace restaurant, handy for exchange and booking rail and bus tickets.

$ Anthy's, Sernabatim Beach (2-min walk south of **Furtado's**), T(0)9922-854566, www.goaguesthomes.com. A tiny collection of simple white cottages with bed, bathroom, mosquito net and not much more, set behind a popular beach café. Simple but nicely done and on a pleasant bit of beach.

$ Failaka, Adsulim Nagar, near Maria Hall crossing, Benaulim, T0832-277 1270, hotelfailaka@hotmail.com. 16 spotless, comfortable rooms, 4 with TV, quieter at rear, excellent restaurant, friendly family set-up.

$ Heaven, north of Benaulim, Sernabatim Beach, T0832-277 2201, www.heavengoa.in. Absolutely stunning views of palm trees and green foliage, but it's 500 m from the beach. Great-value rooms and deservedly popular – book ahead. Also Ayurvedic massage available on site. Recommended.

$ Oshin Holiday Care, House No 126, Vas Vaddo, Benaulim, T0832-277 0069, www.oshins-guesthouse.com. You'll need a bicycle to get to the beach but the peaceful location overlooking egret and buffalo ponds is well worth it. 14 good large rooms with bath on 3 floors (room 11 is best), breakfast, dinner on request, friendly manager, superb well-kept grounds. Recommended.

Agonda *p479*

$$$-$$ Dunhill Beach Resort, towards south end of the beach, T(0)832-264 7328, www.dunhillbeachresort.in. Having had a bit of a facelift, **Dunhill** offers up the most stylish accommodation on the beach with 6 chic wooden cabanas and then cheaper, but large and comfortable rooms at the back. There is a good restaurant serving up all of the usual favourites too.

$$$-$ Shanti Village, towards south end of the beach, T(0)9823-962154, www.shantiagonda.com. With lovely views and chic huts, **Shanti** has chic black huts on the beach and an intimate vibe. It's good value and they have another outpost towards the north end of the beach near **Simrose**, where there are some cheaper huts, although still very nice with tribal masks and textiles to decorate.

$$$-$ White Sand, north end of the beach, T(0)9823-548277, www.agonda whitesand.com. **White Sand** has always been a popular choice in Agonda and

with a new redesign is offering up stylish great-value accommodation. New cabanas have beautiful outside showers and are nicely decorated inside. The menu has also had a rethink and there are great Euro classics and traditional Goan and Indian fare on offer. They also have **Agonda Villas** – 5 boutique-style Balinese-inspired villas which are more expensive but well worth the money. Recommended.

$$ Blue Lagoon Resort, 4 km north of Agonda at Khola beach, T0832-264 7842, www.bluelagooncola.com. Rajasthani tents set up on this secluded beach north of Agonda – blissful. There are also lovely huts, a restaurant and amazing views. You almost have the beach to yourself for romantic moonlit walks as it is mainly a daytripper beach.

$$-$ Common Home, south end of the beach, T(0)9823-367300. Innovatively designed a/c rooms with Rajasthani wooden doors, and beach huts with sleek slate bathrooms and cow dung walls – all with interesting furniture and draped fabrics. There are also huts available.

$$-$ Simrose, towards north end of the beach, T(0)9420-162474, www.simrose-goa.com. Stylish beach shacks and nice rooms at the back. The pretty restaurant has plenty of little nooks for romantic suppers or shady spots for daytime lounging. Good value. Recommended.

$ Dersy Beach Resort, south end of the beach, T0832-264 7503. 50-year-old family house developed to fit 12 clean rooms with bathrooms. Over the road on the beach are 12 basic bamboo huts with a spotless shared wash block. Good value generally, but in high season the huts are not worth the price.

$ Kaama Kethna, 5 km south of Agonda off Palolem Rd, www.kaamakethna.net, phone reception patchy so email

kaamakethna@ymail.com. Beautiful bamboo huts with open-air bathrooms perched in the jungle. Part of an enterprising organic farm there are 5 stylish huts and 2 treehouses and a lot more land to play with for creating new accommodation – really you feel your only neighbour is the jungle itself with just a mosquito net and swaying sari between you and Nature. You will find beautiful land, inspiring people, a yoga platform and a great and nourishing restaurant using the produce from the farm. There is an annual yoga festival, art projects and if you want to get your hands dirty there are opportunities for volunteering. You can walk through the jungle to Agonda beach in 30 mins and to the neighbouring Butterfly beach in 40 mins. Wholeheartedly recommended.
$ Nana's Nook, extreme south end of the the beach, T(0)9421-244672. Simple beach huts dotted around a central café with shared bath. The best huts at the front offer ideal views. Recommended.

Palolem *p479*

Palolem's popularity has soared inordinately and in high season prices go off the scale. Off season, bargain hard and ask around for rooms inside family houses. There is a wide range of accommodation.
$$$-$$ Art Resort, south end of beach in Ourem area, T(0)9665-982344, www. art-resort-goa.com. Colourful seafront cottages with interesting interior design from Riki Hinteregger using khadi natural cotton. Fairly pricey.
$$$-$$ Ciaran's Camp, beach, T0832-264 3477, www.ciarans10.com. Primo glass-fronted wooden huts are spaced wide apart in palm-covered landscaped gardens; many have their own roof terrace with loungers. They have added more rooms so there is more chance of

getting a super-stylish hut here. A library, lovely shop, table tennis and great restaurant plus promises of live jazz all make it the leader in Palolem cool.
$$$-$$ Village Guesthouse, beach, off the main road, T0832-264 5767, www.villageguesthousegoa.com. Stylish renovation of an old house, which, although only 5 mins' walk from beach feels a million miles away. Beautiful rooms with a/c, TV and chic decor. They pride themselves on sourcing everything locally except the washing machine which came from Korea and the tequila from Mexico! Great views across rice fields from the communal veranda, and a courtyard garden in the back.
$$ Bhakti Kutir, cliffside, south end of the beach, T0832-264 3469, www. bhaktikutir. com. This is a hardy perennial of Palolem offering up eco-friendly chic perched on the hilltop above Palolem beach. A relaxing place with 2-tier huts kitted out with antique furniture, compost toilets and bucket baths. There is a popular super-healthy restaurant on-site offering up a selection of every grain you can think of. Renowned yoga teacher Swami Yogananda is based here and has a dedicated following.
$$-$ Cozy Nook, at northern end, T0832-264 3550. Plastered bamboo huts, fans, nets, shared toilets, in a good location between the sea and river, Ayurvedic centre, art and crafts, friendly. Very popular. Getting a bit pricey.
$$-$ Ordo Sounsar, extreme north end of the beach, over a small bridge, T(0)9822-488769, www.ordosounsar. com. Simple yet stylish beach huts nestling north of the estuary away from the busy-ness of Palolem Beach. Exceptional location and restaurant serving up traditional Goan dishes. Highly recommended.

$ Chattai, set back from the beach, behind Bhakti Kutir and Neptune's Point, T(0)9822-481360, www.chattai.co.in. Fantastic coco huts, most with loungey roof terraces. Lovely chilled atmosphere. There is another branch in Agonda.

$ Fernandes, next to **Banyan Tree**, T0832-264 3743. 2 branches of this family-run guesthouse and restaurant on the beach. Lovely wooden cottages with attached bathrooms, good value.

$ Green Inn, on the Agonda road, T(0)9434-053626, www.palolemgreen inn. com. Exceptional location, this 2-storey guesthouse juts out into the vibrant green rice fields offering up almost a 360° view of nature. Nice clean rooms with flatscreen TVs and modern bathrooms, alas no individual balconies, but amazing views from rooftop restaurant.

$ Papillon, south end of beach, T(0)9890-495470, www.papillonpalolem. com. Good-value chic beach huts with laid-back vibe, a cut above the rest.

Beaches further south *p479*

The following places are dotted between Colomb, Patnem and Galjibag. Demand and room rates rocket over Christmas and New Year.

$$$-$$ La Mangrove, Galjibag, T0832 2641243, www.lamangrovegoa.com. Billed as a river lounge, close to the stunning beach of Galjibag you find a unique opportunity to stay in super-chic tipis with kingsize beds, open-air showers and eco toilets. There is a loungey restaurant on site. At the time of writing there were issues with local licenses so fingers crossed that soon gets resolved.

$$ Almond Park, on the road linking Palolem and Patnem, T(0)7875-477788, www.almondpark.com. 5 nice rooms with lovely verandas set amongst, you guessed it, almond trees. Pretty little place and one room has a kitchen. A short walk down to the beach, uphill on the way back!

$$ April 20, next to **Home**, T(0)9960-916989, vickygoan@gmail.com. Smart 1- and 2-tiered beach bungalows with nice balconies and great views, formerly called **Goyam & Goyam**. It's restaurant is recommended by the local Westerners who make south Goa their home.

$$ Hidden Gourmet, Colomb, T(0)9923-686185, www.gourmetpatnem.com. As the name suggests this place is off the beaten track, or at least through the village and tucked away on the promontory overlooking Patnem beach. Beautifully decorated stone rooms all with a stunning ocean view and 2 mango wood and bamboo huts with stylish open-roofed bathrooms. Recommended.

$$-$ Home Guesthouse, Patnem, T0832-264 3916, www.homeispatnem. com Vibey rooms with nice decor make these a cut above the rest – deservedly popular. Quality linen and fairy lights make for good ambience, although opt for a room set back from the kitchen and very popular restaurant. Staying here could affect your waistline.

$$-$ Papayas, Patnem, T(0)9923-079447, www.papayasgoa.com. Eco-friendly huts running on solar power with beautifully kept gardens. Chilled atmosphere set behind small beachfront restaurant.

$ Bonkers, south end Patnem beach, T(0)9822-664026, rocking.bonkers@ gmail.com. Floppy fringed palm huts borrowing their design from neighbours **Lotus Yoga**, laid-back vibe at the quieter end of the beach.

$ Namaste, Patnem, T(0)9850-477189, namaste_patnem@yahoo.in. Variety of wooden huts and bamboo bungalows – good value. Nice vibe and lively restaurant.

$ Solitude Dream Woods, Patnem, T0832-327 7081, solitudedreamwoods@ yahoo.com. Included on www.goa beachhuts.com, which gives more listings for the area. Basic plywood structures, but good value and all with attached bathroom. There is a yoga space here and swinging chairs dotted around.

🍴 Restaurants

Margao *p472, map p472*
$$ Chinese Pavilion, M Menezes Rd (400 m west of Municipal Gardens). Chinese. Smart, a/c, good choice.
$$ Gaylin, 1 V Valaulikar Rd. Chinese. Tasty hot Szechuan, comfortable a/c.
$$ Longuinhos, near the Municipality. Goan, North Indian. Open all day for meals and snacks, bar drinks and baked goodies.
$$ Tato, G-5 Apna Bazaar, Complex, V Valaulikar Rd. Superb vegetarian, a/c upstairs.
$$ Venice Gardens, near Our Lady of Grace Church, opposite Lohia Maidan, T0832-271 0505. Little garden oasis in the middle of Margao offering up the usual fare.

Colva *p474*
$ Joe Con's, 4th Ward. Excellent fresh fish and Goan dishes, good value.
$ Sagar Kinara, 2 mins back from beach overlooking the main road junction. Rare pure-veg restaurant, offering good-value *thalis* and biryanis on a breezy terrace.
$ Viva Goa, 200 m south of roundabout at east end of town. Local favourite, serving proper Goan food on red checked tablecloths. Recommended.

Betalbatim to Velsao *p475*
It's worth coming to Majorda for the food, there are a range of great restaurants.

$$$ Fusion, Majorda Beach Rd, Pacheco Vaddo, T0832-288 1694. Winning a Times Food Award in 2011, this place offers up a lot of meat. Steaks and carpaccio are their specialities, but naturally there are some fish and veg options too. And leave room for their chocolate fondant.
$$$ Martin's Corner, Betalbatim (coming from the south, look for sign on left after village), T0832-648 1518. A huge place in front of an old house, serving great seafood including lobster, tiger prawns and crab. As cricket superstar Sachin Tendulkar has bought a house here, it's become the hangout of choice for holidaying cricket stars and media types.
$$$ Miyabi, Majorda Beach Rd, T(0)9767-704244. Serving up for-real Japanese food – fresh sushi, tasty tempura and all sorts of fish dishes. Beautiful restaurant run by Japanese/Russian couple. Recommended.
$$$ Zeebop, Utorda Beach, follow signs to Kenilworth resort, www.zeebopby thesea.com. Lovely beachfront restaurant offering up a delicious range of seafood, try the crab *papads* and great Goan specialities. Recommended.
$$ Roytanzil Garden Pub, set back from the beach at the end of Majorda beach road past **Martin's Corner** (no sea views). Neat grounds, alfresco and small covered area. Seafood and Indian. One of the best restaurants on the south coast.

Benaulim to Mobor *p476, maps p476 and p477*
Beach shacks all down the coast offer Goan dishes and seafood at reasonable prices.
$$ La Afra, Tamborin, Fatrade. Excellent steaks and fresh fish, sensibly priced. Boatmen ferry holidaymakers to **River Sal**, Betul.
$$ Pedro's, by the car park above the beach, Benaulim. Good seafood and tandoori. Imaginative menu, friendly.

$$ River View, Cavelossim. Tranquil, open-air location, overlooking the river. Wide choice, international menu, good ambience despite being surrounded by ugly hotels. Cocktails Rs 100, sizzlers Rs 150-200, tiger prawns Rs 500.

$ Goan Village, lane opposite Dona Sylvia, Cavelossim. The best in the area for all cuisines.

$ Johncy's, Benaulim. Varied menu, good seafood, big portions, tandoori recommended (after 1830) but service can be erratic. Pleasant atmosphere though; backgammon, scrabble.

$ Malibu, Benaulim. Lush garden setting for spicy fish/meat kebabs.

Cabo de Rama *p478*

$ Pinto's Bar, near the fort entrance. Offers meals and cool drinks on a sandy shaded terrace, may also have rooms available. If there are few visitors about (most likely) order your meal here before exploring the fort to save time waiting later.

Agonda *p479*

Most of the places recommended for accommodation also have good food, especially **White Sand** and **Dunhill**.

$$ Blue Planet, Palolem–Agonda road, 5 km before Agonda, T0832-264 7448, www.blueplanet-cafe.com. This Palolem institution has taken a risk and moved into the countryside just outside Agonda – but it's a beautiful risk to take. The drive is great and there's a lovely view from their new abode. On the menu you will find an array of vegetarian and organic healthy treats.

$$ Kaama Kethna, Palolem–Agonda road, 5 km before Agonda, www.kaama kethna.net. A little bit further up the track than **Blue Planet**, **Kaama Kethna** offers up simple food using the ingredients from their organic farm as much as

possible. Beautiful setting in the jungle. The *thali* is recommended by many.

$$ White Sand, north end of beach. Laid-back vibe and traditional Goan and Indian fare, but with some interesting surprises like sausage and mash and smoked salmon omelettes.

$ Madhu, north end of beach, T(0)9423-813140, www.madhuhuts.com. Always packed, this beach shack serves up a great range of traditional spicy Goan food as well as a range of Indian, Chinese and continental dishes. Also has nice huts available.

Palolem *p479*

$$ Bhakti Kutir (see Where to stay, page 485). Excellent fresh fish dishes, home-grown organic produce and fresh juices. Name any number of obscure nutritious grains and they'll be here.

$$ Café Inn, at the beach road junction. Funky courtyard café serving up quality cappuccinos, a huge array of juices, tortilla wraps and unusual pancakes, such as strawberry and meringue.

$$ Dropadi Beach Restaurant and Bar. Routinely packed out. Lobster and lasagne and North Indian food are the specials – the ex-pat community do rave about the quality of the fish here.

$$ Ordo Sounsar, over bridge at far north end of beach. Simple menu focusing on Goan food – strangely a rarity in these parts. Fantastic stuffed mackerel, calamari masala, Goan-style fishcakes, unique papaya curry, fried plantain chips – exceptional stuff. Highly recommended.

$$ Ourem 88, close to Art Resort in Ourem area, T(0)8698-827679. New player on the Palolem scene offering up exceptional food. With Jodi in the kitchen and Brett out front, there is a relaxed vibe and delicious food with specials like sea bass with rucola mash and great steaks on a menu that changes weekly. And leave room for desserts such as espresso brûlée and an awe-inspiring lemon tart. Booking essential. Highly recommended.

$$ Tavernakki, south end of the beach, Ourem. T(0)8408-090673. With help from the extremely popular **Thalassa** in northern Goa, **Tavernakki** offers up big portions of steak and lots of feta as well as souvlaki.

$ Banyan Tree, north end of the beach. Sitting in the shade of a lovely banyan tree, the menu here focuses on Thai food and mostly gets it just right – good *pad thai* and green curries. Open mic night on Fri.

$ Shiva Sai, off main road. Great cheap *thalis*.

$ Tibet Bar and Restaurant, Main Rd, T(0)9822-142775. Super-fresh ingredients in these excellent Himalayan dishes. Small restaurant that's worth stepping back from the beach for.

Beaches further south *p479*

Nestled between Palolem and Patnem is Colomb Bay with a few huts, restaurants and the main venue, **Neptune's Point**. Most of the places mentioned for accommodation in Patnem also serve up great food.

$$ Hidden Gourmet, Colomb, T(0)9923-686185, www.gourmetpatnem.com. Passionate about their food, the team here serves up a great range of fish and steaks, crisp salads and delicious desserts – all with a stunning view of Patnem beach.

$$ Home, Patnem. Great range of salads, pastas, and veggie specials like beetroot and vodka risotto – make sure you leave room for their legendary desserts such as chocolate brownie or sharp lemon tart – with a very chilled chic beachfront vibe.

$$ Magic View, Colomb, in front of **Hidden Gourmet**, T(0)9960-917287. Remarkably popular Italian restaurant delivering fantastic pizzas served up on tree trunks, deliciously decadent pastas such as gorgonzola and fish specials. Choose from 2 views, one overlooking the rocks at Colomb and the other gazing over Patnem.

$ Boom Shankar, Colomb, T(0)9822-644035. The latest 'in' venue for sundowners, this place also offers a good range of food and rooms to rent; all have great views over the rocks.

$ Mamoos, set back from beach, T0832-264 4261. **Mamoos** has served up excellent North Indian food at great prices for years.

Bars and clubs

Colva *p474*

Boomerang, on the beach a few shacks north of **Pasta Hut**. Appealing sea-view drinking hole with pool table, sociable circular bar, dancefloor (music veers wildly from cool to cheesy), and daytime massages courtesy of Gupta.

Johnny Cool's, halfway up busy Beach Rd. Scruffy surroundings but popular for chilled beer and late-night drinks.

Splash, on beach, 500 m south of main car park. *The* place for music, dancing and late drinking, open all night, trendy, very busy on Sat (full after 2300 Mon-Fri in season), good cocktails, poor bar snacks. May not appeal to all, especially unaccompanied girls.

Benaulim to Mobor *p476*, *maps p476 and p477*

Aqua, **Leela Palace**, Mobor. A gaming room and cigar lounge which turns into a late-night disco after 2000.

Palolem *p479*
Cuba Beach Cafe, Palolem road, behind Syndicate Bank, T0832-264 3449. Cool, upbeat bar for a sundowner with regular sunset DJ sessions.
Hare Krishna Hare Ram, Patnem. Latest place for sunsets and dancing run by old schoolmates, local boys done good.
Laguna Vista, Colomb. Come here on Fri nights for French singer Axailles accompanied by Indian classical musicians – great vibe.
Neptune's Point Bar and Restaurant, T(0)9822-584968. Wide dancefloor nestled between the rocks for a mellow daily chill-out from 1700-2200 with a proper party on a weekly basis. This is also the venue for Silent Noise headphone parties (www.silentnoise.com) – an ingenious way to defy the 2200 curfew. Plugged in via wireless 'phones, you can dance your heart out to a choice of 2 DJs and there's no noise pollution. A giant screen plays movies on Wed nights.

⊛ Festivals

Chandor *p473*
6 Jan Three Kings Festival Crowds gather on each year at Epiphany for the Three Kings Festival, which is similarly celebrated at Reis Magos, with a big fair, and at Cansaulim (Quelim) in southern Goa. The 3 villages of Chandor (Cavorim, Guirdolim and Chandor) come together to put on a grand show. Boys chosen from the villages dress up as the 3 kings and appear on horseback carrying gifts of gold, frankincense and myrrh. They process through the village before arriving at the church where a large congregation gathers.

Colva *p474*
12-18 Oct (Mon that falls between these dates) **Fama of Menino Jesus** when thousands of pilgrims flock to see the statue in the Church of our Lady of Mercy in the hope of witnessing a miracle.

Benaulim to Mobor *p476,*
maps p476 and p477
24 Jun Feast of St John the Baptist (Sao Joao) in Bernaulim gives thanks for the arrival of the monsoon. Young men wearing crowns of leaves and fruits tour the area singing for gifts. They jump into wells (which are usually full) to commemorate the movement of St John in his mother's womb when she was visited by Mary, the mother of Jesus.

Palolem *p479*
Feb Rathasaptami The Shri Malikarjuna Temple 'car' festival attracts large crowds.
Apr Shigmo, also at the Shri Malikarjuna Temple, also very popular.

O Shopping

Margao *p472, map p472*
The Old Market was rehoused in the 'New' (Municipal) Market in town. The **covered market** (Mon-Sat 0800-1300, 1600-2000) is fun to wander around. It is not at all touristy but holidaymakers come on their shopping trip to avoid paying inflated prices in the beach resorts. To catch a glimpse of the early morning arrivals at the **fish market** head south from the Municipal Building.

Books and CDs
Golden Heart, off Abbé Faria Rd, behind the GPO. Closed 1300-1500. Bookshop.
Trevor's, 5 Luis Miranda Rd. Sells CDs.

Clothes

J Vaz, Martires Dias Rd, near Hari Mandir, T0832-272 0086. Good-quality men's tailor.
MS Caro, Caro Corner. An extensive range including 'suiting', and will advise on tailors.

Benaulim to Mobor *p476,*
maps p476 and p477
Khazana, Taj Exotica, Benaulim. A veritable treasure chest (books, crafts, clothes) culled from across India. Pricey.
Manthan Heritage Gallery, main road. Quality collection of art items.

Palolem *p479*
Chim, main Palolem Beach road. Good collection of funky Indian-inspired clothes and *kurtas*, as well as bikinis and accessories.

⊙ What to do

Colva *p474*
Tour operators
Meeting Point, Beach Rd, opposite **William Resort**, T0832-278 8003. Mon-Sat 0830-1900 (opens later if busy). Very efficient, reliable flight, bus and train booking service.

Betalbatim to Velsao *p475*
Watersports
Goa Diving, Bogmalo; also at **Joet's**, and based Chapel Bhat, Chicalim, T0832-255 5117, goadiving@sancharnet.in. PADI certification from Open Water to Assistant Instructor.
Splash Watersports, Bogmalo, T0832-240 9886. Run by Derek, a famous Indian champion windsurfer. Operates from a shack on the beach just below **Joet's**, providing parasailing, windsurfing, waterskiing, trips to nearby islands; during the high season only.

Benaulim to Mobor *p476,*
maps p476 and p477
Body and soul
At **Taj Exotica**, Benaulim, yoga indoors or on the lawn. Also aromatherapy, reflexology.

Dolphin watching
The trips are scenic and chances of seeing dolphin are high, but it gets very hot (take a hat, water and something comfy to sit on). Groups of dolphins here are usually seen swimming near the surface. Most hotels and cafés offer boat trips, including **Café Dominick** in Benaulim (signs on the beach). Expect to pay Rs 250-300 per person.
Betty's Place, in a road opposite the Holiday Inn in Mobor, T0832-287 1456. Offers dolphin viewing (0800-1000, Rs 300), birdwatching (1600, Rs 250) and sunset cruises up the river Sal River (1700, Rs 200). Recommended.

Agonda *p479*
Boat hire and cruises
Monsoon, **Madhu** and **Om Sai** hotels organize trips to the spice plantations and boat trips to Butterfly and Cola beaches. **Aquamer** rents kayaks.

Palolem *p479*
Boat hire and cruises
You can hire boats to spend a night under the stars on the secluded Butterfly or Honeymoon beaches, and many offer dolphin-watching and fishing trips. You can see the dolphins from dry land around Neptune's Point, or ask for rowing boats instead of motorboats if you want to reduce pollution. Mornings 0830-1230 are best. Arrange through **Palolem Beach Resort**, travel agents or a fisherman. Take sunscreen, shirt, hat and water.

Ciaran's Camp, T0832-264 3477. Runs 2-hr mountain bike tours or charter a yacht overnight through Ciaran's bar.

Body and soul

Harmonic Healing Centre, Patnem, T(0)9822-512814, www.harmonicingoa. com. With an enviable location high above the north end of Patnem beach, you can perform your *asanas* while looking out to sea. You can have massage with just the sky and the cliffs as a backdrop. Drop-in yoga, Bollywood and Indian classical dance classes and a full range of alternative treatments are on offer. The owner Natalie Mathos also runs 2-week non-residential reiki courses and yoga retreats from Nov-Mar.
Lotus Yoga Retreats, south end Patnem beach, T(0)9604-290688, www.lotus-yoga-retreat.com. Offering a range of yoga holidays and retreats with guest teachers from Europe, **Lotus** has an enviable location at the relaxed end of Patnem beach. Beautiful yogashala and stylish accommodation made from local materials.

Language and cooking courses

Sea Shells Guest House, on the main road. Hindi and Indian cookery classes.

Tour operators

Rainbow Travels, T0832-264 3912. Efficient flight and train bookings, exchange, Western Union money transfer, safe deposit lockers (Rs 10 per day), good internet connection.

⊖ Transport

Margao *p472, map p472*
Bus All state-run local and long-distance buses originate from the **Kadamba Bus Stand** 2 km to the north

of town, T0832-271 4699. Those from the south also call at the **local** bus stand west of the municipal gardens, and buses for Colva and Benaulim can be boarded near the Kamat Hotel southeast of the gardens. From the Kadamba stand, city buses and motorcycle taxis (Rs 15) can get you to central Margao.

Frequent services to **Benaulim**, **Colva** and non-stop to **Panjim** (1 hr, buy tickets from booth at Platform 1. Several a day to **Betul**, **Cabo da Rama**, **Canacona** and **Palolem**. Daily to **Gokarna** (1500), but trains are much quicker.

Private buses (eg **Paulo Travels**, Cardozo Building opposite bus stand, T0832-243 8531), to **Bengaluru** (**Bangalore**) (15 hrs); **Mangalore** (8-10 hrs); **Mumbai** (**Dadar/CST**) (16 hrs); **Pune** (13 hrs).

Car hire Sai Service, T0832-241 7063. Rs 1000-2000 per day with driver.

Rickshaw Most trips in town should cost Rs 30-40; main bus stand to railway Rs 50. The prepaid rickshaw booth outside the station main entrance has high rates but probably better than bartering on the street. Motorcycle taxi drivers hang around quoting cheaper (but still overpriced) fares. Avoid tourist taxis: they can be 5 times the price.

Train Enquiries, T0832-271 2790. The new station on the broad-gauge network is 1 km southwest of central Margao. The reservation office on the 1st floor, T0832-271 2940, is usually quick and efficient, with short queues. Mon-Sat 0800-1400, 1415-2000, Sun 0800-1400. Tickets for **Mumbai**, **Delhi** and **Hospet** (for **Hampi**) should be booked well ahead.

Konkan Kanya Express (night train) and **Mandovi Express** (day train) from **Mumbai** also stop at **Thivim** (for northern beaches; take the local bus into Mapusa and from there catch another bus or take a taxi) and **Karmali** (for Panjim and Dabolim airport) before terminating at **Margao**. Both are very slow and take nearly 12 hrs. From **Mumbai** (**CST**): *Konkan Kanya Exp 10111*, 1800 (arrives 0550).

To **Delhi** (**Nizamuddin**), fastest train is *Kurj Nzm Exp 02449*, 30 hrs (only Thu), for daily service *Mangala Ldweep Exp 12617*, 33 hrs. Going south to **Ernakulam** (**Jn**): *Mangala Lakshaweep Exp 12618*, 16 hrs. **Hospet** (for **Hampi**): *VSG Howrah Express 18048*, 0750, Tue, Thu, Fri, Sun, 7 hrs. **Thiruvananthapuram** (**Trivandrum**): *Rajdhani Exp 12432*, 135, Mon, Wed, Thu, 18 hrs (via Mangalore, 5 hrs, and Ernakulam, 13 hrs). *Netravati Exp 16345*, 23150, 18 hrs (via Canacona for Palolem beach).

The broad-gauge line between **Vasco da Gama** and **Londa** in Karnataka runs through Margao and Dudhsagar Falls and connects stations on the line with **Belgaum**. There are services to **Bengaluru** (**Bangalore**) *Vasco Chennai Exp 17312*, 1520, Thu.

Colva *p474*
Air From the airport, taxis charge about Rs 800. If arriving by train at Margao, 6 km away, opt for a bus or auto-rickshaw for transfer. Buses pull in at the main crossroads and then proceed down to the beach about 1 km away. Auto-rickshaws claim to have a Rs 30 'minimum charge' around Colva itself.

Scooter hire is available on every street corner, for Rs 200-250 a day; motorbikes for Rs 300 per day, less for long-term rental, more for Enfields. Bicycles are hard to come by – ask at your hotel.

Bus/taxi Bus tours to **Anjuna**, every Wed for the Flea Market, tickets through travel agents, depart 0930, return 1730, Rs 200; to **Margao** half-hourly, take 30 mins (last bus 1915, last return, 2000). Also to **Margao**, motorcycle taxi, Rs 80 (bargain hard); auto-rickshaw, Rs 100-120.

Betalbatim to Velsao *p475*
Bus Buses from Margao (12 km). The **Margao–Vasco** bus service passes through the centre of Cansaulim.

Taxi To/from **airport**, 20 mins (Rs 400); **Margao** 15 mins (Rs 200). From **Nanu Resort**, **Panjim** Rs 700, **Anjuna** Rs 750, or Rs 1000 for 8 hrs, 80 km.

Train **Cansaulim station** on the **Vasco–Margao** line is handy for **Velsao** and **Arossim** beaches, and **Majorda station** for **Utorda** and **Majorda** beaches. Auto-rickshaws meet trains.

From Cansaulim and Majorda there are 3 trains a day to **Vasco** via **Dabolim** for the airport. Westbound trains head to **Kulem** (for Dudhsagar Falls) via **Margao**.

Benaulim to Mobor *p476,*
maps *p476* and *p477*
Bicycle/scooter hire Cycle hire from **Rocks**, outside Dona Sylvia in Cavelossim, cycles Rs 10 per hr, Rs 150 a day; scooters Rs 300 a day without petrol, Rs 500 with 7 litres of fuel. In Benaulim, bikes and scooters for hire, Rs 150 and Rs 300 per day.

Bus Buses from all directions arrive at Maria Hall crossing, Benaulim. Taxis and autos from the beach esplanade near Pedro's and at Maria Hall crossing. Anjuna Wed Flea Market bus 0930, return 1530, Rs 200; you can take it one-way, but still have to buy a return ticket.

From Margao to **Cavelossim**, the bus is slow (18 km); auto-rickshaws transfer from bus stand to resorts.

Agonda *p479*
Bus/rickshaw First direct bus for **Margao** leaves between 0600-0630, last at 1000, takes about 1 hr. Alternatively, arrange a lift to the main road and flag down the next bus (last bus for Margao passes by at around 2000, but it is advisable to complete your journey before dark).

Car/scooter hire Madhu and White Sands in Agonda hire out scooters, motorbikes and cars.

Palolem *p479*
Bus Many daily direct buses run between **Margao** and **Canacona** (40 km via Cuncolim), Rs 20, on their way to **Karwar**. From Canacona, taxis and auto-rickshaws charge Rs 50-80 to Palolem beach only 2 km away. From Palolem, direct buses for Margao leave at around 0615, 0730, 0930, 1415, 1515, 1630 and take 1 hr. At other times of the day take a taxi or rickshaw to the main road, and flag down the next private bus. Frequent private services run to Palolem and Margao as well as south into **Karnataka**.

Train From **Canacona Junction station**, 2 km away from Palolem beach. The booking office opens 1 hr before trains depart. Inside the station there is a phone booth and a small chai stall. A few auto-rickshaws and taxis meet all trains. If none is available walk down the approach road and turn left under the railway bridge. At the next corner, known locally as Chaurasta, you will find an auto-rickshaw to take you to Palolem beach (Rs 50) or **Agonda Beach**; expect to pay double for a taxi.

To **Ernakulam Junction**, *Netravati Exp 16345*, 2325, 15 hrs, and on to **Thiruvananthapuram** (20 hrs); **Mumbai** (quicker to get train from Madgaon otherwise you go into more obscure station not Mumbai CST).

Beaches further south *p479*
Bus/taxi For **Canacona**, buses run to Palolem and Margao and also to Karnataka. You can hire a bicycle for Rs 4 per hr or Rs 35 per day. Direct buses for Margao leave at around 0615, 0730, 0930, 1415, 1515, 1630 and take an hour. Alternatively, take a taxi or rickshaw to the main road and flag down the next private bus. Palolem is 3 km from **Canacona Junction train station**, which is now on the Konkan line.

❶ Directory

Margao *p472, map p472*
Medical services Ambulance T102; Hospicio, T0832-270 5664; Holy Spirit Pharmacy, 24 hrs. **Police** T0832-272 2175; emergency T100. **Post** North of children's park.

Benaulim *p476, map p476*
Medical services Late-night pharmacy near the main crossroads.

Ponda and interior Sanguem

There is enough spirituality and architecture in the neighbouring districts of Ponda and Salcete to reverse even the most cynical notions of Goa as a state rich in beach but weak on culture. Once you've had your fill of basking on the sand you'll find that delving into this geographically small area will open a window on a whole new, and richly rewarding, Goa.

Just over the water lies Salcete and the villages of Goa's most sophisticated and urbane elite, steeped in the very staunchest Catholicism. Here you can see the most eloquent symbols of the graceful living enjoyed by this aristocracy in the shape of palatial private homes, the fruits of their collusion with the colonizers in faith. Ironically, one of the finest – Braganza House in Chandor – is also the ancestral home of one of the state's most vaunted freedom fighters, Luis de Menezes-Braganza.

Ponda and around → *For listings, see pages 503-504.*

Ponda, once a centre of culture, music, drama and poetry, is Goa's smallest *taluka*. It is also the richest in Goan Hindu religious architecture. A stone's throw from the Portuguese capital of Old Goa and within 5 km of the district's traffic-snarled and fume-filled town centre are some of Goa's most important temples including the Shri Shantadurga at Queula and the Nagesh Temple near Bandora. Ponda is also a pastoral haven full of spice gardens and wonderfully scenic views from low hills over sweeping rivers. The Bondla Sanctuary in the east of the *taluka*, though small and underwhelming in terms of wildlife, is a vestige of the forest-rich environment that once cloaked the entire foothills of the Western Ghats.

Arriving in Ponda
Getting there and around Ponda town is an important transport intersection where the main road from Margao via Borlim meets the east–west National Highway, NH4A. Buses to Panjim and Bondla via Tisk run along the NH4A, which passes through the centre of town. The temples are spread out so it's best to have your own transport: take a bike or charter an auto-rickshaw or taxi; you'll find these around the bus stand.
↠ *See Transport, page 504.*

Background

The Zuari River represented the stormy boundary between the Christianized Old Conquests and the Hindu east for two centuries. St Francis Xavier found a dissolute band of European degenerates in the first settlers when he arrived in the headquarters of Luso-India and recommended the formation of an Inquisition. Founded in 1560 to redress the failings within their own community, the Portuguese panel's remit quickly broadened as they found that their earliest Goan converts were also clinging clandestinely to their former faith. So the inquisitors set about weeding out these 'furtive Hindus', too, seeking to impose a Catholic orthodoxy and holding great show trials every few years with the public executions of infidels. Outside those dates set aside for putting people to death, intimidation was slightly more subtle: shrines were desecrated, temple tanks polluted and landowners threatened with confiscation of their holdings to encourage defection. Those unwilling to switch religion instead had to look for places to flee, carrying their idols in their hands.

When the conquistadors (or *descubridores*) took to sacking shrines and desecrating temples, building churches in their place, the keepers of the Hindu faith fled for the broad river banks and the Cumbarjua creek to its west, to build new homes for their gods.

Ponda

Ponda wasn't always the poster-boy for Goa's Hindu identity that it is today. The **Safa Mosque** (Shahouri Masjid), the largest of 26 mosques in Goa, was built by Ibrahim 'Ali' Adil Shah in 1560. It has a simple rectangular chamber on a low plinth, with a pointed pitched roof, very much in the local architectural style, but the arches are distinctly Bijapuri. Because it was built of laterite the lower tier has been quite badly eroded. On the south side is a tank with *meherab* designs for ritual cleansing. The gardens and fountains were destroyed under the Portuguese, today the mosque's backdrop is set off by low rising forest-covered hills.

Khandepar

Meanwhile, for a picture of Goa's Buddhist history, travel 4 km east from Ponda on the NH4A to Khandepar to visit Goa's best-preserved cave site. Believed to be Buddhist, it dates from the 10th or 11th century. The first three of the four laterite caves have an outer and an inner cell, possibly used as monks' living quarters. Much more refined than others discovered in Goa, they show clear evidence of schist frames for doors to the inner cells, sockets on which wooden doors would have been hung, pegs carved out of the walls for hanging clothing, and niches for storage and for placing lamps. The site is hidden on the edge of a wooded area near a tributary of the Mandovi: turn left off the main road from Ponda, look for the green and red archaeological survey sign, just before the bridge over the river. Turn right after the football pitch then walk down the track off to the right by the electric substation.

Farmagudi

On the left as you approach Farmagudi from Ponda is a **Ganesh temple** built by Goa's first chief minister, Shri D Bandodkar, back in the 1960s. It is an amalgam of ancient and modern styles. Opposite is a statue of Sivaji commemorating the Maratha leader's association with **Ponda's Fort**. The fort was built by the Adil Shahis of Bijapur and destroyed by the Portuguese in 1549. It lay in ruins for over a century before Sivaji conquered the town in 1675 and rebuilt it. The Portuguese viceroy attempted to re-take it in October 1683 but quickly withdrew, afraid to take on the Maratha King Sambhaji, who suddenly appeared with his vast army.

Velinga

Lakshmi-Narasimha Templeⓘ *just north of Farmagudi at Velinga, from the north take a right immediately after crossing a small river bridge*, is Goa's only temple to Vishnu's fourth avatar. The small half-man, half-lion image at this 18th-century temple was whisked away from the torches of Captain Diogo Rodrigues in 1567 Salcete. Its tower and dome over the sanctuary are markedly Islamic. Inside there are well-carved wooden pillars in the *mandapa* and elaborate silverwork on the screen and shrine.

Priol

Shri Mangesh Temple ⓘ *Priol, northwest of Ponda on a wooded hill, on the NH4A leading to Old Goa*, is an 18th-century temple to Siva's incarnation as the benevolent Mangesh is one of the most important temples in Goa. Its Mangesh *lingam* originally belonged to an ancient temple in Kushatali (Cortalim) across the river. The complex is typical of Goan Hindu temple architecture and the surrounding estate provides a beautiful setting. Note the attractive tank on the left as you approach, which is one of the oldest parts of the site. The complex, with its *agrashalas* (pilgrims' hostel), administrative offices and other rooms set aside for religious ceremonies, is a good representative of Goan Hindu temple worship: the temple is supported by a large community who serve its various functions. February 25 is **Jatra**.

Mardol

Two kilometres on from Shri Mangesh, the early 16th-century **Mahalsa Narayani Temple** is dedicated to Mahalsa, a Goan form of Vishnu's consort Lakshmi or, according to some, the god himself in female form *Mohini* (from the story of the battle between the *devas* and *asuras*). The deity was rescued from what was once a fabulous temple in Verna at around the same time as the Mangesh Sivalinga was brought to Priol. The entrance to the temple complex is through the arch under the *nagarkhana* (drum room). There is a seven-storeyed *deepstambha* and a tall brass Garuda pillar which rests on the back of a turtle, acting as an impressive second lamp tower. The half-human half-eagle *Garuda*, Vishnu's vehicle, sits on top. A stone 'cosmic pillar' with rings, next to it, signifies the axis along which the temple is aligned. The new *mandapa* (columned assembly hall) is made of concrete, but is hidden somewhat under the red tiling, finely carved columns and a series of brightly painted carvings of the 10 *avatars*, or incarnations, of Vishnu. The unusual dome above the sanctuary is particularly elegant. A decorative arched gate at the back leads to the peace and cool of the palm-fringed temple tank. A palanquin procession with the deity marks the February **Mardol Jatra**, **Mahasivaratri** is observed in February/March and **Kojagiri Purnima** celebrated at the August/ September full moon.

Bandora

A narrow winding lane dips down to this tiny hamlet and its **temple** ① *head 4 km west from Ponda towards Farmagudi on the NH4A, looking for a fork signposted to Bandora*, to Siva as Nagesh (God of Serpents). The temple's origin is put at 1413 by an inscribed tablet here, though the temple was refurbished in the 18th century. The temple tank, which is well stocked with carp, is enclosed by a white-outlined laterite block wall and surrounded by shady palms. The five-storey lamp tower near the temple has brightly coloured deities painted in niches just above the base, the main *mandapa* (assembly hall) has interesting painted woodcarvings illustrating stories from the epics *Ramayana* and *Mahabharata* below the ceiling line, as well as the *Ashtadikpalas*, the eight Directional Guardians (Indra, Agni, Yama, Nirritti, Varuna, Vayu, Kubera and Ishana). The principal deity has the usual *Nandi* and in addition there are shrines to Ganesh and Lakshmi-Narayan and subsidiary shrines with *lingams*, in the courtyard. The **Nagesh Jatra**, normally in November, is celebrated at full moon to commemorate Siva's victory.

In a valley south of the Nagesh Temple lies the **Mahalakshmi Temple**, thought to be the original form of the deity of the Shakti cult. Mahalakshmi was worshipped by the Silaharas (chieftains of the Rashtrakutas, AD 750-1030) and the early Kadamba kings. The sanctuary has an octagonal tower and dome, while the side entrances have shallow domes. The stone slab with the Marathi inscription dating from 1413 on the front of the Nagesh Temple refers to a temple to Mahalakshmi at Bandora. The *sabhamandap* has an impressive gallery of 18 wooden images of Vishnu. Mahalakshmi is special in that she wears a *lingam* in her headdress and is believed to be a peaceful, 'Satvik', form of Devi; the first temple the Portuguese allowed at Panjim is also dedicated to her.

Queula (Kavale)

Just 3 km southwest from Ponda's Central Bus Stand is one of the largest and most famous of Goa's temples; dedicated to Shantadurga (1738), the wife of Siva as the Goddess of Peace. She earns the Shanti (Sanskrit for peace) prefix here because, at the request of Brahma, she mediated in a great quarrel between her husband and Vishnu, and restored peace in the universe. In the sanctuary here she stands symbolically between the two bickering gods. The temple, which stands in a forest clearing, was built by Shahu, the grandson of the mighty Maratha ruler Sivaji, but the deity was taken from Quelossim well before then, back in the 16th century. It is neoclassical in design: the two-storey octagonal drum, topped by a dome with a lantern, is a classic example of the strong impact church architecture made on Goan temple design. The interior of polished marble is lit by several chandeliers. Steps lead up to the temple complex which has a large tank cut into the hillside and a spacious courtyard surrounded by the usual pilgrim hostels and administration offices.

Shri Sausthan Goud Padacharya Kavale Math, named after the historic seer and exponent of the Advaita system of Vedanta, was founded between Cortalim and Quelossim. This Hindu seminary was destroyed during the Inquisition in the 1560s and was temporarily transferred to Golvan and Chinar outside Goa. After 77 years, in the early 17th century, the Math regrouped here in Queula, the village where the Shantadurga deity (which had also originated in Quelossim) had been reinstalled. There is a temple to Vittala at the Math. The foundation has another Math at Sanquelim.

North of Ponda → For listings, see pages 503-504.

Spice Hills

There are a number of spice plantations in the foothills around northeast Ponda that have thrown open their gates to offer in-depth tours that detail medicinal and food uses of plants during a walk through these cultivated forests. These are surprisingly informative and fun. Of these, Savoi Spice Plantation is probably the most popular and the guide is excellent. Taxis from the coastal resorts cost around Rs 700 return from Candolim, but it's better value to ask a travel agent as many offer competitive rates including entrance fees.

Savoi Spice Plantation ① *6 km from Savoi, T0832-234 0272, www.savoiplantation. com, 1030-1730, tour Rs 350, 1 hr, awkward to reach by public transport, ask buses from Ponda or Banastari heading for Volvoi for the plantation,* now over 200 years old, covers 40 ha around a large irrigation tank. Half the area is wetland and the other half on a hillside, making it possible for a large variety of plants and trees to grow. The plantation was founded by Mr Shetye and is now in the hands of the fourth generation of his family, who regularly donate funds to local community projects such as the school and temple. All plants are grown according to traditional Goan methods of organic farming. The tour includes drinks and snacks on arrival, and concludes with the chance to buy packets of spices (good gifts to take home) and a tot of *feni* to 'give strength' for the return journey to your resort. You will even be offered several cheap, natural alternatives to Viagra, whether you need them or not.

Pascoal Spice Plantation ① *signposted 1.5 km off the NH4A, near Khandepar between Ponda and Tisk, T0832-234 4268, 0800-1800, tours Rs 300,* is pleasantly located by a river and grows a wide variety of spices and exotic fruit. A guided tour takes you through a beautiful and fascinating setting. Spices can be bought directly from the plantation.

Sahakari Spice Farm ① *on the Ponda–Khandepar road, Curti, T0832-231 1394,* is also open to the public. The spice tour includes an authentic banana-leaf lunch.

Tropical Spice Plantation ① *Keri, clearly signposted off the NH4A (just south of the Sri Mangesh Temple), T0832-234 0625, tours Rs 300, boats for hire Rs 100,* is a very pleasant plantation situated in a picturesque valley. Guides are well informed and staff are friendly. It specializes in medicinal uses for the spices, the majority of which seem to be good for the skin. At the end of the tour an areca nut picker will demonstrate the art of harvesting by shinning up a tall palm with his feet tied together in a circle of rope. The demonstration ends with the equally impressive art of descent, a rapid slide down the trunk like a fireman. After the tour a delicious lunch is served in the shade overlooking a lake where there are a couple of boats for hire. Visitors arriving in the early morning will find the boats an excellent opportunity for viewing the varied birdlife around the lake.

Bondla Wildlife Sanctuary

ⓘ *20 km northeast of Ponda, mid-Sep to mid-Jun, Fri-Wed 0930-1730. Rs 5, camera Rs 25, video Rs 100, 2-wheelers Rs 10, cars Rs 50. Buses from Ponda via Tisk and Usgaon stop near the sanctuary where you can get taxis and motorcycle taxis. KTC buses sometimes run weekends from Panjim. During the season the Forest Department minibus runs twice daily (except Thu) between Bondla and Tisk: from Bondla, 0815, 1745; from Tisk, 1100 (Sun 1030) and 1900. Check at the tourist office. If you are on a motorbike make sure you fill up with petrol; the nearest pumps are at Ponda and Tisk. Bondla is well signposted from the NH4A east of Ponda (5 km beyond Usgaon, a fork to the right leads to the park up a winding steep road).*

Bondla is the most popular of Goa's three sanctuaries because it is relatively easily accessible. The 8-sq-km sanctuary is situated in the foothills of the Western Ghats; sambar, wild boar, gaur (Indian bison) and monkeys live alongside a few migratory elephants that wander in from Karnataka during the summer. The mini-zoo here guarantees sightings of 'Goa's wildlife in natural surroundings', although whether the porcupine and African lion are examples of indigenous species is another matter. Thankfully, the number of animals in the zoo has decreased in recent years and those that remain seem to have adequate space compared to other zoos in India. The small **Nature Education Centre** has the facility to show wildlife videos, but is rarely used. Five-minute elephant rides are available 1100-1200 and 1600-1700. A deer safari (minimum eight people), 1600-1730, costs Rs 10. The park also has an attractive picnic area in a botanical garden setting and a 2.4-km nature trail with waterholes, lake and treetop observation tower.

Central and southern interior → *For listings, see pages 503-504.*

Sanguem, Goa's largest *taluka*, covers the state's eastern hill borderland with the South Indian state of Karnataka. The still-forested hills, populated until recently by tribal peoples practising shifting cultivation, rise to Goa's highest points. Just on the Goan side of the border with Karnataka are the Dudhsagar Falls, some of India's highest waterfalls, where the river, which ultimately flows into the Mandovi, cascades dramatically down the hillside. Both the Bhagwan Mahaveer Sanctuary and the beautiful, small Tambdi Surla Temple can be reached in a day from the coast (about two hours from Panaji).

Arriving in central and southern interior

Getting there Buses running along the NH4A between Panjim, Ponda or Margao and Belgaum or Bengaluru (Bangalore) in Karnataka stop at Molem, in the north of the *taluka*. Much of the southeastern part of Sanguem remains inaccessible. Trains towards Karnataka stop at Kulem (Colem) and Dudhsagar stations. Jeeps wait at Kulem to transfer tourists to the waterfalls. If you are travelling to Tambdi Surla or the falls from north or central Goa, then the best and most direct route is the NH4A via Ponda. By going to or from the southern beaches of Salcete or Canacona you can travel through an interesting cluster of villages, only really accessible if you have your own transport, to see the sites of rock-cut caves and prehistoric cave art. ➤ *See Transport, page 504.*

Getting around There is no direct public transport between Molem and the sites, but the town is the start of hikes and treks in December and January.

Bhagwan Mahaveer Sanctuary

ⓘ *29 km east of Pondon on NH4A, T0832-260 0231, or contact Forest Dept in Canacona, T0832-296 5601. Open 0700-1730 except public holidays. Rs 5, 2-wheelers Rs 10, cars Rs 250. Or check Goa Tourism (www.goa-tourism.com). Entrance to Molem National Park, within the sanctuary, 100 m east of the Tourist Complex, is clearly signed but the 14 km of tracks in the park are not mapped. Tickets at the Nature Interpretation Centre, 100 m from the police check post in Molem.*

Goa's largest wildlife sanctuary holds 240 sq km of lush moist deciduous to evergreen forest types and a herd of gaur (*bos gaurus*, aka Indian bison). The **Molem National Park**, in the central section of the sanctuary, occupies about half the area with the **Dudhsagar Falls** located in its southeast corner; the remote **Tambdi Surla Temple** is hidden in the dense forest at the northern end of the sanctuary. Forest department jeeps are available for viewing within the sanctuary; contact the Range Forest Officer (Wildlife), Molem. Motorbikes, but not scooters, can manage the rough track outside the monsoon period. In theory it is possible to reach Devil's Canyon and Dudhsagar Falls via the road next to the Nature Interpretation Centre, although the road is very rough and it may require a guide. Make sure you have a full tank of petrol if attempting a long journey into the forest. You can stay overnight.

Sambar, barking deer, monkeys and rich birdlife are occasionally joined by elephants that wander in from neighbouring Karnataka during the summer months, but these are rarely spotted. Birds include the striking golden oriole, emerald dove, paradise flycatcher, malabar hornbill and trogon and crested serpent eagle.

Dudhsagar Falls

ⓘ *There are train day trips organized though Goa Tourism (www.goa-tourism.com) on Wed and Sun. It's a spectacular journey worth taking in its own right, as the railway tracks climb right across the cascades, but trains no longer stop at the falls themselves; to get to the pools at the bottom you can take a road from Kulem, where jeep owners offer 'safaris' through the jungle to the base of the falls. If taking the train simply for the view, it's best to travel through to Belgaum in Karnataka, from where there are good bus and train services back to Goa.*

The Dudhsagar Falls on the border between Goa and Karnataka are the highest in India and measure a total drop of about 600 m. The name, meaning 'the sea of milk', is derived from the white foam that the force of the water creates as it drops in stages, forming pools along the way. They are best seen just after the monsoon, between October and December, but right up to April there is enough water to make a visit worthwhile. You need to be fit and athletic to visit the falls.

A rough, steep path takes you down to a viewing area which allows you a better appreciation of the falls' grandeur, and to a beautifully fresh pool which is lovely for a swim (take your costume and towel). There are further pools below but you need to be sure-footed. The final section of the journey is a scramble on foot across stream beds with boulders; it is a difficult task for anyone but the most athletic. For the really fit and adventurous the arduous climb up to the head of the falls with a guide, is well worth the effort. Allow three hours, plus some time to rest at the top.

You can take the train to Kulem, which is about 17 km from the falls, and then pick up a jeep or motorbike to take you to the falls; but it's a rough ride. By road, motorbikes, but not scooters, can get to the start of the trail to the falls from Molem crossroads by taking the road south towards Kulem. There are at least two river crossings, so is not recommended after a long period of heavy rain. The ride through the forest is very attractive and the reward at the end spectacular, even in the dry season. A swim in the pool at the falls is particularly refreshing after a hot and dusty ride. Guides are available but the track is easy to follow even without one. ➤➤ See also Transport, page 504.

Tambdi Surla

ⓘ A taxi from Panjim takes about 2½ hrs for the 69-km journey. There is no public transport to Tambdi Surla but it is possible to hike from Molem. From the crossroads at Molem on the NH4A, the road north goes through dense forest to Tambdi Surla. 4 km from the crossroads you reach a fork. Take the right fork and after a further 3 km take a right turn at Barabhumi village (there is a sign). The temple is a further 8 km, just after Shanti Nature Resort. Make sure you have enough petrol before leaving Molem. It is also possible to reach the site along minor roads from Valpoi. The entrance to the temple is a short walk from the car park.

This Mahadeva (Siva) Temple is a beautifully preserved miniature example of early Hindu temple architecture from the Kadamba-Yadava period. Tucked into the forested foothills, the place is often deserted, although the compound is well maintained by the Archaeology Department. The temple is the only major remaining example of pre-Portuguese Hindu architecture in Goa; it may well have been saved from destruction by its very remoteness.

For hotel and restaurant price codes and other relevant information, see pages 13-17.

◉ Where to stay

Ponda *p495*
Ponda is within easy reach of any of Goa's beach resorts and Panjim.
$$-$ Menino, 100 m east of bus stand junction, 1st floor, T0832-664 1585. 20 rooms, some a/c, pleasant, good restaurant serves generous main courses, impressive modern hotel, good value.
$ President, 1 km east of bus stand, supermarket complex, T0832-231 2287. 11 rooms, basic but clean and reasonable.

Farmagudi *p496*
$$-$ Atish, just below Ganesh Temple on NH4A, T0832-233 5124. 40 comfortable rooms, some a/c, restaurant, large pool in open surrounds, gym, modern hotel, many pilgrim groups, friendly staff.
$ Farmagudi Residency (GTDC), attractively located though too close to NH4A, T0832-233 5122. 39 clean rooms, some a/c, dorm (Rs 150), adequate restaurant (eat at **Atish**, above).

Spice Hills *p499*
$$ Savoi Farmhouse, Savoi Plantation, T0832-234 0243, www.savoiplantations. com. An idyllic traditional Goan-style farmhouse built from mud with 2 adjoining en suite double rooms each with private veranda. Electricity and hot water; rates are for full board and include plantation tour. A night in the forest is memorable, highly recommended. Ideally, stay 2 nights exploring deep into the forested hills, good for birdwatching.

Bondla Wildlife Sanctuary *p500*
$ Eco-Cottages, reserve ahead at Deputy Conservator of Forests, Wildlife Division, 4th floor, Junta House, 18 June Rd, Panjim, T0832-222 9701 (although beds are often available to anyone turning up). 8 basic rooms with attached bath, newer ones better. Also 1 km inside park entrance (which may be better for seeing wildlife at night) are 2 dorms of 12 beds each.

Bhagwan Mahaveer Sanctuary *p501*
Goa Eco Tourism offer the **Jungle Book Tour** where you can stay in tents or cottages inside the sanctuary (www. goaecotourism.com); take provisions. GTDC accommodation is at the Tourist Complex in Molem, east along the NH4A from the Molem National Park entrance.
$ Molem Forest Resthouse. Book via the Conservator's Office, 3rd floor, Junta House, 18 June Rd, Panjim, T0832-222 4747.
$ Tourist Resort (GTDC), 300 m east of police check post, about 500 m from the temple, Molem, T0832-260 0238. 3 simple but well-maintained, clean rooms, some a/c, dorm, check-out 1200, giving time for a morning visit to Tambdi Surla, restaurant has limited menu serving north Indian food and beer.

Tambdi Surla *p502*
$$ Shanti Nature Resort, 500 m from temple, T0832-261 0012. Emphasis on rest, Ayurvedic treatment and meditation, 9 large mud huts with palm-thatched roofs, electricity and running water in natural forest setting. Restaurant, spice garden visits, birdwatching, hikes, trips to Dudhsagar, etc, arranged (2 nights, US$120). Highly recommended for location and eco-friendly approach.

🍴 Restaurants

Ponda *p495*
$ Amigos, 2 km east of centre on Belgaum Rd.
$ Spoon Age, Upper Bazaar, T0832-231 6191. Garden restaurant serving Goan meals for locals, friendly set up. Occasional live music at weekends.

Spice Hills *p499*
Tropical Spice Plantation offers tasty lunches.
$$ Glade Bar and Restaurant, Pascoal Spice Plantation. Open 1130-1800. Good but pricey.

Bondla Wildlife Sanctuary *p500*
$ The Den Bar and Restaurant, near the entrance. Serves chicken, vegetables or fish with rice. A small cafeteria, inside the park near the mini-zoo, sells snacks and cold drinks.

⏱ What to do

Bhagwan Mahaveer Sanctuary *p501*
Hiking
Popular hiking routes lead to **Dudhsagar** (17 km), the sanctuary and **Atoll Gad** (12 km), **Matkonda Hill** (10 km) and **Tambdi Surla** (12 km). Contact the **Hiking Association**, 6 Anand Niwas, Swami Vivekananda Rd, Panjim.

⊖ Transport

Ponda *p495*
Bus Buses to **Panjim** and **Bondla** via Tisk (enquiries, T0832-231 1050), but it is best to have your own transport.

Bhagwan Mahaveer Sanctuary *p501*
If coming from the south, travel via Sanguem. The road from Sanvordem to the NH17 passes through mining country and is therefore badly pot-holed and has heavy lorry traffic. From Kulem, jeeps do the rough trip to **Dudhsagar** (Rs 300 per head, Rs 1800 per jeep). The journey is also possible by motorbike (Rs 600 per person). This is a very tough and tiring journey at the best of times. From Molem, a road to the south off the NH4A leads through the forested hills of Sanguem *taluka* to **Kulem** and **Calem** railway stations and then south to **Sanguem**. From there, a minor road northwest goes to **Sanvordem** and then turns west to **Chandor**.

Bus Buses between **Panjim**, **Ponda** or **Margao**, and **Belgaum/Bengaluru** (**Bangalore**), stop at Molem for visiting the Bhagwan Mahaveer Sanctuary and Dudhsagar Falls.

Train From the southern beaches, you can get the *Vasco-Colem Passenger* from Vasco at 0710, or more conveniently Margao (Madgaon) at 0800, arriving at **Kulem** (**Colem**) at 0930. Return trains at 1640, arriving **Margao** at 1810; leave plenty of time to enjoy the falls. Jeep hire is available from Kulem Station.

ⓘ Directory

Ponda *p495*
Useful contacts Deputy Conservator of Forests (North) T0832-231 2095.
Community Health Centre, T0832-231 2115.

Contents

Footprint features

Background

History

The first village communities in South Asia grew up on the arid western fringes of the Indus Plains 10,000 years ago. Over the following generations successive waves of settlers – sometimes bringing goods for trade, sometimes armies to conquer territory and sometimes nothing more than domesticated animals and families in search of land and peace – moved across the Indus and into India. They left an indelible mark on the landscape and culture of all the countries of modern South Asia.

The first settlers

A site at Mehrgarh, where the Indus Plains meet the dry Baluchistan Hills in modern Pakistan, has revealed evidence of settlement as early as 8500 BC. By 3500 BC agriculture had spread throughout the Indus Plains and in the thousand years following there were independent settled villages well to the east of the Indus. Between 3000 and 2500 BC many new settlements sprang up in the heartland of what became the Indus Valley civilization.

Most cultural, religious and political developments during that period owed more to local development than to external influence, although India had extensive contacts with other regions, notably Mesopotamia. At its height the Indus Valley civilization covered as great an area as Egypt or Mesopotamia. However, the culture that developed was distinctively South Asian. Speculation surrounds the nature of the language, which is still untranslated.

India from 2000 BC to the Mauryas

In about 2000 BC Moenjo Daro, widely presumed to be the capital of the Indus Valley Civilization, became deserted and within the next 250 years the entire Indus Valley civilization disintegrated. The causes remain uncertain: the violent arrival of new waves of Aryan immigrants (a theory no one now accepts), increasing desertification of the already semi-arid landscape, a shift in the course of the Indus and internal political decay have each been suggested as instrumental in its downfall. Whatever the causes, some features of Indus Valley culture were carried on by succeeding generations.

Probably from about 1500 BC northern India entered the Vedic period. Aryan settlers moved southeast towards the Ganga valley. Classes of rulers (*rajas*) and priests (*brahmins*) began to emerge. Conflict was common. In one battle of this period a confederacy of tribes known as the Bharatas defeated another grouping of 10 tribes. They gave their name to the east of the Indus which is the official name for India today – Bharat.

The centre of population and of culture shifted east from the banks of the Indus to the land between the rivers Yamuna and Ganga, the *doab* (pronounced *doe-ahb*, literally 'two waters'). This region became the heart of emerging Aryan culture, which, from 1500 BC onwards, laid the literary and religious foundations of what ultimately became Hinduism, spreading to embrace the whole of India.

The Vedas The first fruit of this development was the Rig Veda, the first of four Vedas, composed, collected and passed on orally by Brahmin priests. While some scholars date the oral origins as early as the beginning of the second millennium BC, the date of 1300 BC to about 1000 BC still seems more probable. In the later Vedic period, from about 1000 BC to 600 BC, the Sama, Yajur and Artha Vedas show that the Indo-Aryans developed a clear sense of the Ganga-Yamuna *doab* as 'their' territory.

From the sixth to the third centuries BC the region from the foothills of the Himalaya across the Ganga plains to the edge of the Peninsula was governed under a variety of kingdoms or Mahajanapadhas – 'great states'. Trade gave rise to the birth of towns in the Ganga plains themselves, many of which have remained occupied to the present. Varanasi (Benaras) is perhaps the most famous example, but a trade route was established that ran from Taxila (20 km from modern Islamabad in Pakistan) to Rajgir 1500 km away in what is now Bihar. It was into these kingdoms of the Himalayan foothills and north plains that both Mahavir, founder of Jainism, and the Buddha were born.

The Mauryas
Within a year of the retreat of Alexander the Great from the Indus in 326 BC, **Chandragupta Maurya** established the first indigenous empire to exercise control over much of the subcontinent. Under his successors, that control was extended to all but the extreme south of peninsular India.

The centre of political power had shifted steadily east into wetter, more densely forested but also more fertile regions. The Mauryans had their base in the region known as Magadh (now Bihar) and their capital at Pataliputra, near modern Patna. Their power was based on massive military force and a highly efficient, centralized administration.

The greatest of the Mauryan emperors, **Asoka** took power in 272 BC. He inherited a full-blown empire, but extended it by defeating the Kalingans in modern Orissa, before turning his back on war and preaching the virtues of Buddhist pacifism. Asoka's empire stretched from Afghanistan to Assam and from the Himalaya to Mysore.

The state maintained itself by raising revenue from taxation – on everything, from agriculture, to gambling and prostitution. He decreed that 'no waste land should be occupied and not a tree cut down' without permission because all were potential sources of revenue for the state. The *sudras* (lowest of Hindu castes) were used as free labour for clearing forest and cultivating new land.

Asoka (described on the edicts as 'the Beloved of the Gods, of Gracious Countenance') left inscriptions on pillars and rocks across the subcontinent. Over most of India these inscriptions were written in *Prakrit*, using the *Brahmi* script, although in the northwest they were in Greek using the *Kharoshti* script. They were unintelligible for over 2000 years after the decline of the empire until James Prinsep deciphered the Brahmi script in 1837.

Through the edicts Asoka urged all people to follow the code of **dhamma** or dharma – translated by Indian historian Romila Thapar as 'morality, piety, virtue and social order'. He established a special force of *dhamma* officers to try to enforce the code, which encouraged toleration, non-violence, respect for priests and those in authority and for human dignity.

However, Romila Thapar suggests that the failure to develop any sense of national consciousness, coupled with the massive demands of a highly paid bureaucracy and army, proved beyond the abilities of Asoka's successors to sustain. Within 50 years of Asoka's death in 232 BC the Mauryan Empire had disintegrated and with it the whole structure and spirit of its government.

A period of fragmentation: 185 BC to AD 300

Beyond the Mauryan Empire other kingdoms had survived in South India. The Satavahanas dominated the central Deccan for over 300 years from about 50 BC. Further south in what is now Tamil Nadu, the early kingdoms of the Cholas and the Pandiyas gave a glimpse of both power and cultural development that was to flower over 1000 years later. In the centuries following the break up of the Mauryan Empire these kingdoms were in the forefront of developing overseas trade, especially with Greece and Rome. Internal trade also flourished and Indian traders carried goods to China and Southeast Asia.

The classical period – the Gupta Empire: AD 319-467

Although the political power of Chandra Gupta and his successors never approached that of his unrelated namesake nearly 650 years before him, the Gupta Empire which was established with his coronation in AD 319 produced developments in every field of Indian culture. Their influence has been felt profoundly across South Asia to the present.

Geographically the Guptas originated in the same Magadhan region that had given rise to the Mauryan Empire. Extending their power by strategic marriage alliances, Chandra Gupta's empire of Magadh was extended by his son, Samudra Gupta, who took power in AD 335, across North India. He also marched as far south as Kanchipuram in modern Tamil Nadu, but the heartland of the Gupta Empire remained the plains of the Ganga.

Chandra Gupta II reigned for 39 years from AD 376 and was a great patron of the arts. Political power was much less centralized than under the Mauryans and as Thapar points out, collection of land revenue was deputed to officers who were entitled to keep a share of the revenue, rather than to highly paid bureaucrats. Trade with Southeast Asia, Arabia and China all added to royal wealth. That wealth was distributed to the arts on a previously unheard of scale. Some went to religious foundations, such as the Buddhist monastery at Ajanta, which produced some of its finest murals during the Gupta period. But Hindu institutions also benefited and some of the most important features of modern Hinduism date from this time. The sacrifices of Vedic worship were given up in favour of personal devotional worship, known as *bhakti*. Tantrism, both in its Buddhist and Hindu forms, with its emphasis on the female life force and worship of the Mother Goddess, developed. The focus of worship was increasingly towards a personalized and monotheistic deity, in the form of either Siva or Vishnu. The myths of Vishnu's incarnations also arose at this period.

The Brahmins The priestly caste who were in the key position to mediate change, refocused earlier literature to give shape to the emerging religious philosophy. In their hands the *Mahabharata* and the *Ramayana* were transformed from secular epics to religious stories. The excellence of contemporary sculpture both reflected and contributed to an increase in image worship and the growing role of temples as centres of devotion.

Regional kingdoms and cultures

The collapse of Guptá power opened the way for smaller kingdoms to assert themselves. After the brief reign of Harsha in the mid-seventh century, which recaptured something both of the territory and the glory of the Guptas, the Gangetic plains were constantly fought over by rival groups, none of whom were able to establish unchallenged authority. Regional kingdoms developed, often around comparatively small natural regions.

The Deccan The Rashtrakutas controlled much of the central Peninsula between AD 700-950. However, the southern Deccan was dominated by the Chalukyas from the sixth century up to AD 750 and again in the 11th and 12th centuries. To their south the Pandiyas, Cholas and Pallavas controlled the Dravidian lands of what is now Kerala, Tamil Nadu and coastal Andhra Pradesh. The Pallavas, responsible for building the temples at Mamallapuram, just south of modern Madras (Chennai), flourished in the seventh century.

In the eighth century Kerala began to develop its own regional identity with the rise of the **Kulashekharas** in the Periyar Valley. Caste was a dominating feature of the kingdom's social organization, but with the distinctive twist that the **Nayars**, the most aristocratic of castes, developed a matrilineal system of descent.

It was the **Cholas** who came to dominate the south from the eighth century. Overthrowing the Pallavas, they controlled most of Tamil Nadu, south Karnataka and southern Andhra Pradesh from AD 850 to AD 1278. They often held the Kerala kings under their control. Under their kings **Rajaraja I** (984-1014) and **Rajendra** (1014-1044) the Cholas also controlled north Sri Lanka, sent naval expeditions to Southeast Asia and successful military campaigns north to the Ganga plains. They lavished endowments on temples and also extended the gifts of land to Brahmins instituted by the Pallavas and Pandiyas. Many thousands of Brahmin priests were brought south to serve in major temples such as those in Chidambaram, and Rajendra wished to be remembered above all as the king who brought water from the holy Ganga all the way to his kingdom.

The Rajputs The political instability and rivalry that resulted from the ending of Gupta power in the north opened the way for waves of immigrants from the northwest and for new groups and clans to seize power. Among these were the Rajputs (meaning *'sons of kings'*) who claimed descent from a mythical figure who rose out of a pit near Mount Abu. From the seventh century AD Rajputs were always a force to be reckoned with in the northwest, albeit at a comparatively local level. The temples at Khajuraho in Central India, one of contemporary India's most remarkable sites, were built during the Rajput dynasty of the Chandelas (AD 916-1203). However, the Rajputs never succeeded in forging a united front strong enough to establish either effective central government, control internally or protection from external attack.

The spread of Islamic power – the Delhi Sultanate

From about AD 1000 the external attacks which inflicted most damage on Rajput wealth and power came increasingly from the Arabs and Turks. Mahmud of Ghazni raided the Punjab virtually every year between 1000 and 1026, attracted both by the agricultural surpluses and the enormous wealth in cash, golden images and jewellery of North India's temples which drew him back every year. He sacked the wealthy centres of Mathura (UP) in 1017, Thanesar (Haryana) in 1011, Somnath (Gujarat) in 1024 and Kannauj (UP). He died in 1030, to the Hindus just another *mlechchha* ('impure' or sullied one), as had been the Huns and the Sakas before him, soon to be forgotten. Such raids were never taken seriously as a long-term threat by kings further east and as the Rajputs often feuded among themselves the northwest plains became an attractive prey.

Muslim political power was heralded by the raids of Mu'izzu'd Din and his defeat of massive Rajput forces at the Second Battle of Tarain in 1192. Mu'izzu'd Din left his deputy, Qutb u'd Din Aibak, to hold the territorial gains from his base at Indraprastha. Mu'izzu'd Din made further successful raids in the 1190s, inflicting crushing defeats on Hindu opponents from Gwalior to Benaras. The foundations were then laid for the first extended period of such power, which came under the Delhi sultans.

Qutb u'd Din Aibak took Lahore in 1206, although it was his lieutenant **Iltutmish** who really established control from Delhi in 1211. Qutb u'd Din Aibak consolidated Muslim dominion by an even-handed policy of conciliation and patronage. In Delhi he converted the old Hindu stronghold of Qila Rai Pithora into his Muslim capital and began several magnificent building projects, including the Quwwat-ul-Islam mosque and the Qutb Minar, a victory tower. Iltutmish was a Turkish slave – a *Mamluk* – and the Sultanate continued to look west for its leadership and inspiration. However, the possibility of continuing control from outside India was destroyed by the crushing raids of **Genghis Khan** through Central Asia and from 1222 Iltutmish ruled from Delhi completely independently of outside authority. He annexed Sind in 1228 and all the territory east to Bengal by 1230.

A succession of dynasties followed, drawing on refugees from Genghis Khan's raids and from still further to the west to strengthen the leadership. In 1290 the first dynasty was succeeded by the Khaljis, which in turn gave way to the Tughluqs in 1320. **Mohammad bin Tughluq** (ruled 1324-1351) was described by the Moorish traveller Ibn Batuta as 'a man who above all others is fond of making presents and shedding blood'. This period marked a turning point in Muslim government in India, as Turkish Mamluks gave way to government by Indian Muslims and their Hindu allies. The Delhi sultans were open to local influences and employed Hindus in their administration. In the mid-14th century their capital, Delhi, was one of the leading cities of the contemporary world but in 1398 their control came to an abrupt end with the arrival of the Mongol Timur.

Timur's limp caused him to be called Timur-i-leng (Timur the Lame, known to the west as Tamburlaine). This self-styled 'Scourge of God' was illiterate, a devout

Muslim, an outstanding chess player and a patron of the arts. Five years before his arrival in India he had taken Baghdad and three years before that he had ravaged Russia, devastating land and pillaging villages. India had not been in such danger from Mongols since Genghis Khan had arrived on the same stretch of the Indus 200 years before.

After Timur, it took nearly 50 years for the Delhi Kingdom to become more than a local headquarters. Even then the revival was slow and fitful. The last Tughluqs were succeeded by an undistinguished line of Sayyids, who began as Timur's deputies who were essentially Afghan soldier/administrators. They later called themselves sultans and Lodi kings (1451-1526) and moved their capital to Agra. Nominally they controlled an area from Punjab to Bihar but they were, in fact, in the hands of a group of factious nobles.

The Deccan Kingdoms

The Delhi Sultanate never achieved the dominating power of earlier empires or of its successor, the Mughal Empire. It exercised political control through crushing military raids and the exaction of tribute from defeated kings, but there was no real attempt to impose central administration. Power depended on maintaining vital lines of communication and trade routes, keeping fortified strongholds and making regional alliances. In the Peninsula to the south, the Deccan, regional powers contested for survival, power and expansion. The Bahmanis were the forerunners of a succession of Muslim dynasties, who sometimes competed with each other and sometimes collaborated against a joint external enemy.

Across West and South India today are the remains of the only major medieval Hindu empire, the Vijayanagar Empire, to resist effectively the Muslim advance. The ruins at Hampi demonstrate the power of a Hindu coalition that rose to power in the south Deccan in the first half of the 14th century, only to be defeated by its Muslim neighbours in 1565.

For over 200 years Vijayanagar ('*city of victory*') kings fought to establish supremacy. It was an empire that, in the words of one Indian historian, made it 'the nearest approach to a war state ever made by a Hindu kingdom'. At times its power reached from Orissa in the northeast to Sri Lanka. In 1390 King Harihara II claimed to have planted a victory pillar in Sri Lanka. Much of modern Tamil Nadu and Andhra Pradesh were added to the core region of Karnataka in the area under Vijayanagar control.

The Mughal Empire

In North India it is the impact of the Mughal rule that is most evident today. The descendants of conquerors, with the blood of both Tamburlaine and Genghis Khan in their veins, they came to dominate Indian politics from Babur's victory near Delhi in 1526 to Aurangzeb's death in 1707. Their legacy was some of the most magnificent architecture in the world, and a profound impact on the culture, society and future politics of South Asia.

Babur (the tiger) Founder of the Mughal Dynasty, Babur was born in Russian Turkestan on 15 February 1483, the fifth direct descendant on the male side of Timur and 13th on the female side from Genghis Khan. He established the Mughal

Empire by leading his cavalry and artillery forces to a victory over the combined armies of Ibrahim Lodi, last ruler of the Delhi Sultanate and the Hindu Raja of Gwalior, at **Panipat**, 80 km north of Delhi, in 1526. When he died four years later, the Empire was far from secured, but he had laid the foundations of political and military power and also begun to establish courtly traditions of poetry, literature and art which became the hallmark of subsequent Mughal rulers. Babur, used to the delights of Persian gardens and the cool of the Afghan hills, was unimpressed by India. In his autobiography he wrote: "Hindustan is a country that has few pleasures to recommend it. The people are not handsome. They have no idea of the charms of friendly society, of frankly mixing together, or of familiar intercourse. They have no genius, no comprehension of mind, no politeness of manner, no kindness or fellow-feeling, no ingenuity or mechanical invention in planning or executing their handicraft works, no skill or knowledge in design or architecture". Babur's depressing catalogue was the view of a disenchanted outsider. Within two generations the Mughals had become fully at home and brought some radical changes. Babur was charismatic. He ruled by keeping the loyalty of his military chiefs, giving them control of large areas of territory.

Humayun However, their strength posed a problem for Humayun, his successor. Almost immediately after Babur's death Humayun was forced to retreat from Delhi through Sind with his pregnant wife. His son Akbar, who was to become the greatest of the Mughal emperors, was born at Umarkot in Sindh, during this period of exile, on 23 November 1542.

Akbar Akbar was only 13 when he took the throne in 1556. The next 44 years were one of the most remarkable periods of South Asian history, paralleled by the Elizabethan period in England, where Queen Elizabeth I ruled from 1558 to 1603. Although Akbar inherited the throne, it was he who really created the empire and gave it many of its distinguishing features. Through his marriage to a Hindu princess he ensured that Hindus were given honoured positions in government, as well as respect for their religious beliefs and practices. He sustained a passionate interest in art and literature, matched by a determination to create monuments to his empire's political power and he laid the foundations for an artistic and architectural tradition which developed a totally distinctive Indian style. This emerged from the separate elements of Iranian and Indian traditions by a constant process of blending and originality of which he was the chief patron.

But these achievements were only possible because of his political and military gifts. From 1556 until his 18th birthday in 1560, Akbar was served by a prince regent, Bairam Khan. However, already at the age of 15 he had conquered Ajmer and large areas of Central India. Chittor and Ranthambore fell to him in 1567-1568, bringing most of what is now Rajasthan under his control. This opened the door south to Gujarat.

Afghans continued to cause his empire difficulties, including Daud Karrani, who declared independence in East India in 1574. That threat to Mughal power was finally crushed with Karrani's death in 1576. Bengal was far from the last of his conquests. He brought Kabul back under Mughal control in the 1580s and established a presence from Kashmir, Sind and Baluchistan in the north and west, to the Godavari River on the border of modern Andhra Pradesh in the south. Akbar deliberately widened his power base by incorporating Rajput princes into the administrative structure and giving them extensive rights in the revenue from land. He abolished the hated tax on non-Muslims (*jizya*) – ultimately reinstated by his strictly orthodox great grandson Aurangzeb – and ceased levying taxes on Hindus who went on pilgrimage. He also ended the practice of forcible conversion to Islam. Artistic treasures abound from Akbar's court, often bringing together material and skills from across the known world. Akbar's eclecticism had a political purpose; he was trying to build a focus of loyalty beyond that of caste, social group, region or religion. Like Roman emperors before him, he deliberately cultivated a new religion in which the emperor attained divinity, hoping to give the empire a legitimacy which would last. While his religion disappeared with his death, the legitimacy of the Mughals survived another 200 years, long after their real power had almost disappeared.

Jahangir Akbar died of a stomach illness in 1605. He was succeeded by his son, Prince Salim, who inherited the throne as Emperor Jahangir (*'world seizer'*). He added little to the territory of the empire, consolidating the Mughals' hold on the Himalayan foothills and parts of central India and restricting his energies to pushing frontiers of art. He commissioned works of art and literature, many of which recorded life in the Mughal court. Hunting scenes conveyed the real dangers of hunting lions or tigers; implements, furniture, tools and weapons were made with lavish care and often exquisite design.

From early youth Jahangir had shown an artistic temperament, but he also became addicted to alcohol and then to opium. In his autobiography, he wrote: "I had not drunk until I was 18 … a gunner said that if I would take a glass of wine it would drive away the feeling of being tired and heavy … After that I took to drinking wine … until wine made from grapes ceased to intoxicate me and I took to drinking arrack (local spirits). By degrees my potions rose to 20 cups of doubly distilled spirits."

Nur Jahan Jahangir's favourite wife, Nur Jahan, brought her own artistic gifts. Born the daughter of an Iranian nobleman, she had been brought to the Mughal court along with her family as a child and moved to Bengal as the wife of Sher Afgan. She made rapid progress after her first husband's accidental death in 1607, which caused her to move from Bengal to be a lady in waiting for one of Akbar's widows.

At the Mughal court in 1611, she met Jahangir. Mutually enraptured, they were married in May. Jahangir gave her the title Nur Mahal (Light of the Palace), soon increased to Nur Jahan (Light of the World). Aged 34, she was strikingly beautiful and had an astonishing reputation for physical skill and intellectual wit. She was a crack shot with a gun, highly artistic, determined yet philanthropic. Throughout her life Jahangir was captivated by her, so much so that he flouted Muslim convention by minting coins bearing her image.

By 1622 Nur Jahan effectively controlled the empire. She commissioned and supervised the building in Agra of one of the Mughal world's most beautiful buildings, the I'timad ud-Daula ('Pillar of government'), as a tomb for her father and mother. Her father, Ghiyas Beg, had risen to become one of Jahangir's most trusted advisers and Nur Jahan was determined to ensure that their memory was honoured. She was less successful in her wish to deny the succession after Jahangir's death at the age of 58 to Prince Khurram. Acceding to the throne in 1628, he took the title of

Shah Jahan (*Ruler of the World*) and in the next 30 years his reign represented the height of Mughal power.

Shah Jahan The Mughal Empire was under attack in the Deccan and the northwest when Shah Jahan became Emperor. He tried to re-establish and extend Mughal authority in both regions by a combination of military campaigns and skilled diplomacy. Akbar's craftsmen had already carved outstandingly beautiful *jalis* for the tomb of Salim Chishti in Fatehpur Sikri, but Shah Jahan developed the form further. Undoubtedly the finest tribute to these skills is found in the Taj Mahal, the tribute to his beloved wife Mumtaz Mahal, who died giving birth to her 14th child in 1631.

Aurangzeb The need to expand the area under Mughal control was felt even more strongly by Aurangzeb (*'The jewel in the throne'*) than by his predecessors. He had shown his intellectual gifts in his grandfather Jahangir's court when held hostage to guarantee Shah Jahan's good behaviour, learning Arabic, Persian, Turkish and Hindi. When he seized power at the age of 40, he needed all his political and military skills to hold on to an unwieldy empire that was in permanent danger of collapse from its own size. Aurangzeb realized that the resources of the territory he inherited from Shah Jahan were not enough. One response was to push south, while maintaining his hold on the east and north. Initially he maintained his alliances with the Rajputs in the west, which had been a crucial element in Mughal strategy. In 1678 he claimed absolute rights over Jodhpur and went to war with the Rajput clans at the same time embarking on a policy of outright Islamization. However, for the remaining 39 years of his reign he struggled to sustain his power.

The East India Company and the rise of British power

The British were unique among the foreign rulers of India in coming by sea rather than through the northwest and in coming first for trade rather than for military conquest. The ports that they established – Madras, Bombay and Calcutta – became completely new centres of political, economic and social activity. Before them Indian empires had controlled their territories from the land. The British dictated the economy by controlling sea-borne trade. From the middle of the 19th century railways transformed the economic and political structure of South Asia and it was those three centres of British control, along with the late addition of Delhi, which became the foci of economic development and political change.

The East India Company in Madras and Bengal

In its first 90 years of contact with South Asia after the Company set up its first trading post at **Masulipatnam**, on the east coast of India, it had depended almost entirely on trade for its profits. However, in 1701, only 11 years after a British settlement was first established at Calcutta, the Company was given rights to land revenue in Bengal.

The Company was accepted and sometimes welcomed, partly because it offered to bolster the inadequate revenues of the Mughals by exchanging silver bullion for the cloth it bought. However, in the south the Company moved further towards consolidating its political base. Wars between South India's regional factions gave the Company the chance to extend their influence by making alliances and offering support to some of these factions in their struggles, which were complicated by the extension to Indian soil of the European contest for power between the French and the British.

Robert Clive The British established control over both Bengal and Southeast India in the middle of the 17th century. Robert Clive, in alliance with a collection of disaffected Hindu landowners and Muslim soldiers, defeated the new Nawab of Bengal, the 20-year-old Siraj-ud-Daula, in June 1757 at **Plassey** (Palashi), about 100 km north of Calcutta.

Hastings and Cornwallis The essential features of British control were mapped out in the next quarter of a century through the work of **Warren Hastings**, Governor-General from 1774 until 1785 and **Lord Cornwallis** who succeeded and remained in charge until 1793. Cornwallis was responsible for putting Europeans in charge of all the higher levels of revenue collection and administration and for introducing government by the rule of law, making even government officers subject to the courts.

The decline of Muslim power

The extension of East India Company power in the Mughal periphery of India's south and east took place against a background of the rising power of Sivaji and his Marathas.

Sivaji and the Marathas Sivaji was the son of a Hindu who had served as a small-scale chief in the Muslim-ruled state of Bijapur. The weakness of Bijapur encouraged Sivaji to extend his father's area of control and he led a rebellion. The Bijapur general Afzal Khan, sent to put it down, agreed to meet Sivaji in private to reach a settlement. In an act which is still remembered by both Muslims and Marathas, Sivaji embraced him with steel claws attached to his fingers and tore him apart. It was the start of a campaign which took Maratha power as far south as Madurai and to the doors of Delhi and Calcutta.

Although Sivaji himself died in 1680, Aurangzeb never fully came to terms with the rising power of the Marathas, though he did end their ambitions to form an empire of their own. While the Maratha confederacy was able to threaten Delhi within 50 years of Aurangzeb's death, by the early 19th century it had dissolved into five independent states, with whom the British ultimately dealt separately.

Nor was Aurangzeb able to create any wide sense of identity with the Mughals as a legitimate popular power. Instead, under the influence of Sunni Muslim theologians, he retreated into insistence on Islamic purity. He imposed Islamic law, the *sharia*, promoted only Muslims to positions of authority, tried to replace Hindu administrators and revenue collectors with Muslims, and reimposed the *jizya* tax on all non-Muslims. By his death in 1707 the empire had neither the broadness of spirit nor the physical means to survive.

Bahadur Shah The decline was postponed by the reign of Aurangzeb's son. Sixty-three when he acceded to the throne, Bahadur Shah restored some of its fortunes. He made agreements with the Marathas and the Rajputs and defeated the Sikhs in Punjab before taking the last Sikh guru into his service. Nine emperors succeeded

Aurangzeb between his death and the exile of the last Mughal ruler in 1858. It was no accident that it was in that year the British ended the rule of its East India Company and decreed India to be its Indian empire.

Mohammad Shah remained in his capital of Delhi, resigning himself to enjoying what Carey Welch has called "the conventional triad of joys: the wine was excellent, as were the women and for him the song was especially rewarding". The idyll was rudely shattered by the invasion of **Nadir Shah** in 1739, an Iranian marauder who slaughtered thousands in Delhi and carried off priceless Mughal treasures, including the Peacock Throne.

The East India Company's push for power

Alliances In the century and a half that followed the death of Aurangzeb, the British East India Company extended its economic and political influence into the heart of India. As the Mughal Empire lost its power India fell into many smaller states. The Company undertook to protect the rulers of several of these states from external attack by stationing British troops in their territory. In exchange for this service the rulers paid subsidies to the Company. The British extended their territory through the 18th century as successive regional powers were annexed and brought under direct Company rule.

Progress to direct British control was uneven and often opposed. The Sikhs in Punjab, the Marathas in the west and the Mysore sultans in the south, fiercely contested British advances. **Haidar Ali** and **Tipu Sultan**, who had built a wealthy kingdom in the Mysore region, resisted attempts to incorporate them. Tipu was finally killed in 1799 at the battle of Srirangapatnam, an island fort in the Kaveri River just north of Mysore, where Arthur Wellesley, later the Duke of Wellington, began to make his military reputation.

The Marathas were not defeated until the 1816-1818 war. Even then the defeat owed as much to internal fighting as to the power of the British-led army. Only the northwest of the subcontinent remained beyond British control until well into the 19th century. Thus in 1799 **Ranjit Singh** was able to set up a Sikh state in Punjab, surviving until the late 1830s despite the extension of British control over much of the rest of India.

In 1818 India's economy was in ruins and its political structures destroyed. Irrigation and road systems had fallen into decay and gangs terrorized the countryside. Thugs and dacoits controlled much of rural areas in Central India and often robbed and murdered even on town outskirts. The stability of the Mughal period had long since passed. From 1818 to 1857 there was a succession of local and uncoordinated revolts in different parts of India. Some were bought off, some put down by military force.

A period of reforms

While existing political systems were collapsing, the first half of the 1800s was also a time of radical social change in territories governed by the East India Company. **Lord William Bentinck** became governor-general at a time when England was undergoing major reform. In 1828 he banned the burning of widows on the funeral pyres of their husbands (**sati**) and then moved to suppress **thuggee** (ritual murder and robbery carried out in the name of the goddess Kali). His most far reaching change was to introduce education in English.

From the late 1830s massive new engineering projects began to be taken up; first canals, then railways. The innovations stimulated change and change contributed to the growing unease with the British presence. The development of the telegraph, railways and new roads, three universities and the extension of massive new canal irrigation projects in North India seemed to threaten traditional society, a risk increased by the annexation of Indian states to bring them under direct British rule. The most important of these was Oudh.

The Rebellion

Out of the growing discontent and widespread economic difficulties came the Rebellion or 'Mutiny' of 1857. On 10 May 1857 troops in Meerut, 70 km northeast of Delhi, mutinied. They reached Delhi the next day, where **Bahadur Shah**, the last Mughal Emperor, took sides with the mutineers. Troops in Lucknow joined the rebellion and for three months Lucknow and other cities in the north were under siege. Appalling scenes of butchery and reprisals marked the struggle, only put down by troops from outside.

The period of Empire

The 1857 rebellion marked the end not only of the Mughal Empire but also of the East India Company, for the British government in London took overall control in 1858. Yet within 30 years a movement for self government had begun and there were the first signs of a demand among the new Western-educated elite that political rights be awarded to match the sense of Indian national identity.

Indian National Congress Established in 1885, this was the first all-India political institution and was to become the key vehicle of demands for independence. However, the educated Muslim élite of what is now Uttar Pradesh saw a threat to Muslim rights, power and identity in the emergence of democratic institutions which gave Hindus, with their built-in natural majority, significant advantages. Sir Sayyid Ahmad Khan, who had founded a Muslim University at Aligarh in 1877, advised Muslims against joining the Congress, seeing it as a vehicle for Hindu, and especially Bengali, nationalism.

The Muslim League The educated Muslim community of North India remained deeply suspicious of the Congress, making up less than 8% of those attending its conferences between 1900-1920. Muslims from UP created the All-India Muslim League in 1906. However, the demands of the Muslim League were not always opposed to those of the Congress. In 1916 it concluded the Lucknow Pact with the Congress, in which the Congress won Muslim support for self-government, in exchange for the recognition that there would be separate constituencies for Muslims. The nature of the future independent India was still far from clear, however. The British conceded the principle of self-government in 1918, but the reforms already fell far short of heightened Indian expectations.

Mahatma Gandhi Into a tense atmosphere Mohandas Karamchand Gandhi returned to India in 1915 after 20 years practising as a lawyer in South Africa. He

Mahatma Gandhi

Mohandas Karamchand Ghandi, an English-educated lawyer, had lived outside India from his youth to middle age. He preached the general acceptance of some of the doctrines he had grown to respect in his childhood, notably *ahimsa*, or non-violence. On his return the Bengali Nobel Laureate poet, Rabindranath Tagore, had dubbed him 'Mahatma' – Great Soul. From 1921 he gave up his Western style of dress and adopted the hand spun *dhoti* worn by poor Indian villagers. Yet, he was also fiercely critical of many aspects of traditional Hindu society. He preached against the discrimination of the caste system which still dominated life for the overwhelming majority of Hindus. Often despised by the British in India, his death at the hands of an extreme Hindu chauvinist in January 1948 was a final testimony to the ambiguity of his achievements: successful in contributing so much to achieving India's Independence, yet failing to resolve the bitter communal legacies which he gave his life to overcome.

arrived as the government of India was being given new powers by the British parliament to try political cases without a jury and to give provincial governments the right to imprison politicians without trial. In opposition to this legislation Gandhi proposed to call a *hartal*, when all activity would cease for a day, a form of protest still in widespread use. Such protests took place across India, often accompanied by riots.

On 13 April 1919 a huge gathering took place in the enclosed space of Jallianwala Bagh in Amritsar. It had been prohibited by the government and General Dyer ordered troops to fire on the people without warning, killing 379 and injuring at least a further 1200. It marked the turning point in relations with Britain and the rise of Gandhi to the key position of leadership in the struggle for complete independence. **The thrust for Independence** Through the 1920s Gandhi developed concepts and political programmes that were to become the hallmark of India's Independence struggle. Ultimately political Independence was to be achieved not by violent rebellion but by *satyagraha* – a 'truth force' which implied a willingness to suffer through non-violent resistance to injustice. In 1930 the Congress declared that 26 January would be Independence Day – still celebrated as Republic Day in India today. Mohammad Iqbal, the Leader of the Muslim League, took the opportunity of his address to the League in the same year to suggest the formation of a Muslim state within an Indian Federation. Also in 1930 a Muslim student in Cambridge, Chaudhuri Rahmat Ali, coined a name for the new Muslim state PAKISTAN. The letters were to stand 'P' for Punjab, 'A' for Afghania, 'K' for Kashmir, 'S' for Sind with the suffix '*stan*', Persian for country. The idea still had little real shape however and waited on developments of the late 1930s and 1940s to bear fruit.

By the end of the Second World War the positions of the Muslim League, now under the leadership of Mohammad Ali Jinnah and the Congress led by Jawaharlal Nehru, were irreconcilable. While major questions of the definition of separate territories for a Muslim and non-Muslim state remained to be answered, it was clear to General Wavell, the British Viceroy through the last years of the war, that there was no alternative but to accept that independence would have to be given on the basis of separate states.

Independence and Partition

One of the main difficulties for the Muslims was that they made up only a fifth of the total population were scattered throughout India. It was therefore impossible to define a simple territorial division which would provide a state to match Jinnah's claim of a *'two-nation theory'*. On 20 February 1947, the British Labour Government announced its decision to replace Lord Wavell as Viceroy with Lord Mountbatten, who was to oversee the transfer of power to new independent governments. It set a deadline of June 1948 for British withdrawal. The announcement of a firm date made the Indian politicians even less willing to compromise and the resulting division satisfied no one.

Independence arrived on 15 August for India and the 14 August for Pakistan because Indian astrologers deemed the 15th to be the most auspicious moment. Several key Princely States had still not decided firmly to which country they would accede. Kashmir was the most important of these, with results that have lasted to the present day.

Modern India

India, with an estimated 1.21 billion people, is the second most populated country in the world after China. That population size reflects the long history of human occupation and the fact that an astonishingly high proportion of India's land is relatively fertile. About 60% of India's surface area is cultivated, compared with 10% in China and 20% in the US. Although the birth rate has fallen steadily over the last 40 years, initially death rates fell faster and the rate of population increase has continued to be nearly 2% – or 18 million – a year.

Politics and institutions

When India became independent on 15 August 1947 it faced three immediate crises. Partition left it with a bitter struggle between Muslims on one side and Hindus and Sikhs on the other which threatened to tear the new country into pieces. An estimated 13 million people migrated between the two new countries of India and Pakistan.

In the years since Independence, striking political achievements have been made. With the two-year exception of 1975-1977, when Mrs Indira Gandhi imposed a state of emergency in which all political activity was banned, India has sustained a democratic system in the face of tremendous pressures. The contest for power has largely become a two-horse race between two free-flowing coalitions, one led by the right-wing Hindu-aligned Bharatiya Janata Party (BJP), the other based around the centre-left United Progressive Alliance (UPA), a coalition of moderate parties formed in 2004 by Sonia Gandhi and dominated by the Congress Party. The general elections in May 2014 saw the BJP surge to power, a hugely effective and personality-driven campaign by the controversial pro-business leader Narendra Modi winning the party the first absolute majority in Indian national elections for three decades.

The constitution

Establishing itself as a sovereign democratic republic, the Indian parliament accepted Nehru's advocacy of a secular constitution. The president is formally vested with all executive powers exercised under the authority of the prime minister.

Parliament has a lower house (*Lok Sabha* – House of the people) and an upper house (*Rajya Sabha* – Council of States). The former is made up of directly elected representatives from the 543 parliamentary constituencies (plus two nominated members from the Anglo-Indian community), the latter of members elected by an electoral college and nominated members.

India's federal constitution devolves certain powers to elected state assemblies. Each state has a governor who acts as its official head. Many states also have two chambers, the upper generally called the Rajya Sabha and the lower (often called the Vidhan Sabha) being of directly elected representatives. In practice many of the state assemblies have had a totally different political complexion from that of the Lok Sabha. Regional parties have played a far more prominent role, though in many states central government has effectively dictated both the leadership and policy of state assemblies.

States and Union Territories Union territories are administered by the president "acting to such an extent as he thinks fit". In practice Union territories have varying forms of self-government. Pondicherry has a legislative Assembly and Council of Ministers. The 69th Amendment to the Constitution in 1991 provided for a legislative assembly and council of ministers for Delhi, elections for which were held in December 1993. The Assemblies of Union Territories have more restricted powers of legislation than full states. Some Union Territories – Dadra and Nagar Haveli, Daman and Diu, all of which separated from Goa in 1987 when Goa achieved full statehood – Andaman and Nicobar Islands and Lakshadweep have elected bodies known as Pradesh Councils.

Secularism One of the key features of India's constitution is its secular principle. Some see the commitment to a secular constitution as having been under challenge from the Hindu nationalism of the BJP.

Judiciary India's Supreme Court has similar but somewhat weaker powers to those of the United States. The judiciary has remained effectively independent of the government except under the Emergency between 1975-1977.

Civil service India continued to use the small but highly professional administrative service inherited from the British period. Renamed the Indian Administrative Service (IAS), it continues to exercise remarkable influence across the country. The administration of many aspects of central and regional government is in the hands of this elite body, who act largely by the constitutional rules which bind them as servants of the state. Many Indians accept the continuing efficiency and high calibre of the top ranking officers in the administration while believing that the bureaucratic system as a whole has been overtaken by widespread corruption.

Police India's police service is divided into a series of groups, numbering nearly one million. While the top ranks of the Indian Police Service are comparable to the IAS, lower levels are extremely poorly trained and very low paid. In addition to the domestic police force there are special groups: the Border Security Force, Central Reserve Police and others. They may be armed with modern weapons and are called in for special duties.

Armed forces Unlike its immediate neighbours Pakistan and Bangladesh, India has never had military rule. It has around one million men in the army, one of the largest armed forces in the world. Although they have remained out of politics the army has been used increasingly frequently to put down civil unrest especially in Kashmir.

Congress Party The Congress won overall majorities in seven of the 10 general elections held before the 1996 election, although in no election did the Congress obtain more than 50% of the popular vote. In 1998 its popular support completely disappeared in some regions and fell below 30% nationally and in the elections of September-October 1999 Sonia Gandhi, Rajiv Gandhi's Italian-born widow, failed to achieve the much vaunted revival in the Party's fortunes. Through 2001 into 2002 a change began with the BJP losing power in state assemblies in the north and becoming increasingly unpopular nationally, and the Congress picking up a wide measure of support, culminating in their victory in the May 2004 general election, when Sonia Gandhi nominated Manmohan Singh as prime minister. However, despite his successes in liberalizing the Indian economy and presiding over breakneck economic growth during 2007, Singh's time at the helm became indelibly associated with a series of scandals involving allocation of national resources to private corporations; the 'Coalgate' scam allegedly cost the nation the equivalent of US$33.4 billion over eight years, during most of which Singh himself held the portfolio of coal minister. In the 2014 elections the Congress won just 44 seats, suffering its worst ever defeat in a general election.

Non-Congress parties Political activity outside the Congress can seem bewilderingly complex. There are no genuinely national parties. The only alternative governments to the Congress have been formed by coalitions of regional and ideologically based parties. Parties of the left – Communist and Socialist – have never broken out of their narrow regional bases. The **Communist Party of India** split into two factions in 1964, with the Communist Party of India Marxist (CPM) ultimately taking power in West Bengal and Kerala. In the 1960s the **Swatantra Party** (a liberal party) made some ground nationally, opposing the economic centralization and state control supported by the Congress.

At the right of the political spectrum, the **Jan Sangh** was seen as a party of right wing Hindu nationalism with a concentrated but significant base in parts of the north, especially among higher castes and merchant communities. The most organized political force outside the Congress, the Jan Sangh merged with the **Janata Party** for the elections of 1977. After the collapse of that government it re-formed itself as the **Bharatiya Janata Party** (BJP). In 1990-1991 it developed a powerful campaign focusing on reviving Hindu identity against the minorities. In the decade that followed it became the most powerful single party across northern India and established a series of footholds and alliances in the South. Elsewhere a succession of regional parties dominated politics in several key states, including Tamil Nadu and Andhra Pradesh in the south and West Bengal and Bihar in the east.

Recent developments

The attacks on New York and Washington on 11 September and the US-led 'War on Terror' has had major repercussions in India and Pakistan. While the Taliban's rapid defeat brought a new government to power in Afghanistan, strongly supported by India, the Kashmir dispute between India and Pakistan deepened. Both India and Pakistan sought political advantage from the war on terror, and when a terrorist attack was launched on the Indian parliament on 13 December 2001 the Indian government pushed massive reinforcements to the Pakistan border from Gujarat and Rajasthan to Kashmir. India demanded that President Musharraf close down all camps and organizations which India claimed were the source of the attacks in Delhi and Kashmir. Although President Musharraf closed down *Lashkar e Taiba* and *Jaish e Mohammad*, two of the most feared groups operating openly in Pakistan, cross-border firing intensified along the Line of Control in Kashmir and attacks in Kashmir continued. After the change of government in May 2004, however, things improved but the deepening political crisis in Pakistan and the rising strike power of the Taliban has led to increasing fears in India of a collapse of political stability and control in its western neighbour. In parallel there have been increasing reports of terrorist incidents in Kashmir, and a resolution is still nowhere in sight. Encouragingly, though, there are signs that communal violence between Hindus and Muslims elsewhere in India is on the wane. The attacks on central Mumbai of 26 November 2008, carried out by Pakistan-trained militants, did not trigger the reprisals against local Muslims that many feared would occur. Furthermore, several commentators have credited BJP member Varun Gandhi's hate speeches against Muslims for the party's resounding defeat in the 2009 general election.

The change of government in 2014 represents a potential turning point in the perpetually fraught relationship between India and Pakistan. Manmohan Singh's 10 years in office were characterized by a cautious warming in relations. The 2008 terrorist attacks on Mumbai, in which 164 people were killed by Islamic militants of the banned Lashkar-e-Taiba group allegedly operating from bases in Pakistan, caused the suspension of peace talks to resolve the Kashmir situation for more than two years, but the feared backlash against Muslim targets never occurred. Talks resumed in February 2011, with Singh inviting President Asif Ali Zardari to join him for the Cricket World Cup semi-final between India and Pakistan, and the two nations entering into closer trade relations thanks to the removal of restrictions on Pakistani investment in India.

By contrast, since coming to power members of Narendra Modi's right-wing BJP party have indulged in bouts of populist sabre rattling, party elder Subramaniam Swamy touting the prospect of unleashing nuclear weapons on Pakistan. These have been ignored by the government, but Modi's hawkish election campaign promised a low tolerance of Muslim militancy, and greater pressure on the Pakistan government to act against the people behind the Mumbai attacks.

Domestically, much attention has been focused on the corruption and illegality that dominates Indian politics. One in five candidates for the 2014 national election was subject to criminal charges ranging from extortion to murder, and the electorate has become justifiably cynical about official corruption, ministerial scandals and the heavy steering hand of business moguls such as Mukesh Ambani. 2011-2012 saw anti-corruption sit-ins and hunger strikes in North India, leading to the formation of the Aam Aadmi (Common Man) Party by Arvind Kejriwal, which campaigned on the promise of a Jan Lokpal – an independent body to root out corruption in politics. The AAP successfully won government in New Delhi, but found its initiatives stifled by the Congress and BJP – vested interests proving more powerful than the common man – and the party was routed in the 2014 elections.

Culture

Language

The graffiti written on the walls of any Indian city bear witness to the number of major languages spoken across the country, many with their own distinct scripts. In all the states of North and West India an Indo-Aryan language – the easternmost group of the Indo-European family – is predominant. Sir William Jones, the great 19th-century scholar, discovered the close links between Sanskrit (the basis of nearly all North Indian languages) German and Greek. He showed that they all must have originated in the common heartland of Central Asia, being carried west, south and east by the nomadic tribes who shaped so much of the following history of both Europe and Asia.

Sanskrit As the pastoralists from Central Asia moved into South Asia from 2000 BC onwards, the Indo-Aryan languages they spoke were modified. Sanskrit developed from this process, emerging as the dominant classical language of India by the sixth century BC, when it was classified in the grammar of **Panini**. It remained the language of the educated until about AD 1000, though it had ceased to be in common use several centuries earlier.

Hindi and Urdu The Muslims brought Persian into South Asia as the language of the rulers, where it became the language of the politically powerful elite. The most striking example of Muslim influence on the earlier Indo-European languages is that of the two most important languages of India and Pakistan, Hindi and Urdu respectively. Most of the other modern North Indian languages were not written until the 16th century or after. Hindi developed into the language of the heartland of Hindu culture, stretching from Punjab to Bihar and from the foothills of the Himalaya to the marchlands of central India.

Bengali At the east end of the Ganga plains Hindi gives way to Bengali (Bangla), the language today of over 50 million people in India, as well as more than 115 million in Bangladesh. Linguistically it is close to both Assamese and Oriya.

Gujarati and Marathi South of the main Hindi and Urdu belt of India and Pakistan is a series of quite different Indo-Aryan languages. Panjabi in both Pakistan and India (on the Indian side of the border written in the Gurumukhi script) and Gujarati and Marathi, all have common features with Urdu or Hindi, but are major languages in their own right.

Dravidian languages The other major language family of South Asia today, Dravidian, has been in India since before the arrival of the Indo-Aryans. Four of South Asia's major living languages belong to this family group – Tamil, Telugu, Kannada and Malayalam, spoken in Tamil Nadu (and northern Sri Lanka), Andhra Pradesh, Karnataka and Kerala respectively.

Each has its own script. All the Dravidian languages were influenced by the prevalence of Sanskrit as the language of the ruling and educated elite. There have been recent attempts to rid Tamil of its Sanskrit elements and to recapture the supposed purity of a literature that stretches back to the early centuries BC. Kannada and Telugu were clearly established by AD 1000, while Malayalam, which started as a dialect of Tamil, did not develop fully until the 13th century. Today the four main Dravidian languages are spoken by 180 million people.

Scripts

It is impossible to spend even a short time in India or the other countries of South Asia without coming across several of the different scripts that are used. The earliest ancestor of scripts in use today was **Brahmi**, in which Asoka's famous inscriptions were written in the third century BC. Written from left to right, a separate symbol represented each different sound.

Devanagari For around 1000 years the major script of northern India has been the Nagari or Devanagari, which means literally the script of the 'city of the gods'. Hindi, Nepali and Marathi join Sanskrit in their use of Devanagari. The Muslim rulers developed a right to left script based on Persian and Arabic.

Dravidian scripts The Dravidian languages were written originally on leaves of the palmyra palm. Cutting the letters on the hard palm leaf made particular demands which had their impact on the forms of the letters adopted. The letters became rounded because they were carved with a stylus. This was held stationary while the leaf was turned. The southern scripts were carried overseas, contributing to the form of the non-Dravidian languages of Thai, Burmese and Cambodian.

Numerals Many of the Indian alphabets have their own notation for numerals. This is not without irony, for what in the Western world are called 'Arabic' numerals are in fact of Indian origin. In some parts of South Asia local numerical symbols are still in use, but you will find that the Arabic number symbols familiar in Europe and the West are common.

Literature

Sanskrit was the first all-India language. Its literature has had a fundamental influence on the region's religious, social and political life. Early literature was memorized and recited. The hymns of the Rig Veda did not reach their final form until about the sixth century BC.

The Vedas

The Rig Veda is a collection of 1028 hymns, not all religious. Its main function was to provide orders of worship for priests responsible for the sacrifices that were central to the religion of Indo-Aryans. Two later texts, the Yajurveda and the Samaveda, served the same purpose. A fourth, the Atharvaveda, is largely a collection of magic spells.

The Brahmanas Central to the Vedic literature was a belief in the importance of sacrifice. At some time after 1000 BC a second category of Vedic literature, the Brahmanas, began to take shape. Story telling developed as a means to interpret the significance of sacrifice. The most famous and the most important of these were the Upanishads, probably written at some time between the seventh and fifth centuries BC.

The Mahabharata The Brahmanas gave their name to the religion emerging between the eighth and sixth centuries BC, Brahmanism, the ancestor of Hinduism. Two of its texts remain the best known and most widely revered epic compositions in South Asia, the *Mahabharata* and the *Ramayana*.

Dating the Mahabharata

Tradition puts the date of the great battle described in the *Mahabharata* at precisely 3102 BC, the start of the present era, and names the author of the poem as a sage, Vyasa. Evidence suggests however that the battle was fought around 800 BC, at Kurukshetra. It was another 400 years before priests began to write the stories down, a process which was not complete until AD 400. The *Mahabharata* was probably an attempt by the warrior class, the Kshatriyas, to merge their brand of popular religion with Brahmanism ideas. The original version was 3000 stanzas long, but it now has over 100,000; eight times as long as Homer's Iliad and the Odyssey put together.

Good and evil The battle was seen as a war of good and evil, the **Pandavas** being interpreted as gods and the **Kauravas** as devils. The arguments were elaborated and expanded until the fourth century AD by which time, as Shackle says, "Brahmanism had absorbed and set its own mark on the religious ideas of the epic and Hinduism had come into being". A comparatively late addition to the *Mahabharata*, the *Bhagavad-Gita* is the most widely read and revered text among Hindus in South Asia today.

The Ramayana

Valmiki is thought of in India as the author of the second great Indian epic, the *Ramayana*, though no more is known of his identity than is known of Homer's. Like the *Mahabharata*, it underwent several stages of development before it reached its final version of 48,000 lines.

Sanskrit literature

Sanskrit was the language of the elite. Other languages replaced it in common speech by the third century BC, but it remained in restricted use for over 1000 years after that period. The remarkable Sanskrit grammar of Panini helped to establish grammar as one of the six disciplines essential to understanding the Vedas properly and to conducting Vedic rituals. The other five were phonetics, etymology, meter, ritual practice and astronomy. Sanskrit literature continued to be written in the courts until the Muslims replaced it with Persian, long after it had ceased to be a language of spoken communication.

Literally 'stories of ancient times', the Puranas are about Brahma, Vishnu and Siva. They were not compiled until the fifth century AD. The stories are often the only source of information about the period immediately after the early Vedas. Each Purana dealt with five themes: "the creation of the world (*sarga*); its destruction and recreation (*pratisarga*); the genealogy of gods and patriarchs

The story of Rama

Under Brahmin influence, Rama was transformed from the human prince of the early versions into the divine figure of the final story. Rama, the 'jewel of the solar kings', became deified as an incarnation of Vishnu. The story tells how Rama was banished from his father's kingdom. In a journey with his wife, Sita, and helper and friend, Hanuman (the monkey-faced God depicted in many Indian temples, shrines and posters), Rama fought the king Ravana, changed in late versions into a demon. Rama's rescue of Sita was interpreted as the Aryan triumph over the barbarians. The epic is seen as South Asia's first literary poem and is recited in all Hindu communities.

Ravana, demon King of Lanka

(*vamsa*); the reigns and periods of the Manus (*manvantaras*); and the history of the solar and lunar dynasties".

The Muslim influence

Persian In the first three decades of the 10th century AD Mahmud of Ghazni carried Muslim power into India. For considerable periods until the 18th century, Persian became the language of the courts. Classical Persian was the dominant influence, with Iran as its country of origin and Shiraz its main cultural centre, but India developed its own Persian-based style. Two poets stood out at the end of the 13th century AD, when Muslim rulers had established a sultanate in Delhi, Amir Khusrau, who lived from 1253 to 1325 and the mystic Amir Hasan, who died about AD 1328.

Turki The most notable of the Mughal sponsors of literature, Akbar (1556-1605) was illiterate. Babur left one of the most remarkable political autobiographies of any generation, the Babur-nama, written in Turki and translated into Persian. His grandson Akbar commissioned a biography, the Akbar-nama, which reflected his interest in the world's religions. His son Jahangir left his memoirs, the Tuzuk-i Jahangiri, in Persian. They have been described as intimate and showing an insatiable interest in things, events and people.

The Colonial Period

Persian was already in decline during the reign of the last great Muslim Emperor, Aurangzeb and as the British extended their political power so the role of English grew. There is now a very wide Indian literature accessible in English, which has thus become the latest of the languages to be used across the whole of South Asia.

In the 19th century English became a vehicle for developing nationalist ideals. However, notably in the work of **Rabindranath Tagore**, it became a medium for religious and philosophical prose and for a developing poetry. Tagore himself won the Nobel Prize for Literature in 1913 for his translation into English of his own work, Gitanjali. Leading South Asian philosophers and thinkers of the 20th century have written major works in English, including not only MK Gandhi and Jawaharlal Nehru, the two leading figures in India's Independence movement, but S Radhakrishnan, Aurobindo Ghosh and Sarojini Naidu, who all added to the depth of Indian literature in English.

Several South Asian regional languages have their own long traditions of both religious and secular literature which are discussed in the relevant sections of this book.

Science

Views of the universe Early Indian views of the universe were based on the square and the cube. The earth was seen as a square, one corner pointing south, rising like a pyramid in a series of square terraces with its peak, the mythical Mount Meru. The sun moved round the top of Mount Meru in a square orbit and the square orbits of the planets were at successive planes above the orbit of the sun. These were seen therefore as forming a second pyramid of planetary movement. Mount Meru was central to all early Indian schools of thought, Hindu, Buddhist and Jain.

However, about 200 BC the Jains transformed the view of the universe based on squares by replacing the idea of square orbits with that of the circle. The earth was shown as a circular disc, with Mount Meru rising from its centre and the Pole Star above it.

The science of early India By about 500 BC Indian texts illustrated the calculation of the **calendar**, although the system itself almost certainly goes back to the eighth or ninth century BC. The year was divided into 27 *nakshatras*, or fortnights, years being calculated on a mixture of lunar and solar counting.

Technology The only copy of Kautiliya's treatise on government (which was only discovered in 1909) dates from about 100 BC. It describes the **weapons** technology of catapults, incendiary missiles and the use of elephants, but it is also evident that gunpowder was unknown. Large-scale **irrigation** works were developed, though the earliest examples of large tanks may be those of the Sri Lankan King Panduwasa at Anuradhapura, built in 504 BC. During the Gupta period dramatic progress was made in **metallurgy**, shown in the pure iron pillar which can be seen in the Qutb Minar in Delhi.

Mathematics Conceptions of the universe and the mathematical and geometrical ideas that accompanied them were comparatively advanced in South Asia by the time of the Mauryan Empire and were put to use in the rules developed for building temple altars. Indians were using the concept of zero and decimal points in the Gupta period. Furthermore in AD 499, just after the demise of the Gupta Empire, the astronomer Aryabhatta calculated Pi as 3.1416 and the length of the solar year as 365.358 days. He also postulated that the earth was a sphere rotating on its own axis and revolving around the sun and that the shadow of the earth falling on the moon caused lunar eclipses. The development of science in India was not restricted to the Gupta court. In South India, Tamil kings developed extensive contact with Roman and Greek thinkers during the first four centuries of the Christian era. Babylonian methods used for astronomy in Greece remained current in Tamil Nadu until very recent times. The basic texts of astronomy (the Surya Siddhanta) were completed by AD 400.

Architecture

Over the 4000 years since the Indus Valley civilization flourished, art and architecture have developed with a remarkable continuity through successive regional and religious influences and styles. The Buddhist art and architecture of the third century BC left few remains, but the stylistic influence on early Hindu architecture was profound. From the sixth century AD the first Hindu religious buildings to have survived into the modern period were constructed in South and East India.

Hindu temple buildings

The principles of religious building were laid down by priests in the *Sastras*. Every aspect of Hindu, Jain and Buddhist religious building is identified with conceptions of the structure of the universe. This applies as much to the process of building – the timing of which must be undertaken at astrologically propitious times – as to the formal layout of the buildings. The cardinal directions of north, south, east and west are the basic fix on which buildings are planned. George Michell suggests that in addition to the cardinal directions, number is also critical to the design of the religious building. The key to the ultimate scale of the building is derived from the measurements of the sanctuary at its heart. Indian temples were nearly always built according to philosophical understandings of the universe. This cosmology, of an infinite number of universes, isolated from each other in space, proceeds by imagining various possibilities as to its nature. Its centre is seen as dominated by Mount Meru which keeps earth and heaven apart. The concept of *separation* is crucial to Hindu thought and social practice. Continents, rivers and oceans occupy concentric rings around the mountain, while the stars encircle the mountain in another plane. Humans live on the continent of Jambudvipa, characterized by the rose apple tree (*jambu*).

Mandalas The Sastras show plans of this continent, organized in concentric rings and entered at the cardinal points. This type of diagram was known as a mandala. Such a geometric scheme could be subdivided into almost limitless small compartments, each of which could be designated as having special properties or be devoted to a particular deity. The centre of the mandala would be the seat of the major god; they provided the ground rules for the building of *stupas* and temples across India and gave the key to the symbolic meaning attached to every aspect of religious buildings.

Temple design The focal point of the temple, its sanctuary, was the home of the presiding deity, the 'womb-chamber' (*garbhagriha*). A series of doorways, in large temples leading through a succession of buildings, allowed the worshipper to move towards the final encounter with the deity to obtain *darshan* – a sight of the god. Both Buddhist and Hindu worship encourage the worshipper to walk clockwise around the shrine, performing *pradakshina*. The elevations are symbolic representations of the home of the gods. Mountain peaks such as Kailasa are common names for the most prominent of the towers. In North and East Indian temples the tallest of these towers rises above the *garbagriha* itself, symbolizing the meeting of earth and heaven in the person of the enshrined deity. In later South Indian temples the gateways to the temple come to overpower the central tower. In both, the basic structure is usually richly embellished with sculpture. When first built this would usually have been plastered and painted and often covered in gems. In contrast to the extraordinary profusion of colour and life on the outside, the interior is dark and cramped but here it is believed, lies the true centre of divine power.

Muslim religious architecture

Although the Muslims adapted many Hindu features, they also brought totally new forms. Their most outstanding contribution, dominating the architecture of many North Indian cities, are the mosques and tomb complexes (*dargah*). The use of brickwork was widespread and they brought with them from Persia the principle of constructing the true arch. Muslim architects succeeded in producing a variety of domed structures, often incorporating distinctively Hindu features such as the surmounting finial. By the end of the great period of Muslim building in 1707, the Muslims had added magnificent forts and palaces to their religious structures, a statement of power as well as of aesthetic taste.

European buildings

Nearly two centuries of architectural stagnation and decline followed the demise of Mughal power. The Portuguese built a series of remarkable churches in Goa that owed everything to Baroque developments in Europe. Not until the end of the Victorian period, when British imperial ambitions were at their height, did the British colonial impact on public rather than domestic architecture begin to be felt. Fierce arguments divided British architects as to the merits of indigenous design. The ultimate plan for New Delhi was carried out by men who had little time for Hindu architecture and believed themselves to be on a civilizing mission. Others at the end of the 19th century wanted to recapture and enhance a tradition for which they had great respect. They have left a series of buildings, both in formerly British ruled territory and in the Princely States, which illustrate this concern through the development of what became known as the Indo-Saracenic style.

In the aftermath of the colonial period, Independent India set about trying to establish a break from the immediately imperial past, but was uncertain how to achieve it. In the event foreign architects were commissioned for major developments, such as Le Corbusier's design for Chandigarh and Louis Kahn's buildings in Dhaka and Ahmedabad. The latter, a centre for training and experiment, contains a number of new buildings such as those of the Indian architect Charles Correa.

Music, dance and film

Music Indian music can trace its origins to the metrical hymns and chants of the Vedas, in which the production of sound according to strict rules was understood to be vital to the continuing order of the Universe. Through more than 3000 years of development and a range of regional schools, India's musical tradition has been handed on almost entirely by ear. The chants of the **Rig Veda** developed into songs in the **Sama Veda** and music found expression in every sphere of life, reflecting the cycle of seasons and the rhythm of work.

Over the centuries the original three notes, which were sung strictly in descending order, were extended to five and then seven and developed to allow freedom to move up and down the scale. The scale increased to 12 with the addition of flats and sharps and finally to 22 with the further subdivision of semitones. Books of musical rules go back at least as far as the third century AD. Classical music was totally intertwined with dance and drama, an interweaving reflected in the term *sangita*.

At some point after the Muslim influence made itself felt in the north, North and South Indian styles diverged, to become Carnatic (Karnatak) music in the south and Hindustani music in the north. However, they still share important common features: *svara* (pitch), *raga* (the melodic structure) and *tala* or *talam* (metre).

Hindustani music probably originated in the Delhi Sultanate during the 13th century, when the most widely known of North Indian musical instruments, the *sitar*, was believed to have been invented. **Amir Khusrau** is also believed to have invented the small drums, the *tabla*. Hindustani music is held to have reached its peak under *Tansen*, a court musician of Akbar. The other important northern instruments are the stringed *sarod*, the reed instrument *shahnai* and the wooden flute. Most Hindustani compositions have devotional texts, though they encompass a great emotional and thematic range. A common classical form of vocal performance is the *dhrupad*, a four-part composition.

The essential structure of a melody is known as a **raga** which usually has five to seven notes and can have as many as nine (or even 12 in mixed ragas). The music is improvised by the performer within certain rules and although theoretically thousands of ragas are possible, only around a 100 are commonly performed. Ragas have become associated with particular moods and specific times of the day. Music festivals often include all night sessions to allow performers a wider choice of repertoire.

Carnatic (Karnatak) music, contemporary South Indian music, is traced back to Tyagaraja (1759-1847), Svami Shastri (1763-1827) and Dikshitar (1775-1835), three musicians who lived and worked in Thanjavur. They are still referred to as the Trinity. Their music placed more emphasis on extended compositions than Hindustani music. Perhaps the best known South Indian instrument is the stringed *vina*, the flute being used for accompaniment with the violin (played rather differently to the European original), an oboe-like instrument called the *nagasvaram* and the drums, *tavil*.

Dance The rules for classical dance were laid down in the Natya shastra in the second century BC, which is still one of the bases for modern dance forms. The most common sources for Indian dance are the epics, but there are three essential aspects of the dance itself, Nritta (pure dance), Nrittya (emotional expression) and Natya (drama). The religious influence in dance was exemplified by the tradition of temple dancers, *devadasis*, girls and women who were dedicated to the deity in major temples. In South and East India there were thousands of *devadasis* associated with temple worship, though the practice fell into widespread disrepute and was banned in independent India. Various dance forms (for example Odissi, Manipuri, Bharat Natyam, Kathakali, Mohinyattam) developed in different parts of the country. India is also rich in folk dance traditions.

Film Filmgoers around the world are taking greater note of Indian cinema, both home-grown and that produced and directed by Indians abroad. Not all fall into the category of a Bollywood '*masala*' movie or 'curry western' churned out by the Mumbai (Bombay) film industry but many offer an insight into what draws millions to watch diverse versions of Indian life on the silver screen. A few titles, both all-time favourites as well as newer releases include: *Pather Panchali, Mother India; Titash Ekti Nadir Naam; Sholay; Bombay; Kuch Kuch Hota Hai; Lagaan; Kabhie Khushi Kabhie Cham; Monsoon Wedding; The Guru; The Warrior; Rang De Basanti; 3 Idiots; Barfi; A Wednesday* and *Kahaani*.

Religion

It is impossible to write briefly about religion in India without oversimplifying. Over 80% of Indians are Hindu, but there are many minorities. Muslims number about 125 million and there are over 23 million Christians, 19 million Sikhs, six million Buddhists and a number of other religious groups. One of the most persistent features of religious and social life is the caste system. This has undergone substantial changes since Independence, especially in towns and cities, but most people in India are still clearly identified as a member of a particular caste group. The government has introduced measures to help the backward, or 'scheduled' castes, though in recent years this has produced a major political backlash.

Hinduism

It has always been easier to define Hinduism by what it is not than by what it is. Indeed, the name 'Hindu' was given by foreigners to the peoples of the subcontinent who did not profess the other major faiths, such as Muslims or Christians. While some aspects of modern Hinduism can be traced back more than 4000 years before that, other features are recent.

Key ideas

According to the Indian philosopher and former president of India, S Radhakrishnan, religion for the Hindu "is not an idea but a power, not an intellectual proposition but a life conviction. Religion is consciousness of ultimate reality, not a theory about God". There is no Hindu organization, like a church, with the authority to define belief or establish official practice. Not all Hindu groups believe in a single supreme God. In view of these characteristics, many authorities argue that it is misleading to think of Hinduism as a religion. Be that as it may, the evidence of the living importance of Hinduism is visible across India. Hindu philosophy and practice has also touched many of those who belong to other religious traditions, particularly in terms of social institutions such as caste, and in post-Independence India religious identity has become an increasingly politicized feature of life.

Darshan One of Hinduism's recurring themes is 'vision', 'sight' or 'view' – **darshan**. Applied to the different philosophical systems themselves, such as *yoga* or *vedanta*, 'darshan' is also used to describe the sight of the deity that worshippers hope to gain when they visit a temple or shrine hoping for the sight of a 'guru' (teacher). Equally it may apply to the religious insight gained through meditation or prayer.

The four human goals Many Hindus also accept that there are four major human goals; material prosperity (*artha*), the satisfaction of desires (*kama*) and performing the duties laid down according to your position in life (*dharma*). Beyond those is the goal of achieving liberation from the endless cycle of rebirths into which everyone is locked (*moksha*). It is to the search for liberation that the major schools of Indian philosophy have devoted most attention. Together with dharma, it is basic to Hindu thought.

The four stages of life

Popular Hindu belief holds that an ideal life has four stages: the student, the householder, the forest dweller and the wandering dependent/beggar (*sannyasi*). These stages represent the phases through which an individual learns of life's goals and of the means of achieving them.

One of the most striking sights today is that of the saffron-clad *sannyasi* (sadhu) seeking gifts of food and money to support himself in the final stage of his life. There may have been sadhus even before the Aryans arrived. Today, most of these have given up material possessions, carrying only a strip of cloth, a *danda* (staff), a crutch to support the chin during *achal* (meditation), prayer beads, a fan to ward off evil spirits, a water pot, a drinking vessel, which may be a human skull and a begging bowl.

The *Mahabharata* lists 10 embodiments of dharma: good name, truth, self-control, cleanness of mind and body, simplicity, endurance, resoluteness of character, giving and sharing, austerities and continence. In *dharmic* thinking these are inseparable from five patterns of behaviour: non-violence, an attitude of equality, peace and tranquillity, lack of aggression and cruelty and absence of envy. Dharma, an essentially secular concept, represents the order inherent in human life.

Karma The idea of *karma*, 'the effect of former actions', is central to achieving liberation. As C Rajagopalachari put it: "Every act has its appointed effect, whether the act be thought, word or deed. The cause holds the effect, so to say, in its womb. If we reflect deeply and objectively, the entire world will be found to obey unalterable laws. That is the doctrine of karma". See also box, opposite.

Rebirth The belief in the transmigration of souls (*samsara*) in a neverending cycle of rebirth has been Hinduism's most distinctive and important contribution to Indian culture. The earliest reference is in one of the *Upanishads*, around the seventh century BC, at about the same time as the doctrine of *karma* made its first appearance.

Ahimsa AL Basham pointed out that belief in transmigration must have encouraged a further distinctive doctrine, that of non-violence or non-injury – *ahimsa*. The belief in rebirth meant that all living things and creatures of the spirit possessed the same essential soul. One inscription threatens that anyone who interferes with the rights of Brahmins to land given to them by the king will 'suffer rebirth for 80,000 years as a worm in dung'. Belief in the cycle of rebirth was essential to give such a threat any weight!

Schools of philosophy

It is common now to talk of six major schools of Hindu philosophy. *Nyaya, Vaisheshika, Sankhya, Yoga, Purvamimansa* and *Vedanta*.

Yoga Yoga can be traced back to at least the third century AD. It seeks a synthesis of the spirit, the soul and the flesh and is concerned with systems of meditation and

Karma – an eye to the future

According to the doctrine of karma, every person, animal or god has a being or 'self' which has existed without beginning. Every action, except those that are done without any consideration of the results, leaves an indelible mark on that Self, carried forward into the next life.

The overall character of the imprint on each person's Self determines three features of the next life: the nature of his next birth (animal, human or god), the kind of family he will be born into if human and the length of the next life. Finally, it controls the good or bad experiences that the self will experience. However, it does not imply a fatalistic belief that the nature of action in this life is unimportant. Rather, it suggests that the path followed by the individual in the present life is vital to the nature of its next life and ultimately to the chance of gaining release from this world.

self denial that lead to the realization of the Divine within oneself and can ultimately release one from the cycle of rebirth.

Vedanta These are literally the final parts of the Vedic literature, the *Upanishads*. The basic texts also include the Brahmasutra of Badrayana, written about the first century AD and the most important of all, the *Bhagavad-Gita*, which is a part of the epic the *Mahabharata*. There are many interpretations of these basic texts. Three are given here.

Advaita Vedanta holds that there is no division between the cosmic force or principle, *Brahman* and the individual Self, *atman* (also referred to as 'soul'). The fact that we appear to see different and separate individuals is simply a result of ignorance. This is termed *maya* (illusion), but Vedanta philosophy does not suggest that the world in which we live is an illusion. *Jnana* (knowledge) is held as the key to understanding the full and real unity of Self and Brahman. **Shankaracharya**, born at Kalady in modern Kerala, in AD 6, is the best known Advaitin Hindu philosopher. He argued that there was no individual Self or soul separate from the creative force of the universe, or Brahman and that it was impossible to achieve liberation (*moksha*) through meditation and devotional worship, which he saw as signs of remaining on a lower level and of being unprepared for true liberation.

The 11-12th-century philosopher, **Ramanuja**, repudiated ideas of **Vishishtadvaita**. He transformed the idea of God from an impersonal force to a personal God and viewed both the Self and the World as real but only as part of the whole. In contrast to Shankaracharya's view, Ramanuja saw *bhakti* (devotion) as of central importance to achieving liberation and service to the Lord as the highest goal of life. **Dvaita Vedanta** was developed by the 14th-century philosopher, Madhva. He believed that Brahman, the Self and the World are completely distinct. Worship of God is a key means of achieving liberation.

Worship

Puja For most Hindus today, worship ('performing puja') is an integral part of their faith. The great majority of Hindu homes will have a shrine to one of the gods of the Hindu pantheon. Individuals and families will often visit shrines or temples and on special occasions will travel long distances to particularly holy places such as Benaras or Puri. Such sites may have temples dedicated to a major deity but may also have numerous other shrines in the vicinity dedicated to other favourite gods.

Acts of devotion are often aimed at the granting of favours and the meeting of urgent needs for this life – good health, finding a suitable wife or husband, the birth of a son, prosperity and good fortune. Puja involves making an offering to God and *darshan* (having a view of the deity). Hindu worship is generally, though not always, an act performed by individuals. Thus Hindu temples may be little more than a shrine on a river bank or in the middle of the street, tended by a priest and visited at special times when a darshan of the resident God can be obtained. When it has been consecrated, the image, if exactly made, becomes the channel for the godhead to work.

Holy places Certain rivers and towns are particularly sacred to Hindus. Thus there are seven holy rivers – the Ganga, Yamuna,.Indus and mythical Sarasvati in the north and the Narmada, Godavari and Kaveri in the Peninsula. There are also seven holy places – Haridwar, Mathura, Ayodhya and Varanasi, again in the north, Ujjain, Dwarka and Kanchipuram to the south. In addition to these seven holy places there are four holy abodes: Badrinath, Puri and Ramesvaram, with Dwarka in modern Gujarat having the unique distinction of being both a holy abode and a holy place.

Rituals and festivals The temple rituals often follow through the cycle of day and night, as well as yearly lifecycles. The priests may wake the deity from sleep, bathe, clothe and feed it. Worshippers will be invited to share by bringing offerings of clothes and food. Gifts of money will usually be made and in some temples there is a charge levied for taking up positions in front of the deity in order to obtain a darshan at the appropriate times.

Every temple has its special festivals. At festival times you can see villagers walking in small groups, brightly dressed and often high spirited, sometimes as far as 80-100 km.

Hindu deities

Today three Gods are widely seen as all-powerful: Brahma, Vishnu and Siva. While Brahma is regarded as the ultimate source of creation, Siva also has a creative role alongside his function as destroyer. Vishnu in contrast is seen as the preserver or protector of the universe. Vishnu and Siva are widely represented and have come to be seen as the most powerful and important. Their followers are referred to as Vaishnavite and Shaivites respectively and numerically they form the two largest sects in India.

Brahma Popularly Brahma is interpreted as the Creator in a trinity, alongside Vishnu as Preserver and Siva as Destroyer. In the literal sense the name Brahma is the masculine and personalized form of the neuter word Brahman.

In the early Vedic writing, *Brahman* represented the universal and impersonal principle which governed the Universe. Gradually, as Vedic philosophy moved towards a monotheistic interpretation of the universe and its origins, this impersonal power was increasingly personalized. In the *Upanishads*, Brahman was seen as a universal and elemental creative spirit. Brahma, described in early myths as having been born from a golden egg and then to have created the Earth, assumed the identity of the earlier Vedic deity Prajapati and became identified as the creator.

By the fourth and fifth centuries AD, the height of the classical period of Hinduism, Brahma was seen as one of the trinity of Gods – *Trimurti* – in which Vishnu, Siva and Brahma represented three forms of the unmanifested supreme being. It is from Brahma that Hindu cosmology takes its structure. The basic cycle through which the whole cosmos passes is described as one day in the life of Brahma – the *kalpa*. It equals 4320 million years, with an equally long night. One year of Brahma's life – a cosmic year – lasts 360 days and nights. The universe is expected to last for 100 years of Brahma's life, who is currently believed to be 51 years old.

By the sixth century AD Brahma worship had effectively ceased (before the great period of temple building), which accounts for the fact that there are remarkably few temples dedicated to Brahma. Nonetheless images of Brahma are found in most temples. Characteristically he is shown with four faces, a fifth having been destroyed by the fire from Siva's third eye. In his four arms he usually holds a copy of the Vedas, a sceptre and a water jug or a bow. He is accompanied by the goose, symbolizing knowledge.

Sarasvati Seen by some Hindus as the 'active power' of Brahma, popularly thought of as his consort, Sarasvati has survived into the modern Hindu world as a far more important figure than Brahma himself. In popular worship Sarasvati represents the goddess of education and learning, worshipped in schools and colleges with gifts of fruit, flowers and incense. She represents 'the word' itself, which began to be deified as part of the process of the writing of the Vedas, which ascribed magical power to words. The development of her identity represented the rebirth of the concept of a mother goddess, which had been strong in the Indus Valley Civilization over 1000 years before and may have been continued in popular ideas through the worship of female spirits.

In addition to her role as Brahma's wife, Sarasvati is also variously seen as the wife of Vishnu and Manu or as Daksha's daughter, among other interpretations. Normally white coloured, riding on a swan and carrying a book, she is often shown playing a vina. She may have many arms and heads, representing her role as patron of all the sciences and arts.

Vishnu Vishnu is seen as the God with the human face. From the second century a new and passionate devotional worship of Vishnu's incarnation as Krishna developed in the South. By 1000 AD Vaishnavism had spread across South India and it became closely associated with the devotional form of Hinduism preached by **Ramanuja**, whose followers spread the worship of Vishnu and his 10 successive incarnations in animal and human form. For Vaishnavites, God took these different forms in order to save the world from impending disaster. AL Basham has summarized the 10 incarnations (see table, page 538).

Rama and Krishna By far the most influential incarnations of Vishnu are those in which he was believed to take recognizable human form, especially as Rama

Hindu deities

Deity	Association	Relationship
Brahma	Creator	One of Trinity
Sarasvati	Education and culture, "the word"	Wife of Brahma
Siva	Creator/destroyer	One of Trinity
Bhairava	Fierce aspect of Siva	
Parvati (Uma)	Benevolent aspect of female divine power	Consort of Siva, mother of Ganesh
Kali	The energy that destroys evil	Consort of Siva
Durga	In fighting attitude	Consort of Siva
Ganesh/ Ganapati	God of good beginnings, clearer of obstacles	Son of Siva
Skanda	God of War/bringer of disease (Karttikkeya, Murugan, Subrahmanya)	Son of Siva and Ganga
Vishnu	Preserver	One of Trinity
Prithvi/ Bhudevi	Goddess of Earth	Wife of Vishnu
Lakshmi	Goddess of Wealth	Wife of Vishnu
Agni	God of Fire	
Indra	Rain, lightning and thunder	
Ravana	King of the demons	

(twice) and Krishna. As the Prince of Ayodhya, history and myth blend, for Rama was probably a chief who lived in the eighth or seventh century BC. Although Rama is now seen as an earlier incarnation of Vishnu than Krishna, he came to be regarded as divine very late, probably after the Muslim invasions of the 12th century AD. Rama (or Ram, pronounced to rhyme with *calm*) is a powerful figure in contemporary India. His supposed birthplace at Ayodhya became the focus of fierce disputes between Hindus and Muslims in the early 1990s which continue today. Krishna is worshipped extremely widely as perhaps the most human of the gods. His advice on the battlefield of the *Mahabharata* is one of the major sources of guidance for the rules of daily living for many Hindus today.

Lakshmi Commonly represented as Vishnu's wife, Lakshmi is widely worshipped as the goddess of wealth. Earlier representations of Vishnu's consorts portrayed her as Sridevi, often shown in statues on Vishnu's right, while Bhudevi, also known as Prithvi, who represented the earth, was on his left. Lakshmi is popularly shown

Attributes	Vehicle
4 heads, 4 arms, upper left holds water pot and rosary or sacrificial spoon, sacred thread across left shoulder	Hamsa – goose/swan
Two or more arms, vina, lotus, plam leaves, rosary	Hamsa
Linga; Rudra, matted hair, 3 eyes, drum, fire, deer, trident; Nataraja, Lord of the Dance	Nandi – bull
Trident, sword, noose, naked, snakes, garland of skulls, dishevelled hair, carrying destructive weapons	Dog
2 arms when shown with Siva, 4 when on her own, blue lily in right hand, left hand hangs down	Lion
Trident, noose, human skulls, sword, shield, black colour	Lion
4 arms, conch, disc, bow, arrow, bell, sword, shield	Lion or tiger
Goad, noose, broken tusk, fruits	Rat/mouse/ shrew
6 heads, 12 arms, spear, arrow, sword, discus, noose, cock, bow, shield, conch and plough	Peacock
4 arms, high crown, discus and conch in upper arms, club and sword (or lotus) in lower	Garuda – mythical eagle
Right hand in abhaya gesture, left holds pomegranate, left leg on treasure pot	
Seated/standing on red lotus, 4 hands, lotuses, vessel, fruit	Lotus
Sacred thread, axe, wood, bellows, torch, sacrificial spoon	2-headed ram
Bow, thunderbolt, lances	
10 heads, 20 arms, bow and arrow	

in her own right as standing on a lotus flower, although eight forms of Lakshmi are recognized.

Hanuman The *Ramayana* tells how Hanuman, Rama's faithful servant, went across India and finally into the demon Ravana's forest home of Lanka at the head of his monkey army in search of the abducted Sita. He used his powers to jump the sea separating India from Sri Lanka and managed after a series of heroic and magical feats to find and rescue his master's wife. Whatever form he is shown in, he remains almost instantly recognizable.

Siva Professor Wendy Doniger O'Flaherty argues that the key to the myths through which Siva's character is understood, lies in the explicit ambiguity of Siva as the great ascetic and at the same time as the erotic force of the universe.

Siva is interpreted as both creator and destroyer, the power through whom the universe evolves. He lives on Mount Kailasa with his wife **Parvati** (also known as **Uma**, **Sati**, **Kali** and **Durga**) and two sons, the elephant-headed Ganesh and the six-headed

Karttikeya, known in South India as Subrahmanya. In sculptural representations Siva is normally accompanied by his 'vehicle', the bull (*Nandi* or *Nandin*).

Siva is also represented in Shaivite temples throughout India by the *linga*, literally meaning 'sign' or 'mark', but referring in this context to the sign of gender or phallus and *yoni*. On the one hand a symbol of energy, fertility and potency, as Siva's symbol it also represents the yogic power of sexual abstinence and penance. The *linga* is now the most important symbol of the cult of Siva. O'Flaherty suggests that the worship of the *linga* of Siva can be traced back to the pre-Vedic societies of the Indus Valley civilization (circa 2000 BC), but that it first appears in Hindu iconography in the second century BC. From that time a wide variety of myths appeared to explain the origin of *linga* worship. The myths surrounding the 12 **jyotirlinga** (*linga* of light) found at centres like Ujjain go back to the second century BC and were developed to explain and justify *linga* worship.

Siva's alternative names Although Siva is not seen as having a series of rebirths, like Vishnu, he none the less appears in very many forms representing different aspects of his varied powers. Some of the more common are: **Chandrasekhara** – the moon (*chandra*) symbolizes the powers of creation and destruction. **Mahadeva** – the representation of Siva as the god of supreme power, which came relatively late into Hindu thought, shown as the *linga* in combination with the *yoni*, or female genitalia. **Nataraja** – the Lord of the Cosmic Dance. The story is based on a legend in which Siva and Vishnu went to the forest to overcome 10,000 heretics. In their anger the heretics attacked Siva first by sending a tiger, then a snake and thirdly a fierce black dwarf with a club. Siva killed the tiger, tamed the snake and wore it like a garland and then put his foot on the dwarf and performed a dance of such power that the dwarf and the heretics acknowledged Siva as the Lord. **Rudra** – Siva's early prototype, who may date back to the Indus Valley Civilization. **Virabhadra** – Siva created Virabhadra to avenge himself on his wife Sati's father, Daksha, who had insulted Siva by not inviting him to a special sacrifice. Sati attended the ceremony against Siva's wishes and when she heard her father grossly abusing Siva she committed suicide by jumping into the sacrificial fire. This act gave rise to the term *sati* (*suttee*, a word which simply means a good or virtuous woman). Recorded in the *Vedas*, the self immolation of a woman on her husband's funeral pyre probably did not become accepted practice until the early centuries BC. Even then it was mainly restricted to those of the Kshatriya caste. **Nandi** – Siva's vehicle, the bull, is one of the most widespread of sacred symbols of the ancient world and may represent a link with Rudra, who was sometimes represented as a bull in pre-Hindu India. Strength and virility are key attributes and pilgrims to Siva temples will often touch the Nandi's testicles on their way into the shrine.

Ganesh One of Hinduism's most popular gods, Ganesh is seen as the great clearer of obstacles. Shown at gateways and on door lintels with his elephant head and pot belly, his image is revered across India. Meetings, functions and special family gatherings will often start with prayers to Ganesh and any new venture, from the opening of a building to inaugurating a company, will not be deemed complete without a Ganesh *puja*.

Auspicious signs

Some of Hinduism's sacred symbols are thought to have originated in the Aryan religion of the Vedic period.

Om The Primordial sound of the universe, 'Om' (or more correctly the three-in-one 'Aum') is the Supreme syllable. It is the opening and sometimes closing, chant for Hindu prayers. Some attribute the three constituents to the Hindu triad of Brahma, Vishnu and Siva. It is believed to be the cosmic sound of Creation which encompasses all states from wakefulness to deep sleep and though it is the essence of all sound, it is outside our hearing.

Svastika Representing the Sun and it's energy, the svastika usually appears on doors or walls of temples, in red, the colour associated with good fortune and luck. The term, derived from the Sanskrit 'svasti', is repeated in Hindu chants. The arms of the symbol point in the cardinal directions which may reflect the ancient practice of lighting fire sticks in the four directions. When the svastika appears to rotate clockwise it symbolizes the positive creative energy of the sun; the anti-clockwise svastika, symbolizing the autumn/winter sun, is considered to be unlucky.

Six-pointed star The intersecting triangles in the 'Star of David' symbol represents Spirit and Matter held in balance. A central dot signifies a particle of Divinity. The star is incorporated as a decorative element in some Muslim buildings such as Humayun's Tomb in Delhi.

Lotus The 'padma' or 'kamal' flower with it's many petals appears not only in art and architecture but also in association with gods and godesses. Some deities are seen holding one, others are portrayed seated or standing on the flower, or as with Padmanabha it appears from Vishnu's navel. The lotus represents purity, peace and beauty, a symbol also shared by Buddhists and Jains and as in nature stands away and above the impure, murky water from which it emerges. In architecture, the lotus motif occurs frequently.

 Om

 Svastika

 Six-pointed star

 Lotus

Shakti, the Mother Goddess Shakti is a female divinity often worshipped in the form of Siva's wife Durga or Kali. As Durga she agreed to do battle with Mahish, an *asura* (demon) who threatened to dethrone the gods. Many sculptures and paintings illustrate the story in which, during the terrifying struggle which ensued, the demon changed into a buffalo, an elephant and a giant with 1000 arms. Durga, clutching weapons in each of her 10 hands, eventually emerges victorious. As Kali ('black') the mother goddess takes on her most fearsome form and character. Fighting with the chief of the demons, she was forced to use every weapon in her armoury, but every drop of blood that she drew became 1000 new giants just as strong as he. The only way she could win was by drinking the blood of all her enemies. Having succeeded she was so elated that her dance of triumph threatened the earth. Ignoring the pleas of the gods to stop, she even threw her husband Siva to the ground and trampled over him, until she realized to her shame what she had done. She is always shown with a sword in one hand, the severed head of the giant in another, two corpses for earrings and a necklace of human skulls. She is often shown standing with one foot on the body and the other on the leg of Siva.

The worship of female goddesses developed into the widely practised form of devotional worship called Tantrism. Goddesses such as Kali became the focus of worship which often involved practices that flew in the face of wider Hindu moral and legal codes. Animal and even human sacrifices and ritual sexual intercourse were part of Tantric belief and practice, the evidence for which may still be seen in the art and sculpture of some major temples. Tantric practice affected both Hinduism and Buddhism from the eighth century AD; its influence is shown vividly in the sculptures of Khajuraho and Konark and in the distinctive Hindu and Buddhist practices of the Kathmandu Valley in Nepal.

Skanda The God of War, Skanda (known as Murugan in Tamil Nadu and by other regional names) became known as the son of Siva and Parvati. One legend suggests that he was conceived by the Goddess Ganga from Siva's seed.

Gods of the warrior caste Modern Hinduism has brought into its pantheon over many generations gods who were worshipped by the earlier pre-Hindu Aryan civilizations. The most important is **Indra**, often shown as the god of rain, thunder and lightning. To the early Aryans, Indra destroyed demons in battle, the most important being his victory over Vritra, 'the Obstructor'. By this victory Indra released waters from the clouds, allowing the earth to become fertile. To the early Vedic writers the clouds of the southwest monsoon were seen as hostile, determined to keep their precious treasure of water to themselves and only releasing it when forced to by a greater power. Indra, carrying a bow in one hand, a thunderbolt in another and lances in the others and riding on his vehicle Airavata, the elephant, is thus the Lord of Heaven. His wife is the relatively insignificant **Indrani**. **Mitra** and **Varuna** have the power both of gods and demons. Their role is to sustain order, Mitra taking responsibility for friendship and Varuna for oaths and as they have to keep watch for 24 hours a day Mitra has become the god of the day or the sun, Varuna the god of the moon. **Agni**, the god of fire, is a god whose origins lie with the priestly caste rather than with the Kshatriyas, or warriors. He was seen in the Vedas as being born from the rubbing together of two pieces of dead wood and as Masson-Oursel writes "the poets marvel at the sight of a being so alive leaping from dry dead wood. His very growth is miraculous". Riding on a ram, wearing a sacred thread, he is often shown with flames leaping from his mouth and he carries an axe, wood, bellows or a fan, a torch and a sacrificial spoon, for he is the god of ritual fire. The juice of the soma plant, the nectar of the gods guaranteeing eternal life, **Soma** is also a deity taking many forms. Born from the churning of the ocean of milk in later stories Soma was identified with the moon. The golden haired and golden skinned god **Savitri** is an intermediary with the great power to forgive sin and as king of heaven he gives the gods their immortality. **Surya**, the god of the sun, fittingly of overpowering splendour is often described as being dark red, sitting on a red lotus or riding a chariot pulled by the seven horses of the dawn (representing the days of the week). **Usha**, sometimes referred to as Surya's wife, is the goddess of the dawn, daughter of Heaven and sister of the night. She rides in a chariot drawn by cows or horses.

Devas and Asuras In Hindu popular mythology the world is also populated by innumerable gods and demons, with a somewhat uncertain dividing line between them. Both have great power and moral character and there are frequent conflicts and battles between them. The **Rakshasas** form another category of semi-divine beings devoted to performing magic. Although they are not themselves evil, they are destined to cause havoc and evil in the real world. The multiple-hooded cobra head often seen in sculptures represents the fabulous snake gods the **Nagas**, though they may often be shown in other forms, even human. In South India it is particularly common to find statues of divine Nagas being worshipped. They are usually placed on uncultivated ground under trees in the hope and belief, as Masson-Oursel puts it, that "if the snakes have their own domain left to them they are more likely to spare human beings". The Nagas and their wives, the **Naginis**, are often the agents of death in mythical stories.

Hindu society

Dharma Dharma is seen as the most important of the objectives of individual and social life. But what were the obligations imposed by dharma? Hindu law givers, such as those who compiled the code of Manu (AD 100-300), laid down rules of family conduct and social obligations related to the institutions of caste and jati which were beginning to take shape at the same time.

Caste Although the word caste was given by the Portuguese in the 15th century AD, the main feature of the system emerged at the end of the Vedic period. Two terms – varna and jati – are used in India itself and have come to be used interchangeably and confusingly with the word caste.

Varna, which literally means colour, had a fourfold division. By 600 BC this had become a standard means of classifying the population. The fair-skinned Aryans distinguished themselves from the darker skinned earlier inhabitants. The priestly varna, the Brahmins, were seen as coming from the mouth of Brahma; the Kshatriyas (or Rajputs as they are commonly called in northwest India) were warriors, coming from Brahma's arms; the Vaishyas, a trading community, came from Brahma's thighs and the Sudras, classified as agriculturalists, from his feet. Relegated beyond civilized Hindu society were the untouchables or outcastes, who were left with the jobs which were regarded as impure, usually associated with dealing with the dead (human or animal) or with excrement.

Many Brahmins and Rajputs are conscious of their varna status, but the great majority of Indians do not put themselves into one of the four varna categories, but into a **jati** group. There are thousands of different jatis across the country. None of the groups regard themselves as equal in status to any other, but all are part of local or regional hierarchies. These are not organized in any institutional sense and traditionally there was no formal record of caste status. While individuals found it impossible to change caste or to move up the social scale, groups would sometimes try to gain recognition as higher caste by adopting practices of the Brahmins such as becoming vegetarians. Many used to be identified with particular activities and occupations used to be hereditary. Caste membership is decided by birth. Although you can be evicted from your caste by your fellow members, usually for disobedience to caste rules such as over marriage, you cannot join another caste and technically you become an outcaste.

Right up until Independence in 1947 such punishment was a drastic penalty for disobeying one's dharmic duty. In many areas all avenues into normal life could be blocked, families would disregard outcaste members and it could even be impossible for the outcaste to continue to work within the locality.

Gandhi spearheaded his campaign for independence from British colonial rule with a powerful campaign to abolish the disabilities imposed by the caste system. Coining the term *Harijan* (meaning 'person of God'), which he gave to all former outcastes, Gandhi demanded that discrimination on the grounds of caste be outlawed. Lists – or 'schedules' – of backward castes were drawn up during the early part of this century in order to provide positive help to such groups. The term itself has now been widely rejected by many former outcastes as paternalistic and as implying an adherence to Hindu beliefs (Hari being a Hindu deity) which some explicitly reject and today the use of the secular term **'dalits'** – the 'oppressed' has been adopted in its place. There are several websites devoted to dalit issues, including www.dalits.org.

Marriage, which is still generally arranged by members of all religious communities, continues to be dictated almost entirely by caste and clan rules. Even in cities, where traditional means of arranging marriages have often broken down and where many people resort to advertising for marriage partners in the columns of the Sunday newspapers, caste is frequently stated as a requirement. Marriage is mainly seen as an alliance between two families. Great efforts are made to match caste, social status and economic position, although rules governing eligibility vary from region to region. In some groups marriage between first cousins is common, while among others marriage between any branch of the same clan is strictly prohibited.

Hindu reform movements

In the 19th-century English education and European literature and modern scientific thought, alongside the religious ideas of Christian missionaries, all became powerful influences on the newly emerging Western-educated Hindu opinion. That opinion was challenged to re-examine inherited Hindu beliefs and practice.

Some reform movements have had regional importance. Two of these originated, like the **Brahmo Samaj**, in Bengal. The **Ramakrishna Mission** was named after a temple priest in the Kali temple in Calcutta, Ramakrishna (1834-1886), who was a great mystic, preaching the basic doctrine that 'all religions are true'. He believed that the best religion for any individual was that into which he or she was born. One of his followers, **Vivekananda**, became the founder of the Ramakrishna Mission, which has been an important vehicle of social and religious reform, notably in Bengal.

Aurobindo Ghosh (1872-1950) links the great reformers from the 19th century with the post-Independence period. Educated in English – and for 14 years in England itself – he developed the idea of India as 'the Mother', a concept linked with the pre-Hindu idea of Shakti, or the Mother Goddess. For him 'nationalism was religion'. After imprisonment in 1908 he retired to Pondicherry, where his ashram became a focus of an Indian and international movement, see page 105.

The Hindu calendar While for its secular life India follows the Gregorian calendar, for Hindus, much of religious and personal life follows the Hindu calendar (see also Festivals, page 17). This is based on the lunar cycle of 29 days, but the clever bit comes in the way it is synchronized with the 365-day Gregorian solar calendar of the west by the addition of an 'extra month' (*adhik maas*), every 2½ to three years.

Hindus follow two distinct eras. The *Vikrama Samvat*, which began in 57 BC (and is followed in Goa), and the *Salivahan Saka* which dates from AD 78 and has been the official Indian calendar since 1957. The *Saka* new year starts on 22 March and has the same length as the Gregorian calendar. In most of South India (except Tamil Nadu) the New Year is celebrated in the first month, *Chaitra* (corresponding to March-April). In North India (and Tamil Nadu) it is celebrated in the second month of *Vaisakh*.

The year itself is divided into two, the first six solar months being when the sun 'moves' north, known as the *Makar Sankranti* (which is marked by special festivals), and the second half when it moves south, the *Karka Sankranti*. The first begins in January and the second in June. The 29-day lunar month with its 'dark' (*Krishna*) and 'bright' (*Shukla*) halves, based on the new (*Amavasya*) and full moons (*Purnima*), are named after the 12 constellations, and total a 354-day year. The day itself is divided into eight *praharas* of three hours each and the year into six seasons: *Vasant* (spring), *Grishha* (summer), *Varsha* (rains), *Sharat* (early autumn), *Hemanta* (late autumn), *Shishir* (winter).

Hindu and corresponding Gregorian calendar months:

Chaitra	March-April	*Ashwin*	September-October
Vaishakh	April-May	*Kartik*	October-November
Jyeshtha	May-June	*Margashirsh*	November-December
Aashadh	June-July	*Poush*	December-January
Shravan	July-August	*Magh*	January-February
Bhadra	August-September	*Phalgun*	February-March

Islam

Even after partition in 1947 over 40 million Muslims remained in India and today there are around 120 million. Islamic contact with India was first made around AD 636 and then by the navies of the Arab Mohammad al Qasim in AD 710-712. These conquerors of Sindh made very few converts, although they did have to develop a legal recognition for the status of non-Muslims in a Muslim-ruled state. From the creation of the Delhi Sultanate in 1206, by Turkish rather than Arab power, Islam became a permanent living religion in India.

The victory of the Turkish ruler of Ghazni over the Rajputs in AD 1192 established a 500-year period of Muslim power in India. By AD 1200 the Turkish sultans had annexed Bihar in the east, in the process wiping out the last traces of Buddhism with the massacre of a Buddhist monastic order, sacked Varanasi and captured Gwalior. Within 30 years Bengal had been added to the Turkish empire and by AD 1311 a new Turkish dynasty, the Khaljis, had extended the power of the Delhi Sultanate to the doors of Madurai.

The early Muslim rulers looked to the Turkish ruling class and to the Arab caliphs for their legitimacy and to the Turkish elite for their cultural authority. From the middle of the 13th century, when the Mongols crushed the Arab caliphate, the Delhi sultans were left on their own to exercise Islamic authority in India. From then onwards the main external influences were from Persia. Small numbers of migrants, mainly the skilled and the educated, continued to flow into the Indian courts. Periodically their numbers were augmented by refugees from Mongol repression in the regions to India's northwest as the Delhi Sultanate provided a refuge for craftsmen and artists from the territories the Mongols had conquered from Lahore westwards.

Muslim populations Muslims only became a majority of the South Asian population in the plains of the Indus and west Punjab and in parts of Bengal. Elsewhere they formed important minorities, notably in the towns of the central heartland such as Lucknow. The concentration at the east and west ends of the Ganga valley reflected the policies pursued by successive Muslim rulers of colonizing forested and previously uncultivated land. In the central plains there was already a densely populated, Hindu region, where little attempt was made to achieve converts.

The Mughals wanted to expand their territory and their economic base. To pursue this they made enormous grants of land to those who had served the empire and particularly in Bengal, new land was brought into cultivation. At the same time, shrines were established to Sufi saints who attracted peasant farmers. The mosques built in East Bengal were the centres of devotional worship where saints were venerated. By the 18th century many Muslims had joined the **Sunni** sect of Islam. The characteristics of Islamic practice in both these regions continues to reflect this background.

In some areas Muslim society shared many of the characteristic features of the Hindu society from which the majority of them came. Many of the Muslim migrants from Iran or Turkey, the élite **Ashraf** communities, continued to identify with the Islamic elites from which they traced their descent. They held high military and civil posts in imperial service. In sharp contrast, many of the non-Ashraf Muslim

The five pillars of Islam

In addition to the belief that there is one God and that Mohammed is his prophet, there are four requirements imposed on Muslims. Daily prayers are prescribed at daybreak, noon, afternoon, sunset and nightfall. Muslims must give alms to the poor. They must observe a strict fast during Ramadan (no eating or drinking from sunrise to sunset). Lastly, they should attempt the pilgrimage to the Ka'aba in Mecca, known as the Hajj. Those who have done so are entitled to the prefix Hajji before their name.

Islamic rules differ from Hindu practice in several other aspects of daily life. Muslims are strictly forbidden to drink alcohol (though some suggest that this prohibition is restricted to the use of fermented grape juice, that is wine, it is commonly accepted to apply to all alcohol). Eating pork, or any meat from an animal not killed by draining its blood while alive, is also prohibited. Meat prepared in the appropriate way is called *halal*. Finally, usury (charging interest on loans) and games of chance are forbidden.

communities in the towns and cities were organized in social groups very much like the *jatis* of their neighbouring Hindu communities. While the elites followed Islamic practices close to those based on the Qur'an as interpreted by scholars, the poorer, less literate communities followed devotional and pietistic forms of Islam.

Muslim beliefs The beliefs of Islam (which means 'submission to God') could apparently scarcely be more different from those of Hinduism. Islam, often described as having 'five pillars' of faith (see box, above) has a fundamental creed: 'There is no God but God; and Mohammad is the Prophet of God' (*La Illaha illa 'Ilah Mohammad Rasulu 'Ilah*). One book, the *Qur'an*, is the supreme authority on Islamic teaching and faith. Islam preaches the belief in bodily resurrection after death and in the reality of heaven and hell.

The idea of heaven as paradise is pre-Islamic. Alexander the Great is believed to have brought the word into Greek from Persia, where he used it to describe the walled Persian gardens that were found even three centuries before the birth of Christ. For Muslims, Paradise is believed to be filled with sensuous delights and pleasures, while hell is a place of eternal terror and torture, which is the certain fate of all who deny the unity of God.

Islam has no priesthood. The authority of Imams derives from social custom and from their authority to interpret the scriptures, rather than from a defined status within the Islamic community. Islam also prohibits any distinction on the basis of race or colour and most Muslims believe it is wrong to represent the human figure. It is often thought, inaccurately, that this ban stems from the Qur'an itself. In fact it probably has its origins in the belief of Mohammad that images were likely to be turned into idols.

Muslim sects During the first century after Mohammad's death Islam split in to two sects which were divided on political and religious grounds, the Shi'is and Sunni's. The religious basis for the division lay in the interpretation of verses in the Qur'an and of traditional sayings of Mohammad, the Hadis. Both sects venerate the Qur'an but have different *Hadis*. They also have different views as to Mohammad's successor.

The Sunnis believe that Mohammad did not appoint a successor and that Abu Bak'r, Omar and Othman were the first three caliphs (or vice-regents) after Mohammad's death. Ali, whom the Sunni's count as the fourth caliph, is regarded as the first legitimate caliph by the Shi'is, who consider Abu Bak'r and Omar to be usurpers. While the Sunni's believe in the principle of election of caliphs, Shi'is believe that although Mohammad is the last prophet there is a continuing need for intermediaries between God and man. Such intermediaries are termed Imams and they base both their law and religious practice on the teaching of the Imams.

Akbar, the most eclectic of Mughal emperors, went as far as banning activities like cow slaughter which were offensive to Hindus and celebrated Hindu festivals in court. In contrast, the later Mughal Emperor, Aurangzeb, pursued a far more hostile approach to Hindus and Hinduism, trying to point up the distinctiveness of Islam and denying the validity of Hindu religious beliefs. That attitude generally became stronger in the 20th century, related to the growing sense of the Muslim's minority position within South Asia and the fear of being subjected to Hindu rule.

The Islamic calendar The calendar begins on AD 16 July 622, the date of the Prophet's migration from Mecca to Medina, the Hijra, hence AH (Anno Hejirae). *Murray's Handbook for travellers in India* gave a wonderfully precise method of calculating the current date in the Christian year from the AH date: "To correlate the Hijra year with the Christian year, express the former in years and decimals of a year, multiply by .970225, add 621.54 and the total will correspond exactly with the Christian year." The Muslim year is divided into 12 lunar months, totalling 354 or 355 days, hence Islamic festivals usually move 11 days earlier each year according to the solar (Gregorian) calendar. The first month of the year is *Moharram*, followed by *Safar, Rabi-ul-Awwal, Rabi-ul-Sani, Jumada-ul-Awwal, Jumada-ul-Sani, Rajab, Shaban, Ramadan, Shawwal, Ziquad* and *Zilhaj*.

Buddhism

India was the home of Buddhism, which had its roots in the early Hinduism, or Brahmanism, of its time. Today it is practised only on the margins of the subcontinent, from Ladakh, Nepal and Bhutan in the north to Sri Lanka in the south, where it is the religion of the majority Sinhalese community. Most are very recent converts, the last adherents of the early schools of Buddhism having been killed or converted by the Muslim invaders of the 13th century. However, India's Buddhist significance is now mainly as the home for the extraordinarily beautiful artistic and architectural remnants of what was for several centuries the region's dominant religion.

India has sites of great significance for Buddhists. Some say that the Buddha himself spoke of the four places his followers should visit. **Lumbini**, the Buddha's birthplace, is in the Nepali foothills, near the present border with India. **Bodh Gaya**, where he attained what Buddhists term his 'supreme enlightenment', is about 80 km south of the modern Indian city of Patna; the deer park at **Sarnath**,

The Buddha's Four Noble Truths

The Buddha preached Four Noble Truths: that life is painful; that suffering is caused by ignorance and desire; that beyond the suffering of life there is a state which cannot be described but which he termed nirvana; and that nirvana can be reached by following an eightfold path.

The concept of nirvana is often understood in the West in an entirely negative sense – that of 'non-being'.

The word has the rough meaning of 'blow out', meaning to blow out the fires of greed, lust and desire. In a more positive sense it has been described by one Buddhist scholar as "the state of absolute illumination, supreme bliss, infinite love and compassion, unshakeable serenity and unrestricted spiritual freedom". The essential elements of the eightfold path are the perfection of wisdom, morality and meditation.

where he preached his first sermon and set in motion the Wheel of the Law, is just outside Varanasi; and **Kushinagara**, where he died at the age of 80, is 50 km east of Gorakhpur. There were four other sacred places of pilgrimage – **Rajgir**, where he tamed a wild elephant; **Vaishali**, where a monkey offered him honey; **Sravasti**, associated with his great miracle; and **Sankasya**, where he descended from heaven. The eight significant events associated with the holy places are repeatedly represented in Buddhist art.

In addition there are remarkable monuments, sculptures and works of art, from Gandhara in modern Pakistan to Sanchi and Ajanta in central India, where it is still possible to see the vivid evidence of the flowering of Buddhist culture in South Asia. In Sri Lanka, Bhutan and Nepal the traditions remain alive.

The Buddha's Life Siddharta Gautama, who came to be given the title of the Buddha – the Enlightened One – was born a prince into the warrior caste in about 563 BC. He was married at the age of 16 and his wife had a son. When he reached the age of 29 he left home and wandered as a beggar and ascetic. After about six years he spent some time in Bodh Gaya. Sitting under the Bo tree, meditating, he was tempted by the demon Mara, with all the desires of the world. Resisting these temptations, he received enlightenment. These scenes are common motifs of Buddhist art. The next landmark was the preaching of his first sermon on 'The Foundation of Righteousness' in the deer park near Benaras. By the time he died the Buddha had established a small band of monks and nuns known as the *Sangha* and had followers across North India. His body was cremated and the ashes, regarded as precious relics, were divided among the peoples to whom he had preached. Some have been discovered as far west as Peshawar, in Pakistan and at Piprawa, close to his birthplace. From the Buddha's death, or *parinirvana*, to the destruction of Nalanda (the last Buddhist stronghold in India) in AD 1197, Buddhism in India went through three phases. These are often referred to as Hinayana, Mahayana and Vajrayana, though they were not mutually exclusive, being followed simultaneously in different regions.

Hinayana The Hinayana or Lesser Way insists on a monastic way of life as the only path to the personal goal of *nirvana*, see box, page 549, achieved through an austere life. Divided into many schools, the only surviving Hinayana tradition is the **Theravada Buddhism**, which was taken to Sri Lanka by the Emperor Asoka's son Mahinda, where it became the state religion, and spread to southeast Asia as practised in Thailand, Myanmar, Cambodia and Laos today. Suffering, sorrow and dissatisfaction are the nature of ordinary life and can only be eliminated by giving up desire. In turn, desire is a result of the misplaced belief in the reality of individual existence. Theravada Buddhism taught that there is no soul and ultimately no God. *Nirvana* is a state of rest beyond the universe, once found never lost.

Mahayana In contrast to the Hinayana schools, the followers of the Mahayana school (the Great Way) believed in the possibility of salvation for all. They practised a far more devotional form of meditation and new figures came to play a prominent part in their beliefs and their worship – the **Bodhisattvas**, saints who were predestined to reach the state of enlightenment through thousands of rebirths. They aspired to Buddhahood not for their own sake but for the sake of all living things. The Buddha is believed to have passed through numerous existences in preparation for his final mission. Mahayana Buddhism became dominant over most of South Asia and its influence is evidenced in Buddhist art from Gandhara in north Pakistan to Ajanta in Central India and Sigiriya in Sri Lanka.

Vajrayana A new branch of Buddhism, Vajrayana, or the Vehicle of the Thunder bold, appeared which began to lay stress on secret magical rituals and cults of female divinities. This new 'Diamond Way' adopted the practice of magic, yoga and meditation. It became associated with secret ceremonies, chanting of mystical 'mantras' and taking part in orgiastic rituals in the cause of spiritual gain in order to help others. The ideal of Vajrayana Buddhists is to be 'so fully in harmony with the cosmos as to be able to manipulate the cosmic forces within and outside himself'. It had developed in the north of India by the seventh century AD, matching the parallel growth of Hindu Tantrism. The magical power associated with Vajrayana requires instruction from a teacher or *lama*, hence the Tibetan form is sometimes referred to as 'Lamaistic'.

Buddhist beliefs Buddhism is based on the Buddha's own preaching. However, when he died none of those teachings had been written down. He developed his beliefs in reaction to the Brahmanism of his time, rejecting several of the doctrines of Vedic religion which were widely held in his lifetime: the Vedic gods, scriptures and priesthood and all social distinctions based on caste. However, he did accept the belief in the cyclical nature of life and that the nature of an individual's existence is determined by a natural process of reward and punishment for deeds in previous lives – the Hindu doctrine of karma, see pages 534 and 535. In the Buddha's view, though, there is no eternal soul. He denied the identification of the Self with the everchanging Mind-Body (here, some see parallels in the Advaita Vedanta philosophy of Self-*Brahman* in Hinduism). In Buddhism, *Anatta* (no-Self) overcame the egoistical Self, given to attachment and selfishness. Following the Buddha's death a succession of councils was called to try and reach agreement on doctrine. The first three were held within 140 years of the Buddha's death, the fourth being held at Pataliputra (modern Patna) during the reign of the Emperor Asoka (272-232 BC), who had recently been converted to Buddhism. Under his reign Buddhism spread throughout South Asia and opened the routes through Northwest India for Buddhism to travel into China, where it had become a force by the first century AD.

Buddhism's decline The decline of Buddhism in India probably stemmed as much from the growing similarity in the practice of Hinduism and Buddhism as from direct attacks. Mahayana Buddhism, with its reverence for Bodhisattvas and its devotional character, was increasingly difficult to distinguish from the revivalist Hinduism characteristic of several parts of North India from the seventh to the 12th centuries AD. The Muslim conquest dealt the final blow, as it was also accompanied by the large scale slaughter of monks as well as the destruction of monasteries. Without their institutional support Buddhism faded away.

Jainism

Like Buddhism, Jainism started as a reform movement of the Brahmanic religious beliefs of the sixth century BC. Its founder was a widely revered saint and ascetic, Vardhamma, who became known as **Mahavir** – 'great hero'. Mahavir was born in the same border region of India and Nepal as the Buddha, just 50 km north of modern Patna, probably in 599 BC. Thus he was about 35 years older than the Buddha. His family, also royal, were followers of an ascetic saint, Parsvanatha, who according to Jain tradition had lived 200 years previously.

Mahavir's life story is embellished with legends, but there is no doubt that he left his royal home for a life of the strict ascetic. He is believed to have received enlightenment after 12 years of rigorous hardship, penance and meditation. Afterwards he travelled and preached for 30 years, stopping only in the rainy season. He died aged 72 in 527 BC. His death was commemorated by a special lamp festival in the region of Bihar, which Jains claim is the basis of the now-common Hindu festival of lights, Diwali.

Unlike Buddhism, Jainism never spread beyond India, but it has survived continuously into modern India, claiming four million adherents. In part this may be because Jain beliefs have much in common with puritanical forms of Hinduism and are greatly respected and admired. Some Jain ideas, such as vegetarianism and reverence for all life, are widely recognized by Hindus as highly commendable, even by those who do not share other Jain beliefs. The value Jains place on non-violence has contributed to their importance in business and commerce, as they regard nearly all occupations except banking and commerce as violent. The 18-m-high free-standing statue of Gommateshvara at Sravana Belgola near Mysore (built about AD 983) is just one outstanding example of the contribution of Jain art to India's heritage.

Jain beliefs Jains (from the word Jina, literally meaning 'descendants of conquerors') believe that there are two fundamental principles, the living (*jiva*) and the non-living (*ajiva*). The essence of Jain belief is that all life is sacred and that every living entity, even the smallest insect, has within it an indestructible and immortal

The Jain spiritual journey

The two Jain sects differ chiefly on the nature of proper ascetic practices. The Svetambara monks wear white robes and carry a staff, some wooden pots and a woollen mop for sweeping the path in front of them, wool being the softest material available and the least likely to hurt any living thing swept away. The highest level of Digambara monks will go completely naked, although the lower levels will wear a covering over their genitalia. They carry a waterpot made of a gourd and peacock feathers to sweep the ground before they sit.

Jains believe that the spiritual journey of the soul is divided into 14 stages, moving from bondage and ignorance to the final destruction of all karma and the complete fulfilment of the soul. The object throughout is to prevent the addition of new karma to the soul, which comes mainly through passion and attachment to the world. Bearing the pains of the world cheerfully contributes to the destruction of karma.

soul. Jains developed the view of ahimsa – often translated as 'non-violence', but better perhaps as 'non-harming'. Ahimsa was the basis for the entire scheme of Jain values and ethics and alternative codes of practice were defined for householders and for ascetics.

The five vows may be taken both by monks and by lay people: not to harm any living beings (Jains must practise strict vegetarianism – and even some vegetables, such as potatoes and onions, are believed to have microscopic souls); to speak the truth; not to steal; to give up sexual relations and practice complete chastity; to give up all possessions – for the *Digambara* sect that includes clothes.

Celibacy is necessary to combat physical desire. Jains also regard the manner of dying as extremely important. Although suicide is deeply opposed, vows of fasting to death voluntarily may be regarded as earning merit in the proper context. Mahavir himself is believed to have died of self-starvation. The essence of all the rules is to avoid intentional injury, which is the worst of all sins. Like Hindus, the Jains believe in *karma*.

Jains have two main **sects**, whose origins can be traced back to the fourth century BC. The more numerous **Svetambaras** – the 'white clad' – concentrated more in eastern and western India, separated from the **Digambaras** – or 'sky-clad'– who often go naked. The Digambaras may well have been forced to move south by drought and famine in the northern region of the Deccan and they are now concentrated in the south of India.

Unlike Buddhists, Jains accept the idea of God, but not as a creator of the universe. They see him in the lives of the 24 **Tirthankaras** (prophets, or 'makers of fords' – a reference to their role in building crossing points for the spiritual journey over the river of life), or leaders of Jainism, whose lives are recounted in the Kalpsutra – the third century BC book of ritual for the Svetambaras. Mahavir is regarded as the last of these great spiritual leaders. Much Jain art details stories from these accounts and the Tirthankaras play a similar role for Jains as the Bodhisattvas do for Mahayana Buddhists. The first and most revered of the Tirthankaras, Adinatha, also known as Rishabnath, is widely represented in Jain temples.

Sikhism

Guru Nanak, the founder of the religion, was born just west of Lahore and grew up in what is now the Pakistani town of Sultanpur. His followers, the Sikhs (derived from the Sanskrit word for 'disciples'), form perhaps one of India's most recognizable groups. Beards and turbans give them a very distinctive presence and although they represent less than 2% of the population they are both politically and economically significant.

Sikh beliefs The first Guru, accepted the ideas of *samsara* – the cycle of rebirths – and *karma*, see pages 534 and 535, from Hinduism. However, Sikhism is unequivocal in its belief in the oneness of God, rejecting idolatry and any worship of objects or images. Guru Nanak believed that God is One, formless, eternal and beyond description.

Guru Nanak also fiercely opposed discrimination on the grounds of caste. He saw God as present everywhere, visible to anyone who cared to look and as essentially full of grace and compassion. Some of Guru Nanak's teachings are close to the ideas of the Benaras mystic **Kabir**, who, in common with the Muslim mystic sufis, believed in mystical union with God. Kabir's belief in the nature of God was matched by his view that man was deliberately blind and unwilling to recognize God's nature. He transformed the Hindu concept of *maya* into the belief that the values commonly held by the world were an illusion.

Guru Nanak preached that salvation depended on accepting the nature of God. If people recognized the true harmony of the divine order (*hookam*) they would be saved. Rejecting the prevailing Hindu belief that such harmony could be achieved by ascetic practices, he emphasized three actions: meditating on and repeating God's name (*naam*), 'giving' or charity (*daan*), and bathing (*isnaan*).

Many of the features now associated with Sikhism can be attributed to **Guru Gobind Singh**, who on 15 April 1699, started the new brotherhood called the *Khalsa* (meaning 'the pure', from the Persian word *khales*), an inner core of the faithful, accepted by baptism (*amrit*). The 'five ks' date from this period: *kesh* (uncut hair), the most important, followed by *kangha* (comb, usually of wood), *kirpan* (dagger or short sword), *kara* (steel bangle), and *kachh* (similar to 'boxer' shorts). The dagger and the shorts reflect military influence.

In addition to the compulsory 'five ks', the new code prohibited smoking, eating *halal* meat and sexual intercourse with Muslim women. These date from the 18th century, when the Sikhs were often in conflict with the Muslims. Other strict prohibitions include: idolatry, caste discrimination, hypocrisy and pilgrimage to Hindu sacred places. The Khalsa also explicitly forbade the seclusion of women, one of the common practices of Islam. It was only under the warrior king Ranjit Singh (1799-1838) that the idea of the Guru's presence in meetings of the Sikh community (the *Panth*) gave way to the now universally held belief in the total authority of the **Guru Granth**, the recorded words of the Guru in the scripture.

Sikh worship The meditative worship Guru Nanak commended is a part of the life of every devout Sikh today, who starts each day with private meditation and a recitation of the verses of Guru Nanak himself, the *Japji*. However, from the time of the third Guru, Sikhs have also worshipped as congregations in Gurudwaras ('gateways to the Guru'). The Golden Temple in Amritsar, built at the end of the 16th century, is the holiest site of Sikhism.

Christianity

There are about 23 million Christians in India. Christianity ranks third in terms of religious affiliation after Hinduism and Islam.

The great majority of the Protestant Christians in India are now members of the Church of South India, formed from the major Protestant denominations in 1947, or the Church of North India, which followed suit in 1970. Together they account for approximately half the total number of Christians. Roman Catholics make up the majority of the rest. Many of the church congregations, both in towns and villages, are active centres of Christian worship.

Origins Some of the churches owe their origin either to the modern missionary movement of the late 18th century onwards, or to the colonial presence of the European powers. However, Christians probably arrived in India during the first century after the birth of Christ. There is evidence that one of Christ's Apostles, Thomas, reached India in AD 52, only 20 years after Christ was crucified. He settled in Malabar and then expanded his missionary work to China. It is widely believed that he was martyred in Tamil Nadu on his return to India in AD 72 and is buried in Mylapore, in the suburbs of modern Chennai. St Thomas' Mount, a small rocky hill just north of Chennai airport, takes its name from him. Today there is still a church of Thomas Christians in Kerala.

The Syrian church Kerala was linked directly with the Middle East when Syrian Christians embarked on a major missionary movement in the sixth century AD. The Thomas Christians have forms of worship that show very strong influence of the Syrian church and they still retain a Syriac order of service. They remained a close-knit community, who have come to terms with the prevailing caste system by maintaining strict social rules very similar to those of the surrounding upper caste Hindus. They lived in an area restricted to what is now Kerala, where trade with the Middle East, which some centuries later was to bring Muslims to the same region, remained active.

Roman Catholicism The third major development took place with the arrival of the Portuguese. The Jesuit St Francis Xavier landed in Goa in 1542 and in 1557 Goa was made an Archbishopric, see page 423. Goa today bears testimony to the Portuguese influence on community life and church building. They set up the first printing press in India in 1566 and began to print books by the end of the 16th century.

Northern missions Protestant missions in Bengal from the end of the 18th century had a profound influence on cultural and religious development. On 9 November 1793 the Baptist missionary **William Carey** reached the Hugli River. Although he went to India to preach, he had wide-ranging interests, notably in languages and education and the work of 19th-century missions rapidly widened to cover educational and medical work as well. Converts were made most readily among the backward castes and in the tribal areas. The Christian populations of the tribal hill areas of Nagaland and Assam stem from such late 19th-century and 20th-century movements. But the influence of Christian missions in education and medical work was greater than as a proselytizing force. Education in Christian schools stimulated reformist movements in Hinduism itself and mission hospitals supplemented government-run hospitals, particularly in remote rural areas. Some of these Christian-run hospitals, such as that at Vellore, continue to provide high-class medical care.

Christian beliefs Christian theology had its roots in Judaism, with its belief in one God, the eternal Creator of the universe. Judaism saw the Jewish people as the vehicle for God's salvation, the 'chosen people of God' and pointed to a time when God would send his Saviour, or Messiah. Jesus, whom Christians believe was 'the Christ' or Messiah, was born in the village of Bethlehem, some 20 km south of Jerusalem. Very little is known of his early life except that he was brought up in a devout Jewish family. At the age of 29 or 30 he gathered a small group of followers and began to preach in the region between the Dead Sea and the Sea of Galilee. Two years later he was crucified in Jerusalem by the authorities on the charge of blasphemy – that he claimed to be the son of God.

Christians believe that all people live in a state of sin, in the sense that they are separated from God and fail to do his will. They believe that God is personal, 'like a father'. As God's son, Jesus accepted the cost of that separation and sinfulness himself through his death on the cross. Christians believe that Jesus was raised from the dead on the third day after he was crucified and that he appeared to his closest followers. They believe that his spirit continues to live today and that he makes it possible for people to come back to God.

The New Testament of the Bible, which, alongside the Old Testament, is the text to which Christians refer as the ultimate scriptural authority, consists of four 'Gospels' (meaning 'good news') and a series of letters by several early Christians referring to the nature of the Christian life.

Christian worship Although Christians are encouraged to worship individually as well as together, most forms of Christian worship centre on the gathering of the church congregation. Different denominations place varying emphases on the main elements of worship, but in most church services today the congregation will take part in singing hymns (songs of praise), prayers will be led by the minister, priest or a member of the congregation, readings from the Bible will be given and a sermon preached. For many Christians the most important service is the act of Holy Communion (Protestant) or Mass (Catholic) which celebrates the death and resurrection of Jesus in sharing bread and wine, which are held to represent Christ's body and blood given to save people from their sin.

Zoroastrianism

The first Zoroastrians arrived on the west coast of India in the mid-eighth century AD, forced out from their native Iran by persecution of the invading Islamic Arabs. Until 1477 they lost all contact with Iran and then for nearly 300 years maintained contact with Persian Zoroastrians through a continuous exchange of letters. They became known by their now much more familiar name, the **Parsis** (or Persians).

Although they are a tiny minority (approximately 100,000), even in the cities where they are concentrated, they have been a prominent economic and social influence, especially in West India. Parsis adopted Westernized customs and dress and took to the new economic opportunities that came with colonial industrialization. Families in West India such as the Tatas continue to be among India's leading industrialists, just part of a community that in recent generations has spread to Europe and north America.

Origins Zoroastrians trace their beliefs to the prophet Zarathustra, who lived in Northeast Iran around the seventh or sixth century BC. His place and even date of birth are uncertain, but he almost certainly enjoyed the patronage of the father of Darius the Great. The passage of Alexander the Great through Iran severely weakened support for Zoroastrianism, but between the sixth century BC and the seventh century AD it was the major religion of peoples living from North India to central Turkey. The spread of Islam reduced the number of Zoroastrians dramatically and forced those who did not retreat to the desert to emigrate.

Parsi beliefs The early development of Zoroastrianism marked a movement towards belief in a single God. **Ahura Mazda**, the Good Religion of God, was shown in rejecting evil and in purifying thought, word and action. Fire plays a central and symbolic part in Zoroastrian worship, representing the presence of God. There are eight Atash Bahram – major fire temples – in India; four are in Mumbai, two in Surat and one each in Navsari and Udwada. There are many more minor temples, where the rituals are less complex.

Earth, fire and air are all regarded as sacred, while death is the result of evil. Dead matter pollutes all it touches. Where there is a suitable space therefore, dead bodies are simply placed in the open to be consumed by vultures, as at the Towers of Silence in Mumbai. However, burial and cremation are also common.

Land and environment

Geography

India falls into three major geological regions. The north is enclosed by the great arc of the Himalaya. Along their southern flank lie the alluvial plains of the Ganga and to the south again is the Peninsula. The island chains of the Lakshadweep and Minicoy off the west coast of India are coral atolls, formed on submarine ridges under the Arabian Sea.

The origins of India's landscapes

Only 100 million years ago the Indian Peninsula was still attached to the great land mass of what geologists call 'Pangaea' alongside South Africa, Australia and Antarctica. Then as the great plates on which the earth's southern continents stood broke up, the Indian Plate started its dramatic shift northwards, eventually colliding with the Asian plate. As the Indian Plate continues to get pushed under the Tibetan Plateau so the Himalaya continue to rise.

The Himalaya The Himalaya dominate the northern borders of India, stretching 2500 km from northwest to southeast. They are unparalleled anywhere in the world. Of the 94 mountains in Asia above 7300 m, all but two are in the Himalaya. Nowhere else in the world are there mountains as high. The Himalaya proper, stretching from the Pamirs in Pakistan to the easternmost bend of the Brahmaputra in Assam, can be divided into three broad zones. On the southern flank are the Shiwaliks, or Outer Ranges. To their immediate north run the parallel Middle Ranges of Pir Panjal and Dhauladhar and to the north again is the third zone, the Inner Himalaya, which has the highest peaks, many of them in Nepal. The central core of the Himalayan ranges did not begin to rise until about 35 million years ago. The latest mountain building period, responsible for the Shiwaliks, began less than five million years ago and is still continuing, raising some of the high peaks by as much as 5 mm a year. Such movement comes at a price and the boundary between the plains and the Himalayan ranges is a zone of continuing violent earthquakes and massive erosion.

The Gangetic Plains As the Himalaya began their dramatic uplift, the trough which formed to the south of the newly emerging mountains was steadily filled with the debris washed down from the hills, creating the Indo-Gangetic plains. Today the alluvium reaches depths of over 3000 m in places (and over 22 km at the mouth of the Ganga in Bangladesh), and contains some of the largest reserves of underground water in the world. These have made possible extensive well irrigation, especially in Northwest India, contributing to the rapid agricultural changes which have taken place. The Indo-Gangetic plains are still being modified. The southern part of Bengal only emerged from the sea during the last 5000 years. The Ganga and the Indus have each been estimated to carry over one million tonnes of silt every year. The silts washed down from the Himalaya have made it possible for intensive rice cultivation to be practised continuously for hundreds of years, though they cause problems for modern irrigation development.

The Peninsula The crystalline rocks of the Peninsula are some of the oldest in the world, the **Charnockites** – named after the founder of Kolkata, an enthusiastic amateur geologist named Job Charnock, being over 3100 million years old. Over 60 million years ago, when India split from Madagascar, a mass of volcanic lava welled up through cracks in the earth's surface and covered some 500,000 sq km of northern Karnataka, Maharashtra, southern Gujarat and Madhya Pradesh. The fault line which severed India from Africa was marked by a north-south ridge of mountains, known today as the Western Ghats, set back from the sea by a coastal plain which is never more than 80 km wide. In the south, the Nilgiris and Palanis are over 2500 m high. From the crest line of the **Western Ghats**, the Peninsula slopes generally eastwards, interrupted on its eastern edge by the much more broken groups of hills sometimes referred to as the **Eastern Ghats**. The east flowing rivers have created flat alluvial deltas which have been the basis of successive peninsular kingdoms.

Climate

India is divided almost exactly by the Tropic of Cancer, stretching from the nearequatorial Kanniyakumari to the Mediterranean latitudes of Kashmir – roughly the same span as from the Amazon to San Francisco, or from Melbourne to Darwin. Not surprisingly, climate varies considerably and high altitudes further modify local climates.

The monsoon The term monsoon refers to the wind reversal which replaces the dry northeasterlies, characteristic of winter and spring, with the very warm and wet southwesterlies of the summer. The arrival of the monsoon is as variable as is the amount of rain which it brings. What makes the Indian monsoon quite exceptional is not its regularity but the depth of moist air which passes over the subcontinent. Over India, the highly unstable moist airflow is over 6000 m thick compared with only 2000 m over Japan, giving rise to the bursts of torrential rain which mark out the wet season.

Winter High pressure builds up over Central Asia. Most of India is protected from the cold northeast monsoon winds by the massive bulk of the Himalaya and daytime temperatures rise sharply in the sun. Right across the Ganga plains night temperatures fall to below 5°C in January and February. To the south the winter temperatures increase having a minimum temperature of around 20°C; however, the winter is a dry season through nearly all of India.

Summer From April onwards much of India becomes almost unbearably hot. Temperatures of over 50°C are not unknown. It is a time of year to get up to the hills. At the end of May very moist southwesterlies sweep across South India and the Bay of Bengal. They then double back northwestwards, bringing tremendously heavy rain first to the eastern Himalaya then gradually spreading northwestwards.

The wet season The monsoon season lasts from between three and five months depending on the region. Many parts of the west coast get a three-month soaking and the Shillong plateau has received as much as 26 m in one year! If you are travelling in the wetter parts of India during the monsoon you need to be prepared for extended periods of torrential rain and major disruption to travel. However, many parts of India receive a total of under 1000 mm a year. Rainfall decreases towards the Northwest, Rajasthan and northern Gujarat merging imperceptibly into desert. Tamil Nadu has an exceptional rainfall pattern, receiving most of its rain during the retreating monsoon, October-December.

Storms Some regions suffer major storms. Cyclones may hit the east coast causing enormous damage and loss of life, the risk being greatest between the end of October and early December.

Humidity The coastal regions have humidity levels above 70% for most of the year which can be very uncomfortable. However, sea breezes often bring some relief on the coast itself. Moving north and inland, between December-May humidity drops sharply, often falling as low as 20% during the daytime.

Vegetation

India's location ensured that 16 different forest types were represented. The most widespread was tropical dry deciduous forest. However, today forest cover has been reduced to about 13% of the surface area, mainly the result of demand for wood as a fuel.

Deciduous forest Two types of deciduous tree remain particularly important, **Sal** (*Shorea robusta*), now found mainly in eastern Indian and **teak** (*Tectona grandis*). Most teak today has been planted. Both are resistant to burning, which helped to protect them where people used fire as a means of clearing the forest.

Tropical rainforest In wetter areas, particularly along the Western Ghats, you can still find tropical wet evergreen forest, but even these are now extensively managed. Across the drier areas of the peninsula heavy grazing has reduced the forest cover to thorn scrub.

Mountain forests and grassland At between 1000-2000 m in the eastern hill ranges of India and in Bhutan, for example, wet hill forest includes evergreen oaks and chestnuts. Further west in the foothills of the Himalaya are belts of subtropical pine at roughly the same altitudes. Deodars (*Cedrus deodarus*) form large stands and moist temperate forest, with pines, cedars, firs and spruce, is dominant, giving many of the valleys a beautifully fresh, alpine feel. Between 3000-4000 m alpine forest predominates. Rhododendron are often mixed with other forest types. Birch, juniper, poplars and pine are widespread. There are several varieties of coarse grassland along the southern edge of the Terai and alpine grasses are important for grazing above altitudes of 2000 m. A totally distinctive grassland is the bamboo (*Dendo calamus*) region of the eastern Himalaya.

Trees

Flowering trees Many Indian trees are planted along roadsides to provide shade and they often also produce beautiful flowers. The **silk cotton tree** (*Bombax ceiba*), up to 25 m in height, is one of the most dramatic. The pale greyish bark of this buttressed tree usually bears conical spines. It has wide spreading branches and keeps its leaves for most of the year. The flowers, which appear when the tree is leafless, are cup-shaped, with curling, rather fleshy red petals up to 12 cm long while the fruit produce the fine, silky cotton which gives it its name. Other common trees with red or orange flowers include the dhak (also called 'Flame of the forest' or *Palas*), the gulmohur, the Indian coral tree and the Tulip tree. The smallish (6 m) deciduous **dhak** (*Butea monosperma*) has light grey bark and a gnarled, twisted trunk and thick, leathery leaves. The large, bright orange and sweet pea-shaped flowers appear on leafless branches. The 8- to 9-m-high umbrella-shaped **gulmohur** (*Delonix regia*), a native of Madagascar, is grown as a shade tree in towns. The fiery coloured flowers make a magnificent display after the tree has shed its feathery leaves. The scarlet flowers of the **Indian coral tree** (*Erythrina indica*) appear when its branches with thorny bark are leafless. The tall **tulip tree** (*Spathodea campanulata*) (not to be confused with the North American one) has a straight, darkish brown, slender trunk. It is usually evergreen except in the drier parts of India. The scarlet bell-shaped, tulip-like flowers grow in profusion at the ends of the branches from November to March.

Often seen along roadsides the **jacaranda** (*Jacaranda mimosaefolia*) has attractive feathery foliage and purple-blue thimble-shaped flowers up to 40 mm long. When not in flower it resembles a Gulmohur, but differs in its general shape. The valuable **tamarind** (*Tamarindus indica*), with a short straight trunk and a spreading crown, often grows along the roadside. An evergreen with feathery leaves, it bears small clusters of yellow and red flowers. The noticeable fruit pods are long, curved and swollen at intervals. In parts of India, the rights to the fruit are auctioned off annually for up to Rs 4000 (US$100) per tree.

Of these trees the silk cotton, the dhak and the Indian coral are native to India. Others were introduced mostly during the last century: the tulip tree from East Africa, the jacaranda from Brazil and the tamarind, possibly from Africa.

Fruit trees The familiar apple, plum, apricot and cherry grow in the cool upland areas of India. In the warmer plains tropical fruits flourish. The large, spreading **mango** (*Mangifera indica*) bears the delicious, distinctively shaped fruit that comes in hundreds of varieties. The evergreen **jackfruit** (*Artocarpus heterophyllus*) has dark green leathery leaves. The huge fruit (up to 90 cm long and 40 cm thick), growing from a short stem directly off the trunk and branches, has a rough, almost prickly skin and is almost sickly sweet. The **banana** plant (*Musa*), actually a gigantic herb (up to 5 m high) arising from an underground stem, has very large leaves which grow directly off the trunk. Each large purplish flower produces bunches of up to 100 bananas. The **papaya** (*Carica papaya*) grows to about 4 m with the large hand-shaped leaves clustered near the top. Only the female tree bears the fruit, which hang down close to the trunk just below the leaves.

Palm trees Coconut palms (*Cocos nucifera*) are common all round the coast of India. It has tall (15-25 m), slender, unbranched trunks, feathery leaves and large green or golden fruit with soft white flesh filled with milky water, so different from the brown fibre-covered inner nut which makes its way to Europe. The 10-15 m high **palmyra palms** (*Borassus flabellifer*), indigenous to South and East India, have distinctive fan-like leaves, as much as 150 cm across. The fruit, which is smaller than a coconut, is round, almost black and very shiny. The **betel nut palm** (*Areca catechu*) resembles the coconut palm, its slender trunk bearing ring marks left by fallen leaf stems. The smooth, round nuts, only about 3 cm across, grow in large hanging bunches. **Wild date palms** (*Phoenix sylvestris*), originally came from North Africa. About 20-25 m tall, the trunks are also marked with the ring bases of the leaves which drop off. The distinctive leaflets which stick out from the central vein give the leaf a spiky appearance. Bunches of dates are only borne by the female tree.

All these palm trees are of considerable **commercial importance**. From the fruit alone the coconut palm produces coir from the outer husk, copra from the fleshy kernel from which coconut oil or coconut butter is extracted, in addition to the desiccated coconut and coconut milk. The sap is fermented to a drink called toddy. A similar drink is produced from the sap of the wild date and the palmyra palms which are also important for sugar production. The fruit of the betel nut palm is wrapped in a special leaf and chewed. The trunks and leaves of all the palms are widely used in building and thatching.

Other trees Of all Indian trees the **banyan** (*Ficus benghalensis*) is probably the best known. It is planted by temples, in villages and along roads. If it grows in the bark of another tree, it sends down roots towards the ground. As it grows, more roots appear from the branches, until the original host tree is surrounded by a 'cage' which eventually strangles it. The famous one in Kolkata's Botanical Gardens is more than 400 m in circumference. Related to the banyan, the **pipal** or peepul (*Ficus religiosa*) also cracks open walls and strangles other trees with its roots. With a smooth grey bark, it too is commonly found near temples and shrines. You can distinguish it from the banyan by the absence of aerial roots and its large, heart-shaped leaf with a point tapering into a pronounced 'tail'. It bears abundant 'figs' of a purplish tinge which are about 1 cm across. The **ashok** or **mast** (*Polyalthia longifolia*) is a tall evergreen which can reach 15 m or more in height. One variety, often seen in avenues, is trimmed and tapers towards the top. The leaves are long, slender and shiny and narrow to a long point. **Acacia** trees with their feathery leaves are fairly common in the drier parts of India. The best known is the **babul** (*Acacia arabica*) with a rough, dark bark. The leaves have long silvery white thorns at the base and consist of many leaflets while the flowers grow in golden balls about 1 cm across. The **eucalyptus** or **gum tree** (*Eucalyptus grandis*), introduced from Australia in the 19th century, is now widespread and is planted near villages to provide both shade and firewood. There are various forms but all may be readily recognized by their height, their characteristic long, thin leaves which have a pleasant fresh smell and the colourful peeling bark. The wispy **casuarina** (*Casuarina*) grows in poor sandy soil, especially on the coast and on village waste land. It has the typical leaves of a pine tree and the cones are small and prickly to walk on. It is said to attract lightning during a thunder storm. **Bamboo** (*Bambusa*) strictly speaking is a grass which can vary in size from small ornamental clumps to the enormous wild plant whose stems are so strong and thick that they are used for construction and for scaffolding and as pipes in rural irrigation schemes.

Flowering plants

Common in the Himalaya is the beautiful flowering shrub or tree, which can be as tall as 12 m, the **rhododendron** which is indigenous to this region. In the wild the commonest colour of the flowers is crimson, but other colours, such as pale purple occur too. From March to May the flowers are very noticeable on the hill sides. Another common wild flowering shrub is **lantana**. This is a fairly small untidy looking bush with rough, toothed oval leaves, which grow in pairs on the square and prickly stem. The flowers grow together in a flattened head, the ones near the middle being usually yellowish, while those at the rim are pink, pale purple or orange. The fruit is a shiny black berry.

Many other flowering plants are cultivated in parks, gardens and roadside verges. The attractive **frangipani** (*Plumeria acutifolia*) has a rather crooked trunk and stubby branches, which if broken give out a white milky juice which can be irritating to the skin. The big, leathery leaves taper to a point at each end and have noticeable parallel veins. The sweetly scented waxy flowers are white, pale yellow or pink. The **bougainvillea** grows as a dense bush or climber with small oval leaves and rather long thorns. The brightly coloured part (which can be pinkish-purple, crimson, orange, yellow, etc) which appears like a flower is not formed of petals, which are quite small and undistinguished, but by large papery bracts.

The trumpet-shaped hibiscus flower, as much as 7 or 8 cm across, has a very long 'tongue' growing out from the centre and varies in colour from scarlet to yellow or white. The leaves are somewhat oval or heart-shaped with jagged edges. In municipal flowerbeds the commonest planted flower is probably the **canna lily**. It has large leaves which are either green or bronzed and lots of large bright red or yellow flowers. The plant can be more than 1 m high. On many ponds and tanks the floating plants of the **lotus** (*Nelumbo nucifera*) and the **water hyacinth** (*Eichornia crassipes*) are seen. Lotus flowers which rise on stalks above the water can be white, pink or a deep red and up to 25 cm across. The very large leaves either float on the surface or rise above the water. Many dwarf varieties are cultivated. The rather fleshy leaves and lilac flowers of the water hyacinth float to form a dense carpet, often clogging the waterways.

Crops

Of India's enormous variety, the single most widespread crop is **rice** (commonly *Orysa indica*). This forms the most important staple in South and East India, though other cereals and some root crops are also important elsewhere. The rice plant grows in flooded fields called *paddies* and virtually all planting or harvesting is done by hand. Millets are favoured in drier areas inland, while wheat is the most important crop in the northwest. There are many different sorts of millet, but the ones most often seen are finger millet, pearl millet (bajra) and sorghum (jowar). **Finger millet**, commonly known as ragi (*Eleusine corocana*), is so-called because the ear has several spikes which radiate out, like fingers. Usually less than 1 m high, it is grown extensively in the south. Both **pearl millet** (*Pennisetum typhoideum*), known as *bajra* in the north and *cumbu* in Tamil Nadu) and **sorghum** (*Sorghum vulgare*, known as *jowar* in the north and *cholam* in the south) look similar to the more familiar maize though each can be easily distinguished when the seed heads appear. Pearl millet, mainly grown in the north, has a tall single spike which gives it its other name of bulrush millet. Sorghum bears an open ear at the top of the plant. **Tea** (*Camellia* *sinensis*) is grown on a commercial scale in tea gardens in areas of high rainfall, often in highland regions. Over 90% comes from Assam and West Bengal in the Northeast and Tamil Nadu and Kerala in the South. Left to itself tea grows into a tree 10 m tall. In the tea gardens it is pruned to waist height for the convenience of the tea pluckers and forms flat topped bushes, with shiny bright green oval leaves. **Coffee** (*Coffea*) is not as widely grown as tea, but high-quality arabica is an important crop in parts of South India. Coffee is also a bush, with fairly long, shiny dark green leaves. The white, sweet smelling flowers, which yield the coffee berry, grow in groups along the stems. The coffee berries start off green and turn red when ripe. **Sugar cane** (*Saccharum*) is another commercially important crop. This looks like a large grass, up to 3 m tall. The crude brown sugar is sold as jaggery and has a flavour of molasses. Of the many spices grown in India, the two climbers pepper and vanilla and the grass-like cardamom are the ones most often seen. The **pepper** vine (*Piper nigrum*) is indigenous to India where it grows in the warm moist regions. As it is a vine it needs support such as a trellis or a tree. It is frequently planted up against the betel nut palm and appears as a leafy vine with almost heart-shaped leaves. The peppercorns cluster along hanging spikes and are red when ripe. Both black and white pepper is produced from the same plant, the difference being in the processing. **Vanilla** (*Vanilla planifolium*), which belongs to the orchid family, also grows up trees for support and attaches itself to the bark by small roots. It is native to South America, but grows well in India in areas of high rainfall. It is a rather fleshy looking plant, with white flowers and long slender pods. **Cardamom** (*Elettaria cardomomum*) is another spice native to India and is planted usually under shade. It grows well in highland areas such as Sikkim and the Western Ghats. It is a herbaceous plant looking rather like a big clump of grass, with long leafy shoots springing out of the ground as much as 2-3 m in height. The white flowers grow on separate shoots which can be upright, but usually sprawl on the ground. It is from these flowers that the seed bearing capsules grow. The **cashew nut** tree (*Anacardium occidentale*) was introduced into India, but now grows wild as well as being cultivated. It is a medium-sized tree with bright green, shiny, rounded leaves. The nut grows on a fleshy fruit called a cashew apple and hangs down below this. **Cotton** (*Gossypium*) is important in parts of the west and south. The cotton bush is a small knee-high bush and the cotton boll appears after the flower has withered. This splits when ripe to show the white cotton lint inside. The **castor oil** plant (*Ricinus communis*) is cultivated as a cash crop and is planted in small holdings among other crops and along roads and paths. It is a handsome plant up to about 2 m in height, with very large leaves which are divided into some 12 'fingers'. The young stems are reddish and shiny. The well-known castor oil is extracted from the bean which is a mottled brown in colour.

Wildlife

India has an extremely rich and varied wildlife, though many species only survive in very restricted environments. Alarmed by the rapid loss of wildlife habitat the Indian government established the first conservation measures in 1972, followed by the setting up of national parks and reserves. Some 25,000 sq km were set aside in 1973 for Project Tiger, but both tiger and leopard populations are sliding to dangerously low levels, largely due to poaching and conflicts with villagers over livestock kills. The same is true of other less well-known species. Their natural habitat has been destroyed both by people and by domesticated animals (there are some 250 million cattle and 50 million sheep and goats). There are now nearly 70 national parks and 330 sanctuaries, as well as programmes of afforestation and coastline preservation. Most sanctuaries and parks are open from October to March.

The animals

The big cats The **tiger** (*Panthera tigris*), which prefers to live in fairly dense cover, is most likely to be glimpsed as it lies in long grass or in dappled shadow. The **Asiatic lion** (*Panthera leo*) is now found only in the Gir National Park. Less sleek than the African lion, it has a more shaggy coat and a smaller, often black mane. The **leopard**, or **panther** as it is often called in India (*Panthera pardus*), is far more numerous than the tiger, but is even more elusive. The all black form is not uncommon in areas of higher rainfall such as the Western Ghats and Northeast India, though the typical form is seen more often.

Elephant and rhino The **Indian elephant** (*Elephas maximus*) has been domesticated for centuries and today it is still used as a beast of burden. In the wild it inhabits hilly country with forest and bamboo, where it lives in herds which can number as many as 50 or more individuals. They are adaptable animals and can live in all sorts of forest, except in dry areas. Wild elephants are mainly confined to reserves, but occasionally move out into cultivation, where they cause great damage. The **great Indian one-horned rhinoceros** (*Rhinoceros unicornis*) has folds of skin which look like rivet covered armour plating. It stands at up to 170 cm at the shoulder.

Deer, antelope, oxen and their relatives Once widespread, these animals are now largely confined to the reserves. The male deer (stags) carry antlers which are branched, each 'spike' on the antler being called a tine. Antelopes and oxen, on the other hand, have horns which are not branched. There are several deer species in India, mainly confined to very restricted ranges. Three species are quite common. The largest and one of the most widespread is the magnificent **sambar** (*Cervus unicolor*) which can be up to 150 cm at the shoulder. It has a noticeably shaggy coat, which varies in colour from brown with a yellowish or grey tinge through to dark, almost black, in the older stags. The sambar is often found on wooded hillsides and lives in groups of up to 10 or so, though solitary individuals are also seen. The **barasingha** or **swamp deer** (*Cervus duvauceli*), standing about 130 cm at the shoulder, is also quite common. The females are usually lighter and some are spotted, as are the young. The antlers are much more complex than those of the sambar, having as many as 20 tines, but 12 is more usual. Barasingha prefer swampy habitat, but are also seen in grassy areas, often in large herds. The small **chital** or **spotted deer** (*Axis axis*), only about 90 cm tall, are seen in herds of 20 or so, in grassy areas. The bright rufous coat spotted with white is unmistakable; the stags carry antlers with three tines. These animals live in open grasslands, never too far from water. The beautiful **blackbuck** or **Indian antelope** (*Antilope cervicapra*), up to

80 cm at the shoulder, occurs in large herds. The distinctive colouring and the long spiral horns make the stag easy to identify. The coat is chocolate brown above, very sharply demarcated from the white of the underparts. The females do not usually bear horns and like the young, have yellowish brown coats. The larger and heavier **nilgai** or **blue bull** (*Boselaphus tragocamelus*) is about 140 cm at the shoulder and is rather horse-like, with a sloping back. The male has a dark grey coat, while the female is sandy coloured. Both sexes have two white marks on the cheek, white throats and a white ring just above each hoof. The male carries short, forward-curving horns and has a tuft of long black hairs on the front of the neck. They occur in small herds on grassy plains and scrub land.

The very graceful **chinkara** or **Indian gazelle** (*Gazella gazella*) is only 65 cm at the shoulder. The light russet colour of the body has a distinct line along the side where the paler underparts start. Both sexes carry slightly S-shaped horns. Chinkara live in small groups in rather broken hilly countryside. The commonest member of the oxen group is the **Asiatic wild buffalo** or water buffalo (*Bubalus bubalis*). About 170 cm at the shoulder, the wild buffalo, which can be aggressive, occurs in herds on grassy plains and swamps near rivers and lakes. The black coat and wide-spreading curved horns, carried by both sexes, are distinctive. In the high Himalaya, the **yak** (*Bos grunniens*) is domesticated. The wild yak, found on bleak Himalayan hillsides, has a shaggy, blackish brown coat and large horns; the domesticated animals are often piebald and the horns much smaller. The **Indian bison** or **gaur** (*Bos gaurus*) can be up to 200 cm at the shoulder with a heavy muscular ridge across it. Both sexes carry curved horns. The young gaur is a light sandy colour, which darkens with age, the old bulls being nearly black with pale sandy coloured 'socks' and a pale forehead. Basically hill animals, they live in forests and bamboo clumps and emerge from the trees to graze. The **bharal** or **blue sheep** (*Pseudois nayaur*) are found on the open slopes around Ladakh. About 90 cm at the shoulder, it has a grey-blue body and horns that curve backwards over the neck. The rare **Asiatic wild ass** (*Equus hemionus*) is confined to the deserts of the Little Rann of Kachchh. The fawn body has a distinctive dark stripe along the back. The dark mane is short and erect. The **wild boar** (*Sus scrofa*) has a mainly black body and a pig-like head; the hairs thicken down the spine to form a sort of mane. A mature male stands 90 cm at the shoulder and, unlike the female, bears tusks. The young are striped. Quite widespread, they can often cause great destruction among crops. One of the most important scavengers of the open countryside, the **striped hyena** (*Hyena hyena*) usually comes out at night. It is about 90 cm at the shoulder with a large head with a noticeable crest of hairs along its sloping back. The **common giant flying squirrel** (*Petaurista petaurista*) is common in the larger forests of India, except in the northeast. The body can be 45 cm long and the tail another 50 cm. They glide from tree to tree using a membrane stretching from front leg to back leg which acts like a parachute. **In towns and villages** The **common langur** (*Presbytis entellus*), 75 cm, is a long-tailed monkey with a distinctive black face, hands and feet. Usually a forest dweller, it is found almost throughout India. The **rhesus macaque** (*Macaca mulatta*), 60 cm, is more solid looking with shorter limbs and a shorter tail. It can be distinguished by the orange-red fur on its rump and flanks. **Palm squirrels** are very common.

The **five-striped** (*Funambulus pennanti*) and the **three-striped palm squirrel** (*Funambulus palmarum*) are both about the same size (30 cm long, about half of which is tail). The five-striped is usually seen in towns. The two bats most commonly seen in towns differ enormously in size. The larger so-called **flying fox** (*Pteropus giganteus*) has a wing span of 120 cm. These fruit eating bats, found throughout, except in the driest areas, roost in large noisy colonies where they look like folded umbrellas hanging from the trees. In the evening they can be seen leaving the roost with slow measured wing beats. The much smaller **Indian pipistrelle** *(Pipistrellus coromandra)*, with a wing span of about 15 cm, is an insect eater. It comes into houses at dusk, roosting under eaves and has a fast, erratic flight. The **jackal** (*Canis aureus*), a lone scavenger in towns and villages, looks like a cross between a dog and a fox and varies in colour from shades of brown through to black. The bushy tail has a dark tip. The **common mongoose** (*Herpestes edwardsi*) lives in scrub and open jungle. It kills snakes, but will also take rats, mice and chicken. Tawny coloured with a grey grizzled tinge, it is about 90 cm in length, of which half is pale-tipped tail. The **sloth bear** (*Melursus ursinus*), about 75 cm at the shoulder, lives in broken forest, but may be seen on a lead accompanying a street entertainer who makes it 'dance' to music as part of an act. They have a long snout, a pendulous lower lip and a shaggy black coat with a yellowish V-shaped mark on the chest.

Birds
Town and village birds Some birds perform a useful function scavenging and clearing refuse. One of the most widespread is the brown **pariah kite** (*Milvus migrans*, 65 cm). The more handsome chestnut and white **brahminy kite** (*Haliastur indus*, 48 cm) is largely confined to the waterside. The common brown **white-backed vulture** (*Gyps bengalensis*, 90 cm) looks ungainly and has a bare and scrawny head and neck. The smaller **scavenger vulture** (*Neophron percnopterus*, 65 cm) is mainly white, but often has dirty looking plumage and the bare head and neck of all vultures. In flight its wedge-shaped tail and black and white colouring are characteristic. The **house crow** (*Corvus splendens*, 45 cm) on the other hand is a very smart looking bird with a grey body and black tail, wings, face and throat. It occurs in almost every town and village in India. The **jungle crow** (*Corvus macrorhynchos*, 50 cm) originally a bird of the countryside has started to move into populated areas and in the hill stations tends to replace the house crow. Unlike the house crow it is a glossy black all over and has a much deeper, hoarser caw. The **feral pigeon**, or **blue rock dove** (*Columba livia*, 32 cm), found throughout the world, is generally a slate grey in colour. It invariably has two dark bars on the wing and a white rump. The **little brown dove** (*Streptopelia senegalensis*, 25 cm) is bluey grey and brown above, with a pink head and underparts and a speckled pattern on the neck. The **collared dove** (*Streptopelia decaocto*, 30 cm), with a distinct half collar on the back of its neck, is common, especially in the drier parts of India. Bulbuls are common in gardens and parks. The **red-vented bulbul** (*Pycnonotus cafer*, 20 cm), a mainly brown bird, can be identified by the slight crest and a bright red patch under the tail. The **house sparrow** (*Passer domesticus*, 15 cm) can be seen in towns. The ubiquitous **common myna** (*Acridotheres tristis*, 22 cm) feeds on lawns, especially after rain or watering.

Look for the white under the tail and the bare yellow skin around the eye, yellow bill and legs and in flight the large white wing patch.

A less common but more striking bird also seen feeding in open spaces is the **hoopoe** (*Upupa epops*, 30 cm), easily identified by its sandy plumage with black and white stripes and long thin curved bill. The marvellous fan-shaped crest is sometimes raised. Finally there is a member of the cuckoo family, the **koel** (*Eudynamys scolopacea*, 42 cm), which is commonly heard during the hot weather – kuoo-kuoo-kuoo, the double note starts off low and flute-like, rises in pitch and intensity, then suddenly stops, only to start all over again. The male is all black with a greenish bill and a red eye; the female streaked and barred.

Water and waterside birds The *jheels* (marshes or swamps) of India form one of the richest bird habitats in the world. Cormorants abound; the commonest, the **little cormorant** (*Phalacrocorax niger*, 50 cm) is found on most inland waters. An almost entirely black bird with just a little white on the throat, it has a long tail and a hooked bill. The **coot** (*Fulica atra*, 40 cm), another common black bird, seen especially in winter has a noticeable white shield on the forehead. The magnificent **sarus crane** (*Grus antigone*, 150 cm) is one of India's tallest birds. It is widespread all year round across northern India, almost invariably in pairs. The bare red head and long red legs combined with its height and grey plumage make it easy to identify. The commonest migrant crane is probably the **common crane** (*Grus grus*, 120 cm), present only in winter, often in large flocks. It has mainly grey plumage with a black head and neck. There is a white streak running down the side of the neck and above the eye is a tuft of red feathers. The **openbill stork** (*Anastomus oscitans*, 80 cm) and the **painted stork** (*Ibis leucocephalus*, 100 cm) are common too and are spotted breeding in large colonies. The former is white with black wing feathers and a curiously shaped bill. The latter, mainly white, has a pinkish tinge on the back and dark marks on the wings and a broken black band on the lower chest. The bare yellow face and yellow down-curved bill are conspicuous. By almost every swamp, ditch or rice paddy up to about 1200 m you will see the **paddy bird** (*Ardeola grayii*, 45 cm). An inconspicuous, buff-coloured bird, it is easily overlooked as it stands hunched up by the waterside. As soon as it takes off, its white wings and rump make it very noticeable. The **bronze-winged jacana** (*Metopidius indicus*, 27 cm) has very long toes which enable it to walk on the floating leaves of water-lilies and there is a noticeable white streak over and above the eye. Village ponds often have their resident bird. The commonest and most widespread of the Indian kingfishers is the jewel-like **common kingfisher** (*Alcedo atthis*, 18 cm). With its brilliant blue upperparts and orange breast it is usually seen perched on a twig or a reed beside the water.

Open grassland, light woodland and cultivated land The **cattle egret** (*Bubulcus ibis*, 50 cm), a small white heron, is usually seen near herds of cattle, frequently perched on the backs of the animals. Equal in height to the sarus crane is the impressive, but ugly **adjutant stork** (*Leptopilos dubius*, 150 cm). This often dishevelled bird is a scavenger and is thus seen near rubbish dumps and carcasses. It has a naked red head and neck, a huge bill and a large fleshy pouch which hangs down the front of the neck. The **rose-ringed parakeet** (*Psittacula krameri*, 40 cm) is found throughout India up to about 1500 m while the **pied myna** (*Sturnus contra*, 23 cm) is restricted to northern and central India. The rose-ringed parakeet often forms huge flocks, an impressive sight coming in to roost. The long tail is noticeable both in flight and when the bird is perched. They can be very destructive to crops, but are attractive birds which are frequently kept as pets. The pied myna, with its smart black and white plumage, is conspicuous, usually in small flocks in grazing land or cultivation. It feeds on the ground and on village rubbish dumps. The all black **drongo** (*Dicrurus adsimilis*, 30 cm) is almost invariably seen perched on telegraph wires or bare branches. Its distinctively forked tail makes it easy to identify. Weaver birds are a family of mainly yellow birds, all remarkable for the intricate nests they build. The most widespread is the **baya weaver** (*Ploceus philippinus*, 15cm) which nest in large colonies, often near villages. The male in the breeding season combines a black face and throat with a contrasting yellow top of the head and the yellow breast band. In the non-breeding season both sexes are brownish sparrow-like birds.

Hill birds Land above about 1500 m supports a distinct range of species, although some birds, such as the ubiquitous **common myna**, are found in the highlands as well as in the lower lying terrain. The highland equivalent of the red-vented bulbul is the **white-cheeked bulbul** (*Pycnonotus leucogenys*, 20 cm) which is found in gardens and woodland in the Himalaya up to about 2500 m and as far south as Mumbai. It has white underparts with a yellow patch under the tail. The black head and white cheek patches are distinctive. The crest varies in length and is most prominent in birds found in Kashmir, where it is very common in gardens. The **red-whiskered bulbul** (*Pycnonotus jocosus*, 20 cm) is widespread in the Himalaya and the hills of South India up to about 2500 m. Its pronounced pointed crest, which is sometimes so long that it flops forward towards the bill, white underparts and red and white 'whiskers' serve to distinguish it. It has a red patch under the tail. In the summer the delightful **verditer flycatcher** (*Muscicapa thalassina*, 15 cm) is a common breeding bird in the Himalaya up to about 3000 m. It is tame and confiding, often builds its nest on verandas and is seen perching on telegraph wires. In winter it is more widely distributed throughout the country. It is an active little bird which flicks its tail up and down in a characteristic manner. The male is all bright blue green with somewhat darker wings and a black patch in front of the eyes. The female is similar, but duller. Another species associated with man is the **white wagtail** (*Motacilla alba*, 21 cm), very common in the Himalayan summer up to about 3000 m. It is found near water, by streams and lakes, on floating vegetation and among the house boats in Kashmir. Its black and white plumage and constantly wagging tail make it easy to identify. Yet another species common in Kashmir and in other Himalayan hill stations is the **red-billed blue magpie** (*Urocissa erythrorhyncha*, 65 cm). With a long tail and pale blue plumage, contrasting with its black head, it is usually seen in small flocks. This is not so much a garden bird, but prefers tea gardens, open woodland and cultivation. The highlands of India, especially the Himalaya, are the home of the ancestors of **domestic hens** and also of numerous beautiful **pheasants**. These are mainly forest dwellers and are not easy to see as they tend to be shy and wary of man. Last but not least, mention must be made of India's national bird, the magnificent and well-known **peafowl** (*Pavo cristatus*, male 210 cm, female 100 cm), which is more commonly known as the peacock. Semi-domesticated birds are commonly seen and heard around towns and villages, especially in the northwest of India. In the wild it favours hilly jungles and dense scrub.

Reptiles and amphibians

India is famous for its reptiles, especially its snakes, which feature in many stories and legends. In reality, snakes keep out of the way of people. One of the most common is the **Indian rock python** (*Python molurus*), a 'constrictor' which kills its prey by suffocation. Usually about 4 m in length, they can be much longer. Their docile nature make them favourites of snake handlers. The other large snakes favoured by street entertainers are cobras. The various species all have a hood which is spread when the snake draws itself up to strike. They are all highly venomous and the snake charmers prudently de-fang them to render them harmless. The best known is probably the **spectacled cobra** (*Naja naja*), which has a mark like a pair of spectacles on the back of its hood. The largest venomous snake in the world is the **king cobra** (*Ophiophagus hannah*) which is 5 m in length. It is usually brown, but can vary from cream to black and lacks the spectacle marks of the other. In their natural state cobras are generally inhabitants of forest regions. Equally venomous, but much smaller, the **common krait** *(Bungarus caeruleus)* is just over 1 m in length. The slender, shiny, blue-black snake has thin white bands which can sometimes be almost indiscernible. They are found all over the country except in the northeast where the cannibalistic **banded krait** with bold yellowish and black bands have virtually eradicated them.

In houses everywhere you cannot fail to see the **gecko** (*Hemidactylus*). This small harmless lizard is active after dark. It lives in houses behind pictures and curtain rails and at night emerges to run across the walls and ceilings to hunt the night flying insects which form its main prey. It is not usually more than about 14 cm long, with a curiously transparent, pale yellowish brown body. At the other end of the scale is the **monitor lizard** (*Varanus*), which can grow to 2 m in length. They can vary from a colourful black and yellow, to plain or speckled brown. They live in different habitats from cultivation and scrub to waterside places and desert. The most widespread crocodile is the freshwater **mugger** or Marsh crocodile (*Crocodilus palustris*) which grows to 3-4 m in length. The only similar fresh water species is the **gharial** (*Gavialis gangeticus*) which lives in large, fast flowing rivers. Twice the length of the mugger, it is a fish-eating crocodile with a long thin snout and, in the case of the male, an extraordinary bulbous growth on the end of the snout. The enormous, aggressive **estuarine** or **saltwater crocodile** (*Crocodilus porosus*) is now restricted to the brackish waters of the Sundarbans, on the east coast and in the Andaman and Nicobar Islands. It grows to 7 m long and is sleeker looking than the rather docile mugger.

Books

India is a good place to buy English-language books as foreign books are often much cheaper than the published price. There are also cheap Indian editions and occasionally reprints of out-of-print books. There are excellent bookshops in all the major Indian cities.

Art and architecture

Burton, TR *Hindu Art*, British Museum P. Well illustrated; broad view of art and religion.

Cooper, I and Dawson, B *Traditional Buildings of India*, Thames & Hudson.

Michell, G *The Hindu Temple*, Univ of Chicago Press, 1988. An authoritative account of Hindu architectural development.

Ramaswami, NS *Temples of South India*, Chennai, Maps and Agencies, 1996.

KR Srinivasan *Temples of South India*, 3rd ed, New Delhi, National Book Trust, 1985. Good background information.

Sterlin, H *Hindu India*, Köln, Taschen, 1998. Traces the development from early rock-cut shrines, detailing famous examples; clearly written, well illustrated.

Tillotson, G *The Rajput Palaces*, Yale, 1987; *Mughal architecture*, London, Viking, 1990; *The tradition of Indian architecture*, Yale 1989. Superbly clear writing on Indian architecture under Rajputs, Mughals and the British.

Contemporary India

Baru, S *The Accidental Prime Minister*, Viking, 2014. Illuminating insider portrait of the Congress government under Manmohan Singh.

French, P *Liberty or Death*, Harper Collins. Well researched, serious, but very readable.

Guha, R *Patriots and Partisans*, Penguin, 2012. A fine collection of essays on the decline and fall of modern India.

Silver, RB and Epstein, B *India: a mosaic*, New York, NYRB. Distinguished essays on history, politics and literature.

Tully, M *No full stops in India*, Viking, 1991. An often superbly observed but controversially interpreted view of late 20th-century India.

History

Allchin, B and R *Origins of a civilisation*, Viking, Penguin Books, 1997. Authoritative survey of the origins of Indian civilizations.

Basham, AL *The Wonder that was India*, London, Sidgwick & Jackson, 1985. Comprehensive and readable account of the development of India's culture.

Beames, J *Memoirs of a Bengal Civilian*, London, Eland, 1991. A readable insight into the British Raj in the post-Mutiny period.

Dalrymple, W *The Age of Kali*, Penguin 1998.

Edwardes, M *The Myth of the Mahatma*. Presents Gandhi in a whole new light.

Gandhi, R *The Good Boatman*, Viking/Penguin 1995. An excellent biography by one of Gandhi's noted grandson's.

Gascoigne, B *The Great Moghuls*, London, Cape, 1987.

Giridharadas, A *India Calling*. Harper Collins, 2011. Highly readable account of the rapid changes occurring in Indian society.

Guha, R *India After Gandhi*, Picador 2007. Heavyweight but readable history of the nation.

Keay, J *India: a History*, Harper Collins, 2000. A popular history of the sub continent.
Nehru, J *The discovery of India*, New Delhi, ICCR, 1976.
Robinson, F (ed) *Cambridge Encyclopaedia of India*, Cambridge, 1989. An introduction to many aspects of South Asian society.
Spear, P and Thapar, R *A history of India*, 2 vols, Penguin, 1978.
Wolpert, S *A new history of India*, OUP 1990.

Literature

Adiga, A *White Tiger*. Harper Collins India, 2008. Controversial take on the complexities of modern Indian society.
Boo, K *Behind the Beautiful Forevers*. Compelling collection of tales of life in a Mumbai slum.
Chatterjee, U *English August*. London, Faber, 1988. A wry modern account of an Indian civil servant's year in a rural posting.
Chaudhuri, N *The autobiography of an unknown Indian*, Macmillan, London Vivid, witty and often sharply critical accounts of India across the 20th century. Also *Thy Hand, Great Anarch!*
Kanga, F *Trying to grow*, Bloomsbury, 1989. Mumbai life seen through the experiences of a Parsi family.
Mehta, S *Maximum City*. Various shades of the Mumbai underworld brought vividly to life.
Mistry, R *A fine balance*. Faber, 1995. A tale of the struggle to survive in the modern Indian city.
Naipaul, VS *A million mutinies now*, Penguin, 1992. 'Revisionist' account of India turns away from the despondency of his earlier books (*An Area of darkness* and *India: a wounded civilisation*).
Narayan, RK *The Man-eater of Malgudi* and *Under the Banyan tree and other stories*, *Grandmother's stories*, London,

Penguin, 1985. Gentle and humorous stories of South India.
Ramanuja, AK *The collected essays*. Ed by V Dhawadker. New Delhi, OUP, 1999. Brilliant essays on Indian culture and literature.
Roberts, GD *Shantaram*. Scribe Publications, 2003. A compelling, apparently true and often beautifully written account of an escaped convict's life in the Mumbai underworld. A real page-turner.
Roy, A *The God of Small Things*. Indian Ink/Harper Collins, 1997. Excellent first novel about family turmoil in a Syrian Christian household in Kerala.
Rushdie, S *Midnight's children*, London, Picador, 1981. India since Independence, with funny and sharp critiques of South Asian life in the 1980s. *The Moor's Last Sigh*, Viking, 1996, is of particular interest to those travelling to Kochi and Mumbai.
Scott, P *The Raj Quartet*, London, Panther, 1973; *Staying on*, Longmans, 1985. Outstandingly perceptive novels of the end of the Raj.
Seth, V *A Suitable Boy*, Phoenix House London, 1993. Prize-winning novel of modern Indian life.
Shulman, D *Spring, Heat, Rains*. A fascinating and lyrical travelogue of the landscapes, cultures and poetry of Andhra Pradesh.
Weightman, S (ed) *Travellers Literary Companion: the Indian Sub-continent*. Invaluable introduction to the diversity of Indian writing.

Music and cinema

Menon, RR *Penguin Dictionary of Indian Classical Music*, Penguin New Delhi 1995.
Mohan, L *Bollywood, Popular Indian Cinema*, Joshi (Dakini).

People

Bumiller, E *May you be the mother of one hundred sons*, Penguin, 1991. An American woman journalist's account of coming to understand the issues that face India's women.

Dalrymple, W *Nine Lives*, Bloomsbury 2009.

Holmstrom, L *The Inner Courtyard*. A series of short stories by Indian women, translated into English, Rupa, 1992.

Lewis, N *A goddess in the stones*. An insight into tribal life in Orissa and Bihar.

Varma, PK *Being Indian*. Penguin 2004.

Bijapurkar, R *We are like that only*, Penguin 2007. To understand consumer India.

Karkar, S and K *The Indians*, Viking, 2007. Psychoanalyst and cultural commentator take on the Indian identity.

Lloyd, S *An Indian Attachment*, London, Eland, 1992. A very personal and engaging account of time spent in an Indian village.

Religion

Doniger O'Flaherty, W *Hindu Myths*, London, Penguin, 1974. A sourcebook translated from the Sanskrit.

Fernandes, E *Holy Warriors*, Viking, 2006. An overview of religious extremism in India.

Jain, JP *Religion and Culture of the Jains,* 3rd ed. New Delhi, Bharatiya Jnanapith, 1981.

Rahula, W *What the Buddha Taught*.

Singh, H *The heritage of the Sikhs*, 2nd ed, New Delhi, 1983.

Waterstone, R *India, the cultural companion*, Duncan Baird, 2002. India's spiritual traditions, well illustrated.

Zaehner, RC *Hinduism*, OUP.

Travel

Fishlock, T *Cobra Road,* London, John Murray, 1991. Impressions of a news journalist.

Frater, A *Chasing the monsoon*, London, Viking, 1990. Prize-winning account of the human impact of the monsoon's sweep across India.

Keay, J *Into India*, London, John Murray, 1999. Seasoned traveller's introduction to understanding and enjoying India.

Wildlife and vegetation

Ali, S *Indian hill birds*, OUP.

Ali, Sand Dillon Ripley, S *Handbook of the birds of India & Pakistan* (compact ed).

Cowen, DV *Flowering Trees and Shrubs in India*.

Grimmet, R, and Inskipp, C and T *Pocket guide to Birds of the Indian Sub-Continent*. 1999.

Ives, R *Of tigers and men,* Doubleday, 1995.

Kazmierczak, K and Singh, R *A birdwatcher's guide to India*. Prion, 1998, Sandy, Beds, UK. Well researched and carrying lots of practical information for all birders.

Nair, SM *Endangered animals of India*, New Delhi, NBT, 1992.

Polunin, O and Stainton, A *Flowers of the Himalaya*, OUP, 1984.

Prater, SH *The Book of Indian Animals*.

Sippy, S and Kapoor, S *The Ultimate Ranthambhore Guide*, 2001. Informative, practical guide stressing conservation.

Thapar and Rathore *Wild tigers of Ranthambhore* OUP, 2000.

Contents

Footnotes

Language

Hindi words and phrases

Pronunciation
a as in *ah*   i as in *bee*
nasalized vowels are shown
as an *un*
o as in *oh*   u as *oo* in book

Basics
Hello, good morning,
goodbye *namaste*
Thank you/no thank
you *dhanyavad* or
shukriya/nahin shukriya
Excuse me, sorry *maf kijiye*
Yes/no *ji han/ji nahin*
Never mind/that's all right
koi bat nahin

Questions
What is your name? *apka nam
kya hai?*
My name is ... *mera nam... Hai*
Pardon? *phir bataiye?*
How are you? *kya hal hai?*
I am well, thanks, and
you? *main thik hun, aur ap?*
Not very well *main thik nahin
hun*
Where is the...? *kahan hai...?*
Who is? *kaun hai?*
What is this? *yeh kya hai?*

Shopping
How much? *Kitna?*
That makes (20) rupees *(bis)
rupaye*
That is very expensive! *bahut
mahanga hai!*
Make it a bit cheaper! *thora
kam kijiye!*

The hotel
What is the room
charge? *kiraya kitna hai?*
Please show the room *kamra
dikhaiye*
Is there an air-conditioned
room? *kya a/c kamra hai?*
Is there hot water? *garam pani
hai?*
... a bathroom/fan/ mosquito
net ... *bathroom/pankha/
machhar dani*
Is there a large room? *bara
kamra hai?*
Please clean it *saf karwa dijiye*
Are there clean sheets/
blanket? *saf chadaren/
kambal hain?*
Bill please *bill dijiye*

Travel
Where's the railway
station? *railway station
kahan hai?*
How much is the ticket to
Agra? *Agra ka ticket kitne
ka hai?*
When does the Agra bus
leave? *Agra bus kab jaegi?*
How much? *Kitna?*
Left/right *baien/dahina*
Go straight on *sidha chaliye*
Nearby *nazdik*
Please wait here *yahan
thahariye*
Please come at 8 *ath bajai ana*
Quickly *jaldi*
Stop *rukiye*

Restaurants
Please show the menu *menu
dikhaiye*
No chillies please *mirch nahin
dalna*
...sugar/milk/ice ...*chini/
doodh/baraf*
A bottle of water please *ek
botal pani dijiye*
Sweet/savoury *mitha/ namkin*
Spoon, fork, knife *chamach,
kanta, chhuri*

Time and days
right now *abhi*
month *mahina*
morning *suba*
year *sal*
afternoon *dopahar*
evening *sham*
night *rat*
today *aj*
tomorrow/yesterday
kal/kal
day *din*
week *hafta*
Sunday *ravivar*
Monday *somvar*
Tuesday *mangalvar*
Wednesday *budhvar*
Thursday *virvar*
Friday *shukravar*
Saturday *shanivar*

Numbers

1	*ek*	2	*do*
3	*tin*	4	*char*
5	*panch*	6	*chhai*
7	*sat*	8	*ath*
9	*nau*	10	*das*
11	*gyara*	12	*barah*
13	*terah*	14	*chaudah*
15	*pandrah*	16	*solah*
17	*satrah*	18	*atharah*
19	*unnis*	20	*bis*
100/200		*sau/do sau*	
1000/2000		*hazar/
do hazar*	
100,000		*lakh*	

Basic vocabulary
Words such as airport,
bank, bathroom, bus, doctor,
embassy, ferry, hotel, hospital,
juice, police, restaurant, station,
stamp, taxi, ticket, train are
used locally though often
pronounced differently
eg *daktar, haspatal.*
and *aur*
big *bara*
café/food stall *dhaba/hotel*
chemist *dawai ki dukan*
clean *saf*

closed *band*	newspaper *akhbar*	this *yeh*
cold *thanda*	of course, sure *zaroor*	town *shahar*
day *din*	open *khula*	water *pani*
dirty *ganda*	police station *thana*	what *kya*
English *angrezi*	road *rasta*	when *kab*
excellent *bahut achha*	room *kamra*	where *kahan/kidhar*
food/ to eat *khana*	shop *dukan*	which/who *kaun*
hot (spicy) *jhal, masaledar*	sick (ill) *bimar*	why *kiun*
hot (temp) *garam*	silk *reshmi/silk*	with *ke sathh*
luggage *saman*	small *chhota*	
medicine *dawai*	that *who*	

Food and drink

Eating out is normally cheap and safe but menus can often be dauntingly long and full of unfamiliar names. Here are some Hindi words to help you.

Meat and fish
chicken *murgh*
fish *macchli*
meat *gosht, mas*
prawns *jhinga*

Vegetables (sabzi)
aubergine *baingan*
cabbage *band gobi*
carrots *gajar*
cauliflower *phool gobi*
mushroom *khumbhi*

onion *piaz*
okra, ladies' fingers *bhindi*
peas *matar*
potato *aloo*
spinach *sag*

Styles of cooking
Many items on restaurant menus are named according to methods of preparation, roughly equivalent to terms such as 'Provençal' or 'sauté'.

bhoona in a thick, fairly spicy sauce

chops minced meat, fish or vegetables, covered with mashed potato, crumbed and fried

cutlet minced meat, fish, vegetables formed into flat rounds or ovals, crumbed and fried (eg prawn cutlet, flattened king prawn)

do piaza with onions (added twice during cooking)

dum pukht steam baked

jhal frazi spicy, hot sauce with tomatoes and chillies

jhol thin gravy (Bengali)

Kashmiri cooked with mild spices, ground almonds and yoghurt, often with fruit

kebab skewered (or minced and shaped) meat or fish; a dry spicy dish cooked on a fire

kima minced meat (usually 'mutton')

kofta minced meat or vegetable balls

korma in fairly mild rich sauce using cream/yoghurt

masala marinated in spices (fairly hot)

Madras hot

makhani in butter rich sauce

moli South Indian dishes cooked in coconut milk and green chilli sauce

Mughlai rich North Indian style

Nargisi dish using boiled eggs

navratan curry ('9 jewels') colourful mixed vegetables and fruit in mild sauce

Peshwari rich with dried fruit and nuts (northwest Indian)

tandoori baked in a tandoor (special clay oven) or one imitating it

tikka marinated meat pieces, baked quite dry

vindaloo hot and sour Goan meat dish using vinegar

Typical dishes

aloo gosht potato and mutton stew

aloo gobi dry potato and cauliflower with cumin

aloo, matar, kumbhi potato, peas, mushrooms in a dryish mildly spicy sauce

bhindi bhaji okra fried with onions and mild spices

boti kebab marinated pieces of meat, skewered and cooked over a fire

dhal makhani lentils cooked with butter

dum aloo potato curry with a spicy yoghurt, tomato and onion sauce

matar panir curd cheese cubes with peas and spices (and often tomatoes)

murgh massallam chicken in creamy marinade of yoghurt, spices and herbs with nuts

nargisi kofta boiled eggs covered in minced lamb, cooked in a thick sauce

rogan josh rich, mutton/beef pieces in creamy, red sauce

sag panir drained curd (panir) sautéd with chopped spinach in mild spices

sarson-ke-sag and **makkai-ki-roti** mustard leaf cooked dry with spices served with maize four roti from Punjab

shabdeg a special Mughlai mutton dish with vegetables

yakhni lamb stew

Rice

bhat/sada chawal plain boiled rice

biriyani partially cooked rice layered over meat and baked with saffron

khichari rice and lentils cooked with turmeric and other spices

pulao/pilau fried rice cooked with spices (cloves, cardamom, cinnamon) with dried fruit, nuts or vegetables. Sometimes cooked with meat, like a biriyani

Roti – breads

chapati (roti) thin, plain, wholemeal unleavened bread cooked on a tawa (griddle), usually made from ata (wheat flour). Makkaikiroti is with maize flour.

nan oven baked (traditionally in a tandoor) white flour leavened bread often large and triangular; sometimes stuffed with almonds and dried fruit

paratha fried bread layered with ghi (sometimes cooked with egg or with potatoes)

poori thin deep-fried, puffed rounds of flour

Sweets

These are often made with reduced/thickened milk, drained curd cheese or powdered lentils and nuts. They are sometimes covered with a flimsy sheet of decorative, edible silver leaf.

barfi fudgelike rectangles/diamonds

gulab jamun dark fried spongy balls, soaked in syrup

halwa rich sweet made from cereal, fruit, vegetable, nuts and sugar

khir, payasam, paesh thickened milk rice/vermicelli pudding

kulfi cone-shaped Indian ice cream with pistachios/ almonds, uneven in texture

jalebi spirals of fried batter soaked in syrup

laddoo lentil based batter 'grains' shaped into rounds

rasgulla (roshgulla) balls of curd in clear syrup

sandesh dry sweet made of curd cheese

Snacks

bhaji, pakora vegetable fritters (onions, potatoes, cauliflower, etc) deep-fried in batter

chat sweet and sour fruit and vegetables flavoured with tama rind paste and chillies

chana choor, chioora ('Bombay mix') lentil and flattened rice snacks mixed with nuts and dried fruit

dosai South Indian pancake made with rice and lentil flour; served with a mild potato and onion filling (masala dosai) or without (ravai or plain dosai)

iddli steamed South Indian rice cakes, a bland breakfast given flavour by spiced accompaniments

kachori fried pastry rounds stuffed with spiced lentil/ peas/potato filling

samosa cooked vegetable or meat wrapped in pastry triangles and deep fried

utthappam thick South Indian rice and lentil flour pancake cooked with spices/onions/ tomatoes

vadai deep fried, small savoury lentil 'doughnut' rings. Dahi vada are similar rounds in yoghurt

Glossary

Words in italics are common elements of words, often making up part of a place name

A

aarti (arati) Hindu worship with lamps

abacus square or rectangular table resting on top of a pillar

abad peopled

acanthus thick-leaved plant, common decoration on pillars, esp Greek

achalam hill (Tamil)

acharya religious teacher

Adi Granth Guru Granth Sahib, holy book of the Sikhs

Adinatha first of the 24 Tirthankaras, distinguished by his bull mount

agarbathi incense

Agastya legendary sage who brought the Vedas to South India

Agni Vedic fire divinity, intermediary between gods and men; guardian of the Southeast

ahimsa non-harming, non-violence

akhand path unbroken reading of the Guru Granth Sahib

alinda veranda

ambulatory processional path

amla/amalaka circular ribbed pattern (based on a gourd) at the top of a temple tower

amrita ambrosia; drink of immortality

ananda joy

Ananda the Buddha's chief disciple

Ananta a huge snake on whose coils Vishnu rests

anda literally 'egg', spherical part of the stupa

Andhaka demon killed by Siva

anicut irrigation channel (Tamil)

anna (ana) one sixteenth of a rupee (still occasionally referred to)

Annapurna Goddess of abundance; one aspect of Devi

antarala vestibule, chamber in front of shrine or cella

antechamber chamber in front of the sanctuary

apsara celestial nymph

apse semi-circular plan

arabesque ornamental decoration with intertwining lines

aram pleasure garden

architrave horizontal beam across posts or gateways

ardha mandapam chamber in front of main hall of temple

Ardhanarisvara Siva represented as half-male and half-female

Arjuna hero of the Mahabharata, to whom Krishna delivered the Bhagavad Gita

arrack alcoholic spirit fermented from potatoes or grain

aru river (Tamil)

Aruna charioteer of Surya, Sun God; Red

Aryans literally 'noble' (Sanskrit); prehistoric peoples who settled in Persia and North India

asana a seat or throne (Buddha's) pose

ashram hermitage or retreat

Ashta Matrikas The eight mother goddesses who attended on Siva or Skanda

astanah threshold

atman philosophical concept of universal soul or spirit

atrium court open to the sky in the centre In modern architecture, enclosed in glass

aus summer rice crop (Apr-Aug) Bengal

Avalokiteshwara Lord who looks down; Bodhisattva, the Compassionate

avatara 'descent'; incarnation of a divinity

ayacut irrigation command area (Tamil)

ayah nursemaid, especially for children

B

babu clerk

bada cubical portion of a temple up to the roof or spire

badgir rooftop structure to channel cool breeze into the house (mainly North and West India)

badlands eroded landscape

bagh garden

bahadur title, meaning 'the brave'

baksheesh tip 'bribe'

Balabhadra Balarama, elder brother of Krishna

baluster (balustrade) a small column supporting a handrail

bandh a strike

bandhani tie dyeing (West India)

Bangla (Bangaldar) curved roof, based on thatched roofs in Bengal

bania merchant caste

banian vest

baoli or vav rectangular well surrounded by steps

baradari literally 'twelve pillared', a pavilion with columns

barrel-vault semi-cylindrical shaped roof or ceiling

bas-relief carving of low projection

basement lower part of walls, usually with decorated mouldings

basti Jain temple

batter slope of a wall, especially in a fort

bazar market

bedi (vedi) altar/platform for reading holy texts

begum Muslim princess/ woman's courtesy title

beki circular stone below the amla in the finial of a roof

belvedere summer house; small room on a house roof

bhabar coarse alluvium at foot of Himalayas

bhadra flat face of the sikhara (tower)

Bhadrakali Tantric goddess and consort of Bhairav

Bhagavad-Gita Song of the Lord; section of the Mahabharata

Bhagiratha the king who prayed to Ganga to descend to earth

bhai brother

Bhairava Siva, the Fearful

bhakti adoration of a deity

bhang Indian hemp

bharal Himalayan blue sheep

Bharata half-brother of Rama

bhavan building or house

bhikku Buddhist monk

Bhima Pandava hero of the Mahabharata, famous for his strength

Bhimsen Deity worshipped for his strength and courage

bhisti a water-carrier

bhogamandapa the refectory hall of a temple

bhumi literally earth; a horizontal moulding of a sikhara

bidi (beedi) Indian cigarette, tobacco wrapped in tendu leaves

bigha measure of land – normally about one-third of an acre

bo-tree (or Bodhi) *Ficus religiosa*, pipal tree associated with the Buddha

Bodhisattva Enlightened One, destined to become Buddha

bodi tuft of hair on back of the shaven head (also *tikki*)

Brahma Universal self-existing power; Creator in the Hindu Triad.

Brahmachari religious student, accepting rigorous discipline (eg chastity)

Brahman (Brahmin) highest Hindu (and Jain) caste of priests

Brahmanism ancient Indian religion, precursor of modern Hinduism

Buddha The Enlightened One; founder of Buddhism

bund an embankment

bundh (literally closed) a strike

burj tower or bastion

burqa (burkha) over-dress worn by Muslim women observing purdah

bustee slum

C

cantonment planned military or civil area in town

capital upper part of a column

caryatid sculptured human female figure used as a support for columns

catamaran log raft, logs (*maram*) tied (*kattu*) together (Tamil)

cave temple rock-cut shrine or monastery

cella small chamber, compartment for the image of a deity

cenotaph commemorative monument, usually an open domed pavilion

chaam Himalayan Buddhist masked dance

chadar sheet worn as clothing

chai tea

chaitya large arched opening in the façade of a hall or Buddhist temple

chajja overhanging cornice or eaves

chakra sacred Buddhist wheel of the law; also Vishnu's discus

chala Bengali curved roof

Chamunda terrifying form of the goddess Durga

Chandra Moon; a planetary deity

chankramana place of the promenade of the Buddha at Bodh Gaya

chapati unleavened Indian bread cooked on a griddle

chaprassi messenger or orderly usually wearing a badge

char sand-bank or island in a river

char bagh formal Mughal garden, divided into quarters

char bangla (char-chala) 'four temples' in Bengal, built like huts

charan footprint

charka spinning wheel

charpai 'four legs' – wooden frame string bed

chatt(r)a ceremonial umbrella on stupa (Buddhist)

chauki recessed space between pillars; entrance

chaukidar (chowkidar) night-watchman; guard

chaultri (choultry) travellers' rest house (Telugu)

chaumukha Jain sanctuary with a quadruple image, approached through four doorways

chauri fly-whisk, symbol for royalty

chauth 25% tax raised for revenue by Marathas

cheri outcaste settlement; slum (Tamil Nadu)

chhang strong mountain beer of fermented barley maize rye or millet or rice

chhatri umbrella shaped dome or pavilion

chhetri (kshatriya) Hindu warrior caste

chikan shadow embroidery on fine cotton (especially in Lucknow)

chikki nut crunch, a speciality of Lonavla

chit sabha hall of wisdom (Tamil)

chitrakar picture maker

chlorite soft greenish stone that hardens on exposure

chogyal heavenly king (Sikkim)

choli blouse

chorten Himalayan Buddhist relic shrine or a memorial stupa

chowk (chauk) a block; open place in a city where the market is held

chunam lime plaster or stucco made from burnt seashells

circumambulation clockwise movement around a shrine

clerestory upper section of the walls of a building which allows light in

cloister passage usually around an open square

coir fibre from coconut husk

corbel horizontal block supporting a vertical structure or covering an opening

cornice horizontal band at the top of a wall

crenellated having battlements

crewel work chain stitching

crore 10 million

cupola small dome

curvilinear gently curving shape, generally of a tower

cusp, cusped projecting point between small sections of an arch

D

dacoit bandit

dada (dadu) grandfather; elder brother

dado part of a pedestal between its base and cornice

dahi yoghurt

dais raised platform

dak bungalow rest house for officials

dak post

dakini sorceress

Dakshineshvara Lord of the South; name of Siva

dan gift

dandi wooden 'seat' carried by bearers

darbar (durbar) a royal gathering

dargah a Muslim tomb complex

darshan (darshana) viewing of a deity or spiritual leader

darwaza gateway, door

Dasara (dassara/dussehra/dassehra) 10-day festival (Sep-Oct)

Dasaratha King of Ayodhya and father of Rama

Dattatraya syncretistic deity; an incarnation of Vishnu, a teacher of Siva, or a cousin of the Buddha

daulat khana treasury

dentil small block used as part of a cornice

deodar Himalayan cedar; from deva-daru, the 'wood of the gods'

dervish member of Muslim brotherhood, committed to poverty

deul in Bengal and Orissa, generic name for temple; the sanctuary

deval memorial pavilion built to mark royal funeral pyre

devala temple or shrine (Buddhist or Hindu)

devasthanam temple trust

Devi Goddess; later, the Supreme Goddess

dhaba roadside restaurant (mainly North India) truck drivers' stop

dhal lentils, pulses

dhansak Parsi dish made with lentils

dharamshala (dharamsala) pilgrims' rest house

dharma moral and religious duty

dharmachakra wheel of 'moral' law (Buddhist)

dhobi washerman

dhol drums

dhooli (dhooli) swinging chair on a pole, carried by bearers

dhoti loose loincloth worn by Indian men

dhyana meditation

digambara literally 'sky-clad' Jain sect in which the monks go naked

dighi village pond (Bengal)

dikka raised platform around ablution tank

dikpala guardian of one of the cardinal directions mostly appearing in a group of eight

dikshitar person who makes oblations or offerings

dipdan lamp pillar

distributary river that flows away from main channel

divan (diwan) smoking-room; also a chief minister

Diwali festival of lights (Oct-Nov)

diwan chief financial minister

diwan-i-am hall of public audience

diwan-i-khas hall of private audience

do-chala rectangular Bengali style roof

doab interfluve, land between two rivers

dokra tribal name for lost wax metal casting (cire perdu)

dosai (dosa) thin pancake

double dome composed of an inner and outer shell of masonry

Draupadi wife-in-common of the five Pandava brothers in the Mahabharata

drug (durg) fort (Tamil, Telugu)

dry masonry stones laid without mortar

duar (dwar) door, gateway

dun valley

dupatta long scarf worn by Punjabi women

Durga principal goddess of the Shakti cult

durrie (dhurrie) thick handloom rug

durwan watchman

dvarpala doorkeeper

dvipa lamp-column, generally of stone or brass-covered wood

E

eave overhang that shelters a porch or veranda

ek the number 1, a symbol of unity

ekka one horse carriage

epigraph carved inscription

eri tank (Tamil)

F

faience coloured tilework, earthenware or porcelain

fakir Muslim religious mendicant

fan-light fan-shaped window over door

fenestration with windows or openings

filigree ornamental work or delicate tracery

finial emblem at the summit of a stupa, tower, dome, or at the end of a parapet

firman edict or grant issued by a sovereign

foliation ornamental design derived from foliage

frieze horizontal band of figures or decorative designs

G

gable end of an angled roof

gadba woollen blanket (Kashmir)

gaddi throne

gadi/gari car, cart, train

gali (galli) lane; an alley

gana child figures in art

Gandharva semi-divine flying figure; celestial musician

Ganesh (Ganapati) elephant-headed son of Siva and Parvati

Ganga goddess personifying the Ganges

ganj market

ganja Indian hemp

gaon village

garbhagriha literally 'womb-chamber'; a temple sanctuary

garh fort

Garuda Mythical eagle, half-human Vishnu's vehicle

Gauri 'Fair One'; Parvati

Gaurishankara Siva with Parvati

ghagra (ghongra) long flared skirt

ghanta bell

ghat hill range, hill road; landing place; steps on the river bank

ghazal Urdu lyric poetry/love songs, often erotic

ghee clarified butter for cooking

gherao industrial action, surrounding home or office of politician or industrial manager

giri hill

Gita Govinda Jayadeva's poem of the Krishnalila

godown warehouse

gola conical-shaped storehouse

gompa Tibetan Buddhist monastery

goncha loose woollen robe, tied at waist with wide coloured band (Ladakh)

Gopala (Govinda) cowherd; a name of Krishna

Gopis cowherd girls; milk maids who played with Krishna

gopuram towered gateway in South Indian temples

Gorakhnath historically, an 11th-century yogi who founded a Saivite cult; an incarnation of Siva

gosain monk or devotee (Hindi)

gram chick pea, pulse

gram village; gramadan, gift of village

gudi temple (Karnataka)

gumbaz (gumbad) dome

gumpha monastery, cave temple

gur gur salted butter tea (Ladakh)

gur palm sugar

guru teacher; spiritual leader, Sikh religious leader

gurudwara (literally 'entrance to the house of God'); Sikh religious complex

H

Haj (Hajj) annual Muslim pilgrimage to Mecca

hakim judge; a physician (usually Muslim)

halwa a special sweetmeat

hammam Turkish bath

handi Punjabi dish cooked in a pot

Hanuman Monkey devotee of Rama; bringer of success to armies

Hara (Hara Siddhi) Siva

harem women's quarters (Muslim), from 'haram', Arabic for 'forbidden by law'

Hari Vishnu Harihara, Vishnu-Siva as a single divinity

Hariti goddess of prosperity and patroness of children, consort of Kubera

harmika the finial of a stupa in the form of a pedestal where the shaft of the honorific umbrella was set

hartal general strike

Hasan the murdered eldest son of Ali, commemorated at Muharram

hat (haat) market

hathi (hati) elephant

hathi pol elephant gate

hauz tank or reservoir

haveli a merchant's house usually in Rajasthan

havildar army sergeant

hawa mahal palace of the winds

Hidimba Devi Durga worshipped at Manali

hindola swing

hippogryph fabulous griffin-like creature with body of a horse

Hiranyakashipu Demon king killed by Narasimha

hiti a water channel; a bath or tank with water spouts

Holi spring festival (Feb-Mar)

hookah 'hubble bubble' or smoking vase

howdah seat on elephant's back, sometimes canopied

hundi temple offering

Hussain the second murdered son of Ali, commemorated at Muharram

huzra a Muslim tomb chamber

hypostyle hall with pillars

I

lat pillar, column

icon statue or image of worship

Id principal Muslim festivals

iddli steamed rice cake (Tamil)

Idgah open space for the Id prayers

ikat 'resist-dyed' woven fabric

imam Muslim religious leader

imambara tomb of a Shiite Muslim holy man; focus of Muharram procession

Indra King of the gods; God of rain; guardian of the East

Ishana Guardian of the Northeast

Ishvara Lord; Siva

iwan main arch in mosque

J

jadu magic

jaga mohan audience hall or ante-chamber of an Orissan temple

Jagadambi literally Mother of the World; Parvati

Jagannath literally Lord of the World; particularly, Krishna worshipped at Puri

jagati railed parapet

jaggery brown sugar, made from palm sap

jahaz ship: building in form of ship

jali literally 'net'; any lattice or perforated pattern

jamb vertical side slab of doorway

Jambudvipa Continent of the Rose-Apple Tree; the earth

Jami masjid (Jama, Jumma) Friday mosque, for congregational worship

Jamuna Hindu goddess who rides a tortoise; river

Janaka Father of Sita

jangha broad band of sculpture on the outside of the temple wall

jarokha balcony

jataka stories accounts of the previous lives of the Buddha

jatra Bengali folk theatre

jauhar (jauhar) mass suicide by fire of women, particularly in Rajasthan, to avoid capture

jawab literally 'answer,' a building which duplicates another to provide symmetry

jawan army recruit, soldier

jaya stambha victory tower

jheel (jhil) lake; a marsh; a swamp

jhilmil projecting canopy over a window or door opening

-ji (jee) honorific suffix added to names out of reverence and/or politeness; also abbreviated 'yes' (Hindi/Urdu)

jihad striving in the way of god; holy war by Muslims against non-believers

Jina literally 'victor'; spiritual conqueror or Tirthankara, after whom Jainism is named

Jogini mystical goddess

jorbangla double hut-like temple in Bengal

Jyotirlinga luminous energy of Siva manifested at 12 holy places, miraculously formed lingams

K

kabalai (kavalai) well irrigation using bullock power (Tamil Nadu)

kabigan folk debate in verse

kachcha man's 'under-shorts' (one of five Sikh symbols)

kacheri (kutchery) a court; an office for public business

kadal wooden bridge (Kashmir)

kadhi savoury yoghurt curry (Gujarat/North India)

kadu forest (Tamil)

Kailasa mountain home of Siva

kalamkari special painted cotton hanging from Andhra

kalasha pot-like finial of a tower

Kali literally 'black'; terrifying form of the goddess Durga, wearing a necklace of skulls/heads

Kalki future incarnation of Vishnu on horseback

kalyanamandapa marriage hall

kameez women's shirt

kanga comb (one of five Sikh symbols)

kankar limestone pieces, used for road making

kantha Bengali quilting

kapok the silk cotton tree

kara steel bracelet (one of five Sikh symbols)

karma impurity resulting from past misdeeds

Kartikkeya (Kartik) Son of Siva, God of war

kashi-work special kind of glazed tiling, probably derived from Kashan in Persia

kati-roll Muslim snack of meat rolled in a 'paratha' bread

kattakat mixed brain, liver and kidney (Gujarat)

keep tower of a fort, stronghold

kere tank (Kanarese)

keystone central wedge-shaped block in a masonry arch

khadi woven cotton cloth made from home-spun cotton (or silk) yarn

khal creek; a canal

khana suffix for room/office/place; also food or meal

khanqah Muslim (Sufi) hospice

kharif monsoon season crop

khave khana tea shop

kheda enclosure in which wild elephants are caught; elephant depot

khet field

khola river or stream in Nepal

khondalite crudely grained basalt

khukri traditional curved Gurkha weapon

kirpan sabre, dagger (one of five Sikh symbols)

kirti-stambha 'pillar of fame,' free standing pillar in front of temple

kohl antimony, used as eye shadow

konda hill (Telugu)

kos minars Mughal 'mile' stones

kot (kota/kottai/kotte) fort

kothi house

kotla citadel

kovil (koil) temple (Tamil)

Krishna Eighth incarnation of Vishnu

kritis South Indian devotional music

Kubera Chief yaksha; keeper of the treasures of the earth, Guardian of the North

kulam tank or pond (Tamil)

kumar a young man

Kumari Virgin; Durga

kumbha a vase-like motif, pot

Kumbhayog auspicious time for bathing to wash away sins

kumhar (kumar) potter

kund lake, well or pool

kundan jewellery setting of uncut gems (Rajasthan)

kuppam hamlet (Tamil)

kurta Punjabi shirt

kurti-kanchali small blouse

kutcha (cutcha/kacha) raw; crude; unpaved; built with sun-dried bricks

kwabgah bedroom; literally 'palace of dreams'

L

la Himalayan mountain pass

lakh 100,000

Lakshmana younger brother of Rama

Lakshmi Goddess of wealth and good fortune, consort of Vishnu

Lakulisha founder of the Pashupata sect, believed to be an incarnation of Siva

lama Buddhist priest in Tibet

lassi iced yoghurt drink

lath monolithic pillar

lathi bamboo stick with metal bindings, used by police

lena cave, usually a rock-cut sanctuary

lingam (linga) Siva as the phallic emblem

Lingaraja Siva worshipped at Bhubaneswar

lintel horizontal beam over doorway

liwan cloisters of a mosque

Lokeshwar 'Lord of the World', Avalokiteshwara to Buddhists and form of Siva to Hindus

lunette semi-circular window opening

lungi wrapped-around loin cloth, normally checked

M

madrassa Islamic theological school or college

maha great

Mahabharata Sanskrit epic about the battle between the Pandavas and Kauravas

Mahabodhi Great Enlightenment of Buddha

Mahadeva literally 'Great Lord'; Siva

mahal palace, grand building

mahalla (mohulla) division of a town; a quarter; a ward

mahamandapam large enclosed hall in front of main shrine

mahant head of a monastery

maharaja great king

maharana Rajput clan head

maharani great queen

maharishi (Maharshi) literally 'great teacher'

Mahavira literally 'Great Hero'; last of the 24 Tirthankaras, founder of Jainism

Mahayana The Greater Vehicle; form of Buddhism practised in East Asia, Tibet and Nepal

Mahesha (Maheshvara) Great Lord; Siva

Mahisha Buffalo demon killed by Durga

mahout elephant driver/keeper

mahseer large freshwater fish found especially in Himalayan rivers

maidan large open grassy area in a town

Maitreya the future Buddha

makara crocodile-shaped mythical creature symbolizing the river Ganga

makhan butter

malai hill (Tamil)

mali gardener

Manasa Snake goddess; Sakti

manastambha free-standing pillar in front of temple

mandala geometric diagram symbolizing the structure of the Universe

mandalam region, tract of country (Tamil)

mandapa columned hall preceding the temple sanctuary

mandi market

mandir temple

mani (mani wall) stones with sacred inscriptions at Buddhist sites

mantra chant for meditation by Hindus and Buddhists

maqbara chamber of a Muslim tomb

Mara Tempter, who sent his daughters (and soldiers) to disturb the Buddha's meditation

marg wide roadway

masjid literally 'place of prostration'; mosque

mata mother

math Hindu or Jain monastery

maulana scholar (Muslim)

maulvi religious teacher (Muslim)

maund measure of weight about 20 kg

mausoleum large tomb building

maya illusion

medallion circle or part-circle framing a figure or decorative motif

meena enamel work

mela festival or fair, usually Hindu

memsahib married European woman, term used mainly before Independence

Meru mountain supporting the heavens

mihrab niche in the western wall of a mosque

mimbar pulpit in mosque

Minakshi literally 'fish-eyed'; Parvati

minar (minaret) slender tower of a mosque

mitthai Indian sweets

mithuna couple in sexual embrace

mofussil the country as distinct from the town

Mohammad 'the praised'; The Prophet; founder of Islam

moksha salvation, enlightenment; literally 'release'

momos Tibetan stuffed pastas

monolith single block of stone shaped into a pillar

moonstone the semi-circular stone step before a shrine (also chandrasila)

mouza (mowza) village; a parcel of land having a separate name in the revenue records

mridangam barrel-shaped drum (musical)

muballigh second prayer leader

mudra symbolic hand gesture

muezzin mosque official who calls the faithful to prayer

Muharram period of mourning in remembrance of Hasan and Hussain, two murdered sons of Ali

mukha mandapa, hall for shrine

mullah religious teacher (Muslim)

mund Toda village

muqarna Muslim stalactite design

mural wall decoration

musalla prayer mat

muta limited duration marriage (Leh)

muthi measure equal to 'a handful'

N

nadi river

nadu region, country (Tamil)

Naga (nagi/nagini) Snake deity; associated with fertility and protection

nagara city, sometimes capital

nakkar khana (naggar or naubat khana) drum house; arched structure or gateway for musicians

nal mandapa porch over a staircase

nallah (nullah) ditch, channel

namaaz Muslim prayers, worship

namaste common Hindu greeting (with joined palms) translated as: 'I salute all divine qualities in you'

namda rug

Nandi a bull, Siva's vehicle and a symbol of fertility

nara durg large fort built on a flat plain

Narayana Vishnu as the creator of life

nata mandapa (nat-mandir; nritya sala) dancing hall in a temple

Nataraja Siva, Lord of the cosmic dance

nath literally 'place' eg Amarnath

natya the art of dance

nautch display by dancing girls

navagraha nine planets, represented usually on the lintel or architrave of the front door of a temple

navaranga central hall of temple

navaratri literally '9 nights'; name of the Dasara festival

nawab prince, wealthy Muslim, sometimes used as a title

niche wall recess containing a sculpted image or emblem, mostly framed by a pair of pilasters

Nihang literally 'crocodile': followers of Guru Gobind Singh (Sikh)

nirvana enlightenment; literally 'extinguished'

niwas small palace

nritya pure dance

O

obelisk tapering and usually monolithic stone shaft

oriel projecting window

P

pada foot or base

padam dance which tells a story

padma lotus flower, Padmasana, lotus seat; posture of meditating figures

paga projecting pilaster-like surface of an Orissan temple

pagoda tall structure in several stories

pahar hill

paisa (poisa) one hundredth of a rupee

palanquin covered litter for one, carried on poles

palayam minor kingdom (Tamil)

pali language of Buddhist scriptures

palli village

pan leaf of the betel vine; sliced areca nut, lime and other ingredients wrapped in leaf for chewing

panchayat a 'council of five'; a government system of elected councils

pandal marquee made of bamboo and cloth

pandas temple priests

pandit teacher or wise man; a Sanskrit scholar

pankah (punkha) fan, formerly pulled by a cord

parabdis special feeding place for birds

parapet wall extending above the roof

pargana subdivision of a district usually comprising many villages; a fiscal unit

Parinirvana the Buddha's state prior to nirvana, shown usually as a reclining figure

parishads political division of group of villages

Parsi (Parsee) Zoroastrians who fled from Iran to West India in the 8th century to avoid persecution

parterre level space in a garden occupied by flowerbeds

Parvati daughter of the Mountain; Siva's consort

pashmina fine wool from a mountain goat

Pashupati literally Lord of the Beasts; Siva

pata painted hanging scroll

patan town or city (Sanskrit)

patel village headman

patina green film that covers materials exposed to the air

pattachitra specially painted cloth (especially Orissan)

pau measure for vegetables and fruit equal to 250 g

paya soup

pediment mouldings, often in a triangular formation above an opening or niche

pendant hanging, a motif depicted upside down

peon servant, messenger (from Portuguese *peao*)

perak black hat, studded with turquoise and lapis lazuli (Ladakh)

peristyle range of columns surrounding a court or temple

Persian wheel well irrigation system using a bucket lift

pettah suburbs, outskirts of town (Tamil: *pettai*)

pice (old form) 1/100th of a rupee

picottah water lift using horizontal pole pivoted on vertical pole (Tamil Nadu)

pida (pitha) basement

pida deul hall with a pyramidal roof in an Orissan temple

pietra dura inlaid mosaic of hard, semi-precious stones

pilaster ornamental small column, with capital and bracket

pinjra lattice work

pinjrapol animal hospital (Jain)

pipal Ficus religiosa, the Bodhi tree

pir Muslim holy man

pitha base, pedestal

pithasthana place of pilgrimage

podium stone bench; low pedestal wall

pokana bathing tank (Sri Lanka)

pol fortified gateway

porch covered entrance to a shrine or hall, generally open and with columns

portico space enclosed between columns

pradakshina patha processional passage

prakaram open courtyard

pralaya the end of the world

prasadam consecrated temple food

prayag confluence considered sacred by Hindus

puja ritual offerings to the gods; worship (Hindu)

pujari worshipper; one who performs puja (Hindu)

pukka literally 'ripe' or 'finished'; reliable; solidly built

punya merit earned through actions and religious devotion (Buddhist)

Puranas literally 'the old' Sanskrit sacred poems

purdah seclusion of Muslim women from public view (literally curtains)

pushkarani sacred pool or tank

Q

qabr Muslim grave

qibla direction for Muslim prayer

qila fort

Quran holy Muslim scriptures

qutb axis or pivot

R

rabi winter/spring season crop

Radha Krishna's favourite consort

raj rule or government

raja king, ruler (variations include rao, rawal)

rajbari palaces of a small kingdom

Rajput dynasties of western and central India

Rakshakas Earth spirits

Rama Seventh incarnation of Vishnu

Ramayana Sanskrit epic – the story of Rama

Ramazan (Ramadan) Muslim month of fasting

rana warrior (Nepal)

rangamandapa painted hall or theatre

rani queen

rath chariot or temple car

Ravana Demon king of Lanka; kidnapper of Sita

rawal head priest

rekha curvilinear portion of a spire or sikhara (rekha deul, sanctuary, curved tower of an Orissan temple)

reredos screen behind an altar

rickshaw three-wheeled bicycle-powered (or two-wheeled hand-powered) vehicle

Rig (Rg) Veda oldest and most sacred of the Vedas

Rimpoche blessed incarnation; abbot of a Tibetan Buddhist monastery (gompa)

rishi 'seer'; inspired poet, philosopher

rumal handkerchief, specially painted in Chamba (Himachal Pradesh)

rupee unit of currency in India

ryot (rayat/raiyat) a subject; a cultivator; a farmer

S

sabha columned hall (sabha mandapa, assembly hall)

sabzi vegetables, vegetable curry

sadar (sadr/saddar) chief, main especially Sikh

sadhu ascetic; religious mendicant, holy man

safa turban (Rajasthan)

sagar lake; reservoir

sahib title of address, like 'sir'

sahn open courtyard of a mosque

Saiva (Shaiva) the cult of Siva

sal a hall

sal hardwood tree of the lower slopes of the Himalayan foothills

salaam literally 'peace'; greeting (Muslim)

salwar (shalwar) loose trousers (Punjab)

samadh(i) literally concentrated thought, meditation; a funerary memorial

sambar lentil and vegetable soup dish, accompanying main meal (Tamil)

samsara transmigration of the soul

samudra large tank or inland sea

sangam junction of rivers

sangarama monastery

sangha ascetic order founded by Buddha

sangrahalaya rest house for Jain pilgrims

sankha (shankha) the conch shell (symbolically held by Vishnu); the shell bangle worn by Bengali women

sanyasi wandering ascetic; final stage in the ideal life of a man

sarai caravansarai, halting place

saranghi small four-stringed viola shaped from a single piece of wood

Saraswati wife of Brahma and goddess of knowledge

sarkar the government; the state; a writer; an accountant

sarod Indian stringed musical instrument

sarvodaya uplift, improvement of all

sati (suttee) a virtuous woman; act of self-immolation on a husband's funeral pyre

Sati wife of Siva who destroyed herself by fire

satyagraha 'truth force'; passive resistance

sayid title (Muslim)

schist grey or green finely grained stone

seer (ser) weight (about 1 kg)

sepoy (sepai) Indian soldier, private

serow a wild Himalayan antelope

seth merchant, businessman

seva voluntary service

shahtush very fine wool from the Tibetan antelope

Shakti Energy; female divinity often associated with Siva

shala barrel-vaulted roof

shalagrama stone containing fossils worshipped as a form of Vishnu

shaman doctor/priest, using magic, exorcist

shamiana cloth canopy

Shankara Siva

sharia corpus of Muslim theological law

shastras ancient texts defining temple architecture

shastri religious title (Hindu)

sheesh mahal palace apartment with mirror work

shehnai (shahnai) Indian wind instrument like an oboe

sherwani knee-length coat for men

Shesha (Sesha) serpent who supports Vishnu

shikar hunting

shikara boat (Kashmir)

shisham a valuable building timber

sikhara curved temple tower or spire

shloka (sloka) Sanskrit sacred verse

shola patch of forest or wood (Tamil)

sileh khana armoury

sindur vermilion powder used in temple ritual; married women mark their hair parting with it (East India)

singh (sinha) lion; Rajput caste name adopted by Sikhs

sinha stambha lion pillar

sirdar a guide who leads trekking groups

Sita Rama's wife, heroine of the Ramayana epic

sitar classical stringed musical instrument with a gourd for soundbox

Siva (Shiva) The Destroyer in the Hindu triad of Gods

Sivaratri literally 'Siva's night'; a festival (Feb-Mar)

Skanda the Hindu god of war; Kartikkeya

soma sacred drink mentioned in the Vedas

spandrel triangular space between the curve of an arch and the square enclosing it

squinch arch across an interior angle

sri (shri) honorific title, often used for 'Mr'; repeated as sign of great respect

sridhara pillar with octagonal shaft and square base

stalactite system of vaulting, remotely resembling stalactite formations in a cave

stambha free-standing column or pillar, often for a lamp or figure

steatite finely grained grey mineral

stele upright, inscribed slab used as a gravestone

step well (vav) vertical shaft leading down to a well, with elaborately carved walls

sthan place (suffix)

stucco plasterwork

stupa hemispheric Buddhist funerary mound

stylobate base on which a colonnade is placed

subahdar (subedar) the governor of a province; viceroy under the Mughals

Subrahmanya Skanda, one of Siva's sons; Kartikkeya in South India

sudra lowest of the Hindu castes

sufi Muslim mystic; sufism, Muslim mystic worship

sultan Muslim prince (sultana, wife of sultan)

Surya Sun; Sun God

svami (swami) holy man; a suffix for temple deities

svastika (swastika) auspicious Hindu/ Buddhist cross-like sign

swadeshi home-made goods

swaraj home rule

swatantra freedom

T

tabla a pair of drums

tahr wild goat

tahsildar revenue collector

taikhana underground apartments

takht throne

talao (tal, talar) water tank

taluk administrative subdivision of a district

tamasha spectacle; festive celebration

tandava (dance) of Siva

tank lake dug for irrigation; a masonry-lined temple pool with stepped sides

tapas (tapasya) ascetic meditative self-denial

Tara literally 'star'; a goddess

tarkashi Orissan silver filigree

tatties cane or grass screens used for shade

Teej Hindu festival

tehsil subdivision of a district (North India)

tempera distemper; method of mural painting by means of a 'body,' such as white pigment

tempo three-wheeler vehicle

terai narrow strip of land along Himalayan foothills

teri soil formed from wind blown sand (Tamil Nadu)

terracotta burnt clay used as building material

thakur high Hindu caste; deity (Bengal)

thakur bari temple sanctuary (Bengal)

thali South and West Indian vegetarian meal

thana a police jurisdiction; police station

thangka (thankha) cloth (often silk) painted with a Tibetan Mahayana deity

thug professional robber/murderer (Central India)

tiffin snack, light meal

tika (tilak) vermilion powder, auspicious mark on the forehead; often decorative

tikka tender pieces of meat that have been marinated and barbecued

tillana abstract dance

tirtha ford, bathing place, holy spot (Sanskrit)

Tirthankara literally 'ford-maker'; title given to 24 religious 'teachers', worshipped by Jains

tonga two-wheeled horse carriage

topi (topee) pith helmet

torana gateway; two posts with an architrave

tottam garden (Tamil)

tribhanga triple-bended pose for standing figures

Trimurti the Hindu Triad, Brahma, Vishnu and Siva

tripolia triple gateway

trisul the trident chief symbol of the god Siva

triveni triple-braided

tsampa ground, roasted barley, eaten dry or mixed with milk, tea or water (Himalayan)

tso lake (Ladakh)

tuk fortified enclosure containing Jain shrines

tulsi sacred basil plant

tykhana underground room for use in hot weather (North India)

tympanum triangular space within cornices

U

Uma Siva's consort in one of her many forms

untouchable 'outcastes', with whom contact of any kind was believed by high caste Hindus to be defiling

Upanishads ancient Sanskrit philosophical texts, part of the Vedas

ur village (Tamil)

usta painted camel leather goods

ustad master

uttarayana northwards

V

vahana 'vehicle' of the deity

vaisya the 'middle-class' caste of merchants and farmers

Valmiki sage, author of the Ramayana epic

Vamana dwarf incarnation of Vishnu

vana grove, forest

Varaha boar incarnation of Vishnu

varam village (Tamil)

varna 'colour'; social division of Hindus into Brahmin, Kshatriya, Vaishya and Sudra

Varuna Guardian of the West, accompanied by Makara (see above)

Vayu Wind god; Guardian of the Northwest

Veda (Vedic) oldest known Hindu religious texts

vedi (bedi) altar, also a wall or screen

veranda enlarged porch in front of a hall

vihara Buddhist or Jain monastery with cells around a courtyard

vilas house or pleasure palace

vimana towered sanctuary containing the cell in which the deity is enshrined

vina plucked stringed instrument, relative of sitar

Vishnu a principal Hindu deity; the Preserver (and Creator)

vyala (yali) leogryph, mythical lion-like sculpture

W

-wallah suffix often used with a occupational name, eg rickshaw-wallah

wav (vav) step well, particularly in Gujarat and western India (baoli)

wazir chief minister of a raja (from Turkish 'vizier')

wazwan ceremonial meal (Kashmir)

Y

yagya (yajna) major ceremonial sacrifice

Yaksha (Yakshi) a demi-god, associated with nature

yali see vyala

Yama God of death, judge of the living

yantra magical diagram used in meditation; instrument

yatra pilgrimage

Yellow Hat Gelugpa Sect of Tibetan Buddhism – monks wear yellow headdress

yeti mythical Himalayan animal often referred to as 'the abominable snowman'

yoga school of philosophy stressing mental and physical disciplines; yogi

yoni a hole symbolising female sexuality; vagina

yura water channel (Ladakh)

Z

zamindar a landlord granted income under the Mughals

zari silver and gold thread used in weaving or embroidery

zarih cenotaph in a Muslim tomb

zenana segregated women's apartments

ziarat holy Muslim tomb

zilla (zillah) district

Index → *Entries in bold refer to maps*

Credits

Footprint credits

Editor: Jo Williams
Production and layout: Emma Bryers
Maps: Kevin Feeney
Colour section: Leonie Drake

Publisher: Patrick Dawson
Managing Editor: Felicity Laughton
Advertising: Elizabeth Taylor
Sales and marketing: Kirsty Holmes

Photography credits

Front cover: Rene Drouyer/Dreamstime
Back cover: Jameswest/Dreamstime

Colour section

Page i: Shutterstock: Curioso/Curioso
Page ii: Shutterstock: f9fotos/f9fotos
Page v: Superstock: age fotostock/age fotostock
Page vi: Shutterstock: Igor Plotnikov; Superstock:
Travel Pictures Ltd/Travel Pictures Ltd
Page vii: Dreamstime: Jaya Kumar/
Dreamstime.com; Superstock: Alexandra Lande
Page viii: Shutterstock: Murgermari
Page ix: Dreamstime: Sujit Pavithran/
Dreamstime.com; Superstock: Hemis.fr/Hemis.fr
Page x: Superstock: Luis Davilla/age fotostock;
Shutterstock: f9photos

Printed in India by Thomson Press Ltd,
Faridabad, Haryana

Every effort has been made to ensure
that the facts in this guidebook are
accurate. However, travellers should still
obtain advice from consulates, airlines,
etc about travel and visa requirements
before travelling. The authors and
publishers cannot accept responsibility
for any loss, injury or inconvenience
however caused.

Publishing information

Footprint South India
5th edition
© Footprint Handbooks Ltd
October 2014

ISBN: 978 1 910120 033
CIP DATA: A catalogue record
for this book is available from
the British Library

® Footprint Handbooks and the
Footprint mark are a registered
trademark of Footprint Handbooks Ltd

Published by Footprint
6 Riverside Court
Lower Bristol Road
Bath BA2 3DZ, UK
T +44 (0)1225 469141
F +44 (0)1225 469461
footprinttravelguides.com

Distributed in the USA by
National Book Network, Inc.

Footprint Mini Atlas
South India

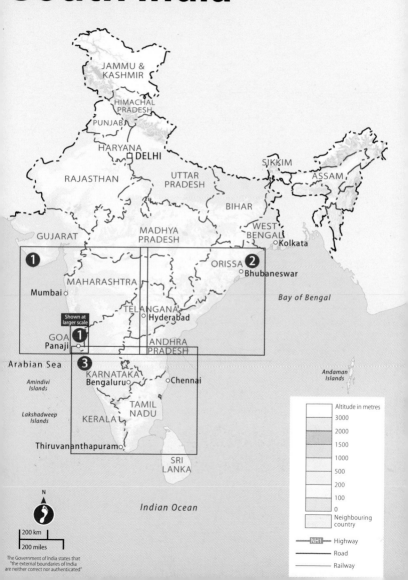

JAMMU & KASHMIR

HIMACHAL PRADESH

PUNJAB

HARYANA

□ DELHI

SIKKIM

ASSAM

RAJASTHAN

UTTAR PRADESH

BIHAR

WEST BENGAL

○ Kolkata

GUJARAT

MADHYA PRADESH

❶

MAHARASHTRA

Mumbai ○

ORISSA ❷
○ Bhubaneswar

Bay of Bengal

TELANGANA
○ Hyderabad

Shown at larger scale

GOA ❶
Panaji ○

ANDHRA PRADESH

Arabian Sea

❸

KARNATAKA
Bengaluru ○   ○ Chennai

Andaman Islands

Amindivi Islands

Lakshadweep Islands

TAMIL NADU

KERALA

Thiruvananthapuram ○

SRI LANKA

N

Indian Ocean

200 km
200 miles

The Government of India states that "the external boundaries of India are neither correct nor authenticated"

	Altitude in metres
	3000
	2000
	1500
	1000
	500
	200
	100
	0
	Neighbouring country

⎯NH1⎯ Highway

⎯⎯ Road

--- Railway

Map 1

① Gondal ② Jasdan ③ Karjan
Velavadhar National Park
Jambusar
Chanod
Rajpipla

Dhoraji
Derdi Babra
GUJARAT
Bhavnagar
Dahej
Andeshwar
Bharuch

Ranavav NH8B
Jetpur
Bagsara
Amreli
Sihor
Gogha

Porbandar
Vanthali
Junagadh
Palitana
Alang
Talaja
Surat
Mandvi Uchchhal
Vyara

Keshod
Visavadar
Dhari
Kundla
Gopnath
Dumas
Ubhrat
Navsari
Vansda
Saputara

Sasan Gir National Park
Chorwad
Veraval
Prabhas Patan
Somnath
Talala Sasan Gir
Tulsishyam
Mahuva
Pip-a-Vav
Dandi
Chikhli
Tithal Valsad

A
Kodinar Diu
Una
Jafrabad
Delwada
Gulf of Khambhat
Pardi
Daman
Silvassa
North Sahyadri Range

N
50 km
50 miles

The Government of India states that the external boundaries of India are neither correct nor authenticated

DADRA & NAGAR HAVELI

Arabian Sea
Jawhar
Nashik
Deolali

Manor
Vada
Igatpuri
Kalsubai Range

Shahpur
Dahisar
Shahpur
Harischandre Range

Kanheri Caves
Bhiwandi
Kalyan
Shivner

Bassein
Manori
Thane

Matheran
Neral
Karjat
Khandala
Karla

Map 1a Goa

+300m
100-300m
50-100m
<50m

To Mumbai
N
10 km
10 miles

Panvel
Mumbai
Kihim
Pen
Lonavla
NH4

A
Tiracol Fort
Keri Tiracol R
Arambol
Najbaga
Parsi Dargalim
Alorna Fort

MAHARASHTRA
Roha
Murud
Janjira
Waki
Bhaja
Sinhagarh
Pune

Siolim Colvale Assenora
Mapusa Bicholim
Carambolin-Brahma

B
Veer
Mahad
Panchgani
Pratapgarh
Mahabaleshwar

Anjuna
Chorao
Sanquelim
Valpoi
Caranzol
Harnai
Khed
Koyna Sagar

Calangute
NH17
Salim Ali Bird Sanctuary
Divar

Aguada Fort
Panjim
Old Goa
Banastari
Savoi-Verem
Bondla Sanctuary
Tambdi Surla

Chiplun

Mormugao
Pilar
Marcel
Usgaon
Molem
Bhagwan Mahaveer Sanctuary

Ganpatipule
Ratnagiri
Hatkamba

Vasco da Gama
Cortalim
Ponda
Tisk
Sancordem
NH4A
Dudhsagar R
Colem
Dudhsagar

B
Dabolim
Loutolim
Borlim
Siroda
Rachol
Calem

Cansaulim
Malkapu

Majorda
Madgaon
Chandol
Sanvorden
Damai

Colva
Benaulim
Varca
Quepem
Sanguem
Cumbari
Vijayadurg
Rajapur
Talera
NH17

Arabian Sea
Cuncolim
Mobor
Betul
Bali
Paroda
Zambaulim
Rivona
Curdi
Netorli

Cabo de Rama Fort
Patorpa
Pirla
Malvan
Sawantwa

NH17
Chaudi (Canacona)
Cotigao Sanctuary
Partagal Math
Vengurla
GOA

C
GOA
Palolem
Galibaga
Talpona R
Mapusa

KARNATAKA
Panjim
Vasco Da Gama
Madgaon

To Mangalore
Cotigao Sanctu

① ② ③

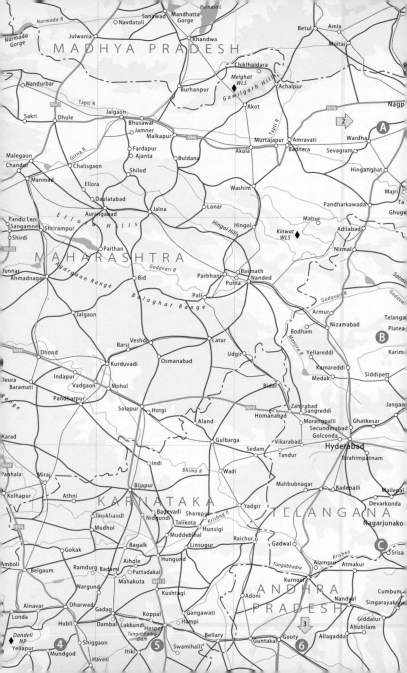

Map 3

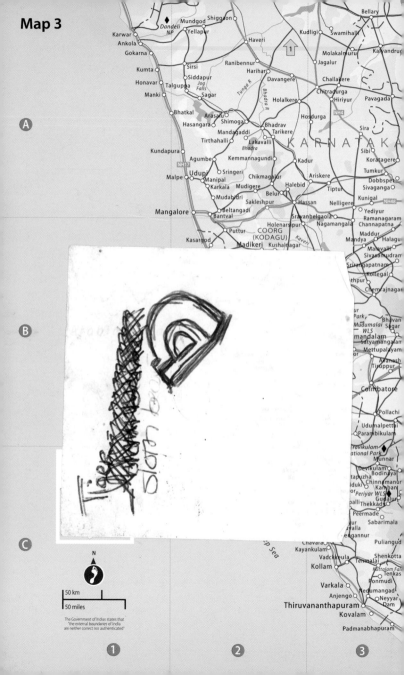

Karwar
Ankola
Gokarna
Kumta
Honavar
Manki
Bhatkal
Hasangara
Kundapura
Malpe Udupi
Manipal
Karkala
Mudabidri
Mangalore
Bantval
Kasargod
Puttur

Dandeli NP
Mundgod
Yellapur
Shiggaon
Sirsi
Siddapur
Jog Falls
Sagar
Talguppa
Arasalu
Shimoga
Mandagaddi
Tirthahalli
Kemmannagundi
Agumbe
Sringeri
Chikmaglur
Mudigere
Belur
Sakleshpur
Beltangadi
Holenarsipur
Madikeri
COORG (KODAGU)
Kushalnagar

Haveri
Ranibennur
Harihar
Davangere
Holalkere
Bhadrav
Tarikere
Lakavalli
Bhadra
Kadur
Ariskere
Halebid
Hassan
Sravanbelgaola
Nagamangala

Bellary
Kudligi
Swamihalli
Molakalmuru
Jagalur
Challakere
Chitradurga
Hosdurga
Hiriyur
Sira
Sibi
Koratagere
Tumkur
Nelligere

KARNATAKA

Kalyandrug
Pavagada
NH4
Dobbspet
Sivaganga
Kunigal
NH48
Yediyur
Ramanagaram
Channapatna
Maddur
Mandya
Malavalli
Sivasamudram
Srirangapatnam
Kollegal
Chemrajnagar

Mudumalai WLS
mandalam
Satyamangalam
Mettupalayam
Avanash
Tiruppur
Coimbatore
Pollachi
Udumalpettai
Parambikulam
Eravikulam National Park
Devikulam
Bodinaya
Chinnamanur
tapuzha
Iduki
Periyar WLS
Kambam
Gudalur
palli
Thekkady
Peermade
Sabarimala
ur
Ayalla
engan
Chavara
Kayankulam
Vadakkeula
Kollam
Varkala
Anjengo
Thiruvananthapuram
Kovalam
Padmanabhapuram
Puliangudi
Shenkotta
Tenmalai
Kuttalam Fall
Tenkas
Ponmudi
Nedumangad
Neyyar Dam

N

50 km
50 miles

The Government of India states that "the external boundaries of India are neither correct nor authenticated"

A   B   C

1   2   3